GANGSTER PRIEST:
THE ITALIAN AMERICAN CINEMA OF MARTIN SCORSESE

Widely acclaimed as America's greatest living film director, Martin
Scorsese is also, some argue, the pre-eminent Italian American artist.
Although he has explored various subjects throughout his lengthy career, the core of his achievement includes five films on Italian American
subjects – *Who's That Knocking at My Door?*, *Mean Streets*, *Raging Bull*,
GoodFellas, and *Casino* – as well as the documentary *Italianamerican*. In
Gangster Priest Robert Casillo examines these films in the context of the
religion, culture, and history of southern Italy and of its people, from
whom the majority of Italian Americans, including Scorsese, descend.

Casillo argues that these films cannot be fully appreciated either
thematically or formally without an understanding of the various facets
of Italian American culture. As a whole, Scorsese's Italian American
films offer what Casillo considers a sustained meditation on the immigrant experience, the relationship between Italian America and southern Italy, the conflicts between generations, and the development of
Italian American identity. Raised as a Catholic and deeply imbued with
Catholic values, Scorsese deals with certain forms of southern Italian
religious practice, which have left their imprint not only on his own
consciousness but also on the spiritually tormented characters of his
Italian American films. Casillo shows how Scorsese challenges the southern Italian code of masculine honour in his exploration of the Mafia,
and discloses its fundamental opposition to Christianity.

Bringing a wealth of scholarship and insight into Scorsese's work,
Casillo's study will captivate readers interested in film and filmmaking,
the rich social history of southern Italy, Italian American culture, and
the sociology and history of the Mafia in both Sicily and the United
States.

(Toronto Italian Studies)

ROBERT CASILLO is a professor in the Department of English at the
University of Miami in Coral Gables, Florida.

ROBERT CASILLO

Gangster Priest

The Italian American Cinema of Martin Scorsese

UNIVERSITY OF TORONTO PRESS
Toronto Buffalo London

© University of Toronto Press Incorporated 2006
Toronto Buffalo London
Printed in Canada

ISBN-13: 978-0-8020-9113-0 (cloth)
ISBN-10: 0-8020-9113-X (cloth)
ISBN-13: 978-0-8020-9403-2 (paper)
ISBN-10: 0-8020-9403-1 (paper)

Printed on acid-free paper

Library and Archives Canada Cataloguing in Publication

Casillo, Robert
    Gangster priest : the Italian American cinema of Martin
Scorsese / Robert Casillo.

(Toronto Italian studies)
Includes index.
ISBN-13: 978-0-8020-9113-0 (bound)
ISBN-10: 0-8020-9113-X (bound)
ISBN-13: 978-0-8020-9403-2 (pbk.)
ISBN-10: 0-8020-9403-1 (pbk.)

1. Scorsese, Martin – Criticism and interpretation.   2. Italian
Americans in motion pictures.   I. Title.   II. Series.   III. Series:
Toronto Italian studies.

PN1998.3.S39C38 2006   791.4302′33092   C2006-901985-1

University of Toronto Press acknowledges the financial assistance to
its publishing program of the Canada Council for the Arts and the
Ontario Arts Council.

University of Toronto Press acknowledges the financial support for
its publishing activities of the Government of Canada through the
Book Publishing Industry Development Program (BPIDP).

To the memory of Louis Casillo

What figure of today aesthetically best suits our streets, what figure aesthetically is best framed by our doorways? The answer is the man in a long overcoat with hand within pocket holding a revolver on which his fingers tighten. There is no gainsaying the aesthetic appropiateness of the thug in our streets and in our interiors. The idea of him saves our town environment from a suggestion of vacuum.

Adrian Stokes, *Color and Form*, 1937

'I'm not talking about Italians. I am talking about criminals.'

Joe Valachi, 1963

'You never stop being a priest. Or a mafioso.'

Judge Giovanni Falcone

Return, Alpheus, the dread voice is past,
That shrunk thy streams; return Sicilian Muse ...

Milton, 'Lycidas'

Contents

Preface

The artistic achievement of film director Martin Scorsese stands unsurpassed in the history of Italian Americans. As is evident from the
prominence of Italian American subjects in his best-known works, including those upon which his reputation most securely rests, Scorsese has gained his popular and critical success not by concealing or
denying his ethnicity but by confronting and exploring it. For Scorsese
is in many ways the cinematic chronicler of the epic of Italian America,
one of the major population movements of modern times. The subject
matter of his Italian American films extends from the earliest days of
immigration, to the ethnic urban neighbourhoods of the Northeast, to
the post–Second World War suburbs, and at last to the transplantation
of Italian Americans to the resort and entertainment capitals of Miami,
Las Vegas, and the Far West. No other artist has equalled Scorsese
in giving a voice to the common experience of this group, whether
social, cultural, or religious, or in interpreting the meaning of that
experience. As Italian Americans enter into what has been called the
'twilight of ethnicity,' they receive from Scorsese a magnificent record
of the earlier generations in their unequal struggle between the pressures of assimilation and the preservation of their predominantly
southern Italian heritage.

Although Scorsese is widely admired as an Italian American director
who frequently focuses on his own ethnic group, it is generally acknowledged that his ethnicity, including his Italian Catholic background,
has imprinted his films even in those many instances in which he has
not treated Italian American subjects. Traces of Scorsese's ethnic origins
appear in the implicitly sacrificial if not redemptive violence at the
climax of *Taxi Driver*, the familial and Pentecostal themes that inform

Cape Fear, and the threatened ritualized society of Tibet that figures in *Kundun* and gives it its distinctive interest and power. Scorsese's ethnicity appears too in his recurrent fascination with the theme of the outsider as well as with certain forms of penitential and even masochistic religiosity. Perhaps most significant, it reveals itself in the characteristically immanentist and analogical Catholic sensibility whereby Scorsese is able to find the sacred in ordinary worldly things and events. It would be easy to provide other examples.

The fact remains, however, that in strict terms Scorsese's Italian American films are those that treat specifically Italian American subjects. These represent the core of his achievement, in which he is most characteristically himself as an artistic personality, and in which the main radicals of his artistic vision stand out most impressively. Scorsese's 'Italian American cinema' consists of a fifteen-minute short, filmed during his student days, entitled *It's Not Just You, Murray!*; a forty-eight-minute documentary, *Italianamerican*, which was shot in his parents' apartment in Manhattan's Little Italy; and five full-length features: *Who's That Knocking at My Door?*, *Mean Streets*, *Raging Bull*, *GoodFellas*, and *Casino*. Scorsese's sixty-page treatment for another Italian American film, *Jerusalem, Jerusalem*, was completed in the mid-1960s but never produced. The justification for examining these works together lies in their thematic unity and almost consistently high quality, in which they contrast with Scorsese's uneven performance in his non–Italian American films. Whenever Scorsese has made films whose subjects are largely unfamiliar to him or in some way foreign to his sensibility, and in which he has shown imperfect control over his materials, he has recovered his bearings and reinvigorated his creative energies by returning to the terrain with which he remains most familiar: Italian America.

Despite the virtues of *Boxcar Bertha*, the B-movie that Scorsese directed in the early 1970s primarily in order to keep his career alive, John Cassavetes rightly encouraged him to make *Mean Streets*, Scorsese's next film, whose Italian American subject matter provided the fullest impetus to his passion and imagination. *New York, New York*, conceived in a musical genre with which Scorsese was less than comfortable, was compensated for by the sublimities of *Raging Bull*, the making of which restored the momentum of his career while enabling him therapeutically to recast his confused personal life. The theological muddle and dramatic misfires of *The Last Temptation of Christ* were recouped by the thematic and technical richness of *GoodFellas*, which ironically has as much if not more to say about the meaning of Christianity than the more self-consciously religious film that preceded it. Likewise the rather static and overly archeological exploration of late-nineteenth-century New York society in *The Age of Innocence* was followed by Scorsese's far more knowing and assured handling of the no less ritualistic and morally ambiguous gambling society of *Casino*, the much misunderstood film with which Scorsese concludes his 'gangster trilogy.' A case can be made that, whatever his successes in other genres, Scorsese has never achieved such sustained intensity or penetration of his materials as in his Italian American films.

These works have attracted serious attention, and a number of critics have treated their ethnic and religious subjects skilfully if only sketchily. Mary Pat Kelly, Richard A. Blake, SJ, and Paul Giles have clarified the ways in which Scorsese's mind and sensibility have been shaped by Catholic sacramentalism, ritualism, liturgy, immanentism, and analogism. Similarly emphasizing the influence of Catholicism upon Scorsese, Leo Braudy reads his Italian American films from this perspective. The Catholic writer Les Keyser shows how these films reflect the sexual and religious attitudes of the ethnic group, including the Italian American 'religion' of the family or domus. Another Catholic writer, Lee Lourdeaux, links Scorsese's spirituality to two competing versions of American Catholicism, the Irish and southern Italian. More recently, Andrew Greeley has discussed the Italian American religiosity in *Mean Streets*. Writing from a more sociological than religious perspective, Richard Gambino finds this film to exemplify the 'dilemma' of young, third-generation Italian Americans in the 1960s and 1970s, trapped in a sort of no-man's land between the ethnic neighbourhood and the daunting challenges of assimilation. Lynn Garafola contextualizes Scorsese's Italian American films by summarizing the social struggles and progress of Italian Americans from the first or immigrant into Scorsese's own third generation.[1]

Nonetheless, there are limitations to all of this criticism and scholarship. No one has ventured a systematic reading of Scorsese's Italian American films both individually and as a whole, fully assessing their ethnic and religious themes and analysing their relation to the social history of the ethnic group. Nor have critics done justice to a crucial element in these films that remains fundamentally apart from Scorsese's Catholicism, namely the Italian American mob. The problem is that most scholars lack knowledge and understanding of this criminal subculture – not only its history, signs, and practices, but the ways in which these shape, enrich, and deepen Scorsese's portrayal of it in his films.

There can be no real comprehension of Scorsese without conjoining the two seemingly incommensurable realms, and the two seemingly irreconcilable components of his sensibility, to which the title of this book alludes: Gangster Priest.

While most would agree that Catholicism has played a central role in southern Italy and Italian America, if only in a folkish and unofficial form, they would be equally likely to argue that the Mafia constitutes a highly anomalous deformation of southern Italian and Italian American life, so that the claims of Scorsese's films to be ethnically representative are gravely weakened by the prominence of the Mafia within them. Yet just as Goethe in his *Italian Journey* says of Sicily that it provides the 'key' to Italy as a whole – by which he apparently means that Italy is an essentially Mediterranean (as opposed to northern European) country whose Mediterranean essence appears most forcefully in Sicily and then in weakened degrees on up the peninsula – so it is arguable that, in similar fashion, the Mafia is the key to southern Italy and Italian America, in that it represents an extreme manifestation of many attitudes and behaviours found in both societies.[2] This is not to say that Italian America is even remotely equivalent to the Mafia. Rather, the choice of the Mafia as subject has enabled an highly imaginative artist like Scorsese to dramatize the qualities and conflicts within his own group with maximum intensity.

Other critics of Scorsese's Italian American films either ignore, underestimate, or misread their ethnic context. Despite its insights, Lesley Stern's *The Scorsese Connection* neither connects the man to his ethnic background nor relates that background to his films. Both Leighton Grist and Lawrence S. Friedman discuss some aspects of Scorsese's ethnicity but fail to give it the emphasis it deserves. Although Mark Nicholls focuses on the mob and to a lesser extent Italian America, he frequently misconstrues both the Mafia and ethnicity. Commenting on Scorsese, Peter Brunette resorts to ethnic stereotypes: 'And as with many working-class Italians, in this country as well as in Italy, Catholicism is also inextricably mixed with the Mafia.'[3] The gross exaggeration and bland assurance of this statement are as breathtaking as its prejudicial ignorance, offensive to any Italian American or Italian (or, for that matter, Catholic) who reads it. Brunette has perpetrated a casual yet serious ethnic slur, linking without evidence a large proportion of Italian Americans and Italians to the Mafia. Yet as Gambino, Ben Lawton, and others have shown, Italian Americans are among the most law-abiding American citizens, according to crime statistics, while the number of Italian American gangsters constitutes less than .03 per cent of the group's population.⁴ Brunette further implies, again without evidence, an intimate connection between Italian American religiosity and Italian American crime. Much in the same vein of smug certitude combined with limited acquaintance with Italian American culture are Pauline Kael's remarks in her 1973 review of *Mean Streets*: 'The zinger [*sic*] ... is the way it gets at the psychological connections between Italian Catholicism and crime, between sin and crime.' She goes on: 'Some editorial writers like to pretend ... [that] there is no basis for the popular ethnic stereotypes – as if crime among Italians didn't have a different tone from among Irish or Jews or Blacks ... But all crime is not alike, and different ethnic groups have different styles of lawlessness.'⁵ To be sure, just as insuperable differences exist between Catholicism and the Italian American criminal ethos, so there are 'psychological' and other links between them, at once subtle and complex. Yet Kael does not specify what these links might be, or how and where they appear in the behaviour of Italian American criminals, or how they can be aesthetically valuable.

An often perceptive interpreter of Scorsese, Robert Philip Kolker believes that his films, including those portraying Italian America, de- pict a world without grace and sanctity – a conclusion at odds with their Catholic immanentism and analogism. According to Lourdeaux, religious grief, penitence, and masochism in Scorsese's Italian Ameri can films reflect his early exposure to a stern, ascetic, and guilt-inducing Irish Catholicism. What Lourdeaux fails to account for is the powerfully masochistic and penitential strain in some versions of Italian American Catholicism, which was carried over from southern Italy, and whose influence upon Scorsese probably equals that of the Irish nuns who taught him in grammar school. Perhaps the most frequent error in the interpretation of Scorsese's ethnicity is that of critics who discern in his Italian American films and more particularly *Raging Bull* a theme of repressed homosexuality. This argument, the most extreme form of which is represented by Robin Wood, reflects a failure to comprehend the difference between homoerotic behaviour and the merely homophilic type characteristic of southern Italian and other versions of Mediterra- nean culture. Finally, Michael Bliss typifies what might be called the anti-Catholic reading of Scorsese, which takes it for granted that Ca- tholicism, and specifically the Italian American variety, is a repressive, life-denying, psychologically retrograde religion imbued with an ar- chaic sexual morality, and that Scorsese's Italian American films, whether

consciously or unconsciously, are dedicated to the exposure of this
pernicious belief system and its traumatizing effect upon the youth of
Italian America.[6]

In general, Scorsese's films have failed to win the admiration of older
Italian American critics, no doubt because they fear that his interest in
the mob must reflect badly upon the group.[7] They apparently assume
that, in the eyes of the public, the portrayal of Italian American gangsters by an Italian American director must give the impression of
authenticated insider information, and thus provide further false justification for the most pernicious ethnic stereotypes.[8] Such fears are understandable, as the older critics have suffered more than their
younger counterparts from the blind prejudice raised by the Mafia. Yet
it also seems to be difficult for them to admit that the gallery of knaves,
low-lifes, and hit-men who populate Scorsese's films really forms the
stuff of worthy art. In those rare instances in which critics of the older
generation have acknowledged Scorsese's Italian American films rather
than bestowing upon them what Dr. Johnson termed the 'superiority of
inattention,' they have tended to show annoyance. To speak from personal experience, I can recall a meeting of the American Italian Historical Association in the mid-1980s in which a second-generation Italian
American scholar rebuked me for raising questions regarding the moral
and spiritual qualities of the boxer Jake La Motta, the scholar's boyhood hero and the main character of Scorsese's *Raging Bull*. Philip V.
Cannistraro writes that since the 1920s, 'Hollywood has sold audiences
the image of the Italian American gangster, most powerfully through
the work of ... Francis Ford Coppola and Martin Scorsese.'[9] Cannistraro
seems to imply that Scorsese is no more than a Hollywood sensational-
ist, selfishly trafficking in injurious ethnic cliches, rather than an artist
of integrity. An example of the older generation's failure to appreciate
Scorsese appears in Jerre Mangione and Ben Morreale's *La Storia*, sometimes regarded as a standard record of the immigrant and later generations. *GoodFellas*, they say, 'draws closer to the Mafia cliches the public
has become accustomed to: the Italian gangster who loves to cook (fat
sausages, veal cutlets)' and 'boring violence' irrelevant to the 'human
condition.' Then, with extraordinary condescension, they add that 'such
violence covers an anger within Scorsese that he has not yet learned to
understand' – as if they grasped the psychology of violence better than
does the director of *Raging Bull*, *GoodFellas*, and *Casino*.[10]

Such attitudes are by no means confined to scholars and critics but
typify the response of many Italian Americans at the present time. This

is evident from the vociferous opposition by the Order of the Sons of Italy to the recent announcement by Italian prime minister Silvio Berlusconi that Scorsese and Robert DeNiro were to receive honorary Italian citizenship in recognition of their contributions to world cinema. Although the furore in the press was directed chiefly at the bestowal of the award upon DeNiro rather than Scorsese, what most angered the protesters was the image of Italian Americans rendered by DeNiro in several of Scorsese's best-known films: *Raging Bull*, whose subject is the sadomasochistic boxer Jake La Motta; *Mean Streets* and *GoodFellas*, in which DeNiro plays Italian and Italian-Irish hoodlums respectively; and *Casino*, whose main character, though Jewish, has the most intimate ties with the Mafia in Las Vegas. Yet it would be a mistake to think that these films have failed to elicit annoyance in some younger Italian American critics as well. That is the tone of Luisa del Giudice's remark to her Italian American readers that they need to visit Italy, which will 'contribute richness to a cultural identity far beyond the abilities of a *Mean Streets* or *Goodfellas*.'[11] Although no one will want to compare such films to the masterpieces of Michelangelo or Donatello, del Giudice has needlessly insulted two of the finest works of art produced by an Italian American since the days of immigration. Another younger critic, Frank P. Tomasulo, complains that Scorsese presents to the 'entire world ... unflattering self-portraits' of Italian American ethnicity that are all the more damaging in that they carry the 'cachet of insider knowledge and legitimacy.' Apparently Scorsese should have presented ennobling images of his group.[12]

The following pages offer a comprehensive reading of Scorsese's Italian American films both in themselves, as coherent, individual works of art, and as an unfolding and internally consistent whole. These works must remain imperfectly understood unless the depth and variety of the Italian American ethnic background is brought to bear upon the films themselves, including a knowledge of the immigrant generations that have had a lasting impact upon Scorsese. One also needs to elucidate the 'anthropology' or 'sociology' of the mob that these films intentionally provide. This in turn necessitates a throrough examination of the Mediterranean and more particularly southern Italian ideal of masculine honour upon which the code of the Sicilian as well as the Italian American Mafioso ultimately rests. I concur with Fred Gardaphe on the need for a 'culture-specific' criticism, and propose to read Scorsese's Italian American films in terms of the 'Italian American signs' of which they are composed, as the basis for further comprehension.[13] Yet far from treating Italian America simply as local colour, as a pretext for personal nostalgia, or as the object of merely anthropological or ethnological interest, these films contain Scorsese's increasingly mature evaluation of his own ethnic group, which he views both sympathetically and critically. The force and seriousness of his criticism will become evident over the course of this study.

However much Scorsese's Italian American films are embedded within their ethnic milieu, he endows them with an interest and significance transcending their comparatively parochial origins. He has achieved this partly through his Catholicism, situating his characters and narratives within the moral context of a universal religion. His absorption in the subject of Italian American gangsters and boxers, of which his critics complain, is no mere product of a perverse craving for melodrama or excess, or an attempt to magnify his personal recollections of a boyhood spent in an ethnic neighbourhood among aspiring toughs and hoodlums. What Scorsese has attempted in these Italian American films, with the mob as his chief example, is a general statement on the psychology and sociology of violence, and specifically its relationship to the sacred. A non-practising Catholic but a Catholic nonetheless, he has always been concerned with the central religious problem of violence, sometimes extolling bloody redemptive sacrifice and sometimes absolute religious pacifism. Few artists are as aware as Scorsese of the role of violence not only in creating order and sanctity, but in undermining them through acts of provocation and transgression. In more recent statements he implies that the only permanent antidote to the apparently endless cycles of human violence lies in the imitation of Christ as the absolute model of non-retaliation. His portrayal of the southern Italian code of masculine honour, whose essence lies in pride and retaliatory violence, thus exposes its long-standing opposition to Christianity.[14] This conflict is at the heart of Scorsese's Italian American films.

Acknowledgments

This book is the product of many years of thinking about Martin Scorsese and Italian America both in themselves and in their unbroken connection. It also reflects my continuing concern for questions of ethnicity and national identity, whose relevance has only increased over the last several decades in a climate of multiculturalism and globalization. And, finally, *Gangster Priest* represents the first of an in-progress two-volume study of the films of Martin Scorsese, the second volume being intended to treat those of his films that focus on subjects outside Italian America.

In a sense this book originated in my discovery of Scorsese's *Mean Streets* when, in the summer of 1974, and amid a neighbourhood as rough as that in the film, I found it in a run-down and virtually empty Boston moviehouse. From that moment I realized that Scorsese's presence in American cinema could not be ignored. His was a talent that, as I watched it develop over the next several decades, proved to be at once various, unpredictable, and dazzling, though always returning to Italian America for creative replenishment.

Gangster Priest makes use of materials from several essays that previously appeared in *Italian Americana* and the publications of the American Italian Historical Association. Of great help to me in the writing of this book have been my conversations with numerous scholars and friends, who in not a few instances have invited me to lecture on Scorsese in both the United States and Italy. It is therefore a pleasure for me to be able to thank all those who, in one way or another, have contributed to the making of this book: Carol Bonomo Albright, Massimo Bacigalupo, Casey Nelson Blake, Robert Bock, Mary Jo Bona, Jerome Bongiorno, Michele Bottalico, the late Philip J. Cannistraro, Andrea

Carosso, Giuseppe Castorina, Frank Cavaioli, Simone Cinotto, Maria Vittoria D'Amico, Paul G. Degler, Tony di Nonno, Mary Dulik, Deborah Falik, Joseph Falik, Ferdinando Fasce, Thomas J. Ferraro, Avrom Fleishman, Giovanna Franci, Patrizia Fusella, Fred Gardaphe, Shelagh Geoghegan, Paul Giles, Cristina Giorcelli, Paolo Giordano, Edvige Giunta, Iain Halliday, Brianna Herzog, Anna Camaiti Hostert, Bruce Kawin, Salvatore La Gumina, Elena Lamberti, Catherine Lederman, Valeria Gennaro Lerda, Giuseppe Lombardo, Mario Maffi, Salvatore Marano, Andrea Mariani, Mario Mignone, Mark Crispin Miller, Laura Mullaney, Gigliola Nocera, Maria Parrino, Gordon Poole, Ross Posnock, Jacqueline Reich, Caterina Ricciardi, Simonetta Romagnolo, David Rosen, William Rothman, Ilaria Serra, Giuseppe Sertoli, David Simpson, Federico Siniscalco, Thomas F. Skipper, Maria Galli Stampino, Lydia Starling, Anthony Julian Tamburri, Marylou Tibaldo-Bongiorno, Maurizio Vaudagna, and Robert Viscusi.

Ron Schoeffel, my editor at the University of Toronto Press, has been exacting, clear-headed, and judicious. To my colleague John Paul Russo I owe a special debt of gratitude, as he has helped me to sharpen and clarify my ideas on points too numerous to recall. My daughter Jane, whose enthusiasm for Scorsese equals mine, has watched the unfolding of this project with unfailing interest from start to finish. The thought of being able to present this book to my mother, brother, and Italian American relatives has been a steady source of inspiration in the writing of it. I regret only that my father was not able to see the completion of my book, which he would have greeted with the warmest interest and delight, not only because of his Italian American background, but because of his keen admiration of Scorsese, whose *Mean Streets* he first urged me to see over three decades ago.

GANGSTER PRIEST:
THE ITALIAN AMERICAN CINEMA OF MARTIN SCORSESE

1 The Immigrant Generations:
Italianamerican

Martin Scorsese was born in Flushing, Queens, on 17 November 1942 to Charles and Catherine Scorsese, both Italian Americans of Sicilian immigrant parentage. Martin's paternal grandfather, Francesco Scorsese, was born in Polizzi Generosa, a town near Palermo, around 1880. His mother having died when he was six or seven, Francesco upon his father's remarriage was sent to live with a local farmer who raised him. Unwilling to remain in Sicily, Francesco chose to emigrate to the United States. After his arrival in New York City in 1901, he married a young immigrant woman named Teresa who had arrived in the same year from Polizzi Generosa and had nearly died in passage. The Scorseses took an apartment at 241 Elizabeth Street, on the outer reaches of Manhattan's Little Italy, where Charles Scorsese was born in 1912.[1]

Martin Scorsese's maternal grandfather, Martin Cappa, was an orphan who joined the Italian cavalry after having been raised by a kindhearted family and is said to have cut a handsome and dashing figure on horseback. He and his future wife Domenica immediately fell in love as he rode with his company through her home town of Cimmina. After his marriage Martin sailed to America in search of better conditions for his wife and young daughter Sarah. Within a short time he was so desperate for his wife and children that he insisted they join him. His wife initially refused, terrified of the passage, but was tricked into going by a brother-in-law. Catherine Cappa, Martin Scorsese's mother, was born in New York City in 1913, apparently not long after her family's arrival. At first the Cappas lived on Third Street, but moved to an apartment on the fourth floor of 232 Elizabeth Street, where Fanny Scorsese, the sister of Charles, lived directly beneath them. Their apartment was nearly directly across the street from that of Francesco

Scorsese's family. Martin Cappa made good money for those days as a scaffolder in Springfield, New Jersey, but this required him to spend weekdays away from home; moreover, his income had to go a long way, as there were fourteen people, including boarders and relatives, in the three-room apartment.

During visits to his sister Fanny's apartment Charles Scorsese was noticed by Catherine Cappa, whom he wooed. After he repeatedly serenaded her on his guitar, which she believed him incapable of actually playing, Catherine finally consented to date Charles, a gesture that in Italian American communities of those days definitely pointed towards marriage. Charles had already dropped out of grammar school and was working in the rag trade as a presser. Although business was seasonal, leaving him jobless for several months per year, piecework rates gave him a decent income. Catherine had wanted to go on to high school but was stymied by economic circumstances, and at the age of seventeen was already working as a machinist in the nearby garment industry after having previously found work making dolls' dresses. After a period of courting, Charles and Catherine married on 19 June 1934, the wedding celebration taking place on the roof of the tenement house since the apartment was too small.

The Scorseses settled in at 253 Elizabeth Street, only four doors down from the parental grandmother's residence at 241. In 1936 Martin's brother Frank was born, and by the time of Scorsese's birth in 1942 the family had already moved to Flushing, Queens, settling in with relatives in Corona, an Italian American neighbourhood.[2] Charles Scorsese was in search of more lucrative employment and better housing for his family, and had enabled young Martin to spend his earliest years in a backyard amid sunlight, fresh air, and trees. But because of unspecified business and financial difficulties, Charles and the family had to return to their former address on Elizabeth Street in 1949.[3] Both parents again found work in Manhattan's garment industry. Martin Scorsese was only eight years old at the time of the return, and found himself in an almost entirely Sicilian American neighbourhood – a 'Sicilian village' as he later called it.[4] Here he found his playmates and friends, went to school, received his religious training, and showed the first signs of his cinematic vocation.

Critics have generally been most interested in Scorsese's personal experience of growing up in Little Italy or his directorial interest in contemporary Italian America. One must keep in mind, however, that he is closely linked through his parents and grandparents to the first and second generations of Italian Americans, that is, the immigrants and their children, and that their attitudes, values, and way of life have powerfully influenced him. Nor has Scorsese disavowed or ignored these family and more generally ethnic origins, but interrogates and in a sense rediscovers them in his 1974 documentary *Italianamerican*. The failures and successes of this group's immigrant experience form the essential basis by which to comprehend his ethnicity as it relates to his life and art. In some ways the first- and second-generation members of Scorsese's immigrant family convey a strong individuality, yet in many others they typify their ethnic group.

Italian immigration to the United States was part of a larger, global movement of population from the peninsula. Although relatively few Italian immigrants came to the United States before 1880, the average annual number of immigrants to other countries had risen to 117,596 in the late 1870s.[5] The next thirty-four years, terminating with the start of the First World War, would constitute its peak period. By the early 1890s America had surpassed Europe as the favoured destination of Italian immigrants. According to Richard Alba, two million immigrants arrived in the United States between 1901 and 1910, with 1907 marking the high point, when nearly 300,000 Italians were admitted.[6] For the period between 1907 and 1916 the total is 1,892,155. From 1900 to 1914 somewhere between 20 and 30 per cent of immigrants to the United States were Italians.[7] Overall, approximately 5.7 million Italians have immigrated to the United States since 1820, with the peak period of 1880–1920 accounting for roughly four million of the total. The tide would have continued had not the Immigration Act of 1924, passed amid a nativist furor against southern and eastern European 'invasion,' legally blocked immigration from southern Europe.[8] In 1900 an enumeration found that 484,000 persons of Italian birth were living in the United States; in 1910 the figure had risen to 1,343,125, making up 10 per cent of the foreign population of that country; if one includes American-born children, the number of Italians had reached 2,098,360. Ten years later the number of Italian-born was somewhat over 1.6 million, rising to 1,790,000 in 1930.[9]

The great increase of Italian migration around the turn of the century was largely the result of the severe economic crisis in many regions of Italy in the decades after 1870. Although northern Italy experienced hardship, causing many northerners to emigrate, the fact that southern Italians made up about 80 per cent of Italian immigrants to the United

States reflects the extraordinary miseries of the ill-favoured, underdeveloped, and overpopulated Mezzogiorno, which includes southern Italy and Sicily.[10] Nowhere were its miseries more acutely felt than in the agrarian sector, among the peasants or *contadini*. Contrary to its reputation for fertility, southern Italy is ill suited for agriculture, as it is formed largely of rugged mountains and contains relatively little good arable land. The summers are ferociously hot, and the heaviest rainfall occurs in winter, when it is least needed. Moreover, the deforested hillsides are incapable of retaining water, with their erosion resulting in malarial pools in the obstructed river valleys.[11] For reasons of defence but also to avoid the insect-ridden lowlands, the peasants typically congregate in densely populated hilltop 'agrotowns' from which family members descend daily to work on plots of land distant from home.[12]

Although feudalism had been officially abolished in southern Italy in the early 1800s, and although ecclesiastical holdings were put up for sale by the national state after the 1861 unification, hopes for land redistribution were thwarted by the fact that most peasants were too poor to buy their own shares. A disproportionate amount of land came to be owned by rich absentee landlords, who felt little incentive to improve their holdings or to farm them intensively. Instead, they assigned their supervision to managers whom they employed to collect rents from impoverished tenant farmers and sharecroppers. Many peasants settled on small plots of land with short-term leases that encouraged the overexploitation rather than improvement of properties.[13] Tenants' rents were often fixed and, owing to their inelasticity, sometimes proved impossible to pay; usury was widespread. It was no help to the peasants that their methods of cultivation were hopelessly antiquated.[14] As there was little agricultural surplus from these ill-cultivated lands, the peasantry remained close to starvation. Because of partible inheritance, even those few peasants who owned land lacked sufficient amounts to rise above the subsistence level, and furthermore holdings were often divided into small, inconveniently separated lots.[15] Peasants did not receive the right to vote until the early 1900s.[16]

The southern Italian economy deteriorated industrially and agriculturally after 1870. The abandonment of protectionist policies following Italian unification proved the inability of the underdeveloped southern Italian industries to compete with their more developed rivals in northern Italy and abroad. Southern Italy was thus flooded with cheap industrial manufactures.[17] In the late nineteenth century southern Italian agriculture, including Sicilian wheat production, declined sharply in the face of challenges from the economically and technologically more advanced North Atlantic world. The lemon and orange growers of Calabria, Basilicata, and Sicily could not compete with California and Florida. As the landlords sought to expand at the peasants' expense, many villagers became wage labourers.[18] To help fledgling northern Italian industries, the government adopted protectionism in the early 1880s, but so far as Italian agriculture was concerned, this only caused other countries – most significantly France – to raise their own trade barriers, so that southern Italian export goods dammed up, barred from international markets. The southern Italian wine trade went into a tailspin. The new protectionist policies led as well to a decline in the conditions of the peasantry, as the tariff on wheat and new milling techniques caused big landowners to encroach increasingly upon peasants' land.[19] In addition to a high public debt, the considerable expense of the national government's upkeep and of the misguided foreign ventures into which it was being led by nationalistic vanity caused it to impose unusually high taxes upon the Mezzogiorno, in a proportion far above its contribution to national wealth. Ironically, the tax increase coincided with the depression of southern Italian agriculture in the 1880s and 1890s.[20] During the last decades of the nineteenth century the traditional but technologically outmoded Sicilian sulphur industry succumbed to foreign competition, even as the attempt of Sicilian peasants to form *fasci* or labour unions met with government repression. By this point the southern Italian economy was incapable of absorbing the Mezzogiorno's overpopulation.[21] The peasants were fully aware of the absence of industry in the Mezzogiorno and, despairing of reform, sought their fortunes elsewhere. However, they derived typically not from the very lowest social strata, the *giornalieri* or day labourers, but from small landowners, who could pay for the passage and set themselves up abroad.[22]

Notwithstanding that most southern Italian immigrants were landless peasants, they included some artisans and skilled workers such as masons, carpenters, miners, bakers, blacksmiths, shoemakers, and barbers. There were also traders and entrepreneurs and a small percentage of professional people such as doctors, lawyers, accountants, pharmacists, and teachers.[23] The immigrants represented all of southern Italy, but of the mainland regions Campania (Naples), Abruzzi, Molise, and Calabria were strongly represented, while Sicilians formed the largest group, over a quarter of the whole.[24] Yet whatever their class, local origin, or economic condition, a very high percentage were young working-age males who planned to rejoin their families in Italy after taking the quickest possible advantage of the higher wages and employment opportunities in the United States, at least during boom periods.

Many of these immigrants were bachelors, but a considerable number were married men separated from their families. The majority appear to have been peasants whose goal was to work in American industry until they had accumulated enough capital to invest in land at home. While they worked in America these immigrants typically sent money home to their families. There were nuclear families among them, although these were rare. Some immigrants, the so-called birds of passage, criss-crossed the Atlantic several times, alternating between visits to the home country and bouts of work and cash acquisition. Of every five Italians who emigrated between 1892 and 1896, two returned; the percentage fell off over the next five years but rose to a high level between 1902 and 1916. Of the four and a half million Italians who arrived on American soil between 1880 and 1924, fewer than half remained. According to Lopreato, 1,215,998 immigrants repatriated between 1908 and 1916. The high ratio of males to females persisted into the 1930s. In not a few cases repatriation was necessitated by economic failure.[25] Despite these repatriations, there was much re-emigration to the United States, and many immigrants came or chose to settle on American soil. Over the long run bachelors and birds-of-passage yielded to a more family-oriented movement exemplifying what ethnologists term 'chain-migration.' By around 1900 many Italian males were either marrying fellow Italians in the United States or, in the case of men already married, summoning Italian wives and children to join them in the host country, where they resettled. An additional link in the chain was provided when transplanted individuals and families invited friends and relatives to join them in the the United States.[26] For these latecomers, the difficulties of settlement were eased by the help and knowledgeable advice offered them by their predecessors, with whom they often moved in temporarily or for a longer term. For pre-established households, the advantage lay in the formation of closer kinship ties and reassuring contacts within the emerging ethnic neighbourhood.

Although one might expect southern Italian immigrants, with their largely peasant origins, to have settled in the agrarian countryside, they tended to establish themselves primarily in urban areas of the Northeast. This occurred not only because previous immigrants had occupied much of the nation's farmland, but because many Italians were too poor to acquire lands that often had the disadvantage of being at a costly distance from their place of arrival.[27] Nor were the Italians, having left an agrarian culture of *miseria*, inclined to sentimentalize farming. Contrastingly, the expanding American urban and industrial centres promised a wide variety of quickly available jobs paying what the immmigrant saw as good wages.[28] These wages were by American standards quite low, and forced the immigrants to live in pre-existing slum areas, in which they often replaced the Irish and blacks. In Manhattan's Fourteenth Ward, where Elizabeth Street is located, by 1890 two-thirds of the residents were Italian as against a third Irish; ten years later the Italians had taken it over entirely.[29]

Besides kinship, a key factor in the southern Italian settlement of American cities was *campanilismo*, loyal identification with the community of one's origin, which was typically a small or modest-sized village. Thus a villager was often expected to marry within his or her native community. In some cases he or she also identified, though less so, with the region of origin, which had its distinctive Italian dialect. In short, most southerners did not see themselves as Italians. In attempting to recreate their native villages within the American city, newcomers preferred initially to settle with fellow townspeople or co-regionalists.[30] An Italian neighbourhood populated by residents from every region of southern Italy typically formed an aggregate of village-like subcolonies, with each 'village' concentrated in a particular street or area of a neighbourhood and sometimes even a specific building. Not surprisingly, feuds often broke out between the groups.[31] As Thomas Kessner writes of Manhattan's Little Italy just after 1900: 'Mott Street between East Houston and Prince held the Napoletani; the opposite side of the street was reserved for Basilicati. Around the corner the Sicilians settled Prince Street, while two blocks away the Calabresi lived in Mott between Broome and Grand.' He continues: 'Mulberry Street was strictly Neapolitan, and Hester Street, running perpendicular to Mulberry, carried the local color of Apulia.'[32] Donna Gabaccia likewise remarks the impulse to social fragmentation in that part of Manhattan's Little Italy where Martin Scorsese's family settled. The settlement of Palermitans in Little Italy is determinable by the number of households with members named Rosalia, after the patron saint of Palermo, and is concentrated on Elizabeth Street between Prince and East Houston and around the corner between Mott and Elizabeth. Whereas Sicilians from the Sciacca region, in the southwestern part of the island, settled in lower and middle Elizabeth Street, those from the Palermo area congregated in its northern blocks. The latter territory includes the residence of the Scorseses, who came to the United States from near Palermo.[33] Many immigrants from Sciacca were named or named their children after their Old World patron, San Calogero, whose feast was celebrated annually in the neighbourhood, and who as late as 1984 continued to be honoured not only with a local feast but with a shrine and office on Elizabeth Street. This office, with its window sign, is visible in an early scene of Scorsese's *Who's That Knocking at My Door?*, which was shot from his grandmother's apartment on Elizabeth Street, and which shows the characters J.R. and Joey as they walk along its sidewalk.

One should not exaggerate *campanilismo* or regional loyalty, or imply that the Italian neighbourhoods remained static, as is often assumed. Circumstances often prevented Italian immigrants from living with their former co-villagers or co-regionalists, and such loyalties could only diminish through de-ethnicization and Americanization. Because of the constant influx of new immigrants up to 1924, the make-up of the neighbourhoods was constantly changing. Research of recent decades discloses that, contrary to expectations, Italian immigrant families even of the early period were surprisingly mobile geographically, not only out of a desire to improve their material conditions but because of an equally surprising occupational mobility upward on the social scale.[34]

Yet being of peasant origin, most Italian immigrants of the earliest period arrived in the United States without the skills required in an industrial society and inevitably found themselves working long hours as low-paid labourers. This was especially true of those Italians who intended to repatriate. Above 80 per cent of the immigrants had to take unskilled jobs, while three out of four Italians were manual labourers.[35] Crispino estimates that a full third of Italian males in 1900 worked as general labourers, digging canals and sewer lines, laying railroad tracks, mining coal, and working menially in steel plants and meat-packing houses. Italians also frequently worked as longshoremen, bootblacks, street-sweepers, ragmen, junkmen, hod-carriers, street-pavers, tunnel-diggers, and drainers of swamps.[36] A very much smaller percentage of better-educated Italians retained their former professions as doctors, lawyers, engineers, teachers, actors, musicians, and priests. These people usually settled in Italian neighbourhoods where the possibility of work was greater than elsewhere. Some immigrants earned their living in low-level white-collar entrepreneurial jobs as undertakers, traders, dealers, hucksters, and pedlars of groceries, wines, liquors, and other commodities. In 1905 in New York City, 18 per cent of Italian workers fit this category. The immigrants included a relatively low proportion of skilled labourers who became prominent in their respective trades: among them were stonecutters, carpenters, mechanics, mariners, fishermen, masons, tile-setters, barbers, shoemakers, shoe repairers, cooks, lumbermen, and small manufacturers such as candymakers, tailors, dressmakers, and seamstresses.[37] A small number of Italian men rose to become skilled blue-collar and even white-collar workers, including successful manufacturers, bankers, merchants, and businessmen.[38] Not only was there substantial Italian representation in the garment industry in both New York and Chicago, but by around 1910 these employees included a fair percentage of women who had entered the sweatshops at low rates of pay in order to provide an indispensable supplement to their meagre family income. Since southern Italian husbands greatly feared spousal infidelity, they allowed their wives to work outside the home only because female employees in the garment industry laboured in the company not of men but of other women. Italian women soon became the single largest group in the garment trades, where they worked as tailors, seamstresses, and dressmakers. Outside the domestic setting women also made lace, candy, paper, pins, plumes, tobacco products, cheap jewellery, and other items. At least in the first decade of the twentieth century, however, wives and daughters preferred to finish clothing at home, or else earned small sums making artificial flowers, which was their specialty.[39]

Again to consider Elizabeth Street, Donna Gabaccia writes that in 1905 a large percentage of its Sicilian male residents performed unskilled work, and that of these, three-quarters dug tunnels, excavated subway passages, worked in construction or on the docks, or shined shoes. A third of the male workers were artisans, while others were small-scale entrepreneurs, working as pushcart vendors of fruit and vegetables. A relatively small but important component of the male workforce was concentrated in the nearby garment industry, where the men were employed as pressers, cutters, or independent tailors; the pay was relatively good even if jobs were available for only ten or eleven months of the year. Within a few decades Charles Scorsese, Martin's father, would be earning respectable wages as a presser in the same seasonal rhythm. Yet what is perhaps most notable about employment patterns on Elizabeth Street is that, contrary to Sicilian rural tradition, which limited women to the domestic sphere, some local women took jobs as factory operatives, especially in the garment industry. In other cases, in which jealous Sicilian husbands feared to allow wives to work at non-domestic jobs, they permitted them and their daughters to supplement the family income by working at home, where they finished garments at piecework rates for local factories. Two decades later, in 1925, the occupational distribution on Elizabeth Street was much the same, the southern blocks consisting of immigrants from the Sciacca region forming a concentration of dockworkers and fishpedlars, and the northern ones – where the Scorseses resided – showing among the Palermitans a concentration of day labourers, building trades, and artisans.[40] Although homework gradually declined, the persistent occupational connection between the neighbourhood and the garment industry is reflected in the fact that, as Scorsese's father pressed haute couture gowns, so his mother became a seamstress after having been taught by her mother to sew piecework at home.

Most Italian immigrants lived in multifamily walk-up slum tenements, whose low rents were all they could afford, and were preferably located close to the workplace. These buildings were usually five to six storeys high and occupied the whole of the property save for a narrow strip at the back, where toilet pits or, at best, covered toilets could be found.[41] Consisting normally of railroad flats or dumbbell-shaped tenements, the buildings were quite close together and often had narrow airshafts as substitutes for courtyards. The residents were densely packed into small rooms affording little light and air, especially on the apartment interior.[42] Nearly a quarter of Italian households in Manhattan occupied two-rooms each, and nearly three-eighths, three rooms; in the case of Italians engaged in mining and manufacturing, each sleeping room held 2.62 persons. In a typical two-room flat, one room served as a kitchen, dining room, and general living room and the other as a bedroom.[43] Not only were the tenements cold and dirty, especially the hallways, but they normally had no bathtubs, and the water supply – including hot water – was generally deficient; often the only heat was provided by the kitchen stove, and it was not unusual for residents to sleep in kitchens. During the heat of the summer they slept on fire escapes. Under such conditions one out of nine children died before the age of five. As most tenements could hold from ten to thirty families, Foerster justly likens the Italian settlements to anthills or beehives. For the sake of a modest contribution many families took in boarders, usually relatives or friends from the native village. Although this practice had begun to decline not long after the beginning of the century, it continued beyond the period of immigration.[44] For playgrounds children had only the streets, congested with crowds and pushcart-pedlars.

The Italians were prepared to adapt to the American slum, whose population density somewhat resembled that of the agrotown. In New York in 1910 there was little residential mobility, with over forty thousand Italians living in a seventeen-block area. Yet many other Italian colonies were in constant flux, owing to the steady supply of new immigrants and residential mobility from neighbourhood to neighbourhood. They were in search of better or cheaper housing, of nicer, less congested neighbourhoods, or of higher-paying or more conveniently located jobs. Nonetheless, most transplantations involved the exchange of one Italian American working-class neighbourhood for another.[45]

The housing situation on Elizabeth Street seems fairly typical of Italian American immigrant experience in urban neighbourhoods. As Gabaccia notes, there had been considerable residential dissatisfaction among the residents of the Sicilian agrotowns, who, besides enduring the high population density of the towns themselves, usually lived with few amenities in restricted, crowded, and cramped quarters, often among farm animals. Nor were initial housing conditions on Elizabeth Street much better than those of Sicily. By 1905 the New York census recorded 8,200 immigrants packed into its tenements. Around the turn of the century the street had various kinds of tenements, including the old-style barracks type, which was entered through the kitchen, where the toilet was often located. These cramped apartments were dark and airless, as they had few windows. Some apartments lacked running water, while toilets often consisted of pits in the back yard. The new housing law of 1901 required landlords to construct vents and to insert internal windows in the barracks apartments, as well as to replace the toilet yard-pits with sanitary toilet facilities; they were also required to introduce fire escapes. Even with these reforms, not a single apartment on Elizabeth Street had a bath. A further drawback was that these apartments were often located amid stores, shops, manufacturing establishments, and other places of work. By 1915 many factories had moved out, and the number of apartments increased.[46]

Although most nuclear families on Elizabeth Street would have preferred to lodge within their own homes, their low purchasing power forced them into paying rents that, though cheap by New York standards, were costly for these low-wage earners. This helps to explain the flexible and economical use of space in their apartments, in which two and sometimes three families lived in the so-called partner household. Such arrangements almost entirely disappeared by 1915. A more popular and durable method by which nuclear families met their high rents was by taking in boarding relatives who shared expenses and normally ate with the members of the nuclear family – an important step in the development of extended kinship ties on American soil. Rental costs were also met by taking in mostly male boarders, a system lasting at least into the 1920s. Yet already in the previous decade high rents and increasingly crowded conditions resulting from the increasing size of families had led many residents to look elsewhere for better housing – not home ownership, which remained largely beyond their reach, but larger apartments, often in the boroughs. The goal was often to move closer to the workplace, for instance the garment district, which had moved uptown. Those who remained on Elizabeth Street enjoyed better sinks, toilets, and general hygiene than previously, but still complained about their living conditions. They knew nonetheless that their rents were comparatively cheap and that neighbourhood social life was warmer and more satisfying than that of the agrotown.[47]

What enabled most Italian immigrants to endure their entry into an alien social and cultural environment was the southern Italian family, which they brought with them from Italy and which long retained its structure on American soil despite important modifications. Because of political and social oppression in southern Italy, and also because of the pervasive atmosphere of rivalry and distrust arising from the lack of a real community, the family rather than the individual has been been what Richard Alba calls the 'basic social atom' and 'only social unit' in southern Italian life, the individual's chief protection against a hostile world. Or as Francis A.J. Ianni puts it, Italy is a 'nation of families,' while in the south 'the family *is* the social structure.'[48]

In southern Italy, including Sicily, the family is identified with two groups: the procreative nuclear family, known as the *casa*, consisting of blood kin; and the extended family, or *famiglia*, which includes all nearest blood relations and in-relations – the so-called *parenti* – to the third and fourth degree. The family thus forms an inclusive social world, and in some cases consists of several households in the same town. At least as a cultural ideal, the nuclear family is seen as linked to the *parenti* through love and obligation, and the groups are expected to help each other out in hard times. Nor has the typical nuclear family been in a position to ignore relatives, as it has lacked self-sufficiency and therefore has in some instances needed their aid.[49] Besides relatives, southern Italian society has supplemented the nuclear family through the Latin tradition of fictional parentship known as *compareggio*, which is centred on the *compare* or *comare* (godfather or godmother). A godparent should set a worthy example for the godchild as well as show concern for his or her development, yet though some scholars stress the seriousness of the ties established by *compareggio*, others hold that it is usually sufficient for the godparent to take a friendly interest. Godparents are sometimes chosen from among the brothers and sisters of a baby's parents, although they also derive from outside the family, in which case godparenthood implies a permanent spiritual connection as strong as kinship.[50]

This is not to say that the southern Italian family has necessarily met its members' ideal expectations. For the impoverished working classes the extended family would consist ideally of all blood relations and other relatives up to the fourth degree living under the same roof and engaged in a common economic pursuit. But though many southern Italians have desired families of the extended type, with all their mutual helpfulness and protection, and though Leonard Covello believes such families to have flourished around 1900, they have proved difficult to achieve in the Mezzogiorno.[51] The problem has been that as a result of divided inheritances the land plots have been too small, scattered, and unyielding to allow for a large familial residence, but rather have required nuclear families to live apart, without much cooperation. Nor could a farm labourer on a short-term lease survive save in a nuclear family household. Therefore the marital unit typically resides under its own roof.[52] Another problem has been the poverty of the peasant families, which has impaired the reciprocal gift-giving, hospitality, and entertaining upon which extended family life depends. Another difficulty is that the general scarcity of land and money in the Italian south tends to make relatives suspicious and rivalrous of each other rather than cooperative, and leads the individual to concentrate on improving his own fortunes and those of immediate kin, whom he can trust, and even to prefer friends or neighbours over relatives. The nuclear rather than the extended family has thus been the main focus of social loyalty and cooperation in the Italian south.[53]

The southern Italian nuclear family is often seen as a patriarchal hierarchy in which the husband and father stands morally, economically, and physically supreme. His authoritarian regime perhaps based ultimately on fear, the husband demands respect and obedience from a wife whose power, in Sicily as in many other regions of southern Italy, is limited by the expectation that she will not work outside the home. Her role is largely to interpret the wishes of her husband. The possibility of divorce hardly enters the mind of either spouse, whose lives are nonetheless pursued in sexually segregated spheres. The father strictly disciplines his children and does not avoid verbal and physical punishment. Since they are to respect and obey him whether at first hand or through their mother, he can count on their uncomplaining performance of their assigned household tasks or extra-domestic jobs. Not only must male children receive their father's permission before any major enterprise but, up to their marriage, which is normally arranged by their parents, they lack all economic independence, as they must contribute their entire earnings to the family store. Until their marriage sons are indispensable economic assets in an essentially adult-centred family.[54]

Yet one should not exaggerate a southern Italian husband's power and influence over a household that is best described as father dominated but mother centred. Far from being totally servile, the wife claims a measure of freedom and authority while enjoying considerable prestige and influence over her husband and children.[55] For instance, she can withdraw her dowry as a protection against a husband's abuses. Family finances are customarily treated as a husband-wife decision, and the wife disposes of the household budget. While her husband is in town or working in the fields, she controls the household and supervises the older daughters and young children of both sexes in domestic as in religious matters. The raising of children is largely left to her.[56] When a daughter-in-law enters the family, she defers to the mother of the house, for the sake of harmony. In the case of all major decisions or dangerous enterprises a mother's children will come to her, rather than their father, in order to receive her blessing. Like Covello, Nelli believes that the respect accorded the maternal figure has made it hard for the husband to be a genuine patriarch. In the view of Mangione and Morreale, the superficially submissive southern Italian wife typically out-talks her only nominally patriarchal husband in a stream of eloquence, wearing him down and manipulating him to the point where she becomes family manager.[57]

As a condition of family loyalty, the individual is seen as subordinate to group interests and needs. He or she is expected to live up to the reputation of the family, defend it if necessary, and avenge offences to its honour – the latter being almost entirely determined by the judgment of the surrounding community. As a wife or unmarried daughter must protect her chastity lest family honour be sullied, so all insults to her sexual reputation impugn the family and must be avenged by its adult males.[58] The worst situation for an individual is to be excluded from one's family for having dishonoured it, for instance by disobeying or criticizing the father or by neglecting one's obligations. Symbolically, this is felt by the outcast as banishment from the family dinner table, where the communal feast prepared by the mother embodies and affirms group solidarity.[59]

Contrary to Oscar Handlin's assumption that immigrant families disintegrated in their encounter with American society, the southern Italian family not only remained structurally intact but, even as it became what Tricarico calls the 'regulating principle of immigrant experience,' flourished as never before.[60] As in southern Italy, the family still defined the basic roles of its members, with the first-generation father retaining, though in a reduced degree, his authority as leader and provider. Yet unlike in Italy, where fathers often worked far from home, in the United States the father-absent household was less frequent. The wife often had to enter the workforce to supplement the family income, whereas in Italy, or at least Sicily, she was likely to have stayed home. Yet she continued to receive the respect of family members for directing the household while wielding unofficial influence behind the scenes. Children were expected to work as soon as possible in order to contribute to the family income. The reputation of families was upheld by their members, sometimes through vendettas but often less dramatically through tidy houses and gardens and a refusal to accept public welfare.[61]

The immigrant family was most sharply distinguished from its Old World predecessor by the development of extended kinship ties as the norm of Italian American life. Not only did related households come to America, but they often followed each other in 'migration chains' and settled in the same neighbourhoods. More established groups customarily helped the new arrivals materially and socially and thus laid the basis for lasting loyalties and obligations. Sometimes nuclear families took on relatives as boarders.[62] In time these nuclear family households established firm links with larger kinship groups and thus strengthened an emerging family-centred network. Unlike Sicily, America witnessed the emergence of 'malleable' households formed increasingly of both *casa* members and *parenti* or relatives. The greater available wealth in the United States, and its superior housing conditions, fostered the hospitality, reciprocal visitation, and gift-giving upon which extended family ties depended and which had exceeded the reach of most southern Italian peasants. Families became larger and their members grew closer on American soil, while the kinship group became the chief reference point in defining a person's identity within the neighbour-hood.[63] As Nelli notes, the ideal of the extended family, which many southern Italians had only dreamed of, approached reality in the immi-grant neighbourhoods of urban America.[64] Ironically, the American stereotype of the 'traditional' Italian American family, supposedly an Old World transplant and typified by extended kin of several genera-tions gathered at a lavish banquet, originates on American soil. Yet the family most often took an intermediate form between the nuclear and the extended type. For whereas the classical extended family functions as an economic and residential unit, the Italian American household was usually nuclear and formed an economic and residential unit in its own right. Surrounding it were relatives with whom visits were fre-quently exchanged and holidays celebrated, but whose nuclear families likewise lived in separate households.[65]

The southern Italian family proved to have serious hindrances, espe-cially within an American context. The most troublesome of these in-cluded persistent Old World attitudes towards literacy and education, attitudes that could only impede the educational and occupational opportunities of the group. The southern Italian peasantry from which the immigrants largely derived had small reason to value education for either itself or its children. Not only were the southern Italian village schools of poor quality, owing to government indifference towards public education, but occupational advancement through education was available almost exclusively to the sons of the rich, who could afford to attend good schools. What was the value of teaching a peasant boy standard Italian when he would spend his life speaking a local dialect?[66] Nor was it customary to promote a child's intellectual curios-ity. Being practical minded, the peasant saw little value in educating a son, let alone a daughter, but put them to work as soon as possible. The peasant furthermore preferred the relative security of the status quo to the risk of change, fearing that to educate a child above the parents' own level would undermine familial hierarchy and solidarity.[67] Around 1900, southern Italy had perhaps the highest illiteracy rate in western Europe. Although it is sometimes wrongly assumed that southern Ital-ian immigrants were overwhelmingly illiterate, it is true that roughly half could neither read nor write.[68]

During the period of settlement some immigrants grasped the value of education as a means of acculturation and occupational advance-ment, while some children defied their parents' attempts to cut short their schooling. But the general parental attitude was that children –

and more especially girls – should abandon school at the legal age of fourteen and take low-level jobs so as to pursue the short-term goal of supporting the family. Frequently the penalty of making such choices was to remain in the working class.[69] As Martin Scorsese's mother recalls in an interview, upon graduating from junior high school she had 'wanted to ... go to high school and become something.' But then her mother told her that family finances made it impossible for her to attend high school: '"You have to go to work."' Mrs. Scorsese comments that there were 'nine children' in the family and 'we all had to help out. So naturally, I looked for work.'[70]

Lacking an ideology of change, most immigrant parents feared the American school as the source of ideas that would Americanize their children and turn them against the family. It was seen as better to maintain familial tradition and loyalty even at the price of remaining at a low occupational level than to betray that tradition by aspiring educationally to a professional career.[71] Thus, the first and to a lesser extent the second immigrant generation acquired a deserved notoriety for lack of appreciation of education. Not a few Italian American parents tolerated and even encouraged truancy.[72] Given the oral and visual bias of the southern Italian culture, immigrant households contained few books, and children received little encouragement to read. Mario Puzo recalls that his mother 'looked on all this reading with a fishy Latin eye. She saw no profit in it.'[73] Writing of second-generation Italian Americans in the 1960s, Carla Bianco noticed much television watching and little reading, as did Herbert Gans among the Boston West Enders.[74] This helps to explain the at best mediocre educational performance for the group over several decades.[75] However, these tendencies began to be reversed in the second generation, especially after the Second World War, as the drop-out rate declined and Italian Americans entered college in greater numbers.[76] Such changing educational attitudes and practices naturally correlated with increased occupational mobility and assimilation.

Another limitation that the southern Italian family brought to the United States was its demand for the exclusive loyalty of its members. Not only has this impeded, if not precluded, other forms of allegiance, whether to the national state or to other voluntary groups and institutions, but it has often limited possibilities for civic involvement and social cooperation within the group as a whole. In southern Italy the importance of the family results in large degree from a weak yet oppressive government that, in failing to protect its people against injustice and exploitation, has never won their respect, trust, or allegiance.[77] As Scorsese remarks of the Sicilian police: 'How could you trust them?'[78] Even as individuals looked to their families as their sole dependable protection against the state, they developed a long-standing hatred for centralized authority, pledging their absolute loyalty not to law but to the family code of honour. The self-reliant and internally cohesive family, besides refusing to cooperate with the government, would take the law into its own hands if necessary.[79] These atomistic conditions would prove to be a fertile breeding ground for the criminal organizations known as Mafia. At the same time, southern Italian society was marked by such intense competition for scarce material and social goods that the tightly knit families found it very difficult to trust or cooperate with each other. The one-sided concentration on the family inhibited social interests, as altruistic acts as well as associations outside the family were discouraged save where self-interest was also involved.[80] In such a climate of general mistrust, there was a weakened sense of communal responsibility or desire to cooperate with non-family members as part of a public or as members of institutions in the long-term pursuit of common civic objectives. In the eyes of the southern Italians, formal organizations and public causes seemed impossibly abstract, universalist, and impersonal, and they found it more reassuring to define their social preferences and affiliations in personalist terms.[81]

It is important to determine the degree to which southern Italians and Italian Americans have been family centred and to what extent this has impeded their participation in a wider communal and national life, with all that it allows for acculturation, assimilation, and occupational mobility. Edward C. Banfield identifies southern Italian social behaviour with an ethos of 'amoral familism,' meaning the inability to engage in cooperative activity apart from the interests of the immediate or nuclear family and for only short-term goals. The amoral familist does not reject all activities that benefit the community, but only those from which he believes he or his family have nothing to gain. Banfield acknowledges that material scarcity, insecure land tenure, and the absence of the extended family have contributed to such attitudes, yet he finds no pathological hatred of the state among the southern Italians he studied, and in any case he sees amoral familism as a cultural and mental phenomenon woven of many causes. Here, he claims, is the deepest explanation for the lack of voluntary action and cooperation, distrust of power, and failure to create organized charities and civic improvement associations that have long plagued southern Italy.[82] Were Banfield's argument valid, southern Italians would be utterly anarchistic in the Hobbesian sense and thus without social morality. His conclusions would also have major implications for the immigrant generations, whose familial attitudes remained close to parental norms.

Banfield's study has found supporters, especially in the decade following its publication. They include Herbert Gans, Nathan Glazer and Daniel Patrick Moynihan, and Joseph Lopreato, for whom amoral familism helps to explain Italian American behaviour. In his 1965 study *The Italian South*, Gustav Schachter cited Banfield on the amoral familism and war of all against all in southern Italy. Writing in 1970, Humbert S. Nelli noted that, were Banfield's thesis correct, it would mean that the Italian American sense of community and ethnic consciousness had arisen not in the Old World but in the United States. Thomas Kessner agrees that the prevailing attitude of the Mezzogiorno has been amoral familism. As late as 1992, Robert D. Putnam used the concept to contrast northern Italian civic culture and its inferior southern counterpart.[83]

Yet even before Banfield's book appeared, Florence Gower Chapman in her study of a Sicilian village had remarked the limited yet 'constant cooperation between individuals in the ordinary business of getting a living.' Not only was this facilitated through the exchange of favours, but villagers cooperated in annual *feste*, or festivals, which required committee work.[84] Writing in 1948, Paul Campisi refers similarly to 'that strong family and community culture which had long been an indispensable part of the Old World peasant family.'[85] Subsequently, Banfield's thesis was criticized by those who agreed with him on the social atomism and familial centredness of southern Italian behaviour but thought he had mistaken its real causes. Other scholars claimed he had misrepresented that behaviour by ignoring counterexamples to his thesis.

Like Frank Ciancian, Sydel Silverman accepts amoral familism as a description of southern Italian life yet locates its origin less in values than in economic and social conditions of poverty, scarcity, and land distribution. Pino Arlacchi's studies of contemporary Calabria show that Banfield's thesis is much too reductive, falsely presuming the existence of an homogenous southern Italy but accurately describing only one among the many types of social structure in the region. In addition to the amoral familism of impoverished peasant holdings, Arlacchi identifies the great estate, the *latifondo* or small peasant holding, heavy industry, family workshops, kinship and market, the classic village *Gemeinschaft*, modern commercial systems, primitive systems of reciprocity, the Mafia, and Prussian-style statism. Henner Hess finds the concept of amoral familism too narrow, as it ignores ritual relationships, friendship, clientelism, bandit groups, and other clique relationships typical of Sicilian society. It also fails to account for the Sicilian's habit of withdrawing into self-help systems, such as clientelistic groups. Contrary to Bondanella's claim that amoral familialism 'certainly describes perfectly' the Mafia, this voluntary and cooperative activity itself contradicts Banfield's thesis.[86]

In a review of Banfield's book, John Davis not only points out the irrationality of joining cooperatives in the small and undifferentiated economies of southern Italy, but notes that the southern Italian individual often interlocks with his or her neighbourhood through patron–client relations and general social estimations of personal honour and prestige. William Muraskin holds that southern Italian peasants have no desire to be amoral familists, but their environment leaves them little choice. In a more local study of southern Italians at carnival time on the island of Pantelleria, Anthony H. Galt acknowledges the normal familial and individualistic atomism of this society, yet sees the carnival as a cooperative event whose participants momentarily transcend social fragmentation. Although Leonard W. Moss locates a 'morsel of truth' in Banfield's argument, he sees no evidence of anarchy at the village level, adding that Banfield had ignored *compareggio*, patron–client relations, trade networks, peer groups, and circles of intimacy among friends. Donna Gabaccia shows that Sicilians have not been familist in their social ideals but have desired ties outside their nuclear families, as witness the word *famiglia*, referring to the lineal group of closest relatives. Nineteenth-century Sicilian proverbs stress the give-and-take among nuclear families, while migration from southern Italy is now seen as an organized social movement in which extended family ties played a key role. Nor did the Sicilians Gabaccia studied lack a desire for friendship.[87]

Nonetheless, in the United States the tendency of many Italian Americans to concentrate upon the interests and activities of their own families is often seen as having limited their participation in the institutions of the larger Italian American society, including the church. Primary family allegiances have also been regarded as an obstacle to occupational mobility and assimilation, which require an ability to associate and cooperate freely with mainstream Americans outside the family and ethnic group, as part of a general public in pursuit of universalistic goals. Even before Banfield had formulated the concept of amoral familism, Leonard Covello had noted the inextricably related positive and negative aspects of the Italian American family, which, though it provided the immigrants with a protective shell and a means of social control and moral regulation, posed a barrier to Americanization.[88] Lydio F. Tomasi holds that the assimilation and acculturation of Italian Americans required them to become individuals in the American sense, sufficiently free from family ties and obligations to be able to interact cooperatively with the larger American society.[89]

Although Herbert Gans found second-generation Italian Americans to have developed ties outside the nuclear family, most notably in the extended family and its peer group, he held Banfield's thesis to be at least partially applicable to the working-class Italian Americans he studied in the late 1950s. He found in them a strong familial centredness and personalism along with a related incapacity to join together for objective or non-personalistic public goals, whether within the peer group, neighbourhood, or wider community. Gans concluded that, at least for this group of Italian Americans, community participation was secondary to participation in a peer group based in the extended family. Italian Americans also had difficulty comprehending or entering into the world beyond their own ethnic community, and had even retained something of the southern Italian familial suspicion of government and law.[90] According to Virginia Yans-McLaughlin, writing in 1979, the Italian Americans of Buffalo were still affected by familism into the 1930s. In 1964 Rudolph Vecoli found amoral individualism to apply to many contemporary Italian Americans. Commenting on less assimilated second-generation Italian Americans, James A. Crispino cited Gans on their lack of social cooperation, distrust of authority, and difficulty in thinking outside the family. For Alba, the kernel of truth in Banfield's flawed argument lay in the Italian Americans' familial-based suspicion of strangers, which remained strong in the early decades of immigration.[91]

The persistence of familist attitudes among the first- and second-generation immigrants does not erase the fact that they developed new forms of familism and sociability extending to the local community and even beyond. Many recently arrived southern Italian immigrants helped to bring other Italians, who were often relatives, to American shores in the heyday of chain migration. The new arrivals in turn found work and housing for kin who would soon make the transatlantic passage. Kinship connections affirmed and solidified in this period, leading the nuclear family to evolve into a more cooperative and communal structure. Immigration was aided by other kinds of networks, not just familial but communal and associational, including labour organizations.[92] Gianfausto Rosoli refers to the 'collective mechanism' linking 'the immigrant with the larger economic and political structures in places of origin and destination.'[93] Like Yans-McLaughlin, Gabaccia finds the immigrants to have expanded their social networks, with the artisans forming voluntary associations on a professional rather than familial basis. Families took in boarders who were not relatives, a practice virtually unknown in the Old Country.[94] The immigrant communities also cooperated in the organization of their annual *feste*.[95] Such activities suggest that Italian Americans were by no means mired in familism, but were creating a sense of ethnic community as the foundation for entry into the mainstream. The question thus arises, to what extent had Italian Americans changed in the transition to the second generation, which is that of Scorsese's parents, and in the midst of which he himself came of age?

Some scholars believe the Italians changed comparatively little for many decades following their arrival. Though, in Gans's view, considerable acculturation into American society occurred between the first and second generations, the basic cultural and social structure, centred in the family, remained largely intact. Indeed, the 'society and culture of the West Enders are quite similar to those of the Southern Italians, past and present.'[96] For Vecoli, the comparative absence of change reflected the tenacity of peasant customs and a defensive withdrawal into family and community.[97] Glazer and Moynihan, however, refer to the rapid Americanization of Italians following immigration. Yans-McLaughlin doubts that Old World culture was imported wholesale into the United States, while Gabaccia stresses the changes experienced by Sicilians after 1910, even referring to a fundamental cultural change. Nelli perhaps occupies a middle position on this issue, as he sees both acculturation and assimilation and a persistence of Old World habits and attitudes.[98]

It is impossible in any case to ignore a crucial change that occurred between the first and second generations, namely the emergence of Italian American ethnicity itself. It is now widely accepted, according to the concept of ethnogenesis, that ethnicity, far from being a fixed attribute or essence of arriving immigrants, has been constructed or 'invented' historically on American soil as a new social form. Rather than being permanent or final, this form is reconstructed from generation to generation, as the ethnic group interacts with and adjusts to the host country.[99] Upon their arrival in the United States, and owing to their lack of national consciousness, the immigrants typically thought of themselves not as Italians but as representatives of a village or region. Yet through their exposure to the host society they came to realize their *italianità* and ultimately their half-conferred, half-chosen identity as Italian Americans, with a newly acquired hybridized culture neither altogether Italian nor altogether American. In responding to novel and challenging experiences, many immigrant groups have also 'invented' traditions so as to establish links to an imagined or idealized historic past – a tendency not uncommon among Italian Americans.[100]

The original form of Italian American ethnicity, especially visible in language and clothing, disappeared quickly in the encounter with the host culture. The Italian American family also underwent significant changes in its composition during the first and second generations, most notably a transformation from the nuclear to the extended type (or rather its approximation), which came to be regarded by Italian Americans as well as by the host culture as a marker of Old World tradition and Italian American identity.[101] The quasi-extended family in turn gave rise to peer groups consisting in many instances of extended family members as a sort of supplement and offshoot of the original nuclear grouping. However, these peer groups retained the fundamental value of loyalty to kin.[102] Less happily, the first-generation family became the scene of major conflicts where immigrant parents, resisting Americanization, were confronted by their Americanizing sons and daughters.[103]

Lacking education and often refusing to learn English, and frequently confined to unskilled working-class jobs, the parent generation tended to hang together in ethnic and familial enclaves while attempting suspiciously to hold mainstream culture at bay.[104] For the parents, the American schools their children were required to attend deprived the family of an economic asset while exposing those children to notions of individual freedom, choice, and self-realization, all of which clashed with the southern Italian idea of the person as an extension of the family.[105] The father's difficulties were compounded by the fact not only that his wages were uncertain, but also that, owing to the entry of his wife and children into the workforce, his domestic authority had become tenuous.[106]

Many second-generation Italian American schoolchildren found their home environment, with its lack of privacy and demand of absolute submission, impossibly claustrophobic. Through their exposure to teachers, non–Italian American playmates and classmates, settlement houses, and media messages, they acquired yearnings for extra-familial independence while being made to feel ashamed of their parents' Old World ways.[107] The capitalist individualism taught in the schools led Italian American children to consider keeping their earnings rather than turning them over to their families. At the same time the schools exposed girls to more liberal notions of feminine behaviour in an environment that, unlike the Old World, was no longer sex-segregated, in which casual dating and a variety of boyfriends were possible, and in which arranged marriages were seen as archaic. Children, especially males, now entertained the idea of dating and perhaps even marrying non-Italians, which many parents regarded as unthinkable and punishable by exclusion.[108] Outside the school and family, boys were forming long-lasting peer groups that provided an escape from parental authority. For young women, working outside the house awakened dreams of financial and sexual independence beyond the imagination of their housebound mothers.[109] Many second-generation children refused to learn Italian and showed hostility or indifference to Italian culture, including cuisine.[110] Yet the father of the family recognized, however dimly, that with their superior command of English and higher degree of acculturation, his children held a distinct advantage over himself.[111] These generational conflicts often came to a head in heated arguments at the family dinner table, the traditional ritualized scene of paternal authority and filial obedience.[112]

Writing in 1943, Irwin L. Child groups the responses of the second to the first generation into three main categories.[113] The most extreme is that of the 'rebel,' who largely abandons the parents' way of life, including their language, culture, and neighbourhood, in order to assimilate within the mainstream society with which he or she identifies. Such individuals are often motivated by a desire to dispose freely of their own earnings. They acknowledge the existence of anti-Italian prejudice but strive to overcome it. Disdaining most things Italian, they would prefer that Italian American ethnicity dissolve into the mainstream, and hold Italian Americans themselves responsible for negative attitudes towards them. Not only do such individuals often change their names and marry non–Italian Americans, but they also value education and frequently become middle-class, white-collar professionals. They form only a minority, approximately one-fourth, of second-generation Italian

Americans, and were relatively rare in the 1930s, although increasing in the post-war period.[114]

The category of the 'apathetic' applies to those second-generation Italian Americans who, though regarding the parental culture as irrelevant to their situation, quietly tolerate it, their complaints remaining at the level of polite disagreement. These individuals see themselves as neither Italian nor American, and do not commit to one or the other identity. They marry Italian women, often locals, reside in their old neighbourhoods, and continue, if only grudgingly, to turn their earnings over to their parents, at least before marriage. Besides maintaining close relationships with their parents, they often live near them. Although apathetic individuals see Americanization as an antidote to anti-Italian prejudice, they ignore the reality of that prejudice or accept it uncomplainingly, as part of a general strategy of avoiding frustration and reducing tension. This category probably includes most of the second generation into the 1930s.[115]

Child's third category is the 'in-group,' consisting of working-class Italian Americans who, though resenting the family as a barrier to Americanization, remain loyal to it. These individuals regard themselves as Italian and, in addition to preferring Italian cuisine, want to speak the language. Even into their adult lives many individuals of this type turn over their earnings to their parents. As they identify with first-generation culture, they choose with little regret to live in the older Italian neighbourhoods alongside parents, relatives, and friends, their preferred associates. This blue-collar community clings to family-based social practices, with a focus on the nuclear family and the family-based peer group. Not only do members of the in-group prefer to marry Italian Americans, but they maintain Old World attitudes towards child-rearing, sexual behaviour, and sex segregation. They also place small value on education and, owing partly to the preservation of a familist and personalist heritage, find political organization and participation difficult. They share a continuing fear and suspicion of outsiders and an insularity so strong that any community member who attempts to enter the middle class is seen as a traitor. Although the in-group acknowledges anti-Italian prejudice, it resents it less than do the rebels, as it lacks the same social and professional aspirations.[116]

The second-generation Italian American family is of special interest, as Scorsese's parents belonged to this category. In general, it appears that familial loyalty and unity survived only through compromise, as the children retained merely a small part of the Old World culture, while the Italian language began to fall into disuse. Yet though the children of first-generation parents rejected many Old World values, attitudes, and behaviours, they retained a family-centred social structure. On the other hand, their generation restructured the Italian American family so as to correspond more closely to the American type – in short, a considerable acculturation was achieved within a basically southern Italian framework.[117] Tomasi refers to the second generation as an overt or conscious patriarchy that disguised the fact that the father's power had decreased and that in some ways the family constituted a hidden matriarchy. Although the mother avoided face-to-face confontations with her husband, the home was her domain and she greatly influenced her children. Yet even if the father was no longer consciously feared or imitated, he continued to be respected.[118] Whereas *compareggio* continued to be practised, the husband and wife differed from the earlier generation in practising birth control, smaller families being the consequence.[119] Within the family individual rights were increasingly recognized so that, though still required to follow rules, children now had the right to live their own lives outside the home. They not only kept their earnings but dated freely and chose their own spouses. Most marriages nonetheless remained within the group, while in some neighbourhoods sex segregation persisted, causing children to complain of suffocation.[120] Like wives, daughters worked outside the home, and there was increasing esteem for education, so that children were much less frequently removed from school at the legal age.[121] Charles Scorsese, who never finished grammar school, typifies this attitude: 'I always looked at the NYU college buildings and I used to say, "I hope some day one of my sons will go there." Sure enough, God granted me that wish.'[122]

By the second generation, according to some accounts, the Italian American family had abandoned most of its cultural traditions save for food and eating habits. For food is closely connected with family and group life and helps to hold a group together with minimum strain. In the acculturation of an ethnic group, cooking skills and preferences last a bit longer than other cultural forms, since they form a part of the group's extrinsic culture and are easiest to retain.[123] Not only did southern Italian cooking acquire major symbolic significance both within and outside the Italian American family, but it underwent some significant modifications through Americanization. As Simone Cinotto notes, the scene of generational conflict was the family dinner table, at which second-generation cultural rebellion was signified by a preference for

American cuisine. As part of the compromise between the generations, children were allowed a substantial increase in their freedom, mobility, choice of friends, and forms of cultural consumption, but with the understanding that they must join the extended family in the ritual of the family dinner, especially on Sundays. Normally prepared by the mother of the major household, the southern Italian fare consumed on these occasions embodied and affirmed a successfully defended familial solidarity. Food signified ethnic identity and the supposed continuity of a cultural tradition. For as Cinotto also shows, it was through these family dinners that the older generation mythified the Italian past, leading its children to conceive of southern Italy, where in reality the nuclear family had prevailed, as the ideal realm of a unified, disciplined, harmonious, and multitudinous extended family that was claimed to have been carried across the sea, but whose ideality could never be recaptured in the United States. Thus emerged the false notion, accepted by many Italian Americans as well as Americans generally, of the supposedly 'traditional' Italian American extended family, which developed largely on American soil in a classic example of what Hobsbawm terms the 'invention of tradition.'[124]

Another questionable assumption regarding Italian American food and eating habits is that the food consumed by this ethnic group is of the 'traditional' or 'original' type, carried over intact from the old country. In reality it too results uniquely from the interplay of southern Italian cooking practices and the special alimentary conditions and possibilities of the host environment. America has produced a hybrid known as Italian American food, a creation that, like the ethnic group, mingles Old World and American elements. To begin with, no 'traditional' or codified southern Italian cuisine exists, but only a wide variety of regional and familial cooking practices. The Mezzogiorno was furthermore an impoverished economy in which the peasant's diet consisted chiefly of home-cooked grain, vegetables, and fruits, with very little meat, fish, wine, and spices. For reasons of economy a housewife often added animal gizzards and other organs to the family fare. Industrialized foods – canned, bottled, or wrapped – were not commonly consumed, and only on feast days did the cuisine approach richness or abundance. All this, however, changed in the United States, where immigrants took advantage of the novelty, variety, and sheer abundance of American foods, especially meat, fish, and eggs. In some cases old staples were unavailable and gave way to American substitutes. As new ingredients were added to traditional recipes, the cuisine became more lavish and rich than ever before, and in some cases new recipes were devised. Families of immigrants from one region even appropriated regional specialties other than their own. And whereas in the Mezzogiorno food had been preserved, prepared, and cooked manually, the Italian American housewife relied increasingly on industrialized forms of food. Companies like La Rosa and Ronzoni, founded by Italian Americans, specialized in such products.[125]

All this confirms Cinotto's point that Italian American cuisine was largely created between the wars from ingredients of American manufacture.[126] As Arthur J. Vidich remarks, the pizza eaten by mainstream Americans is a 'new culinary creation, adapted for the American market and unknown as such in Italy and brandmarked as an American "ethnic" cuisine.' The southern Italian penchant for individuality in culinary preparation also resurfaced in the United States, for as Tricarico notes, 'family cohesion was expressed in the manner in which food was prepared. Certain dishes, especially tomato sauce for pasta, conveyed the sense of family solidarity and singularity,' and 'it was traitorous to like someone else's sauce.'[127] On ordinary occasions, Italian Americans ate American-style foods, often preparing them with Italian spices and accompanying them with Italian side dishes.[128]

The question arises whether, from the first to the second generation, the Italian American family developed a sense not simply of ethnic consciousness, but of ethnic community transcending kin and household. It also needs to be determined to what extent, during this period, Italian Americans transcended their restrictive ethnic designation through assimilation into American society. Such an achievement would require a high degree of acculturation as well as considerable occupational, residential, and social mobility.

If the formation of quasi-extended families indicates a capacity and willingness to widen the boundaries of the nuclear type, the formation of a specifically Italian group consciousness was hindered by the immigrants' tendency to settle among *paesani*, people from the same villages or regions, which could only reinforce the insular, anti-cooperative tendencies brought from the Mezzogiorno.[129] However, the influence of these older patterns was weakened by the fact that most immigrants found themselves amid a fluctuant population of Italians from other villages and regions. Frequently their neighbours included people of other nationalities, as few neighbourhoods were over 50 per cent Italian. Not only was it impossible to live alongside 'strangers' without some amity and cooperation, but the immigrants came to realize that, whatever their local and regional differences, mainstream society regarded them collectively as Italian – a crucial moment in the formation of ethnic consciousness.[130] Already in this period Italians from different regions and villages were attending the same schools as well as intermarrying. Also contributing to the new consciousness was the establishment of national parishes for Italian Catholic worshipers.[131]

Gradually the immigrants recognized that the family, and the patterns of isolated group life typical of the Old Country, failed to meet all their needs in the new and complex American environment. In order to survive they could either depend on the favours of the ward bosses and initiatives of the settlement house workers, or, without eliminating the family-centred society, join with their now-acknowledged fellow Italians in the creation of community institutions.[132] Whereas in southern Italy mutual aid societies had appeared infrequently, they became popular among the immigrants, with over 150 springing up in New York City alone. Intended to help immigrant families in time of need, these societies provided accident insurance, health services, and a decent funeral and burial in the event of death; they also offered opportunities for socializing. In the long run they solidified into national organizations and gave rise to numerous fraternal lodges, orders, and recreational associations. This, though, was the only type of formal institution in which the first generation participated, and the societies were often organized on the basis of *campanilismo*. Furthermore, the very large number of such societies itself testifies to social fragmentation.[133] The early decades of immigration also witnessed the emergence of padrone labour systems, churches, the Knights of Columbus, the Dante Alighieri Society, and the Sons of Italy, which was founded in 1905 and by 1923 had three hundred thousand members.[134] Nor did the immigrants fail to establish voluntary associations and labour unions in a great variety of trades, although, with their village mentality, they were initially reluctant to do so.[135] The wealthier and more socially minded individuals of the community launched business enterprises intended to meet the needs of their co-ethnics, such as banks, insurance companies, travel agencies, employment agencies, boarding houses, import houses, real estate firms, legal agencies, and the like. The heyday of the Italian-language press extends from the later nineteenth century at least into the 1920s. First-generation Italian Americans also came to realize the advantages of political participation as a source of jobs and favours, yet they enjoyed only limited political success up to the 1920s, at the ward and occasionally the city level.[136]

Italian Americans thus acquired in the United States a community and group consciousness for which there was no equivalent in southern Italy, and which provided them with what Humbert S. Nelli terms a 'staging ground' for their adjustment to America.[137] There were limits, though, to the development of communal or cooperative organizations among the first generation, as family-centredness in most instances probably precluded 'deep involvement in extra-familial groups,' with the result that their organizational life lacked the richness to be seen in some other nationalities.[138] In her study of Italian Americans in Buffalo up to 1930, Yans-McLaughlin finds their society to have been adversely affected by familism, though it was combined with more communal patterns of behaviour.[139] Similarly, the Mezzogiorno tradition of political suspicion and apathy hindered Italian Americans' capacity for political organization and participation. For instance, many immigrants never became American citizens even after living for decades in the United States, long after deciding not to repatriate.[140]

As the second generation came to maturity, *campanilismo* had largely faded and Italian American ethnicity emerged as a separate, self-conscious, and hybrid identity.[141] Although the extended family had prospered, familist attitudes were receding, making it possible to enlarge one's circle of friends and neighbours outside the family to the point where a separate peer group society developed, sometimes lasting throughout its members' lives. By now Italian Americans felt much less suspicious of strangers, Italian American or otherwise.[142] Yet the evaluation of the degree of community attained by Italian Americans during this period varies depending on the neighbourhood observed. According to Tricarico, Banfield's ideas have kept many scholars from realizing that ethnic family patterns have coexisted with a high degree of communal solidarity, as witness the Italian Americans of Greenwich Village. Tricarico finds that following the First World War this neighbourhood became the locus for family group life, as the ethnic family radiated outwards to take in friendship networks and cliques, mutual aid societies, male clubs, parish organizations, various recreational societies, and voluntary associations such as the American Legion and the Knights of Columbus. Tricarico calls it an integrated ethnic community, where people feared not to leave their doors and windows open at virtually any time, and where the boundaries between apartment, apartment house, and community were highly fluid.[143] Despite predictions of its disintegration in 1930, the neighbourhood regenerated itself for many more decades – a fact that Tricarico attributes to the stability of its population.[144]

Other assessments of the second generation accent its limited capacity for communal and cooperative effort, partly owing to the persistence of the southern Italian suspicion of government. Italian Americans had not yet won political power and influence proportionate to their population.[145] In Gans's view, the Italian Americans of Boston's West End resembled their immigrant and southern Italian ancestors in their insularity and personalism, which prevented them from working together for long-term political goals. Perhaps more surprisingly, Gans found in them an underdeveloped sense of neighbourhood and community, with little participation, interaction, or integration. Tricarico contends that this resulted from the fact that the West End, unlike South Greenwich Village, lacked residential stability. In any case, both neighbourhoods were doomed, the West End by forced demolition in the late 1950s, the South Village by slow dissolution into the 1980s. They shared the fate of other Italian neighbourhoods of these decades, many of which became casualties of urban flight or renewal, occupational and residential mobility, and increasing assimilation.[146]

The assimilation of Italian Americans into the mainstream has largely depended on their residential and occupational mobility as well as their rate of intermarriage outside their ethnic group, which taken together indicate the group's relative success or failure in winning social acceptance. The capacity of Italian Americans to move up the social and occupational ladder is further related to their level of education. It is therefore obvious that the Italian American family, with its habits of intimacy, devaluation of education, and suspicion of the larger society, has somewhat retarded the pace of the group's assimilation. The first generation consisted primarily of badly educated blue-collar workers who gravitated towards the ethnic ghetto.[147] Yet one should not exaggerate the group's insularity even at this time, as the early communities witnessed instances of marriage between Italians and outsiders, that is, non-Italians.[148] Still more surprising is the fact, revealed in recent decades, that first-generation Italian Americans achieved a surprising degree of occupational and residential mobility, so that assimilation was already discernible. This occurred notwithstanding that many immigrants initially had no intention of staying in the United States, and were therefore content with lower level, low-paying jobs and not concerned with occupational and social mobility. As Thomas Kessner shows for 1880–1915, corresponding to the first generation, a significant number of blue-collar workers advanced from the ranks of the unskilled to the skilled. Because of negative attitudes towards education within the group, Italian American white-collar workers were unusual and typically to be found at the lower end of that category, yet there was improvement in the kinds of white-collar jobs they held. Thus, although a large percentage of Italian workers remained unskilled, and although female workers fell behind males, others had tangible proof of the possibility of occupational mobility, and this was reflected in their improved residential and social opportunities as they moved in significant numbers from their ghettos into better urban neighbourhoods.[149] Kessner's research builds on the findings of Humbert S. Nelli, who denies that Italian Americans' rate of assimilation was slow at this time. As he remarks, already in Chicago of the 1920s they were occupationally and residentially mobile in substantial numbers, and so became increasingly Americanized.[150]

By comparison with some other ethnic groups, such as the Jews, first- and second-generation Italian Americans showed a slow rate of occupational advancement. This has been attributed to slum crowding, large families, and culturally determined attitudes towards education, work, savings, and career planning. In some cases, second-generation Italian Americans fell to a lower occupational level than that of their parents, from white to blue collar.[151] Nonetheless there is evidence of increasing occupational and residential mobility, along with assimilation, in the second generation through the interwar period and beyond. This partly reflected the influence of schools and settlement houses, which stressed education, and the Americanization of parents. Public schools offered the opportunity to enter commercial, trade, and professional classes. Although Kessner notes that many earlier members of the second generation remained at the level of unskilled workers, the group generally held better blue-collar jobs than did the preceding generation, as many went from unskilled to skilled status. There was, moreover, some professionalization, and an increase in the quality of white-collar jobs, so that the early second generation made a notable advance.[152] Between 1916 and 1931 the number of Italian American common labourers dropped from about 50 to 31 per cent; during the 1930s the group's occupational structure in New York City approached the national norm.[153] Its upsurge coincided with a very large amount of residential mobility between the wars, which explains the decline of some older immigrant settlements at this time.[154] This pattern of demographic shift and neighbourhood decline persisted after the Second World War.

The degree of assimilation among second-generation Italian Americans relates to their response to the conflict between themselves and their first-generation, immigrant parents. As Child argues, they had to decide whether they wanted to be Italian or American – either to return to the group, with its satisfactions of belonging, or to identify with mainstream society. The latter choice would point the way to mobility and assimilation, but entailed few emotional comforts and serious risks.

Crispino observes that loss of Italian identity occurred quickly after the first generation, citing statistics that show that, whereas 30 per cent of the first generation claimed to be Italian, the figure had dropped to 5 per cent in the second generation, which clearly desired to Americanize.[155] However, the desire to assimilate is not the same as assimilation, before which stood obstacles. Within the second generation, the most assimilated Italian Americans were undoubtedly Child's 'rebels,' who rejected their ethnic neighbourhoods in favour of educational advancement, outgroup marriage, upward mobility, and Americanization. In the case of the 'apathetic,' their desire to live close to their parents generally limited their occupational possibilities and thus their opportunities to assimilate. Yet despite their attempt to accommodate their parents, the apathetic tended ultimately to leave their old neighbourhoods even while keeping up their ties with them, if only loosely.[156] And finally, there is the 'in-group,' consisting of working-class Italian Americans who identified with first-generation culture and chose with little regret to live alongside their parents and relatives in their ethnic communities. These seem to have been the least assimilated of all Italian Americans. As Lopreato suggests, the in-group corresponds to the urban villagers Herbert Gans studied in Boston's West End in the late 1950s, which he believed to typify Italian Americans as a whole.[157]

For all his insight into the urban villagers, Gans made two related errors. First, he assumed that Italians have remained basically the same in their social and familial patterns, in both Italy and the United States. Second, he assumed that urban villages typified Italian Americans of around 1960. What Gans failed to realize was that such communities were by then atypical of second-generation Italian Americans, whose upward mobility had enabled them to achieve a substantial – and increasing – degree of assimilation into the American middle class.[158]

Alba speculates that the rise of the Italian American middle class in the postwar period perhaps eroded the older ethnic culture more than is known, as the assimilating Italians remained unstudied at this time.[159] Between 1925 and 1945 Italian Americans experienced a rise in social and structural mobility, as the second generation gained in professional standing and class position and developed contacts outside the ethnic group. An even stronger drive for assimilation occurred after the Second World War, thanks to the educational opportunities made available to Italian Americans through the G.I. Bill. The group's improving social condition was manifest in its educational level, which more or less equalled that of WASPs, as well as in the large increase in intermarriage with members of other, mainly Catholic ethnic groups, from the late 1950s onward.[160] Admittedly, Italian Americans have had a reputation for residential immobility in ethnically homogeneous urban neighbourhoods even into the second generation, but this applies chiefly to blue-collar and older families; by 1970 a significant percentage of the second generation had dispersed into the suburbs in quest of homeownership and middle-class status.[161] That year's census revealed that many Italian Americans had acquired white-collar jobs and that the group's income was comparable to that of other ethnic groups. Writing in 1970, Joseph Lopreato characterized the Italian American middle class as practically indistinguishable from the American middle class, adding that the first and second generations tended to live near each other. By 1980 Americans of Italian descent were almost evenly divided between the suburbs and the working-class areas of the Northeast.[162]

The drama of the Italian immigration, the challenge of acculturation and assimilation on American soil, the formation of Italian American ethnicity, the social and cultural conflict between second-generation Italian Americans and their immigrant parents – these sociological and ethnological abstractions take on a special vividness and immediacy in Scorsese's *Italianamerican*, which he completed in 1974, and which he terms the 'best film I ever made.'[163] While some may challenge this judgment, it would be harder to dispute Les Keyser's observation that the 'material in *Italianamerican* constitutes the bedrock of Scorsese's art.'[164] Ironically, the idea for the project came not from Scorsese but from the National Endowment for the Humanities, which, as part of a television series entitled *Storm of Strangers*, had asked him to make a twenty-eight-minute documentary on Italian Americans.[165] The time was the early 1970s, with the ethnic-consciousness movement in full swing, and Scorsese had already made two films, *Who's That Knocking at My Door?* and *Mean Streets*, with Italian American characters, settings, and themes. Nonetheless, he initially turned down the project, and then agreed to participate only if he was allowed not to rely primarily on archival and other traditional documentary-type materials. Instead, the film would emerge from questions Scorsese asked his parents, Charles Scorsese, a presser in the garment district, and Catherine Scorsese, a garment industry seamstress.[166] In response to their son's questions (and in some instances those of the camera crewmen) they would recount the story of their families and their Elizabeth Street neighbourhood from the days of immigration into their adulthood. The film was shot in six hours over two days while the Scorseses and their son had dinner in the family apartment on Elizabeth Street; in its final cut it runs forty-five minutes, its original sixteen-millimetre film having been blown up to thirty-five millimetre. The attraction of the project for Scorsese lay not in factual history but in his parents' tendency to 'stick to the emotions. That's what I wanted to hear, some emotion.' He says that the film 'tells a series of stories. But because of the structuring of the questions, and ... [his parents'] answers, a bigger story came out overall' – a representative story of an Italian American family and neighbourhood.[167]

Most viewers are unaware of the improbability of an Italian American family of this period allowing itself to form the subject of a documentary. Nor are they likely to realize the degree of Scorsese's success in persuading his parents to participate so freely and openly in his enterprise. Even in this phase of their ethnicity, Italian American families, individuals, and neighbourhoods remained suspicious of outsiders and jealously protected their domestic spaces and histories against public scrutiny. The ideal of *omertà*, which dictates secrecy, reserve, and silence in the presence of non-family members and non-friends, still influenced Italian American behaviour, especially that of males, into the second generation.[168] Mr. Scorsese's demeanour, at least initially in the documentary, exemplifies the reserve typical of southern Italian males. However, that Scorsese's parents chose to discuss their lives and families on camera suggests a considerable degree of Americanization.

In contrast to most documentaries, which avoid calling attention to themselves so as to suggest the transparent rendition of fact, *Italianamerican* discloses the process of its own fabrication in the scene before the title, which shows Scorsese, his camera crew, and their lights and other equipment deployed in the living room in preparation for filming. As Kelly remarks, the revelation of this recording apparatus deliberately nullifies the distance between the viewer and what he or she sees. One is made aware not simply of the documented material but of the fact that it is being documented and, ultimately, constructed.[169]

The setting consists of a moderately sized living room with a dining room adjoining it and a kitchen off the dining room. The living room contains a slipcovered sofa, coffee table, air conditioner, curtained windows, a television against the narrower wall and, on the wall above the sofa, a framed reproduction of Sir Thomas Lawrence's *The Calmady Children* (1823). Characterized by the artist's high technical proficiency, this painting enjoyed popularity among Italian Americans of earlier generations, perhaps for its not excessive sentiment but almost certainly for its exalted treatment of beautiful children in movement, a theme congenial to the Italian sensibility. Some Italian Americans may have favoured it because it affords an example of the Italianate style in English painting, which flowered belatedly under Italian influence. The presence of this painting in the home of an acculturated Italian American family thus suggests certain ironies of cultural transmission and borrowing between the Italian and Anglophone worlds. Not only has Lawrence created a *tondo*, a painterly form perfected in Renaissance Italy, but his sensitivity to the form and movement of children is surely indebted to those Italian models that Lawrence studied and later saw at first hand during his Italian visit. Conjoined with the air conditioner and the television set, the painting testifies unintentionally to the mutual indebtedness of two societies and cultures that, whatever their differences, belong to a unitary Western civilization. Yet what is also noticeable is that the apartment lacks books. The television set and *tondo* imply a culture that is primarily oral and visual rather than one of literacy.

The living room is occupied by Charles and Catherine Scorsese. Their son now and then appears in the film, accompanying his mother into the kitchen or sitting with his parents at the dinner table, where he eats and listens to their stories. Yet he mainly appears at the margins of the frame and, apart from a few questions, remains unobtrusive. In this way he enables his parents to be themselves. One receives, moreover, an immediate impression of a typical pattern of interaction between his parents as the film begins, with Mrs Scorsese sitting at the far left end of the sofa and Mr Scorsese claiming its far right. Aware of the large space between them, Mrs Scorsese urges him to approach her (and the camera), his reluctance to do so eliciting her comment that 'he's bashful.'

Finally, after some coaxing, Mr Scorsese changes position until he is sitting next to his wife at her end of the sofa. She has contented herself with no more than a concessionary token shift of position in the direction of her husband, who yields much the greater amount of space. These seating rearrangements and the verbal exchange that accompanies them reflect the social and more especially domestic dynamics of this married couple, which become further evident as the documentary proceeds: the vivacity of the wife, her husband's comparative shyness and reticence, their relative equality within the domestic sphere as within their marriage, and the considerable powers of persuasion Mrs Scorsese wields over him – all of which qualify as classic traits of Sicilian married couples.

Mrs Scorsese enters the kitchen to prepare the tomato sauce whose recipe will, in a circular structure, conclude the documentary. Not only does she talk about making the sauce, but we see her performing part of this task, which culminates in Sunday dinner. The sauce is cooking, moreover, while the interview is being recorded. As the sauce figures as the film's chief marker for Italian American ethnicity, so its preparation stands for the creation of the film and the many elements that go into it. This is suggested by Mrs Scorsese, who, beginning her work in the kitchen, remarks, 'To begin with,' whereupon the title *Italianamerican* appears on the screen with accompanying ethnic music.

The title chosen by Scorsese, and more particularly its spelling, requires comment, as it might have been written in a variety of ways, each with its own semantic valence. The orthography is significant since, for Daniel Aaron and Anthony Julian Tamburri, the relation of Italian Americans to their larger society as well as its general attitude towards them are implicated in the adjectival form (or rather forms) of the group's name. Aaron and Tamburri show that these issues have centred on the possible hyphenated forms of the adjective; for Tamburri especially, the hyphen is not a 'neutral' but an 'ideological construct.'[170] Thus Scorsese might have called his documentary 'Italian-American,' with the hyphen separating as well as linking the two adjectives and the worlds they define. Yet as Aaron and Tamburri observe, this hyphenated form tends, as a result of the space created by the hyphen, to imply Italian Americans' distance from the mainstream and its partial rejection of them – the problem of incomplete assimilation. Whereas Aaron sees the hyphen primarily as a distancing device, Tamburri sees it as mainly disjunctive, a colonializing sign that under its pretentions to grammatical correctness conceals a subjugating force. Another possibility, 'Italo-American,' contains a hyphen but, in reducing 'Italian' to an abbreviated adjectival form, amounts to what Tamburri regards as a violation or 'castration' of ethnic identity. The limitations of these forms, in either stressing Italian Americans' distance from the mainstream or in limiting the Italian component of their identity, lead him to propose that the hyphen be replaced by the diagonal slash, which narrows the space between the two terms yet, without eliminating that space, implies the increasingly narrow gap between the ethnic group and the mainstream.[171]

Scorsese adopts neither the forms that Tamburri disapproves nor that which he favours. Nor does he call his documentary 'American Italian,' in the manner of the American Italian Historical Association. Founded in 1966, that organization apparently chose its name to emphasize its Americanness, but since in English a second adjective weighs more than than a first, the title actually highlights the group's Italian-ness rather than its assimilation. Scorsese, however, may have rejected such a title because his documentary gives due value to acculturation and assimilation. He might also have titled his film 'Italian American,' so as to stress the group's American-ness, with the adjective 'Italian' importing secondary, vestigial, or residual qualities; indeed, in these decades of increasing assimilation, this has been a favoured form, perhaps even supplanting its hyphenated predecessors.[172] Apparently Scorsese did not view the process of assimilation as having extended so far in 1974, and therefore rejected such a title in favour of 'Italianamerican,' an unusual form rarely if ever used. For while its majuscule underscores the priority of Italy as the origin of ethnic identity, Scorsese not only avoids capitalizing 'American' but eschews the spatial separation and hyphenation whereby the problematic relation – linked yet separated – between the Italian and American are conventionally signified. Instead, he suggests the merging of two identities, in which the Italian flows uninterruptedly into the American, but through which the temporal and perhaps ontological priority of the 'Italian' is asserted too.

Italianamerican is neither thematic nor logically sequential in presentation. Yet as it unfolds, one may piece together from its anecdotes, recollections, and images a coherent conception of the formation of Italian American ethnicity: the first generation, with its aspirations and Old World limitations; the centrality of the patriarchal family; its economic pressures and domestic circumstances; the surrounding neighbourhood and a new sense of community; encounters with other ethnic groups; husband-wife relations and roles; generational conflict, including the struggle over acculturation; and, finally, the passing down of a substantial part of southern Italian tradition from the first to the second generation.

Like many second-generation Italian Americans, the Scorseses have no doubt as to what compelled their parents to emigrate. Commenting on their recent visit to Italy, Mr Scorsese remarks, 'The land is beautiful but there's no work over there.' This is because, apart from the big cities, 'they have no industries.' To which his wife adds: 'That's why they came to America.'[173] She subsequently refers to the sixteen-year-old Neapolitan met on her visit, who vainly begged the Scorseses to take him to America: 'I felt so sorry for him, because there's no work over there.'

Although Catherine Scorsese's parents largely conform to a classic first-generation type, the circumstances of their meeting have the flavour of Old World romance. Her mother fell in love with her father at first sight as he rode into her home town as a member of an Italian cavalry troop. Yet because of her parents' disparate social origins – her father hailed from Baucina and her mother from Cimmina, both towns lying somewhat inland from the northern coast of Sicily – she curiously describes them as being of 'different nationality.' Such a statement reflects southern Italian *campanilismo*, that is, loyalty to one's native village and a corresponding inability to identify with Italy as a collectivity. After his marriage Mr Cappa left for the United States in the hope of improving the family fortunes, his wife having refused to follow him for fear of the hardships of the ocean voyage. Finding his loneliness unbearable, yet being unwilling to repatriate, he demanded under threat of permanent abandonment that his wife and new-born daughter, Catherine's older sister, come to America. The Cappas settled in New York City and, in a characteristic example of chain migration, were followed by a number of relatives who moved in with the family. Born in 1913, Catherine Scorsese grew up among Italian-born adults and mainly native-born siblings.

In another typical first-generation story, which begins somewhat south of Palermo in his family's hometown of Polizzi Generosa, Mr Scorsese tells of how his father, after his mother's death and father's remarriage, had been taken in by a farmer, among 'goats and things like that.' Though the farmer had hoped to marry him to one of his three daughters so as to keep him on the premises, Mr Scorsese's father came to America in 1901 at the age of nineteen. His future wife, Teresa, was also

Sicilian born, and, as Charles Scorsese reports, nearly died on the voyage to America. In 1903 Mr Scorsese's mother and father were married in St Patrick's Church in Manhattan's Little Italy, the same church where young Martin Scorsese attended school and served as an altar boy. His father Charles was born in 1912.

It is unclear from the documentary whether the Scorsese family settled initially on Elizabeth Street, but Mrs Scorsese mentions that her family made its first home on 3d Street and only later moved to Elizabeth. Such geographical mobility was common among immigrant families, as they were often dissatisfied with housing or rents or both. The marital destinies of Charles and Catherine Scorsese depended on the convergence of their families on Elizabeth Street, about which they reminisce freely. The neighbourhood was, she recalls, already inhabited by the Irish, who at first 'resented' the Italian newcomers and whose presence, comments Mr Scorsese, was signalled by six or seven bars. These recollections are accompanied by archival shots – infrequent in this documentary – of streets and sidewalks crowded with pedestrians and vendors. The chief sellers of goods were Jews, notes Mr Scorsese, and there were also pushcart vendors (many probably Italian) from whom local children often stole, usually for fun but sometimes from 'necessity.' Mr Scorsese also mentions the Chinese, who then occupied the Chinatown area across Canal Street, but who in more recent decades have taken over Little Italy. Indeed, New York's Little Italy was already declining by around 1930, as a result of the flight of locals to the suburbs. At present it is no longer a real Italian American neighbourhood, but a tourist attraction featuring Italian cafes and restaurants, and with a predominantly Chinese population.[174] Mr Scorsese very possibly alludes to the beginnings of this demographic transformation in noting that, whereas the neighbourhood in its earliest days had been filled with many prosperous stores, some of which specialized in Italian American imports, 'They faded away, they got a sort of depression like, you know, and people started to move.' Mrs Scorsese retains a similar impression of the closing of many neighbourhood businesses.

Mr and Mrs Scorsese's report of the housing conditions they encountered on Elizabeth Street conforms closely to Donna Gabaccia's documentation. They lived in tenements in which, 'if you were lucky,' as Mrs Scorsese says, the bathrooms were in the hallway. Otherwise they were in the backyard – the so-called backhouse, a word she pronounces with an Italian inflection, and which Italian Americans, in their hybrid language, continued to apply to the more sophisticated toilet facilities they found in America. The apartments had no gas stoves, but cold stoves that had to be heated up. The chief cause of the extraordinary crowding was the inclusion of extended family members as well as boarders within these small rental units. Mrs Scorsese remembers that when her aunt arrived in the United States, she and her husband and son were invited to board in the family apartment. With three relatives joining the family (husband, wife, and nine children), there were fourteen people in three rooms. Mrs Scorsese adds that her maternal grand- mother came to make her home in the same apartment. The residents of Mr Scorsese's parental home at 241 Elizabeth Street included two board- ers who lived in the kitchen and whose cooking and washing were done by Charles Scorsese's mother, Teresa. He recalls that the four small rooms of his family apartment housed seven people, although he ac- knowledges that Catherine's family experienced worse conditions.

As in so many immigrant reminiscences, the Scorseses portray the family as an integrating force of order and discipline. Mrs Scorsese refers unequivocally to her father as 'the master of the house' while suggesting the formidability of this scaffold-maker and former cavalry- man. With his old-style handlebar moustache, he qualifies as a 'Mus- tache Pete,' the name given in the early Italian communities to those immigrants who, in their grooming, dress, carriage, and deportment, exemplified the reserve and toughness of the southern Italian male. Yet if Mrs Scorsese's father calls to mind the power and command conven- tionally attributed to southern Italian paternity, especially in the first generation, *Italianamerican* suggests the nearly equal power of the ma- ternal figure in the immigrant households. That the domestic life of the second-generation Scorseses is no masculine tyranny may be inferred from the interchange between Mr and Mrs Scorsese, in which she criticizes her husband's shyness and remoteness from the camera, and then coaxes him into joining her on her side of the sofa. Yet as a display of feminine formidability, this is nothing compared to Mr Scorsese's mother, Teresa, who, in arguments with outsiders, substituted for her husband: 'As far as my mother goes,' says Mr Scorsese, 'she was a strong woman. My father would never get into arguments with any- body. She would face them. She would push my father away.' He also notes the most important role of the southern Italian mother, that of commanding and disciplining the household: 'She was a real whip ... She was always a strong woman, even with us. She hadda say some- thing, she told you, that was it, you couldn't answer her.'[175]

In their recollections of their parents, characterized as much by realism as by nostalgia, Mr and Mrs Scorsese remain aware of the differences between themselves and a first generation raised elsewhere and
impelled by hopes and aspirations more limited than those of their
American-born children. 'Our fathers and mothers were from a different world,' says Mr Scorsese; 'they were different.' He adds, 'As long as
we ate and were healthy, that's all that counted. They couldn't afford to
send us to school, they didn't have that kind of money. They had all to
do to survive.' Raised in the impoverished Sicilian society, their parents
limited their ambitions to the preservation and continuity of their families. Having achieved this, they died with the sufficient satisfaction of
seeing their children, to quote Mr Scorsese, 'all get married and settled
up with families and that's it.'

In America, as in Sicily, family survival depended on work. Charles
Scorsese's father was at first a tailor and later a not particularly successful small shopkeeper, never becoming more than a low-level white-
collar worker. As Mr Scorsese mentions in the documentary, his father
lost his business 'just at the time the Second World War started.'[176] Mr
Scorsese's employment as a presser in the garment industry thus indicates a drop in economic status from the first to the second generation, a
decline not uncommon in the data for New York City that Kessner
studied and that probably reflects Mr Scorsese's business failure; had
he succeeded, his son would probably have inherited the business. Mrs
Scorsese's father constructed scaffolds and for one stretch during the
First World War worked on the interior of ships in a naval yard; with
little education to speak of, he commanded a hundred men at the height
of his career. The male parents of Charles and Catherine Scorsese were
thus skilled labourers and small entrepreneurs. Typical of this period,
Catherine Scorsese's mother also worked to support the family. As her
daughter comments: 'She hadda help out too.' Although Sicilian tradition opposed the notion of a working woman, economic necessity left
no alternative for many families. Yet it was hard to dispel the fear
among Sicilian husbands that a wife who worked outside the house in
the company of males could not avoid seduction. The solution, in the
case of Catherine Scorsese's mother as in that of many other Sicilian
women, was to work at home. This was feasible owing to the proximity
of the garment industry, the seamstressing skills of Sicilian women, and
the willingness of businessmen to accept piecework performed outside
the factory. 'My mother,' says Catherine Scorsese, 'used to sew pants,'
and after finishing the work at home, she used to 'fold them all up

nicely, make a bundle, and carry them to Ninth Street.' After she delivered them, 'they would give her another batch, and she'd come back [home]. You had to bring them and deliver them.' Mr Scorsese recalls that his mother 'did the same thing.' However, Mrs Scorsese describes her mother as 'a very fine handsewer' whom a clothing store customarily assigned the task of sewing the pants of a famous millionaire.

As in Sicily, the children had to work. When Mr Scorsese says that his and his wife's parents could not afford to send their children to school, since survival was their main goal, he means that it was expected that children would curtail their education at the legally permissible age of fourteen and henceforward contribute their labour and wages to the family welfare. What Mr Scorsese does not say, and cannot be faulted for not saying, is that such devaluation of education in favour of short-term gains impaired family members' long-term occupational advancement and mobility. For his part, Mr Scorsese mentions his after-school job delivering vests. He exemplifies the frugality of the Italian Americans of those days in recalling that he would avoid paying car fare by hitching a ride on a horse cart.[177] One assumes that his profits went into a family pool rather than being reserved for his use. He mentions that he made extra money lighting gas stoves in the houses of the Jews of Delancey Street on the Sabbath day, when Jewish law forbade them to do so. He had become what the immigrant Jews called a 'Shabbas Goy.'[178] As for Mrs Scorsese's family, she recalls that her brother took his first job, as a messenger, at the age of fourteen, and that subsequently she and her other siblings found jobs. Her comment that 'we started to earn some money' suggests that these earnings were collective, perhaps surrendered by each sibling to the parents. Mrs Scorsese mentions too that her mother taught her and her sisters 'how to sew, how to knit, how to crochet, how to embroider, everything. We watched and we learned, but it was tough.' Mrs. Scorsese helped her mother in her home-based work until she was old enough to enter the garment industry.

Not to be discounted in this picture of the Italian American immigrant family is the amount of unpaid domestic work performed. Consistent with southern Italian tradition, such work was assigned to the wife, who was aided by her obedient children. It consisted of constant and unvarying domestic tasks carried out without modern conveniences. The family clothes had to be cleaned by scrubbing them against washboards, and Mr Scorsese mentions wooden floors that were hand scrubbed and polished until they sparkled. The most important maternal task was to cook for a large family, which, to judge from Mr Scorsese's comments, included people of demanding as well as different tastes: 'But as far as cookin' it was a big job.' His wife agrees: 'The women really worked.' Regarding women's labour, Mr Scorsese comments that 'they never cried that they were tired. There was no such thing as being tired.' Contrastingly, today's women have it 'soft ... They got washing machines, they got this, they got that.' It was also customary, Mr Scorsese recalls, for the father of the family to make wine at home. This was done by stomping rubber-booted in the barrels, or with a strainer. When Mrs Scorsese's faulty memory leads her to think that these methods were applied together, Mr Scorsese corrects her, which suggests that wine-making was very much a male sphere.

These lives had relieving diversions and pastimes, however limited. Mr Scorsese mentions that the absence of radio and television was compensated for by the art of storytelling, which the Sicilians had transported to America from their oral village culture: 'Years ago they were great storytellers, because ... you had no radio and television.' These men would visit individual tenements with 'fantastic stories' that would 'keep you on your toes.'[179] The other diversion he mentions is eating, which he apparently pursued not simply as a necessity but as a pastime: 'Eating ... always eatin'.' Besides family dinners and cooking practices, he mentions visiting a local Jewish neighbourhood where, for only fifteen cents, he ate with a cup of coffee the 'original' Jewish potato knishes. One has the impression that eating had become a pastime for Italian American immigrant families because of the increasing dietary variety of America's industrial abundance, and also because their increasing purchasing power enabled them to sample a variety of hitherto unavailable foods whose consumption the families encouraged as a visible token of escape from the other world of *miseria*.

Still other sources of compensation were provided not only by the extended family, which had rooted itself in the tenements, but through the development of stronger ties with neighbours and to some extent the neighbourhood – a more communal form of life than is typical of the Italian south. A major site of this new sense of community was the tenement house, where the extended family and its neighbours lived in surprising harmony, with little of the middle-class demand for privacy and solitude. Mr Scorsese remembers that apartment doors were always open, with constant comings and goings of family members, tenants, and local people on the tenement stairs. When the dinner fare in his family's apartment dissatisfied him, he always found something more to his taste in a relative's apartment, where he was welcome. In his recollection the tenement formed 'one big happy family' apparently extending beyond the nuclear household or even the extended family to the fourth degree. Yet for all their success in strengthening kinship ties in their new environment, the Scorseses and their neighbours had not achieved the Old World dream of the extended family as a single economic unit living under the same roof. On the other hand, Mr Scorsese's description of life on Elizabeth Street in this era, presumably the 1920s, supports Donna Gabaccia's point that, though not perfectly pleased with living conditions in Little Italy, the families found them more satisfying – materially and socially – than those left behind.

Nonetheless, the way of life followed by the Scorseses had its limitations. In recalling that eating had been his chief pastime, Mr Scorsese gives the impression of limited aspiration, curiosity, and contentment. What not only explains but perhaps largely justifies such attitudes is the *miseria* of the older culture and the immigrants' astonished discovery of American abundance. For them, the difference between their former and present conditions was so enormous that, given the depths from which they had risen, they were largely unaware of the low ceiling they had set for themselves. Another deficiency was that, while the Sicilian art of storytelling survived, shaping the storytelling abilities of Charles and Catherine Scorsese, the written word languished. Mr Scorsese preferred eating to reading newspapers, of which he complains that there was 'nothing' in them. His statement may reflect weak education, lack of interest in reading within his community, and ethnic self-absorption and familial insularity, which offered no basis by which to evaluate the news. A tendency to insularity may underly the fact that neither Mr nor Mrs Scorsese mentions local associations or cooperative organizations linking them or their families to the neighbourhood or the outside world. What apparently counted were the primary links to the family and relatives and the informal give-and-take with neighbours. Indeed, Mrs Scorsese's father spent three decades in America before claiming citizenship, an omission that implies long-term inability to identify with the nation.

The Little Italy depicted in *Italianamerican* is neither ethnically self-encapsulated nor historically static. As Mr. Scorsese recalls, he had met Jews not only while performing as a 'Shabbas goy' but while visiting Jewish cafes and restaurants. Given the loyalty of many Italian immigrants to their own cuisine, his gastronomic experimentation seems adventurous. In recollecting that Italian and Jewish shopkeepers came to dominate the neighbourhood, Mr Scorsese gives the impression that the two ethnic groups enjoyed generally amicable relations while 'working together.' Perhaps reflective of Martin Scorsese's earliest experiences of the Lower East Side, his films could explore the interpenetration of Italian and Jewish cultures within not only New York's neighbourhoods but the more specialized society of the underworld, in which Italians and Jews have often been associates. Mr Scorsese mentions as well the adjoining community of Chinatown, adding that during its 'Tong Wars' the Chinese had preyed only upon themselves, so that a non-Chinese could go there safely. This observation seems to indicate that Mr Scorsese visited to the area, perhaps to sample its restaurants. A long-term consequence of this initial contact between the two cultures can be seen in Martin Scorsese's films, whose Italian American characters favour Chinese food. In *Who's That Knocking at My Door?* Joey proclaims his fondness for the cuisine in neighbouring Chinatown; in *Mean Streets* Charlie Civello and Johnny Boy make plans to 'eat chink' in the same locale; and in *Raging Bull* Jake La Motta and his brother devour Chinese spare ribs and other items from cartons. As for the Irish, Mr Scorsese mentions that Elizabeth Street was lined by six or seven Irish bars. Conversing with her son in the privacy of the kitchen, Mrs Scorsese objects to her husband's remark, apparently for its implied stereotype of the drunken Irish. Seemingly to minimize Italian–Irish conflicts, she claims that though their relations 'were a little tough' initially, the two groups came to form 'one big happy family.' As a description of the often strained relations between Italians and Irish in New York City, this statement sounds sentimental.[180] In New York's Little Italy some degree of tension persisted between the groups until the Irish left the neighbourhood. And yet the fact remains that many Italian Catholics came to accept a 'Hibernian' Catholicism, just as they intermarried increasingly with the Irish. Indeed, Martin Scorsese's first wife was named Eileen Brennan.

The more important changes signalled long-term Americanization of Italian Americans and their future entry into the mainstream. Mr. Scorsese mentions the arrival of a radio within the household and the struggles it provoked over the choice of programming. To judge from Mr Scorsese's comments, he and his fellow family members responded to the radio far more enthusiastically than to books and newspapers, very possibly because it was more in keeping as a medium with the mentality and rhythms of the oral village culture in which these families had originated. Yet with this invasion of their domestic space, they were now willing targets of a homogenizing mainstream.[181] In *Italianamerican* a key indicator of Americanization appears in the adoption of the custom of Christmas, which was less popular in Italy, where emphasis was given to the Feast of the Epiphany or Befana in early January, and still more to Easter.[182] Although Mr Scorsese cannot remember his parents ever introducing a Christmas tree within their household, he does recall the celebration of a southern Italian–style Christmas in his family, whose members attended midnight mass, ate sausages and bread immediately afterward at home, and went to bed in expectation of a family feast the following day. Contrastingly, Mrs Scorsese recalls that the younger members of her family pitched in to buy a Christmas tree, after which, confirming the reputation of Italians as practical jokesters, they filled their siblings' Christmas stockings with worthless items.[183] These anecdotes are accompanied by a photograph in which the young cowboy-suited Martin Scorsese and his older brother Frank pose before a Christmas tree. By this point – the mid-1940s – Christmas was a 'tradition' for the Scorseses.

Other signs of change, and with it tension and conflict, appear in connection with the first-generation male parent. His difficulties arose partly through the humiliations of prejudice and the challenge of Americanization. With advancing years he became aware not only of his physical limitations, including mortality, but of challenges to his authority from within the family itself. Martin, Mrs Scorsese's father, had begun his life in America as a 'Mustache Pete' whose handlebars proclaimed proud masculinity and stubborn *italianità*. Linguistically he was a diehard, for as she reports, when her sister took him to receive his citizenship papers thirty years after his arrival in this country, the clerk was annoyed by his failure to learn English, to which he responded with a stream of curses in that language. Mrs Scorsese also recalls the time when her father, having unexpectedly shaved off his handlebar moustache, frightened his children upon returning home, as they failed to recognize him. His removal of the moustache may indicate a concession to the American norm, but in any case, his new clean-shaven presentation cannot have had that air of Old World patriarchal authority one associates with the mythically all-powerful Italian American father-figure. Mrs Scorsese further mentions the on-the-job injury suffered by her father, because of which the 'master of the house' was prevented from working, apparently for a long time. What she does not say is that such a work-curtailing injury would probably have resulted, if only tacitly, in a reduction of her father's familial authority and prestige. As in Italy, the Italian American father's dominance within the family has depended chiefly on his supremacy as a breadwinner. Thus his authority was likely to decline through an incapacitating injury or old age.[184]

This loss of power by Catherine Scorsese's father is revealed in an anecdote from her adolescence. It exemplifies some of the ways in which the southern Italian father, formerly assured of unquestioning obedience and respect, was being challenged by his Americanizing second-generation children as a result of their exposure to American ideas of domestic propriety and boy–girl relationships. Mrs Scorsese reports that, as she and her sisters grew older, they acquired 'boy-friends': 'You brought them up to the home. You wanted the home to look nice. So we painted the apartment.' Given the social practices of the southern Italian society and its first-generation American offshoot, in which boys and girls were typically segregated, and in which parents controlled later premarital connections between the sexes, the acquisition of 'boyfriends' by Mrs Scorsese and her sisters as well as their freedom to invite them into the family residence indicates Americanization and therefore some degree of independence from parental authority. Mrs Scorsese remarks that the job of painting the apartment required the temporary removal of her father's portrait – a remembrance of his days as a cavalry trooper – from its place of prominence. But though the sisters intended to replace the portrait after completing their job, they failed to do so, an omission Mrs Scorsese attributes to their desire to please their boyfriends. She seems to mean that they all felt more comfortable, and more American, without this reminder of Old World parentalism. At first Mrs Scorsese's father failed to notice the removal of his portrait, but a meddlesome neighbour called it to his attention. This set off an 'enormous row in the house,' with the father demanding the return of the picture in order to break it, although, as Mrs Scorsese recalls, she and her sisters held on to it for safekeeping. The father's response to these events implies confusion and ambivalence. That he had ignored the picture's disappearance shows that this challenge to his authority had occurred almost invisibly. Yet instead of demanding that the picture be returned to its former place, he wanted to destroy it, as if in bitter confirmation of his seriously diminished authority. Although the sisters never returned the picture to its former setting, they not only preserved it but distributed small copies of it to various relatives in a belated acknowledgment of the lapsed authority they had already challenged.

The passing from the first to the second generation is evoked in Mrs Scorsese's report of the circumstances of her father's death following his and his wife's transfer to a house and spacious yard on Staten Island.[185] Showing mobility even in the first generation, the move was presumably motivated by a desire for space, closeness to nature and, not least, home-grown produce, as Italian Americans have shown a special fondness for kitchen gardens. Another possible motivation was the desire of a former *contadino* to own land, a 'dream' that, as Malpezzi and Clements observe, 'had seldom been fulfilled in Italy.'[186] Nor is it surprising that Catherine's father planted fig trees, as they were very much favoured by immigrants. Indeed, Nat Scammacca goes so far as to describe them as the 'symbol of Sicily.' They were, however, ill suited to the cold climate of the Northeast, and therefore had to be kept covered, for instance by rugs and linoleum, lest they perish in the winter.[187] Though Catherine's father delighted in cultivating his fig trees, his wife never liked them, and had all the more reason for her dislike when her husband, attempting to cover them in the winter, fell from a ladder and sustained a mortal injury. Soon after his wife had cursed the fig trees, she too died, after which they never bloomed again. 'It was just like she took them with her,' says Mrs Scorsese, who, as if conscious of her sentimentality, recovers the hard realism that is as Italian as Sicilian: 'And that was that.' Considered symbolically, the death of the fig tree can be taken to stand not only for the passing of the father (and more generally that of the first generation), but for the transplantation of the entire group to American soil, where many of its most familiar customs and practices proved incapable of surviving in the new environment. Recalling the place on Staten Island, Mr Scorsese remarks that 'now that he's gone they destroyed everything,' since 'nobody could take care of it.' He continues: 'It's all gone. That goes to show you. One day you build it up, one day the fathers and mothers build it up and nobody else wants to take care of it.'

Actually, it is an exaggeration for Mrs Scorsese to say that the second generation did no more than destroy or neglect the creations of its predecessor. For the outcome of generational conflict was often a compromise between Italian and Americanizing attitudes and thus the formation of a self-consciously Italian American lifestyle typified by urban dwellers like Mr and Mrs Scorsese. They combine the two co-adopted cultures and societies, with a tilting perhaps to the Italian side of the combination, as is reflected by their continued residence in the same Italian American neighbourhood as their parents. This statement needs qualification, however, as it is known that during the 1940s Mr Scorsese attempted unsuccessfully to move his family to Corona, in Flushing. It is unclear why the film ignores this period of the family's life, and one hesitates to speculate on the omission. Nonetheless, Corona was at that time a heavily Italian American community only partially assimilated into the mainstream. In moving there for the sake of a more comfortable and spacious residence with trees and a yard, the Scorseses found themselves in an environment not that different from Little Italy. In any case, the family's next major move following its return to Little Italy from Corona occurred twenty years later and amounted to a transfer to a refurbished and more attractive apartment on Elizabeth Street directly across from their former residence. The Scorseses, then, belong in the category of what Herbert Gans terms 'urban villagers.' They exemplify not those upwardly mobile middle-class Italian American families who moved out of the old urban neighbourhoods in an attempt to enter the American mainstream, and whose social behaviour conforms closely to the American norm, but those working-class families who remained in the declining but still viable ethnic neighbourhoods in which they had been raised. Although these working-class families had acculturated considerably, their social structure still reflected southern Italian norms, which entailed the centrality of the authoritarian family, its ideals of honour, respect, and deference, and its moral values, not least regarding sexual behaviour.

Italian social traditions are in evidence early in the documentary as it becomes apparent that Mr Scorsese espouses Old World conceptions of family hierarchy, clear-cut distinctions between masculine and feminine roles, and male dominance within the hierarchy. On the subject of cooking, Mr Scorsese observes that 'it's known that a man can cook better than a woman any time.' Stung by this mildly insulting remark, Mrs Scorsese rejoins: 'Why aren't you in the kitchen?' He responds: 'It's not my line.' His implication is that gender roles ought to be strictly separate, the domestic sphere being the wife's domain. Accordingly, Mr Scorsese expects his wife to cook for him after work, and cannot entertain any other possibility. Yet it is wrong to think that, in the terms of this ethnic society, he has shown disrespect for his wife; rather, he has defined and affirmed the special realm within which she deserves respect. For instance, in remarking that his father-in-law 'set a bad example by cooking for himself,' Mr Scorsese implies that he had exceeded the masculine role assigned to him.

Something of the husband–wife relations in Sicilian households of the older type is discernible in the interactions of Charles and Catherine Scorsese. Traditionally the approved deportment of the Sicilian male, in public as in private, has combined reserve, reticence, and even silence – behaviours necessitated by an atmosphere of risk and danger. A Sicilian male is expected to show gravity and discretion, suppressing rather than expressing his in her most feelings. In traditional Sicily, wives generally exhibit a greater talkativeness and expressiveness than their husbands, being free from their fears and inhibitions. A certain awkwardness, diffidence, and even stand-offishness characterizes the relations between the sexes, partly because of their social segregation beginning in childhood, but also because of the superior verbal skills acquired by women in their more voluble and expressive groups. Indeed, Sicilian women may have developed their verbal fluency as a compensation in a male-dominated society.[188] Customarily, Sicilian males feel disadvantaged in the face of the superior verbal abilities of women, and fear being manipulated by them. These cultural patterns may help to explain why, as the film opens, Charles Scorsese sits at the opposite end of the sofa from his wife. It is as if he were keeping her at a safe distance. Nor is there any doubt that Mrs Scorsese surpasses her husband in verbal facility. Having succeeded in persuading her reluctant husband to move to her end of the sofa, she mentions that, following her work, he customarily lapses into long silence. 'Why don't you talk?' she had often asked him, to which he responds: 'What can you say to a woman you're married to for forty-two years?' As Scorsese says of his parents: 'My mother talks a great deal, and my father is quite reticent, usually.'[189]

Whereas Mrs Scorsese objects to her husband's silences, he complains of her style of speech in the opening scene. In his view, his wife is 'not talkin' natural' but 'puttin' on airs.' 'She's not an actress,' says the slightly annoyed Mr Scorsese, adding that she would be 'better off [if she spoke] naturally.' Actually, rather than being affected or theatrical, Mrs Scorsese is simply delighted to have a chance to express her personality, including her verbal fluency, before an audience. Unlike her husband, who initially shrinks from the camera, she wants to shine. He seems to sense this, moreover, and perhaps fears to be eclipsed by his wife, as he lacks the verbal skills to meet her on even terms. Yet Mr Scorsese may have cause to attribute theatrical ambitions to his wife, who had already appeared in three of her son's films, and would appear in several others.

That Mrs Scorsese's verbal facility gives her an advantage over her husband seems to be acknowledged by Mr Scorsese himself. Recalling the move to their present apartment, he mentions that at first he had resisted the idea. Yet he adds: 'You always give in.' Mrs Scorsese's fluency, combined with her personal charm and outgoing nature, must have influenced his decision. This minor episode illustrates the point that the Sicilian male, though officially a patriarch, is often dominated or at least met on equal terms by his spouse, who works behind the scenes while letting her husband enjoy fantasies of superiority in public. The impression of Mrs Scorsese's formidability is reinforced in the film's final scene, in which, after announcing her return to her housework, she notices that the camera is still recording. She then says in mock rage, 'I'll kill you, you won't get out of this house alive.' Even in joking she expresses her strong personality, which calls to mind that of Mr Scorsese's mother, to whom her husband entrusted all arguments and with whom no one would tangle.

The centrality of Mrs Scorsese within the household results in no small degree from her role in cooking the tomato sauce – although, typical of northeastern Italian Americans, she calls it 'gravy.' The film's major action, with which it begins and which coincides with its unfolding, is the cooking and consumption of the sauce, whose ingredients are specified in the recipe at the film's conclusion. The film thus portrays Mrs Scorsese as nurturer, provider, and maker of the family's substance. While his father remains in the living room, the camera follows Martin Scorsese when, on two occasions, he moves through a narrow hallway into the kitchen to speak with his mother as she prepares the sauce. It is as if he were entering the family's inner sanctum, its secret core of power, the ultimate source of its providence. Beyond any merely biological or utilitarian considerations, her act has ritualistic significance, with overtones of the sacred. This is the heart of the 'mother-centred' household.

Symbolically central to the film, the tomato sauce and Italian American cuisine more generally figure as markers for the ethnic group and its many elements. As noted above, no single southern Italian traditional cuisine has ever existed, but only a multitude of regional, local, and familial variations. Though building on Old World traditions, Italian American cuisine came into being on American shores, partly through the greater abundance and variety of foods, and also through the technologization of food production, which changed cooking and to some extent the foods themselves. In *Italianamerican*, these culinary factors are discernible in the ingredients of the sauce as in its preparation.

The documentary shows that the sauce is in no sense a manifestation of some generic, collectively based and agreed-upon tradition of southern Italian or Italian American cooking, but a distinctive product deriving from a recipe that blends two family traditions. When Martin Scorsese asks his mother how she 'learned' the sauce, she refers not to a traditional Italian cookbook but to her mother and mother-in-law. As an indicator of the culinary variety that often prevailed even within individual families, Mr Scorsese mentions that his father-in-law cooked for himself. As a further indicator of the variety of Italian American cooking, Mrs Scorsese says that her mother-in-law had shown her the 'secret' of softening her meatballs by adding a touch of tomato sauce, whereas the meatballs prepared by her friends are often 'hard.' Her mother, she recalls, taught her cooking 'one way,' while her mother-in-law had a 'different slant.' She also mentions that her father 'had to have a certain gravy' and cooked 'his own tomato paste,' the ingredients of which her mother combined in summer and then preserved. On family occasions her father would 'call everybody in to taste his kind of paste.' The overall impression is of culinary variety, so that, as Scorsese recognizes, one may speak of family and even individual cuisines.[190]

The recipe for tomato sauce with which the film concludes testifies to the great variety of 'Italian American' cuisine and, in its specific ingredients, is perhaps unique to Mrs Scorsese.[191] Her recipe differs from comparable ones in nineteenth-century Sicily not only in the richness, variety, and abundance of its ingredients but in its reliance on industrially produced foods. The recipe includes such flavouring meats as veal, beef, pork sausage, and lamb neckbone, a richness rarely to be seen in Sicily; the neckbone alone calls to mind those days when impoverished Sicilian wives used discarded scraps of meat to flavour soups and sauces. The benefits of American abundance appear in the pride of the recipe, Mrs Scorsese's meatballs, a dish that did not exist in southern Italy (except in the basically different Neapolitan *polpette*) but became popular in the United States thanks to the availability of meat. Women of the Old Country often made their own pasta, tomato paste, and other items, and the persistence of such customs is shown in Mrs Scorsese's mention that her mother hand-made a special tomato paste for her husband. Contrastingly, Mrs Scorsese's recipe lists a 'can of packed whole tomatoes,' while its tomato paste is almost certainly of the canned type. Her tomato sauce is therefore a hybrid entity, combining native Italian and familial with American and industrial elements, and as such it affords Scorsese with a metaphor for the hybridity of Italian America itself, as it existed on the cusp of the second and third generations. He justly describes the 'preparation of the tomato sauce as the most important moment in the film.'[192]

2 Scorsese as Third-Generation Italian American Artist

As a man and artist, Martin Scorsese belongs to the third generation of Italian Americans and exhibits many of the characteristic conflicts and ambivalences that come with external as well as internal pressures to resist or embrace acculturation and assimilation. Among the first to explore the problems of third-generation Italian Americans were Rudolph J. Vecoli and Richard Gambino. In Vecoli's view, second-generation parents produced ambivalence in their third-generation children by requiring a commitment to both family values and hard work for the sake of upward mobility. The children thus received the contradictory message: 'Get an education but don't change.' This conflict typifies the Italian American 'dilemma' analysed in Richard Gambino's *Blood of My Blood*.[1] Vecoli also holds that Italian Americans came of age in the early 1970s, with the maturation of the third generation. Yet it was also at this time that the more assimilated suburban Italian Americans began to lose touch with their counterparts among lower-class urban dwellers.[2]

During the 1980s, James A. Crispino and Richard Alba closely analysed third-generation samples, which according to Crispino fall into two basic categories. One includes blue-collar dwellers who, like their parents and grandparents, continue to live in ethnic neighbourhoods, usually urban. These individuals, though appreciative of education, have a low educational level and therefore a low social and professional status. Although acculturated in the sense of accepting the host society's values, they adhere to a fair number of traditional Italian social and cultural patterns. They also remain comparatively unassimilated by the larger society, that is, unincorporated within its social organization, but prefer to find their friends and institutional affiliations among either relatives or fellow ethnics. These preferences are encouraged by the fact of living in Italian American neighbourhoods. The ethnicity of the first and second generations remains alive, but as a working-class phenomenon, and closely correlates with a low educational level.[3]

The other category is that of the more assimilated middle-class Italian Americans, who, notwithstanding the media cliché of the working-class Italian American, now make up the greater percentage of their ethnic group. These individuals value education and are educated at least at the college level:[4] 45 per cent of Italian Americans attended college in the 1970s as compared with 21 per cent in the 1940s.[5] With their comparatively high educational attainment, these individuals have become middle-class white-collar workers and live dispersed in multiethnic suburbs rather than tight-knit urban ethnic enclaves. They tend, moreover, to be highly assimilated as well as acculturated. Not only have they largely shed most remaining Italian cultural patterns, including the Italian language and even, to a considerable degree, cuisine, but they prefer to derive their friends, associations, interests, values, and lifestyles not from relatives or fellow ethnics but from like-minded people of their class. Thus class proves more powerful than culture or ethnicity. Moreover, a substantial portion of this group claims half-Italian parentage. As a further indicator of assimilation, these individuals tend very much to marry outside their ethnic group, usually to fellow Catholics, and, unlike their parents and grandparents, they are tolerant of divorce. The data strongly suggest that, like their parents, Italian Americans of the third and fourth generation follow the pattern of 'straight-line' assimilation, their ethnicity being continually eroded through upward mobility, rising middle-class status, and out-group marriage, all of which lead to increasing assimilation.[6] Alba thus places Italian Americans in the 'twilight of ethnicity,' which implies the gradual dwindling and fading away of their ethnic consciousness.[7]

This is not to imply that middle-class Italian Americans lack consciousness of or pride in their ethnic identity. Many of them conform in their attitudes and behaviour to the 'law' that Marcus Hansen, writing in the late 1930s, discerned in the third-generation descendants of nineteenth-century immigrants. As Hansen notes, first-generation immigrants can only remain what they are, representatives of a foreign culture on American soil. Their second-generation offspring desire to become assimilated and therefore want to forget as much as possible their connection with the ethnic group. But in the third generation the immigrants' grandchildren seek in a 'spontaneous and almost irresistible' fashion to remember the Old World origins – the 'heritage of blood' – their parents had left behind, and to which they can now 'return' in confidence and security, having already become largely assimilated. Their reasons for doing so mingle pride of origin with a desire for self-identification so as not to be lost in a homogeneous American mass.[8] Applying Hansen's law to third-generation ethnics in the 1950s, Will Herberg found the rediscovery of ethnicity to be reflected in their renewed interest in and embrace of the religion of their grandfathers, rather than the total complex of the ethnic culture.[9] In the case of third-generation Italian Americans, one must also consider as a factor in their return to ethnicity the ethnic revival of the 1960s and 1970s, which not only legitimated ethnic consciousness as never before, but in the case of the Italian Americans coincided with the maturation of the third generation. Their newly found acceptance and security as Americans had made them less defensive about their ethnicity, enabling them to assert it with a confidence unknown to earlier generations.[10]

Yet one should not overestimate the force of the Italian American ethnic revival. Those middle-class Italian Americans who assert their ethnicity do so on a highly selective basis peripheral to their class interests. They show attitudinal support for Italian culture but little support in terms of actual practice. For the dyed-in-the-wool ethnic, ethnicity is something encountered and expressed in daily activities and implies a comprehensive pattern of life. But for most middle-class Italian Americans, ethnicity exists at the non-behavioural level, not as a permanently ascribed status or absorption in group life but as a state of mind that one may turn on and off voluntarily as the occasion allows. Few Italian Americans join ethnic organizations, which they regard as low status, but prefer to confine their ethnicity to Italian cooking and vacations.[11] Both Crispino and Alba agree with Gans that most current expressions of ethnicity are purely 'symbolic' or 'low cost,' carrying no threat of social divisiveness, involving no social risk for an individual, and serving expressive rather than instrumental purposes.[12] To quote Crispino: 'The symbols of Italian descent, rather than the traditional social structure, ... are the hallmarks of the "New Ethnicity."'[13] Ironically, the ethnic revival betokens a decline in ethnicity, its largely middle-class exponents having become diminished in their *italianità*. The revival amounts to an nostalgic, illusory attempt to reverse the assimilatory trend. One must allow, though, that a depth of identification and commitment to ethnicity sometimes appears among members of the highly educated Italian American middle class.[14]

In assessing Scorsese's third-generation identity, one is struck by the fact of its having been formed, atypically, of working- and middle-class experiences dissociated and radically different from each other. One is also struck by the strength of his ethnicity and the rapidity of his acculturation and assimilation beyond his original environment. Apart from his earliest years in Corona, Queens, Scorsese spent much of his childhood and youth as an urban villager whose social contacts and spatial boundaries were largely confined to Manhattan's Little Italy. It is almost hard to believe the cultural insularity of his early environment: 'I never went to the Village until I enrolled at NYU in 1960. I grew up on the East Side. From 1950 to 1960, for ten years, I never ventured past Houston Street, past Broadway and Houston.' He adds: 'I think my father took me on a bus when I was five years old or something. I remember Washington Square.' On another occasion a friend's mother took him on a 'little tour' of Greenwich Village, which seemed to him 'a wonderland, because they had flowers. It was a very different culture.' Although Scorsese acknowledges that 'growing up down there [in Little Italy] was like being in a Sicilian village culture,' he did not see it as a limitation at the time: 'It was great,' he says. Yet Scorsese also acknowledges the disadvantages his background posed as he attempted to educate himself and move up in the world: 'Certainly it was having come from that neighborhood and living there completely closed in, like in a ghetto area, not really leaving till the early sixties to go to the West Side. So I had one foot in the university and the other foot in ... that world, that life-style.' It was only 'much later,' says Scorsese, that he 'became aware of other people in the world and other life-styles, other views, political and otherwise. But [in Little Italy] I was quite closed off. It was like somebody coming out of the Middle Ages going to a university.'[15] That his parents felt ambivalence towards Scorsese's college career with all its possibilities of social mobility is suggested from the fact that, though Charles Scorsese was fulfilled in his hope that his son would be able to attend NYU, he and his wife feared that he would become morally and politically corrupted by the books he brought from school into their apartment.[16] The young Scorsese was receiving the contradictory signals noted by Gambino and by Vecoli in his analysis of the 'dilemma' of young Italian Americans during this period.

In view of Scorsese's background, one cannot see him as a typical example of the third-generation 'return' to ethnicity. His chief object as he entered adulthood was not to return to his ethnic origin but to 'escape' from Little Italy into the American mainstream.[17] The effort of acculturation and assimilation was all the greater given the social gulf that had to be crossed and the lost time to be made up in crossing it. In describing Scorsese's life and career as a 'journey,' Mary Pat Kelly refers partly to his gradual upward mobility, to the point where, as a Hollywood player, he entered the American upper middle class. His *éloignement* from his former, ethnically defined world was marked by his rejection of the institutional Catholicism of his youth and formation of friendships among a great variety of people, many of whom are non-Italian Americans and the majority of whom seem to enjoy similar class status. His assimilation is further evident in his five marriages, in four instances to non-Italian American women.[18]

Yet it would be wrong to think of Scorsese as perfectly assimilated, or as desiring complete assimilation. Not only has he never disavowed his ethnic origins, but, even while strengthening his ties to the mainstream, he has 'returned' to his ethnic past. His interest in his own ethnicity was perhaps encouraged to some degree by the ethnic revival of the 1960s and 1970s, but its chief explanation lies in the intensity of his initial exposure to the parent culture as well as his emotional loyalty to the social world that gave him his earliest formative experiences. He mentions the contrary claims of ethnicity and assimilation in a 1998 interview recalling his days as a 'streetcorner' boy in Little Italy: 'I think all my life has been wanting to get out. And I'm interested in a lot of the people who "got out" and what they took with them. Because without the streetcorner, I have nothing.' He says of Little Italy: 'I don't go down there very often now that my parents are gone, but that's what I am ... I went another way – but I'm still there.'[19]

Scorsese often visited his now deceased parents in the old neighbourhood during the several decades after his departure. Although these visits served chiefly to renew old connections, he also made interesting discoveries typical of the 'returning' third-generation ethnic. Mary Pat Kelly writes that during the filming of *Italianamerican* Scorsese 'discovered' his parents. 'I had seen them as parents, not as people,' recalls Scorsese. Then 'suddenly they became people, and it was a love story.' He adds: 'I was able to learn things about my parents I didn't know. I learned where they came from. I learned how they lived in the twenties and thirties in New York.' Another sign of Scorsese's growing curiosity towards his own ethnicity is Mrs Scorsese's report that, during the filming of *The Color of Money*, her son 'got us back in touch with the family in Italy' – a gesture that follows up Scorsese's investigation of his family's Sicilian backgrounds in *Italianamerican*. His closeness to his parents is evident too in their frequent appearance as actors in his films, to the point where Mrs Scorsese remarks of her son, her husband, and herself that 'we made *The Color of Money*,' as if it were their collaborative product.[20]

The strongest evidence of Scorsese's ethnic identification lies in his feature films, five of which over a period of three decades have involved Italian American settings and themes. It would be unfair to say that Scorsese has attempted simply to cash in on the ethnic revival and the enormous success of *The Godfather* (1971), which awakened a vast popular interest in Italian America, including its underworld. Even before ethnicity became fashionable, Scorsese was making student films and writing treatments for a projected trilogy concerning his own ethnic group. These works include *It's Not Just You, Murray!* (1964), *Who's That Knocking at My Door?* (1969), the unrealized treatment for *Jerusalem, Jerusalem*, and another project that in revised form appeared as *Mean Streets* (1973). These works are based on Scorsese's experiences in Manhattan's Little Italy, and at the time had small promise of financial reward. His mentor at the NYU film school, Haig Manoogian, told him after the disappointing release of *Who's That Knocking?* that it would be advisable commercially not to make any more films about Italian Americans. Scorsese can hardly be blamed for the fact that, by the time he was able to make *Mean Streets*, public attitudes had changed.

Nor would it be fair to say that Scorsese's Italian American films exemplify his indulgence in symbolic or 'low-cost' ethnicity, adopted for casually expressive purposes. Rather, the stakes have always been much higher than that. Film-making requires not only an enormous sustained act of imagination but a great investment of time, will, and effort; and these demands have weighed all the more heavily on the frail and asthmatic Scorsese. He has had physical difficulties in making some films, including *Raging Bull*, which so exhausted him that he checked into a hospital upon its completion. At the same time, insofar as Scorsese's Italian American films constitute not simply a representation but a judgment of Italian America, including the Mafia, he has risked both the resentful opprobrium of his fellow ethnics and embarrassing misunderstandings by the host community, with its stereotypical notions of Italian Americans. And finally, what is at stake in Scorsese's

Italian American films is collective and personal: to determine whether Italian American experience can serve the highest cinematic art, and to strengthen his bid to become America's greatest director since John Ford.

In order to comprehend Scorsese's circumstance as a third-generation Italian American artist, it is useful to compare him with Italian American artists of earlier and present generations. As Jerre Mangione rightly limits the concept of Italian American literature to works on Italian American subjects, rather than the totality of works produced by writers within the ethnic group, so the term 'Italian American cinema' properly applies to the work of directors who overtly treat their own ethnicity on screen.[21] By this standard, one must exclude the works of Gregory La Cava, Vincente Minnelli, and even Frank Capra, three first- or second-generation Italian Americans who enjoyed distinguished careers in Hollywood. Save for rare exceptions, these directors do not treat specifically ethnic subject matter, nor is their ethnicity much evident in their works.[22]

Frank Capra claims that when he left Sicily at the age of seven, he forgot it entirely.[23] Actually, rather than forgetting his past, Capra found his ethnicity troublesome throughout his career: he feared not fitting into Hollywood and desperately sought mainstream success.[24] As Raymond Carney suggests, Capra shows his desire for assimilation in the wilful suppression of ethnicity in his films, which transfer to American characters and settings the unhappy circumstances of his youth. These include poverty, social emargination, and family catastrophe, chiefly the unexpected death of his father and the sale of the family farm as the precipitating factor of emigration to America. The last incident is reflected in many Capra films, including *It's a Wonderful Life* (1946).[25] Capra's inclination to populist fantasies may also reflect his yearning to belong to the American 'mainstream.' Yet it is probably wrong to attribute the omission of Italian subjects from Capra's films to self-censorship alone, since a film director under the studio system lacked freedom in the choice and handling of subject matter. Although Capra, whose motto remained 'one man, one film,' enjoyed considerable creative freedom as the reward for his box-office success, commercial exigencies could hardly have encouraged him to make films about Italian Americans, as the public had little interest in what was then a peripheral group.

Nonetheless, Lee Lourdeaux holds that Capra manifests only 'surface assimilation,' for though he normally portrays Americans rather than Italian Americans, his characters have an intensely ethnic vision of America. In Capra's films, argues Lourdeaux, such positive Italian values as warm familialism, community, political participation, and compassion challenge WASP economic individualism, the success ethic, and political hierarchy and centralization. Even if some of Lourdeaux's arguments carry weight, they are often exaggerated, as his rigid antithesis between Italian and WASP values prevents him from seeing that many of the 'Italian' values he attributes to Capra also appear in American folk culture and politics. On the other hand, certain values that Lourdeaux attributes to Italians, such as voluntary, grass-roots types of associations, had little part in their Old World culture.[26] John Paul Russo shows that one of Capra's earliest efforts, a lost film of the pre-sound era, possibly encrypts Italian American themes; that some of his later films portray Italian Americans; and that these works, even when treating non-Italian American characters, sometimes contain religious and social values rooted in Capra's ethnicity. Russo further demonstrates the richness of Capra's later comedy *A Hole in the Head* (1959), the only Capra film in which Italian American ethnicity defines the characters and their situation, and which Capra hoped to follow with a film on Jimmy Durante. However, Russo acknowledges that ethnicity remains peripheral to the main line of Capra's work.[27] For Vito Zagarrio, Capra cannot be faulted for neglecting Italian American ethnicity, Zagarrio rightly sees such self-censorship as a typical response of the first- or second-generation immigrant seeking assimilation.[28]

Capra's films stand not so much in an antithetical as a dialectical relation to those of Scorsese and Francis Ford Coppola. The emergence of the Italian American cinema of which the latter are the most distinguished practitioners is inseparable from the 'arrival' of the Italian Americans, their attainment of unprecedented social, political, cultural, and economic importance. Both directors' willingness to explore their ethnic origins cinematically reflects their high degree of acculturation and assimilation as well as confidence in their identity as successful third-generation ethnics. Social and historical distance from the original culture has afforded them a margin for reflection upon themselves and their group, which they are secure enough to contemplate with aesthetic detachment.

However, Scorsese's situation as film-maker is better understood in relation to the development of Italian American literature from the first to the third generation.[29] According to Daniel Aaron, first-generation writers have tended to focus narrowly on ethnic themes and characters largely to acquaint the host culture ingratiatingly with their ethnic situation as well as to explode pernicious stereotypes. Too often this kind of writing, in which the writer 'represents' the ethnic group, limits itself to local colour and detail while subordinating artistic form to a social agenda. Second-generation writers are usually conciliatory towards the host culture yet risk alienating mainstream and Italian American readers through their sometimes cantankerous protest against the contradictions of the American dream.[30] Whereas for Fred Gardaphe these are the first Italian American writers to exhibit an 'articulate voice,' Helen Barolini complains that they sacrifice style and technique to narrative realism.[31] In any case, they remain hyphenated Americans, for like their predecessors they are imperfectly assimilated and self-consciously outside the social mainstream. In Aaron's third stage, which, borrowing a term from Thomas J. Ferraro, he calls the 'ethnic passage,' the third-generation writers move from the periphery to the centre of the 'majority society,' where they no longer feel hyphenated. These writers have appropriated American culture as 'deserving beneficiaries' and linked themselves with its illustrious representatives. Yet they are still aware of their marginal perspective, as they have not completely lost their ethnic consciousness. Through this double awareness, they are liberated from narrow parochial allegiances and identifications and, neither desiring to please the host culture nor regarding themselves necessarily as representatives of their ethnic group, may operate freely in the 'republic of the spirit' and 'province of the imagination.'[32]

Where these critics most disagree is on the potential universality of Italian American literary texts. Citing Werner Sollors, Gardaphe thinks it mistaken to impose upon ethnic literature a pattern of development from 'parochial' marginality to 'universal' significance in the literary mainstream. If one reads Gardaphe correctly, he relies on Sollors's ethnic theory to argue for a historically relativistic or 'culture-specific' criticism. The critic's main task is to interpret the 'ethnic signs' in an artist's work through the cultural codes that determine their significance, and on that basis to formulate a special aesthetic for ethnic, in this case Italian American, texts. Yet though Gardaphe favours such an aesthetic, his approach to his chosen texts is by his own admission mainly 'ethnographic,' the text being conceived as a 'communicative event determined by the cultural constraints within which the writer performed.' The success of an 'ethnographic critic' depends on his or her ability 'to read the culturally specific signs generated in the multicultural text.' While Gardaphe rightly emphasizes competence in reading ethnic signs as a preliminary to the evaluation of ethnic texts, a 'communicative event determined' by a writer's 'cultural' constraints allows for little imaginative freedom in handling such signs. The text sounds like a mere product of external conditions. The interpretive activity Gardaphe describes seems to call not so much for aesthetic judgment as for sociological and anthropological comprehension, with no indication of how to arrive at the former. In legitimating ethnic literature on relativistic grounds, Gardaphe seems to see no necessity for the ethnic work to rise above its narrow origins and self-enclosed system of signs to a more general interest.[33] Ferraro similarly denies that the quality of hyphenated writings depends on the author's transcendence of ethnicity so as to achieve a more universal aesthetic value. Instead, the aesthetic quality of the best ethnic writing is never stronger than when the writer is most determinedly ethnic.[34]

By contrast, Daniel Aaron envisions the minority writer as breaking out of his or her self-determined or enforced segregation into a larger United States, and thence into a universal republic of letters. He means that such writers' works have moved beyond a primarily ethnic interest or political agenda to a wider appeal and significance. For such writers, ethnicity is but one 'colour' of their 'palette.' Aaron finds the most successful dehyphenated ethnic writers to be those who, being neither 'insiders' nor 'outsiders,' move easily between their ethnic and mainstream identities and inheritances. He finds, though, that whereas some Jewish writers have done this, Italian American writers exploit their identity less imaginatively. He instances Mario Puzo, who lacks Saul Bellow's 'blend' of ethnic and American 'flavors,' and Don DeLillo, who largely avoids Italian American subjects.[35]

If one may invoke an analogy between literature and film, Aaron's paradigm remains the best by which to understand Scorsese's filmmaking and the nature of his cinematic achievement. Being neither an ethnic outsider nor fully assimilated insider, whether in American society or the film industry, he has never been bound by the claims of his ethnicity but has repeatedly demonstrated his artistic freedom, curiosity, and daring.[36] Many of his films have nothing to do with Italian America. He has directed urban melodramas, satires of contemporary life, thrillers, surrealistic fantasies, costume dramas, historical biographies, musicals, and biblical films. To be sure, these works reflect Scorsese's background as an Italian American Catholic, but he has also brought to them an awareness formed outside Italian America, including a lifelong immersion in American and European cinema. The rich texture of Scorsese's non-Italian American films testifies to this interweaving of cultural strands.

Yet though Scorsese managed to escape the 'Family' and the Church, meaning the totalizing claims of his ethnicity, 'his would never be a mainstream American life.'[37] And this is largely because Scorsese, as he fashioned an independent artistic career, remained loyal to Italian America as man and artist, drawing upon it repeatedly for inspiration. Italian America has been the subject of five of his feature films – arguably the core of his achievement quantitatively and qualitatively. In these films Scorsese has refused to ingratiate himself with either Italian America or the mainstream. Whatever failings he finds in Italian America he presents without apology or extenuation, with the critical detachment afforded by his position between minority and majority culture. Nor has Scorsese's chief interest in these films been ethnographic, although they are dense with what Gardaphe calls 'Italian signs' and remain imperfectly comprehensible without their deciphering. Despite his description of *GoodFellas* and *Casino* as an 'anthropological' portrait of Italian American gangster society, Scorsese has never been interested in ethnic details for their own sake but has sought to find in them a larger significance, to project them onto a universal plane. He has done this partly by observing the Italian American world from the perspective of a universal religion: that Catholic optic whereby, in his films, Italian American signs rise through immanentism to sacred analogy. Though imbedded within an ethnic milieu, the themes and behaviours that continue to attract Scorsese in his Italian American films have been neither trivial nor purely ethnic, but rather of the more widely significant and comprehensible type, such as pride, vanity, envy, rivalry, prepotency, and retaliatory violence. At the very core of Scorsese's Italian American cinema is a fascination with ritual in its capacity to prevent as well as provoke transgression and disorder – a universal theme applicable to all societies. Few artists equal Scorsese in exposing the Mediterranean cult of masculine honour in its longstanding conflict with Christianity. In doing so Scorsese has achieved insights into individual and social violence that are anthropological in the broad sense.

Yet it is a mistake to think that Scorsese's Italian American films consist solely of Italian signs, or that comprehension of their meaning and quality would depend solely on an elucidation of those signs, following a strictly culture-specific criticism. As Scorsese's cinematic career has paralleled his increasing assimilation into mainstream society, so his sequence of Italian American films has coincided with the stages of that process and amounts to his ongoing revaluation of his own ethnic background. The films themselves broadly coincide in their depicted behaviours and geographies with the process of Italian American acculturation and assimilation, manifest in migration from the Little Italies to the suburbs, and from the urban Northeast to Florida, Las Vegas, and California. What interests Scorsese in these films are not simply ethnic signs but his co-ethnics, the bearers of those signs, in their ever-changing interaction with the host culture and its powerful sign-system. The meaning of Scorsese's Italian American films is largely generated through this interaction. Though unmistakeably Italian American, his characters are deeply influenced by American culture even as they conflict with it.

In *Who's That Knocking at My Door?* J.R. listens to rock and roll, admires John Wayne and Lee Marvin, and endures a traumatic struggle between Italian American Catholic sexual attitudes and those of the sexual revolution. Like J.R., Charlie Civello in *Mean Streets* loves rock and roll and John Wayne yet cannot escape the moral and behavioural entrapment of Manhattan's Little Italy, where Mafia dons watch American gangster films on television and Sicilian songs play on jukeboxes in local bars. Charlie's girlfriend Teresa has been affected by feminism and intends, at the risk of ostracism, to leave Little Italy for an uptown apartment; Teresa's and Charlie's clandestine sexual encounters in uptown hotels likewise violate Old World norms. In *Raging Bull* Jake La Motta, despite his ghetto origin, plays miniature golf with his prospective non–Italian American bride, forsakes boxing for stand-up comedy, and comes to recite monologues in imitation of Marlon Brando. Two leading characters in *GoodFellas* and *Casino*, the half-Italian Henry Hill and Nicky Santoro, disconcertingly resemble ordinary suburbanites notwithstanding their criminal careers. They live in comfortable suburban houses, buy expensive cars and Christmas trees, wear sports clothes, play golf, attend Little League games, and indulge in a distinctly non–Old World reckless consumerism. That Henry Hill is only half-Italian is significant, for not only does this keep him from becoming a full-fledged member of the mob, but out-group marriage is a key indicator in Alba's 'twilight' of Italian American ethnicity.

What holds for Scorsese's characters holds for Scorsese himself, as man and artist. Despite his tendency to refer to Little Italy as a hermetically sealed enclave, he did not live even then exclusively within Italian America, but was exposed continually and unavoidably to signs transmitted from American mainstream culture and Italy. Aside from movie houses, the chief medium for their transmission was the family TV set where, besides Italian-language films, young Martin Scorsese was exposed through 'Million Dollar Movie' and other programs to the great tradition of American cinema, which was everywhere available for television viewing in those decades. Thus television not only contributed to Scorsese's Americanization but, in its best offerings, gave him standards of cinematic excellence he has always sought to honour. When he came to make 'ethnic' films of his own, Scorsese never supposed that these should be judged in 'culture-specific' terms, with aesthetic concessions bestowed tacitly as the reward of ethnicity, but in relation to the universal standard set by his great American predecessors, some ethnic, others of the mainstream: Ford, Welles, Hitchcock, Hawks, Lang, Capra, Vidor, and the rest. This is the standard by which Scorsese's Italian American films – the core of his achievement, and the foundation of his directorial excellence – demand to be judged.

3 The First World of Martin Scorsese

A major influence on Martin Scorsese, of an impact nearly equal to that of his family, was his local neighbourhood on Elizabeth Street and more generally Little Italy – the environment evoked in *It's Not Just You, Murray!*, *Who's That Knocking?*, *Mean Streets*, and *Italianamerican*. Acknowledging that these films perhaps overemphasized the grimness of the neighbourhood, Scorsese recalls that it was made up largely of 'decent, hardworking people' and in some ways resembled a true community.[1] Yet this neighbourhood was seriously flawed, as the southern Italian immigrant groups preferred to live with people from their native towns and regions and thus came to engage in bitter, sometimes violent feuds. Not only was there 'rivalry between the Neapolitans and Sicilians and Calabrese,' but these groups warred against their compatriots on the East and West Side, 'even down to the buildings.' 'It was always crazy that way,' remarks Scorsese of these intra-ethnic conflicts, which disappeared with Americanization.[2] Another cause of disorder in the neighbourhood was that there were 'some tough guys around,' so that fights broke out 'all the time,' the streets being then transformed into the 'Wild West,' although people were normally safe in their apartments.[3] 'It could be terrifying in your own backyard,' recalls Scorsese, who mentions having seen a baby falling from a roof.[4] While going to school as a child he often witnessed 'guys in the Bowery beating each other up with bottles. There was blood all over the street and you'd just step into it. I mean, that's normal.'[5] His brother Frank similarly describes the neighbourhood as 'very violent. There were gangs and fights [which could] ... break out instantly. In the middle of the night you could hear all kinds of fights and violence ... People lived by the sword and died by the sword.'[6] Apart from these local disturbances, many residents felt 'an irrational hatred of outsiders,' and Italian American gangs often clashed with 'Puerto Ricans who were moving into the area.'[7]

At least some of the violence observed by the young Scorsese would have involved local Italian American gangsters. At the same time, however, he came to comprehend the role of the Mafia in settling local disputes and providing security within the neighbourhood.[8] Since the criminal syndicate or Mafia regards the local ethnic neighbourhood as a field or fiefdom for its activities, it seeks not only to minimize violence but to monitor all incoming strangers, so as to deflect police attention while preventing trouble. The syndicate's goal is to establish and maintain a 'market peace' for itself in its own backyard. It furthermore thinks of its neighbourhood paternalistically, providing employment for local people, settling local disputes, dispensing favors, making donations to local organizations and the parish. So the Mafia often acquires an ennobled image in the eyes of the locals. And yet the fact remains that many of its gambling, loan-sharking, and protection rackets target neighbourhood people with violence and intimidation. According to Tricarico, the syndicate's benevolent functions are 'overshadowed' by its parasitism and exploitativeness.[9] Nor was the young Scorsese unaware that the Mafiosi preyed on each other as well as their Italian American neighbours. Concerned for their son's safety, Martin's parents taught him to follow the Sicilian custom of *omertà* or silence – that is, the refusal to report any lawlessness he may have witnessed in the neighbourhood. As his brother recalls, 'In the event that you opened your mouth then you were next.'[10] Scorsese was also told by his streetwise father that he must never borrow money, as indebtedness to a local loan shark often signals the beginning of a downward spiral into crime.[11] Nonetheless, Scorsese admits that he 'always had a morbid fascination with gangsters. Some of them were my role models despite what my father told me.'[12]

Scorsese's more immediate society consisted of a male peer group gathered at streetcorners: 'I'd been on the streetcorner a lot when I was young.'[13] His participation in such an informal organization was typical for his class and generation. In a classic study of Italian American 'streetcorner society' among children of first-generation immigrants, William Foote Whyte shows how these youths formed peer groups that supplemented or replaced their families, and in which some members continued to participate into their late years. Herbert Gans notes similar behaviour among the Italian American 'urban villagers' of Boston's

West End in the late 1950s.[14] Writing in the early 1980s, Richard Alba stresses the continuing importance of the peer group, formed of individuals of the same sex, age, life style, and status, as a supplement (and to some extent challenge) to the family, although he acknowledges the importance of loyalty to kin. In Robert Orsi's view, the streets of Italian American neighbourhoods are a 'theater of male posturing and demand,' where young men challenge familial authority by organizing themselves into gangs whose satisfying friendships would last a lifetime.[15]

In contrast to the typical Italian American male peer group, Scorsese's associates included juvenile delinquents as well as future criminals, including mafiosi. His, then, was a rough and violent society, where fighting was taken for granted and where a small and physically weak boy like Scorsese was greatly disadvantaged. 'There was always fighting going on ... always blood in the streets,' he recalls, since he and his friends saw violence 'as the answer to most problems.'[16] To quote a childhood friend of Scorsese's, the code of Little Italy was that 'If you weren't able to give a beating, you had to take one.' He adds that 'Marty was always the littlest guy, the weakest, but he fought.'[17] Or as Scorsese puts it, 'the only way I was able to defend myself was to be able to take punishment. Then I got a lot of respect. They said, "Oh, he's okay, he can take it. Don't hit him."' Scorsese also recalls the extraordinary egotism of these hot-headed types, proud of their muscle and highly sensitive to insults real or imagined: 'In the old days, in those neighbourhoods, certain people, if you stepped on the guy's *shoe*, you could die, let alone come over and insult him. He'd kill you ... Oh you'd be surprised how the insults come.'[18]

Scorsese's recollections of his peer group call to mind his Italian American films, in which aspiring hoodlums, seasoned gangsters, boxers, and other tough guys carouse at all hours of the night in bars and nightclubs apart from their wives and families. Sometimes they gather in all-male groups and in other instances are joined by girlfriends or prostitutes. Whatever the circumstance, they fill the screen with their overbearing bluster, swagger, and insult. Obsessed with personal honour, they not only demand but receive the respect to which they believe their toughness entitles them. Their local reputations rest invariably upon the threat of violence, which they never hesitate to use in avenging real or imagined affronts. Sometimes their quarrels erupt over possessions or prerogatives; in other instances what is at issue is the favours or honour of a particular woman. So far removed from mainstream standards, such behaviour reflects the fact that Scorsese's Italian American films depict typical features of southern Italian or, more generally, 'Mediterranean' masculinity.[19] This is not to say that these films treat Mediterraneans or southern Italians, as Scorsese's special cinematic province is Italian America. However, as I have noted, in the several decades following immigration Italian Americans continued to retain customs and attitudes deeply rooted in the face-to-face peasant communities, the farms, towns, and villages, of their southern Italian (and Sicilian) homeland. In order to understand the male–female relations that once typified Italian America, as well as the peculiar cult of masculine honour that figured prominently among its first and second generations, one needs to consider the relations between the sexes, patterns of behaviour, and ideals of masculinity as they had existed in the Old Country.

Since, in the agricultural communities of southern Italy, the fields have usually been distant from the familial residence in the village or agrotown, fathers have often had to spend the night close by the workplace and therefore away from home. The great distance between the towns and the peasant's workplace results from the towns having been built on hilltops so as to avoid the malaria that threatened the lower areas from dawn to dusk. Furthermore, the large estates or *latifundia* normally ringed the towns, leaving the poorer, smaller holdings on the periphery. As day labourers usually accepted any work they could find, employment necessitated long separation from families. However, the father-absent household of southern Italian society results not simply from work conditions but from ingrained social habit, as a southern Italian husband typically spends his evenings in the company of male friends, leaving his wife to perform her domestic duties. This pattern, which enables a husband to spend maximum free time in the public arena, exemplifies the sex-segregated character of work and leisure in the southern Italian household – a pattern also to be seen in northern Italy, though perhaps less than in the south. There is little mixing of boys and girls, while girls, removed from public view or else closely watched by chaperones, avoid talking to men, and do all they can to seem modest, industrious, and domestically inclined. In Lopreato's view, these social practices, as well as the southern Italian male's lack of acquaintance with his wife before marriage, have produced emotional distance and poor communication between marital partners.[20]

Until recent times Italian American males have resembled their southern Italian counterparts in tending to spend their free time in male peer groups segregated from women, including their wives. Donna Gabaccia observes that the Sicilian immigrant husbands of Elizabeth Street frequently left the house between supper and bedtime, and that in good weather they gathered outside in small groups. Herbert Gans finds emotional distance and poor communication among the Italian American couples of Boston's West End in the late 1950s, although in his view their father-absent households typify the American working class. By contrast, Lopreato attributes such behaviour in large degree to Old Country habits. In the view of Glazer and Moynihan, Italian American husbands of the 1960s customarily returned to their groups of friends after marriage.[21] However, Donald Tricarico remarks of Greenwich Village that the first- and second-generation husbands usually reined in their socializing with friends so as to perform their parental duties. According to Gans, the habits of aggregation among males were fading in Boston's West End in the late 1950s. In recent decades Italian Americans have if anything become more centred on their families.[22]

Scorsese's first feature film, *Who's That Knocking at My Door?*, depicts the Italian American male peer group of the 8th Ward Pleasure Club, where J.R. and his Italian American cronies play cards, smoke cigarettes, get drunk, and drown their sorrows in an all-male environment into which 'broads' alone are allowed, though only for casual sex. J.R.'s mother is portrayed in the film, but his father neither appears nor is mentioned. Like J.R., Charlie Civello of *Mean Streets* spends his nights in bars among male friends; his mother is only a vague presence, while his father is dead – perhaps Scorsese's way of emphasizing the father-absent family. That J.R., Charlie, and their friends adhere to a pattern set by the older, married males of their community is suggested by the all-male Debonair Social Club, which figures in *Raging Bull* as the watering hole of the gangster Tommy Como, where Tommy and his associates talk, drink coffee, smoke, and play cards. Early in the film, as the brothers Jake and Joey La Motta depart for a local dance hall, leaving behind Jake's disgruntled wife, she denounces them as 'queers' and 'faggots.' Sociologists more accurately describe the Italian American peer group not as homosexual but as homophilic.[23] Just before Jake's marriage falls apart, he is shown in his nightclub where, in the absence of his wife, he consorts with male friends and unmarried women. The half-Italian gangster Henry Hill in *GoodFellas* spends most nights away from his home, children, and wife in the company of his peer group and assorted girlfriends, behaviour Scorsese contrasts with what he implies to be the uxoriously housebound habits of the typical

Jewish male. In *Casino* Nicky Santoro is a kind of male witch who loves to fly at night; it is then that, as his wife falls sleep watching television, he performs his assorted loan-sharking, card-sharping, burglarizing, philandering, and murdering operations. These occupy him until the morning hours, when he arrives home in time to make his young son breakfast.

The Mediterranean cult of masculine behaviour cannot be understood apart from the related values of honour and shame. Building on the research of J.G. Peristiany, Julian Pitt-Rivers, and others, David Gilmore notes that Mediterranean societies, including the southern Italian, exemplify the shame as opposed to the guilt culture. This is not to imply that the distinction between shame and guilt cultures is absolute; these categories function as ideal types at the extremes of a continuum, whereas actual cultures and societies exemplify mixtures of types of behaviour, with one or the other tending to predominate. At the risk of considerable simplification, in guilt cultures conduct follows the private conscience as it adheres to moral values esteemed for their own sake as universally binding imperatives – an internalized morality that may have its fullest (and perhaps even unique) embodiment in England, northern Europe, and North America. These cultures exhibit a high degree of impersonality as well as being imbued with the Protestant heritage of self-examination, with the conscience performing at least ideally as an exacting inner tribunal in all moral decisions. Yet in the small, face-to-face communities of the Mediterranean, the moral and behavioural code is primarily determined and imposed externally, by public opinion, the approval or disapproval of the entire society conceived as an audience gathered in the piazza, plaza, or agora. A man who fulfils the social code has won honour and status for himself, family, and friends; to do otherwise is to suffer shame, the antithesis of honour, which means humiliation in the eyes of the community. To be sure, Christianity has attempted to replace honour with virtue in the sense of an impersonal, non-socially determined, absolute moral standard, but Mediterranean societies have resisted it. A person's excellence – honour more than virtue – needs to be recognized and confirmed by the community, without which no person has a right to pride. The chief imperative for the typical southern Italian male, his very reason for being, is to preserve and increase his personal honour, and that of his family and associates, by meeting the community's expectations, in public, of masculine behaviour. In view of Scorsese's interest in Italian American gang life, it is interesting that Peristiany and Pitt-Rivers find the honor-and-shame complex typical of streetcorner societies, in which violence is employed in cases of dishonour. Pitt-Rivers also links the cult of honour with the sacred, noting that prohibitions or taboos surround the man of honour, and that the code of honour 'derives ... from a sacred quality of persons, not from ethical or juridical provisions.'[24]

In Mediterranean societies masculine honour may be achieved through non-aggressive and non-competitive traits and activities such as honesty, sociability, hospitality, generosity, personal integrity, and the fulfilment of duties to one's peers, family, or community. It may also be won through economic success and the prestige and respect it brings to oneself, family, and friends. Contrariwise, a person may suffer dishonour through failings of sociability and conviviality as well as by engaging in fraud and other disreputable dealings. Yet because community expectations require the Mediterranean male to be a 'real' rather than 'effete' man, the code of honour often issues in a *machismo* complex characterized by intensely aggressive, competitive, and exhibitionistic masculinity. The southern Italian male feels the socially imposed necessity of being strong, tough, and hard, of controlling his emotions in public, and of constantly enacting, as the token of personal triumph, a phallic display of physical prowess. The honourable man surrounds himself with an invisible barrier carrying the message '*Nemo me impune lacessit*,' while the ultimate vindication of his honour, continuous with that of his family and associates, lies in retaliatory physical violence. These values may explain why southern Italy had the highest homicide rate in Europe around 1900. As a further stimulus to exhibitionistic violence, the Mediterranean code tends to foster not the healthy, controlled rivalry that modern nations have more or less achieved in their civic life, but vain and desperate competition over a common object, namely honour. In such a rivalrous society, one's honour often depends on the shaming of one's opponents: to win honour is to defeat and thus to bring shame upon them. In a world where honour is in very short supply, competition for honour takes the form of a zero-sum game, in which it can be gained only by taking it from others. As a value, then, it carries a built-in aggressive component. And because in Mediterranean societies shame is identified especially with women, whose social and ontological status is defined as inferior to that of men, to suffer shame is for the Mediterranean male the most humiliating of all fates. Yet no matter how much honour he may have inherited or achieved on his own, the Mediterranean male lives in a state of embattled masculinity, for no display of prowess, no public esteem, can ever confer honour permanently. Masculinity is always ready (and even seeking) to be tested by greater and greater challenges, and always about to evaporate in an unforeseen moment of shame and humiliation. The contests of honour involve what Maria Pia di Bello terms a 'progressive raising of the stakes' whereby the honourable individual is incited constantly by rivals to prove himself, a situation that can lead to competition 'so frenzied' that 'even murder may be envisaged.' Thus the vendetta.[25]

The point of vulnerability in the southern Italian cult of honour is that, while honour is male, shame is female. No matter how well he proves his prowess in other realms, a Mediterranean man's honour requires him to preserve the chastity of his wives and daughters. Mediterranean society practises a double sexual standard, so that little or no shame falls upon a philandering husband; in some instances his reputation will thereby increase. Yet should his wife or daughters dishonour themselves sexually, the shame falls equally upon him and his family. This ethos, which originates in the fact that, in these patriarchal societies, women have been a comparatively scarce commodity, underlies the protectiveness of the southern Italian (and Italian American) male towards his womenfolk. Such anxieties are intensified by his deeply conflicted attitude towards women. As the cult of the madonna requires a southern Italian woman to conform to a desexualized ideal of maternity and femininity, so the male displaces his erotic wishes onto the madonna's antithesis, the shameful prostitute. Nonetheless, the southern Italian male typically assumes, possibly through projection, that women cannot control their sexuality, so that, given the opportunity, they would couple with the nearest man. These anxieties have been especially intense in southern Italy, where many husbands work long hours and even months and years away from home. In angry moments southern Italian males have accused even 'respectable' women of promiscuous impulses. Southern Italian and Italian American women have also had to endure domestic isolation and close surveillance by their fathers and husbands as well as being made to conform to male-imposed standards of behaviour, the assumption being that, lacking internal restraints, they require the external control of the shame culture.[26] Scorsese's *Italianamerican* affords a glimpse of these social tensions when Mrs. Scorsese, reporting on her and her husband's trip to Palermo, recalls the Piazza della Vergogna, which is adorned with a multitude of nude female statues – a display that she describes as 'great' but of which her husband clearly disapproves.[27] It is hardly surprising that the madonna-whore complex as well as the rigid distinction between 'good' and 'bad' girls have played a prominent role in the sexual attitudes of the Italian American males in Scorsese's films.[28]

In Mediterranean societies, as in Italian America, honour is closely bound up with sex.[29] Not only is there a sexual component in male rivalries, which are often inspired by women or carried on to impress them, but sex defines the style by which one man dishonours another. As is exemplified by Jake La Motta's irrational doubts of his wife's fidelity in *Raging Bull*, perhaps the greatest fear known to the Italian American male is that of being cuckolded. A male thus dishonoured is known as the *cornuto* (the horned one), whose imaginary horns symbolize castration and defeat by a sexual rival. They may also be regarded as the symbolic inversion of the no-less-imaginary bull's horns that Jake claims for himself as the sign of his phallic mastery as a boxer. To suffer such indignity, and by extension any other indignity from a rival, is for the southern Italian male identical to being reduced to the passive, feminine position of being victimized and penetrated, and thus to experience the shame associated with women.[30] A man thus disgraced will either avenge the insult to name and family, or will remain, with his family members, a laughing stock of the community.

Another crucial factor in Scorsese's development was the asthma he suffered as a young child and that troubles him to this day. Even as a toddler Scorsese had respiratory problems, and at the age of four, after the traumatic removal of his tonsils, he became asthmatic, a condition that required injections and almost constant treatment. Because of it he spent many hours by himself first in his family home in Corona, Queens, and subsequently in his parents' and grandmother's apartments on Elizabeth Street. 'Right from the beginning,' recalls Scorsese, 'I couldn't join in and play stickball. In the summer they'd open the hydrants and water would go all over the street, and I was never allowed to go into that.' He adds that his self-description calls to mind 'some poor little kid behind a window staring at kids playing, but that's really what it was.'[31] The chief positive result of Scorsese's illness was that he precociously discovered movies as a source of mental stimulation and inspiration. 'During the first five or six years of my life I was mainly in the movie theater,' he recalls. 'I wasn't able to participate in any children's sports or games, so my parents took me to the movies. My brother did too. It became a place to dream, to fantasize, to feel at home.'[32]

Besides asthma, Scorsese suffered another handicap, less obvious than the first, and of a cultural rather than physical origin. For though he often recalls how his illness helped to foster his interest in film, he seems not to have relied on books to enrich his hours as a young invalid. Nor was this option likely to have been encouraged in an Italian American boy of the 1940s and 1950s, especially of the lower class. As noted above, not only were the Italian immigrants who arrived in the United States largely illiterate, but they strongly suspected education and reading as threats to family solidarity; thus it required more than a single generation for their descendants to become fully acclimatized to the American culture of literacy and to aspire to university educations. As Scorsese recalls, 'I grew up in a house without books, and basically everything I learned was visual.'[33] In an interview he mentions having lived in 'a home where the only things that were read were the *Daily News* and the *Daily Mirror*,' two tabloids. When he first brought a book into his home, 'there were discussions' between his parents, neither of whom had finished high school, over whether it should be allowed. They were 'worried' that his exposure to books would expose him to strange ideas and thus alienate him from the family.[34] However, the adolescent Scorsese was increasingly aware of the value of books and education, for as he reports, by around 1960 he was 'reading a lot' and thinking seriously of studying English at NYU.[35] His parents' worries only increased when, as an NYU undergraduate, he continued to bring books into the house, which they feared as a possible source of liberal or communist influences.[36]

Critics such as Stanley Kaufman attribute the supposed limitations of Scorsese's early films to his lack of a strong literary foundation.[37] For his part, Scorsese as late as 1992 complained (with historical inaccuracy) that 'there has always been the tyranny of the word over the image,' and that it is generally assumed that 'anything that's written has got to be better.' Yet from college onward he has continued to be a dedicated reader, trying to make up for what he perceives as lost time, and has written or co-written some of the best scripts of recent decades.[38] Arguably Scorsese has the best ear for dialogue – balanced between idiomatic realism and expressive stylization – among contemporary scenarists. Moreover, the lack of books in Scorsese's household was partly counterbalanced by the bias of the southern Italian working-class culture for visual, oral, auditory, tactile, and olfactory experience. The young Scorsese responded powerfully to the sensory plenum of Catholic services, and ultimately excelled in the visual and auditory medium of cinema.

Although Scorsese disliked sports, neither illness nor physical frailty detached him from his Italian American peer group. Not only did he have friends among the neighbourhood tough guys, but he sometimes joined them in their gang fights: 'I couldn't do it personally,' he recalls, 'but as a boy of thirteen or fourteen I had to harden my heart against the suffering. I had to take it. My friends go to beat someone up, I went with them. I didn't jump in, but I watched or set it up.'[39] He admits that, to compensate for his physical weakness, he attempted 'to be a nice guy to have around.'[40] Nonetheless, his asthmatic condition distanced from his peers, who called him 'Marty Pills' because of his frequent use of medication.[41] Often unable or unwilling to leave the family apartment, he became introverted and learned to spend much of his time in solitude, his imagination his only companion. He recalls 'how lonely I was as a kid. My parents worked, and I came home from school at three and sat at the kitchen table making up stories on my drawing board, or watching TV or escaping to the movies.'[42]

By now it is a cliché that Scorsese's illness afforded him a unique perspective that shaped his films. He admits that his asthma 'left him with the solitary sense that he was somehow different, set apart by nature from others.'[43] The young Scorsese had become an outsider, capable of observing his peer group and community with a detachment and objectivity unavailable to most Italian Americans of that generation. This sense of detachment perhaps originates at the moment when, as an asthmatic child, he began to observe events on Elizabeth Street from the window of his grandmother's apartment. A further explanation for Scorsese's distanced perspective on reality lies in the fact of his having been a working-class Italian American at a time when his ethnic group was much less assimilated than now. Such feelings of apartness also help to explain his persistent interest in the theme of emarginated individuals or groups attempting to maintain solidarity while in conflict with mainstream society. To quote Scorsese, his films are concerned with 'the outsider struggling for recognition,' a person with whom he identifies.[44] As Robert Philip Kolker puts it, his films take place within a 'tightly circumscribed area that has no exit,' and hold 'no triumph for his characters,' all of whom are ultimately lost to their isolation or their antagonism.[45] One thinks of the all-male group in *Who's That Knocking at My Door?*, the aspiring gangsters in *Mean Streets*, boxer Jake La Motta in *Raging Bull*, the 'wiseguys' in *GoodFellas*, and 'Ace' Rothstein and the other Mafiosi in *Casino*. Scorsese's debilitating asthma would also seem to underlie his cinematic fascination with gangsters whom he could never hope to emulate and whose physical prowess he in some way had envied.

Scorsese's experience of illness calls to mind Herbert Gans's findings in his study of Italian American 'urban villagers' following the Second World War. Those who had the courage to escape the community, including the conformist values of their peer group, had usually experienced a personal crisis that caused them to withdraw from the community and thus to see it from 'outside.' Among such crises Gans mentions illness.[46] Francis Ford Coppola, the Italian American director, attributes his heightened self-awareness and critical detachment from his environment to his childhood bout with polio, which taught him how to be alone. 'The popular kid,' observes Coppola, 'doesn't sit around thinking about who he is or how he feels. But the kid who is ugly, sick, miserable or schlumpy sits around heart-broken and thinks.'[47]

The most significant influence on Scorsese has been the Catholicism in which he first sought his vocation. He has often commented that, because of his asthma, his life came to be centred on movies and the church, the latter initially taking first place. There is no understanding Scorsese's mind and personality, or the world portrayed in his films, apart from basic features of Catholic theology and experience.

One way of comprehending Catholicism is through its differences from Protestantism. For the Protestant, God is a transcendent being whose absolute removal from nature makes Him the object of forbidding mystery: the *mysterium tremendum*, 'totally other,' whose divine reality can never be identified with the human. Consistent with the Protestant principle of segregation, which divides the realm of transcendent grace from fallen nature, an irreconcilable distance exists between the Creator and His creation. Sacraments are kept to a minimum; there is little or no belief in routine miracles; and saints are unavailable as a means of intercession with the divine. Protestant theology distrusts metaphor and emphasizes dialectical and logical distinctions between and among entities, ever keeping in mind the absolute uniqueness of God. But for the Catholic, God is at once transcendent, a figure of mystery and awe, and immanent within nature through the free operation of divine grace. God makes himself locally present within daily life through the sacraments and various intercessors that form a complex hierarchical system of mediations between the divine and material realms.[48]

The sacraments are the chief means by which the church mediates the divine to humankind. In the classic Augustinian definition, a sacrament is a visible sign of invisible grace enabling one to see the divine in the human, the infinite in the finite, the spiritual in the natural, in accordance with the Catholic belief in the sanctity of reality. Not only does a sacrament visibly signify that grace has penetrated the natural realm, it causes what it signifies. The body and blood of Christ are present in the Eucharistic Host at the moment of its blessing, this being the major example of the Catholic belief in immanence; however, Christ is present too in all the other sacraments. Divine grace is further mediated to humanity through the Virgin Mother, the church (equivalent to Christ), priests, ritual, saintly intercessions, prayer, works of mercy, and holy celebrations. Like the seven sacraments, these are the signs and means of personal salvation.[49]

In contrast with the Protestant principle of segregation, Catholicism, in assuming the presence of the divine on earth, favours an analogical mode of thought whereby theologians and artists assert the existence of physical and moral correspondences between God and nature. The world is conceived as an objective hierarchy or series whose elements are related analogically in terms of similarity and difference, with these correspondences bridging the gap between material reality and divine grace. It is thus possible to gain spiritual illumination through sense experience of the visible and concrete. For instance, God is not a father, but is like a father, and an individual father's or priest's behaviour may be judged accordingly. Such analogies differ from the normal non-theological use of metaphor and simile, which presumes no dependence of the related terms upon a hierarchical arrangement of being. Yet from the Catholic point of view, just as material objects may intercede in the relations between God and man, in a cosmic hierarchy reaching from earth to the divine, so they are capable of illuminating other material objects and actions. Analogy is of two kinds: parallelism, as in Dante, or contraries in analogy, whereby spirit is revealed by what opposes it, and which resembles spirit parodically or ironically.[50]

Not all critics are convinced that Scorsese's Catholic background counts for much in his view of everyday things or in his films themselves. In a discussion of *Taxi Driver*, Robert Philip Kolker attributes to Scorsese a viewpoint that could be described as Protestant. As Kolker says, although scenarist Paul Schrader had 'intended *Taxi Driver* to be an inquiry into spiritual isolation and redemption, the loneliness and transcendence of the outcast,' the film 'presents no such transcendental material, for this is not the way Scorsese sees individuals inhabiting their world.' Kolker adds that Scorsese 'has rooted his film in the very earthbound context of a lonely, barely coherent individual who cannot make sane associations between the distorted fragments of his perceptions.'[51] It is probably true that, given its character and subject matter, and Schrader's role as scriptwriter, *Taxi Driver* is among the least overtly Catholic of Scorsese's films, and much less so than his Italian American works. Nonetheless, Kolker's notion that Scorsese depicts a world where the possibilities of transcendence are absent, and where all is reduced to 'earthbound' literalism, untouched by redeeming metaphor, misses the centrality of Catholic immanence, sacramentalism, mediation, and grace in his work. Scorsese envisions a reality in which spirit penetrates and illuminates the surface of things, if not directly then through analogical parallel and parody. Or as Mary Pat Kelly says, from an early age Scorsese 'imbibed a sacramental view of the world,' and this is the proper vantage from which to examine him.[52]

Given the significance of the theme of chance in Scorsese's films, whether in the recreational gambling of his Italian American 'wise guys' or in a film concerned specifically with the gambling industry, like *Casino*, it is worth contrasting the Catholic attitude towards gambling with that of Protestantism. For the Protestant, not only does chance violate the divine providence and predestination that governs reality, it opposes the Protestant assumption that hard work and a disciplined life are the proper path to worldly wealth. Hence Protestants strongly disapprove of gambling in itself and as a source of gain. Yet Catholics like Scorsese are more inclined to see earthly success, as well as failure, as involving luck. Instead of thinking of themselves as predestined, his characters see the combination of skill and luck as the secret to worldly triumph. Sometimes their lives depend entirely on the whims of chance, while for the fortunate ones the lucky break carries overtones of divine favour.[53]

More than simply Catholic in their orientation, Scorsese's films reflect the peculiar type of southern Italian Catholicism that Italian immigrants brought with them from the Old Country. This version of Catholicism contained many features that sharply distinguish it from the more orthodox type of Catholicism their Irish predecessors had already established on American soil. The stubborn unwillingness of Italian immigrants to adapt to the Irish form of Catholicism led to what many Catholic prelates – mainly though not exclusively Irish – referred to as the 'Italian Problem' within the Church, a problem that persisted up to around 1930.[54]

Southern Italians brought with them a syncretic folk religion that showed considerable cultic variety and in which beliefs grounded in

Christianity mingled with anthropomorphizing pagan holdovers. Although these beliefs exemplify the immanentist and sacramental outlook typical of Catholicism generally, they also exhibit a strongly materialist, occultist, and visual emphasis that awakens in unsympathetic observers – not always without justification – suspicions of pagan idolatry, animism, polytheism, fetishism, magic, and other forms of superstition. Preferring human forms of intercession, the peasants normally prayed not to God or Jesus but to the Virgin and saints figured as visual images and devotional icons made of clay or metal and even plastic.[55] Such cultic practices, which included festivals and processions in honour of the sacred icon, reveal the lasting influence of pagan polytheism and often amounted to image worship or a belief in magic, as the images of the madonnas and saints were thought to have supernatural powers. Devotion often consisted of half-imploring, half-threatening conversations with religious images and statues that had to be propitiated and upon whom the southern Italians lavished kisses and caresses, but whose worship they angrily abandoned when their prayers went unfulfilled. The immanentist and visual character of southern Italian Catholicism appears in the use of crosses, rosaries, holy cards, scapulars, ex votos, blessed palms, rings, miraculous waters, shrines (edicole), crèches, decorative frescoes, colourful processions, and roadside shrines. The lighting of candles was especially popular, though frowned upon by the Irish clergy. The immanentist conception allows for typical southern Italian beliefs in magic, witchcraft, and sorcery, which involved the use of holy cards and amulets for the evil eye and horns (the corno) to visit evil on one's enemies.[56] So far as the official church is concerned, southern Italians have for a variety of reasons distrusted institutional Catholicism and to some extent even disregarded its official teachings and representatives.

Unlike southern Italian Catholicism, the Irish version that had won hegemony in the United States by around 1900 was English speaking and Anglicizing. The mainly Irish clergy desired a 'formalized and cold' ecclesiastical structure, in imitation of White Anglo-Saxon Protestant churches. Like northern European and American Protestantism, Irish American Catholicism emphasized 'transcendence, juridical formalism, neo-puritanism, [and] a concentration on instruction,' all of which has led to its being compared with Jansenism, a version of Catholicism reminiscent of the severity of Calvinist morality. Rejecting popular and traditional forms of devotion, Jansenism is Christocentric and conceives of the transcendent God as an entity who reveals himself

to the worshipper only rarely and only after the worshipper's strenu-
ous preparation. With its focus on the Trinity, Irish Catholicism carries a
strongly patriarchal emphasis in contrast with the prominence of the
Virgin Mother in southern Italian worship. Whereas southern Italians
approached religion individualistically, iconically, emotionally, and yet
somewhat casually, sometimes disrespecting priests and even church-
going, the Irish stressed the hierarchical unity of the church, the supremacy of doctrine, unquestioning support of churchmen and church
policy, ritualistic displays of faith free from folkish or 'superstititous'
elements, and rationality over emotion. Catechism and abstract dogma
define what it is to be a Catholic.[57]

For reasons partly of economy but even more of attitude, Italian
immigrants sent their children to public rather than to Irish-run and
tuition-charging parochial schools.[58] What they encountered in Irish
American Catholicism was to them remote, unfeeling, and impersonal.
The dry legalism and abstract formalism of the Irish-dominated church
alienated the immigrants in the extreme, as did its doctrinalism, emphasis on the word, and transcendentalist lack of appreciation of
religious imagery. The immigrants were offended by its use of English, supernationalism, and fund-raising. Still another cause for their
disapproval of the Irish church was its puritanical joylessness, marked
by asceticism and sexual repression.[59] Yet because southern Italian religiosity also exhibits asceticism and penitential masochism, it would be
misleading to attribute such religious impulses, whether in Scorsese or
in Italian America generally, solely to Irish influence.

Sebastian de Grazia writes that the American Catholic clergy succeeded over the long run in imprinting the religion of Catholic immigrants with 'American hues' – an anti-hedonic, work-oriented ethos
like that of Protestantism.'[60] In assessing the Irish American response to
southern Italian Catholicism, it should be noted that the Irish clergy had
only recently overcome the lack of religious discipline and persistence
of an animistic folk religion in the Irish peasantry, the chief source of
Irish Catholic immigrants. The reappearance of such traits on American
shores in the form of the southern Italian immigrant reminded the Irish
all too uncomfortably of their own recently surmounted past. Both Irish
priests and laymen disdained the Italian newcomers, if not as pagans,
then as disorderly, noisy, superstitious idolators of icons, greeting these
apparent deviants from true Catholicism with scowls and insults. For a
long time they were allowed to worship only in church basements.
Italian immigrant families were to be taught by Irish priests and nuns in

Irish-supported churches, to adapt them to the Irish model of Catholicism. Though the Italians wanted their own priests and churches, their national parishes flowered only after the First World War, as the second generation came of age.[61]

A main cause of friction between Italian immigrants and the Irish American clergy was the distrust and even scorn the former exhibited towards the church and many of its doctrines and practices, including the assumption that institutional Catholicism monopolizes religiosity. These divergences reflect varying historical circumstances between Ireland and southern Italy. In Ireland, the church protected the people against the English Protestant oppressor while giving them a rallying point by which to define their national identity. Irish life focused intensely upon the church, and Irish families often contributed at least one son to the priesthood. In southern Italy, the peasant distrusted the church as an instrument of political, social, and economic oppression. Such anticlericalism was reinforced on American shores when the Italian Americans encountered an insensitive Irish-American Catholic church. At the same time, Irish Americans resentfully identified Italian immigrants with a newly formed Italian state that had recently divested the Pope of his temporal power.[62]

The southern Italians' comparative detachment from official Catholicism is shown in the fact that, in the home country, the Virgin Mary and saints belonged less to the official church than to the towns and villages (or *paesi*) of which they were patrons and protectors. Sometimes local saints were not even recognized by the official church.[63] In doctrinal interpretation, southern Italians have been stubbornly individualistic in Italy as in the United States. Whereas southern Italian women and children often attend church, southern Italian males have a poor record of attendance in both Italy and the United States, especially in the first generation.[64] Not only have they regarded church-going and religious observances as 'cose *femminile*,' that is, feminine matters, but they exhibit a basic indifference to the mass and sacraments. The highest rate of Italian American church attendance corresponds to major holidays and family events such as weddings, christenings, holy communions, confirmations, and funerals. Southern Italian immigrants scandalized the Irish by their seeming lack of piety, as they spoke during mass, showed boredom during sermons, and showed impatience and even disrespect for priests. Naturally, the Irish were offended by the Italians' poor church attendance.[65] Yet for southern Italians, with their worldly realism, the overly pious person is '*troppobuono*' – too good. Into the

1970s Italian Americans remained the least pious of all Catholic groups, as only 30 per cent of their population regarded church attendance as important.[66] The Italian record of donations to the church has been unimpressive.[67] Nor have Italian American families remotely equalled their Irish counterparts in the percentage of sons entering the priesthood. This is largely because celibacy is disfavoured in southern Italian culture, which identifies masculinity with sexuality, marriage, procreation, and physical toughness.[68]

As late as the 1950s, the conflict between Irish and Italian Catholic religiosity was being played out in American cities, including Martin Scorsese's Little Italy. This is not to deny that the Catholicism practiced by Italian Americans increasingly resembled the Irish type, that they had probably increased their church donations, and that middle- and working-class Italian Americans were now less reluctant to send their children to Irish-dominated parochial schools.[69] Indeed, Scorsese's parents exemplify the latter trend, having enrolled him in St Patrick's School in Little Italy. Nonetheless, Herbert Gans notes of Boston's West End during the late 1950s that the Italian American residents complained the parochial schools were teaching their children Irish Catholicism.[70] As a young boy at St Patrick's School, Scorsese was 'acutely aware of the distinction between his ancestors' faith and the Catholicism promulgated by his school's Irish clergy and nuns.'[71] Even at this late date, St Patrick's Church and its convent reflected older attitudes, as they were still partly administered by Irish priests, while Irish nuns taught the Italian American children. Scorsese comments that St Patrick's Church had been built in the early nineteenth century and had originally served what had been the local Irish population. He adds that even during his childhood 'they sent over Irish nuns to work in that parish – right from Ireland, with Irish brogues.' However, 'the neighbourhood was all Italian, so you had a little enclave of Irish mafia religious thinking in the school which conflicted with the home lives of the Italian kids.'[72]

The Italian American immigrants' refusal to allow the official church a monopoly of piety is related to the powerfully immanentist outlook that, to the consternation of the Irish American clergy, extended the realm of spirituality beyond the church itself, so that conventional religion ceased to define genuine religiosity. To quote Philip Kayal, religion is 'fused' with the 'overall cultural mentality' of southern Italians and Italian Americans, whose 'everyday behavior is grounded in a

Catholic "idea," principle or thought.'[73] Primeggia and Varacalli concur that, for this group, the church is not the starting point, nor is the mass 'of ultimate signifance.' Instead, greater emphasis is assigned to institutions and social realities outside the official church, the ritualized street festival being the chief means of mediating the sacred to the individual and community.[74]

The southern Italian immigrants to the United States had a tradition of annual celebrations or *feste* characterized by processions, holy icons, and various outdoor events. Defying the Irish clergy, who accused them of paganism, they would not allow religious authority to alienate them from their sense of the sacred.[75] The *feste* and *feste* societies competed successfully with the clergy for the people's loyalty, devotion, and donations. It is reported that on festival days priests held mass before empty pews, as the people were outside celebrating; and only following World War II have the church and its rituals predominated over the *feste*.[76] The feast of San Gandolfo, which was formerly held annually on 14 September in Manhattan's Little Italy, and which continues as an annual celebration, though now scheduled for June, honoured the patron saint of Polizzi Generosa, the home of Martin Scorsese's paternal grandfather. It is fair to assume that Charles Scorsese, his father, and the young Martin Scorsese attended this event,[77] which was celebrated by the Jesuits with a high mass in the Church of Our Lady of Loreto on Elizabeth Street, but whose high point was a procession to Prince, Bleeker, and Mott streets. It concluded 'with a flight of angels, two girls dressed up as angels suspended by pulleys over the statue of the saint as they gave recitations to the patrons while the icon completed its journey through the neighbourhood.'[78]

Despite modifications in the postwar period, the *festa* remains a major outdoor and collective event that takes place within the carefully defined boundaries of the neighbourhood whose precincts it sanctifies. To ensure the orderliness of the crowd, whether at religious services or during outdoor events, individuals are assigned hierarchical roles. The *festa* aims to affirm collective identity and communal membership through ritualized actions that raise it from the quotidian to the sacred. Contributing to this feeling of extra-worldly sanctity is the fact that the festival continues at all hours, rejecting familiar temporal boundaries, including the everyday work schedule. At the centre of the *festa* is the patron saint or holy figure whom it commemorates in the form of an icon or icons carried in procession.[79] One thinks of the Madonna of Mount Carmel, whose feast is celebrated annually in Italian East Harlem, or the tower of lilies (Giglio tower), centrepiece of the Giglio feast in the Williamsburg section of Brooklyn. The ritual procession marks various neighbourhood sites so as to affirm a sacred topography; as in the Giglio feast, the life of the saint is re-enacted.[80] For many Italian Americans, festival promises a cure for their ailments and those of their loved ones. They throw themselves upon the mercy of devotional icons such as the Madonna of Mount Carmel, imploring her to remove their pain. Lucky charms are sold at the *festa*, and sacred wax images of body parts can be bought by people suffering from diseases that affect those organs. Others who have been cured of such diseases regard themselves as miraculously blessed, and in gratitude to their patron saints buy wax corporeal images as gifts to be placed in their chapels. Orsi refers to the *mysterium tremendum* experienced in the *festa*, the atmosphere of love and fear pervading these holy days.[81]

The spirit of the *feste* depends on the elements of sensuousness, hedonism, aestheticism, and merrymaking that normally accompany them, and that contribute to their sacred character. The *festa* is a total event the sum of whose activities produces the healing its participants passionately desire. The consumption of vast quantities of food and drink unites the neighbourhood in what amounts to a communal feast, food being regarded as a virtually sacramental substance on these occasions. The rich smells of cooking combine with songs, fireworks, musical performances, people in costume, dancing, and coloured lights in decorative patterns strung from sidewalk to sidewalk. A bazaar-like atmosphere is created by the presence not only of many stalls where holy cards and other items are sold, but of fortune-tellers, games of chance, wheels of fortune, and competitions for prizes.[82] These games of chance, writes Orsi of the feast of the Madonna of Mount Carmel, were played before the madonna, the participants 'wagering their pain and discomfort to win some prize they had long been hoping for,' so that she 'became the symbol of fate.' John Paul Russo refers to the 'rich plenum of sensation' which is as much a part of the experience of the festival as its specifically religious performances.[83]

For southern Italians, as for Italian Americans, the sacred overflows the church and extends beyond to the family itself, where sanctity crystallizes in the most essential and intimate form of Italian American spirituality. This is the religion of the house or domus conceived as both an enclosed spatial entity and a hierarchical system of relationships, each invested with sacred significance. To quote a statement made in 1912 by the Italian American priest Louis Giambastiani: 'It is not far from the truth to say that for many Italians whatever religion they possess is narrowed within the walls of the home; for the home of the Italian is essentially religious,' and 'people always imagined the divine in relation to the domus.'[84] Indeed, a main reason for southern Italian anticlericalism is that a priest lacks a domus.[85]

Within the immigrant family the domestic hierarchy was dominated by the father, whose authority was supplemented by that of the mother. What maintained the hierarchy was respect or *rispetto*, a mixture of love, fear, duty, and loyalty towards the family order. As Orsi says, '*Rispetto* was the essential and fundamental value of the domus-centered society.'[86] Children had to accept the parental will even when they disagreed; to do otherwise was to bring shame to the family and oneself. Each individual was furthermore pledged to protect, defend, and avenge the honour of his or her family as embodied in its sanctified hierarchical relationships. This hierarchy defined the way in which the family presented itself to other families and thus was known to the outside world. To quote Russo, 'the religion of the family extends in concentric circles outward from the home to the neighbourhood, city and country, ultimately to the natural universe.'[87]

The holiness of the interior space of the domus was underscored by an abundance of holy shrines, objects, figures, and images whose presence had less to do with their inherent sanctity than with that of the home. These included statues and pictures of saints; lithographs with religious subjects; crucifixes, which often appeared over beds; and pillows with religious medals. Holy cards were displayed in many homes, while holy candles were lit ritualistically before images of saints.[88] Important holy days as well as *feste* were celebrated as major events of the domus. The idea of the Holy Family strengthened blood ties as well as providing a model for imitation. But of all the rituals of the domus, probably the most significant were the weekly and Sunday dinners where family members customarily gathered. Occupying the head of the table, with his wife at his right hand and children ringed about him, the father served the meal, during which conversation was minimal.[89] Because the food had sacred significance, the family dinner resembled a holy feast. To quote Orsi: 'Eating was the sacrament of the home, and the Sunday meal was more important to immigrants than regular attendance at Mass.' He adds that 'food was symbol and sanction and sacrament, integrating the home, the streets, and the sacred.' Or as Richard Gambino writes: 'I was made to feel that food was the host of life ... In a very poignant way, meals were a "communion" of the family, and food was "sacred" because it was the tangible medium of that communion.'[90] These remarks apply equally to the family dinner represented in Scorsese's *Italianamerican*.[91]

As the sacred never exists without fear, so the religion of the domus had its dark side, which Orsi designates as the suppression of anger, especially that of female family members.[92] Since the maternal ideal of the Virgin Mary was held as the highest ideal of womanhood, and since Italian American males desired a woman who most closely approximated this ideal, chastity was deemed essential in an unmarried woman. Otherwise, a woman was scorned as the virtual equivalent of a prostitute. Yet like their counterparts in the Old World, as we have seen, many Italian American males thought women incapable of controlling their sexual impulses.[93] Immigrant families thus expected young men and women to keep a formal distance until they were engaged. As Gambino notes, this reflected the value system of peasant society, where 'male and female roles were distinctly separated,' where 'warmth and tenderness were classified entirely as feminine roles,' and where 'aggression and impassiveness were masculine characteristics.'[94] Young men and women often grew up with little knowledge or understanding of each other, and their courting behaviour was hedged by prohibitions. Not only were young women expected to protect their sexual reputations, but families guarded against as well as punished violations of their chastity.[95] As Scorsese remarks: 'I grew up in a certain kind of culture: Sicilian, Roman Catholic; women were separate entities; and the madonna-whore dichotomy encouraged fear of them, distrust, and, because they didn't seem to be like real human beings, difficulty in relating to them.'[96]

The Italian American sense of the sacred included the neighbourhood or community, where family and church were intermingled, and which too was governed by *rispetto*. This 'indicated a general attitude toward life, affirming the dignity of the person respected as well as the person respecting.' In its neighbourhood manifestation, *rispetto* implied the 'complex ... weaving together' of 'love and fear, intimacy and distance,' as people of different families interacted socially. Since the lines between the domus and neighbourhood were defined imprecisely, it was normally expected and indeed insisted upon that individuals in the streets should treat each other respectfully, according to their social status, lest disgrace fall upon them or their families. Thus *rispetto* 'was the most serious criterion' by which to 'judge the quality of another person.'[97] Its violators risked shame or violent punishment and even death.

A disturbing side of southern Italian Catholicism appears in the strongly penitential and masochistic component to be found in some of its versions, and which has apparently left its imprint on Scorsese's life and work. He states hyperbolically that 'punishment for everything you ever felt sexually ... is the basic moral battleground of Christian ethics.'[98] When asked to define the influence of Catholicism upon him, Scorsese replied: 'Guilt. A major helping of guilt, like a lot of garlic.'[99] These attitudes originate at least partially in the puritanical views of the Irish clergy and nuns, whom the Italian American immigrants considered to be sexually repressive, masochistic, and life-denying in their teachings. However, comparable attitudes appear in Italian American Catholicism itself, tracing back to the Old Country.[100]

Michael Carroll shows that some forms of southern Italian religious ritual and festival processions display a penitential and masochistic cast. The chief object of southern Italian worship is not Christ but the madonna and saints, who conjoin beneficence and punitive sadism. Whereas in northern Italy the Counter-Reformation terminated public displays of ritualistic masochism, Catholic rituals and processions in southern Italy have been characterized up to recent times by public self-mutilation and self-flagellation: tongue-dragging over rough ground, walking barefoot over long distances on hot pavements and stones, the slashing of one's head with knives, and the hanging of a heavy stone around the neck. These acts of self-punishment serve to propitiate a madonna perceived by penitents as a punitive and unpredictable woman of extraordinary ferocity; Carroll thus writes of 'Madonnas that maim.' Such masochism may reflect the fact that, for southern Italians, Christ is much less an exemplar of the moral conscience, or a figure of compassion, than the ideal of sincerely penitential good son, the martyred child for whom the madonna sorrows.[101]

Italian American Catholicism has been influenced by its southern Italian counterpart in its emphasis on suffering as the mark of both atonement and closeness to the divine, with the saintly martyr or crucified Christ figuring as the ideal spiritual model. This masochistic syndrome is evident in the annual *feste* of many Italian American neighbourhoods, including the Madonna of Mount Carmel in Italian East Harlem. During the festival female participants made vows to the madonna to assume penitential suffering and sacrifice on behalf of another suffering person, usually a family member. Such sacrifice demonstrates *rispetto* towards the madonna, who must be propitiated with pain, and who thus elicits love and fear. The participant drags her tongue on stone in crawling up the steps and down the aisle of the church, or walks barefoot on burning pavement for many miles to the festival. Those who lift the heavy processional icon during the Giglio feast do so as penance for their relations in purgatory.[102] The atmosphere of suffering at the feast of the Madonna of Mount Carmel is reinforced by images of St Francis receiving the stigmata, the Pietà, and street-corner images of Christ in the *Ecce Homo* tradition: the 'face of the man-god ... is bathed in blood – redemptive, life-giving blood,' according to immigrant beliefs.[103] Reflecting their assumption that suffering and sacrifice are 'essential links between themselves and the divine,' the participants' self-punishments affirm their connection with divine suffering so as to gain liberating access to the sacred. The participants want to manipulate suffering so as to win the attention of the divine and to receive special favours, including redemption. Yet Orsi finds more questionable aspects in these proceedings, as the self-laceration of women on behalf of family members reflects their sense of powerlessness within the domus. Their very idea of divine power seems 'pathological in its origins and consequences,' as they seem 'to want to bind themselves to the divine with a covenant of pain.'[104] The behaviour described by Carroll and Orsi calls to mind such typically Scorsesean characters as J.R., Charlie Civello, and Jake La Motta.

For all their anticlericalism and comparative indifference to church attendance, observes Gambino, Italians see themselves as Catholics. Primeggia and Varacalli note that despite their rejection of the 'legitimacy of magisterial authority to normatively define the standards of the Catholic faith,' Italian Americans 'believe their form of religious adherence to be a legitimate variation of authentic Catholicism.'[105] Yet given the sometimes residually pagan and idolatrous worship of southern Italians and Italian Americans, and given their ambivalence towards official religion, cannot one conclude, with Vecoli, that they are only 'nominally' Catholic or, with Primeggia and Varacalli, that they are only 'marginally' Catholic and even non-Catholic?[106] John Paul Russo holds that one should neither exaggerate the anticlericalism of the Southern Italians nor claim, as does Leonard Covello, that they are Catholic only unofficially. Nor should one accept Vecoli's contention that southern Italian and Italian American religion are essentially independent of the church. It is an error, says Russo, to mistake anticlericalism for a consistent anti-Catholicism, or to forget that the church, which allows considerable latitude in the forms and practice of Catholicism, has never repudiated its popular southern Italian versions. Michael

Carroll asserts that Italian popular Catholicism, though often quite different from the official variety, remains Catholicism, as it adapts its conventional forms under local conditions.[107]

Scorsese's characterization of his parents' and relatives' religiosity holds few surprises. In an interview of 1987 he remarks that his grandparents had 'very old, traditional, more European icons,' including the large crucifix that appears over Jake La Motta's bed in *Raging Bull*. However, his parents were 'never really very religious,' for whereas his grandparents were certain to attend mass on Palm Sunday, his mother would only sometimes attend, and his father never. Nor did his parents announce publicly that their children 'should become priests and nuns.' To be sure, when young Martin behaved badly and his parents wanted to 'pull out all the stops,' they would tell him to inform the priest of his 'disgrace.' Yet on major ethical issues, such as birth control, his parents followed the typical Italian American pattern in regarding their decision as 'none of his [the priest's] business.'[108] In an interview in the late 1980s, Scorsese doubted that 'the church figured into [*sic*] their life that much,' adding that they were 'pagans' who put the church in a 'certain perspective' so as to control their major personal choices. His family, including his grandmother, thought of the church chiefly in terms of what Keyser describes as 'icons and rituals, ... statues and sacramentals, ... feast days and festivals.' Scorsese further recalls that his grandmother had a picture of the Sacred Heart, a 'niche with the statue of the Virgin Mary grinding the snake under her foot,' and the aforementioned 'gigantic crucifix over the bed.' Nor did Scorsese think that neighbourhood attitudes towards religion differed much from those of his family.[109] Within this social context, the young Martin Scorsese must have been anomalous, for though by his own admission he had 'no religious upbringing' before his family returned to Little Italy, he began to take official Catholicism 'seriously' soon after their return. He needed some kind of order amid the 'chaos,' as he says of the transplantation from Queens back to the old neighbourhood.[110]

Growing up in Little Italy in the 1950s, Scorsese had at least two major career possibilities available to him – organized crime and the church. Yet though he had friends among the local tough guys, he realized that, because of asthma, he 'couldn't do it in the streets – the kids were really rough.' Asthma seems to have initiated Scorsese's church attendance, as a way of filling his time, but he soon found that the nuns 'liked' him and that he 'needed to be accepted somewhere.'[111]

Unusually among the local boys, he found himself drawn to the church and began to attend mass regularly beginning at the age of seven or eight. His parish church was St Patrick's on Little Italy's Mulberry Street, which by then was staffed by some Italian priests as well as Irish nuns. Commenting in 1973 on his earliest attitude towards church dogma and liturgy, Scorsese remarks: 'Well, I did believe it, every word of it. I wouldn't touch meat on Friday, and I believed I would go to hell if I missed Mass on Sunday.'[112] He fasted during Lent, observed the Easter obligation, and often followed the Stations of the Cross. Not only did Scorsese become an altar boy, but by the age of eight or nine he had decided to become a priest.[113] In a 1987 interview he recalls as his motivation a desire for 'some peace or an answer of some sort,' and initially he showed special interest in missionary work.[114] Whatever Scorsese's later objections to the Irish nuns of his parish, they had instilled in him a highly inward, scrupulous, rigorous, disciplined, and church-centred conception of Catholicism atypical of Italian Americans.[115]

In choosing his new vocation Scorsese was fascinated by Father Damien, the missionary to Hawaii who cared for lepers and eventually died of leprosy himself. There was fascination too in a visiting missionary's report of his exorcism of a boy in the Philippines.[116] Yet what most attracted Scorsese was Catholic ritualism as the embodiment of spiritual order and sacramentalism. As he says, 'I loved the ritual.'[117] This was partly because, to quote Mary Pat Kelly on the Catholic mass, 'everything carried special significance: Gold was for great feasts such as Christmas, purple for the seasons of penance, red for the martyrs, white for the Blessed Mother and the great saints, and green for ordinary Sundays and days when no special saint was commemorated.'[118] For Scorsese, the high point of the mass was the moment of the transubstantiation of the communion wafer through the priest's blessing into the real presence of the Eucharist – he calls it that 'special moment when God came down to the altar.'[119] Yet as Kelly explains, a perfect enactment of the rite was required: 'when all the [ritual] actions were performed correctly, and the sacred words spoken, the bread and wine were no longer what they appeared to be. They had become the body and blood of Christ, who was truly present, just as he had been at the Last Supper, on the cross, at his birth.'[120]

Yet the motives behind Scorsese's choice of career were less than pure, selfless, or compassionate. He confesses awe of the 'theatrical' spectacle of Catholicism, its colour, icons, music, solemnity, and beautiful liturgies – what he terms the 'trappings of religion.'[121] There was furthermore in Scorsese's attraction an element of egotism and vanity, that of being at the centre of a sacred spectacle. As he reports, he became an altar boy because he 'loved ... the chance to be close to that special moment when God came down to the altar.'[122] He refers to the priest's role at the moment of transubstantiation, when his words render Christ sacramentally present. As Andrew Greeley remarks, in Catholic tradition the priest is himself a 'sacrament. When he presides over the Eucharist, he stands in the role of Jesus the high priest and is touched therefore lightly but permanently by the transcendent,' and for this reason, though human, is also 'someone special.'[123] A further attraction of becoming a priest lay in taking out insurance for salvation while enjoying a privileged position of intimacy with the Saviour. 'It seemed,' says Scorsese, 'that the best guarantee of being saved was to become a priest, which would be like being able to pick up a phone any time and talk to God.'[124] He recalls believing that 'at least with a religious vocation a priest or a nun might have more of an inside line to heaven – into salvation, if you want to use that word.' He mentions 'really wanting that vocation, selfishly, so that I'd be saved.'[125] That vanity or social status figured in his choice of vocation is suggested by his observation that priests had great prestige in Little Italy, equal to that of local gangsters. The latter 'would tip their hats to a priest and watch their language, and they would have their cars and pets blessed.' Scorsese adds that this may have influenced his decision to become a priest.[126] One thinks of Charlie Civello in *Mean Streets*, whose attempt to play lay priest to his thuggish associates reflects his morally and spiritually compromising vanity. In considering the long-term debilitating effects of Scorsese's asthma, one wonders whether he sought the priesthood because he was unable to become a gangster. In any case, his choice of calling further distanced him from his community while deepening his understanding of the experience of the outsider.

Over the long run Scorsese's desire to become a priest came to nothing. In 1956, at the age of thirteen or fourteen, he enrolled at Cathedral College, a junior seminary school on the Upper West Side. A year later, however, he was expelled. According to his parents, Scorsese was unable to apply himself to his Latin lessons. He attributes his expulsion to academic failure, classroom misbehaviour, rock and roll, and a growing preoccupation with girls that led to guilt-inducing bouts of masturbation. There are reports of roughhousing in class and brandishing of fake guns. At some point during this period Scorsese was terminated as an altar boy because of tardiness.[127]

Despite these setbacks Scorsese still seriously considered the priest-hood and enrolled at Cardinal Hayes High School in the Bronx with the intention of entering the Jesuit University at Fordham and ultimately becoming a Jesuit.[128] Influenced by Catholic familialism, which condemned premarital sex, as well as by the puritanism he had imbibed from Irish nuns, the adolescent Scorsese suffered extreme guilt over his erotic desires. Yet it was also during his adolescence that, according to Scorsese, he 'constantly' felt himself to be 'communicating directly with God' and 'having spiritual experiences.'[129] These experiences of guilt and mysticism culminated in a three-day religious retreat that seems to have been only one of several Scorsese attended with high-school classmates. Having arrived at the retreat in a disturbed state, he attempted to overcome his guilt by participating in the Stations of the Cross.[130] He also heard sermons in which the priests discussed sex, the Ten Commandments, the Shroud of Turin, and the punishment and suffering of Jesus. Scorsese responded with 'a vision of some sort, which was really more a fright vision than anything else because I was feeling guilty about things.' Not only did he experience an 'auditory hallucination,' the sounds of the night growing unbearably loud, but the 'smudges on the window became like the face of the Shroud.' As 'this happened about three times during the night,' Scorsese walked the halls of the monastery 'trying to get out of it,' after which he 'went to a special grotto to pray.' These prayers failed, for as he remembers, 'I wound up in a very bad state for which the priest's only advice' was that he should 'see ... a very good Catholic psychiatrist.'[131] This experience was to inspire Scorsese's 1966 film treatment *Jerusalem, Jerusalem*, which he never filmed; and traces of it appear in *Mean Streets*, in which Charlie Civello, unlike his friends, remains affected by high-school retreats.

Scorsese graduated from high school in 1960 but was disappointed when Fordham rejected him because of low grades; he chose NYU as an alternative.[132] It appears that he remained devoted to official Catholicism into the early 1960s, when he still thought seriously of becoming a priest. Yet with Scorsese's enrolment in the NYU film program under Professor Haig Manoogian, the study and making of films began to occupy much of his time, and ultimately cinema would replace the priesthood as Scorsese's vocation.

During the mid-1960s Scorsese came to question official Catholicism and gradually drifted away from the official church. He was troubled by the division between Catholic teaching and the moral and physical reality of Little Italy, where brotherly love had little place amid prideful displays of violence and desire. What also disturbed him was the morally ambiguous role of priests, for as he had seen in Little Italy, they had no objection to baptizing the children of gangsters who genuflected in church yet murdered outside it.[133] Scorsese was coming to suspect the moral insufficiency of the church, its willingness to compromise with the evil it had failed to defeat. Such suspicion of the church was common among Italian Americans at this time, or at least the 'urban villagers.'[134] Scorsese was further troubled by orthodox church teachings on sexuality, which he saw as unreasonable and life denying; various dogmas concerning mortal sin, such as the prohibition against eating meat on Friday, which lacked biblical foundation; the apparent role of the church in promoting intolerance of other groups; and not least the attitude of some churchmen towards the Vietnam War. The decisive moment in his repudiation of official Catholicism came during a sermon in which a priest justified American's participation in Vietnam as a 'holy war.'[135] By the time he had made *It's Not Just You, Murray!* Scorsese had no intention of returning to the seminary, and by 1965 or 1966 he was no longer a practising Catholic, having stopped going to mass and made his last confession.[136]

In a 1983 interview Scorsese describes himself as an 'agnostic' who had 'lost ... faith in the man-made aspects of the religion,' adding that his films are concerned with 'how to live and find an honest, non-institutional faith.'[137] In subsequent statements Scorsese repudiates agnosticism in favour of belief in God, but his quest for non-institutionalized religious experience remains constant. As a self-described 'Catholic layman,' he adheres in his films as in his life to a distinction between the formal and official requirements of Catholicism and the daily practice of Christian ethics.[138] To quote a 1986 interview, 'living the good life,' which for Scorsese is the same as 'practicing the tenets of Christianity,' is achieved 'through love, rather than making Mass on Sunday.' Contrary to the idea that mere religious routine provides an 'inside line' to salvation, Scorsese finds such formalism insignificant as compared with the moral challenges of daily life. 'You don't make up for your sins in church,' says Scorsese, 'you make up for them in the street.' Again, it is insufficient simply to perform one's penance in church; the 'idea is ... [to] do it outside, you do it out in the streets, you do it with your family, you do it with your friends.' These statements, reminiscent of the opening voiceover in *Mean Streets*, show the extent to which Scorsese, for all his indebtedness to Irish American Catholicism, came to reject its legalism, formalism, and institutionalism for a more personal style of worship.[139] In this he exemplifies a common tendency of Italian American religiosity, which apparently had a more lasting impact upon him than his first teachers among the Irish American nuns. Nor does Scorsese identify his abandonment of a religious vocation with spiritual weakness, for as he remarks of his own secular discipline: 'Mine was harder. I had to do it in the street.'[140]

Despite Scorsese's disavowals of Catholicism and his desire for a non-institutionalized religion, it is a mistake to think that he sees himself as being outside Catholicism, or that it fails to influence his life and work. Although he categorizes himself as a 'lapsed Catholic,' he adds the qualification that 'I *am* a Roman Catholic.'[141] Such statements make more sense if one considers Scorsese's Italian American background. Having, as he says, 'never gotten over the ritual of Catholicism,' he remains haunted by recurrent 'images' from the time of his religious indoctrination.[142] In a 1991 interview he states that though he has made his final confession, he still 'can't help being religious' and that he is 'looking for the connection between God and man.'[143]

Scorsese's discovery of cinema and his ultimate choice of film-making as a vocation contributed to both his abandonment of the priesthood and declining devotion to official Catholicism. The more time he devoted to film, the less time he had for religion. And yet these spheres are by no means absolutely divided in Scorsese's practice as a filmmaker, as he has diverted into film many of the spiritual interests and energies he had formerly focused on Catholicism. Scorsese recalls that Professor Manoogian had seen that he would be able to carry out 'whatever good I would be doing with a vocation ... through my films.' As soon as he heard Manoogian lecturing, Scorsese realized that he could put his 'passion' for religion into making movies, and that the 'Catholic vocation was, in a sense, through the screen for me.'[144] He later remarks that the 'passion' he 'had for religion wound up mixed with film,' and that, following his final confession, he had been 'confessing most of the time' on the screen.[145] Or as he puts it, 'My whole life has been movies and religion. That's it. Nothing else.'[146]

As a career choice, film-making afforded Scorsese a unique opportunity to bring together the two seemingly incompatible vocations by which he had been tempted in his youth: organized crime and the church. Not only does the Catholic belief system inform most if not all of his cinema, but it figures in his Italian American films as the chief basis by which he evaluates the underworld, its sanctities, loyalties, perfidies, brutalities. Out of this mingling of two incommensurable moral realms within Scorsese's directorial consciousness springs the most revealing of his comments on his own version of Italian American cinema: 'I was raised with them, the gangsters and the priests ... As an artist, in a way I'm both gangster and priest.'[147]

Scorsese's films, and especially those treating Italian American subjects, testify to basic elements of the Catholic worldview – immanentism, sacramentalism, analogism, and community, whereby the sacred is conceived as existing visibly within the physical world in a complex web of correspondences, some related in parallel, others ironically or parodically. To quote Andrew Greeley: 'the works of Martin Scorsese are the quintessential illustration of the use of the Catholic sense of community and Catholic symbols in American filmmaking.'[148] In acquiring this view of reality, Scorsese was perhaps indebted less to the Irish nuns of his parish, who would have held a transcendentalizing concept of the Creator as hidden, than to his good friend Reverend Frank Principe, who characterizes Scorsese as 'incarnational in his approach to religion,' being 'able to find God in all things.' Rev. Principe adds that, for Scorsese, 'as to most Italians, religion is incarnational, earthly.'[149] Thus, when Scorsese says that the 'whole idea of faith fascinates me,' he exemplifies this fascination with earthly examples: 'I have faith in this project. I have faith in this person.' For him, 'These are material matters, and you could look at them concretely, but I tend to feel they're spiritual.'[150]

Although Scorsese's choice of a career may seem a radical deviation from the priesthood, he thinks of the two analogically, stressing in Catholic fashion their similarity in difference. As an altar boy Scorsese found in Catholic icons and rituals a theatrical spectacle he likens to that of cinema.[151] 'For me Holy Week was always a very powerful time,' recalls Scorsese; 'it was even more dramatic than Christmas. The rituals were dramatic. The liturgies were beautiful. The Stations of the Cross were very dramatic. This colored my whole sense of God.'[152] He remarks of the missionaries who visited St Patrick's School that 'what they were doing was really *theater*. It was a holdover from the medieval period.'[153] Peter Boyle, the Irish American actor whom Scorsese directed in *Taxi Driver*, comments on the interplay of Catholic ritualism and cinema in the experience of the young Scorsese: 'And if Marty spent a lot of time in the movies as a kid, he also spent a lot of time in church. They're both big and dark, and they're full of mystery, and the rites of purification and of life and death are acted out in the same way.'[154] Sacrilegious though such comparisons may seem, Paul Giles observes that, as early as the 1910s and 1920s, the identification of film and Catholic ritual had become commonplace: both Protestants and Catholics compared movie houses with cathedrals and liturgical devotion. But whereas some Protestants denounced cinema for its seductive visual illusions, its 'gods and goddesses,' Catholics have tended, in keeping with the analogical, mimetic, sacramental, universalizing, and pictorial orientation of their religion, to favour cinema and the mass appeal of its iconography.[155]

As Scorsese associates Catholicism with cinema, so he regards his films as dramas of salvation and damnation, in which visual representations transmit transcendental truth. Abounding in the sacramental images, icons, and festivals of Italian America, Scorsese treats these not simply as local colour but as behavioural and psychological influences upon his main characters, whose aggression, however, they often prove unable to control. Consistent with Catholic teaching, Scorsese's Italian American films typically find analogues of the sacred in the quotidian, for instance in the ritualization of behaviour, vain pretentions to divinity to be seen in Jake La Motta and various gangsters, and underworld substitutes for priestly mediation. Scorsese's films further call to mind the Catholic worldview in assigning a major role in the lives of characters not to predestination but to chance, which often determines their success or damnation while carrying implications of divine favour or disfavour. As Les Keyser notes, 'Scorsese puts little trust in a rational universe progressing in orderly ways to a preordained goal.' Instead, 'his fictional universe frequently lacks causality and structure, and his characters depend more on the final mercy of God than on any day-to-day evidence of divine Providence.'[156] This sense of dependence on chance, regarded ultimately as a divine manifestation, is even revealed in Scorsese's film-making practice, as witness the conclusion of his 1970 political documentary *Street Scenes*, which breaks off abruptly because the film ran out: 'I just left it that way. I thought "Perfect, it was God sent."'[157] His Italian American films likewise reflect his assumption that the true site of moral and spiritual testing lies not in the church but in the streets, place of work, and family, as witness such characters as Charlie Civello and Jake La Motta. There is further evidence of the indebtedness of these films to Catholicism in their concern with penitential suffering, whether in the sexual-ascetic form of the madonna-whore dichotomy, or in the characters' mistaken tendency to identify self-elected pain or martyrdom as the mark of spiritual success. This appears in Charlie Civello and even more so Jake La Motta, whose religiosity takes the form of self-punishing masochism – a pathology to which the director seems half-attracted even as he condemns it.

Besides noting that Scorsese's films imply the failure of religion to control aggression, Michael Bliss remarks his fascination with purgative and redemptive violence. For Chris Hodenfield, 'blood sacrifices' are 'essential' to Scorsese's plots.[158] According to Bliss, not only does Scorsese see violence as a 'necessary prerequisite of self-awareness,' but his films portray it as a 'redemptive force ... alleviating socially induced tensions.' Bliss further claims that the 'depicted regenerative capabilities of violence' in Scorsese's films aim to show that violence is 'an essential part of existence' that, 'through its curative powers, affirms society's basic healthiness.'[159] There is some support for Bliss's view in Scorsese's explanation of why his characters 'always bleed from the neck in his movies': 'it's ... really like a purification,' says Scorsese, 'you know, the fountains of blood.'[160] His references to the centrality of blood (he calls it the 'life force') in Catholic ritual, and to the importance of human sacrifice in 'practically every culture' (which seems an exaggeration) might imply, untenably, the identity of primitive blood rites and the Crucifixion.[161] In a 1976 interview he compares the violent conclusion of *Taxi Driver*, in which Travis Bickle (Robert De Niro) attempts to pacify and purify society through a series of random murders, with the Crucifixion and the 'ritualistic, religious experience' of the 'Mass.'[162] Such an interest in violence partly stems from Scorsese's awareness of his own impulses: 'I know the killing feeling. The feeling of really being angry.'[163] Or as he rephrased it fifteen years later: 'I'm just an angry guy ... I'm angry about – you name it, I'm angry. You get to a point where the anger in you can explode. You go into little pieces. And then what – you're dead.'[164] These admissions are confirmed by observers such as Jonathan Taplin who, as the producer of *Mean Streets* (1973), saw the young Scorsese at close hand: 'He had a bad temper,' recalls Taplin, and 'gave it full rein' – not, however, among men, but in the company of women.[165] 'To me,' says Scorsese, 'I like the idea of spurting blood ... I like the idea of getting shot.'[166] Nor does he exempt his audiences from violent emotions: 'You can't stop people from getting an exhilaration from violence, because that's human.' He apparently refers to violence both actual and cinematic. As for the latter, he acknowledges that such exhilaration requires aesthetic detachment, the 'creation of ... [the] scene in the editing.'[167] In yet another interview Scorsese remarks: 'Violence is a form of expression ... It's how people live.'[168]

Nonetheless, Scorsese speaks of a 'civilizing process' through which, over history, religion has advanced from the child sacrifices of the Carthaginians, to Hebrew blood sacrifice, to the bloodless sacrifice of the mass.[169] In the same interview in which he rashly compares Travis Bickle's violence to the mass and the Crucifixion, Scorsese characterizes the latter as an ultimate sacrifice whereby Christ terminates the 'ritualistic blood sacrifice of lambs.'[170] Scorsese has also made statements disavowing all violence while testifying to his acceptance of fundamental Catholic values. In a mid-1980s interview he identifies the 'good life' not with materialism but with 'practicing the tenets of Christianity,' which he summarizes as 'love. Not hate, not retribution, not revenge. Love.'[171] In another interview he observes that 'I always think it's much harder to deal with the idea of love without retribution, as opposed to Mosaic law. I think that's the thing everybody has to go for: forgiveness.' Invoking the example of Gandhi, he states that 'what [he] ... did was extremely hard, obviously. Much easier for everybody to run around and start retaliating, like the Hindus and Moslems all killing each other.' Scorsese mentions his film *The Last Temptation of Christ* (1988), then in preparation, whose purpose was 'to make people begin to see that maybe the best philosophy is the way Gandhi took it and to give people something to hope for.'[172] Not surprisingly, Scorsese went on to direct *Kundun* (1998), which celebrates Tibetan Buddhist pacifism. Commenting on *The Last Temptation*, Scorsese states that despite his moral struggles he remains a 'believer,' that he believes in 'love,' and that Jesus had the 'right idea.' His reputation as a poet of redemptive violence consorts oddly with his advice to 'turn the other cheek,' although he agrees that 'it's hard' to do so.[173] At once contradictory, exploratory, and tentative, Scorsese's statements raise the issue of the relation between sanctity and violence, which stands at the centre of his Italian American films.

Located outside the ordinary, profane world, and attaching to certain objects, beings, places, and times, the sacred manifests itself as a mysteriously capricious duality. Roger Caillois observes that it conjoins the beneficence of life enhancement and rejuvenation with a terrifying, death-dealing power of destruction, chaos, and panic. To derive its benefits while avoiding its dangers, humanity must surround it with taboos, the violation of which causes the offending person to become the polluting pariah whose expulsion purifies society. Yet society must also draw upon the life-giving power of the sacred through controlled contact with it – the task of ritual and the priest. Another desirable means of contact is the festival, for though its topsy-turvy world is only temporary, it allows for revivifying invasions of the sacred in the form of violations of the social order. Games of chance figure typically amid such misrule, as signs of the gods' power to deal out good and bad unpredictably.[174]

René Girard bases his interpretation of social and religious behaviour on the idea that desire, far from being instinctive, as is commonly believed, is imitative, mediated by human models from whom the human subject learns the objects of his or her desire. Deriving from Girard's early work on the novel, this idea forms the basis for his studies of violence and the sacred. He defines imitation as of two main types. In the first, imitation focuses on an external mediator, spatially or temporally beyond the reach of the subject, so that the subject's imitation of the model's desires cannot result in acquisitive and mimetic rivalry with the latter. Such mediation, though delusive, does not destroy the subject. But in the second or 'internal' type, individuals regard each other as gods and thus become the mediators of each other's desire – a situation fraught with potential for conflictual mimesis. Especially vulnerable are those individuals who, feeling ontological deprivation, choose as models of desire individuals seeming to embody god-like autonomy and self-sufficiency, Because the subject needs the model in order to designate worthy objects of desire, the latter hypnotizes the former. But then the originally worshipped model becomes the subject's rival and ultimately obstacle in their shared desire for the same object. Seeming to hold the key to success or salvation, the mediator incites an intense attraction as well as hatred in the subject who, in the presence of this sadistic being, luxuriates in a masochistic humiliation that ironically keeps his or her hopes of acceptance alive. For Girard, masochism results from the subject's need for a superior model as the object of a repetitive, enslaving, self-defeating rivalry. Sadism is the mark of god-like autonomy, the pretence that one is not enslaved to others' desires. Homosexuality originates precisely in the subject's obsessive fascination with the model become rival and obstacle.[175]

Such a relation may change, however, as the model can substitute for the subject, making the latter into a model and imitating his or her desires, so that the model and subject become gods of each other. All autonomy is lost, even for the original model or mediator, who had feigned haughty self-sufficiency. Girard's name for this state of affairs is 'double mediation,' meaning that, in their repetitive, unacknowledged imitation of each other, the rivals have unwittingly become each other's doubles. As their envious rivalry intensifies, they forget the original objects of their desire and become absorbed in mimetic conflict to the point of actual violence. Girard characterizes internally mediated desire as 'metaphysical' because, at once vain, abstract, empty, and pleasureless, it originates in the subject's lack of being and in the false belief that the mediator can fill that void. On the other hand, such desire constitutes a distorted reflection of the individual's inarticulate hunger for the authentically transcendent, the divine in its real form. Thus, even in Girard's early study of the novel one detects his implicitly Christian orientation. What he terms 'deviated transcendence' refers to the process whereby individuals in deifying each other fall into soul-lacerating mimetic desire and rivalry. The only escape lies in the Imitation of Christ, a figure of non-conflictual mimesis and an unapproachably transcendent model.[176]

Unexpectedly, Girard's later works extend his concept of mimetic or 'triangular' desire to anthropology and religion. He uses it as a template by which to grasp the relation between violence and the sacred, the subject of his study of 1972. Girard assumes that any society requires an operative system of hierarchical distinctions – in short, a differentiated structure. Vendetta and other retaliatory forms of violence have often endangered and sometimes even undermined traditional societies, a breakdown he attributes partly to the failure of religious forms and prohibitions, but also to the fact that, unlike their modern successors, these societies have not assigned to the state, police, and judiciary a monopoly of violence. Girard emphasizes the role of mimesis not only in the breakdown of social order but in its re-establishment following a violent internal crisis. Such a crisis originates in mimetic and acquisitive rivalry, that is, centred on common objects of desire. As rivalry yields to conflict, insults and accusations pass back and forth until cycles of retaliatory violence break out between the antagonists and their supporters. Since their behaviour is imitative, the more the embattled individuals assert their differences through violence, the more they unwittingly resemble each other. Violence is also contagious, sucking more and more people into the swirling tide of the original rivalry, so that escalating hostilities further undermine the social distinctions upon which order depends. For Girard, the feuding doubles or brothers traditionally symbolize undifferentiating conflict rooted in mimetic rivalry. The plague is another standard metaphor for the random, seemingly uncontrollable spread of mimetic, undifferentiating violence within a community. Kings, priests, aristocrats, children, paupers, outcasts, and a host of others are all potentially victims. Nor can the crisis be checked by religious or legal controls, since general violence has robbed them of their power. As the conflict rages each combatant seeks by violence to bring it to an end, yet he or she only fuels its flames. A society at this point of dissolution has entered the 'sacrificial crisis.' Its situation is all the more serious given that, unlike animals, human beings and societies lack a built-in braking mechanism to control their aggression.[177]

Nonetheless a mechanism exists by which to resolve the crisis. An individual is singled out arbitrarily and transformed into the monstrous embodiment of the crisis in all its violent undifferentiation. This is accomplished by heaping the individual with false accusations identifying him or her as a violator of those prohibitions that, before its breakdown, the community deemed sacred. Typical accusations include incest, parricide, and the spreading of plague. The unacknowledged double of his or her accusers, such an individual is chosen from among those on the social margins, such as kings, women, orphans, paupers, cripples, and foreigners, as these types not only conform easily to a pariah role but, because of their marginal social position, are readily identifiable with undifferentiation. Whatever his or her origin, the individual in question is the scapegoat, whose unexpected and seemingly miraculous elimination through an act of unanimous violence is followed by a return to social order. Yet the notion of a collective founding murder is intolerable to the community and is concealed through mythical and ritual distortions testifying to the community's *méconnaissance*, its misunderstanding of its own origins. The scapegoat becomes a god-saviour; the gods, identified with 'good' violence, are held responsible for saving the community; and ritual is established with animal victims substituting for the foundational human victim. Mediated by priests, ritual is the controlled mimesis, in disguised form, of the crisis that issued in peace and harmony.[178]

The institutionalization of ritual has far-reaching social effects. There is, apart from the recovery of social unity, a restoration of order in the sense of a hierarchical, differentiated system based on ritual. All that the sacrificial crisis had endangered has been regained, with ritual observances now serving to keep violence from the community. Such rituals also become the foundation for a whole complex of distinctions, representations, and symbolic substitutions that constitute not ritual alone, but the mimetic system of culture. These offshoots of ritual include laws, art, theatrical performances, games, and a host of what

Victor Turner would term 'social dramas,' essentially secular events whose aim is to achieve social redress, reconciliation, propitiation, and pacification. In its more immediate effects, ritual differentiates between good and bad violence, both of which are mimetic, but the first of which is ritualistic and therefore controlled and contained, the other being uncontrolled and potentially all-destroying. Also arising from ritual order is the idea of the sacred in the sense of a complex system of fearful yet provocative prohibitions whose chief aim is to discourage mimetic desire with all its potential for violence, and the violation of which carries harsh penalties. The taboo against incest typifies such a prohibition. In this way the community claims the sacred power to punish transgressions against its own taboos. Thus violence, whether in the form of ritual prohibitions, punishments, or mimetic conflict, is the 'heart and secret soul of the sacred.'[179]

The ritual commemoration of the sacrificial crisis includes the festival or holiday, which is of considerable significance to Scorsese and to Italian Americans generally. Rituals and the *feste* attached to them aim to recreate, for purposes of social rejuvenation, the circumstances under which, in panic, fear, anger, and uncertainty, the community united itself as if by chance and miracle upon the murdered body of the scapegoat. This explains the frequent, virtually obligatory presence of games of chance in both festivals and rituals. Not only is ritual the origin of play, whose relation to the sacrificial crisis appears in the arbitrary nature of prizes, but games of chance first appear in ritualistic form and only later lose their sanctity. The link between ritual and chance is that the sacrificial crisis had been characterized by a levelling of distinctions through random violence, arbitrary victimization, and the community's miraculous recovery, interpreted as divine. Like ritual itself, the function of games of chance in ritual is to commemorate and imitate the crisis – the vertiginous atmosphere of hope and panic, and the unpredictable potential of violence for destruction or salvation.[180]

Unfortunately the system of the sacred is of limited efficacy, as the cycles of violence inevitably recur and gradually undermine the power of ritual and taboo to control them. However necessary as a check against mimetic desire and its attendant violence, prohibitions awaken not just fear but desire, and thus by their very existence provoke transgression.[181] Where the system of the sacred prevails, certain people will be invested with divine attributes or else claim for themselves godlike autonomy and self-sufficiency, which can only inspire envy, imitation, and rivalry. People will become fascinated by and enslaved to seemingly superior individuals, appropriating their desire and transforming them into punishing rivals and hypnotizing obstacles to their happiness. Inevitably antagonism expands into open mimetic hostility with the usual train of accusations and retaliations – a vortex of undifferentiating violence into which more and more people are swept. The possibility of violence further increases as gigantic human aggregates, such as the nation-state, claim to incarnate divine violence. Yet the most important factor in the decline of ritual has been the critique contained in the Old and especially the New Testament. These texts have exposed the underpinnings of ritual and ritually generated social order in scapegoating violence, with all its arbitrariness, injustice, and hypocrisy.[182] On the negative side, the demystification of ritual greatly diminishes its powers of social control, so that humanity may lose its most reliable buffer against its own violence.[183]

For Girard, the alternative to ritual and the system of the sacred based upon it is to follow the teachings that have called them into question. Not only does the Old Testament show an unusual sympathy for victims, but it partly reveals the workings of mimetic violence and sacrificial victimization. In turn, the Gospels totally unmask the sacred, including its complicity with the scapegoating mechanism. In a controversial interpretation of the Crucifixion in non-sacrificial terms, Girard claims, contrary to the orthodox interpretation, that this apparently sacrificial act supposedly required for humanity's salvation was neither foreordained nor necessary theologically. It resulted from the inability of a depraved world to accept Jesus's revelation of mimetic violence and persecution. The murder of Jesus, a totally innocent man, shows once and for all the moral bankruptcy of the sacrificial mentality, rooted in the violence of mimetic rivalry and false accusation. Exclusively human in its causes, and entirely comparable to all previous human sacrifices, the Crucifixion belies the characteristic tendency of human communities to attribute the killing of the scapegoat to a divine source rather than to their own violence. Henceforward societies find it increasingly difficult and finally impossible to sanctify and worship their victims. In the Gospels, the alternative to sacrificial victimization lies in the worship of a God altogether removed from that human violence which human beings falsely attribute to the divine. However, the most important remedy for violence in the Gospels is the *Imitatio Christi*, which demands both total abstention from mimetic conflict and total rejection of social violence. As the unapproachable model of a non-rivalrous and non-acquisitive life, Jesus opposes suffering for its own sake, as he comprehends that masochistic debasement at the hands of the mimetic obstacle in no way confers spiritual election; yet if suffering is the alternative to violence, and if it entails a greater human good, he gladly takes it upon himself, as in the Crucifixion.[184]

Girard recognizes a common tendency to misconstrue the *Imitatio*, which he attributes to the fact that the Gospels themselves have been misconstrued as celebrating Christ's death as a necessary act of penitential, self-sacrificial suffering. Affording ammunition to those who deride Christianity as a masochistic and self-sacrificial religion of life denial, many Christians have made a 'fetish' of the Passion by interpreting it as a uniquely sanctifying and divinizing event and have thus come to imitate Jesus's victimization and torture as signs of their spiritual election. These Christians assume that immolation of the 'flesh' in the Pauline sense is essential to their liberation from bondage to mimetic desire and violence. Yet for Girard, these self-martyring individuals are trapped unwittingly in a triangular relationship in which salvation is the prize and in which the subject and Christ confront each other as imitator and model respectively. For them, Jesus is the torturing model-rival-obstacle who incites desire yet withholds the desired object, namely salvation, even as he proffers it. The subject identifies with the model's sufferings and seeks through pride and vanity to outdo the model in the misery that he believes himself to suffer at the model's hands. Suffering remains the token of possible grace, indicating that the model still pays attention to the subject and may bestow upon him the salvation long withheld. For Girard, this masochistic interpretation of the *Imitatio* falsely displaces mimetic desire and conflict onto the spiritual plane. Suffering is not to be pursued deliberately and pridefully but, as with Jesus, will come to the good soul in a world of woe.[185]

The value of Girard's schema to Scorsese's Italian American films is that the religious, social, and cultural values of southern Italian and Italian American society provide an especially rich and dramatic breeding ground for the phenomena Girard describes.

The Italian American world in which Scorsese grew up, and which he depicts in his films, is a highly sacralized and ritualized society within which individuals are hierarchically defined and differentiated. Each individual is entitled to *rispetto*, which may be defined as a mixture of attraction and fear, intimacy and distance, and in whose prohibitions lie discernible traces of the sacred. The highest *rispetto* attaches to institutions and individuals essential to the community. These include the church and its priests, custodians of the ritual order and its prohibitions. There is also the family, a hierarchical arrangement based partly on religious beliefs and attitudes and ruled over by an authoritarian father whom other family members honour and obey. The father guards the family order while enforcing those taboos, sexual and otherwise, by which its integrity is maintained. The Italian American mob plays an important unofficial and clandestine role in the community, as its leaders not only help to maintain peace but, as men of honour and power, gain respect in doing so. The social drama of *rispetto* unfolds every day on the neighbourhood streets, in the constant show of honour and deference among individuals and families.

However, the most potent affirmation of communal order and harmony appears in the periodic outdoor *feste* by which the streets themselves become sanctified. As with rituals and festivals generally, one can discern in these occasions traces of the sacrificial crisis in which, in remoter times, the *feste* themselves very possibly originated, and of which they are the controlled mimetic representation. Two major examples include the Giglio feast of the Williamsburg section of Brooklyn and the feast of the Madonna of Mount Carmel, celebrated in Manhattan's Italian (now largely Spanish) Harlem.

The Giglio feast was probably founded on an originally pagan ritual celebration involving Dionysus. It ostensibly celebrates and re-enacts the safe return of St. Paulinus to Nola after he had offered himself as a sacrifice to save the city from the Arabs. The main event is a procession in which male community members carry an enormous image of the saint placed upon the so-called Giglio Tower. This consists of a display of lilies raised on steeples weighed down by a multitude of large and heavy candles. The feast is characterized by a hierarchical and orderly disposition of the participants, holy processions with stops at wayside shrines, and abundant sacred representations and offerings, including papier mâché saints, angels, and flowers placed upon the Giglio Tower; there is also much singing and eating in a communal atmosphere. All this exemplifies the good and orderly mimesis of ritual. However, probable vestiges of the festival's originating violence appear in the fireworks that accompany the proceedings, and which represent that violence in a safely conducted and aestheticized form. A competitive spirit also prevails among the men especially chosen to lift the heavy lily tower. Although their competition is friendly, it may unconsciously commemorate remoter times when the community was engulfed in violent mimetic rivalries.[186]

Regarding the feast of the Madonna of St Carmel, Orsi notes many features that invite interpretation as mimetic and controlled representations of the sacrificial crisis and its unpredictably salvific conclusion in human victmization. Not only are the participants in the festival assigned specific roles within it, but the event occurs within well-defined boundaries marking a sacred space. Such activities continue at all times, thus simulating the topsy-turvy world of the crisis, in which basic social differentiations cease to matter. Here one finds, though tempered by the anti-carnivalistic modern industrial world, some evidence of that transgressive element which Girard, Mikhail Bakhtin, and Natalie Zemon Davis find typical of the carnival. The event is sacred, a 'high time' (*Hohe Zeit*) altogether out of time, and from which work is therefore banished. Partaking of a communal feast, which has a sacramental import, the participants buy religious icons while engaging in various games of chance, whose presence amid the festival activities represents indirectly the random violence which brought the crisis to its climax. Reminiscent of the 'lifters' who compete with each other at the Giglio feast, the Madonna of Mount Carmel is pulled through the streets of Italian Harlem by devotees who had vied for that honour. Another link with the sacrificial crisis is suggested by Orsi's remark that the festival expresses cultural rage, but in contained fashion. This is largely manifest in the penitential self-laceration or self-victimization of the participants, who among other acts of penitence walk barefoot in procession for many miles to the festival. If such activities recall the crisis in its aspect of victimization, its salvific character for the community is reflected in the fact that those who punish themselves have come not simply as penitents, but to be healed. Implicitly, the festival cures the ills of the community. Festivals like the Giglio feast and the feast of the Madonna of St Carmel are an intensified expression of those values of *rispetto*, backed up by annual ritual commemorations, that preserve communal order and harmony.[187]

Italian American *feste* have exerted a unifying and pacifying influence upon a community very much in need of it. Not only have the inhabitants of southern Italian regions suspected and hated those of other regions, but strong animosities have often arisen between and among the inhabitants of local villages. Clannishness and insularity also prevailed in the early days of immigration, as southern Italians preferred places of residence on the basis of regional and local loyalties, thus reproducing Old World hatreds. As Mangione and Morreale remark, 'there were some difficulties when a celebration honoured the patron saint of a village, who was not held in high esteem by immigrants from another village.' They add that the 'tensions that existed in Italy were no less intense in the urban Little Italies of America' where, amid a festival, 'insults were [sometimes] exchanged and traffic blocked as a quarrel gained momentum and police were summoned to restore order.'[188] On the positive side, Mangione and Morreale note that the 'annual religious festival was an occasion when animosities between Italians from different villages and regions were temporarily put aside as a mark of respect for the holy personage being celebrated.'[189]

To judge only from Scorsese's films, Italian American festivals are imperfectly efficacious, as their ethnic world is constantly threatened with violent disruption. Not only are religious prohibitions ignored or flouted in his films, but violence explodes within the family itself, as in *Who's That Knocking at My Door?*, *GoodFellas*, and *Raging Bull*. It also undermines those more extended 'families' that constitute the Italian American mob, as in *GoodFellas* and *Casino*. Besides transgressing against their fellow ethnics, Scorsese's gangsters occupy the margins of mainstream society, whose laws and taboos they deliberately violate by supplying it with illicit goods and services. Nor is the society of Italian American gangsters immune to internal violence, being afflicted with frequent power struggles marked by insults and provocations. The inevitable result is betrayal, transgression, and vendetta.

What explains the volatile behaviour of such typically Scorsesean characters as J.R., Johnny Boy, Michael, Jake La Motta, and the gangsters of *GoodFellas* and *Casino*? It derives from such phenomena as Girard describes: mimetic desire leading to rivalry leading to violence, with the conflicted individuals contending ultimately not so much for material goods as for such intangibles as social prestige and reputation. Amounting to a whole behavioural complex partaking of the sacred, the southern Italian ideal of masculinity not only impels the characters' fantasies of prepotency but incites them to mimetic and transgressive violence.

Thus far honour and *rispetto* have been related to the southern Italian masculine ideal, sexual code, and cult of the family. We have emphasized the fact that, in southern Italian communities, both honour and respect depend on external estimations, as they are conferred by the community in public upon those who live up to its values. Honour is identified with the male and shame with women. What still needs to be elucidated is the extreme and unusual development of the concept of honour within the specifically Sicilian society from which Scorsese and most Italian American gangsters derive. To grasp what Sicilians mean by a 'man of honour' or 'man of respect,' one must define the semantic weight of two terms with which the Sicilian man of honour is associated: 'omertà' and 'Mafia.' What also needs clarification is the social presentation of personal honour in the Sicilian male: in short, those public characteristics that, fascinating, attractive, fearful, and provocative, justify the name of Mafioso.

Although Americans and northern Italians often identify the Sicilian dialect word *mafia* with a secret society or centralized criminal organization supposedly dominating the island, Sicilian crime, however extensive, has always been loosely organized. The word *mafia* refers not to a criminal organization but to a state of mind and style of behaviour shared and prized by the Sicilian (and Calabrian) people. It also crystallizes a variety of social attitudes regarding the male individual's proper public presentation. Nor is there doubt that the complex of attitudes and behaviours that constitute *mafia*, especially those encouraging disrespect for the government, provide a fertile breeding ground for criminal activity and loosely knit criminal organizations. Pitrè traces *mafia* to Sicilian Arabic and finds it to have already existed as a dialect word in pre-1860 Palermo. Even then it signified 'beauty and excellence' united with the notions of 'superiority and bravery.' Regarding men, it referred to the consciousness of being a man, 'assurance of mind,' 'boldness,' 'protection against the arrogance of the powerful,' 'remedy to any damage,' 'sturdiness of body,' and 'strength and serenity of spirit.' According to Hess, in Palermo of 1880 the word *mafia* carried the above meanings, to which he adds 'pride,' 'grace,' 'perfection,' 'self-confidence,' and 'vainglorious behaviour'; adjectivally it connoted 'outstanding,' 'manly,' 'handsome.'[190]

The subcultural code providing the pattern of manliness is known as *omertà*, deriving from the Sicilian *omu*, meaning 'man.' This code arose in response to the fact that Sicily has been oppressed for centuries by foreign governments and rapacious and reactionary feudal aristocracies. In Sicily, wealth and prestige were in very short supply and were therefore the objects of harsh competition among the inhabitants. Thus the 'honourable' Sicilian distrusted official authorities and refused to cooperate with them.[191] Such distrust and non-cooperativeness also pervaded society, as each group and individual feared to be taken advantage of by others.

Nonetheless the Sicilians have developed social and behavioural strategies for survival in a hostile environment. Uncooperative with and disloyal to the outside world, they have found loyalty and solidarity in private organizations.[192] These include the nuclear and, rarely, the extended family, fictional kinship relationships or godparenthood, and fictional kinship organizations in which friends unite for common purposes. The members of a group must aid each other but never cooperate with the authorities. Although *omertà* is often mistakenly believed to refer solely to vows of silence rather than the code of manliness as a whole, the Sicilian man of honour is expected to guard the secrets of the groups to which he belongs and thus to remain close-mouthed before government officials, even under brutal interrogation. More generally, children are taught to keep silent and to mind their own business. Hence the contempt of garrulity throughout Sicily, where, proverbially, 'a man who is really a man never reveals anything.'[193] Indeed, it is regarded as a 'sacred duty' not to inform on one's friends. Contrariwise, an informer or person who relies on the law in settling a dispute is universally hated and disrespected. To the vow of silence *omertà* adds the further requirement of self-control in the presence of others, including the authorities. The 'man of honour' is tough, courageous, and unyielding under pressure, so as never to reveal his passions or weaknesses.[194] As crime boss Joe Bonanno says, the 'archetypal Sicilian' is 'stoic' and 'self-possessed': 'An aspect of manly behaviour, according to my Tradition [*sic*], is strict control over one's emotions.' This reflects the norms of *contadino* society, in which, to quote Gambino, male and female roles were distinctly separated, and 'warmth and tenderness were classified entirely as feminine roles' while 'aggression and impassiveness were masculine characteristics.'[195]

Omertà further requires that the man of honour exhibit absolute self-reliance and self-sufficiency in personal affairs. Filled with a 'proud awareness' of his 'own personality' and its 'independence,' he fears nothing, bows to no one, and punishes the 'superiority' or 'arrogance' of others.[196] Nor will he allow himself and his associates – his family or friends – to be slighted, insulted, or challenged by another person. In punishing those who offend his name and reputation, the honourable man never depends on the police or judiciary, least of all when the offence has been delivered in public and against his family. Rather, he relies entirely upon his own power to administer retaliatory violence. It matters not whether he or his friends are in the wrong and his enemies are in the right; however long it takes, he will exact his vengeance.[197] Embodied in the successful criminal leader, *mafia* is, to quote Pitrè, 'an exaggerated idea of the power of the individual, the sole power of decision in each conflict and in each clash of interests.'[198]

The reward of being a *mafioso* in the sense of a leader or participant in a criminal organization is to receive *rispetto* from the entire Sicilian community. As with other forms of honour within the Mediterranean world, *rispetto* is socially rather than inwardly conferred and depends on satisfying external standards. To quote a Sicilian doctor: 'a *mafioso* is not the man who regards himself as one, but the man who is regarded as one. It is the public that makes a *mafioso*.'[199] The Mafioso sees it as highly important to cut a good figure – *fare figura* – in public. As he enjoys wielding power, so he delights to receive the respect his quasi-sanctity demands. However, the foundation of such honour and respect lies in his capacity to use threat, intimidation, and physical violence.[200] For Hess, 'a mafioso, *che se fa rispettarsi* [who makes himself respected], must avenge any violation of the integrity of his own person ... [and property] by his own efforts, which means resorting to violence.'[201] Such violence is never more awe-inspiring than when it bursts forth unexpectedly, in an astonishing display of cunning, toughness, and murderousness.[202] On the question of how a Mafioso becomes respected, Barzini says that people must be made to know that he will retaliate for any offence done to him, so that his social position depends 'ultimately' on the 'amount of fear he can generate, the halo of fear that surrounds him.' To scare and intimidate, this is the 'way of the Mafia.'[203] A Sicilian saying states that the Mafioso will not tolerate a fly on his nose. Likewise, '*mafia* in all its forms means the commission of an act of violence against another person.'[204]

One might think that the Mafioso, who craves social recognition, favours arrogant, boastful, overbearing, and ostentatious forms of public be-haviour as a means of imposing his will upon others. Actually, he cunningly adjusts his public image so as to satisfy his simultaneous need for pride and secrecy.[205] For Barzini, the Mafioso is 'anybody bearing himself with visible pride.' Nicola Gentile recalls that in early-twentieth-century Palermo men walked the streets in a 'slow strut' so as to 'appear solemn,' with their hats tilted over the right eye, thus creating 'an arrogant air that should command respect.'[206] Yet though, as Ianni remarks, the Mafioso's 'self-assured strut' implies a 'general air of self-reliance,' he displays 'bravura not bragodoccio.' In Sicilian tradition, a major Mafioso eschews the flashiness typical of insecure, lower echelon criminals.[207] Given to what Gambino calls 'reserve' rather than to 'emotions or passions,' he normally shuns the showy and passionate swagger one conventionally (yet incorrectly) associates with Spanish *machismo* and prefers to express his manliness through 'aloofness from outsiders ... self-reliance and self-control.'[208]

According to Hess, the true Mafioso favours modesty and restraint. Should he suffer a public insult, he responds with characteristic emotional detachment and patiently awaits his chance for vengeance.[209] Normally, though, he neither encounters insult nor resorts to violence. As Joseph Bonanno says, the 'archetypal Sicilian' is 'given to violence only to restore order, not out of self-display.'[210] No marginal, rebellious, or iconoclastic type, the Mafioso rightly sees himself as a conservator and guarantor of community values such as honour and respect.[211] He exerts his power in an understated, veiled, and mysterious fashion, settling all sorts of local problems through a word, glance, or gesture. To quote V. Titone, the 'true man reveals himself above all by his silence, by the secret presence of a hidden power ... [working] in the shadows.' Wilhelm Emil Muhlmann says of the Mafioso that 'what most creates the impression of awe in the charismatic personality is an icy impenetrability or a mysterious lurking, cunning, or uncertain element,' for instance by punctuating sentences with 'deliberate pauses' and 'mysterious silences' so as to create a 'sense of insecurity' in the listener.[212] The mysterious understatement typical of the Mafioso only adds to his fascination and terror as a lethal being invested with power and sanctity. He exemplifies the 'honourific dimension of murder,' which, 'as an expression of the arrogance and capacity for revenge of the killer, wrapped in an aureole of glory every homicide.'[213] As if he were the unmoved mover, keeping all others at a distance, the Mafioso embodies the autonomy and self-sufficiency, impassivity, and indifference of the pagan gods.

How do native Sicilians respond to the full-fledged Mafioso and his constant public display, however muted, of godlike prepotency and proud superiority? Since, as Hess remarks, most Sicilians are poor, powerless, and downtrodden people suffering a constant round of humiliations, and since they cannot punish their abusers, they are 'fascinated by the image of the independent, powerful, and influential gentleman.' In their envious eyes the Mafioso absolutely embodies the masculine ideal, the *omu* par excellence.[214] Accordingly, the Sicilians pay him their awed homage, either seeking his help or avoiding him out of fear. 'A man's position in [Sicilian] society,' says Barzini, 'ultimately depends on the fear he casts in the hearts of envious people.' Again, Sicilians 'admire the kind of beauty that is flaunted as a challenge ... the fatal beauty that will damn timid people who try to conquer it.'[215]

Surrounded by an invisible boundary that none dare transgress, the death-dealing Mafioso partakes of the sacred. And yet there is another possible response to the Mafioso, less deferential and submissive, and by no means common. For what if in his public presentation the Mafioso awakens admiration and envy but without the added element of fear? And what if in flaunting his challenge the Mafioso fails to intimidate but only provokes the envious observer to act transgressively against his person? The Mafioso's low-profile and unostentatious lifestyle is one means by which he attempts to suppress the threatening fires of envy among potential rivals. Nonetheless, the very autonomy and untouchability of the Mafioso, like those taboos that hedge the sacred, constitute a standing provocation to transgressive violence aiming to usurp all that the Mafioso possesses. Another source of danger is that, despite underworld taboos, an ambitious Mafioso will flout all rules when power and status are at stake. This, then, is a formula for mimetic rivalry, conflict, and mayhem that, given the strong group loyalties within Sicilian society, often spread beyond the initial dispute. This likelihood is all the greater given that in Sicily power, prestige, and wealth are in short supply and are the objects of ferocious envy and competition. As Hess observes of the 'young mafiosi' low in the criminal hierarchy: 'The young man of violence ... [has] always been anxious to displace the established ... old mafioso ... from his position because otherwise, in view of the inevitable shortage of positions of power, no advancement is possible to him.'[216] Contrastingly, the older Mafioso as a conservator of community values and aspirant to social and political legitimacy would 'freeze' or at least control the distribution of honour, so as to die peacefully in bed.[217]

Yet can the phenomena of Mafia, *omertà*, and *rispetto* serve to explain the behaviour of Scorsese's Italian American characters? It has often been noted that Little Italy is not Sicily, and that southern Italians have undergone a process of Americanization – and ethnicization – in the United States. It therefore seems risky to propose close parallels, in crime as in much else, between Italian Americans and their Old World counterparts. So great are the structural differences between the Sicilian Mafia and Italian American criminal organizations that Italian American criminals continue to be called Mafiosi for no better reason than their Sicilian background.[218] Not only do Scorsese's films indicate his awareness that the attitudes, habits, and behaviour of his Italian American characters are more American than Italian or Sicilian, but he dramatizes the clash between the traditional and American ways of doing crime. And yet the fact remains that Sicilian and southern Italian codes of criminality and masculinity can help to illuminate Scorsese's characters. As crime experts Ralph Salerno and John Tompkins put it: 'The rules [of the Mafia] are an American invention, but they are based heavily on the attitudes toward life and the world that the Southern Italian peasants brought with them to this country.'[219] These attitudes include that disrespect for government which drives much Mafia activity. In reading the autobiography of Joseph Bonanno, a traditional-minded Italian American crime boss, one is struck by such values as respect, honour, silence, stoic toughness, and other elements of the Sicilian code of masculinity. And the same impression is produced by other Mafia biographies, from Peter Maas's *The Valachi Papers* (1964) to Charles Rappleye and Ed Becker's *All-American Mafioso: The Johnny Rosselli Story* (1994).

It is appropriate that the rivalries of the young thugs in Scorsese's *Mean Streets* are played out to the accompaniment of old-style Sicilian music; that Mascagni's *Cavalleria Rusticana*, on the theme of southern Italian or 'rustic chivalry,' provides the score of *Raging Bull*; and that the crime bosses in *GoodFellas* and *Casino*, though second-generation Italian Americans, maintain the rituals of honour and respect, deference and subservience, passed down from the Old Country. Southern Italy and more particularly Sicily provide the ideal of masculinity adopted by Uncle Giovanni, Michael, Jake La Motta, and other Scorsesean characters. This ideal calls to mind that pose of god-like superiority which, according to Girard, the sadistic person adopts in order to convince the world of his freedom from enslavement to other people, and which inevitably attracts the admiring, envious, and secretly resentful gaze of others who would find their model, lacerating obstacle and, ultimately, rival in such a person.

That Scorsese is acutely aware of this behavioural complex is suggested not only by his friend and teacher Father Frank Principe, but by his own comments in an interview. According to Father Principe, Italian American Catholics see the 'worst sins' as those of pride: 'The sins of the flesh are signs of human weakness. But pride, putting man in God's place, that was very serious because it's a direct rejection of God.'[220] Scorsese remarks similarly that the 'great sin is pride. It's the undoing of everyone. It's the sin that created Lucifer because he was the angel that felt he could be as important as God and was cast into Hell. He was a favourite up to that point, but thought he could take over.' Scorsese adds that reflecting on Lucifer's relation to God has made him 'very interested in a [type of] character who consciously makes the effort to deal with every problem with a solution in which his pride is ten steps ahead of him.'[221] Scorsese thus links pride to Lucifer's envy of God, whom Lucifer, choosing God as his model of desire, attempts to replace. Scorsese also speaks of this rivalry in terms appropriate less to the Old Testament than to the lexicon of Al Capone. Lucifer wanted to 'take over,' as if he were a gangland underling jealous of his boss.

As Lucifer challenges God, his model, for his possessions, so in Scorsese's films those who pretend to god-like autonomy are bound to attract not only imitators but violent rivals. And just as the rivalry between God and Satan caused the angelic hosts to divide themselves into factions behind one or the other contestant, so in Scorsese's cinematic world such rivalries draw other people within their violent orbit. The problem is partly that the *rispetto* the godlike individual claims for himself is in both great demand and short supply, and can only be had by taking it from its possessor. Another problem in the films is that the *rispetto* attaching to esteemed persons and institutions invites transgression by the fact of its existence, as is true of all sacred prohibitions. Although *rispetto* continues to be observed under normal circumstances, the unleashing of mimetic rivalries creates a transgressive atmosphere into which more and more people are drawn by a kind of contagion. In these instances Scorsese's films powerfully exemplify the Girardian theme of the 'holiday-gone-wrong.'[222] With the spread of random, undifferentiating violence, more and more people are endangered, formerly accepted limits and boundaries collapse, and a small-scale example of the sacrificial crisis, complete with the doubles of violence, comes into being. This situation typifies the climactic moments of several of Scorsese's Italian American films.[223]

Scorsese's awareness of mimetic phenomena, including their relation to violence and undifferentiation, originates in his early childhood, when he took film and television characters as his models. According to Scorsese, at the age of three he had 'dreamed of becoming a cowboy,' and indeed in *Italianamerican* a very young Scorsese appears in a family photo wearing a cowboy outfit in the company of his brother. He also observes that his 'training in handling actors came from watching a lot of movies and being thrilled by them. That's how a lot of mirror scenes in my movies came about. I used to fantasize in front of the mirror, playing all my heroes.'[224] In playing this childhood game, Scorsese was not only imitating in his imagination a model of violence but seeing himself in the place of that person, as his own mirror image. To the extent that he desired at some level to become his model, he was experiencing in these moments mimetic desire with all its potential for rivalry and undifferentiating violence. The entanglement of subject and mediator in violent mimetic reciprocity betokens undifferentiation, and is implied in the doubling of Scorsese's image in the mirror; he was at once himself, himself imitating his model, and himself replacing that model. Yet Scorsese avoided the dangerous possibilities of such mimesis for two reasons. One is that, whereas the mimetic rivalries depicted in his films stem from what Girard calls internal mediation, meaning that the rivals belong to the same world, Scorsese's experience before the mirror exemplifies external mediation, as he was imitating a cinematic model more imaginary than real, and with which it was impossible to enter into rivalrous conflict. The other reason is that Scorsese put aside his childhood desire to imitate literally the action heroes of his youth and replaced it with a different and less harmful form of mimesis, the distanced representation of violence on the screen. This is not to suggest, however, that a childhood obsession with cinematic cowboys must fail to produce violent results simply because it arises from external mediation. In *GoodFellas*, gangster Tommy DeVito sprinkes his tough-guy patter with the lingo of cowboy films, thinks of himself as a Western outlaw during his hijacking raids, and commits a senseless and unprovoked murder while under the momentary delusion of being Humphrey Bogart in *The Oklahoma Kid*. In scenes like these Scorsese reshapes the violent fantasies of his childhood.

Also contributing to the reckless transgression and collapse of order in Scorsese's films is the marked propensity of his Italian American characters to engage in two distinctive yet closely related types of play defined by Roger Caillois. One is *alea* or chance, typified by the throw of the dice, lotteries, many card games in one degree or another, and racetrack betting. Reminiscent of the sacrificial crisis, *alea* requires each player to abdicate his or her will to the miraculous workings of chance, whose decision the player awaits on a 'democratic' level with other players. Accordingly, the individual allows him or herself to 'drift' and has the intoxicating feeling of being 'possessed by strange powers.' Since both lucky and unlucky players are hardly aware of their surroundings, being so absorbed by the mysterious play of chance, they are seized by a 'special kind of vertigo.' Yet what makes *alea* disturbing in Scorsese's films is that his characters allow its tyrannous power to extend beyond the gaming table to the whole of their lives, which come to be characterized increasingly by highly dangerous risk-taking and the testing of social limits, in the hope that chance will prove the agent of a miraculous success or salvation. In this respect *alea* shares many features with what Callois terms *ilinx*, the most primitive form of play. Meaning 'whirlpool' and implying vertigo, *ilinx* is a whirling movement that produces a sense of overwhelming speed, spatial projection and disorientation, rapid rising or falling, rotation, acceleration, and gyration. Caillois sees it as 'intoxication of the moral order,' causing a person to adapt vertigo to daily life, and thus to experience a permanent need for drugs and alcohol. Such a person disregards all rules and lives in a topsy-turvy panic-driven state where vertical movement at ever-increasing speed promises total triumph but leads to self-destructive collapse.[225]

The combination of random violence born of mimetic desire and rivalry, of *alea*, with its inducements to greed, self-oblivion, and constant risk-taking, and of *ilinx*, characterized by a delirious loss of identity, indifference to rules, and a disorienting experience of speed and intoxication, defines the typical conclusion of Scorsese's Italian American films. Their essential rhythm is that of a world which, beginning in comparative order however precarious and threatened, gradually spins out of control through violence and desire. Appropriately, the theme of chance, symbolized by either the wheel of fortune or the gaming table, figures prominently at the climax of most of these films, as nothing better suggests their hectic confusion, restless movement, and unpredictable acts of victimization.

Does Scorsese entertain the possibility of checking the violence he depicts? The church, with its rituals, ceremonies, and festivals, may seem to offer a corrective, yet this is precisely what the films call in question. Another possible solution lies in the *Imitatio Christi*, which is largely absent from the films but which certain Scorsesean characters such as J.R. in *Jerusalem, Jerusalem* and Charlie Civello in *Mean Streets* attempt to follow. Charlie's failure to adhere to this form of non-acquisitive and non-violent imitation only underscores the difficulty of his task.

There is, moreover, the pronounced tendency in characters such as Charlie and Jake La Motta to misinterpret the *Imitatio* as a masochistic absorption in sacrifice, martyrdom, and penitential punishment, as if these were essential to the Christian life, and as if sanctification and salvation required the choice of martyrdom. Charlie consciously seeks divine punishment as a means not simply of assuaging his guilt over his enslavement to mimetic desire but of demonstrating his spiritual superiority over other Christians, so that masochism, ostensibly the sign of his abjection, covertly reveals his pride. In a highly confused version of the *Imitatio*, not only does Jake La Motta aim for absolute sporting and sexual triumph, but he is led by feelings of abjection and unworthiness to derive his desires from models who then become his obstacles and punishing rivals in both the ring and bedroom. Yet like Charlie, the masochistic Jake regards suffering, which in his case consists of beatings by real ring opponents and periodic bouts of suspicion and jealousy towards imagined sexual rivals, as acts of penitence and even as tokens of spiritual worth. In each case, the characters have interpreted the *Imitatio* as rivalry with Christ, whom they attempt either to surpass in penitential suffering or to transform into a punishing obstacle. As he inflicts punishment upon them the obstacle withholds the salvation they seek, yet in bestowing attention upon them at least keeps the hope of it alive. In short, the *Imitatio* is falsely interpreted as the sadomasochistic relation between subject and model-obstacle-rival described by Girard. Both Charlie and Jake are enslaved to a conception of Christ answering primarily to their own self-destructive impulses. Scorsese's implicit rejoinder to such spirituality appears in the quotation he intended for his never-completed film *Jerusalem, Jerusalem*, and which he derived from Robert Bresson's *Diary of a Country Priest* (1951): 'God is not a torturer ... He only wants us to be merciful with ourselves.'[226]

The other possibilities of the control of violence implied by these films paradoxically involve recourse to the thing itself, in accordance with the sacrificial logic that good violence drives out bad. In order to prevent the spread of violence throughout their society, the gangster in-group will banish or exterminate certain dangerous individuals. Examples from *Mean Streets* and *Casino* come readily to mind. In other instances, even when violence has been allowed to proliferate, its increasing scope and randomness paradoxically hold out the possibility that the next victim will be the last, and that the seemingly uncontrollable crisis will then miraculously come to a halt. This also helps to explain the mixture of laughter and violence in Scorsese's Italian American films, the laughter being a kind of anticipation of that exultant moment when violence has finished its job of pacification. Sometimes, though, when the violence of the Italian American in-group gets completely out of hand and threatens the core community, the state must correct this potentially Hobbesian situation by singling out at least some offenders for special punishment. In such cases, the state acts in bad faith, as the films show it to be complicit with the ostracized gangsters, in the form of bribes, pay-offs, secret alliances with the mob, and common commercial interests, as in *GoodFellas* and *Casino*. Scorsese realizes, however, that expulsive violence of whatever type, though expedient and temporarily successful, cannot pacify society in the long run, so that the violent cycles must begin again.

4 'Where's the Action?': Early Projects and *Who's That Knocking at My Door?*

Scorsese's first film on Italian American themes is *It's Not Just You, Murray!*, which he made in his final year as an undergraduate at NYU with partial financial backing from his father.[1] Filmed in stark black and white and only fifteen minutes long, this low-budget production had been encouraged by Scorsese's mentor, Professor Haig Manoogian, then director of the NYU film program, who had urged him to make films based on personal experience. For Scorsese, this meant a return to the streets of Little Italy.[2] Besides parodying the tradition of the gangster film, for instance Raoul Walsh's *The Roaring Twenties* (1939), *It's Not Just You, Murray!* contains many documentary-like scenes of Little Italy as it existed in the 1960s, before it declined into a tourist site known chiefly for its restaurants.[3] Scenes were shot in Scorsese's parents' apartment, in the apartments of his grandmother and uncle, and in the cellars and fire escapes of the Lower East Side, with the aim of capturing the distinctive look and texture of the neighbourhood walls, hallways, and basements. 'Of all my films,' says Scorsese, *Murray!* is the 'one that shows the old neighborhood, the way it looked in the early sixties, right before it began to die out.' He drew his inspiration from stories concerning local people, including his uncles, so that the film's mood and subject matter look forward to *Who's That Knocking at My Door?* and *Mean Streets*. In Scorsese's view the film shows 'how Italian Americans lived in the early sixties.' In another interview he describes *Murray!* as an 'attempt to portray just the way I was living.'[4]

Like some of Scorsese's other efforts from this period, *It's Not Just You, Murray!* shows the influence of the French New Wave in its use of the freeze frame, borrowed from Truffaut. The film's weaknesses include lack of variety in locations, obscure lighting, and overuse of voice-over, all reflecting its low budget. It also shows sophomoric self-reflexivity along with too obvious imitation of European models, including Fellini. As the film opens Murray winks into the camera and begins to give directorial instructions, while the conclusion feebly echoes Fellini's *8 1/2*. On the whole, the film lacks thematic and narrative focus and tends towards diffuseness after its effective first scene. Concerning his desire to portray his own way of life, Scorsese complains: 'I couldn't really get it together.'[5] Nonetheless, *It's Not Just You, Murray!* was honoured as the finest student film of 1964 with an award from Producers Guild, the Edward L. Kingsley Award, and the Jesse L. Lasky Intercollegiate Award. It premiered at the Fourth New York Film Festival on 13 September 1966.

A heavily ironic satire on the pretentions of neighbourhood Mafiosi, *It's Not Just You, Murray!* anticipates many of the characters, relationships, and situations of Scorsese's later Italian American films. It is worth recalling that Italian American organized crime had in the four preceding decades traced the trajectory followed in the film. During Prohibition Italian American criminal groups increased in their organizational complexity and, having extended their operations through bootlegging, possessed enormous amounts of ready cash. Following Prohibition, these same groups took the form of interlinked family-based syndicates as they branched out into various illegal operations, including gambling, racketeering, and loan-sharking. Thanks to further expansion and profiteering during the war years, Italian American crime syndicates entered a low-profile halcyon period that ended in the 1950s, with the televised Kefauver hearings in 1950–1; the ill-fated Mafia summit meeting at Apalachin, New York, in 1957; the Senate hearings on racketeering chaired by Arkansas senator John McClellan, which extended into the early 1960s; and the televised revelations of criminal underling Joseph Valachi to the U.S. Senate, which, however, followed the completion of *Murray!* Many Americans came to fear an organized crime conspiracy against the nation while mistakenly identifying all Italian Americans with organized crime.[6] This was partly owing to the television show *The Untouchables*, to which Scorsese alludes in *It's Not Just You, Murray!* and which enjoyed great popularity from the late 1950s into the early 1960s. Although pretending to document the struggle between Al Capone and lawman Eliot Ness during Prohibition Chicago, the show consisted of historical fabrications given the patina of authenticity through narration by crime columnist and radio personality Walter Winchell. This show contributed mightily to the negative stereotyping against which Italian Americans were now protesting.[7]

Murray, the film's Italian American narrator and main character, pretends to be an ordinary businessman but in reality is an incompetent and unapologetically materialistic second-rate gangster: 'I always wanted to live good, ever since I was a kid.'[8] He calls to mind the worldly interests of Charlie Civello, the would-be priest in *Mean Streets*, of Henry Hill in *GoodFellas*, who had wanted to be a gangster 'ever since ... [he] could remember,' and of the high-living Mafiosi in *Casino*. As the film opens, Murray sits at his business desk with cigarette in hand and leans forward, smiling ingratiatingly at the viewer. An American flag appears prominently to his left, a detail consistent with the professed patriotism of Italian American gangsters after World War II, in recognition that their wealth depended upon the free enterprise system.[9] Having stood up, Murray proudly shows off his tie, which he proclaims with great self-satisfaction to have cost twenty dollars. Next there is a shot of his shoes, which by his report cost fifty dollars, and then the camera takes in the remainder of his five-hundred-dollar suit. In *GoodFellas* the camera, as it descends from the adolescent Henry Hill's tailored suit to his polished shoes, signals his arrival as a gangster. The scene then shifts to an outdoor urban setting as Murray invites us to join him for a ride in his brand new white Cadillac convertible with predatory-looking fins, which he boasts cost five thousand dollars. In Scorsese's later Italian American films, for instance *GoodFellas* and *Raging Bull*, the purchase of a flashy new car, preferably a Cadillac, marks the gangster's social arrival. But Murray's vanity also exposes his incompetence, as he needs to restart the film upon realizing that, in his zeal to display his clothes and car, he had failed to introduce himself. It is as if his identity had been entirely absorbed in his possessions.

Back in his office as if to restart the film, Murray gives his name and announces clumsily: 'The reason I'm here is to tell you how I got here.' There follows a perverted Horatio Alger story in which, as in Scorsese's other Italian American films, crime exemplifies what Daniel Bell terms a 'queer ladder of social mobility.' Murray's progress is reflected in both his dress and improved base of operations, for whereas in his initial career as a bootlegger he wears a vest and pinstripe shirt and works in a dingy basement distillery, now as a middle-aged Mafioso he wears conventional businessman's attire and operates out of a high-rise office far above the streets.

Like Scorsese's later gangster films, *It's Not Just You, Murray!* acknowledges not only the value Italian American criminals place upon useful connections, which for them include both corruptible individuals and sheer luck conceived as a 'connection' with divine grace or favour, but their concealment of their criminal lives under euphemistic doubletalk, until they convince themselves of their normality and even legality. The presence on Murray's desk of a large pair of scales and a statue, apparently of the appropriately blindfolded Justice holding the scales that bear her name, imply that the judiciary is in Murray's pocket, and indeed he later receives cash pay-offs. According to Murray, he is 'very rich ... very influential ... very well-liked,' as witness his 'going places, meeting people,' this being the way to 'live good.' Yet Scorsese punctures Murray's pretentions while exposing the truth of his criminal career. Shots of Murray in a tugboat in New York harbour and on the Staten Island Ferry with nondescript Mafiosi belie his claim to have travelled widely among influential friends. Next recalling his highly undignified arrest during a police raid on his distillery, Murray remarks that 'in this life you only got so much luck,' and that 'events happen in life, they take a turn.' Thus there occurred in the 'course of business this event, a misunderstanding, in which due to circumstances' beyond his 'control' Murray was 'misunderstood.' He refers circumlocutorily to his arrest and conviction because of which 'he didn't exactly have a great amount of free time to go many places for a while,' although he 'did see Ossining, New York,' the site of Sing Sing; to which Murray adds: 'It wasn't bad up there.' Subsequently testifying before a racketeering committee, Murray unwittingly says the opposite of what he means: 'I refuse to answer on the grounds that I might incriminal myself ... I mean that I might be discriminated.'

Normally, though, Murray maintains his self-deception. In claiming to belong to 'one of the great financial syndicates in America,' he means racketeering and the investment of the profits gained from it. The money that enables Murray and Joe, his partner, to enter the rackets derives from a string of Broadway hits backed by their production company, JOMURRAY. This turn of the plot enables Scorsese to parody Hollywood and Broadway musicals of the 1930s and 1940s, including those of Busby Berkeley.[10] In the biggest of the company's hits, the ridiculously titled *Love Is a Gazelle*, a tuxedoed crooner with a chipped tooth is accompanied by a string of chorus girls one of whom stands out immediately for her fat legs. Reminiscent of such musicals as *The Great Ziegfeld* and *Yankee Doodle Dandy*, a hackneyed montage of neon marquees along the Great White Way advertises hit JOMURRAY productions with such impossible titles as *Hello, Harriet, Goodbye, Sam* and *Tomatoes Are Cheap*, which tilt the titles of actual Broadway musicals into absurdity.[11]

The mood turns to sleazy and sinister when Murray reports on the impact he and his partner Joe, as racketeers, have had upon American life. As if to minimize his agency, Murray employs the passive form, stating that 'sports were affected by us,' as were 'hotels,' 'motels,' 'undertaking operations,' 'television,' 'foreign aid,' and 'imported products.' These claims are given their real value in scenes of athletes accepting bribes, motels with cheap prostitutes parading their wares, and a gangland assassination in which the victim, reminiscent of *Little Caesar* (1930), the earliest example of the gangster film in its classic form, is shot dead running up the steps of a building. To exemplify Murray's effect on television, Scorsese includes a shot of Robert Stack, who played Eliot Ness in *The Untouchables*, examining a piece of paper marked with the conventional symbol of the Black Hand, extortionists and blackmailers who worked either individually or in small gangs during the period of Italian American immigration. Given that the Black Hand had nothing to do with the syndicate-like criminal organizations Ness confronted, but confined its activities to the Italian American community, this image perhaps comments on the historical inaccuracy of Stack's television show.[12] Yet if Scorsese acknowledges public misconceptions of the Mafia, he also identifies it, if only parodically, with political conspiracies in both foreign nations and the United States. As an example of 'foreign aid' there appear Arabs, possibly revolutionary terrorists, receiving a shipment of rifles from the syndicate, which, to paraphrase Aristophanes, makes its true home wherever it can do business. In another shot the Lincoln Memorial bears the imprint 'Made in Japan,' Japanese products being a byword for low quality in those days.

Like Murray, later Scorsesean gangsters such as Charlie Civello make a point of wooing influential people while promoting their own popularity, chiefly out of self-interest. For Henry Hill, as for Murray, the good life entails cultivating those who can enable him to 'go places' such as the Copacabana. Another prominent theme in Scorsese's gangster films is luck, to which the gangsters yield their lives yet which ultimately disappoints them, the turn of their fortunes being signalled by an unexpected prison term or legal obstruction, as in *GoodFellas* or *Casino*. Yet just as Murray's mother brings him spaghetti in Sing Sing, which according to Murray 'wasn't bad,' so the Mafiosi of *GoodFellas* find that prison 'wasn't that bad,' to quote inmate Henry Hill, as they continue to be supplied with Italian delicacies by their Mafia wives and associates. Nor can the characters in Scorsese's later films accept the truth of their criminality, as witness Charlie Civello, who rationalizes his involvement with the Mafia, and Karen Hill, Henry's wife, who believes that she, her gangster husband, and their associates lead 'normal' lives.

Also reminiscent of the main characters of Scorsese's later Italian American films, Murray's chief emotional ties are with his mother, wife, and gangster friends, especially Joe. His mother, played by Catherine Scorsese, wears a black wig and black shawl suggestive of long-suffering Sicilian matrons. In reality she is an obtuse and deliberately one-dimensional figure whose sole parental 'psychology' is to force upon Murray large plates of spaghetti with the accompanying injunction quite consistent with the alimentary ethos of the mob: 'Eat first.'[13] For Murray's mother eating is a ritualized event, as in Scorsese's *Italianamerican* and his feature films on Italian America. Yet because she has no interests beyond the kitchen, she has no idea of her criminal son's career. Also played by Catherine Scorsese, J.R.'s mother in *Who's That Knocking?* exhibits considerable dignity and authority in the opening scene in which she prepares a meal for the small children of the family, thus affirming the religion of the domus and the social harmony that springs from it. In *Mean Streets* Charlie Civello receives gifts from his absent mother, who probably remains unaware of her son's criminality. In *GoodFellas* Tommy DeVito's mother (Catherine Scorsese) serves a lavish breakfast to Tommy and his gangster friends without realizing that their most recent victim lies concealed in the trunk of their car; indeed, she unwittingly lends them the carving knife with which they dismember and bury the body. The aged Mafia mother in *Casino*, Catherine Scorsese's final appearance in her son's films, dutifully cooks sumptuous meals for the Mafia leaders at their Kansas City headquarters, scolds her gangster son for his profanity, and either ignores or remains oblivious to his involvement in the skimming of Las Vegas casinos. Such scenes reflect the fact that Italian American gangsters totally dissociate their criminal activities from the domestic sphere, so that Mafia wives neither ask about their husbands' work nor know anything of it.[14]

Murray's relation to Joe anticipates those instances in Scorsese's Italian American films in which a presumed friendship between gangsters issues in a betrayal that utterly shatters the betrayed party – except that in *Murray* the betrayal is mitigated by denial and materialistic distraction. Murray's fellow racketeer Joe is his idolized best friend, of whom he says: 'I will tell you, this good livin', is all due I must admit, to one person, and that's my friend, my pal, Joe.' Yet though, according to Murray, their 'empires of wealth and security' testify to the 'love of one's fellow men in friendship,' the reality is that Joe requires his friend to do most of the work connected with their bootlegging business, and that after their operation is broken up by police it is Murray who takes the bootlegging rap and goes to prison while Joe avoids arrest. Murray thus pays the price for observing the Mafia code of *omertà*, which requires a gangster to be a 'stand-up guy,' silent concerning all criminal operations. Not only does Joe bum cigarettes from his imprisoned friend, but he subsequently appears before a fleeting image of the Last Supper while offering Murray advice contrary to his own interests. As Judas betrayed Christ, so Joe betrays his friend (and indirectly Christ). Images of the biblical betrayal appear in *Who's That Knocking?* and in the scene in the mother's house in *GoodFellas*, a foreshadowing of Henry Hill's betrayal of his associates. In *Murray!* as in Scorsese's later gangster films, the presence of religious imagery within the gangsters' domestic or professional surroundings contrasts ironically with the characters' depraved lives and the unthinking conventionality of their religious beliefs and practices: a contradiction typical of the Mafia.[15] Thus in one scene of statue of Christ appears behind Murray's desk as he counts his racketeering money while, indifferent to sanctity, Joe lights a cigarette from a holy candle that burns alongside the icon. The theme of profanation will also appear in connection with a holy candle in *Who's That Knocking?*, though with a different inflection.

Joe's chief act of betrayal is his adulterous affair with Murray's voluptuous wife, a nurse who attends to Murray during a hospital stay and whom he mistakes for an 'angel of mercy' apparently because she is clothed in innocent white. Yet even in the hospital room she not only smokes cigarettes, indifferent to Murray's health, but makes eyes at Joe. Scorsese thus satirizes the Italian American – including Mafioso – preference for virginal and modest wives of unblemished reputation. He also underscores Joe's deception of Murray by extending it as far as adultery, a major infraction of the Mafia code, which punishes with death members who carry on with other members' wives. Joe's refusal to accept second place to Murray in any sphere is suggested by his primacy in the title of their company, JOMURRAY. During a performance of *Love Is a Gazelle*, Murray remains oblivious to the two adulterers cuddling in the wings. At the Senate hearings, Joe sits next to his 'friend' but does nothing other than to provide Murray with whispered advice before the latter speaks publicly through a microphone. It is as if Murray were a front for Joe, who continues to work behind the scenes, even in public; or as if Joe, a criminal, were acting as Murray's lawyer before the investigators. Murray's subsequent remarks concerning his and Joe's family, that 'Everything we did we did together,' is accompanied by stills of family outings, with close-ups of children. What the audience knows by now, but which Murray does not yet suspect, is that Joe, whom Murray describes as 'like a second father' to his children, is probably their real father. One thinks of *GoodFellas*, in which stills from family albums evoke the Mafia families as a tight-knit, insular society, which finally collapses amid suspicion and betrayal. One thinks too of *Casino*, in which the leading characters, initially best friends and allies in the same gangland operation, fall into a bitter rivalry with one cuckolding the other.

Apparently realizing that his 'good-looking' children have most likely been fathered by Joe rather than himself, Murray summons his friend to his office for what ought to be a major confrontation. The presence of Murray's black-clad mother in this scene, predictably with yet another proffered plate of comforting spaghetti, can do nothing to assuage her son's outrage or distress. Instead, his first response to Joe's admission of betrayal is angrily to order the film technician to 'cut the sound.' It is implied that Murray, in a manner typical not just of Mafiosi but of Italian Americans, is ensuring that his sexual disgrace – the worst possible form of dishonour – will not be publicized. Yet the removal of the sound also indicates Murray's desire to ignore or deny the unwelcome truth of his friend's treachery. Thus, unexpectedly, Murray neither retaliates against Joe nor terminates their friendship. As previously with his prison sentence, whose cause and significance he had been loath to admit, Murray refers to the betrayal as a mere 'misunderstanding.' Although he confesses to having been 'embarrassed' by Joe, he is satisfied to observe that 'times change, things change, you gotta move with the times' – to which he adds that his wife and 'good-looking kids' still live in his house, 'they're my kids.' Murray thus anticipates *GoodFellas* in providing the first instance in Scorsese's Italian American cinema of the theme of the Sicilian *cornuto contento* – the contented cuckold.

What seems most of all to repair the broken friendship between these Mafiosi is that Murray allows himself to be bribed by the offer of a Cadillac that, notes Murray, cost ten thousand dollars. For the materialistic Murray this represents an advance in life, as his previous Cadillac cost only five thousand. He remarks of his new car that its interior is of 'imported naugahyde,' with a 'formica bar in the trunk.' Now armed against despair, Murray attempts to overcome his disappointments by inviting the cast members and film audience to a public exhibition of his new Cadillac on a forlorn plain in the suburbs. Naturally his mother shows up, black clad and carrying a plate of spaghetti. In a scene too reminiscent of the ending of *8 1/2*, though lacking its joyfully redemptive overtones, Murray carries a megaphone with which he directs the cast members in a circular procession around his car – a scene of unrepentant materialism and circular futility reminiscent of earlier shots of Murray's car and its turning wheels. Unlike the director Marcello in Fellini's film, Murray's behavior rings hollow, and his hypocrisy and crass realism elicit no sympathy. Nor is he even now free from his friend's dominance, as Joe appropriates the megaphone and takes the role of director himself. In the final shot, in which Murray and Joe pose for a formal photograph before the Cadillac, Murray's outstretched arm rests upon Joe's shoulder. Nothing has changed between them.

It's Not Just You, Murray! parodies two types of behaviour which Scorsese would treat more seriously in his later Italian American films, and that, despite their differences, superficially resemble each other. On the one hand is the exaggerated self-possession or 'cool' of the gangster, who never shows emotion, who remains aloof from the violence around him, who stoically endures all that he suffers, and who, resisting needless provocations, engages in violence only when necessary. On the other hand there is the pacificity of the self-possessed Christian, who also seeks detachment from violence though for different reasons, who suffers patiently in the manner of Christ, and who, turning the other cheek, shuns violent retaliation and even allows himself to be victimized. Joe informs Murray that 'you gotta control yourself,' advice Murray ignores after he is assaulted by two hoodlums and attempts to defend himself. Joe is insistent: 'Don't do anything, don't say a word' – advice whose authority is emphasized by a low-angle shot of Joe looming with drink in hand. 'In other words,' continues Joe, 'when people bother you, abuse you, curse you, you know what I mean, Murray, really, really bother you, well, Murray, don't do nothing.' These statements, parodying at once tough-guy fortitude and Christian non-retaliation, accompany a shot of Murray collapsing on a coffee table, as if struck by a bullet from behind, followed by a sequence of shots in which he is hit on the head, beaten by two thugs, and cursed behind his back during a card game. Next appears a bag of dry cement lying on the ground followed by a shot of the unflappable Murray in his dinner suit; though tied up and gagged, he smokes a cigarette through the gag as if unaffected by his situation. Actually he is standing in a bucket as wet cement is poured into it – a standard Mafia method of disposing of murdered enemies. Murray has fallen for advice that, without danger to Joe, allows the latter to exploit him. Joe's final advice to Murray anticipates a familiar theme and situation in Scorsese's later Italian American films, namely the quest for the victim, who can at least pacify the community by focusing its diffuse hostilities: 'Remember that one day, Murray, one day you're gonna see somebody, some guy who's all those guys rolled into one, and then you can give him all he deserves.' This person is none other than Murray, who looks at himself in a mirror, which he then smashes in self-loathing. At least two of Scorsese's Italian American films, Mean Streets and Raging Bull, contain similar scenes in which a leading character confronts himself in a mirror in a moment of fleeting and troubled self-recognition.

During the mid-1960s Scorsese began envisioning a cinematic trilogy, based largely on his own experiences, about Manhattan's Little Italy. The three films were to follow the same characters from adolescence into early manhood. Completed on 29 March 1966, while Scorsese was still an NYU graduate student, the treatment for the first installment was titled Jerusalem, Jerusalem; its successor received the working title of Bring on the Dancing Girls; and the third was projected as Season of the Witch.[16] Unfortunately Jerusalem, Jerusalem, which was intended to run for about an hour and fifteen minutes, was never produced, though the treatment survives.[17] The reason for Scorsese's failure to complete the project was a presumed lack of popular interest in what many saw as a socially retrograde upbringing. However, the remaining two parts of the trilogy made it to the screen, the second in 1969 under the title Who's That Knocking at My Door?, the third in 1973 under the revised title of Mean Streets, and with a differently named main character.

Thematizing the conflicting demands of flesh and spirit, Jerusalem, Jerusalem is inspired by Scorsese's own adolescent experiences of Catholic retreats, when the priests warned him and his friends of infernal punishment for their earthly desires. On one such occasion the sleepless Scorsese, worked up to a kind of religious hysteria by the total experience of the retreat, suffered a harrowing auditory hallucination while kneeling alone in a chapel. In the treatment the eighteen-year-old high-school senior J.R., Scorsese's protagonist and alter ego, joins with his classmates Bud and Mikey for a three-day visit to a Jesuit retreat house under the supervision of Father McMahon. To quote Dominic Lo Faro, a friend of Scorsese's who accompanied him on these occasions: 'A retreat is a time when through praying, meditating, and listening to sermons one is supposed to examine the spiritual aspects of life to see if they've been neglected.' He adds that the 'atmosphere of the silent and cloistered retreat house is overpowering, and the sermons, which tend to the hellfire-brimstone variety, are totally effective,' so that 'one knows one's spiritual life has been neglected after a weekend retreat.'[18]

Since *Jerusalem, Jerusalem* remains a treatment, any analysis of it must remain somewhat speculative, as it is impossible to determine precisely what would in the film have been a complex interplay among visual, auditory, and thematic components. The epigraph to the treatment derives from Robert Bresson's version of George Bernanos's 1938 novel *Diary of a Country Priest*: 'God is not a torturer ... He only wants us to be merciful with ourselves.' Yet rather than providing a pat commentary on what follows, the epigraph raises questions about the theology portrayed in the treatment. It can even be argued that the retreat teaches J.R. a penitential, masochistic form of Catholicism, with an overemphasis on Christ's suffering, which leads the worshipper to withold mercy from himself.

The film opens on a more joyous note, with J.R. and Bud sitting and joking in a Chinese restaurant. As Bud 'cradles' his hot tea in his hands 'as a priest would a chalice,' he 'smiles at J.R., raises the cup, and intones': '*Introibo ad altare dei*.' His familiarity with the Latin, meaning 'I will go unto the altar of God,' taken from the Ordinary of the Mass, suggests that both J.R. and Bud have been altar boys, and indeed J.R. signs up to serve mass at the retreat. They are well aware that the mass commemorates the Last Supper, in which Jesus offered himself as sacrifice for humanity – the Crucifixion without which, in the orthodox interpretation, humanity cannot receive salvation from sin. In the older version of the mass, superceded by Vatican II, a celebrant was required to say the Latin phrase at the opening of the ritual, with the minister or server responding: '*Ad deum qui laetificat juventum meam*' – 'To God who giveth joy to my youth.'[19]

The inspiration for the scene in the restaurant, however, is not the mass alone but the opening page of James Joyce's *Ulysses*, in which the irreverent Buck Mulligan intones, '*Introibo ad altare dei*' as, with a bowl of lather, mirror, and razor, he prepares to perform his morning shave. After greeting the arrival of Stephen Dedalus, the lewd and blasphemous Mulligan proceeds with a parody of the mass and Eucharist in which Dedalus reluctantly plays the role of server. But whereas in Joyce's novel the effect is one of scandalous impiety, Scorsese's adolescents show at worst a mild irreverence, while the projected soundtrack accompanying the restaurant scene would seem, without blasphemous intent, to take the role of the server who praises God as the joy of his youth. Scorsese writes that J.R. and Bud 'both laugh at the joke and the frame freezes as a joyous piece of Vivaldi music smashes in on the soundtrack' simultaneously with the first title. Both adolescents participate in this mood, and apparently identify it with Catholicism. Vivaldi's music is especially appropriate not only because he was himself a priest but because, in composing both religious and secular music, he bridged the ecclesiastical and everyday worlds – this being for Scorsese a major problem for religion. His music may also evoke the colour and ebullience of Italian Catholic piety as against the grimly severe version of it that the boys encounter at the retreat, directed by Irish priests.

In the next scene J.R., Bud, and other boys board the bus taking them to the retreat. They show muted rebelliousness in refusing to 'honour' the Irish American Bob McDonald, president of their senior class, whose 'All-American' image offends them though it pleases the priests. During the bus trip the music of Vivaldi, 'very joyous and very loud,' carries over from the opening, perhaps in ironic interplay with the boys' 'mocking' statements about McDonald and their 'self-aimed' ethnic jokes. Upon arriving at the monastery the boys meet the surprisingly informal Father McMahon, who instantly wins them over. Besides three meals a day in the dining room, they are allowed one free hour a day during which they can buy candy at the candy shop, which suggests an ungenerous rationing of 'sweets' literally and metaphorically. After J.R. and some of the others sign up as altar boys, Father McMahon distributes postcards of the monastery, which are to be collected and mailed the next day. Then, to J.R.'s and Bud's annoyance, he chooses McDonald as the group's captain so that it 'runs true to schedule.' Although the rule of silence is in effect, the boys have the one hour a day for talking and recreation. Upon completing evening prayers they are to line up for confession, and will then be assigned rooms. Since Scorsese intends for scenes of these activities to be juxtaposed with Father McMahon's announcement of the boys' schedule, he apparently wants to emphasize priestly authority and the boys' passive obedience. The monastery's internal practices give the impression of time-bound regimentation devoid of individuality or spontaneity. This is reinforced when the priest tells the boys to be ready for morning prayers at 7:15. Each boy must prepare private 'petitions' with resolutions enabling him to live a more 'Christ-like' life.

By this point J.R. has been reminded of his spiritual shortcomings after saying confession in a small room, 'very dark, very quiet.' Having initially confessed his disobedience, tardiness at mass, and distraction during mass, he works up the courage to mention what he sees as his worst sin, masturbation, or 'self-impurities.' The priest urges J.R. to resolve this problem on retreat, suggesting that sermons and prayer should help.

The tone moves from spiritual urgency to triviality and vanity as J.R. is shown in his room where, after unpacking and putting on his pyjamas, he is much annoyed to discover that his mother had failed to pack his favourite pair of pants – so annoyed that he complains to her in a postcard. But before he places the postcard on the desk blotter he notices that it contains inscriptions in ink, including 'Listen to this guy because he's right' and 'When I first came here I thought this guy was crazy, but I found out he wasn't.' Since J.R. does not appear to mail the postcard, the blotter inscriptions may have called him to higher things and thus saved him from petty pique towards his mother. On the other hand, since it is revealed later that the priests deceive their tutees, apparently for a spiritual aim, the inscriptions may be forgeries. In any case, J.R. turns the light out, climbs into bed and, finding the room to be 'pitch-black,' like the night outside, puts the light back on and returns to bed. That he cannot endure the dark suggests both spiritual timidity and an unwillingness to face the confessional, which is also 'very dark.' But that J.R.'s mind is distracted from spiritual austerities is evident when, after he returns to bed, the camera focuses on his suit hanging on the wall – the cut of the lapels, shape of its sleeve, weave pattern, floridly designed collar and pockets, French cuffs and cufflinks. J.R.'s watch, ring, and belt are also magnified on the tabletop beyond their actual size. In short, J.R. is both a spiritual seeker and a materialist, much like the character into whom he metamorphoses, Charlie Civello. The image of J.R.'s fancy dress suit takes on an added irony the next day as J.R. sits in the main hall of the monastery reading *Lives of the Saints*. He imagines a Roman soldier who, riding along a dusty road at night, is stopped by a beggar. Despite the harsh wind, the soldier dismounts and cuts his cloak in two with his sword. After giving the larger part to the beggar, he remounts and rides off. The story, which is obviously that of St Martin and the beggar, ironizes not only J.R.'s foppish dress suit but the highly clothes-conscious Martin Scorsese, who though named for the saint finds his alter ego in J.R.[20]

The late afternoon of the next day is reserved for the Stations of the Cross, fourteen devotional commemorations of Christ's suffering and death from his condemnation to his interment. Although these often appear within churches, it is also customary, as on the retreat, to represent them as wayside shrines leading up a hillside, to be visited in procession. The climax of the procession in both physical elevation and spiritual significance is the twelfth station, representing Jesus's death.

Led by Father McMahon, the procession observes no formal order, but J.R.'s and Bud's position towards the end of the line may suggest their at least initially qualified enthusiasm for the exercise. Following tradition, the boys sing the 'Stabat Mater' after the first station. When they come to a station they kneel wherever they can find level ground, but this fails to alleviate the growing pain in J.R.'s knees, which parallels, however disproportionately, Jesus's miseries. At the second station, where Christ receives his cross, Father McMahon in his homily says that Jesus takes his 'heavy cross ... with meekness, nay, with a secret joy, for it is the instrument with which he is to redeem the world.' At this point, consistent with Catholic analogism, Scorsese juxtaposes Father McMahon's sermonizing and the stations of the cross with scenes set in Manhattan. The treatment thus calls to mind those later Italian American films in which Scorsese finds analogies of the Christian life, parodic or otherwise, in the underworld. When the procession reaches the second station, Scorsese (or perhaps J.R.) responds with an inward vision of a daytime city street in New York City. Two police place a large wooden log upon the shoulders and a cap of barbed wire upon the head of a beaten and bloodied young criminal who, analogous to Christ's agony, is forced to walk the streets, as soldiers and policemen hold back jeering crowds.

At the fourth station, just before Father McMahon announces Jesus's meeting with his mother, the boys praise the Saviour: 'Because by Thy holy cross Thou has redeemed the world.' In the parallel narrative, not only is the criminal beaten and scourged by the crowd, but his mother resembles the Virgin Mary: 'He sees a middle-aged woman wearing a black coat and a veil over her head. She is crying silently, face contorted. Other women in black are holding her and crying with her.' It is as if Murray's spaghetti-bearing and black-clad mother had become the Mater Dolorosa, with eyes 'penetrating and awesome.' As the eleventh station depicts Jesus being nailed to the cross, so the young criminal appears before a cross whose horizontal is formed by the log he had been carrying. The crowd remains unruly as two policemen nail the young man's hands into the crossbeam. Visible in the distance is the Empire State Building.

Located on a hilltop above a valley, the twelfth station depicts the death of Jesus with the sorrows of Mary. J.R. is now 'tired and sluggish,' while in the parallel narrative the young criminal suffers the torments of crucifixion. When the procession reaches the summit the boys pray before the twelfth station, although each of them, save J.R., who remains 'extremely intent' upon praying, steals a glance at the valley. When Bud calls J.R.'s attention to the view, J.R. shows annoyance and returns to his prayers. Following Father McMahon's recounting of Jesus's death agony, the boys respond: 'O Jesus, I devoutly venerate that honored cross upon which Thou didst love me even unto death.' Weakly reflecting Jesus's agony, J.R.'s knees trouble him increasingly, but now the criminal suffers real death throes. The crowd thins out, his mother comforted by two friends while two policemen play cards – modern analogues to the scene at Golgotha.

As J.R. moves 'sluggishly' to the next station, the boys sing: 'Let me share with thee his pain, Who for all our sins was slain, Who for me in torment died.' The young criminal looks skyward and then dies, whereupon a policemen fires a revolver into his right side, from which, recalling the Johannine text significant in Scorsese's later Italian American films, blood and water gush forth. The thirteenth station, where Jesus is laid in the arms of his mother, is paralleled by a scene in which the criminal's mother is consoled by black-clad friends as the police take down her son's body and place it in her arms. The crowd disperses and the police clean up the area. At the last station, the boys sing the 'Stabat Mater' and pray with Father McMahon. A still shot shows men, women, and young disciples surrounding the criminal and his mother, who recall a Pietà grouping.

The procession in *Jerusalem, Jerusalem* affords clues to Scorsese's fascination with the penitential and self-tormenting – even masochistic – form of Catholicism to be seen in later characters such as J.R., Charlie Civello, and Jake La Motta. Throughout the procession stress is placed upon the orthodox teaching of the absolute necessity of Jesus's death for humanity's salvation. At the second station the boys say: 'Because by Thy holy cross thou hast redeemed the world' – which they repeat identically at the fourth and thirteenth stations. Before the thirteenth station the boys describe Jesus as dying in 'torment' after having been 'slain' for 'our sins.' As in the orthodox interpretation, emphasis is given not only to the cross but to the 'excruciating suffering,' as Father McMahon terms it, that Christ experiences in his redemptive role. Because such suffering is redemptive, it provides Jesus with what Father McMahon calls 'secret joy.' The procession further reflects the orthodox teaching that worshippers must take Christ as model (the *Imitatio Christi*). Implicit in the very observance of the stations of the cross, this idea is revealed at the second station in the boys' response: 'Oh Jesus, grant me, by virtue of Thy cross, to embrace with meekness and cheerful submission the difficulties of my state, and to be always ready to take up my cross and follow Thee.' To fulfil the *Imitatio*, the worshipper must emulate Jesus in self-sacrificial suffering even to death. Appropriately, on their way to the twelfth station the boys ask the Holy Mother to 'pierce me through, In my heart each wound renew, Of my Savior crucified.' The boys next pledge to 'venerate the honored cross' while placing all their 'confidence' in Christ's 'death,' to which they add: 'Henceforth let me live only for thee and when I die, let me die loving only thee.'

Although nothing in the procession violates orthodoxy, it could conceivably foster a misunderstanding of the *Imitatio*. Suffering would then be seen as being in itself the badge of spiritual election and thus sought for its own sake. The worshipper would embrace suffering not for a redemptive aim but out of pride or vanity. He or she would seek out penitential suffering not from sincere contrition but to advertise his or her spiritual superiority, or as proof of inner worthiness otherwise doubted. Under these circumstances Christ must take on for the masochist the aspect of a 'torturer.' The pleasure a worshipper receives from pain deliberately pursued perverts the 'secret joy' Father McMahon attributes to Christ as he freely sacrifices himself for the salvation of mankind. Such a worshipper may also fall unwittingly into rivalry with Christ, the model, whom he or she attempts self-destructively to equal or outdo in stoicism, as if this were the true seal of spirituality. In a one-sided evaluation of pain and torment as the sole authentic spiritual markers, the masochist may also forsake life for an extreme ascetic discipline, but only to gain ashes and bitterness. All or most of these impulses drive the self-abnegating, self-punishing, life-denying behaviour of Scorsese's characters, whose masochistic spirituality, instead of yielding the desirable results of self-sacrifice pursued for a vital human good, proves sterile and self-destructive.

In representing the Stations of the Cross in the analogical mode,

Jerusalem, Jerusalem anticipates Scorsese's use of Catholic theology in his later films. Yet by comparison with such works as *Mean Streets, Raging Bull,* and *GoodFellas,* his use of analogy in *Jerusalem, Jerusalem* seems contrived and heavy handed, especially in the wearying parallel between the stations of the cross and the suffering criminal. To be sure, Scorsese introduces urban scenes for the sake of realism and timeliness as well as to convey through biblical analogy the immanence of spirit in everyday life. Unfortunately, the parallels seem all too schematic and predictable. Scorsese's later films more successfully satisfy the demands of realism by only implying theological analogues to an object or event, so that each retains its concrete particularity and natural rhythm, with the effect of immanence being thereby enhanced.

Following the procession, J.R. and his friends are shown at recreation time, complaining of their aching knees and the monastery fare. These pampered boys are far from fulfilling the self-abnegating requirements of the *Imitatio.* When Bud mentions the beauty of the valley as seen from the twelfth station, J.R., who had previously been annoyed by his friend's attempt to deflect his attention from his prayers to the landscape, insists that the plaques at each station are also very beautiful. Bud thus speaks for material and secular beauty and J.R. for its even greater divine and sacred counterpart. For though Bud finds the plaques beautiful, he holds that the best 'art work' has been created by the true artist – 'the scenery, courtesy of God.' When J.R. expresses doubts whether God qualifies as an artist, Bud instances the creation of man, which leaves J.R. speechless. Yet he hesitates to allow the created world equal weight with divine and holy imagery. Although the debate remains unsettled, it is worth noting that in *Who's That Knocking at My Door?* a somewhat older and romantically smitten J.R. appears in another climbing scene, although instead of participating in a retreat he now ascends a mountain overlooking a sunlit valley. And whereas in the treatment J.R. downgrades natural beauty, now his delight in it is contrasted with the bored indifference of his friend Joey. This moment can be read, if not as J.R.'s repudiation of the sacred in its otherworldly manifestation, then as his recognition of the need for worldly happiness – which in his case would involve love and marriage.

Not accidentally, marriage and sexuality form the subject of Father McMahon's chapel sermon after the procession. He explains that, since marriage is the layman's vocation, which most members of the audience will inevitably choose, Christ had greatly emphasized marital relationships. Reminiscent of the earlier scene in which the stages of

Christ's suffering were paralleled by Manhattan scenes, Father McMahon's sermon is intercut with scenes from the Bible and the world of the urban poor. The Marriage at Cana is juxtaposed with a wedding in a tenement apartment where bottles of new wine are placed before a bride and groom, whose nuptial feast culminates with a 'surrealistic, overflowing, creamy, white cake.'

Alternately calm and agitated, Father McMahon needs to convince the boys that, though celibate, he is competent to talk about real life, including sex. Accordingly, he reports his experiences as a war chaplain and urban social worker amid the 'screaming nihilism' of drug addicts and drunken child-abusing couples. Father McMahon then tells a story exemplifying the Catholic view of premarital sex. It concerns a couple that, just before marriage, could no longer resist desire for intercourse. After having parked at the roadside for a petting session, they yielded to their passion. At that moment two trucks collided alongside their car, engulfing it in an 'infernal mass of flames.' Then, in a demonstration of God's wrath, 'the young couple was killed ... burned to death in each other's arms.' Mary Pat Kelly notes that Father McMahon's sermon resembles that of the priest Father McNamee in Joyce's *Portrait of the Artist as a Young Man*, who warns Stephen Dedalus of infernal punishments in the meditative style of St Ignatius Loyola. But Scorsese, though struck by the resemblance, read Joyce's novel only after completing his treatment.[21]

The priest's story of the couple destroyed for engaging in premarital sex strongly impresses the boys, and J.R. and Bud find it 'very effective.' J.R. especially 'liked' the story. His naivety is quickly punctured by Mikey, who mentions that on another retreat his girlfriend had been told the same story by a different priest. When J.R. doubts that priests would deceive him, Mikey dismisses their deception as insignificant, as they employ interchangeable 'form sermons.' This scene prefigures that in *Mean Streets* in which Charlie Civello – J.R. under another name – is reminded by his friend Tony that while on retreat Charlie had taken seriously priestly sermons against premarital sex. Like Mikey, Tony discredits the priests by revealing that they used interchangeable form sermons.

After lunch on the final day of retreat, J.R. meets Father McMahon. Hurrying to ensure that the boys are on the bus, the priest apologizes for not having been able to speak to J.R. personally about his masturbatory problems, but tells him to see a 'good Catholic psychiatrist.' Like the form sermon, this statement undercuts priestly authority, for besides having failed to give J.R. the attention he needs, Father McMahon has to some extent abdicated his role to a mere layman with a different belief system. It is not irrelevant that Scorsese himself underwent quite a few years of psychoanalysis following his abandonment of official Catholicism. That Father McMahon's concern for the boys collectively hinders the fulfilment of his obligations to them individually is suggested when, just before boarding the bus, he musters them for a group picture. The final shot of the retreat consists of a freeze-frame of the group photo, with the boys arranged according to height, and with the overall impression one of anonymity and regimentation.

However, the conclusion of *Jerusalem, Jerusalem* remains ambiguous. Having returned to his family's apartment, J.R. appears with his mother and father and then prepares for bed. First he turns on the overhead light; next, after turning on the double-bulb table lamp next to his bed, he turns out the overhead light. Beside his bed is a prayer manual and the resolution envelope he had prepared while on retreat. After getting into bed he turns out one of the lights of the double lamp and points the other towards the wall so as to keep it out of his eyes. One recalls that, following his confession, J.R. had kept a light on to dispel his fear of the darkness. Nervous and uncomfortable, he turns on the remaining double light and rolls back into bed with the covers 'practically hiding his face.' But though J.R. may seem as troubled as before, the presence of light may also indicate that of God. Spiritual striving is also implied in J.R.'s resolution envelope. And finally, in a joyous mood like that of the opening, the 'fairly well-lit' room is flooded with the 'glorious and beautiful' music by Vivaldi with which it began. A title proclaims not only 'The End' but 'For the Greater Glory of God.' What remains to be seen is whether the next installment of Scorsese's projected trilogy can sustain such confidence.

Whereas *Jerusalem, Jerusalem* was never realized, Scorsese had better luck with *Bring on the Dancing Girls*, which, initially financed by a student loan of six thousand dollars, began as his master's project at NYU film school in 1965 and took four years to make. After a disastrous debut and major revisions, it was released in expanded form in 1969 as *Who's That Knocking at My Door?*, Scorsese's first feature film and his first work to attract a larger public. The film's protagonist is a somewhat older J.R. in love with a beauty known only as 'The Girl.' The film itself explores the sexual attitudes of Italian American youth of Scorsese's generation. His aim was 'to portray just the way I was living' and 'to actually record the daily life of the neighborhood.'[22]

Filming began in 1965, with Harvey Keitel, then an aspiring amateur actor, in the role of J.R., which he received only after three tryouts. The film's co-producers were Joe Weil and Haig Manoogian, professor of film at NYU, who later admitted to having too hastily approved Scorsese's outline for the film, which probably needed work. The production was slowed down by a minuscule budget as well as the fact that, since most of the actors worked during the week, shooting took place mainly on weekends; actors occasionally failed to show up or switched jobs and were unable to work, and sometimes their recent haircuts made matching shots impossible. Another difficulty arose from the decision to shoot in thirty-five millimetre, which prevented Scorsese from moving the camera to achieve desired angles.[23] Still unfinished and running about sixty-five minutes, the film was shown in 1967 at the NYU Film Festival, where it was poorly received. The problem, says Manoogian, was a weak story line and some 'real bad actors.'[24]

Nonetheless Manoogian believed that parts of the film were brilliant, especially those treating Little Italy, and that the project could be salvaged by eliminating weak scenes and adding new ones. Scorsese was also trying to raise funds to complete the film. After Manoogian rounded up some money, shooting resumed with new actors and a totally revised script six months in the making and interwoven with the old. Scorsese had liked Keitel's original performance, retaining him as J.R., but the part of The Girl was reassigned to nineteen-year-old Zina Bethune, a former child actress who had starred in the television series *The Nurses*. Michael Wadleigh, who later made *Woodstock* with Scorsese as his assistant, replaced the unavailable Richard Cole as cameraman, while Thelma Schoonmaker was brought in as editor, thus initiating her long collaboration with Scorsese. The film's new segments were shot in sixteen millimetre and blown up to thirty-five millimetre to conform to the pre-existing segments. The entire project, including *Bring on the Dancing Girls*, cost about seventy-five thousand dollars. Upon its completion at a length of ninety minutes, and under the title *I Call First*, Scorsese and Manoogian hoped to enter the film in the Venice Film Festival or the New York Film Festival, but failed in both instances. It premiered in September 1969 at the Chicago Film Festival, where it was awarded Best Student Film. At its debut Roger Ebert described *I Call First* as an American classic, but other critics were more reserved, and it played in only a few theaters. To enhance its commercial possibilities, Manoogian persuaded Scorsese to add a nude scene, and so Keitel was flown to Amsterdam to meet Scorsese, who was there directing commercials. Thus originated the scene in which J.R. fantasizes his own private orgy in a loft. Not only does Scorsese regard this as the worst part of the film, but critics dismiss it as unmotivated and abruptly inserted, with inappropriately overactive camera work.[25]

Scorsese remains dissatisfied with the technique of *Who's That Knocking?*, which pleases him only in its 'emotional aspects.'[26] Like many of his films, *Knocking* exhibits documentary, naturalistic, and improvisatory features, in this case partly attributable to budgetary limitations. The frequent use of the hand-held camera is a documentary or realistic feature showing the influence of the French New Wave, which enjoyed great popularity in the United States during the 1960s. Scorsese anticipates his later films in combining documentary realism with a highly stylized and expressionistic presentation including jumpcuts, freeze-frames, slow-motion sequences, and restless, whirling camera movements. Thus is created a fictional reality where the characters' subjective responses are accentuated and that stands counterposed to the 'real' or documented world of the film, consisting of actual interiors that, as Kolker remarks, continue to exist after it is over.[27] The limitation of Scorsese's expressionistic style, in *Knocking* at least, is that it calls attention to the techniques he had learned in film school. There he had also acquired the art of cinematic allusion to be seen, for instance, in Godard's *Breathless*, where references to the films of Humphrey Bogart and Randolph Scott comment on the action. In *Who's That Knocking?* J.R. and The Girl leave a double bill with *Rio Bravo* and *Scaramouche* on the marquee, and during their initial encounter J.R. discusses Ford's *The Searchers* and *The Man Who Shot Liberty Valance*. Yet though they add to the thematic interest of *Who's That Knocking?*, these discussions of film are also clumsily discursive and dramatically inert, and Kolker and Friedman rightly complain of their imperfect integration with the dramatic action. Scorsese's later works incorporate cinematic allusions much more deftly.[28]

The main character of *Who's That Knocking?* calls to mind Scorsese's self-description as 'gangster' and 'priest' in being drawn to gang society yet troubled by religious scruples, chiefly in sexual matters. J.R.'s peer group consists of thuggish ne'er-do-wells who, though possibly candidates for a life of crime, share his Catholic upbringing and its sexual attitudes. This is not to say that they are regular churchgoers, as their disorderly lives seem not to allow for it. J.R. spends most of his time with his homophilic peer group, which favours drinking, gambling, roughhousing, and gang warfare. He and his friends belong to that portion of the working-class Italian American urban community that Gans designates as 'action-seekers.' Their favourite activity is the collective pursuit of promiscuous women, whom they disdain as 'broads,' and whom they even share among themselves, sometimes in serial copulation. For them, these women are undeserving of love and altogether unmarriageable.[29] The young men of the peer group are mired in sexual squalor, without emotional connection or commitment, sinking into a desperation they dimly recognize yet cannot articulate. As J.R., Joey, and Sally Gaga ride silently in an elevator to the upper floor of a parking garage, the elevator's blank walls and noisily grinding machinery suggest the prospectlessness and mechanical repetition of their lives. Such futility is also implied by the circular repetition of their forays around town, which return as if inevitably to their point of departure, the dismal and ironically named Eighth Ward Pleasure Club.[30] The sense of confinement is already present at the opening, as the camera, initially focused on a butcher shop on Elizabeth Street, draws back, pans right down the street, picks up J.R. and Joey as they round the distant corner, and then follows them *back* down the sidewalk to the Pleasure Club. It is as if the camera were blocked by the limits of the neighbourhood and, failing to 'escape' it, were falling in with the main characters' predictable pattern of life. Also contributing to the feeling of claustrophobia are the many images of entrapment: the padlocking of the doors of the Pleasure Club, shots of the closing of the doors and automatic windows of Joey's car, the confessional to which J.R. finally retreats.[31] Yet despite the routine of life in Little Italy, the peer group members seem to prefer it. J.R. takes no joy in his trip to Staten Island, and Joey, during his brief visit to Copake, New York, longs for Manhattan.[32]

J.R. has a chance to abandon his pointless existence when he meets a beautiful young woman answering his desires for a madonna-like image of virginal femininity. His sexual life having been limited to casual encounters, he regards his new acquaintance as marriageable so long as her virginity can be attested to. The unreality of his conception of her is suggested by the fact that she remains nameless, the credits referring to her only as 'The Girl.' Unlike the Italian American girls J.R. is likely to have known, she lives alone in an apartment and has thus won a certain independence from her family. Her undoubtedly upper-middle-class background places her at a considerably higher social level than J.R., who apparently derives from the lower middle class.[33] The social distance between the lovers is conveyed effectively at the level of everyday speech, for whereas the inarticulate J.R. liberally sprinkles his conversation with the expression 'you know,' The Girl employs the much tonier idiom of the English and American upper and upper-middle classes. Thus, when asked by J.R. whether her magazine is French, she responds, 'I'm afraid it is,' resorting to the apologetic locution by which well-bred Anglophone speakers indicate their extreme unwillingness to displease or give offence.[34]

Although their romance blossoms into love, J.R. rejects her attempts to initiate sex partly out of respect for her virginity but also to prevent her from becoming a tainted 'broad.' However, their romance collapses upon her revelation that she had lost her virginity as a result of rape. Angered by her 'defilement,' J.R. doubts her story, implying that she had engaged in voluntary sex, whereupon she breaks off their romance. Alone once more, he returns to his peer group until his growing dissatisfaction with its lifestyle drives him to visit The Girl in an attempted reconciliation. When he proposes to 'forgive' her loss of virginity as a condition of marriage, she realizes the impossibility of marrying him. Her rejection leads him to denounce her as a 'whore' who sees herself as the 'Virgin Mary or something' but fails to realize that, in her degradation, J.R. is the only man magnanimous enough to marry her. With great restraint she dismisses him from her apartment, after which he takes refuge in church in a vain effort to quell his emotional turmoil.

As a study of Italian American mores, including sexual attitudes, *Who's That Knocking?* is conscious of its cinematic precursors and invites comparison with them. The most obvious example is the Academy Award–winning *Marty* (1955). Based on the television play by the non–Italian American Paddy Chayefsky and directed by Delbert Mann, *Marty* was shot on Arthur Avenue in the Bronx and in the surrounding Italian American neighbourhood.[35] Like Scorsese's film, *Marty* not only stresses Italian American motherhood but represents the Italian American community, typified by the male peer group, as insular and entrapping. In both films, the protagonist's salvation from the moral, social, and cultural limitations of his ethnic background depends on marriage with a northern European woman marked by superior manners and a higher educational level.

Played by Ernest Borgnine, an Italian American actor, in an Oscar-winning performance, Marty is a heavy-set, unprepossessing, and unmarried Italian American butcher who, fast approaching middle age, has failed with women and fears he will never find a wife. Many younger members of his peer group have married, and it is assumed by Marty's widowed mother (Esther Minciotti), in whose apartment he lives, that he should follow the pattern. Marty belongs to a homophilic peer group consisting of directionless, loveless, and unmarried Italian American males, the boredom and futility of whose existence is typified by repeated exchanges between Marty and his friend Angie: 'So whaddya wanna do tonight, Marty?' 'I dunno, Angie, whadda you wanna do?' For Marty's friends, the favoured pastime consists of sexual encounters with available 'broads,' whom they hunt together, hold in misogynistic contempt, and regard as thoroughly disposable. Although the film is guarded on this point, Marty for all his good-natured decency has participated in these sexual expeditions, nurses being the preferred targets. When not pursuing casual sex, the peer group feasts its eyes upon pornography or escapes into the misogynistic lowbrow fiction of Mickey Spillane, whose detective hero, Mike Hammer, follows his shooting murder of a perfidious 'broad' with the throwaway line: 'It was easy.'[36] To quote a simian member of Marty's peer group, 'Mickey Spillane, he could really write.' Despite these pastimes Marty and Angie attend Sunday mass regularly.

Against all odds, Marty falls in love with a non–Italian American woman named Clara Snyder (Betsy Blair), a homely chemistry teacher. Yet their path to marriage is strewn with difficulties. In contrast with Marty's maternal devotion, his relatives find their own widowed mother impossible to deal with and arrange for her to live in Marty and his mother's apartment. Through conversations with the forsaken widow, Marty's mother comes to fear abandonment by her son and loses all desire to see him married. She behaves rudely to Clara Snyder on their introduction, and subsequently tries to poison the relationship with remarks concerning the young woman's homeliness and non-Italian background. Marty's relationship with Clara is also opposed by his friends, who deride her as a 'dog' unworthy of their pornographic standard. Actually, they resent his success in love and fear his departure from the group. In the final scene Marty's desire for personal happiness conquers his conformism, and it is understood that he and Clara will marry.

Scorsese alludes to *Marty* in the opening scene, with a high-angle shot into a butcher shop on the ground floor of an urban building, where the butcher chops meat with a cleaver.[37] One recalls the opening of *Marty* in which the camera, at ground level, records street traffic along Arthur Avenue and then continues into Marty's butcher shop, where he cuts and packages meat while greeting customers. It is also likely that Scorsese, known to his friends as Marty, sees a parallel between Borgnine's butcher and himself. The connection rests partly on the fact that the young Scorsese lacked confidence in his physical appearance and despaired of success with women. And just as Marty the butcher cuts meat for a living, so Martin Scorsese cuts celluloid.[38]

It is more useful to consider the differences between *Marty* and *Who's That Knocking?* Although Borgnine's Marty cuts meat, he performs his task unemphatically, whereas Scorsese's butcher is 'whacking a slab,' to quote Lourdeaux.[39] Scorsese thus implies a continuity between the ordinary violence of the butcher's shop and that of the surrounding Italian American society. To the extent that this butcher stands for the director, then what is suggested is Scorsese's identification, in cutting his film, with its depicted violence. Scorsese would later characterize film directing and editing as a form of physical aggression upon actors and characters.[40] Some of his later films suggest his strong emotional investment in their represented violence, for instance *Mean Streets*, in which Scorsese plays the assassin Shorty, and *Taxi Driver*, in which he portrays a husband planning to kill his adulterous wife and her lover. By comparison with *Who's That Knocking?*, *Marty* with its cautious realism amounts to a sanitized representation of Italian American life, written from outside its subject matter, with characters too close to stereotypes. Virtually every main point in the film is made with clumsy insistence. Its heart-warming intent is expressed in the vaguely Italianate and cloyingly upbeat title song 'Marty,' by the Italian American composer Harry Warren.[41] The misogyny, emotional squalor, and potential violence, sexual and otherwise, of the peer group are toned down in *Marty* so as to suit popular taste, being little more than suggested through such details as the characters' fondness for Mickey Spillane. But in Scorsese's film the sexual and social pressures reach deeper, the milieu impinges far more claustrophobically, the anguish lacerates more intensely and desperately, and the road to happiness proves to be more troubled and obscure. The key difference is that the non–Italian American woman fails to provide the salvation the protagonist longs for, weighed down as he is with cultural, social, and psychic baggage.

What is it that condemns J.R. and his cronies to unbroken rounds of futility, violence, promiscuity, and sexual dissatisfaction? Some critics, including Michael Bliss, seconded by Grist, find these characters' frustrations to result from their 'religiously polluted' Catholic upbringing, whose culpability is implied in the opening scenes.[42] The first scene begins with a middle-aged mother of an Italian American family – Catherine Scorsese in the second of her appearances in her son's films – making a meat pie or *calzone* in her rather run-down tenement kitchen. Not only does the kitchen contain a devotional candle and religious icons shot in close-up, but the mother and maternal icon appear together in the opening shot, each reflected in a mirror against the kitchen wall. Scorsese implies a resemblance and even a doubling of the maternal figures, one secular, one sacred. He also calls attention to the fact that his portrayal of the mother is itself a representation, like the icon – a representation of idealized Italian American maternity. The shot from behind the statuette of the Virgin and Child suggests a sacred feminine presence, reflected in the maternal figure, presiding over the kitchen itself. Emphasis is given as well to the making of the pie, as in successive shots the mother rolls, pounds, and kneads the dough, fills it with meat, and places it in an oven. This physically strong woman appears to have shaped her family as authoritatively as she forms the thick but yielding dough. The pie having been cooked, she calls five young children, two boys and three girls, to the kitchen table, where they assemble patiently and in orderly fashion, after which she divides and distributes their food equally with a knife. It seems that this scene derives from J.R.'s boyhood, that these are his brothers and sisters, and that the woman is his mother. Her relation to J.R. is later implied insofar as the religious icons resemble those in J.R.'s mother's bedroom during the scene of his sexual failure. The kitchen scene is followed by a cut to the streets, where a now-grown-up J.R. appears as part of a five-member Italian American street gang about to do battle with two Puerto Ricans. One of the Puerto Ricans crosses himself and kisses the crucifix around his neck as invoking divine help. It does little good, as the Italians beat the outnumbered Puerto Ricans mercilessly with sticks and fists.[43]

Bliss's analysis of the kitchen scene relates both the mother's presence and the icons of the madonna to the madonna-whore dichotomy. The Catholic-based glorification of motherhood, marriage, and their concomitants of feminine virginity and chastity have enslaved the film's male characters to an 'essentially unrealistic, polarized view of women,' divided between the 'redeemed and damned, the virgins and the whores.' This 'poisons' their minds and causes them to become 'trapped' in a rigidly dualistic conception of good and evil. At the same time, an upbringing that 'condemns' the male characters' 'physical desires' provides only the 'supposed solace of the church.'[44] Grist accepts Bliss's view of the kitchen scene, adding that Scorsese shoots the kitchen from behind the madonna, which suggests that she not only presides over but dominates the room.[45] For Bliss, the family scene and ensuing gang fight exemplify the same anti-Christian thematic, the point being that Catholicism yields 'violence, not peace.' He then reads the violence of the gang members back into the kitchen scene. The distribution of bread, he claims, passes on the 'heritage of violence'; the bread being broken is the stuff of not life but 'death.' Similarly, the distribution of the bread signifies the transmission of the Catholic view of polarized good and evil. Bliss resumes this condemnatory tone in commenting on the Catholic elements abounding in the final scene, when J.R., dismissed from The Girl's apartment, runs to church, enters a confessional, and performs contrition amid bloody, grotesque, and sadomasochistic icons of penitential suffering. According to Bliss, the title of the song that accompanies this scene, and that provides the film's title, admits of only one answer. It is the 'Catholic-corrupted, Catholic-appropriated Jesus, the god of pain and destruction, ... the God of morbidity who demands entrance.'[46]

To claim that Catholicism satisfies all the needs of the film's characters would be contrary to Scorsese's purposes. Commenting on the film, and especially the unrealistic moral dichotomies governing the characters' sexual behaviour, Scorsese remarks that 'it's that whole Italian-American' – and thus to some extent Roman Catholic – 'way of thinking, of feeling.'[47] The making of *Who's That Knocking?* coincided with Scorsese's growing dissatisfaction with the church, including doubts of its relevance to everyday morality, as a result of which he became a self-described 'Catholic layman.' Nonetheless, Bliss's uninformed and one-sided criticisms of Italian American and Catholic culture show yet again that anti-Catholicism remains the 'anti-Semitism of the intellectuals.'[48] Not only does Bliss ignore the positive moral influence of Catholicism in the film, obvious to all but a prejudiced observer; he also blames Catholicism for attitudes and behaviours for which it is not responsible, but seeks to counteract.

The most flagrant example of Bliss's misreading is his interpretation of the kitchen scene. Like other commentators, he ignores the commemorative image that, placed high on the wall above the mother, depicts a moustached male figure, clearly paternal and of immigrant times. This image, along with the icons and ritualization of the meal, betoken not official Cathlicism alone, but the Catholic-based Italian American 'religion of the domus.' The *calzone* the mother cooks for her children is both the Eucharist of Italian American family life and the embodiment of her maternal love, consistent with the Italian American saying, '*Buono come il pane* [as good as bread].'[49] The bread is distributed peaceably among a group of apparently happy yet disciplined children gathered not in quarrelsomeness but harmony. The mother's attitude towards her children, and that of the children towards her and each other, testifies to that *rispetto* – combining distance and intimacy – essential to the religion of the domus. This not to imply that, in the film or actuality, such a religion is utopian; the element of fear that Orsi notes in the domus, as a complement to love, is implicit in the paternal image high on the wall, as in the commanding images of the mother, Madonna, and Child. Also not to be ignored is the non-diegetic music accompanying the kitchen scene. With its tight and steady staccato drumbeat combined with a no less steady clicking or rattling metallic sound, reminiscent of the beating of sticks, the score has an almost militaristic insistence, perhaps suggesting disciplined rigidity and monotony in the Italian American experience of growing up. These inhuman sounds recall other moments when the repetitive dullness of the adult characters' lives is evoked by machine-like grinding noises, as in the elevator. Yet only an ideologically motivated observer could hold that threat and menace, and an education into sexual and other vio-lence, prevail in the kitchen scene. Contrary to Bliss's claim that the children learn violence at home, they are being taught its opposite. Far from being thematically continuous with the gang fight, as Bliss claims, the peaceable kitchen scene contrasts with it.

Bliss may seem on stronger ground in arguing that the sexual miser-ies of the film's male characters – as well as their propensity to sexual and other violence – result from the madonna-whore dichotomy, lead-ing to the unreasonable distinction between virgins and 'broads.' Such criticisms of Italian American and Roman Catholic sexual morality, which often appear in discussions of the film, reflect the common assumption that expressions of sexuality are basically instinctual and largely healthy, and should be liberated from long-standing prohibi-tions that are inherently repressive, enslaving, and life denying. In fairness to the Catholic position, one should keep in mind that these sexual prohibitions, and particularly the rule against sex outside of marriage, were never instituted so as to promote sexual misery. The assumption has been that love and promiscuity are radically different forms of experience, that the former is preferable emotionally and morally to the latter, and that love typically flourishes within the context of marriage, with sexuality in subordination to it, rather than in momentary passion and free-floating desire, as with promiscuity. From the Catholic point of view, sexuality when it fails to come under the sway of reason and self-control shows a natural tendency towards concupiscence, a form of malice towards the other person in which sex and physical pleasure are pursued solely for themselves, without any serious (in the sense of permanent) commitment, and under the sway of uncontrolled but fleeting passion. In such instances sex is characterized by violence in the form of an aggressive, acquisitive, dominating, and selfishly exploitative attitude towards the object of desire, who as a sexual partner is reduced to the status of a merely pleasurable object, with his or her sexuality abstracted from the totality of the person.[50] By contrast, sex within marriage is conceptualized within Catholicism as a form of rational self-mastery or self-control through which the self, being truly possessed by the individual, can then be given freely and exclusively to the love object in a lifetime commitment founded in neither malice nor exploitation but in mutual love and respect for each other's dignity. In this way, marriage itself becomes a form of the *Imitatio Christi.*[51]

From such a standpoint, it might be argued that the lifting of the hated prohibitions against the free pursuit of sexual pleasure has unexpectedly sanctioned as well as unleashed those forms of sexual desire that, contrary to the naive view of sex as an unalloyed natural good, tend towards exploitativeness, aggressiveness, and even emotional violence towards the other person. The currently high divorce rate as well as the frequent fleetingness of many so-called relationships at the present time might well support such a view.[52] A defender of the Catholic prohibitions might further argue that the supposed instinctual and free expressions of sexuality recommended as the counter to those prohibitions are frequently neither purely instinctual nor free, but originate in various mimetic cues and other social mediations, including the popular media, advertisements, desire of status, desire of transgression, conformism, envy, jealousy, rivalry, resentment, ambition, sadism, masochism, scandal, and flight from boredom.[53] The prohibitions have prevented at least some individuals from being swept up in the vanity, frustration, and delusiveness of the many forms of mediated sexual desire. An advocate might further argue that it remains for critics of Catholic prohibitions to prove that their removal has actually rendered individuals, in their sexual relations, less scarred, wounded, deluded, and prey to envy, compulsion, and disappointment than when the prohibitions exerted their strongest power – something unprovable, certainly, but at least open to doubt.[54]

Perhaps the strongest objection against such prohibitions, as Girard observes and as Scorsese's film suggests, is that, being founded on the sacred, their very existence provokes transgression, so that the prohibition is bound to produce the behaviours it seeks to prevent. Regarding the film's characters, and more especially J.R., two points need emphasis. One is that the characters' sexual promiscuity and violence against non-Italians and each other are disapproved by Catholicism. It is therefore hard to see how its prohibitions could lead intentionally to such behaviour. Second, the characters' violence and sexual promiscuity, far from being Catholic inspired, result from their mimetic, de-individuated, pack-like behaviour.

This latter can be seen in the gang fight between the five Italian and two Puerto Rican males at the film's beginning. Despite Bliss's claim that their violence derives from Catholicism, all of these thugs dishonour church teachings – unless one believes that the church condones gang warfare. The Puerto Rican's gesture in crossing himself, from which Bliss falsely concludes that violence results from Catholicism, reveals only the error of falsely claiming divine sanction for human violence – an error exemplified by practitioners of many religions. The characters' motivations are revealed not in the Catholic trappings with which they falsely invest their behaviour, but in that behaviour itself. It is purely mimetic. As the Italian American gang members are all dressed in similar pants, shoes, jackets, and sweaters and have similar haircuts, making it hard to distinguish them from even a short distance, so they converge pack-like upon their victims, each performing the same gestures of beating and kicking. The mimetic nature of their actions is again revealed when J.R. and his friend Joey return to the gang after having beaten a Puerto Rican man. In a closer shot of the two men moving along the sidewalk, J.R. unexpectedly and without provocation throws a mock left hook in the direction of Joey, in an unconscious and imitative overflow of the violence he has witnessed and in which he has participated. Such a gesture reinforces the impression of the contagious – that is, mimetic – power of the violence that has overtaken the gang members.

Not only does J.R. contribute to violence in this scene (and presumably others like it), but his participation is inspired by models of violence by whom he is fascinated. Were Catholicism responsible for J.R.'s violence, these models would derive from the church, yet they originate entirely outside it, in the popular media and more especially the Western film. As J.R. tells The Girl during their first meeting, he and his Italian American friends enjoy 'John Wayne epics,' three of which J.R. comments on during the film. These are John Ford's masterwork *The Searchers* (1956), which provides J.R.'s gambit in his initial conversation with The Girl on the Staten Island Ferry, when he notices her copy of *Paris Match* with pictures of Wayne in the title role; Ford's *The Man Who Shot Liberty Valance* (1962), whose villainous title character J.R also discusses with her; and Howard Hawks's *Rio Bravo*, which J.R. takes her to see on a date, and stills of which flash on the screen as they leave the theater. Unlike the Ford films, this latter one is significant to J.R. less for its themes of violence than for its analogues with his peer group. Yet it also resembles the Ford films in the light it sheds on J.R.'s sexual attitudes.

It is hardly surprising that J.R. and his friends admire the Wayne persona. As Herbert Gans remarks, Wayne, along with Humphrey Bogart, was the most popular male movie star among the Italian Americans of Boston's West End in the 1950s, which Gans views as a typical working-class Italian American community of that time. Like J.R. and his peers, the West Enders conflated Wayne and his portrayed characters, referring to the latter as 'John Wayne.'[55] The special appeal of Wayne to this ethnic group is partly explained by the fact that the traits of Wayne's screen personae – impassivity; self-control; patient, unflinching endurance; a strict personal code of honour; retaliatory violence – closely resemble those prized by Italian American males. For J.R., Wayne's primary appeal lies in his violence, for as he tells The Girl, 'Wayne can get pretty nasty.' Yet J.R. is nearly equally fascinated by Wayne's opponent, the savage Liberty Valance, whose very name, and whose enlistment in the cattle barons' defence of the 'open range,' link him to values J.R. admires as the antithesis of his social imprisonment: violence, personal autonomy, unbridled freedom. Thus he tells The Girl that the world would be a better place if everyone liked Westerns. He fails to realize that these anachronistic models of behaviour add to his delusion and entrapment.

Not only is J.R. drawn to models of violence, he is fascinated especially by mimetic violence as embodied in the agon between Ethan Edwards, Wayne's character in *The Searchers*, and the Comanche chief, Scar. The source of their hatred is that Scar, in vengeance for the killing of his two sons, has led a raid on the settlements during which he killed Edwards's brother, sister-in-law, and nephew, raped and murdered his eldest niece, and abducted the younger one, Debbie, whom Scar later includes among his Comanche wives. Besides seeking vengeance against Scar, Edwards aims to kill Debbie because of what he sees as her tainted purity. In *Who's That Knocking?*, J.R. practically initiates his conversation with The Girl by quoting an unpleasant exchange between Edwards and Scar – a Wild West version of the Southern Italian *passatella* or ritual trading of insults described by Richard Gambino.[56] Thus Edwards: 'You speak pretty good American for a Comanch' – someone teach ya?' To which Scar replies: 'You speak pretty good Comanch', someone teach ya?' The nearly perfect symmetry of this retaliatory exchange, implying the mimetic equivalence of the characters, contributes to the escalating violence between them. Subsequently J.R. calls attention to this retaliatory symmetry: 'Scar was a very nasty Indian ... He was more nasty than Wayne could ever get.' Yet realizing that to assert Scar's superior nastiness (read violence) lessens Edwards's masculinity vis-à-vis his rival, J.R. adds: 'But then again, John Wayne could get pretty nasty too when he wanted to be,' thus maintaining Wayne's violent equivalence with Scar.[57]

J.R.'s interest in mimetic rivalry is evident from another of his cinematic favourites. Directed by George Sidney and starring Stewart Granger, *Scaramouche* (1952) is set against the backdrop of the French Revolution, when civil war threw a whole nation into undifferentiating fraternal conflict. Ignorant of fencing, Andre Moreau (Granger) is humiliated in a duel by the Marquis de Maynes (Mel Ferrer), the best swordsman in France. After finding refuge in a theatrical troupe in the guise of the buffoon Scaramouche, Moreau receives a lesson in retaliatory mimesis as he takes fencing lessons so as to avenge himself against the Marquis. The film climaxes with a six-minute swordfight in which Moreau defeats the Marquis but spares his life at the last moment upon discovering that they are half-brothers. If, as Girard argues, the spread of civil war within a community is most adequately symbolized by the feuding brothers, doubles of each other's undifferentiating violence, then, symbolically speaking, Moreau and the Marquis would seem to have been exempted by such violence – in this case that of the French Revolution – owing to this small difference in their genealogies.

Although J.R. somewhat grasps Ethan Edwards's mimeticism, he fails to comprehend the doubling or undifferentiation resulting from Edwards's vengeful exchanges with enemies and rivals, Comanches in general and Scar particularly. Nor does J.R. realize that repeated acts of retaliation can rob an individual of autonomy even as he imagines himself to be asserting it through oppositional violence. *The Searchers* reveals the link between mimetic violence and undifferentiation in showing how Edwards, the Indian hater, unwittingly resembles his Indian enemies more than the white community with which he identifies. He favours a nomadic, outdoors existence; wears Indian clothing; lends credence to Indian superstitions; prides himself on his knowledge of Indian military tactics, customs, and language; makes mimetic animal noises; gestures in sign language; and, at the climax, scalps Scar. Such behaviour testifies to Edwards's unacknowledged loss of autonomy born of his obsessive vengefulness, which dominates his personality. Yet J.R. ignores this deformation, thinking that Edwards maintains his autonomy: 'Wayne could get pretty nasty when he wanted to be.'[58]

Mimeticism is crucial to J.R.'s personality, especially his difficulty in achieving autonomy over his own desires. His problem is signalled by The Girl during their first meeting, although the implications of her question elude him: 'Do you always do what you want to do?' An appraisal of his social and sexual behaviour reveals that, contrary to his imagined self-autonomy, his desires are mediated by others. This is not chiefly because J.R. and his friends vaguely model themselves on John Wayne, since, as an unapproachable model situated in an imaginary West, Wayne can inspire only external mediation, like Amadis de Gaul for Don Quixote.[59] But J.R. is actually amid a peer group whose emotionally confused and weak-willed members normally gather together to mediate and reinforce each other's desires through mimetic suggestion. It may be objected to the claim that J.R. finds it hard to think and desire for himself that, when depressed over the loss of The Girl, he rejects Joey's proposal that they visit a convenient 'broad'; instead, J.R. would drown his sorrows in drink. On the same occasion he also shows his emerging dissatisfaction with the whole business of the collective pursuit of available women when he says with mocking condescension to Joey, 'Got any more toys to play with?' This moment, though, is atypical of J.R.'s behaviour within the peer group. Normally he, like the others, relies on mimetic cues from his friends, as witness the *Marty*-like exchange between J.R. and Joey: 'What are we gonna do tonight? ... What do you wanna do? ... What do you wanna do?' These young men have difficulty desiring on their own, and rely on others' hints and suggestions. Hence they socialize and fight in packs, their minds pretty much interchangeable, being driven by conformist interests.[60] This is seen when J.R., Joey, and Sally Gaga, sitting together at a bar, get drunk and behave incredibly childishly, even squirting drinks at each other. They have regressed to a stage of unformed personality in which mimeticism predominates. Appropriately, the accompanying soundtrack consists of rock-and-roll versions of 'Mary Had a Little Lamb' and 'Humpty Dumpty.'

Inasmuch as the peer group members favour sameness within the group, they resent marked assertions of personal difference that might endanger its ethnic insularity and pack mentality – as for instance in J.R.'s atypically serious affair with The Girl, whom he apparently never introduces to his friends. However, the peer group members disfavour excessive sameness within the group, reacting against their own conformism through assertions of individual difference within a loosely defined pecking order. This tendency is reinforced by models such as the John Wayne persona, a prepotent, competitive individual who likes to stand out. In *The Man Who Shot Liberty Valance*, Tom Doniphon, played by Wayne, announces swaggeringly: 'Liberty Valance is the toughest man south of the Picketwire – next to me.' Such copying leads to what Keyser terms the 'boyish antics' of the peer group – exaggerated gestures, macho display, and the ritual insults of the *passatella*.[61] Within the peer group, Sally Gaga functions to introduce an element of reassuring difference by playing the role of despised pimp, thief, and generally marginal individual. As the passive butt of insults and jokes, and even of Joey's violence, he canalizes the internal tensions within the group. In the opening scene in the Pleasure Club, after denouncing Gaga for playing cards while owing him money, Joey gives Gaga a beating to which he passively submits. Joey rejects Gaga's apology, saying, 'tell your priest if you're sorry, not me' – a statement that, incidentally, shows not how close the group is to Catholicism, as Bliss contends, but its distance from it.[62] When J.R. asks Joey why he has given Sally the nickname 'Gaga' (accented on the second syllable), he is told that Sally is 'stupid.' A possible motivation for this disdainful epithet is suggested in a later scene in Joey's car when, having been described by J.R. as stupid, Joey protests that he is every bit as intelligent as his friend. Joey's insistence upon Gaga's stupidity thus defines a difference between him and a despised person he fears to resemble. At the same time, Joey resents J.R. for his affair with The Girl, a non-'broad' outside the peer group's shared sexual conquests. When Joey complains that J.R.'s sadness over the recent break-up robs the group of its festive spirit, J.R. experiences vanity in having attracted a woman of such quality, and with it feelings of sexual superiority over Joey: 'I'd like to see you get a girl without paying five dollars.' Finding this too great an insult, and annoyed by J.R.'s excessive independence, Joey throws him out of his car.[63] But though J.R. leaves willingly, he shortly returns upon Joey's invitation, the need for belonging, sameness, and familiarity winning out over the desire for individuality, novelty, and freedom.

The tensions within the peer group, arising from conformist pressures in conflict with desperate and ineffectual assertions of individuality, climax in the later scene at the stag party. Unfolding to the primitive and hypnotic rhythms of Ray Barretto's 'Watusi,' whose title appropriately connotes tribalism, this scene exposes not only the disturbing lack of differentiation within the peer group, but the lure of violence as its antidote. The guests are all young, Italian American, dark haired, and dressed in the same fashion – dark or gray jacket, white shirt, and tie. Two of the young men look like brothers or even twins; twins are often regarded as harbingers of violence because they represent absence of difference and thus evoke the doubles of undifferentiating conflict.[64] Initially the guests are shown talking, drinking, or reading newspapers, some in the living room, others in the kitchen. The black-and-white photography de-emphasizes the chromatic differences in their clothing and thus accentuates their sameness. As it takes in the group, the camera pans through the rooms dreamily, one scene fading into another, so that the interior space of the apartment is encompassed several times. This continuous inclusive movement traces an invisible circular enclosure suggestive of the external boundaries and hence limits of the group. It also suggests the equality of its members, as the camera rests on no single individual.

The possibility of violence arises when an unidentified guest produces a revolver. He gives it to Joey, who drops it into J.R.'s lap, whereupon J.R., smiling with the exhilaration of holding so potent an object, opens the chamber to find it empty. The revolver is then passed in nervous fascination among the members of the group as a kind of sacred object, a cause of attraction but also fear, so that no one dares to claim it. Yet the violent impulses lurking within the celebration emerge when a tall young man appropriates the gun, walks past Sally Gaga into the kitchen, takes a drink, and loads the chamber. He walks back into the kitchen dining area and points the gun randomly at the guests, including Gaga, Joey, and the two seated brothers or twins. His cocking of the hammer causes the guests to respond ambiguously. On the one hand there is ebullient laughter, which J.R. shares, based on the assumption that what is being witnessed is only a harmless mimesis of violence; indeed, Joey and the others imitate holding a gun by pointing their fingers mockingly at the gunman. On the other hand, the guests fear that this joke will turn tragic, that real violence will claim a random victim, and that the circle of friends will become a fatal wheel of fortune. Not taking any chances, the guests flee to the furthest limits of the living room. Yet some of them, including J.R. and Joey, are half-laughing in the lingering suspicion that the gunplay remains only a game. Meanwhile, the gunman collars Gaga and, pointing the gun in his face, drags him into the living room. Gaga's laughter turns to terror. That he should become an object of aggression is hardly surprising, for if there is anyone present who cries out for victimary status, it is Gaga. This is not only because of his marginal place within the community, but because of his despised (yet necessary) function as pimp for the peer group. He is an all-purpose whipping boy, with connections among the despised 'broads,' a thief, and possibly a homosexual. If the gunman fails to shoot Gaga, the reason may be that, as was revealed earlier, he has brothers, so that to harm him would invite retaliation. However, the gunman only pretends to threaten violence, and indeed part of the scene's unsettling effect arises from our prolonged uncertainty on this point. Finally the gunman shoots not Gaga but a liquor bottle, so that the scene amounts to a mere letting off of steam, a joke after all.

As the guests flee from the gunman, the camera takes in casually, in three separate shots, a small picture resting upon a console. Examination reveals it almost certainly to represent Frank Sinatra, whose image is predictable in this setting. For J.R. and his peer group, as for Scorsese and his generation, Sinatra exemplifies Italian American masculinity par excellence. Making no secret of his ethnicity, but flaunting it as an essential component in his social and professional success, Sinatra appeared to many Italian Americans of those days as the very model of rebellious nonconformity vis-à-vis the core culture. Such a persona could only be highly attractive to a peer group such as J.R.'s, in which rampant conformism, however unconscious, needs to be compensated for by romantic fantasies of individualistic self-assertion.[65] Sinatra's mystique of personal autonomy was expressed in his vocal performances and, by the late 1960s, in his signature song, Paul Anka's 'My Way.' In its refrain Sinatra boasts of having, against all obstacles, lived life after his own fashion. He thus calls to mind the protagonists in Scorsese's Italian American films, including Charlie Civello, Jake La Motta, Henry Hill, and Sam 'Ace' Rothstein, each of whom, notwithstanding his actual bondage to group values and unwittingly slavish imitation of other people, states explicitly or implicitly his desire to do it 'his way.'[66]

Sinatra's appeal for J.R. lies as well in his reputation for sexual predation, his associations with the Mafia and Las Vegas, which he publicized rather than hid, and his leadership of a predominantly male peer group – the Rat Pack, a high-profile brother- and sisterhood of high livers and ne'er-do-wells. In the late 1950s and early 1960s the Rat Pack gained a reputation for nonconformity notwithstanding that its members formed an acknowledged 'pack' and, as the so-called Kings of Cool, exemplified a new kind of conformity later phased out by the conformist youth culture of the 1960s.[67] The name 'Rat Pack' suggests predation upon women in the orally aggressive manner of rodents, chewing them up; interestingly, J.R. says admiringly of Liberty Valance that he's so mean he even bites. 'Rat Pack' also plays on 'rat' as informer, implying that its members boast of their many sexual conquests.[68] For Gans, the Rat Pack amounts to a middle-aged deluxe version of a streetcorner group.[69] This is to say, Sinatra and his cronies, for all their apparent rebelliousness, are a magnified and idealized version of what J.R. and his friends would like to be – a perfect combination of apparent iconoclasm and unthinking devotion to group values. The Rat Pack may also have held the same appeal for the young Martin Scorsese, who acknowledges his admiration for Sinatra and more especially his interest in Dean Martin. Even more than Sinatra, Martin was characterized in his behaviour by extreme *lontananza*, that is, emotional distance or detachment from the world around him, as well as by *menefreghismo*, an attitude that best translates as 'I don't give a damn.' Scorsese had been captivated by both performers in the 1960s, and remains fascinated by Martin's coming to terms with himself simultaneously with his abandonment of the Rat Pack.[70] Were Scorsese to film his long-projected biography of Martin, one would expect to find in Martin's gradual detachment from the Rat Pack a more mature, middle-aged analogue to J.R.'s desire to extricate himself from the likes of Joey and Sally Gaga.

The stag party in *Who's That Knocking?* initiates a formal, thematic, and spatial pattern typical of Scorsese's Italian American films, including *Mean Streets*, *GoodFellas*, and *Casino*. Each depicts an increasingly chaotic situation that, in an atmosphere of vertiginous elation and anxiety fed by gambling, alcohol, drugs, sex, and various internal conflicts and rivalries, escalates into random and undifferentiating violence within the depicted groups, which then succumb to mini-versions of the sacrificial crisis. These situations are identified variously with an all-encompassing circular or vortex-like motion: the wheel of fortune, the revolving chamber of a pistol, successive panning shots around a room, the vertiginous experience of extreme drunkenness, the rotation of helicopter blades, the stirring of a pot of spaghetti sauce, and increasingly frenetic camera movements, as the director aims to convey kinetically the experience of a world spinning out of control. Amid escalating hostility, the members of the community or peer group gather in apparent amity and goodwill around a circular table where they feast, gamble, play cards, and engage in simulated gunplay. Then the seething tensions within the group issue unpredictably in a quest for victims, who are chosen more or less arbitrarily and whose removal temporarily pacifies the community. Exemplifying the Girardian motif of the 'holiday-gone-wrong,' this is the formula for some of the most powerful scenes in Scorsese's oeuvre.

The party in *Who's That Knocking?* calls to mind Scorsese's other Italian American films in portraying a seemingly inexplicable mingling of laughter and violence. This disturbing combination typifies the behaviour of such tough guys as Johnny Boy and Charlie in *Mean Streets*, Tommy DeVito and Jimmy Conway in *GoodFellas*, and Nicky Santoro in *Casino*. Yet for all its apparent irrationality, such seemingly contradictory behaviour is perhaps explicable anthropologically if one recognizes violence and laughter as two components, inextricably related, not only of the sacrificial crisis but of its subsequent ritual celebration in disguised form. Although the sacrificial crisis elicits only fear from its participants, its successful conclusion, celebrated upon the death of the scapegoat, produces joyful laughter within the now reunited community. So too elements of simulated violence and joyful laughter figure in the ritual performances and holiday festivals that, in recreating the sacrificial crisis in controlled mimetic form, discharge social violence in a 'healthy' fashion. As is suggested in Scorsese's films, including *Who's That Knocking?*, such laughter may also arise where violence is perceived to be only a game, in which case it resembles the simulated and delight-inducing violence of rituals, festivals, and holidays. In those of Scorsese's films where laughter precedes or accompanies lethal gunplay, it anticipates the joy that, upon the scapegoat's elimination, suddenly floods the community. It is a kind of celebration before the fact.

Not only is J.R.'s peer group mimetic in its expression of violence, it is imitative in its pursuit of 'broads.' Just as J.R. has difficulty in feeling desire without suggestions and reinforcement from his peer group, so his friends require mimetic cues, including those provided by J.R., to awaken, confirm, and support their own desires. The Pleasure Club has a *Playboy*-like foldout over the bar, while Sally Gaga sits in a corner reading the magazine itself. At this moment his gaze converges with that of tens of thousands of other males upon a common sexual object, the desire of each being intensified by the collective desire of the others. It is as if Gaga were training himself for his role of pimp, determining desirable objects for his friends by investigating the mimetic preferences of other males. In another scene Joey himself plays pimp for the peer group, announcing: 'I got a new broad uptown, supposed to be very nice.' That the peer group settles for communal, sequential sex is apparently intended as a precaution, not necessarily reliable, against in-group rivalry, so that competing desires cannot endanger the group's solidarity. Such solicitude does not however extend to their sexual partners, towards whom they are aggressively exploitative. Thus Gaga steals forty dollars from the pocketbook of a 'broad' even as he necks with her.

The convergence of male desires upon the same object carries the risk of levelling the differences among those males through mimetic rivalry and hostility. For instance, a dispute may arise over the sequence of fornications. In the scene of the gang-bang towards the end of the film, as five males await their turn with one or another of two available 'broads,' who are occupied individually with two other males behind closed doors, J.R. announces that he has called 'first.' (His line provided the title under which the film had appeared at the Chicago Film Festival in 1968: *I Call First*.) Joey, however, protests J.R.'s claim to first choice of the available women, insisting that they 'choose.' His notion of choice is to leave the decision to chance, for the order in which the five males are to visit the women is determined by means of a version of the old playground game of throwing fingers.[71] Ironically J.R., who had 'called first,' loses the game and ends up last. The further irony is that, in its randomness and levelling democratism, the peer group's appeal to chance as arbiter of its desires only reveals the fundamental sameness of its members, each alike in the objects of desire as in willing submission to unknown, unpredictable forces.

As for the 'broads,' what counts is not their individuality but that they are 'supposed to be very nice' – that is, they have won the approval of other males as sexual objects. There is irony in Joey's praise of a 'very nice broad,' as if she had special distinction. Her attraction lies only in her promiscuity, the fact that she has in the past and will in the future awaken the desires of other males – this being the condition of a 'broad.' If anything, the 'broads' whom the peer group members play around with form an anonymous, interchangeable lot. They call to mind the photo of the horizontally posed woman over the bar at the Pleasure Club, her face invisible, her back and backside prominently displayed – a dehumanized come-on. The woman whose money Gaga steals during their necking session stretches out horizontally in his arms, her back to the viewer, with her head pointing in the opposite direction from that of the pin-up. Some women, however, like Susan at the near-gang-bang, rebel at such impersonal treatment, for though she accepts the friends sequentially she is angered when, led by the impatient J.R. in his unwillingness to forgo his claim to 'call first,' they all pile into her room in what seems a collective assault. When Susan scratches Joey, he threatens to kill her, thus revealing his latent violence towards the despised 'broads.' Indeed, Susan is immediately dismissed from the party so as to preserve peer group solidarity.

That J.R. and his friends regularly share the same women raises the question of whether some critics rightly characterize the group as homosexual or repressed homosexual. Grist refers to the male characters' 'displacement of inadmissible homoeroticism' while apparently regarding their sequential sex with 'broads' as one step away from homosexuality. For Keyser, 'J.R.'s real love affair centers on the guys in the street.'[72] The film contains moments that might confirm Grist's interpretation, as when J.R. first mentions Sally Gaga to The Girl and she says, 'Who's she?' There follows a cut to Sally Gaga, who raises his head as if he were being referred to. Gaga's characterization as 'homosexual' or 'latent homosexual' is perhaps justified by his pretty-boy looks, his role as the butt of his friends' jokes, and his playing the pimp for his buddies, with the 'broads' performing what he might otherwise be required to do. And when at the stag party a hood collars Gaga and levels a pistol at his head, the gesture is suggestive of oral sex.

Nonetheless, the imputation of homosexuality to these hoods is at once too easy, too predictable, and too boring. The problem is partly that such an interpretation makes the film's examination of behaviour less subtle and interesting than it is. The interpretation must also rely inevitably on a now increasingly quaint Freudianism, with its elusive, arbitrary, and infinitely malleable categories of repression and the unconscious – neither of which is accepted by most psychologists, never having been observed or confirmed in a laboratory. Another reason for rejecting such an interpretation is that it reflects an erroneous interpretation of Italian American behaviour. Sociologists commonly refer not to the homosexual but to the homophilic character of male behaviour in southern Italy and Italian America, tracing it to the custom of sex segregation, which encourages individuals to frequent same-sex company. Such close and exclusive grouping and habits of physical affection among Italian males, including kissing on the cheek, have given emotionally contained northern European visitors to southern Italy the false impression that Italian males are somehow effeminate or 'queer.'[73] Yet there is another reason – in this case Girardian – that a hasty or prejudiced observer might identify the film's characters with overt or repressed homosexuality. In a group where mimetic desire and rivalry appear so obviously, to the point where the members take turns with the same woman, considerable possibility exists for what might be termed a 'homosexual effect,' as the desiring individuals, in taking each other as models, become at least as interested in each other as in their objects of mutual desire.[74] Yet there is no more reason to say of J.R. that his behaviour within the peer group denotes homosexuality than to claim that his impotence with The Girl indicates an essential sexual malfunction. It is best to accept Bliss's cautious formulation in speaking of the characters taking refuge in 'deadly' homophilic rather than heterosexual love.[75]

J.R.'s obsession with 'broads' culminates in the scene in the loft, which must be taken as his fantasy. Since this scene was added in the hope that its sexual content would increase box-office clout, many critics see it as gratuitous and inorganic. Grist says that Scorsese intercuts it 'almost contemptuously' in a conversation between J.R. and The Girl as they stroll along a sidewalk after seeing *Rio Bravo*.[76] However, closer examination shows that, whatever Scorsese's motivation in adding the scene, he intregrated it organically within the film. This is suggested by that fact that, just as J.R. and The Girl discuss 'Feathers,' the Angie Dickinson character in *Rio Bravo*, a typical 'broad,' so the loft fantasy concerns J.R. and women of that type. Nor is it accidental that, even as J.R. denounces the sexual promiscuity of broads to a woman he clearly thinks of as his prospective wife (that is, the very opposite of a broad), he and The Girl pass by the steps of a local church, which implies the possible sanctification of their romance, and the legitimation of its sexuality, through marriage. This outcome is further suggested by the fact that, as the couple moves from left to right on the sidewalk, they are passed by a woman with a baby carriage walking in the opposite direction – a symbol of the marital future that perhaps awaits J.R. On the other hand, that the woman with her baby carriage follows a path counter to that of the couple may portend the ultimate breakup of their romance. In any case, the loft scene portrays the absolute antithesis of all that The Girl represents for J.R., namely the possibility of the termination of his emotionally dissatisfying promiscuities, and with it a commitment to a more generous, productive, and fulfilling existence.

As the scene opens, individual parts of J.R.'s face – eye, nose, and lips – appear in close-up in separate shots. J.R. is thus introduced as a creature of the senses but also as a divided, fragmented being. He lies on his back naked in bed, with his arms stretched out behind him, in a posture reminiscent of the crucified Christ yet also suggestive of submission and enslavement. In analogical parody of Christian teaching, his pain comes from bondage to imitative desire in contrast with its transcendence through the *Imitatio*. Next come images of 'broads' in a rapid and bewildering multiplicity, conveying the instability of J.R.'s hyperstimulated desires. One of these women, fleetingly shown, seems even to bear a vague resemblance to The Girl. The women are nude or scantily dressed, well formed, seductive, Caucasian, Oriental, nameless, interchangeable, often with their backs to the viewer or their faces concealed by hair, so that they remain undifferentiated, as are J.R.'s desires. In several instances women remove stockings in a pose reminiscent of Feathers; others are shot horizontally in bed and from behind, with buttocks displayed – a pose reminiscent of the pin-up in the Pleasure Club. However, this scene is not concerned exclusively or even primarily with orgiastic sexuality, as the lack of differentiation among these women is linked to a larger theme of undifferentiation resulting from transgressive violence against not only 'broads,' but the system of sanctities and prohibitions by which J.R. has been raised. The theme is introduced on the soundtrack, as sixties Dionysian icon Jim Morrison intones his rock anthem 'The End,' a paean to liberation from (actually transgression against) identity and family: 'He took a face from the ancient gallery ... put on his boots ... and walked on down the hall.' The speaker than announces his intention of committing various enormities – the rape of his sister, murder of his father, rape and possible murder of his mother. The mask signifies loss of identity, the doubles of violence, and the undifferentiation of the sacrificial crisis.[77] As a symbol of masculine power and authority, the boots align the song's protagonist with J.R.'s cowboy heroes, some of whom – Edwards in *The Searchers*, Liberty Valance – embody antisocial violence to the point of desecration. The hall mentioned in Morrison's lyric evokes the domestic space of the family home, while the threats against family members imply an assault against the very domus that stood for peace and harmony in the film's opening. J.R. is thus perhaps on the verge of repudiating his family – if not by actual violence, then by a major sundering in favour of a life devoted to 'broads' – a life driven by uncontrolled mimetic desire.

In accompaniment to the music, the scene becomes increasingly frenzied in its cutting, with more shots of provocatively posed nude women. Morrison urges, 'Come on baby take a chance with us,' as if he, the androgynous 1960s Dionysus, spoke for the orgiastic crew of women. As J.R. embraces a 'broad,' the camera as it moves around them at increasing speed creates the impression of vertiginous spinning or whirling. At one point it even reverses direction unexpectedly. This evokes the restless, ever-turning, and increasingly painful career of mimetic desire in all its pathology, as it rushes from mediator to mediator, object to object, by mere suggestion – in short, by chance. The individual women alternate uncontrollably with ever-increasing speed, their faces and bodies merging in a chaotic blur. These whirling camera movements suggest the *turba* of the sacrificial crisis, that all-engulfing vortical chaos at whose climax violence focuses on its terminal victim, whose sacrifice permits a temporary return to order and distinction. The Morrison song climaxes with a demand for such a victim: 'Kill! Kill! Kill!'

Rather than responding violently against the women in his fantasy, J.R. surprises us. No longer naked, no longer resembling a primitive about to perform multiple social transgressions, he appears clothed in a vest, white shirt, and tie. In his right hand is a pack of cards symbolizing the random confusion of his life and desires. But that he holds the cards also symbolizes his mastery of the chance that had formerly ruled him, and he throws them down in a chaotic flurry onto the naked body of a woman who lies stretched out on the bed where he had lain.[78] Then

J.R. walks away from left to right, entirely out of the scene. If only temporarily, he has repudiated 'broads' in favour of The Girl, the object of a different form of desire than he has known.

One wonders to what extent Catholicism causes the miseries that afflict J.R. in this scene – obsessive and dissatisfying promiscuity, lack of human concern, and the impulse to murder and desecrate. Is Bliss correct that in this scene, as elsewhere, Catholicism causes J.R.'s rage, frustration, morbidity, and life denial? Actually, the scene in the loft shows that J.R. has come under the influence not of Catholicism, but of the youth movement of the 1960s as represented by one of its leading gurus, Jim Morrison. Although this movement is conventionally identified with liberation of sexual 'instinct' and rebellion against paternal prohibitions, Scorsese's film apparently identifies it – or at least its incarnation in Morrison – with sacrilege, anti-familial transgression, and violence, each implying a loss of identity. This movement seems to be associated with the destruction of the Italian Catholic familial order, which – as Bliss himself recognizes – the film links inextricably to Catholicism. One can hardly imagine a thematic less likely to win a young director favour in the late 1960s.[79]

J.R.'s apparent surmounting of promiscuous desire in the loft fantasy betokens his recognition of his love for The Girl. He now experiences the possibility of love in the sense not of intense passion – so often confused with love but frequently bound up with acquisitive mimesis and the frustrating model-obstacle relationships born of mediated desire – but of devotion to another person.[80] J.R.'s new willingness to escape old contacts and pursuits is suggested in the fact that, soon after the loft fantasy, an aquaintance drives him and Joey into rural Copake, New York, for a three-day weekend. As Bliss rightly notes, Gaga's absence from the party may imply J.R.'s and Joey's increasing maturity.[81] Their flight from Manhattan occurs in early spring, a time suggestive of renewal, as the trees are about to show their leaves. That the entire out-of-town episode has spiritual implications seems likely in view of the fact that J.R.'s trip to the country is a pared-down, modest, secularized version of the religious retreat in *Jerusalem, Jerusalem*. To be sure, J.R. has not totally banished the past, as Joey tries to draw him and his friend into rounds of drinking and the hunt for women. When the friend proposes to show them 'something really beautiful,' Joey can only ask: 'What's her name?' He cannot feel alive unless he is in a state of aroused desire suggested by another person. Despite Joey's reluctance, the three friends climb a low mountain in order to wait for sunset over the Catskills. At the summit Joey finds nothing of interest in the landscape, remarking, 'Big deal.' He means that this landscape contains nothing for him to desire intensely or appropriate, and so he is left with the void of himself. J.R.'s response differs from Joey's, however, for not only does he seem uncustomarily serene and happy in this quiet setting, but he appreciates its beauty for its own sake. It is as if he had been freed from his aggressive and acquisitive impulses. While this experience of nature testifies to J.R.'s *askesis*, his self-purging of his desire for 'broads,' it parallels his growing devotion to The Girl, whom he loves not as an object of acquisition but for her self, and whose radiant beauty he finds mirrored in that of the sunset.[82]

J.R.'s relations with The Girl remain fraught with complications, suspicions, doubts, and ambivalences. Not least, he feels crippled by sexual incapacity, as he cannot have sex with her for fear of violating her purity. At the same time, he feels an unacknowledged and only gradually manifested impulse of sacrilegious violence against her. Nor are his feelings free of mimetic interferences, and these too contribute to the failure of his love.

Some of these suspicions are already suggested in their initial meeting in the waiting room of the Staten Island Ferry where, as they sit alongside each other on a bench, J.R. repeatedly moves towards and away from The Girl. She is an object of attraction and fear born of prohibition – in short, the sacred. His latent suspicions of her are conveyed in his response to her remark that she sometimes rides the ferry for fun. J.R.'s comment, 'I never thought of it as a cruise,' shows Scorsese's mastery of colloquial language, for J.R. knows that from one point of view this refined young lady could be seen as his pick-up. This may explain why, as they await the ferry, a trash can appears behind her, portending J.R.'s ultimate discarding of her as a 'broad.'

For a time, though, J.R. surmounts these worries, investing The Girl with heavenly attributes. Scorsese frequently backlights her face so that her light skin and blond hair seem etherealized and even spiritualized, as if surrounded by a halo. With this image fixed in his mind, J.R. invites The Girl to his family's apartment and then into his mother's bedroom, where religious icons appear on a dresser before a mirror, with the Madonna and Child presiding over the interior space. This icon recalls, and is perhaps identical with, the statuette in the opening kitchen scene. The sanctity of the Virgin, and her identification with J.R.'s mother, are accented when The Girl touches the icon, whereupon

J.R. says: 'Don't touch it or my mother will pass out.' This statement further implies that, under the watchful eyes of the madonna, the virginal young lady is off-limits, untouchable, sacred. Nonetheless she initiates kissing, which seems to be leading to sex on the mother's bed, but though at first J.R. seems to cooperate, he is soon paralysed by inhibition. Scorsese conveys his emotional state by framing the bed as it appears in the mirror, so that, surrounded impingingly by the mother's icons, the lovers seem hemmed in by Catholic sanctities and taboos. The mirror implies both the tyranny of religious representations over J.R.'s mind and the repetition of the madonna in his mother and The Girl. Another reason for his paralysis is that the sexual act performed on his mother's bed, especially before her watchful icons, would amount to sacrilege. Indeed, even before his attempted lovemaking J.R. had removed his mother's pillow and placed his girlfriend's head upon it, another implicit identification of these idealized figures. Now drained of desire, he draws back from The Girl, finally confessing his love for her and thus his sexual incapacity. He pleads for her to 'understand if you love me,' and she seems willing to do so. Scorsese remarks that J.R. has avoided sex with The Girl out of respect, by which he also means *rispetto* in the Italian sense, encompassing attraction and fear.[83] But now this respect is put to a stronger test as sex enters the picture. Not only does the prohibition arise as an obstacle, but so does J.R.'s secret, unacknowledged desire for transgression and sacrilege.

The scene in the mother's bedroom is followed by the couple's viewing of *Rio Bravo* and *Scaramouche*, which enables J.R. to announce his sexual values. *Rio Bravo* depicts a homophilic peer group much like his own in its sexual attitudes, though far more courageous and harmonious. The group includes the deputy sheriff Dude (Dean Martin), who endures a two-year bout of alcoholism following a failed romance with a faithless woman, and the significantly named Sheriff John T. Chance (John Wayne), whom the peer group members respect for his responsible and sensitive leadership – something entirely lacking among J.R.'s friends. In a situation similar to Dude's, Chance must decide whether to risk marrying the former dance-hall girl Feathers (Angie Dickinson), whose character he fears resembles that of the woman who nearly ruined Dude – the character of a 'broad.' The romantic themes of *Rio Bravo* prompt a conversation between J.R. and The Girl as they leave the theater, when J.R., appropriately in front of a church, remarks of Feathers: 'That girl is a broad.' He explains: 'There are girls and there are broads. A broad isn't exactly a virgin. You play around with a broad. You don't marry a broad.'[84] To which The Girl replies: 'You don't mean that.'

The testing of his avowal comes soon after J.R.'s return from Copake. J.R. and The Girl are in his mother's apartment, and it is understood that he has enjoyed his recent liberating visit to the country. Yet a discordant note is struck when The Girl lights a votive candle and places it on the kitchen table, to which J.R. objects: 'You don't do that with a holy candle.' Bliss rightly notes that this implies J.R.'s failure to integrate religious values with everyday life.[85] Sensing that the time is ripe for a most intimate revelation, The Girl informs J.R. for the first time of her experience of date rape. She tells how a seemingly 'nice boy,' whom she had dated previously, had driven her in wintertime to an isolated stretch of road amid dark woods. As she tells the story of her rape, we see it through J.R.'s eyes, as if in a nightmare. Contrasting with the portrayal of nature in Copake, where the arrival of spring corresponded to J.R.'s emergence into a new life, the winter scene, with its snow and dark woods and the violence that transpires there, suggests the death of his relationship with The Girl. Moreover, J.R. suspects that she is lying about the rape, that she had yielded to sexual desire on this and other occasions, repeating the same false story to successive partners and now to him. Thus the spectre of mimetic rivalry enters into their romance, as he imagines The Girl attracting former admirers, who enter the picture retroactively as models and obstacles of his own desire, preventing his possession of that fetishized virginity without which he regards her as nothing. His love thus dwindles into a vain and hopeless possessiveness.[86]

In envisioning the rape J.R. imagines The Girl as not only falling but rolling on the ground and then, in an overhead shot with her head upside down, forced down upon her back by the rapist in the front seat of the car. This implies the total inversion of her formerly exalted status, as J.R. now locates her at the bottom of the feminine hierarchy. There is strong irony here, for he and The Girl had appeared at the beginning of their love affair on the sunlit roof of an apartment house, their refuge from the noise and dirt of the streets. When she sat too close to the roof edge, J.R. had warned her to 'be careful.' She is also connected implicitly with J.R.'s ascent to a kind of beatific vision at the mountaintop in Copake. These ironies are compounded following the revelation of the rape, as J.R. appears in a three-shot with his cronies in a local bar. The drunken J.R. falls from the bar stool, leaving an empty space between Joey and Gaga. Thus his impugnment of The Girl's virtue is his fall as well. Further ironies are generated by the soundtrack, consisting of a rock and roll version of 'Mary Had a Little Lamb' and 'Humpty Dumpty.' The former song connotes the Virgin Mary, the innocence of Christ the Lamb, and J.R. as the lamb who would have faithfully followed The Girl, his hoped-for stand-in for the Virgin Mary. Humpty Dumpty, who had a great fall and who cannot be repaired, refers both to the fall suffered by J.R. and The Girl and the fact that their romance can never be patched up. After leaving the bar, the drunken J.R. enters the lobby of his apartment house, braces himself against a wall, and slides to the ground.

The question remains whether the virgin-whore syndrome that afflicts J.R. and ruins his romance with The Girl, derives exclusively, as some critics hold, from his Catholicism. In reality, J.R. thinks and feels in accordance with a sexual dichotomy that, though common among Catholics, also appears in popular culture, the media, and Western civilization generally, and he need not have gone to the Catholic Church or Mediterranean Europe to acquire it.[87] In his initial meeting with The Girl he remarks: 'You must have something to do with movies ... How 'bout TV commercials? I swear to God you look familiar.' Rather than identifying The Girl solely with the virginal sanctity of the madonna, J.R. finds in her the remoteness and quasi-divinity of a media icon. Appropriately, he swears to God that she, his object of worship, must derive from that fictitiously 'sacred' space now defined by the media or entertainment. The Girl aligns in this instance less with the madonna than with images of pristine femininity manufactured by movies and television. Such images seem 'familiar' to J.R. because, in their elevation of the feminine to a position of untouchable but tantalizing sanctity, they call to mind uncannily the madonnine images of his Italian American background.

J.R.'s identification of The Girl with movies and television is all the more interesting in that he judges her character and desirability on the basis of his favourite films; and these, without being particularly Catholic in orientation, conform basically with J.R.'s dualistic views towards women. The chief example in *Rio Bravo* is Feathers, who inspires J.R.'s definition of a 'broad.' Although the film sidesteps the question of whether Feathers has been a prostitute, which is only suggested, she confesses to having worked as a dance-hall girl, that is, in the realm of entertainment and mimesis, where she wore provocative costumes to attract the desire of male customers.[88] Besides continuing to wear feathers as an attention-grabber, she operates in parnership with a crooked gambler, having formerly been married to another gambler with whom she took up the reckless, nomadic existence she has yet to abandon. Initially suspicious of Feathers as a card sharp and worse, Sheriff Chance acknowledges his attraction to her but has doubts about her past, which calls in question her suitability as a wife. In short, he has to transform Feathers from a 'broad' into a respectable woman. This takes place in the film's final scene in which Feathers, dressed in black tights and about to perform in the local saloon, is forbidden to do so by Chance, who tells her that henceforth such costumes are reserved for the marital bedroom. This statement amounts to a proposal, which she accepts. But Chance changes his mind about her costume, for after she removes it he throws it out the window. Her transformation into a respectable wife requires her divestment of all mimetic sexual cues and trappings. A busy man, Chance cannot spend the better part of his time fending off his wife's admirers. The coda concerns the two deputies, Dude and Stumpy (Walter Brennan), who find Feathers' tights on the street outside her window. Stumpy, a toothless old man, picks them up, recognizes them as belonging to Feathers, and, thinking of the pleasures Chance must now be enjoying, asks Dude: 'Do you think I can get to be a sheriff?' To which Dude replies: 'Only if you mind your own business' – that is, avoid those desires that destroy social harmony by promoting vain and bitter rivalries.

In two other instances J.R.'s favourite films afford parallels to the madonna-whore syndrome without revealing any special connection with Catholicism per se. Andre Moreau, the hero of *Scaramouche*, works in a theatre troupe as he plots vengeance against the Marquis de Maynes, and is attracted to two markedly different women. One is the blonde, demure, and virginal Anne de Gavrillac (Janet Leigh), whom Moreau believes to be his half-sister and hence non-marriageable. The other is the beautiful but tempestuous Lenore (Eleanor Parker), a sexually experienced stage performer who plays leading lady to Granger's Scaramouche. In the final scene, as Lenore's costume goes from a full-length dress to a tutu with tights, thus placing her among the 'broads,' Moreau fortunately discovers that Anne de Gavrillac is not his sister, so that he can marry the high-born woman. The film concludes with a sight-gag in which Lenore, clearly a figure of roving desire, goes on to greater conquests, her next admirer being the young Napoleon Bonaparte.

In a much grimmer vein, the theme of exalted and degraded womanhood appears in Ford's *The Searchers*. Captured by Comanches as a young girl during a raid in which her family is exterminated, Debbie Edwards becomes a wife of the polygamous Comanche chief Scar. Although she has not been raped, as was her sister, her marriage to Scar results from a catastrophe and in ultimate terms is against her will. Debbie's uncle Ethan and adoptive brother Martin Pauley (Jeffrey Hunter) set out on a five-year search in order to find her, but with different motives. Whereas Pauley aims to return Debbie to the settlements, Edwards intends to kill her in the belief that she has been defiled through her membership in an Indian tribe. The scene in which she confronts Edwards and Pauley, urging them to 'go,' that is, return home, reflects her realization that, now stigmatized by white society, she will find full reacceptance within it very difficult if not impossible. Indeed, within seconds Edwards attempts to kill her. Not only does J.R. quote Debbie's dismissal of Pauley in his first conversation with 'The Girl,' but in the penultimate scene, she dismisses J.R. once and for all with the words 'Go home,' realizing that he will always hold her as impure and that their marriage is on that basis impossible. Underscoring the resemblance between The Girl and Debbie, this dismissal also carries a powerful irony, as it calls to mind Edwards's words at the moment when, surmounting his murderous impulses against his niece, he chooses to accept her: 'Let's go home, Debbie.' In *The Searchers*, the 'impure' woman is restored to her original society rather than suffering permanent rejection. In *Who's That Knocking?* she rejects her offended suitor, who can only rejoin a group he would prefer to leave.

These examples show that J.R.'s bondage to the virgin-whore opposition cannot be attributed solely to his Roman Catholic or Italian American upbringing. This opposition appears in European and American culture in varying degrees even to this day, although much less so than in the past. Yet even if this opposition receives special emphasis in Italian American culture, it would be prejudicial to think that Italian Americans monopolize it. Rather, their sexual attitudes, like those of J.R., are partly reinforced by mainstream culture.

As critics treat the provenance of the virgin-whore complex onesidedly, so they miss a key aspect of its effect upon J.R. To be sure, they recognize that J.R. freely engages in sex with women to whom his value system attaches no prohibition. They also point to his blocked impulses in the presence of feminine purity and the prohibitions attached to it, so that his fears of sacrilege lead to impotence and frustration. Yet what goes unnoticed is that the very existence of the prohibition against contact with the sacred object itself becomes a major incitement to violent transgression and sacrilege.[89] In short, for all his avowals to respect The Girl, J.R. experiences concealed feelings of violence against her.

This side of J.R.'s personality can be inferred from not only his behaviour but the actions and attitudes of his Western action heroes. In *The Searchers*, Ethan Edwards's return to the family homestead following the Civil War is complicated by the secret love between him and his brother's wife Martha. Shortly after Edwards's arrival, however, the family is almost totally wiped out by Scar, who rapes and kills Martha. Besides these enormities, Scar rapes Edwards's niece, Lucy, or at least allows his warriors to do so. This is the Indian of whom J.R. says half-admiringly: 'He was more nasty than Wayne could ever get.' Although Edwards never commits rape in the film, events nonetheless suggest that he harbours violence towards women, and even barely contained impulses to rape. In one scene Martin Pauley is exasperated by the attentions of the Indian 'bride' he had mistakenly bartered for and wants nothing to do with. When Pauley literally kicks her out of bed, causing her to roll down a hillside, the amused Edwards remarks that Martin 'plays really rough' and that such behaviour affords 'grounds for dee-vorce in Texas.' Yet as much as Ethan Edwards resents the violation of his brother's homestead, the film suggests an underlying and potentially transgressive antagonism between the two brothers as a result of rivalry over the sister-in-law. Had not Edwards's thwarted passion been rendered unfulfillable through the Comanche raid, it could have issued in an attack upon his brother and violent appropriation of Martha. Moreover, not only does Edwards adopt many Indian ways, but he has been shown to resemble mimetically the rapist Scar, who desecrates the forbidden woman Edwards desires.

A further indication of J.R.'s unacknowledged impulse towards the sexual desecration of The Girl appears in his fascination with Liberty Valance, whose name suggests not just violence but freedom from taboos and a licence to transgress. J.R.'s attraction to Valance and his type is noted by the girl: 'You always like the bad guys, huh?' To which J.R. replies, 'Now Lee Marvin, there's a real bad guy,' alluding to Marvin's role as Valance. As in his discussion of John Wayne's personae, J.R. identifies Valance and the actor who plays him. Refusing to 'do anything normal,' Marvin 'just doesn't play tough guys, he goes all the way. He comes into a room ... just imagine what women think of him ... the worst kind of bad guy ... He not only kills people but breaks furniture.' What, then, *do* women think of him? Ford answers this question in the scene in which Valance, with his two henchmen behind him, enters a restaurant filled with townsmen, homesteaders, and cow-hands, where Hallie (Vera Miles), the girlfriend of Tom Doniphon (Wayne), waits on tables. Valance throws several patrons out of their chairs and even appropriates their food, but what is most disturbing is the moment that his and Hallie's eyes unexpectedly meet. She stands terrified by his gaze, well aware that this man is a rapist. The aura of sexual violence surrounding Valance helps to disclose the deeper impli-cations of J.R.'s statement that Marvin, as tough guy, goes all the way – a phrase referring colloquially to sexual consummation. There is also the curious phrasing of J.R.'s praise of Valance, who 'not only kills people but breaks furniture': the grammar suggests that breaking furni-ture is more serious than murder. For what most fascinates J.R. in Valance is his 'liberty' in violating the sanctities of the domus, signified by furniture and domestic appurtenances generally, and presided over by respectable women like Hallie or J.R.'s mother. The theme of domes-tic violation previously appeared in J.R.'s loft fantasy, in the lyrics to the Doors' 'The End.'

However obliquely rendered, J.R.'s fascination with the character of a rapist helps to explain why, as Grist notes, the rape of The Girl is presented through J.R.'s eyes, thus aligning him with the attacker.[90] J.R. even possibly identifies with the rapist, as if envisioning the way he himself might perform such an act. Also worth considering is The Girl's initial impression of the rapist as a 'nice boy.' The same description also fits J.R., at least as he presents himself to her, as she knows nothing of his peer group, 'broads,' drinking, gunplay, and inter-ethnic brawling. His complaint to The Girl, that she rode in a car with her rapist – 'and you go with some one and you don't know what he's like' – applies nearly equally to him. A hint of his potential for violence appears in their last meeting, when J.R., in desperately embracing her, causes her to protest: 'You're hurting me.' (Ironically, her bedtime reading had been Fitzgerald's *Tender Is the Night*.) Had J.R. acted out his fascination with Liberty Valance, he would have broken her furniture and even inflicted physical harm.[91]

The cinematic allusions in the film, and to John Wayne's characteriza-tions in particular, ironically contrast the adolescent sexual behaviour and attitudes of J.R. with the greater degree of maturity towards which the Wayne characters struggle in *The Searchers* and *Rio Bravo*. As we have seen, Ethan Edwards intends to kill his niece for having in his eyes become defiled through contact with the Comanches, even if against her will. But at the end of the film, instead of killing Debbie, he accepts and embraces her, altogether surmounting his reservations about her supposed loss of purity: 'Let's go home, Debbie.' For all his admiration for Wayne in his role of Ethan Edwards, J.R. fails to imitate his hero when placed in a comparable situation. Ironically, his difficulty at the end of the film more closely resembles that of Martin Pauley, of whom The Girl had previously observed that 'he winds up trading for an [unacceptable] Indian bride and he doesn't know what to do with her.' J.R.'s failed romance with The Girl is also reflected inversely in the relation between John T. Chance and Feathers. For though Chance, despite his attraction to Feathers, holds her disreputable past against her for much of the film, he overcomes his reservations and is able to marry her, thus turning the 'broad' into a respectable wife. J.R. is perhaps thinking of Chance's romance with Feathers when, in his final meeting with The Girl, he announces, 'I forgive you,' a statement redolent of vanity, pride, and condescension rather than love. He has mistaken Chance's act of acceptance for one of forgiveness. In so doing he remains faithful to his own sexual code, with its prohibitions and exclusions – the system of the sacred.

After their final meeting, having been told by The Girl to 'go home,' J.R. takes refuge in church, by implication his true home. He enters a confessional and prays to a crucifix in its dark and cramped interior. The intercut shots of J.R. kissing The Girl in recollection contrast with his fervent, desperate kissing of the crucifix, showing the irreconcilable conflict between devotion and desire. Scorsese also introduces rapid shots of the rape and orgy scenes. Besides seeking consolation in his misery, J.R. seems to suffer an oppressive sense of wrongdoing in his treatment of women, and would thus 'repent of his sins and resolve with divine grace to sin no more.'

For many critics, J.R.'s flight to the church only repeats and confirms his entrapment in a distorted system of religious values, one that offers no solutions but only returns him to the source of his difficulties. Nor can these arguments be totally discounted, despite the error of blaming J.R.'s unhappiness entirely upon Catholicism. That the conventional ritualistic form of Christianity affords no solution to J.R.'s problems is suggested when he is shown several times alternately in the confessional receiving his penance and at the altar in the act of performing it. It is implied that this pattern will be repeated again and again, but with no alleviation of J.R.'s anguish, or clarification of sexual or moral values, or change in his way of life. In Scorsese's next Italian American film, *Mean Streets*, Charlie Civello eschews Catholic ritualism, including the routine of confession and penance, for a religion centred ethically in the streets. It is also true that Catholicism tends to promote a radical antithesis between virgins and 'broads,' wives and 'broads,' chaste and impure sexuality, with no middle ground. This is partly responsible for J.R.'s unhappiness, contributing unintentionally to both his depersonalized relations and his unacknowledged violent impulses towards virgins. Thus Scorsese reintroduces in the final scene images not only of rape but of his mother in her domestic role.

Critics further object to the type of Catholicism, penitential and even masochistic, to which J.R. is drawn, and which forms the core of his religious feeling. Like Charlie in *Mean Streets*, Jake La Motta in *Raging Bull*, Max Cady in *Cape Fear*, and Jesus in *The Last Temptation of Christ*, J.R. seems to seek self-martyrdom both to punish himself and, in unacknowledged pride, to prove his worthiness. His devotions in church are performed amid abundant imagery of fleshly lacerations, the *Imitatio Christi* construed as inseparable from self-inflicted suffering in imitation of and even rivalry with the Saviour's atonement for humanity. We see icons with images of the stigmata; the Saviour reclining in death or hanging from the cross in a posture reminiscent of J.R. in the orgy scene; a gashed thigh suggestive of both punishment and menstrual blood with its traditional associations of impurity, so that sexuality is identified with desecration and retribution; and the martyred Santa Lucia, patron saint of Sicily and guardian of eyesight, with her two excised eyes upon a platter.

It would probably be a mistake to attempt a univocal reading of the figure of Santa Lucia, whose legend, going back to early fourth-century Sicily, appears in various versions and whose multiple meanings seem to reflect, through similarity and contrast, the confused state of J.R.'s mind.[92] As tradition has it, the saint had taken a vow of chastity and, to satisfy a suitor who admired the beauty of her eyes, plucked them out and gave them to him, whereupon an angel immediately restored her sight by giving her a new pair of eyes. The story implies that the divine power rewards those who refuse sexuality to the point of self-punishment. Insofar as Santa Lucia guards eyesight, her presence suggests J.R.'s need for protection against desire itself, which, in most people, arises through visual stimuli. The orgy scene, which exemplifies J.R.'s bondage to the *Venere Oculis*, begins with a shot of his eyes – individually, as if each were excised.[93] Yet though the name 'Lucia' (from the Latin *lux*) connotes light, which is necessary to vision, her presence is ironized by the darkness of the church and confessional in which J.R. undergoes his torment. Somewhat reminiscent of J.R.'s situation is the legend telling of Santa Lucia's refusal of marriage to a suitor who then denounced her as a Christian, the saint having made a vow of chastity to the Lord. J.R. has similarly been refused marriage by The Girl, yet he denounces her not as a Christian but as a whore; however, the parallel between J.R. and the suitor may also imply the former's lack of Christian charity in his cruel and unjustified recriminations. And finally, J.R. resembles the pagan governor who, following the suitor's disclosure, sentences Santa Lucia to a brothel as punishment for her Christianity and chastity. The alignment of J.R. with the governor, and The Girl with the saint, may mean that, as J.R. fails in his Christianity, so he has implicitly forced The Girl unjustly into the imagined role of prostitute.

Adding to the penitential mood is an image of the Pietà, and not least the blood that gushes from the confessional crucifix as J.R. kisses it – a not especially unusual display of southern Italian Baroque piety. In Girardian terms, J.R. has perversely transformed Christ into not just his model but his punishing rival-obstacle, trying to equal or outdo him in the suffering that J.R. takes as the mark of the divine. In this sadomasochistic complex, salvation is constantly withheld from the sufferer by the sadistic model-obstacle – Jesus as J.R. conceives him – yet the sufferer maintains his hope of salvation so long as the model-obstacle – ultimately God – continues the torture.

The soundtrack in this climactic scene is provided by the Genies, playing the eponymous rock and roll song of the title, *Who's That Knocking at My Door?*[94] It is not altogether mistaken for Bliss to say of J.R. that the God knocking at his door is a Christian 'God of morbidity,' the God of death and suffering, the life-denying God.[95] Yet Bliss errs in suggesting that mode of worship represents the better part of Catholicism. Nor is he right to suggest that Scorsese considers the essence of Catholicism necessarily to lie in such sadomasochistic configurations of creature and Creator. Lawrence Friedman correctly identifies Scorsese's intention in this as in other films when, specifying the God who knocks at J.R.'s door, he cites the epigraph of *Jerusalem, Jerusalem*, taken from Robert Bresson's *Diary of a Country Priest*: 'God is not a torturer. He only wants us to be merciful with ourselves.'[96] The God whom J.R. needs is a model of non-acquisitive, non-mimetic, and non-rivalrous desire, a deity capable of saving him from the soul-lacerating transgressions and punishments, sadistic and masochistic impulses, into which he has fallen.

Does J.R. find such a God? The final scene forms a brief and muted coda pervaded by a sense of frustrating circularity, with J.R. and Joey meeting at night on a familiar neighbourhood street. *Jerusalem, Jerusalem* was planned to conclude with joyful music, a mood of resolution, and a scene of J.R.'s bedroom fully illuminated; such optimism has now given way to darkness. 'I'll see you tomorrow,' the friends say to each other. The accompanying song, 'I Love You So,' underlines ironically the sterile homophilism now to resume. Implicitly, J.R. has returned to the same cycle of rivalries, parties, 'broads,' the same deformed desires. His world of futility and entrapment resembles that of Charlie Civello, the protagonist of *Mean Streets*, Scorsese's next film on Italian American themes.

5 Season of the Witch: *Mean Streets*

Mean Streets was initially conceived by Scorsese as the third instalment of a trilogy including *Jerusalem, Jerusalem* and *Who's That Knocking at My Door?* But though he and Mardik Martin had already written a script by 1966, the project remained long suspended, partly under Haig Manoogian's advice that 'nobody wants to see films about Italian Americans.'[1] Scorsese was also occupied in bringing *Who's That Knocking?* to the screen as his first feature film, which required a radical reworking of his original student effort. Subsequently Scorsese took on various directorial and editorial tasks in order to make ends meet, including the direction of *Boxcar Bertha* (1972), a B-movie produced by Roger Corman. Although this film has its virtues, Scorsese's friend John Cassavetes, an exponent of a personal cinema, dismissed it as 'shit' and urged Scorsese to do something he 'really wanted to do.'[2] The attractiveness of tackling what came to be known as *Mean Streets* was perhaps all the greater in the early 1970s owing to the success of *The Godfather*, which, whatever its differences from Scorsese's work, had proved America's interest in Italian Americans, especially criminals. As with *Who's That Knocking?*, Scorsese confronted major budgetary limitations and decided largely on a cast of unknowns, including Harvey Keitel, Robert De Niro, Richard Romanus, Amy Robinson, and David Proval; Cesare Danova and David Carradine were the best-known actors in the film. Given his budget as well as a tight shooting schedule of twenty-seven days, Scorsese achieved the required authenticity by shooting interiors and exteriors – chiefly apartment hallways and the San Gennaro festival – in lower Manhattan over a six-day period; but most of the film, including many night scenes, was shot in Los Angeles. It was completed at a cost of about three hundred thousand dollars and enjoyed critical if not commercial success upon its release in 1973.[3]

The trilogy for which *Mean Streets* was to be the final instalment was never completed. In retrospect, *Mean Streets* figures as the first instalment of a trilogy focusing on Italian American gangsters. Initially they appear centred in the Italian American neighbourhoods of the Northeast, as in *Mean Streets* and the earlier parts of *GoodFellas*. In the latter film they move from the older ethnic enclaves into the suburbs of Miami, New York City, and other parts of the Northeast, including Pittsburgh. Finally, *Casino* portrays the mob in its Midwestern manifestation (Chicago and Kansas City) as it reaches to the gambling mecca of Las Vegas. Unlike *The Godfather* series, these films eschew a mythifying treatment of Italian American criminals in favour of a disturbingly realistic presentation clearly reflecting the vicissitudes of Italian America.[4] Consistent with recent theories of the 'twilight of ethnicity' and the decline of the Mafia, Scorsese's gangster films depict not only the disintegration of the ethnic community through intermarriage and transplantation, but the deterioration of the mob through increased police surveillance, betrayals, and corporate competition.

Part of Scorsese's intention in *Mean Streets* is to document the Italian American subculture as it then existed in Manhattan's Lower East Side. He calls the film 'an anthropological or sociological tract' showing 'what life was like in Little Italy.'[5] The film's realism is owed in large measure to its documentary and naturalistic style, with frequent use of the hand-held camera along with rapid and abrupt editing. Another factor contributing to the realistic impression is the highly spontaneous acting, often the result of on-the-set improvisations.[6] Of these, perhaps the most memorable is the scene in which Johnny Boy initially explains to Charlie his inability to pay Michael's debt. This documentary 'feel' is not entirely premeditated, though, as it reflects the material exigencies under which Scorsese struggled. He remarks that those critics who dwell on his nervous hand-held camera work fail to realize that he had no time to lay down tracks. Nor in most instances did he have a chance to set up establishing shots.[7] It is also a mistake to exaggerate the documentary elements in *Mean Streets*, which like Scorsese's other works combines naturalism and expressionism. There are oblique camera angles, exaggerated lighting, slow-motion sequences, long tracking shots as in the pool hall scene, and restless camera movements. Sometimes Scorsese employs a hand-held camera and expressionistic jump-cuts inspired by the French New Wave.[8] *Mean Streets* also resembles Scorsese's later works in the essential role it assigns to music, which typically comments on the action and characters. The latter, moreover, are differentiated partly through music, as the Old World gangster types appear in conjunction with florid Sicilian songs sung in Italian, while their more Americanized counterparts are associated with brash and pulsating rock and roll.

Displeased with the rough technique of *Mean Streets*, Scorsese is also dissatisfied with its former and present titles.[9] The original title, *Season of the Witch*, derives from a 1960s song of that name by Mike Bloomfield and Al Kooper, to which Charlie refers in remarking the hazardous and violent period he and his friends are living through. Scorsese's journalist-and-screenwriter friend Jay Cocks persuaded him to adopt the present title, inspired by a passage in Raymond Chandler's 'The Simple Art of Murder.' A manifesto stating Chandler's concept of detective fiction, the essay calls for a detective hero at once noble, well rounded, and courageous: 'Down these streets a man must go who is not himself mean, who is neither tarnished nor afraid. He must be a complete man and yet an unusual man. He must be, to use a rather hackneyed phrase, a man of honor – by instinct, by inevitability, without thought of it, and certainly without saying it.'[10]

The present title, which Scorsese finds a 'little pretentious,' may nonetheless seem justified as a comment on both the morally squalid lives of the film's characters and the spiritually and materially impoverished environment they inhabit.[11] It has shortcomings, however, including the implicit and rather excessive claim that the everyday streets of Little Italy were at that time typified by hatefulness to the point of violence. This is not to challenge Scorsese's recollections of having grown up in a neighbourhood in which brutal confrontations sometimes flared up between local youths and youth gangs as well as between rivalrous hoodlums. Yet it also seems likely that Scorsese somewhat exaggerated the degree of malice within this neighbourhood. As Tricarico points out, the social psychologist Ann Parsons wrongly characterizes Italian American urban neighbourhoods as 'inherently dangerous, tempting and freely accessible only to men.' In his study of South Greenwich Village, an Italian American community not far from Scorsese's Little Italy, Tricarico calls that area a 'protective enclosure' with the 'sheltering properties associated with the home.'[12] He mentions among other things the Mafia's role in protecting children and elderly people – a role of which Scorsese himself is by no means ignorant. Thus the title probably exaggerates the ordinary cruelty of the streets and plays to upper-middle-class expectations concerning Italian 'slum' neighbourhoods. Another failing of the title is that the film has nothing to do with the detective genre with which, given its association with the writings of Raymond Chandler, the viewer connects it. So too, Chandler's ideal detective hero defines standards met by no one in the film, including Charlie, the protagonist. Although Uncle Giovanni appeals to the Mafia code of honour, this is hardly the chivalric example Chandler has in mind, while Giovanni's mention of it aloud violates Chandler's requirement that the code be unspoken. The current title has the further disadvantage of identifying Charlie too intimately with a morally degrading milieu that he partly transcends, since for all his failings his spiritual struggles reveal a personal dignity that sets him apart from his peer group. Scorsese characterizes Charlie as a 'false' or 'modern saint' whose society 'happens to be gangsters' and whose life raises the question whether one can be both 'saint' and 'hoodlum' simultaneously.[13]

With its clashing loyalties and pressures deriving from multiple sources, Charlie Civello's life calls to mind Scorsese's own coming-of-age in Manhattan's Little Italy, and is based loosely upon it. His father having died, Charlie lives in the family apartment with a mother who, though seldom present, spoils him with spending money and clothes. Essentially unmoored from parental authority, Charlie moves freely about a neighbourhood whose traditions and values he basically respects but that confines him within its insular and oppressive environment. Like many third-generation Italian Americans of the urban neighbourhoods, he understands some Italian but does not speak it, as is shown in his periodic meetings with top-ranking gangster Giovanni, his uncle and patron. His loyalties and interests are divided among Teresa, his girlfriend, whom he may intend to marry; his peer group of young hoodlums and ne'er-do-wells; and the mob itself. A numbers runner and collector in Giovanni's protection racket, Charlie is being groomed to take over the family business. He also expects Giovanni to turn a restaurant over to him as soon as the uncle finishes driving the owner into bankruptcy. The remaining influence upon Charlie's values and behaviour is the church, as he respects priests and has even gone on religious retreats, although this side of his character clashes with his aspirations as a gangster.

As the film opens, Charlie's spiritual musings are heard in voice-over against a black screen, although the voice is actually that of Martin Scorsese. The doubling of Scorsese's and Charlie's voices implies the director's identification with his character, whose religious attitudes and ambivalences he shares. The theme is religious morality and the proper setting for penance: 'You don't make up for your sins in church. You do it in the streets. You do it at home. The rest is bullshit and you know it.' These statements are amplified in the later scene that closes the introductory section, in which Charlie appears in church, shot from behind and moving towards the altar. In voice-over, he complains that the ritual of penance has been routinized without real moral effect: 'I just come out of confession, right? Right? And the priest gives me the usual penance, right? Ten Hail Marys, ten Our Fathers, ten whatever.' And yet 'next week I'm gonna come back and he's gonna give me another ten Hail Marys and another ten Our Fathers, and I mean you know how I feel about that shit.' What Charlie claims to prefer, if only for himself, are more stringent – and self-imposed – religious standards. 'Those things,' meaning ritualized penance, 'don't mean anything to me, they're just words. Now that may be okay for the others, but it just doesn't work for me ... If I do something wrong I just want to pay for it in my way so I do my own penance for my own sins.'[14]

Despite Charlie's assumption that institutional Catholicism applies only to others, his individualistic religiosity is hardly atypical of Italian Americans. They have regarded the sacred as present not in church alone but in the world, and they also have viewed the home and streets as the testing ground of faith and morality. Scorsese implies the presence of this belief system in a later shot of the roofline of Little Italy, from which rises the tall and imposing statue of Christ in the act of blessing the streets below. Charlie's statements gain further point from the fact that the film's action coincides with a major expression of the Italian religion of the streets, the annual San Gennaro festival, transplanted from Naples to lower Manhattan. The festival is introduced several times in the film, initially in an overhead shot of the main stage, whose pedimented arch and framing pinnacles with their coloured lights suggest the facade of a Romanesque church – again, the religion of the streets. Another shot portrays the main street of the *festa* as seen from a tall building, with the illuminated archways forming a river of light amid the surrounding blackness. Other scenes of the festival include musicians and milling crowds of visitors, while the film's bloody climax coincides with the last night's celebration. There is irony in this, however, for in Girardian terms rituals and festivals commemorate and simulate sacrificial violence so as to inoculate society against it. The festival fails to do so, and violence erupts among the young men of Little Italy in another part of town.

Following the voice-over, the film's opening scene conveys restless disturbance through Scorsese's use of a hand-held camera. As Charlie awakens in bed from a troubled sleep, the window admits a dim light along with the sound of cars and sirens. An anticipation of the police sirens at the climax, in which Charlie pays the price for adhering to his religion of the streets, these sounds also suggest that impinging external world where salvation is to be worked out. Charlie wears a T-shirt, boxer shorts, and a crucifix; another crucifix adorns the wall. Having risen from his bed and gone to the mirror, he stares at his reflection for several seconds, as if thinking of the two selves that war within him: Charlie the ambitious mobster and Charlie the Catholic. He returns to the bed where, as he reclines face up to rest his head upon the pillow, our sense of his spiritual anguish is intensified by three rapid jump-cuts, each progressively closer to his troubled face. A drum roll simultaneously introduces the Ronettes' 'Be My Baby,' whereupon Scorsese cuts to a darkened room containing a home movie projector that, as the camera pans from right to left, comes into frontal view, its beam of light pointing towards the viewer. Besides implying his intention of illuminating the lives of both his characters and his audience, Scorsese calls attention self-reflexively to his medium. There follows an eight-millimetre home movie, parts of which derive from the Scorsese family collection but most of which was filmed so as to introduce Charlie, his chief friends and contacts, and his social and physical environment. There are shots of a baptism; of family celebrations involving Charlie, Teresa, and his best friend Johnny Boy, uncustomarily dressed in a coat and tie; of his cigar-smoking uncle and godfather Giovanni, whose opening a door and entering a room implies his control over this social world, and who has apparently been chosen as the godfather of the newly baptized child; of Charlie and another friend, the small-time but well-dressed young gangster Michael; and another of Charlie in a full-length coat standing with a priest on the steps of a local church. Initially the two men are within the shadow cast by the facade, but then Charlie steps down into a sunlit area, puts on dark glasses, and shakes hands with the priest. There are also scenes of local people, streets, sidewalks, and buildings, and the lights of the San Gennaro festival strung like glowing coloured beads in the darkness. These festive images are followed by the title and credits, the former printed in red so as to suggest urban mayhem, the sacrificial blood of Christ as its corrective, and the passion of Charlie caught between these two forms of violence.

The entire opening sequence, its title, images, and music, introduce the film's persistently ironic view of the characters, especially Charlie. From the outset Scorsese implies the spiritual ambiguities of Charlie's existence, living as he does in a world of deviated transcendence, where the sacred in the Christian sense is mainly parodied and where higher spiritual impulses are replaced by lower. It has been noted that the song 'Be My Baby,' which can only be addressed to Charlie, presents an 'uncomplicated view of male/female relationships' and thus comments on Charlie's sexual attitudes.[15] Though by no means wrong, such a reading ignores the song's broader commentary on Charlie's religiosity and pretentions thereto. Accompanied by images of a baptized child and Charlie eating cake, its title suggests his immaturity, dependence on his family, and appetite for the goodies with which his mother pampers him. Analogically, the title parodies Christ's statement in the Gospels that his followers must 'become as little children' to enter the kingdom of heaven.[16] In relation to the film as a whole, the christening contrasts with Charlie's baptism of fire at the climax. The first stanza, sung by a female singer passionately devoted to her beloved, suggests that the love that most interests Charlie is directed towards not the divine but himself, in displaced self-idolatry: 'That night we met I knew I needed you so / And if I had the chance I'd never let you go / So won't you say you love me / I'll make you so proud of me / We'll make them turn their heads every place we go ' The idea of Charlie and his woman turning all heads – not simply attracting but *compelling* envious admiration – implies Charlie's vanity and thus a concern for others' estimation over that of Christ. This is evident in later scenes where Charlie shows an exaggerated concern to maintain his immaculately well-tailored *bella figura*, to attract a certain awed respect, and to adapt his life to the social code of Little Italy. In the opening of the next stanza the singer announces: 'I'll make you happy, baby, just wait and see / For every kiss you give me, I'll give you three / O since the day I saw you, I have been waiting for you / You know I will adore you until eternity.' The happiness for which Charlie is asked to wait in confidence not only parodies Christian faith – the Pauline 'substance of things hoped for' – but calls to mind his hopes for the restaurant.[17] Likewise, the disproportion in affection between the singer and her beloved – three kisses to one – again suggests that Charlie is less interested in loving than in being loved. The singer's avowal to 'adore' him 'until eternity,' although using a sacred lexicon, works equally ironically, implying that the adoration Charlie properly owes Christ he prefers to bestow upon himself. Not merely traduced in a jukebox lyric, divine love has found its measure in Charlie's narcissism.

Charlie's Catholicism is ironized in the concluding images of the home movie, as he stands with a priest on the steps of a church. Charlie thus occupies an intermediate space, neither within the church nor on the sidewalk or streets, in keeping with his divided spiritual and material loyalties. Although Robert Lee Kolker rightly observes that *Mean Streets* refuses to build on the 'firm generic base' of the gangster film, of which it contains only 'some elements,' Charlie calls to mind Mervyn Leroy's *Little Caesar* (1930), the inception of the modern gangster film, in which a gangland murder occurs on the steps of a church.[18] In shaking hands with the priest Charlie seems to have reached an accommodation, a sort of 'gentleman's agreement.' Nonetheless, the dark glasses Charlie puts on as a shield against the sunlight conform to the Mafioso image, and thus imply his imitation of the gangster over the priest.[19] Also applicable ironically is the Pauline text: 'When I was a child, I spake as a child, I understood as a child, I thought as a child; but when I became a man, I put off childish things. For now we see through a glass darkly, but then face to face.'[20] This passage concerns spiritual maturity, the abandonment of childishness, and the perception of essentials. One thinks too of the Gospel According to John: 'And men loved darkness rather than light.' Charlie's dark glasses symbolize the obscurity of his spiritual vision. Indeed, the film's bloody conclusion occurs at night.

The rendition of Charlie's milieu in the home movie is followed by a more formal introduction of the film's main characters in the reverse order of their importance both to the story and to Charlie. Each belongs to Charlie's peer group, and none is connected with the church. Tony, a prosperous local bar owner, upon discovering a junkie in the men's room of his bar, removes the offender bodily from the premises and then berates his bartender for having ignored him. Next appears Michael, a tall and carefully dressed young gangster who stands between two trucks beneath an elevated railway with New York Harbor in the background. He thinks he is closing a smuggling deal, but soon learns from his prospective buyer that instead of German telescopic lenses, he has bought Japanese adapters. The deal having fallen through, Michael gazes into the distance with his characteristic look of pained frustration and ineffectuality. The next scene begins with an exterior shot of a mailbox with Johnny Boy entering the frame from the left in a deliberately imbalanced composition evocative of both his oddball nature and generally disturbing presence. Dressed like an overgrown street urchin in a thuggish jacket and pork-pie hat, Johnny Boy drops a bomb into the mailbox, edges away from it along a storefront, and then takes off at full speed as the mailbox explodes. Of the four characters introduced at the opening of the film, Johnny Boy is the only one who does not speak. The apparent implication is that he is a non-verbal, sub-rational person who chiefly expresses himself through acts of destruction.

Charlie's centrality is emphasized by the fact that, just as he appears singly in the opening, so he is reintroduced as the last of his peer group. Now, however, he kneels at the church altar as he attempts to justify his individualistic form of morality and penance. What spiritual models sustain him in these mean streets? The crucifix around his neck, like that upon the wall of his bedroom, suggests the *Imitatio Christi* with its pacifism, selflessness, and freedom from vanity. To supplement this all too demanding model, Charlie turns to St Francis of Assisi, of whom he says: '[he] had it all down.' Not only is St Francis associated with a boundless love of nature, but his stigmata signify extraordinary fidelity in imitating Christ.[21]

Nonetheless Charlie's later conversation with Teresa at the seashore ironizes his identification with St Francis, whom he mentions in nearly the same breath as he reveals his dislike of nature: he 'hate[s]' grass and trees and likes mountains only because they resemble skyscrapers. The seriousness of Charlie's dedication to St Francis is called in question by the saint's trivializing inclusion in a list of Charlie's favourite things, such as 'spaghetti with clam sauce,' 'chicken with lemon and garlic,' and John Wayne. Reminiscent of J.R.'s (and Scorsese's) admiration for the film actor, Charlie's fondness for Wayne ill consorts with Franciscan piety. Far from embodying Christian meekness and pacifism, Wayne stands for physical toughness, swaggering bellicosity, and heroically violent masculinity. In films such as *The Searchers* he is associated with retaliatory violence, which fails to qualify as a Christian virtue. Given that Charlie and his peer group take in *The Searchers*, one assumes that they admire Wayne's personae as much as does J.R. in *Who's that Knocking?* There is further irony in that, as Charlie cannot fulfil the model of St Francis, so he and his friends cannot hope to equal Wayne's cinematic incarnations. This is suggested by the inserted sequence from *The Searchers*, in which not Wayne but two lesser characters – Martin Pauley and Charlie McCorry – kick and gouge each other as they roll in the dust in their quarrel over a woman. This scene, which within *The Searchers* affords a low mimetic parody of Wayne's high mimetic agon with the

Commanche chief Scar, parallels the low mimetic street-brawling of Charlie and his friends. Their lack of heroic stature is further accentuated when Charlie and Johnny Boy engage in an impromptu late-night mock battle with garbage can covers, like two would-be knights errant of the urban wilderness.[22] A similar reduction appears later when Charlie and Johnny Boy are framed by a restaurant window advertising 'hero sandwiches.'

The deeper cause of Charlie's failure to meet the Christian ideal is suggested by Teresa's cutting remark that St Francis 'didn't run numbers,' an accusation he feebly denies. She has reminded him painfully of his role as small-time but aspiring gangster with influential connections, chiefly his Uncle Giovanni. Charlie's exploitative and parasitic relation to Little Italy and its residents is implicit in the opening sequence of home movies, in which Charlie, standing on a sidewalk and joking with an anonymous middle-aged male friend, playfully places his hand into the friend's coat pocket and then withdraws it, as if having commited an act of theft. The mutual amusement this gesture elicits cannot disguise what the remainder of the film reveals, that Charlie, like his uncle, preys upon the local neighbourhood. Charlie not only runs numbers but includes loan-sharking among his illegal activities. He also benefits from other people's illegalities, as when he receives cartons of stolen cigarettes from Michael, even complaining about the prices. Later, when Charlie visits his uncle's restaurant, a cashier informs him of the 'right combination' in a numbers operation. Nor is Charlie free from mimetic desire and rivalry, as he expects to receive the uptown restaurant as soon as its current owner declares bankruptcy owing to his failure to pay the uncle protection payments. As Charlie waits, he justifies his refusal to join Teresa in leaving Little Italy by employing a telling predatory image: 'I'm closin' in on somethin.'' In the meantime he serves as his uncle's go-between with the restaurateur, towards whom he is less than helpful. When the restaurateur says, 'Will you tell your uncle that I have nothing?' he replies: 'You talk to Giovanni, not me.' Subsequently Charlie tells his uncle self-servingly that the restaurateur is concealing his prosperity so as to avoid protection payments. That Charlie is torn between two codes, of the church and of the streets, is suggested by his remark to Johnny Boy, who offers psychological excuses for his non-payment of debts to Michael: 'Michael doesn't care if you're depressed. What is he, your fuckin' priest?'

Charlie's divided motives help to explain another aspect of his spirituality, namely its penitential and even masochistic character, marked by a guilty abjectness and unworthiness before God. In the initial scene of Charlie in church, he says in voice-over: 'Lord, I am not worthy to eat your flesh, not worthy to drink your blood.' Charlie evokes in his mind's eye images of infernal punishment: 'That's all bullshit except the pain, right? The pain of hell, the burn from a lighted match increased a million times. Infinite.' When Charlie looks up at the altar, he sees images of suffering that only confirm his view of Catholicism as a penitential religion: a Pietà, with Christ's hand clutching a red rose symbolic of shed blood. According to Scorsese, Charlie, 'being me, has to grapple with a sense of guilt,' to which Friedman adds that Charlie 'wants not so much to mend his sinful life as to cauterize his guilty conscience.'[23] The images of immolation reflect Scorsese's adolescent experience of a Catholic retreat, when he still aspired to the priesthood, and when the priests told him to place his fingers in fire so as to comprehend infernal torture.[24] In the film this gesture is repeated not only in the scene in church, as Charlie strokes the flame of a devotional candle, but in the later barroom scene where, to the astonishment of his cronies, he lets a match burn down to his finger. In a later scene, during a visit to the coveted restaurant, Charlie places his hand over a kitchen grill to feel its licking flame. If anything, this outstretched hand signifies the acquisitive desire that blindly drives him.[25]

As the conscience is especially devious in deceiving itself, alternative explanations of Charlie's penitential behaviour have been suggested. It has been argued that Charlie is insincere in his penance, and that, being committed to the restaurant, he assuages his conscience through periodic visits to the church and largely symbolic gestures of self-punishment.[26] As he says, 'You don't fuck around with the infinite.' His highly individualistic religion may also signify his vain belief in the superiority of his form of spirituality over that of his neighbours and ordinary churchgoers. He remarks, in voice-over, of confession and acts of contrition: 'These things, they're just words. Now that may be okay for the others, but it just doesn't work for me ... I just want to pay for it in my own way so I do my own penance for my own sins.' There is a tone of spiritual pride – for Scorsese as for Italian Catholics the worst of sins – in these statements, amounting to Charlie's declaration that he wishes to be his own priest. Charlie thus figures with Jake La Motta, Henry Hill, Ace Rothstein, and Nicky Santoro as a typically vain and hubristic Scorsesean character afflicted with what may best be described as the 'Sinatra syndrome,' the fantasy of doing it 'my way.' And finally, Charlie's verbal and psychological self-lacerations stem from a masochistic complex marked by two contradictory impulses. On the one hand is the desire to suffer in abject penitence for one's sins. Although he thinks of God as a torturer and obstacle to salvation, the masochist in him finds this comforting, for as long as he suffers, he knows that God at least pays attention to him and may someday confer the long-withheld gift of salvation. On the other hand, in a religion where divine election is so closely associated with the death of the saviour and the martyrdom of the saints, the masochistic desire for martyrdom may also mask spiritual pride and vanity, in advertising one's superiority over other worshippers.[27] Seemingly inspired by the imitation of the suffering Christ, such behaviour may originate in rivalry with him, with the individual seeking martyrdom not for a higher good but from vanity, so as to equal and even surpass Christ in suffering.

The challenge to Charlie's Christian values comes not only from the pagan materialism of his environment, but from the gangsters who figure as local authority figures and in whom he and his friends find their models. The values of the criminal organization are embodied primarily in Giovanni (Cesare Danova), a local mob boss and godfather (*compare*) to many families, who also happens to be Charlie's uncle and patron. A tall, distinguished, soberly dressed man who wields his familiar cigar as a symbol of authority, Giovanni represents an ideal of the southern Italian male. He seeks to convey the impression of autonomy, authority, and self-sufficiency – a god-like remoteness from the dirty world of ordinary human affairs. Self-possessed in all situations, he rarely relaxes his impassivity, and then only to reveal himself with great guardedness and restraint. As a *compare* and local leader, Giovanni has obligations to which he attends out of *rispetto*, but much of this is merely maintaining appearances, while his real attitude, compounding detachment and calculated self-interest, appears in his advice to Charlie: 'Don't get involved.' Giovanni shows that he, in reality as in appearance, is himself eminently deserving of *rispetto* – a man simultaneously to be loved and feared, whose authority is to be neither transgressed nor challenged. He corresponds to what Scorsese, using his neighbourhood idiom, calls a 'dun.' It refers to a 'man of respect' and an 'honourable man,' and is equivalent to 'don' or 'Mafia leader.'[28]

Not that Giovanni himself lacks models. His public presentation apparently copies that of Lucky Luciano, of whom Giovanni speaks in reverent tones to Charlie, and who qualifies as the most important

Italian American gangster of the last century.[29] Luciano's mystique is partly reflected in his nickname, implying his mastery of chance; for luck is important to any gangster, and is something neither Charlie nor his cronies will be able to control. Concerning Luciano's activities during the Second World War, when the U.S. government softened his imprisonment in exchange for his help in maintaining the security of the New York docks, Giovanni says simply: 'He was there.' Giovanni implies the preferability of economy in the use of violence, the mere presence of the gang leader being sufficient to guarantee peace through the power of respect.[30] When Charlie pretends to have attended a social event where his presence was required, his uncle reminds him sternly: 'You were not there.'

Giovanni can maintain his image and reputation only if *rispetto* and its peaceful harmonies continue to be honoured locally, and this means that sometimes he cannot avoid becoming 'involved,' if only to keep the lid on violence. In a key scene Giovanni orders the expulsion to Miami for at least six months of a local hood who had committed an unprovoked public murder, and whose reckless behaviour endangers the local peace. Thus the strength of Scorsese's film derives partly from its moral ambiguity, for even if the audience acknowledges Giovanni's criminality, it also comprehends that without his intervention the San Gennaro festival cannot proceed undisturbed in the traditional manner.[31] Despite Giovanni's vilification of local politicians as 'dishonest' and 'all blackmailers' – an insult very possibly typical of urban villagers of those years – and also notwithstanding his boastful claim that the local people prefer to solicit the help of his underworld organization rather than the government, his fundamental conservatism is suggested by the juxtaposed portraits of Pope John Paul XXIII, Robert Kennedy, and President John F. Kennedy in his restaurant, which taken together testify not only to pro-Catholicism but to loyalty, however qualified, to the national state. Such mingling of piety and patriotism typifies many mob bosses.[32]

Under Giovanni's tutelage Charlie is learning not simply how to be but how to appear as a top-echelon gangster. Like Giovanni, he dresses formally, in jacket, tie, and overcoat, his clean well-tailored clothes and careful grooming signifying outwardly his unflappable personal autonomy and cool remoteness from the ordinary world. As Charlie watches Giovanni exchange cordialities with a party of guests at the coveted restaurant, he receives a lesson in how to conceal a cold and unyielding interior under a superficial amiability that reveals nothing. Charlie also learns the importance of economy in violence, and of the leverage afforded by the intimidating power of *rispetto*, as when he proposes to help Giovanni hasten the turnover of the restaurant, only to be told: 'Do nothing.'

Like Charlie, Michael desperately wants to enjoy the substance and appearance of a don, but is much less successful in doing so. Therein lies the main source of the insecurity that troubles Michael and that his expression reveals even in ordinary moments. This is not to say that he fails to adopt appropriate mimetic cues in his attempt to appear personally autonomous and thus worthy of respect. He dresses as carefully as Charlie, shows measure in gesture and speech, and assumes a formal Old World manner worthy of the Mafiosi of earlier periods. In one scene Scorsese heralds Michael's arrival at Tony's bar with a rich Sicilian melody, in contrast with the rock and roll normally commenting on the antics of Michael's associates. Yet finally, Michael remains a small-time hood who fails repeatedly to fulfil the exalted image he projects in public. Having initially embarrassed himself by botching a smuggling deal, he steals cartons of cigarettes to sell at discount, which episode is followed by the revelation of his illegal sale of toilet paper stolen from a U.S. Army PX. 'I got a good buy on toilet paper. I got Scotts,' says Michael, to which Tony replies: 'So now you're stealin' from the army.' Among Michael's other embarrassments is to have been 'stiffed' by two adolescents from Riverdale, who give him only twenty dollars rather than the forty he had expected. Nor is Michael socially adroit, as he attempts to interrupt Giovanni and Charlie during a private conversation in the uncle's restaurant: 'Doesn't he see that we are talking?' says the annoyed Giovanni. But Michael's greatest embarrassment is in not enjoying sufficient respect to compel Johnny Boy, a mere punk, to repay a loan-sharking debt, which shames him increasingly in the eyes of the neighbourhood. To quote Scorsese on Michael: he 'doesn't manage to become a real tough guy, the kind that you don't get too near to, but whom you respect and offer allegiance in embracing him.'[33] His characteristic obscurity within the underworld is suggested when, having been cheated by the Riverdale adolescents, he sits in the front seat of Tony's car only half visible amid a mass of shadows.

More than Charlie or Michael, Johnny Boy generates the film's action – a wild-card figure capable of turning this small world topsy-turvy. Again to quote Scorsese: 'Johnny Boy was going to blow up the whole system.'[34] This results from the fact that he, unlike his friends, claims absolute autonomy, entailing complete indifference to the *rispetto* that normally governs the neighbourhood. As Johnny Boy says to Michael in their final confrontation: 'I don't give two shits about you or anybody else.' In an early scene, Johnny Boy arrives at Tony's bar to the accompaniment of the Rolling Stones' 'Jumpin' Jack Flash,' whose title suggests Johnny Boy's violence, volatility, and – given the increasing hostility towards him – likely ephemerality. The song's opening line – 'I was born in a cross-fire hurricane' – identifies Johnny Boy quite appropriately not only with the random violence in which he participates (and largely causes) at the film's conclusion, but also with the turbulent and all-engulfing circular motion that most adequately represents in symbolic terms the violent climaxes of the majority of Scorsese's Italian American films. Dressed self-consciously as a raffish thug, in contrast to Charlie and Michael, Johnny Boy belongs to their peer group yet, because of his behaviour, remains its most emarginated and dispensable member. In this, as in his compulsion to spend money while in debt, he resembles Sally Gaga in *Who's That Knocking?* Yet unlike the passive and victimized Gaga, Johnny Boy is dangerous and a potential victimizer. His irrationally offensive behaviour may result from the head injury that, as we learn in one of the film's few clumsily expository moments, he suffered in defending Charlie during an adolescent gang fight. Apart from this uncharacteristically selfless action, Johnny Boy's conduct is a series of transgressions and provocations against the community.

In keeping with Johnny Boy's role as joker, some of his offences are comical or relatively harmless, as when, upon entering Tony's bar, he pretends to check his pants at the door, and when, in Joey's pool hall, he gratuitously insults the girls at the jukebox: 'You call those skags girls?' (although this insult helps to provoke the subsequent brawl).[35] He shows his contempt for the national government when in his opening vignette he blows up a mailbox. That he has no respect for the larger community of Manhattan is shown when he stands on a rooftop and fires his pistol at the summit of the Empire State Building. Disdainful of the neighbourhood and its pieties, Johnny Boy by his own admission 'hates' the feast of San Gennaro 'with a passion,' as it congests traffic in Little Italy. In a later scene he 'accidentally' shoots out a window in the apartment of a local whom he also 'hates ... with a passion.' After setting off a small bomb on a rooftop, Johnny Boy tells Charlie that 'he wants an atom bomb to wake up the whole neighbourhood.' The scene in which Johnny Boy stretches out on a tombstone shows that he disrespects the dead as much as the living. When Charlie mentions his terminally ill grandmother, Johnny Boy finds his friend's sadness curious. His disrespect extends to his own family, as witness his plan to break into his grandmother's house in search of a snack. One has the impression that the chief aim of the break-in, which Charlie wisely prevents, is to provide Johnny Boy with a pretext for entering the apartment of his epileptic cousin Teresa, towards whom Johnny Boy feels a forbidden sexual interest, and with whom Charlie is himself carrying on a clandestine affair. Subsequently, in the presence of Teresa the envious and inquisitive Johnny Boy questions Charlie concerning Teresa's sexual behaviour, going so far as to ask his friend whether she experiences an epileptic fit during orgasm.

The most scandalous and dangerous of Johnny Boy's transgressions is that he is a chronic deadbeat who, to quote Michael, 'owes money right and left' in the neighbourhood, and whose movements are increasingly constricted by his need to avoid his creditors. What infuriates them is that he fails to clear his debts yet continues to borrow and spend money with reckless abandon. At Tony's bar Johnny Boy's tab is a standing joke, as he continues to buy drinks there without any intention of settling his account. As he remarks quite accurately yet without any hint of irony: 'I'm not payin' for these drinks, they're all on the tab.' His flashing of money calls to mind 'Jumpin' Jack Flash,' and indeed Michael refers to him as 'Flash.' As the local black sheep, Johnny Boy would already have been expelled save for Charlie's cautious protection.

Notwithstanding Johnny Boy's extreme unattractiveness, many critics praise his supposed authenticity in the sense of freedom from falsifying social demands and constraints, while others at least prefer his energy and outspokenness to the more contained behaviour of his friends. For Douglas Brode, Johnny Boy is the only one 'who is his own man ... the true hero.' Michael Bliss sees him as the 'rebel' of the community. Hosvey, Wollman, and Engdahl describe him as the 'vital element' in an otherwise deadened world. In the words of Pauline Kael, Johnny Boy 'flouts all the rules ... [but] is not really crazy.' In her view he 'is the only one ... who is his own man; he is the true hero, while Charlie ... is the director's worst vision of himself.' Marilyn Yaquinto favours Johnny Boy over Charlie, claiming that the former sees the truth clearly, and even exculpating his gunplay with the argument that 'shooting guns gives him a thrill, and what more harm can it do to the beaten tenements?'[36] 'Romantic' in the Girardian sense, these readings mistake a compulsive and exhibitionistic transgression of prohibitions, and enslavement to others' desires, for autonomy, freedom, and the liberation of repressed instincts.[37]

Though Johnny Boy claims and may even seem to be self-sufficient, refusing to give 'two shits' about anyone save himself, he is driven by desires that rob him of autonomy. His professed indifference only pathologically exaggerates the gangster pose of self-mastery cultivated with varying success by Giovanni, Charlie, and Michael. Notwithstanding this apparent indifference, the very existence of social prohibitions awakens in Johnny Boy a compulsive need to transgress them, as if they were in themselves a provocation. His refusal to acknowledge such prohibitions thus enslaves him to blindly transgressive impulse. Nor is Johnny Boy indifferent to other people or to the community at large, despite what he claims, but is highly conscious of the impression he makes upon other people – the more shockingly transgressive the better. His more outrageous actions – pretending to check his pants at the bar entrance, shooting out windows, blowing up mailboxes, setting off bombs – aim to advertise his individuality and prepotency. In the poolroom brawl, Johnny Boy climbs onto the pool table from which he kicks and flails at his attackers. When Charlie reminds Johnny Boy of his debts in public, he complains that Charlie has made him 'look bad' – not the complaint of an indifferent person. Actually, Johnny Boy envies his friends their greater ambition, prospects, and material success. Rather than having achieved self-mastery, he is in bondage to desire, and more specifically mimetic desire, failing to pay his debts partly because he needs to keep up his sartorial image in competition with Charlie, Michael, and other locals. So much is suggested when he insults Joey's two-dollar sneakers. In another scene, Johnny Boy wears a double-breasted overcoat in the style favoured by Charlie and Michael. The question arises how Johnny Boy, whose weekly salary as a dockworker amounts by his own admission to $110 a week, and who is required to give a portion of those earnings to his mother, finds the means to buy such a coat in an obvious attempt to keep up with his friends. One further wants to know how it is possible for him to frequent such undoubtedly expensive Greenwich Village hotspots as Cafe Bizarre, where he picks up the two middle-class Jewish women whom he brings to Tony's bar. The answer is that he borrows money he has no intention of repaying. Yet his compulsive spending only increases his obligations to his creditors and is against his best interests. Is this freedom? Is this rebellion in any meaningful sense? Jealous of the advantages enjoyed by his peers, Johnny Boy not only shows sexual interest in Teresa, Charlie's girlfriend, but resents the fact that Charlie has no need to work. Subsequently, Michael reports that Johnny Boy has quit his job. His mimetic rivalry with Michael, which enslaves each to the other, originates partly in his resentful awareness of Michael's don-like pose, which Johnny Boy reads as a personal insult and thus as a provocation for counter-insult.

Despite his colossal egotism, Johnny Boy experiences inarticulate self-hatred because of his indebtedness. This is subtly established in parallel scenes, the first of which takes place in Tony's bar when Michael attempts to collect his debt from Johnny Boy, and the second in Joey's pool hall when Charlie, Johnny Boy, and their friends attempt to collect a debt from Joey. In the first scene the embarrassed Johnny Boy pretends to have forgotten the day of payment, and his oversight is charitably forgiven. In the second scene Joey, having been reminded of his failure to pay on time, not only remarks that 'a mistake can be made' but announces his intention to pay up on the spot. The only person to show annoyance over Joey's behaviour is Johnny Boy, who glares at him with resentful hatred much in excess of the situation, as Johnny Boy is no creditor of Joey. Nonetheless he refuses Joey's gesture of friendship, derides Joey as a 'scumbag,' mocks his cheap sneakers, and urges his friends to count the payment so as not to be cheated. The best explanation for Johnny Boy's behaviour is that he projects onto Joey the hatred he feels for himself.

Charlie's peer group resembles as well as contrasts with the male peer groups described by Herbert Gans in *The Urban Villagers*. Gans found an interest in social conformism and competitive display among the males he observed, who showed off verbally, physically, sartorially, and in other ways, yet he found no bitterly rivalrous antagonism or violence among them. Each male was satisfied to play an accustomed and acknowledged role within the group, and none needed to shine inordinately at another's expense; indeed, it was considered bad form to stand out, as this led to envy or jealousy.[38] Something similar prevails among Charlie and his friends, who are basically social conformists, and who engage in their own version of the southern Italian *passatella*, or trading of ritualized insults, to let off steam and establish parity among themselves. Yet unlike the individuals Gans observed, these young men show intense mutual aggression and violent rivalry, partly because they are eager to gain *rispetto* or prestige, the acquisition of which normally requires its loss by another person, who thereby declines in status within the peer group.

Charlie, Michael, and their friends adopt a pose of unflappability and arrogant self-sufficiency, as if already enjoying the respect they crave. Yet as with Michael in his dealings with Johnny Boy, such a pose can itself be read as an insult and provoke transgressive counter-insult against the person who adopts it. Moreover, Charlie's friends vie with each other not only for honour and prestige but for the material possessions and success upon which they depend. Far from being autonomous, they measure their own worth and status in relation to prospective rivals and the opinion of others. One sees this in Charlie's home movies, where he and Michael, ostensibly friends, appear dressed in the same fashion but with Charlie in the forward position. Michael comes forward, pushes Charlie aside, and takes his place – all in good fun, yet foreshadowing their ultimate conflict.

That conflict occurs when Charlie, having played both sides against the middle, takes Johnny Boy's side in the matter of his debt to Michael. Initially Michael and Johnny Boy had been quarrelling over the withheld money, as Johnny Boy's refusal to pay had entangled Michael unexpectedly in acquisitive mimesis with him. Ultimately, not only does Michael lose his pretence of autonomy under the growing pressure to redeem his loan, but his quarrel finally has less to do with money than with intangibles Girard would term metaphysical. It has to do with his embarrassing inability to collect from a mere 'punk' – which can only lessen Michael's local prestige. Johnny Boy is thus transformed from Michael's rival into his obstacle, the entity who prevents him from enjoying what he most craves: respect. Nor is Michael wrong to think that Johnny Boy has sought deliberately to insult and injure him. In the aftermath of the unexpected killing in Tony's bar, when Charlie and his friends are scrambling to escape in Tony's car with Michael at the wheel, Johnny Boy refers to the latter with casual contempt as 'chauffeur.'

A major problem of violence within this community is that the supply of prestige falls short of the demand. As a result, occasions must be created artificially so as to provide an opportunity for those displays of violent prowess by which respect is gained – although nothing guarantees that this strategy will work. The most outrageous example in *Mean Streets* concerns the young Italian American hoodlum who kills a drunk in Tony's bar on the pretence that he is avenging the murdered man's insult of Mario, a top gangster. In this warped case of violent mimesis, the thug imitates the presumed violent desire of another man for vengeance. As Charlie tells Teresa, no personal grudge was involved in the killing, only the hope of gaining prestige with the higher-ups. Adjudicating the matter, Uncle Giovanni rejects the notion that an insult had been given and, fearful that the hoodlum's bad example will inspire bloody imitations, sends him to Miami until the whole thing blows over.

A similiar hypersensitivity to obscure insults, and the same need for an excuse for violence, appear if only in low comic form when Charlie and his friends, having visited Joey's poolroom in another part of the city for the purpose of collecting a debt, find themselves brawling with Joey and his group. One explanation for this brawl is that Charlie's group is Sicilian and Joey's Neapolitan: Scorsese reports that in his neighbourhood feuds raged between buildings and streets simply because their residents came from different areas of southern Italy and naturally disliked 'outsiders.'[39] However, what sets off the brawl is Johnny Boy's insulting behaviour, to which Joey responds by calling him a 'mook.' Although the meaning of this word, 'big mouth' in Neapolitan dialect (from *boca*), remains a mystery to everyone, including Joey, Charlie and his friends take it as a grave insult and instantly retaliate: 'You can't call me a mook.'[40] The word's meaninglessness implies that, for these young men, the insult could have arisen as easily from some other cause, as what they want is a pretext for fighting, so as to confirm or inflate honour and ego.

The significance of *Mean Streets* largely eludes critics who fail to grasp that its violence originates not so much in the characters' harsh or anomic environment as in the vain egoism of their rivalries. Projecting onto the film the wrongs of the earlier immigrant generation, Mangione and Morreale mistakenly interpret Johnny Boy's antics as a manifestation, however confused, of social protest. For them, he and his aimlessly violent friends typify the children of immigrants who feel trapped in a dead-end situation with no access to mainstream America.[41] Lee Lourdeaux identifies the film's violence with youthful yet futile 'democratic' rebellion against a 'rigid,' 'superstitious,' 'insensitive,' and 'oppressive' patriarchal order that determines employment and thus marital opportunities.[42] These arguments ignore not only the hostilities generated from within Johnny Boy's peer group but the complacent insularity of most of the film's characters, who remain content to live and work in Little Italy. Charlie Civello has the means and intelligence to attend college, yet he finds his criminal career more enjoyable and lucrative as well as less demanding. The same applies to Tony and Michael. Although the older generation of gangsters acts coercively and oppressively, the younger generation shows no interest in democracy, being either anarchic or hierarchical in its attitudes. However flawed, the male elders prove to be an indispensable force for order within the volatile Italian American community, especially its hot-headed young males.[43] As in his other works, Scorsese's portrayal of individual characters in *Mean Streets* remains elusive owing to its avoidance of simplistic notions of behavioural or environmental causality. Philip Lee Kolker says of *Mean Streets* that its depiction of 'disenfranchised ethnics ... does not attempt to comment on a social or economic class.'[44] Joseph Kanon similarly notes the 'absence of protest or even rebellion' in the film, which is 'about a society of walls that are going to be neither jumped over nor smashed through.'[45]

Like J.R., Charlie's sexual attitudes are strongly influenced by Catholicism, and he too subscribes to the madonna-whore dichotomy, distinguishing marriageable good girls from licentious 'broads.' These values figure implicitly in the early scene where Charlie kneels in church before an altarpiece representing the dead Christ in the arms of the Virgin Mary. Although Teresa intends to marry Charlie, their clandestine sexual encounters in mid-town hotels lead him to doubt her respectability, and indeed he states outright that he cannot marry a 'cunt.' He quickly retracts this statement, but at some level he means it. When during the same bedroom scene he calls her 'Wild Woman,' he suggests her unfitness for marriage while implying half-ironically and half-self-deceptively that she, rather than he, had initiated their sexual relationship: 'Wild Woman, let me alone! Get your fingers off me!'[46] Charlie had previously shown lack of respect for Teresa in spying upon her as she undressed in the apartment adjoining his. In being reduced visually to corporeal fragments in this scene, she becomes a voyeuristic object. In a later scene in their hotel room, Teresa asks Charlie to close his eyes as she dresses, but he disrespectfully ignores her request for privacy. That he identifies sex with Teresa with sinfulness and penitential suffering is evident when he stretches out upon their hotel bed as if crucified, and also when he reports a dream of intercourse with Teresa in which he ejaculated blood. His latent hostility towards her is evident when, lying in bed in their hotel room, he forms his hand into the shape of a gun, points it at her, and pretends to fire, with the imaginary explosion provided by the sound track. This is not to suggest, however, that Charlie's friends necessarily share his conflicted sexual attitudes. Johnny Boy apparently disrespects all women, and Tony mocks Charlie's credulity when, during a Catholic retreat, he falls for a priest's hackneyed story about a young betrothed couple who, on the eve of their wedding, impatiently engage in intercourse only to be obliterated by a train as their divine punishment.

The peer group's sexual attitudes, and more particularly the male characters' frequent congregating in all-male company, raise the issue of their possible homosexuality, as with the peer group in *Who's That Knocking?* The assassination in Tony's bar, in which a young thug, apparently for reasons of disguise, unloosens his long hair before murdering the drunk in the lavatory carries homosexual undertones, and this too is suggested by the Italian song playing simultaneously on the jukebox: 'La Femina.' In the confused aftermath of the assassination, as Tony's patrons flee to the streets amid the wail of police sirens, Michael allows Charlie and Johnny Boy to take refuge in his car, whereupon two homosexuals pile into the backseat, attracted by male company.[47] These homosexuals, one of whom is comparatively reserved and the other outrageously flamboyant and libidinous, seem like doubles of the sober-minded Charlie and the unruly and demonstrative Johnny Boy. The more effeminate of the homosexual pair, dressed in loud yellow, seems especially to resemble Johnny Boy, if only in his self-identification with absolutely unrestricted desire: 'I want it all.' This scene also reveals that the two homosexuals are acquainted with Michael, although he pretends not to know them. Possible homosexual undertones are again suggested in the following scene in which, on the morning after the assassination, Charlie and Johnny Boy share the former's bed. Johnny's remark 'Why don't you tuck me in, sweetie?' may seem homoerotic, although it may also mean nothing.[48] Yet when Teresa suffers an epileptic fit during an altercation between Charlie and Johnny Boy, Charlie abandons her and runs off to make up with his friend, as if she were less important. The only possible justification for such unfeeling behaviour is that at this moment Charlie must determine whether Johnny Boy intends to inform Uncle Giovanni of Charlie's romance with Teresa, which the uncle had forbidden. Yet in James F. Maxfield's questionable view, Johnny Boy's jealousy towards Charlie for his sexual relationship with Teresa masks his feelings for Charlie.[49] During an earlier scene in a movie theatre, Charlie and his friends are distracted by a homosexual encounter in another row of seats. An anonymous voice exclaims, 'Take your hands off me,' at which another protests: 'You're a fruit.' This exchange makes Michael uncomfortable, although Charlie and his other friends find it amusing.[50] Michael's response is all the more interesting in view of the rather effeminate gesture – raising the palm of his hand to his head – in the film's opening home-movies section. During the early scene in Tony's bar, where the majority of the male patrons cast admiring glances at the beautiful dancer Diane, only Michael appears to show no interest in her. At the conclusion, when Johnny Boy announces to Michael his refusal to pay his debt, he compounds it with homosexual insults. His statement 'I fuck you where you breathe,' an allusion to oral sex, is followed by a humping gesture, signifying anal rape.

Yet is the characters' behaviour really homoerotic, or only homophilic in the southern Italian style? While a homosexual aura perhaps attaches to Michael, there is no actual homosexual behaviour among the other characters, and in the absence of such evidence, it is best to relate their close friendships to ethnic homophilism. Moreover, the characters' apparent homoeroticism must be evaluated in cultural or ethnic terms, so as to clarify its real content. When Johnny Boy makes 'homoerotic' gestures towards Michael, he in no way expresses erotic attraction towards him. He is, rather, expressing a form of insult typical of southern Italian society in which reduction to the passive homosexual position is for a man the worst possible degradation. Other seeming instances of homosexual interest or attraction are best understood as symptomatic of the atmosphere of mimetic rivalry within the peer group, and more particularly Girard's observation that the male subject's prolonged fascination with the male model-rival often produces a kind of 'homosexual effect,' with the rival increasingly receiving the interest inspired initially by the desired object.

The spatial, social, cultural, and spiritual claustrophobia of Charlie's world resembles that of *Who's That Knocking?*, whose characters are likewise trapped in Little Italy. In that film, when Joey weekends in rural Copake, he disdains the countryside and wants only to resume his urban habits and pleasures. Likewise, Charlie enjoys neither his visit to the beach nor the outdoors generally. When he and his friends drive into another part of Manhattan, they lose their way; for Johnny Boy, Brooklyn is a 'jungle,' terra incognita. Charlie's confessed dislike of nature ironizes his attempt to conceal the targeted Johnny Boy at 'Greenwood Lake,' which Michael's ambush prevents them from reaching. In addition to spatial confinement, there is the characters' cultural and social claustrophobia resulting from their inability to think beyond the code of *rispetto* and its rituals of insult, rivalry, and aggression. A further sign of insularity is the characters' ethnocentrism and even xenophobia, chiefly directed towards Jews and blacks. Not only do Charlie and his friends regard all Jewish women as 'broads,' but Michael attempts to defraud the Jewish adolescents from Riverdale who come to the San Gennaro festival in search of firecrackers. Blacks are referred to contemptuously in Sicilian dialect as *'mulinjan,'* meaning eggplant (from *melanzane*), alluding to their colour. The isolation of Little Italy is evoked in a remote overhead shot of the neighbourhood, its brilliantly illuminated main street dwarfed by the massive blackness of Manhattan surrounding it.

This is not to say that all the characters consent to confinement in Little Italy, for Teresa has announced her intention of moving to an uptown apartment and hopes that Charlie will join her as a prelude to marriage. He hesitates to do so, however, not simply because of his reservations regarding Teresa's sexual freedom but for fear of losing the restaurant. Nonetheless, Charlie also dreams of breaking out of the neighbourhood, and never more adventurously than in attempting to date Diane, the black dancer in Tony's bar. Charlie realizes that to do so risks disaster, as he would be betraying not just Teresa but the values of his community. He would also disgrace himself before his uncle and lose the restaurant he dreams of.

Teresa's ignorance of Charlie's potential betrayal provides the basis for two of the film's ironic moments. In the first, Teresa informs a black hotel maid that her and Charlie's room is ready for cleaning. 'I only have two hands, ma'am,' says the woman, to which Teresa responds rudely: 'Well use 'em.' One can only imagine Teresa's outrage were she aware that Charlie has already shown interest in Diane, whose slender hands had appeared in a previous scene framed in a single shot, weaving a web of sexual fascination for Charlie and other onlookers. The second instance of irony comes when Michael, seeking information concerning Johnny Boy, follows Teresa, laden with groceries, into her apartment house. Her groceries having spilled in their nasty exchange, Teresa asks Michael angrily: 'Would you please get me my eggplant?' To rephrase her statement, she asks Michael to pick up her eggplant. The irony is that, unbeknownst to Teresa, Charlie had earlier attempted to pick up Diane the *mulinjan'*. Yet Teresa need not fear her rivalry, as Charlie, terrified of being seen in the Village with a black woman, cancels his date at the last minute and orders the cabdriver to return to the point of departure, thus confirming the circular futility of his existence.

The chief site of Charlie's spiritual testing is Tony's bar, which the peer group members treat as their second home. It first appears following the scene in which Charlie, while in church, comments on the two pains of hell, one material, the other spiritual. In addition to the pain 'you can touch with your hand,' says Charlie, there is the 'kind you can feel with your heart, your soul, the spiritual side' – to which he adds that 'you know the worst of the two is the spiritual.' In saying this, he reaches out to touch the flame of a votive candle. There follows a cut to the red interior of Tony's bar, which, according to Kolker, may appear to be 'Charlie's hell' but, 'unless Scorsese is adopting a literal Sartrean position, is not hell, but merely the place where Charlie hangs out.'[51] Actually, Scorsese's analogical imagination finds parallels to as well as parodic inversions of spiritual realities within everyday things. In a further example of Catholic analogism pervading *Mean Streets*, the bar represents the infernal world. So much is suggested by the fact that, whereas Charlie is portrayed previously in a forward tracking shot as he strides in a straight path down the aisle of the church to the altar, the corresponding scene of his entrance into Tony's bar depicts him, first, as he weaves his way through its crowded, confused, and shadowy spaces, and then, in another forward tracking shot, follows his winding progress into the deeper interior of the bar until he finds himself at last not at an altar, but at a stage enlivened by two prancing go-go dancers. Analogically, the viewer is being asked to think not of those righteous ones who choose the straight path of rectitude, but of those mentioned in Proverbs and Psalms, whose 'paths are crooked' and 'who turn aside upon their crooked ways.' So too it is said in Proverbs that the 'way of the guilty is crooked,' while Luke proclaims that the 'crooked shall be made straight.'[52]

Being hell, the bar stands for both mimetic desire, material and sexual, and the temptation to transgress against community norms – the whole system of *rispetto*. That desire is incited mimetically within this setting is suggested by the opening shot of a mirror adorned with the representation of a nude woman in silhouette, and at the same time reflecting the images of the women of flesh and blood who dance before it on the stage. Next appears Diane, who dances virtually in the nude and whose gestures aim to attract and seduce. Incapable of resisting, Charlie leaps onto the stage, removes his jacket, and begins dancing with Diane in what is actually a controlled display of fearful attraction. Returning to his table, he twice remarks to himself, 'She's really good lookin,' but adds the crucial qualification: 'But she's black.' His resistance to the prohibition is indicated in voice-over, as he proposes that little real 'difference' exists between himself and Diane. He then lights a match to his fingers, as if punishing himself for his transgressive desire.

The bar is the scene not simply of mimetic desire but of mimetic conflict, with the second often following fast upon the first. Such conflicts arise over women, money, and prestige, with ensuing insult, accusation, and violence. To judge from Charlie's response, it seems ordinary for a fight to break out behind him as he watches the stage. In a later scene at the bar, at a party held in his honour, a Vietnam veteran named Jerry goes berserk when he finds his girl dancing with a guest. Towards the film's climax, as Charlie anxiously awaits the chance to mediate Johnny Boy's dispute with Michael, he provokes a near-fight by claiming a patron's date as his own and daring him to reclaim her. Completely uninterested in the woman, Charlie merely wants a pretext for provoking a competition in which he can demonstrate his prepotency. Tony's bar also hosts the murder in which a young thug, hoping to please a mob boss, kills a local drunk, an act motivated by a false accusation. In another scene, Johnny Boy and Tony nearly come to blows when the former proposes a game of cards for money despite his enormous tab. Their quarrel amounts to an innocuous version of Johnny Boy's dispute with Michael, which later, amid a bitter exchange of insults, culminates in this setting.

Having come under priestly influence, and attempting to live by the *Imitatio*, Charlie adopts a quasi-priest-like role in dealing with his godless friends. He attempts to intercede in Michael's grievance against Johnny Boy, and later announces upon arriving at Jerry's party: 'I have come to create order.' Subsequently, as Tony pours him a J&B and soda, he intones: 'May God be with you.' Charlie feels a priest-like responsibility for Johnny Boy, who, as the neighbourhood deadbeat, has many enemies and whose behaviour constantly embarrasses Charlie. The price of bearing such a cross is suggested when Charlie observes Johnny Boy enter Tony's bar with two 'broads' after having pretended to check his pants at the door: 'All right, thanks a lot, Lord,' says Charlie in voice-over, 'thanks a lot for opening my eyes. We talk about penance and you send this through the door.'

Yet Charlie's 'sanctity' is repeatedly ironized, as he combines moral ineffectuality with considerable bad faith. Even his desire to play secular priest is parodied, at one point by himself. Thus, upon entering the pool hall he fulfils Joey's sacrilegious request to 'bless my balls' and blesses the pool cues, billiard lamp, and pool players for good measure, and then, after the ensuing gang fight, announces dubiously that 'we're

Italianamerican. The young Martin Scorsese sits with his parents, Charles and Catherine Scorsese, in the living room of their apartment in Manhattan's Little Italy.

It's Not Just You, Murray! Murray (Ira Rubin) counts his ill-earned money, his wife (Andrea Martin) sucks her thumb, and Joe (Sam DeFazio), Murray's 'best friend,' who is having an affair with Murray's wife, lights his cigarette from a votive candle.

Who's That Knocking at My Door? As horseplay turns into gunplay, the stag party exemplifies the Scorsesean theme of the 'holiday-gone-wrong.' Warner Brothers Entertainment.

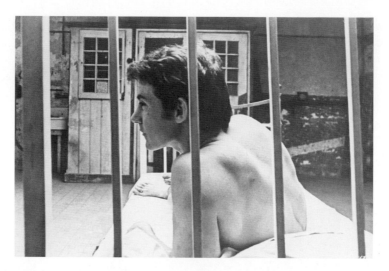

Who's That Knocking at My Door? Enslaved by an uncontrollable flood of promiscuous desire, J.R. (Harvey Keitel) appears as if imprisoned behind bars in the film's controversial orgy scene. Warner Brothers Entertainment.

Who's That Knocking at My Door? The images of a young man and a young woman are reflected in a mirror, with the young man dominating the foreground. His erotic ambivalence rooted in the madonna-whore complex, J.R. (Harvey Keitel) experiences simultaneous attraction to and withdrawal from 'The Girl' (Zina Bethune), who appears with him in J.R.'s mother's bedroom amid icons of feminine purity. Warner Brothers Entertainment.

Mean Streets. Half-heartedly appeasing his troubled conscience during a visit to the local church, Charlie Civello (Harvey Keitel) dismisses the mechanical routine of prayer and penance in favour of his own 'religion of the streets.' Warner Brothers Entertainment.

Mean Streets. Charlie Civello (Harvey Keitel) attempts in vain to intercede at the climax of the quarrel between Michael (Richard Romanus) and Johnny Boy (Robert De Niro, offscreen). Warner Brothers Entertainment.

Mean Streets. Having followed imperfectly the *Imitatio Christi* and the Christ-like pattern embodied in St. Francis of Assisi, his favourite saint, Charlie Civello (Harvey Keitel) suffers not the stigmata but a traumatic hand wound in the film's climactic scene, and thus learns the cost of his self-elected version of non-institutional Catholicism. Warner Brothers Entertainment.

Raging Bull. In the film's 'emblematic' opening, Jake La Motta (Robert De Niro) appears as if self-encapsulated within a boxing ring where, remote from a shadowy, amorphous crowd, and reminiscent at once of a monk and predatory beast, he confronts imagined rivals and personal demons. MGM Home Entertainment.

Raging Bull. Having abandoned the violent mimesis of boxing for standup comedy, a considerably milder substitute, Jake La Motta (Robert De Niro) practises his routine only moments before going on stage. MGM Home Entertainment.

Raging Bull. Jake La Motta meets his future wife Vickie (Cathy Moriarty) for the first time - a radiant image seemingly unapproachable behind a chain-link fence. MGM Home Entertainment.

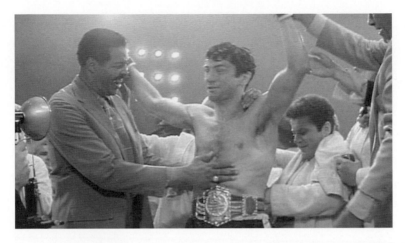

Raging Bull. Joe Louis, Jake La Motta's role model and rival, congratulates Jake (Robert De Niro) immediately after his conquest of the middleweight championship of the world. MGM Home Entertainment..

Raging Bull. Moments after their unexpected encounter on a Manhattan street, Jake La Motta (Robert De Niro) makes an inconclusive attempt to reconcile with the apparently still resentful Joey (Joe Pesci), his long-estranged brother. MGM Home Entertainment.

GoodFellas. Martin Scorsese directs Robert De Niro in the role of Jimmy Conway. Warner Brothers Entertainment.

GoodFellas. Initiating his future wife Karen (Lorraine Bracco) into mob violence, and thus providing her with a hitherto unknown addictive thrill, Henry Hill (Ray Liotta) hands her the pistol with which he has just beaten her would-be boyfriend, and which she then conceals in her mother's milkbox. Warner Brothers Entertainment.

GoodFellas. Following the murder of Billy 'Batts,' Henry Hill (Ray Liotta), Tommy DeVito (Joe Pesci), and Jimmy Conway (Robert De Niro) sit down to an impromptu breakfast at the house of Tommy's mother (Catherine Scorsese). Warner Brothers Entertainment.

GoodFellas. As he and his fellow gangsters sit around their clubhouse card table playing poker, Tommy DeVito (Joe Pesci) angrily berates mob gofer Spider (Michael Imperioli, offscreen) for having failed to bring him the Scotch he had ordered. Warner Brothers Entertainment.

GoodFellas. Jimmy Conway (Robert De Niro) casts the evil eye (*mal occhio*) on his latest victim. Warner Brothers Entertainment.

Casino. Known as a 'queen around the casino,' high-class hooker Ginger McKenna (Sharon Stone) rolls dice for her latest 'john' while surreptitiously stealing his chips and dropping them into her purse. Universal Home Entertainment.

Casino. 'Ace' (Robert De Niro) and Nicky Santoro (Joe Pesci) find their friendship turning sour as a result of their conflicting ambitions within the Las Vegas gambling industry. Universal Home Entertainment.

Casino. In fearful anticipation of his rendezvous with Nicky Santoro (Joe Pesci) in the hinterlands of Las Vegas, 'Ace' Rothstein (Robert De Niro) enters a desert terrain filled with the unmarked graves of underworld victims. Universal Home Entertainment.

all friends here.' Joey's mocking characterization of Charlie as 'St Charles,' alluding presumably to St Charles Borromeo, who fought the plague in sixteenth-century Milan, calls to mind Girard's characterization of the plague as a transparent metaphor for the spread of violence within a community.[53] Soon after Joey identifies Charlie with his saintly namesake, the first of two fights erupts in the pool hall. Yet Charlie's spiritual failings are most deeply rooted in his compromised position between the church and mob, an interstitial identity in some ways similar to that of 'Ace' Rothstein in *Casino*, torn between his obligations to the mob and state. Eagerly expecting his uncle's gift of a restaurant, Charlie had not expected that Groppi, the co-owner, would kill himself after losing his business. When Charlie, in the men's room of his uncle's restaurant cafe, overhears Giovanni ordering the banishment of a thug to Miami, he washes his hands in a gesture reminiscent of Pilate's disavowal of moral responsibility. Or perhaps he is attempting to remove the taint of his fallen world.

Charlie's bad faith and moral compromise stand out most glaringly in his dealings with Johnny Boy. With atypical astuteness, the rather stupid Johnny Boy comprehends what Charlie cannot see, that worldly policy largely governs his supposedly selfless conduct: 'Charlie likes everybody, everybody likes Charlie. Fuckin' politician.' Realizing that his friend promotes social harmony chiefly for personal advantage, so as to win popularity, Johnny Boy also knows that he can expect only limited help and protection from Charlie, who fears that their friendship will offend his uncle. Yet the underlying dishonesty of Charlie's role stems not from worldly interests alone, but from his moral vanity in wanting to be a priest, an emotion from which the young Scorsese was not immune. (Indeed, he embraced the priesthood selfishly, thinking that it would increase his chances of salvation.) When Charlie says to Teresa of Johnny Boy, 'Who's gonna save him if I don't,' his statement smacks of a spiritual superiority and exhibitionism that helps to explain why Scorsese himself numbers Charlie with the Pharisees. As it 'serves his [Charlie's] needs to keep Johnny Boy dependent on him,' remarks Scorsese, so the Pharisees would 'blow trumpets' to advertise their almsgiving.[54] In another interview Scorsese says of Charlie's conduct that 'he acts like he's doing it for others, but it's a matter of his own pride – the first sin in the Bible.'[55]

Unimpressed by Charlie's religiosity, the pragmatic Tony sees only its impracticability. For him, Charlie's problem is that, having let 'those guys' – namely the priests – 'get to' him, he wants to be 'saved.' Instead, he needs to realize that the church, like the Mafia to which both Charlie and Tony are connected in one way or other, is nothing more than what Tony describes as a 'business,' an 'organization.' 'You gotta be like me,' he counsels Charlie, proposing worldly cunning and self-interest as an alternative to the *Imitatio*. So much is suggested by Tony's surname – Volpe, the fox. He is very definitely an Italian type, what the Italians would call *furbo*. Whereas Charlie would answer anger with understanding, mediation, and reconciliation, Tony, like Giovanni, favours tidily efficient expulsive violence, as when he kicks a drug addict out of his bar. His opinion of pacifism is plain in his complaint to his bartender that the latter 'didn't do nothin'' to remove the addict. Whatever one thinks of Tony's values, they contain worldly wisdom, for whereas Michael allows Johnny Boy's escalating debt to provoke a nearly lethal dispute, Tony cuts his losses by revoking the deadbeat's tab. On the night of Michael's final attempt to settle his grievance with Johnny Boy, Charlie sits in Tony's bar and nervously lights a match to his drink, whereupon Tony orders him to put out the flames. As in the earlier scene in Groppi's restaurant, Charlie is both literally and figuratively playing with fire, something Tony would never do. At the climax of Johnny Boy's quarrel with Michael, Tony looks on calmly while eating a late-night snack; he then provides Charlie and Johnny Boy with a getaway car not simply out of friendship but to avoid violence in the neighbourhood. Unlike his peers, Tony knows how to live amid bloodshed without being drawn into it, as one infers from his absence in the final shoot-out. His ease in dealing with violence is implied when he unveils his two illegal tiger cubs hidden in covered cages in a backroom of his bar. While his friends withdraw in terror, Tony enters a cage, where he showers kisses and caresses upon its occupant – an analogical parody of the Johannine idea that love drives out fear.[56] His ability to negotiate the competing value systems of Little Italy is indicated in the items he has collected in the backroom of his bar: the tigers in their cage, signifying the violence and brutality of the streets; the *Playboy* foldout pinned to the wall (which resembles the one in *Who's That Knocking at My Door?* save that this playmate looks towards the viewer), which connotes the sexual promiscuity of the peer group; and a religious statuette of a saint, this being a reminder of and weak concession to the Catholic religious system Tony has abandoned in favour of what he terms the 'business' of the local crime syndicate.

The film affords many other examples of Christian analogy, the sanctities appearing mainly in negative or deviated form. Uncle Giovanni figures as the unofficial God of this universe, its unmoved mover, conferring benefits only upon his favourites. With a wave of his cigar he embodies the expulsive violence by which the community distinguishes between acceptable and unacceptable, sacred and profane. The uncle also inverts the idea of God as the provider of sustenance, as witness the scene in the restaurant he intends to take over. The uncle orders tripe on this occasion, for as Rudolph Bell notes, quoting the analysis of Mikhail Bakhtin, the bowels and belly represent the 'very life of man' insofar as they are associated with both death and what Bell terms the 'generative belly.'[57] The uncle's feast of tripe thus signifies his devouring of the two restaurateurs, whom he drives out of business. In ironic contrast to the uncle's feasting, Groppi commits suicide by placing a gun in his mouth, his response to his humiliation by Giovanni. Again, in providing Charlie with a model of worldly conduct, Giovanni inspires a warped version of the *Imitatio*. When Charlie volunteers to help in securing the restaurant, Giovanni advises, 'Don't do anything. His business is bad ... You can help by waiting.' 'Doing nothing' parodies Christian non-aggression, while the 'help' Charlie offers yields only personal advantage. The uncle's counsel of patience sounds like a corrupted version of Christian faith, the substance of things hoped for. Christian charity is present only by its absence, as when it becomes known that Michael charges Johnny Boy usurious interest, and when Charlie and Johnny Boy abandon the epileptic Teresa to a neighbour (played by Catherine Scorsese) whose bitter 'Thank you' (*Graziate*) shows only annoyance while parodying the idea of grace.

Analogical parody operates by other means, as when the use of religious language in profane contexts indirectly calls attention to its transcendental significance. Johnny Boy's assertion that he 'hates that feast [of San Gennaro] with a passion' displays an aggressive ill will antithetical to the Passion of Christ and the deeds of the martyr whom the feast commemorates. When Michael in rage against Johnny Boy 'swear[s] to Jesus Christ on the goddamn cross,' he undercuts his avowal by cursing the very symbol of the religion. In the same spirit of unintentional parody, Michael orders his gunman Shorty to shoot at Johnny Boy with the words: 'Now is the time.' This statement inverts Jesus's declaration, 'The time is at hand,' showing his willingness to die on the cross.[58] That the biblical statement is being parodied is suggested by the fact that Shorty kisses his gun before firing, as if it were his crucifix.

Christ would also seem to be present analogically in the scene in which Charlie and his cronies, having stopped at an interminable red light during their trip into an unknown neighbourhood to collect on a debt, encounter an unwashed, tattered, bearded, and beggarly old man, a bum in fact, who, presumably in the hope of a modest tip, offers unrequested to clean Tony's windshield. Despite his professions of Christianity elsewhere in the film, Charlie shows no sympathy for this abject person, but speaks of him with undisguised disdain: 'Look at this character, he hasn't taken a bath since last Christmas ... He's probably an ex-judge.' As Tony waits with growing impatience for the light to change, he becomes increasingly annoyed with the old man's attempted helpfulness, remarking to Johnny Boy: 'John, you wanna keep your father away from the car, please.' Finally, to demonstrate his utter lack of concern for the old man. Tony closes the automatic windows in his face. Yet what Charlie and his friends have failed to realize is that at this moment they have encountered Christ, and his lesson of charity, in analogical form. It is worth noting in this context that the friends' drive into a strange part of town begins with a high-angle overhead shot in which the most prominent object is a white full-length statue of Christ placed on the roof of a tall building, from which he blesses the streets below. There follows Charlie's description of the old man as having gone without a bath since the previous Christmas, which implies that in that entire period he has met with a total refusal of Christian fellow feeling. At the same time, Tony says much more than he realizes in telling Johnny Boy to keep his father away from the car. If only analogically, the old man stands for the abject and repudiated Christ and is therefore Johnny Boy's real or ultimate father, whose message Johnny Boy is incapable of realizing. Whereas in *Who's That Knocking?* the closing of the automatic windows of Joey's car had chiefly signalled the claustrophobic self-imprisonment of the ethnic peer group, in *Mean Streets* the same gesture is more aggressive and defiant, as it represents a deliberate hardening of heart against human sympathy. And finally, there is Charlie's identification of the old man as an 'ex-judge,' which at one level reflects his Mafioso (and southern Italian) disdain for the agents of the law, but which in a much more important sense carries with it the idea of Christ as the temporarily rejected yet ultimate judge of humanity. The relevant text is Matthew 25, in which Christ, predicting his ascension to the throne of judgment at the end of the world, announces his aim of punishing all who have failed to act charitably towards those unfortunate persons who, unbeknownst to the hardhearted, were the analogues and embodiments of Christ on earth.[59]

Throughout *Mean Streets* analogies of the transcendent appear in the form of chromatic symbolism, red being easily the most significant colour overall. Its importance is emphasized towards the conclusion when Charlie, having run a red light in flight from Michael's vengeance, asks: 'What does the colour red mean?' Red appears in multiple contexts within the film. One thinks of the film's title; the stigmata of St Francis, mentioned by Charlie; the represented wounds of the icons in his local church; the infernal interior of Tony's bar, a scene of bloody assassination; the interior of the restaurant Charlie covets; the red lights of the festival; the hellish flames and bloodstained shirt of Vincent Price in Roger Corman's *The Masque of the Red Death* (1964), which Charlie and Johnny Boy watch at a local theatre during their flight from Michael's vengeance; the red carpeting of the hotel corridor; the blood Charlie ejaculates in his dream of intercourse with Teresa; and the bloodshed immediately after his running a red light. Red is also the colour of the martyrs in the Catholic mass, and as such foreshadows Charlie's 'martyrdom.' It furthermore signifies blood sanctified by sacrifice, whether that of the martyr San Gennaro or of Jesus Christ, whose Passion Charlie misinterprets as a secretly prideful self-aggrandizing masochism. Red also signifies profane passion – the tumult of desires that fuel each other in Tony's bar, or Charlie's yearning for a business that does not belong to him. Again, red is a universal danger sign, calling to mind profane violence: the blood of the murder in Tony's bar, the wounding of Charlie, Teresa, and Johnny Boy at the conclusion. On the Italian mainland red signifies counter-magic against evil, while in Sicily the red *corno* or horn is the most popular amulet against the evil eye.[60] Notwithstanding his status as a third-generation Italian American, Tony is sufficiently superstitious to attach such an amulet to his car's rear-view mirror, which suggests that Mezzogiorno folk beliefs had by no means disappeared from the Little Italy of the 1970s.

Charlie's hopes for the restaurant, which require him to satisfy his uncle, are endangered by his friendship with Johnny Boy and his cousin Teresa, of neither of whom the uncle approves, notwithstanding his obligations towards them. As Giovanni explains to Charlie, not only is he *compare* or godfather to Johnny Boy's family, a relation normally entailing responsibilities, but Johnny Boy's very name honours his godfather. The uncle's sense of obligation may be compounded by the fact that he himself bears the name of San Giovanni, patron saint of *comparaggio*.[61] Giovanni must therefore 'take an interest' in Johnny Boy, or at least pretend to. Yet actually he warns Charlie against associating with 'that kid Johnny Boy,' describing him as 'a little bit crazy' and adding: 'I understand that you try to take an interest' but 'watch yourself, don't spoil anything.' The uncle deplores Johnny Boy's erratic behaviour, random violence, and lack of respect for the neighbourhood. He would probably prefer to expel him from Little Italy, but family loyalty prevents him. Fearing that such a person may dishonour Charlie, Giovanni reminds him that 'honourable men go with honourable men' – *uomini simili attiro a ogni simili*. He uses the word 'honour' not in the Anglo-Saxon sense of virtue based on a code of internalized universal morality, independent of social opinions and estimations, but in the southern Italian sense of outward behaviour conforming to a community standard, with an emphasis on appearances and external evaluations.

According to Giovanni, not only does Teresa's family have 'problems,' but she resembles Johnny Boy in being 'sick in the head' and is therefore off-limits to Charlie. When Charlie explains that Teresa suffers from not mental illness but epilepsy, the uncle reiterates his 'diagnosis.' It was typical for ignorant Italian Americans of that generation to view this disease as a mental disorder. The uncle's lack of sympathy for Teresa's malady, which divides her from the community while inviting its hostility, is interesting given that epilepsy is a classic victimary sign.[62] Nor is the uncle pleased by Teresa's intention to leave Little Italy, which he reads as a further sign of her mental illness.[63] He would prefer to tell her parents to 'lock her up,' but as with Johnny Boy he must observe *rispetto*, and will not violate its externally imposed code by an overt act of disloyalty towards her family. So far as Charlie is concerned, he advises: 'Keep an eye on them' but 'don't get involved.'

Although after receiving this advice Charlie initially avoids Teresa, he resumes seeing her, and indeed she joins him and Johnny Boy in the final scene. Charlie's loyalty to Teresa is one of his chief redeeming qualities, all the more so because she behaves unattractively. To be sure, one appreciates her courageous desire to escape Little Italy and her realism in puncturing Charlie's Christian pretensions. Yet these virtues are offset by her foul mouth, her petty stealing in the mid-town hotel, her rudeness to Michael and the black maid, and her espousal of a selfish personal outlook, as when she tells Charlie to 'help yourself first.' Nor has her epilepsy made her sensitive to social misfits, for rather than sympathizing with her cousin Johnny Boy, she sees him mainly as a hindrance to Charlie's prospects. No less ironically, she sees Johnny Boy as Giovanni sees him and herself, as mentally disturbed: 'He's like an insane person,' she tells Charlie. 'Fuck him.'

Johnny Boy remains Charlie's greatest cross, as he continues to associate with and grudgingly protect him for various reasons, including a
sense of obligation. It is suggested that Charlie helps Johnny Boy partly
out of guilty gratitude for the protection he had received from him
during a street fight, when Johnny Boy suffered a serious head wound
while enabling his friend to escape unharmed. The irony is that the
neighbourhood scapegrace has performed an act of self-sacrifice greater
than any Charlie, with all his moralizing, has ever achieved. In maintaining this friendship Charlie risks the disapproval not only of his
uncle but of Michael, who increasingly resents his disappointing reas-
surances of Johnny Boy's ability to pay the debt. After denouncing
Johnny Boy as the 'biggest jerk-off around,' Michael cannot comprehend why Charlie 'hang[s] around that punk kid.' In his view, Charlie
shows insufficient 'care' regarding the unpaid interest.

For his part, Johnny Boy never lacks for an insult for Michael, as
when, standing rounds of drinks on an escalating tab, he answers
Michael's request for a drink with the affirmative: 'Does a bear shit in
the woods?' Typifying Scorsese's Italian American films in its mingling
of humour and aggression, this insult anticipates Michael's later mention that he deals in toilet paper stolen from the army – a revelation that
only underscores Michael's status as a punk, the lowly position he
assigns Johnny Boy. And in comparing Michael to a bear, Johnny Boy
signals that confusion of human and animal that portends violence.[64]
By now Johnny Boy is both Michael's rival for the withheld money and
the immovable obstacle to his attainment of it, and as such, the object of
sadomasochistic fascination and hatred. Increasingly exasperated by
Johnny Boy's behaviour and embarrassed by the loss in prestige it has
cost him, Michael offers an extension on the payment of the loan only to
learn that Johnny Boy has quit his job. He and Charlie then plan to settle
the matter at a party for the Vietnam veteran Jerry.

In approaching its climax, *Mean Streets* exhibits a number of themes and
motifs that, anticipated in *Who's That Knocking?*, come to typify Scorsese's
Italian American films, particularly in their concluding phases. In the
earlier work, the members of J.R.'s Italian American peer group have
lost their individuality through mimetic conformism and unacknowledged rivalry. Each member is hardly distinguishable in physical
appearance, dress, and desire from any other. The latent desire for
differentiating violence reveals itself at a stag party, where the members
gather non-hierarchically in a circle and an unloaded gun – symbol of

masculine prepotency – is passed around among them at once jokingly and fearfully. The terrifyingly attractive gun signifies the sacred, and tempts every member to assert his difference from the others by claiming and using it. Although, in the presence of this intimidatingly auratic object, no one is initially willing to do so, an unidentified guest finally comes forward, loads the gun, and waves it in the air. Other partiers flee to the remote corners of the apartment, again half-jokingly and half-seriously. The gunman then collars the despised pimp Sally Gaga, a logical candidate for victimization, yet a killing is avoided when the gunman contents himself with shooting a liquor bottle to pieces. In the loft scene, J.R.'s fantasy of a one-man orgy, his enslavement to mimetic desire is identified variously with the donning of masks, promiscuous or serial copulation with a crowd of 'broads,' and cards as a symbol of submission of the will to chance. J.R.'s loss of personal identity, and the general atmosphere of undifferentiation and profanation, are conveyed through the camera's rapid and repeated turning and swirling, the visual equivalent of the vertiginous tumult of J.R.'s experience. In the final example, a stag party offering serial sex with two women, competition over the few available women is averted through the throwing of fingers so as to determine – that is, differentiate – the sequence of copulations. Thus the group's inner tensions as well as its misogynistic hostility are more effectively directed against these 'broads,' its customary object of sexual victimization. Yet the underlying violence of this occasion bursts forth when one of the 'broads' resents her mistreatment and lashes out against her abusers.

Like Scorsese's other Italian American films, *Mean Streets* exemplifies the 'holiday-gone-wrong' – the failure of conventional social forms, including rituals, festivals, and other celebrations, to control the spread of violence within a community. Among the causes of this failure are acquisitive and mimetic desire leading to rivalries in which the behavioural model becomes a hated obstacle and hostility issues in retaliation. Another incentive to conflict is the very existence of social prohibitions, which provide unintended provocations to transgression. As the embattled individuals perform repeated acts of mutual hostility, the differences between them erode to the point where they become each other's violent doubles. Traditional sanctities and prohibitions prove powerless to check undifferentiating violence, which shows no respect for persons, customs, or anything else. As the crisis escalates, it involves more and more people, so that anyone in its vicinity risks becoming a random victim. In Scorsese's Italian American films, mimetic desire and violent undifferentiation are sometimes identified with the mask, but more typically they appear in conjunction with images of spinning or whirling, a dizzying experience in which identity and reality are lost. The films also connect these phenomena with the increasing power over the depicted events of chance, identified with cards or the wheel of fortune as the very symbol of undifferentiating violence. There is, however, a crucial difference between *Who's That Knocking?* and *Mean Streets* in treating these themes. In the first, for all its brutality, the rivalries never really carry a lethal threat. But in *Mean Streets* they explode into potentially deadly retaliatory violence that, detached from its intended targets, claims random victims.[65]

The climax of *Mean Streets* begins with a reunion in Tony's bar in honour of Jerry, newly returned from the Vietnam War. On this occasion, moreover, Michael and Johnny Boy plan to settle their debt at last. In addition to 'Welcome Home' posters, there are festive streamers and a cake, while the guest of honour shows up richly bemedalled in his military uniform to receive a large American flag as a gift from his assembled friends. The scene thus has a quasi-ritualistic significance, for not only is the American flag a symbol of peace and harmony, but Jerry's medals imply sanctified violence, the protection of the nation against its enemies, and personal sacrifice for the general good. Yet the fact remains that, like all returning war veterans, Jerry carries the contagion of bad violence, and all the more so as he has participated in a highly unpopular war marked by its own desecrations, including flag burnings. His party is thus vulnerable to the violence it ought to prevent, which is ready to break out at the least opportunity, without choosing its targets.

Apparently Scorsese had intended the party as a costumed affair with Charlie appearing in the guise of the crucified Jesus Christ, complete with stigmata.[66] Like the mask in *Who's That Knocking?*, Charlie's masquerade would evoke the confusion of identity portending the sacrificial crisis. In Charlie's case the masquerade would also culminate his confused fascination with the *Imitatio Christi*. For though Charlie identifies with Christ as a peacemaker, there is an unmistakable element of falsity or hypocrisy in his pursuit of the *Imitatio*, which he falls short of in many ways. Nor can one discount the element of pride and vanity in Charlie's overly masochistic interpretation of the *Imitatio*, as he seems to want to prove his spiritual election by rivaling Christ in penitential suffering. In any case, Scorsese preferred for Charlie, like the other guests, to attend the party undisguised, although not without sacred associations of the parodic type. Charlie dresses for the occasion with a slow, ritualistic solemnity, as if he were a priest preparing for mass.[67] The irony lies in the idolatrous delight he exhibits in gazing upon the expensive new shirt his mother has left for him, whose blazoned monograph, shot in close-up, betokens its wearer's vanity. (J.R., who figures as Scorsese's alter ego in the treatment of *Jeruselem, Jerusalem*, and who ultimately metamorphoses into Charlie Civello, is similarly identified with a sartorial exhibitionism that ironizes his ostensible dedication to Christianity.) Upon entering the bar, Charlie announces, 'I come to create order.' In a parody of the Communion rite, he holds his hands over a glass of J&B while Tony pours water over them. Then, to Tony's query, 'Art thou King of the Jews?' Charlie repeats Christ's words to his tormentors: 'My Kingdom is not of this world.' All this betokens sacrilege, loss of difference between the transcendental and profane. When Charlie proclaims his other-worldly kingdom, he refers ironically to his imminent drunkenness, which only increases during the party. After playing pool on the bartop, using whisky glasses as billiard balls, he appears in extreme close-up as, with the barroom seeming to swirl around him, he experiences an increasing loss of orientation and even identity. Scorsese produces this effect by placing Harvey Keitel (Charlie) and the camera on a dolly that was then moved through the bar. The vertiginousness results from the fact that, even as the background seems to move, Charlie appears stationary and in close-up, as if the world were swirling around him.[68]

Charlie's vertigo is accompanied by verbal nonsense, the linguistic equivalent of his mental confusion. The song 'Rubber Biscuits,' which plays on the soundtrack, tells of a so-called 'wish sandwich,' which consists of two pieces of bread and no meat, leaving the consumer to wish for something more substantial. The song also mentions the 'ricochet biscuit,' which, if it fails to ricochet off a wall, leaves one hungry. However nonsensical, these lyrics comment on Charlie's condition. As the wish sandwich implies both the intensity and futility of his desires, so the ricochet biscuit suggests not only his lack of spiritual sustenance but the random violence soon to issue from Michael's vendetta against Johnny Boy, which, by a kind of ricochet, claims Charlie and Teresa as its victims. So too, in its utter vanity and senselessness, as in its failure to provide real nourishment, the Rubber Biscuit must be taken to parody the Eucharist, the sanctified bread that for the Catholic stands for the ever-nourishing incarnate Word in which ultimate meaning resides and in which all subsidiary meanings are peaceably resolved and reconciled.

Sleeping off his drunkenness in the back of Tony's bar, Charlie is awakened by Michael's report that Johnny Boy has put him off yet again. For his part, Charlie is displeased to learn that Michael has charged Johnny Boy, a fellow local, 'vig' or interest of three thousand dollars, and persuades him to lower the figure.[69] This small detail, mentioned in passing, implies the increasing lack of solidarity and fellow feeling within a neighbourhood formerly characterized by personalism but now increasingly dominated by the impersonal American business mentality. At the same time, Charlie's growing sense of the seriousness of Johnny Boy's and Michael's quarrel is manifest in his quotation from Matthew, 'till thou hast paid the last penny.' The quotation derives from a section of the Sermon on the Mount in which Jesus, seeking to extend the range of the Jewish law, urges his followers to avoid not just murder but anger, which leads to murder. He further advises them to reconcile quickly with their adversaries, lest they suffer escalating penalties to the absolute limit of their capacity to pay. The passage thus reflects on Charlie's and Michael's relationship, the former attempting to reconcile two friends before they come to bloodshed, the latter reluctant to exact anything but the maximum from his creditor, even to the point of attempted murder.[70]

Upon returning to the party, Charlie and Michael find themselves unexpectedly in the midst of violence sparked by jealous rivalry. Outraged to discover his girlfriend dancing with a guest, Jerry the guest of honour sets off a brawl in which his celebratory cake splatters in all directions. Earlier at the party Michael had attempted to maintain his familiar look of detachment and unflappability, blowing smoke rings insouciantly and gazing into the distance in a display of *lontananza*, as if unaffected by ordinary things. Yet now, flecked ignominiously with cake fragments and surrounded by chaos, he struggles visibly to maintain his composure. Soon enough, as his quarrel with Johnny Boy comes to a head, he will be forced to abandon his affectation of cool remoteness and self-sufficiency.

The violence inside the bar has its reflection out of doors. For though the San Gennaro festival coincides with the events of the main narrative, this ritualized event does not pacify the main characters, whose violence finally enters the streets. At the party's conclusion Teresa informs Charlie that Johnny Boy has taken to the roof of a tenement building with gun in hand. Having failed to keep his appointment to meet with Michael at Jerry's party, and apparently seeking random victims as substitutes for Michael, he expresses his titanic yet impotent pride by shooting at the Empire State Building. He next shoots out a window in the apartment of a local woman, initially apologizing for his 'mistake' but then confessing his vengeful yet apparently unmotivated hatred for her. After telling Charlie of his desire for an atomic bomb to awaken the neighbourhood, he sets off an explosion on the rooftop, from which he and Charlie scamper off like two overgrown juvenile delinquents.

In *Mean Streets* the motif of chance figures both in conjunction with and as a sign of increasingly unpredictable violence. Ironically, the backroom of Tony's bar contains a sign announcing: 'Positively No Gambling.' When Johnny Boy proposes a card game for money, a fight nearly erupts between him and Tony, who naturally resents this misuse of what is, after all, his money. In another scene, Charlie's futile effort to round up participants for a game of blackjack is followed by the unexpected killing of a local drunk. As the film draws to a close, Scorsese includes a shot of the wheel of fortune at the San Gennaro festival, a feature typical of festivals generally. This hardly seems surprising if one recalls that, as part of their effort to contain social violence, festivals simulate in controlled form the chaos of the sacrificial crisis upon whose violent climax the community is returned to peace and order. Accordingly, festivals typically incorporate themes of chance. At the same time, however, Scorsese implies desacralization, as the wheel of fortune connotes not just simulated violence but the random violence of the conclusion.

The film's climax, in which Johnny Boy and Charlie suffer neck and hand wounds respectively, and Teresa multiple contusions, seems from another perspective to unfold by an ominously inexorable fatality. When Michael raises his hand to his neck in the home movie at the film's beginning, his gesture portends the climax. Not only does Charlie place his hand close to fire, but he rubs his neck on several occasions. That he does so at the very moment his uncle asks him whether he likes restaurants connects Johnny Boy's suffering with Charlie's ambition.[71] Charlie's hand wound is anticipated in his mock fisticuffs with Johnny Boy, in which he excuses himself because of his 'bad hand,' and in the pool hall brawl, in which he uses the same excuse in order to avoid a pummelling. In the final scene Charlie appears on his knees with his wounded hand outstretched as if in prayer. Likewise Johnny Boy seems marked by fatality when he stands beneath a gigantic pistol advertising the gun shop where he and Charlie stop by night to admire the merchandise. Adding to the ominousness, Johnny Boy notices his creditor Joe Black in the vicinity and hides from him. The grimly named Joe Black is a death symbol, representing all of Johnny Boy's unpaid debts. A similar gloom surrounds Johnny Boy when, during a late-night consultation with Charlie in the local cemetery, he stretches out upon a tombstone, perhaps anticipating his own death, and seeming almost resigned to it. The uproar and apparent violence that erupt unexpectedly during a party in a nearby apartment house seem likewise to portend the mayhem at the conclusion, while the possible fate of Charlie and Johnny Boy is suggested when, as they leave the cemetery, they appear in a long shot as if lost among or swallowed up by the graves and funeral monuments. Later, when they attempt to evade Michael, they hide out in a movie theatre where, appropriately, John Boorman's *Point Blank* is showing.

Charlie's and Johnny Boy's flight from Little Italy follows upon the last failed attempt to settle the debt with Michael. Although Johnny Boy wants Charlie to request Uncle Giovanni's intervention, Charlie will not do so for fear of offending his uncle. Instead, he plans for Johnny Boy to meet Michael at Tony's bar with enough money to appease him temporarily, restore his public reputation, and convince him that the debt will ultimately be paid. Michael would probably accept a steady flow of reasonable partial repayments, as loan sharks know that something is better than nothing.

Nonetheless, the mood on the night of the meeting is anxious and recriminatory. When, on his way to Charlie's apartment Johnny Boy beats up a pedestrian who accidentally bumps into him on the sidewalk, one has a foretaste of the climax, in which innocent victims suffer. After revealing that he has only thirty dollars for Michael, the tearful Johnny Boy rebukes Charlie: 'You didn't do nothin' for me.' This accusation proves unfair, as Charlie increases the sum by a small amount in the hope of placating Michael. At Tony's bar they learn that Michael has left the premises but will later return. The theme of random violence reappears just before Michael's arrival when Charlie, at least partly to discharge his nervous tension, makes advances to an allegedly Jewish (and therefore supposedly promiscuous) woman who sits alone at the bar following a quarrel with a boyfriend. Within moments Charlie provokes a confrontation with the boyfriend, whom he insults as a Jew though he has no knowledge whatsoever of his origin, and whom he encourages his friends to remove bodily from the premises. This sudden and casual outburst of anti-Semitism gives the impression of a desperate attempt to find a safety valve – conveniently but arbitrarily located in an out-group – for the violence about to explode among members of Charlie's ethnic community. At the same time, his anti-Semitic baiting affords a further indication of the limits of his Christianity.

Michael's arrival is accompanied by old-style Sicilian music, as if announcing a don. However, during Michael's absence Johnny Boy has been buying rounds of drinks and now has only ten dollars – an insulting amount. He asks Michael tauntingly whether he thinks himself 'too good for this ten dollars' and mocks him as the 'only jerk-off' to lend him money. Their mimetic rivalry is evident in that Michael had originally called Johnny Boy a 'jerk-off,' and that Charlie had later warned Johnny Boy not to make Michael look like a 'jerk-off.' The differences between the rivals have been eroded by reciprocal hatred, pointing to the obliteration of those differences in mutual violence. Announcing his refusal to 'give two shits' for anything, Johnny Boy pulls a gun and heaps Michael with homosexual insults, including a humping gesture and the imputation that he performs fellatio. His most insulting provocations aim at Michael's vanity, his self-doubts regarding his prestige as a gangster. For Johnny Boy, Michael is a would-be 'big shot' and a 'disappointed dunsky,' the second insult alluding to his failure to be a don, rubbed in through a mocking diminutive.[72]

Michael having sworn vengeance for this unforgivable public insult, Tony lends Charlie and Johnny Boy his car as their means of escape out of town. Before they leave the bar, Johnny Boy remarks to Charlie, 'You got what you wanted,' thus raising the key question: is Charlie committed to saving his friend or only pretending to do so out of vanity? As Charlie sits at the wheel his patience is further tested by Johnny Boy, who instead of entering the car performs a rock and roll war dance to the accompaniment of 'Mickey's Monkey' by the Miracles. The title comments ironically on the mimetic rivalry between Michael ('Mickey') and Johnny Boy, implying that, far from being an autonomous being, Johnny Boy has become the ape of Michael. Each mirrors the other in acquisitive as in conflictual mimesis.

Teresa having joined Charlie and Johnny Boy, they set out for Brooklyn with Charlie reflecting on the night's events: 'I guess you can safely say that things haven't gone too well tonight.' His detached, even bemused tone is that of one who thinks himself out of danger, an impression reinforced by his casual use of the word 'safely.' Calling to mind his earlier statement to Johnny Boy that the latter should have 'run safely like me' during the fight in which Johnny Boy sacrificed himself for his friend, Charlie seems to think that flight will work again. He monologizes on his moral responsibilities – 'I'm tryin', Lord, I'm tryin' – which Johnny Boy and Teresa find inexplicable but amusing. Then, as they enter Brooklyn, they are ambushed by Michael and Shorty. Their car goes out of control and crashes into a fire hydrant, from which a geyser leaps high into the air. Amid the sound of ambulances and police cars, Charlie extricates himself from the demolished car and falls to his knees with hands outstretched, as if in supplication. His hand wound recalls the stigmata of St Francis of Assisi, his model of the Christian life.[73] The combination of water and shed blood evokes the Gospel passage in which blood and water flow from Christ's side as the sign of divine sacrifice, and with it the cleansing of sin through the release of Spirit into the world.[74] Yet that Charlie has not received the full complement of divine wounds suggests that, unlike St Francis, he has followed the *Imitatio* imperfectly. As Charlie is helped to an ambulance, the medical unit removes Teresa slowly from the car; she is in shock, her hand having gone through the windshield. Johnny Boy limps away with his hand to his neck, indicating a serious non-lethal wound; Michael had previously threatened to break his legs.[75] A classic victimary sign, Johnny Boy's limp implies that, apart from his actual physical injuries, his career in the neighbourhood is over.

Coinciding with the closing ceremonies of the San Gennaro festival, the conclusion of *Mean Streets* is densely ironic. A festival intended to pacify the community has concluded with an eruption of 'pure random violence,' as Scorsese calls it, among its younger members.[76] Absent from the festival on its final night, Uncle Giovanni, the real master of the neighbourhood, appears in his living room with cigar in hand, watching Fritz Lang's *The Big Heat* (1953) on television. The screen shows a firebombing, with Glenn Ford, in the role of police detective, removing his dying wife from a burning car.[77] This mirrors the mayhem taking place that night, yet the self-sufficient Giovanni is as coolly detached from one as from the other. As the festival concludes, the master of ceremonies cautions the audience to drive safely – *'Guidate con molto cautela'* – on its way home, an unintentionally ironic comment on the evening's shootings. The emcee then signs off with 'Arrivederci' rather than 'Addio' or farewell, as the festival will return in succeeding years. The music following the closing ceremonies is 'No Place Like Home,' played by a festival band, which is accompanied by the credits superimposed upon the image of a window shade being pulled down in a local apartment. Scorsese thus suggests the circular futility, insularity, and entrapment of the residents of Little Italy. At the same time, the evident indifference of Charlie's friends to the festival confirms Gans's observation regarding young Italian Americans of this period, namely that they had usually lost their identification with Italian culture, especially street *feste*.[78]

Mean Streets raises questions concerning both the implications of its climactic violence and Charlie's sincerity in helping Johnny Boy. Although such violence contaminates the San Gennaro festival, Scorsese remarks of the characters that 'they all learn something at the end of *Mean Streets*, only they have to get it from, again, the hand of God.' He compares the climactic bloodshed to a 'fountain, washing,' as if it were sacrificial and purificatory.[79] Les Keyser sees a 'hopeful lesson' in the ending, while Michael Bliss finds in it a 'lesson' like that of Scorsese's other films. He adds, 'we can conclude ... that violence is meant to act as a redemptive force in these films' by reintegrating the 'aberrant individual' within the community.[80] Bliss can hardly be faulted in noting Scorsese's interest in purificatory violence, which often figures in his Italian American as in his other works. However, Bliss mistakenly sees the climactic violence in *Mean Streets* as restoring its victims within the community. Rather, it marks Johnny Boy permanently as an outsider while terminating Charlie's hopes as a gangster and restaurateur. Having offended his uncle irreparably by his involvement in mayhem with two interdicted people, he has proved unworthy of the mob. Yet Bliss rightly notes that the ending shows 'selfless sacrifice' to be 'impossible ... if one is to endure' in the neighbourhood – an insight relevant to Charlie's dealings with Johnny Boy.[81]

Some critics regard Charlie as a totally self-serving hypocrite who sells out Johnny Boy while pretending to help him. Pauline Kael characterizes him as 'Judas the Betrayer because of his careful angling to move up the next rung of the ladder.'[82] Yet though Charlie's worldly interests and Pharisaism prevent him from helping his friend wholeheartedly, he does not abandon Johnny Boy at the conclusion. Rather, he risks his own life during their escape and is present at Johnny Boy's wounding. Insisting that Charlie 'never' sold out his friend, Scorsese finds Charlie's error to lie elsewhere, in his excess of moral zeal coupled with lack of street smarts. When 'somebody does something wrong' in Little Italy, 'you've got to break his head or you shoot him. It's as simple as that.' Unfortunately, Charlie 'refused to acknowledge' this reality and 'eventually did the worst thing he could do which was to put everything off, put all the confrontations off, until everything explodes.' Scorsese adds that Charlie 'just waited too long so that everything blows up in his face.' He also acted 'very irrationally' in taking his friends 'out of town,' especially Teresa, whom he exposed to violence, which was the 'worst thing he could have done.'[83]

Mean Streets ends on a note of moral ambiguity and worldly realism characteristic of Scorsese. Charlie, a would-be Christian, however ambivalently, follows a course that only increases the final quotient of violence. Had he observed the local code, fewer people would have been injured and Johnny Boy would have learned his lesson all the sooner.[84] The film's realism derives partly from one's awareness that it is not Christian teachings, but Giovanni's intimidating and watchful presence, that affords the best guarantee of peace within the community. Yet by the time Charlie grasps this truth, it is useless to him.

6 The Abject God: *Raging Bull*

Probably the finest of Scorsese's films, *Raging Bull* is inspired by the identically titled autobiography of Jake La Motta, who reigned as middle-weight champion from 1949 to 1951. La Motta was born in New York's Lower East Side on 20 July 1921 to a Sicilian immigrant father who peddled goods for a living and an Italian American mother. The family moved to Philadelphia when he was six but ultimately settled in a Bronx slum. As a child and adolescent La Motta not only experienced the poverty, squalor, and misery of lower-class life but, like his brothers, was often beaten by his demanding and insensitive father, who encouraged him to fight for money. The young La Motta learned to steal and left school after the eighth grade. By the age of sixteen he was a juvenile delinquent and, by his own admission, had assaulted and robbed a neighbourhood bookie named Harry Gordon, whom he mistakenly believed himself to have killed. By this point La Motta had become friends with Peter Petrella (Savage), a small-time thug who later pursued his own boxing career and who through all the vicissitudes of their friendship remained loyal to La Motta, even helping him with his autobiography. The sixteen-year-old La Motta was sent to Coxsackie Reformatory for a term of one to three years as punishment for attempted burglary. While in reform school he renewed his friendship with fellow inmate Rocky Graziano, another middleweight champion of the 1940s; La Motta had known him previously on the Lower East Side, where they joined in acts of theft and sometimes fought each other, though remaining on good terms. After attempting to escape reform school, La Motta was placed for a period in special confinement. It was at this time that, encouraged by a priest named Father Joseph, he learned to box. After receiving early parole he began boxing as an amateur, and in 1941, not yet twenty years old, he won his first professional bout. His decision to become a professional boxer may have saved him from a life of crime.

La Motta was soon advancing in the middleweight division, although he often fought as a light heavyweight. During his long career he gained a reputation for toughness and stamina, for though not especially strong as a puncher, he had an incredibly strong chin and could take extraordinary amounts of punishment in order to gain a victory. He was also virtually impossible to knock down. La Motta's legendary rivalry with Sugar Ray Robinson, which extended to six bouts over nine years, began on 2 October 1942 when Robinson won a ten-round decision. On 8 February 1943 La Motta handed Robinson his first professional loss, knocking him down (through the ropes) for a nine-count. They fought four more times, culminating in the middleweight title match of 1951, with Robinson winning all four matches, of which three were extremely close. Some boxing experts think these three should have gone to La Motta.

Although La Motta's boxing ability was never in dispute, and although he willingly took on any opponent, he was long denied his shot at the title. This resulted from his refusal to cooperate with the mob, which, through its assigning and fixing of fights, could determine a fighter's career. Ultimately, La Motta was forced to compromise his integrity. As he later informed a Senate investigative committee, on 14 November 1947 with the connivance of Italian American gangsters he threw a fight to long shot Billy Fox, who 'won' a fourth-round technical knockout whose fraudulence was all too evident. According to La Motta, only through a fix would the mob guarantee him a championship bout. Following the fix, La Motta's doctor informed boxing authorities that he had fought with a ruptured spleen, which was stretching the truth, whereupon La Motta was fined a thousand dollars and barred from the ring for seven months for concealing an injury. On 16 June 1949 at Briggs Stadium in Detroit, La Motta defeated defending middleweight champion Marcel Cerdan of France in ten rounds by technical knockout. However, he was unseated by Robinson in Chicago Stadium on 14 February 1951. The fight was stopped in the thirteenth round, but only after La Motta had absorbed a superhuman beating without being knocked down.

Thereafter La Motta's career declined, partly because he was aging but also because of his difficulties in keeping down his weight, so that he sometimes fought as a light heavyweight. A sign of his career's approaching end came on 31 December 1952 in Coral Gables, Florida, when in the eighth round he was knocked down for the first time by Danny Nardico. In 1953, by which point La Motta and his family were living in Miami Beach, he was inactive as a boxer, and his attempted comeback in 1954 fizzled after three fights. His last bout was a ten-round loss to Billy Kilgore in Miami Beach on 14 April 1954. His career record was eighty-three victories, thirty by knockout; nineteen losses; and four draws.

La Motta's personal life rivals his boxing career in tumultuousness. His marriage at the age of twenty to a nineteen-year-old Bronx girl ended in divorce, without children. His next wife, known only as Vickie in his autobiography, was a beautiful blonde whom he wooed passionately yet came to suspect, unjustifiably and to the point of paranoia, of sexual betrayal. Their marital troubles were compounded by his sexual abstemiousness while training for fights and his frequent wife-beating. Their marriage, which produced three children, remained intact until the early 1950s, when the collapse of La Motta's personal life followed that of his boxing career. As owner of Jake La Motta's, a well-appointed nightclub and package store on Miami Beach, La Motta began to drink heavily and betrayed Vickie with numerous women. She sued for divorce and won custody of their children. Following his arrest on a morals charge, for having (probably unwittingly) allowed a fourteen-year-old prostitute to operate in his establishment, La Motta was sentenced to six months on a Florida chain gang.

During his isolation in the Dade County Stockade in 1957, La Motta experienced a self-illumination that enabled him to begin to come to terms with his colossal egotism and self-destructiveness. He resolved to regenerate his life. His helpmate at this time was Sally Carlton, a young woman whom he met in Miami and later married. Upon leaving jail, La Motta took up Rocky Graziano's suggestion that he perform, with Graziano, on Martha Raye's television comedy show. He subsequently appeared in plays in the Miami area and took acting lessons in New York City, followed by his participation in a movie and a road company tour of *Guys and Dolls*. Unfortunately, his testimony before the Kefauver Senate subcommittee in 1960, by which he hoped to contribute to the clean-up of boxing through his report of his participation in a fix, transformed him into a pariah for about six years. His finances nearly dried up and his marriage failed; but after 1966 La Motta recovered. Besides film appearances in *A House in Naples* (1969) and *The Cauliflower Cupids* (1970), he became a popular after-dinner speaker and nightclub performer – the 'George Jessel of the sports circuit.' Public attention focused on La Motta with the 1970 publication of his autobiography, *Raging Bull*, which garnered generally favourable reviews and continued to attract attention following Scorsese's interpretation of the book a decade later. La Motta's boxing career has been revaluated, and he is now recognized as one of the greatest middleweights. In 1987 he was inducted – with some reservations regarding his ethics – into the *Ring Magazine* Boxing Hall of Fame. Married six times by this point, La Motta has won permanent status as a minor celebrity.[1]

Scorsese credits Robert de Niro with alerting him to La Motta's autobiography, which he first read in California while completing *Alice Doesn't Live Here Anymore*. Though De Niro grasped its cinematic possibilities from the start, having on several occasions asked Scorsese to join him in transforming the book into a film, Scorsese lacked enthusiasm for the project, and it required a long 'personal crisis,' as he calls it, for him to see both its artistic potential and relevance to his own life.[2] During the late 1970s Scorsese entered a two-year period of wild partying and drug-taking, as a result of which his life and career disintegrated and he nearly died. The casualties included his marriage to Julia Cameron, whom he had wed in 1975. Scorsese attributes his deterioration partly to his depression over the failure of *New York, New York*, during the filming of which he was already taking drugs. He was also exhausted from overwork, as the completion of *New York, New York* coincided with that of his rock documentary *The Last Waltz*. Another factor, by his admission, was his arrested emotional development under a controlled upbringing, which prompted a belated quest for fun and thrills.[3]

Jamie Robbie Robertson, the lead guitarist for The Band, who had gone to Hollywood in hopes of becoming a film star, and who lived with Scorsese in Hollywood in these years and shared his lifestyle, joined with him in an increasingly reckless and self-destructive indulgence in sex, pills, cocaine, and alcohol. Their emotional cycles ran from megalomania to incapacity, abjection, and self-doubt: 'At first you felt you could make five films at once – then you were exhausted,' remarks Scorsese: 'It was a matter of pushing the envelope, of being bad, seeing how much you can do ... to see what it would be like getting close to death.'[4] The strain was aggravated by Scorsese's emotional immaturity, including his susceptibility to anger and even violence. As Peter Biskind writes, Scorsese was 'still extremely fragile' and 'easily hurt; he was quick to feel slighted and slow to forgive. He nursed grudges for years.

He built a wall around himself.' Scorsese himself recalls that 'I was always angry, throwing glasses, provoking people, really unpleasant to be around. I always found, no matter what anybody said, something to take offense at.'[5] Finally Scorsese's always delicate health succumbed to the pressure of his lifestyle. For much of late summer 1978 he was in bed unable to function, and by Labour Day he was in the hospital, where he suffered internal bleeding and nearly died from bad cocaine. Scorsese comments: 'I was pretty self-destructive. I was lucky to get out of it alive. I nearly died. But I did it; it's over.'[6]

The crucial phase of Scorsese's hospital convalescence was a four-day period of isolation during which he 'went through some kind of trans-formation.'[7] While in hospital he was visited by Robert De Niro, who again proposed to make La Motta's autobiography into a film. Whereas Scorsese had previously failed to identify with the subject, his masoch-istic brush with death now revealed its potential: 'I finally understood that for me I had found the hook – the self-destructiveness, the destruc-tion of people around you, just for the sake of it. I was Jake La Motta.'[8] Not only was Scorsese 'fascinated' by this 'side' of La Motta's character, as he terms it, but, to quote another interview, 'Jake La Motta, at least as he appears in the film ... allowed me to see more clearly.'[9] Indeed, 'I understood then what Jake was, but only after having gone through a similar experience myself.' He also understood that *Raging Bull* '[had] to be made,' partly as a means of comprehending his own ordeal, but also as a personal exorcism. 'I was just lucky,' he recalls, 'that there happened to be a project there for me ready to express this.'[10]

The original script of *Raging Bull* was supplied by Paul Schrader and Mardik Martin, but Scorsese and De Niro were dissatisfied with it, especially a scene written by Schrader in which the jailed La Motta soliloquizes to his penis while regretting his abuse of a multitude of sexual partners. As Scorsese and De Niro knew, the scene would guar-antee a commercially ruinous X-rating.[11] Yet like Schrader, Scorsese and De Niro in rewriting the script realized the necessity of modifying La Motta's autobiography: the 'real Jake had to be set off to the side.'[12] Not only is the book, as Dougan remarks, a 'rather self-serving piece' of self-justification, but it offers a simplistic explanation of La Motta's charac-ter and motivation extending back into his youth.[13] Nonetheless, *Raging Bull* contains powerful moments as well as extraordinary situations and characters. Scorsese perceived that, for all its shortcomings, it contained the seeds of a tighter, more profound creation.

Although La Motta admits that he 'never went to church,' he claims that, for all his pretended atheism, his mother's Catholicism had instilled in him a fear of punishment for his sins. He also mentions the support he received at key points in his life from Father Joseph. La Motta portrays himself as weighed down by sinfulness and driven to atone for his moral failings by absorbing inhuman amounts of punishment in the ring. As mentioned, for many years he feared that he had killed a bookie in a hold-up and that he would 'pay' for the killing. (Actually, the bookie survived to become a fan of La Motta's and astonished him by appearing in his dressing room after his championship.)[14]

Eliminating all references to La Motta's disadvantaged upbringing, and thus avoiding all simplistic and extenuating explanations for his behaviour, Scorsese makes La Motta's motivation and sense of guilt much more 'opaque' and 'diffuse' than in the autobiography.[15] The mother disappears (along with the father), and the Catholic moral atmosphere is only suggested. Father Joseph and the bookie are omitted, while Jake's guilt is detached from any event or individual so as to acquire a vague brooding presence suggestive of original sin. Scorsese's *Raging Bull* thus diverges from the book in refusing to be an 'apology and justification' for La Motta's life.[16] Yet perhaps Scorsese's most perceptive transformation of the novel was to give a prominent place to La Motta's brother. In the autobiography, Joey La Motta is little more than his brother's boxing manager, figuring peripherally in the narrative.[17] La Motta's closest friend, Peter Petrella, serves as a sounding board and commentator. Preceded by Martin and Schrader, Scorsese combined Joey and Petrella in the character of Joey La Motta, who figures as his brother's manager but also his confidante, sparring partner, spiritual adviser, and best friend. These distortions of La Motta's biography are justifiable aesthetically as a means of dramatic compression. They also bring out the Christian themes of fraternal love and hatred, since Scorsese regards La Motta as less a historical character than a moral exemplum.

Raging Bull stands out among Scorsese's films for its genre, subject matter, and style. His only work to qualify as a boxing film, it shows its awareness of its Hollywood precursors in its final scene, as La Motta recites Terry Molloy's speech from Elia Kazan's *On The Waterfront* (1954). Yet Scorsese resists generic clichés and conventions. Unlike those many boxing films which, combining brutality and sentimentality, portray a hard-nosed fighter who proves emotionally soft and likeable, often through the help of a tender-hearted woman whom he ultimately marries, Jake La Motta remains brutally hard nearly to the conclusion, abuses the woman who might redeem him, and never ingratiates himself with the audience. Whereas the clichéd hero's championship victory often coincides climactically with his worldly success, as in Robert Wise's *Somebody Up There Likes Me* (1956), based on the autobiography of Rocky Graziano, La Motta's life goes downhill immediately after he wins the middleweight championship, the quest for which nearly destroys him.[18] In Robert Rossen's *Body and Soul* (1947), Robert Wise's *The Set Up* (1949), and Mark Robson's *The Harder They Fall* (1956), demonic promoters and gangsters pressure boxers to fix fights and rob them of their earnings. Some cinematic boxers, like the Kirk Douglas character in *Champion*, are punished for their corruption, while others, like the characters played by Robert Ryan in *The Set Up* and John Garfield in *Body and Soul*, win moral victories.[19] Yet in *Raging Bull* La Motta throws a fight and wins his title only by doing so.[20] Nor does the film demonize gangsters, but portrays them in some respects as a helpful, pacifying force within the ethnic community.

Nonetheless, *Raging Bull* has little to do with boxing per se, in which Scorsese had no interest before making the film.[21] Nor is it simply a study of an aberrant and unappealing individual, or a disguised autobiography in which La Motta doubles for Scorsese. Besides investing boxing with religious associations, Scorsese treats it as a metaphor for life, the soul's struggle for redemption. La Motta's greatest success takes place outside the ring, in mastering his demons. Contrary to Pauline Kael's claim that Scorsese has sought universality and ended up with 'banality,' *Raging Bull* makes a universal statement on the psychology of violence.[22] As Scorsese says: 'to call it a boxing picture is ridiculous. It's sports but it's something to do with living. Jake La Motta takes on the aspects of everybody.'[23] Friedman correctly interprets La Motta as Everyman, quoting Scorsese's statement that 'the ring becomes an allegory of whatever you do in life.'[24]

Raging Bull resembles many of Scorsese's other films in its episodic structure, as it has little narrative continuity and almost no plot. He has also relied on both new and familiar means of achieving his characteristic combination of realism, expressionism, and stylization. The film has a documentary 'feel' at many points, achieved through black-and-white photography, the inclusion of Jake's home movies in colour, and the use of titles and actual dates. Scorsese chose black-and-white over colour when his good friend, the director Michael Powell, noted excess red in the boxing gloves.[25] David Denby remarks that the boxing scenes accentuate realism over atmosphere, since the flat and stark images lack the chiaroscuristic depth and mystery typical of forties boxing films.[26] Yet given that colour photography was standard for films by the late 1970s, the use of black-and-white implies stylization. The viewer experiences it as essentialism, recognizing that Scorsese 'leaches a life of distracting pigments to expose its essence.'[27] Stylization is prominent in the boxing scenes, which are shot almost entirely from within the ring, and each of which avoids formulization in being assigned its own distinctive form of presentation. Scorsese renders boxing as a solemn ceremony or ritual, with its own vocabulary of gestures, vestments, and paraphernalia. The energy and violence of boxing are sometimes expressed by means of 'even more movement than I normally have and a frenetic quality.'[28] There are deliberate violations of realism as Jake delivers and receives beatings beyond any fighter's capacity to withstand. In other instances realism is eschewed in favour of close-up slow-motion shots of the grotesquely distorted faces of fighters, such as Tony Janiro, as they absorb a barrage of dead-on punches. In the climactic bout the pace of the fight is reduced to a lingering slow-motion shot of Robinson as he prepares a right-hand overhand assault more reminiscent of cave-man tactics than modern boxing, while Jake, standing before the ropes, seems passively to invite punishment. The soundtrack in the boxing scenes consists of screams, grunts, and other animal noises that seem to emanate from a primeval jungle rather than the ring.[29]

The credits are accompanied by a shot of Jake La Motta on the left side of a boxing ring, as if trapped by the three dark and thin horizontals of the ropes in the foreground. Wearing his imitation leopard-skin robe, Jake shadowboxes before an audience that, barely visible in the smoky distance, calls to mind his imagined, phantom-like opponents. The appropriateness of the accompanying sound track, the intermezzo from Pietro Mascagni's *Cavalleria Rusticana*, which is based on the identically titled story by Giovanni Verga, lies in the close thematic connection between the opera and Scorsese's film, the former concerned with Sicilian villagers, the latter with their Italian American counterparts. The two share the theme of masculine honour or rustic chivalry, which the opera exemplifies in the climactic duel between Alfio and Turridu, the former fatally stabbing the latter in revenge for having been cuckolded. Jake's fears of betrayal by his wife similarly drive him to violence, though with neither justification nor lethal result. Dramatizing the clash between Catholicism and the Sicilian code of masculinity, Turridu's death at the hands of his rival occurs on Easter Sunday, the time of resurrection. *Cavalleria Rusticana* thus explores a Girardian theme dear to Scorsese, that of the 'holiday-gone-wrong,' undermined by violence born of mimetic rivalry. In similar fashion, Scorsese emphasizes the disparity between Jake's code of violent behaviour and the Christian ethos of fraternal compassion and forgiveness, which is most conspicuous in the film by its absence. Yet whereas the opera ends with Turridu's death, *Raging Bull* concludes with Jake La Motta's symbolic resurrection, if not redemption.

Following the credits, the scene switches to the Barbizon-Plaza Hotel. The year is 1964, and an older and much heavier La Motta, now a nightclub entertainer, appears in jacket and tie and with cigar in hand as he practises a comedy routine. Like the poverty of his monologue, which is doggerel throughout, his halting and ill-timed delivery suggests that he has yet to master his new profession, although he takes it seriously: 'I remember those cheers, they still ring in my ears, and for years they remain in my thoughts.' He goes on: 'And though I'm no Olivier, if he fought Sugar Ray, he would say, the thing ain't the ring it's the play. So give me a stage where this bull here can rage, and though I can fight I'd rather recite.' As we come to learn, La Motta has partly redeemed himself from a self-destructive and tumultuous past, upon which he now looks with detachment and thus a degree of freedom.

The remainder of the film shows that Jake had formerly lived among competing value systems, of which the most important is Catholicism with its icons, rituals, and priestly mediations. This is not to forget Joey's comment regarding the stubbornly self-absorbed Jake, that 'Jesus Christ could come off the cross sometimes and he don't give a fuck.' Nor is there anything to suggest that Jake or Joey attends church regularly, or that they or their friends hold priests in any special regard. Their attitude towards the clergy is suggested in the early scene filmed in Webster Hall, a ballroom popular among Italian Americans of those decades, where Joey, Jake, and their male co-ethnics encounter a local priest moving among the tables offering benediction. The irreverent question asked of him – 'Hey Father, wanna get laid?' – would not likely have been ventured at an Irish Catholic gathering. However, it is entirely credible coming from Italian American males, given the traditional irreverence towards priests carried over from southern Italy. And yet as Michel Henry rightly notes, the Catholic iconography of *Mean Streets* 'keeps popping up' in *Raging Bull*.[30] When Jake brings Vickie

(Cathy Moriarty) to his father and mother's apartment for the first time, their dining room is shown to contain an image of the Virgin Mary to the right and that of a dark-clad female saint to the left. The parents' bedroom also contains a statue of St Francis of Assisi in addition to the crucifix over the bed. A rosary is visible draped over the picture of Jake and Joey on their dresser. In the scene of Jake and Vickie's interrupted lovemaking in their urban apartment before the Robinson fight, there appears a representation of Christ to the left and another of the Virgin Mary to the right of the bathroom door. Subsequently in their suburban house a small crucifix is seen on the wall over Jake's and Vickie's bed, implying the sexual *askesis* he suffers there.

The image of the Virgin Mary is significant in that, like J.R. and Charlie Civello, Jake subscribes to the madonna-whore dichotomy, absolutely distinguishing between chaste and therefore marriageable women and mere 'broads,' that is, promiscuous women suitable only for casual and impersonal encounters.[31] This distinction is present in Jake's mind when he sees Vickie for the first time at the neighbourhood pool. In her association with water, a cleansing agent, and with her blonde hair radiating a halo-like light, Vickie embodies the feminine purity Jake is looking for. So strong is her impact upon him that, despite his own frequent use of profanity, Jake objects to his brother's foul language: 'Joey, how many times I gotta tell you? Why're you always cursin' when I'm talkin' to you? Don't do that around me.' It is as if Vickie had momentarily opened up Jake's awareness to a realm beyond the profane and the violent. When Jake, with his brother's help, speaks to Vickie for the first time, she addresses him through an ugly mesh fence; behind him is a local church, protected by iron railings. Scorsese implies a resemblance, though not an identity, between these two forms of sanctity, one erotic, the other spiritual, each requiring reverential distance, worship, difficulty, penance, and self-abnegation. On the other hand, the sexual betrayal Jake comes paranoically to suspect in Vickie is indicated by her fondness, after their marriage, for wearing turban-like hats of the type favoured on screen by Lana Turner, a classic forties femme fatale – headdresses that by their very shape suggest a serpentine or labyrinthine duplicity.[32] What Jake fails to see is the falsity of both images, negative and positive, which he has projected upon Vickie.

Reminiscent of *Who's That Knocking?* and *Mean Streets*, Jake's world is shaped by a masculine code centred in all-male peer groups where honour and *rispetto* are the highest values. These groups gather in gyms, social clubs, sporting arenas, and nightclubs. The man worthy of respect wants to produce the impression of autonomy and self-sufficiency so as to awaken in his audience both attraction and fear, akin to what one feels before the sacred. Normally such a person will quickly punish violations of his honour, including sexual betrayal. The male peer group is also a chief site, surpassed only by the family and church, for the reinforcement of the community's sexual values, including the madonna-whore dichotomy. As Joey says to Jake when he first sees Vickie: 'She's not a broad. You don't bang her and forget about her.' Yet for all their praise of chaste women, Jake and Joey have no compunction about betraying their wives. Over Joey's feeble objections, Jake unhesitatingly pursues Vickie while still married to his first wife, and later at his Miami nightclub he apparently consorts with women while Vickie stays home with the children. Likewise, Joey visits the Copacabana with a woman other than his wife. Yet curiously, in view of their esteem of the madonna type, the brothers concur that Vickie, like any woman, will engage in sex with any man if given the opportunity – a misogynistic prejudice consistent with traditional southern Italian male attitudes. Jake therefore watches Vickie closely, ultimately becoming so pathologically jealous that her own house seems to her a 'prison.' Her confinement is foreshadowed during Jake's and Vickie's initial visit to his parents' house, where he shows her an empty birdcage whose former occupant had died.

Given the male characters' misogyny, and their frequent congregating in the absence of women or with women assigned an accessory or decorative role, some critics assume a homosexual undercurrent in their behaviour. This interpretation consorts with the enraged accusations of Jake's first wife, who, as Jake and Joey depart in search of Vickie, denounces them publicly: 'Faggots! Queers!' Critics also note that, in greeting Jake at the Copacabana, the mobster Como kisses his cheek and puts his arm around him, and that Joey kisses his friend Salvy (Frank Vincent) on the cheek after their reconciliation at Como's club.[33] However, kissing among southern Italian males conventionally expresses affection and friendship. As in *Who's That Knocking?*, the all-male peer groups in *Raging Bull* are homophilic rather than homosexual.[34]

This survey of Jake's world cannot omit the Italian American gangsters of the neighbourhood, who supplement and even compete with the local priests. Centred in the Debonair Social Club, where its members converse, drink coffee, sip liqueurs, and play cards, this peer group consists of the *capo* Tommy Como, his assistant Salvy, and underlings.

These criminals prey parasitically upon the surrounding society and their Italian American neighbours, offering or withholding protection and other privileges. And yet, as in *Mean Streets*, they may well surpass the local priests in preserving peace and order. For if the task of the priest is to promote Christian ethics, the gangsters in their own fashion maintain the well-being of the community by limiting transgressive violence within it. Their local activities include helping and protecting residents, mediating disputes, and settling grudges, lest violence proliferate. Commenting on Jake's defeat under the unfamiliar Ohio points system, Salvy tells Joey that if 'Tommy [Como] had been there, this wouldn't have happened.' When Salvy leaves a local gym, he pauses to address an old and infirm Italian American man who sits against a wall. 'How's your wife?' asks Salvy: 'Listen, anybody bothers you let me know.' Tommy Como similarly intervenes to patch up the quarrel between Joey and Salvy, which had led to an embarrassing brawl at the Copacabana.[35]

Accustomed to influencing local affairs, the mob encounters a special problem in Jake La Motta. Intending to succeed entirely on his own, he refuses, at least initially, to comply with its demand that he throw a fight. The parodic analogy between priests and gangsters is patent. As a priest would 'deliver' a soul to God, so Tommy Como informs Joey, as Jake's manager, that unless Jake throws a fight Tommy will never 'deliver' him a shot at the championship, which Jake views as the earthly equivalent of salvation. The irony is partly that Jake's championship victory, the worldly prize he overvalues, precedes rather than coincides with his self-regeneration, in which the mob plays no part.

The film invests boxing, and Jake's all-consuming commitment to it, with a quasi-ritualistic significance. Anthropologically, the origins of boxing may be traced to the sacrificial crisis, which is both recalled and disguised in the 'rituals' of boxing and other sports. Born of acquisitive mimesis and mimetic rivalry, the sacrificial crisis exhibits the ever-increasing spread of retaliatory and random violence throughout society, so that no person or thing is safe, and the whole social order is threatened with undifferentiation. At the climax of the crisis, the collective murder of the scapegoat victim returns society to peace and order. Originating in this phase of recovery, ritual commemorates the sacrificial crisis in a disguised and controlled mimetic form, so as to re-enact safely the community's renewal. In boxing, the match occurs within a 'sacred area' accessible only to the boxers and to officials, who play a priest-like role. Stripped down and equipped for combat, the oppo-

nents recall the mimetic doubles of the sacrificial crisis, in which reciprocal violence plunges society into the chaos for which the scapegoat is
the only remedy. Yet far from being a free-for-all, a boxing match
proceeds 'ritualistically' in a contained fashion, with definite rules and
at regular intervals called rounds. As rituals and festivals incorporate
elements of chance, so as to represent the random violence of the crisis
and the surprise of its resolution, so in boxing prizes are arbitrary and
the action inspires rampant betting.[36]

In *Raging Bull* Scorsese links boxing with Catholic ritual through
Catholic analogism. The vestments Jake wears in performing the rite of
boxing include a robe resembling a monk's hood and cassock. The long
Steadicam shot that follows Jake and his entourage from his dressing
room into the ring on the night of his championship victory calls to
mind a priestly procession from aisle to altar. During one fight Jake's
trainer makes hand gestures like those of the priest who had blessed
Jake's table at a church dance. His trainers resemble priests as they
sponge down his bloodied body between rounds – a mingling of water
and blood with Christian overtones. Jake's mouthpiece, as Tomasulo
notes, is offered to him as if it were a Communion wafer.[37] Commenting
on Jake's final match with Robinson, Scorsese remarks that the 'trainer
was putting vaseline onto Jake's face, but it looked like some sort of
blessing almost. It looked as if this guy was anointed to be sacrificed.'[38]
At the conclusion of the bout, the decision is accompanied by a shot of
the ropes where Jake has undergone his agony. They drip with his
blood, each drop resembling a rosary bead. Scorsese, who says of Jake
that he sees boxing as a 'religious ritual' and who refers to his 'martyrdom' and 'body that they're preparing for the sacrifice,' parallels Jake
and Christ. Yet in noting that Jake uses Robinson 'to punish himself,'
Scorsese raises the question to what extent Jake adheres to a masochistic conception of Catholicism, with God and Christ as his torturers and
himself as their victim.[39]

A further resemblance between Catholic ritual and boxing is that, just
as the former fails to prevent domestic and underworld violence in
Little Italy, so boxing fails to confine violence to the restricted, ritualized, and 'sacred' space of the ring. This is evident in the crowd's
dissatisfaction after Jake's loss of his first fight. Although he has knocked
down Jimmy Reeves twice in the final round, Jakes loses in accordance
with Ohio Boxing Commission rules, as he had needed a knockout.
Already during the fight a woman had screamed in response to the
sudden outbreak of a fight between two male spectators. Upon the

announcement of the decision, the mainly pro-Jake audience erupts in anger. Chairs and popcorn are thrown into the ring in disregard of the demarcation between the properly segregated realms of violence and non-violence. Hoping to reverse the decision, Jake flings his totemic robe to the crowd so as to incite it to protest in his favour. This act similarly collapses the distinction between the interior space of the ring where violence is permitted and the exterior space in which it is forbidden. A woman in the audience is trampled, while supporters of Jake and Reeves pummel each other in both the stands and the ring itself, which has become chaos. People are even thrown from the ring into the stands, and the police are powerless to stop the all-engulfing brawl. Struggling to appear unruffled at the centre of the ring, the tuxedoed master of ceremonies orders the organist to play the national anthem in the futile hope that this 'sacred' affirmation of national solidarity will restore harmony to the arena.[40]

Boxing rituals are equally ineffective in preventing violence from spilling over into Jake's domestic life, where, as in the ring, he is as destructive to others as to himself. In an early scene, Jake and his first wife enter into a nasty argument because of an overcooked steak. At the height of his career, Jake customarily abuses his wife verbally, and in one instance allows himself not simply to slap her but to beat her with his fists. Nor is Joey's household free of violence. Immediately before Jake beats him up on suspicion of adultery with Vickie, Joey tells his son at the dinner table: 'If you put your hands in that plate one more time, I'm gonna stab you with this fork.' The general mood of everyday violence is accentuated by the characters' casual profanity, their speech being punctuated constantly with 'shit' and 'fuck,' and even more so by the recurrent identification of human beings with animals, which portends violence. Properly, the loss of this distinction between species should be permitted only within the ring, where contestants may freely exhibit the inhuman brutality that Scorsese accentuates through animal noises on the soundtrack. Yet such inhumanity extends beyond the ring, for as Stanley Kaufman puts it, *Raging Bull* is 'like visiting a human zoo.'[41] Salvy regards Jake as a 'gorilla.' In demanding a bloody steak Jake sounds like a predatory beast, and not for nothing is he called the 'Bronx Bull.' When a neighbour objects to Jake's noisy argument with his first wife, shouting, 'What's the matter with you out there, you animals?' Jake responds with: 'I'm gonna eat your dog for lunch.' To this the neighbour retorts, 'Crazy animal,' whereupon Jake threatens animal sacrifice: 'You're gonna find your fuckin' dog dead in the doorway.' When Jake deems Joey unworthy of the radiant Vickie, he calls him an animal. Vickie in turn calls Jake a 'sick animal' when he accuses her of adultery with Joey. And in the film's crucial moment, Jake cries out in his jail cell: 'I am not an animal!'

Jake La Motta seems colossally enigmatic. A mystery surrounds his nearly psychopathic indifference to other beings, sadomasochistic violence, obsession with boxing rivals, self-hatred and abjection, sexual paranoia, physical abuse of his wife and brother, and the guilt his own behaviour induces in him. La Motta's character has called forth various interpretations, including those of critics who see Jake's behaviour as inexplicable, and of others who regard Scorsese's apparent failure to explain that behaviour as a thematic and aesthetic flaw. David Denby objects that 'we never do discover why Jake is such a surly crumb-bum,' adding that, whereas La Motta's autobiography reveals the causes of his behaviour, 'the mean obsessive Jake' of the film 'isn't given a past or any particular motives, drives, ideas.' Robert Hatch remarks that 'no one concerned with the picture ... attempts to explain Jake La Motta, and that may be felt as a lack.' Gary Arnold finds hardly a 'trace of a sustained motive' in Jake's actions, except that his wife's beauty feeds his jealousy, although this 'can't explain where La Motta's aggression originated and why he began boxing.'[42]

Other critics think it a mistake to seek explanations for Jake's behaviour, since Scorsese typically portrays character as fundamentally mysterious. As David Friedkin remarks, the film refuses the typical Hollywood 'explanatory approach to character.'[43] To quote Kolker: 'In none of his films will Scorsese opt for the psychological realism of explained actions, defined motivations, or identifiable characters.' Preferring lack of clarification to facile analyses, Andrew Sarris observes: 'There are no glib rationales – Freudian, Marxist, Gothic, or whatever – for La Motta's self-debasement.' According to Louis Menand, Jake resists 'traditional modes of explanation,' while, except for his paranoid fantasy of Vickie's infidelity, the film implies no 'motivating cause for Jake's violent behaviour.'[44] That Scorsese aimed for such an impression is suggested by his interview with Michel Henry, who notes that, in contrast with the autobiography, the film omits La Motta's youth and thus, through the removal of all apparently 'extenuating circumstances,' affords no clear explanation for his guilt. Concurring with Henry, Scorsese describes Jake's guilt as 'part and parcel' of his character from birth. Nor does Scorsese challenge Henry's point that 'Jake's environment doesn't really explain his character' and that 'there's something irreducible, which escapes analysis, that interests' the director.[45]

Other critics suppose that a simple explanation exists for Jake's behaviour but that Scorsese perversely withholds it. For Richard Coombs, the autobiography contains the key to Jake's brutality.[46] Commenting on the characters' lack of illumination, Arnold laments the absence of sufficient biographical information, including the influence of 'Mom and Pop La Motta.' Ronald Bergan complains that *Raging Bull* is 'virtually an anti-biopic, [which] ... tells us nothing of ... [Jake's] past.' Kathleen Carroll faults Scorsese for ignoring Jake's reform-school background, which she implies explains his antisocial behaviour.[47]

Must one agree with Kolker on the impossibility of any deep understanding of Jake La Motta? Kolker is excessively sceptical, ignoring the ethnic elements in Jake's behaviour. This is not to challenge Stanley Kaufman's claim that Jake is more than simply 'reactive to the Italian American atmosphere' in which he lives; yet Kaufman goes too far in claiming that the script would have been exactly the same in another ethnic context – a statement ignoring the extent to which Italian American views of masculinity, sexuality, and religion shape Jake's attitudes and behaviour.[48] Kolker also discounts the influence of Catholicism upon not only Jake but the main characters of Scorsese's earlier Italian American films. 'If his often commented-upon Catholicism does appear in his work,' claims Kolker, 'it is in the form of a purgatorial sense of his characters' serving in the world, not looking for grace.'[49] Lawrence Friedman claims similarly that Jake shows 'no discernible imprint' of Catholicism.[50] Neither critic's judgment can stand the test of the evidence. Other critics seek a deeper answer to Jake's character and motivation but adopt a mistaken approach, by either inculpating Jake's Catholic background or attempting to understand him in Freudian terms.

In Gerald Early's view, Jake's troubles derive from a bad father, while his violence targets father-surrogates. Reminiscent of Bliss's attempt to attribute J.R.'s miseries in *Who's That Knocking?* to a life-denying, punitive Catholicism, Brode writes that 'it is as if ... [Jake] had entered the ring in part because of some self-loathing, coupled with guilt and a basic sense of worthlessness growing out of his Catholic-inspired ideals.' A *Variety* reviewer observes that Scorsese and his screenwriters portray 'an extreme form of Catholic masochism.' There follows a Freudian interpretation implicating Catholic-based sexual repression: 'La Motta's violence toward himself and other people seems to stem from the deep repression of his sexual tendencies,' while 'all of the unsatisfactory encounters between [Jake and Vickie] ... take place underneath prominently displayed crucifixes and religious paintings, providing a pervasive feeling of guilt and frustration.'[51]

The most strenuously argued explanation for Jake's behaviour locates his sadomasochism and paranoia in repressed homoerotic impulses of which boxing is alleged to provide the most typical sporting expression. Joyce Carol Oates's *On Boxing* conforms with the ideas of those critics who – sometimes relying on Oates – argue for Jake La Motta's homoeroticism. For her, 'no sport appears more powerfully homoerotic' than boxing, with its 'sweaty heated combat that is part dance, courtship, coupling' and the 'frequent urgent pursuit by one boxer of the other in the fight's natural and violent movement toward the "knockout."' She goes on: 'Surely boxing derives much of its appeal from this mimicry of a species of erotic love in which one man overcomes the other in an exhibition of superior strength and will.' Likewise, the 'heralded celibacy of the fighter-in-training' requires that, 'instead of focusing his energies on and fantasies upon a woman,' he concentrate them 'upon an opponent.' Accordingly, Oates modifies a passage from Freud's *Ego and the Id*: 'Where Woman has been, opponent must be.' Oates quotes boxing manager Bundini Brown, who equates a boxing performance with the ability to maintain an erection as well as to achieve a timely ejaculation. She also claims that the public embrace of two contestants at the climax of a match affords the only admissible expression of their 'passion.' Although Oates mentions La Motta's autobiography and Scorsese's rendition of it, she treats not La Motta's sexuality but his guilty masochism in the ring; yet she probably expects us to see these as masking homosexual impulses.[52]

Such an overstimulated interpretation necessitates a return to balance and proportion through respect for the evidence. That boxing, like sex, generates much sweat and heat does not imply a close resemblance between the two activities. The exertions of boxing could produce no other result. Similarly, that a beautiful woman is called a 'knockout' does not justify an intimate identification of boxing with sex, and would seem so only to those who take metaphors for realities and think not by logic but by association. Although beautiful women are also known as 'bombshells,' no one seriously imagines ballistics or pyrotechnics to have any deeply relevant connection with them. By the same token, to refer to a beautiful woman as a 'dish' only remotely identifies her with cooking or gastronomy. When Bundini Brown parallels boxing and sex, he means not that both activities are erotic, but that they both require skill, patience, and stamina. If, as some contend, boxing is the 'meta-sport,' revealing energies and motivations other sports exhibit only when their discipline breaks down, then part of this revelation lies in the boxers' near-nakedness, accenting not their eroticism but their ferocity.[53] That a prizefighter avoids sex before a match does not normally imply his expectation of a sublimated sexual encounter with a male opponent, a dubious notion frequent in writings on *Raging Bull*. Rather, the practice derives from the notion that physical strength resides in the seminal substance, and that a boxer requires maximum energy and power during a fight.[54] The fighter thus sacrifices sexual gratification for the greater ego-satisfaction of victory. This is usually done under economic (hence rational) incentives, as most professional boxers derive from disadvantaged minorities.

Were Oates's theory correct, most boxers would be either homosexuals or latent homosexuals. In the absence of statistical evidence, the very notion violates probability and common sense. Based on his own experience among amateurs in a gym, Lawrence de Garis characterizes that site as not a homosexual but a homosocial environment where the object is 'somatic' rather than sexual intimacy.[55] For Michael Messner, boxing promotes not emotional closeness but aggression, domination, and the destruction of bodies. The boxer's desire to impose his will prohibits emotional reciprocity.[56] Noting that professional boxers routinely insist that they fight for money, Ronald Levao quotes Mike Weaver's statement that 'there's nothing to love about being hit in the head.'[57] Like many boxers, Roberto Duran never befriended an opponent before a fight, but fueled his own antagonism.[58] And to quote George Garrett, 'most of the fighters I knew were wounded people who felt a deep, powerful urge to wound others at real risk to themselves.'[59] Weaver's and Garrett's statements weaken Oates's claim that boxing has more to do with masochism than sadism. Few boxers, save Jake La Motta and his type, want to be hit, as this can hardly prolong a career; yet a boxer must risk being hit to land punches effectively. Since a good boxer knows how to slip punches, he is usually identifiable by the relative lack of permanent marks on his face and body.

Nonetheless, critics argue not only for the homoeroticism of boxing but for latent homosexuality as the source of La Motta's violence and sexual miseries. Paul Schrader, who succeeded Mardik Martin as the scenarist of *Raging Bull*, was perhaps the first to call attention to this supposed homosexual thematic, remarking the 'hidden sexual bond between the brothers.'[60] This kind of argument was extended by Robin Wood in *Hollywood from Vietnam to Reagan*. A proponent of the Freudian theory of original and instinctive bisexuality, and certain of gay liberation as the answer to gender construction under a repressive patriarchal civilization, Wood looks forward to the 'liberation of heterosexuals' into homosexuality (or bisexuality) while reading *Raging Bull* as an 'eloquent sermon on the urgency of such a project.' Jake's repressed homosexuality supposedly feeds the film's 'relentless and near hysterical intensity,' while Jake's homophobia and that of the other characters is explicable *only* psychologically, as the hatred of one's own homosexual instincts. Far from loving Vickie, Jake embraces a plastic image of femininity modelled on Lana Turner. As the director of his home movies, which, being in colour, contrast with the film's black-and-white realism, Jake constructs a fantasy image of himself as the happily married heterosexual patriarch. Yet the reality of Jake, says Wood, is that of a repressed homosexual whose instincts appear only in the displaced form of attacks on rival boxers and in his paranoid preoccupation with Vickie's presumed admirers. Wood follows the Freudian line that paranoid delusions originate in repressed homosexuality. However, he believes that Jake's original and strongest homosexual desire is for his brother Joey, a passion he claims to be intensified by the intimacy of the Italian family – the only instance where Wood resorts not to Freud but to ethnology. Having denied his sexual love for Joey by assaulting him, Jake attempts to make up for this in the parking garage, showering Joey with kisses in belated recognition of his own homosexuality. Regarding the theme of Christian 'grace,' which is suggested during Jake's solitary confinement, Wood sees it as secondary to the film's concerns, outweighed by the pointless unredeemed pain of Jake's sexual behaviour. Wood is therefore pleased to report that, in conversation with him, the director belatedly recognized the presence of a 'homosexual subtext,' as Scorsese calls it, in *Raging Bull*.[61]

Later critics have extended Wood's arguments. Drawing upon Freud, Michael S. Kimmel characterizes boxing as 'transformed homoerotic passion, fusing gendered rage and the sexualized terrors of being dominated,' and in which more bodily fluids are exchanged than in any homosexual act. Although Jake attacks boxing opponent Tony Janiro in 'an orgy of displaced homoerotic rage,' he unconsciously evokes the 'erotic equation of boxing and sex' through his 'homophobic displacement of homoeroticism,' as Janiro's body 'becomes the mechanism to purge the body of its own homoerotic desires.'[62]

Commenting that the 'nature of Jake's conflict is never specifically addressed in the film,' David Friedkin finds a clue in the slow-motion scenes that, shot from Jake's point of view, show Vickie's image occluded by his presumed sexual rivals. For Friedkin, this indicates unconscious sexual fascination with her male admirers. Jake's hostility towards rivals, like his need to imagine Vickie with other men, indicates repressed homosexuality. Homoerotic anxiety also appears in Jake's comedy routine, in which he mentions his dream of appearing in the ring without boxing shorts, while Jake's complaint of having 'little girl's hands' reveals his fear of his own femininity. Thus, to prove his toughness, he orders Joey to punch him, and when Joey refuses Jake calls him 'faggot.' When Joey punches Jake feebly, Jake insults him: 'You throw a punch like you take it up the ass.' Yet in telling Salvy to 'go fuck yourself,' claims Friedkin, Joey also shows repressed sexual affection. While Jake and Joey spar in the gym, Salvy's gangster associate remarks perceptively that 'they look like two fags up there'; later, as the brothers leave for the dance hall, Jake's wife rightly calls them 'faggots and queers.' For Friedkin, Jake's homoeroticism is founded on his relationship to his brother, so that the kisses and embraces of their belated reunion not only resemble boy-girl 'necking' but reveal their long-hidden sexual bond.[63]

Friedman's reading of the sexual themes of *Raging Bull* fuses the ideas of Schrader, Oates, Wood, and Friedkin. Convinced that the film contains a 'homosexual subtext,' Friedman isolates Jake's perplexity in not knowing whether to 'fuck or fight' Janiro as possibly 'one of those all-too-revealing Freudian slips.' By the same token, boxing and sex 'conflate' in the Janiro fight, where Jake 'imprints his homoerotic desires on his opponent's body.' Jake's sexual failure with Vickie, like his worries over his 'little girl's hands,' indicate homosexual repression. Friedman accepts not only Wood's argument that Jake directs his home movies to verify his heterosexuality, but Wood's and Friedkin's view of Joey as the original object of Jake's desire. 'It was Jake's own unresolved sexual conflicts that contributed to the formation of his obsessively jealous, violent, and self-destructive nature,' says Friedman, while the resolution of those conflicts 'is prefigured in the kiss he gives Joey.'[64]

The same objections invited by Wood's essay apply to those of his successors. Scorsese's acknowledgment of a homosexual subtext does not mean that he accepts the dubious notion that Jake is a repressed homosexual in love with his brother. If Jake's acceptance of his supposed homosexuality were enough to resolve his problems, one would expect him to proclaim himself a homosexual at the conclusion. Yet the ending suggests that he has experienced something like a Christian redemption, in which homosexuality plays no role. Like other critics, Wood has little understanding of Italian America and fails to comprehend how its homophilic social patterns often produce a false impression of homosexual behaviour.[65] He denatures *Raging Bull*, transforming it into a gay liberation tract; and he does so through hackneyed and all-too-obvious Freudian interpretations along with the whole tired apparatus of repression and the Freudian conception of the unconscious, notions rejected by many psychologists and whose very existence remains unproven.[66] As for the contention that *Raging Bull* offers a 'sermon' for gay liberation, Scorsese never indulges in cinematic sermons, except perhaps in *The Last Temptation of Christ*, arguably his most muddled film; the very idea of a sermon implies the sacrifice of art to propaganda. Were *Raging Bull* a sermon supporting homosexuality, it would lose its organic unity as a work of art, since this theme is impossible to integrate not only with the film's Christian concerns but with its concluding New Testament passage – the nearest thing to a sermon in the entire film. Since Wood, as a Freudian, apparently regards religion as a mere derivative of repressed instinct, and since *Raging Bull* interests him mainly as propaganda, such a lack of artistic unity is not likely to trouble him. Nonetheless, the recovery of the unity of *Raging Bull* demands a reading that subsumes its sexual under its religious themes, as it is obvious that, for Scorsese, the former can neither encompass nor explain the latter. More precisely, what is needed is an interpretation of Jake's behaviour that, as it accounts for his sexual paranoia and masochism, avoids reducing them to repressed instinct, but reveals their spiritual dimension while connecting them with the film's religious concerns.

In life as in boxing, Jake oscillates between two behavioural poles: divine presumption and sadism on the one hand and masochistic abjection on the other. In the first case he claims what he regards, whether consciously or not, as the equivalent of god-like status as manifest in repeated demonstrations of self-sufficiency, inner plenitude, and violent mastery over others. This is not to say that Jake lacks human needs or a desire for compassion, for in the interrupted sex scene with Vickie he reveals his vulnerability in asking her, almost as a child to its mother, not only to touch his wounds but to give him a 'boo-boo kiss.' But Jake rejects these feelings, and normally responds to others mistrustfully.[67] This attitude arises from his fear not only of being exploited but of revealing his vulnerability. Accordingly, Jake combines distrust of others with a compensatory desire to awaken in them an overwhelming fear of the physical and psychological violence of which he is capable. His behaviour thus demonically parodies the Johannine formula that love casts out fear; for Jake, fear casts out love. He aims to create for others a terrifying impression of predominance through his remoteness from normal human need and compassion as in his ability to punish all rivals and obstacles. According to Hemmeter and Hemmeter, the scenes of Jake in the ring 'suggest that he sees himself as a man with a divine mission' – although they fail to clarify what that might be.[68] What Jake embodies is the perennial human desire to achieve that complete autonomy which, in its fearful power, remoteness, and indifference to human beings and desires, pagan and secular religions identify as divine. Seeking to become an invulnerable monolith, the ultimate 'big shot,' Jake pursues spiritual transcendence not through the selfless charity of the *Imitatio*, but through the exultant transport of megalomaniac conquest in the ring. He would be the favoured one of the gods, the last one standing when all others have fallen.[69] He imagines that in defeating all opponents he will guarantee his god-like status in the form of total independence from other people. This explains Jake's sadistic streak, antisocial behaviour, adamantine stubbornness, and hostility to mediators, whether gangsters, Catholic priests, or Jesus Christ.

Jake's behaviour carries to an extreme features of the southern Italian (and therefore to some extent Italian American) ideal of masculinity as manifest in the very gangsters he despises. As we have seen, the ideal southern Italian male cultivates an image of impassive and silent self-possession as a means of winning that *rispetto* which combines attraction and fear – the sacred. Not only does he remain detached from others' affairs, but others tremble to approach him too closely, knowing that violations of *rispetto* will elicit punishing retaliation. Yet southern Italian and Italian American males, even gangsters, normally pursue such behaviour within a community where they have their assigned niche and whose personal and institutional sanctities they more or less respect. Nor are they unwilling to trust and cooperate with some members of their group, whatever their suspicions towards mainstream society. What makes Jake so unusual is his pathological isolation from and indifference to others, the distance he sets between himself and them, his paranoid distrust even of intimates, and, not least, his abnormal readiness to retaliate against insults imagined or otherwise.

The most striking sign of Jake's desire for autonomy, and of his indifference to others, is Joey's remark to Tommy Como that 'Jesus Christ could come off the cross sometimes and he don't give a fuck.'[70] Joey had previously told Salvy that Jake 'wants to do things for himself' and that it is impossible to 'talk' to him. Nonetheless, Salvy urges Joey to persuade Jake to negotiate with Tommy for the sake of his career, adding that if Joey cannot communicate with his brother, no one can. This forecasts Jake's ultimate break with Joey, marking the onset of his professional and personal decline. Subsequently Salvy and several gangsters appear at Jake's gym to determine his willingness to accept Tommy's patronage. Immediately arousing Jake's displeasure, the gangsters leave the gym, whereupon Jake bitterly assaults his brother, who doubles as his sparring partner: 'They'll take my money. Don't ever send them up here again.' Jake's refusal of help or concern extends to his wife, who angers him by offering useful advice regarding his bout with Janiro. 'She was talkin' on your behalf,' says Joey, but Jake ignores him. In another scene,[71] a sit-down meeting with Tommy Como at the Debonair Social Club, Joey says that Jake 'doesn't even say hello to anybody,' adding that he 'likes to do it his own way.' Or as Tommy puts it, he has a 'head of rock.' As Tommy realizes, in refusing help Jake makes it needlessly 'hard on himself,' so that here, in contradiction to Jake's proud desire for brutal mastery, one glimpses that masochistic self-destructiveness, that desire to find and invent obstacles, which is the other side of his pathology.

His problem, though, encompasses more than excessive self-reliance and stubbornness, for when Joey assures Tommy of Jake's respect, the gangster rightly denies it: 'He's got no respect. He respects nobody.'[72] This is as true for Jake's wife and brother as it is for Christ. In part a hubristic disregard for social limits and hierarchies, Jake's lack of respect reveals itself in his ambition to fight Joe Louis, adding: 'I'm better than him.' Reminding Jake that he and the heavyweight Louis fight in mutually exclusive weight classes, Joey issues a caution: 'You're crazy to think like that. It's not normal. You'll go crazy.' Yet woe betide those who deny Jake the respect he feels he deserves. When Vickie innocently allows Tommy Como to kiss her, Jake threatens: 'You don't ever have disrespect for me.' When Joey comes to her defence, Jake says: 'I'm disgusted with the both of yuz,' slamming his bedroom door behind him. As the camera lingers briefly on the shut door, white, flat, and blank, one senses the isolation into which Jake's egoism leads him.

Understandably, Tommy Como and other local gangsters resent Jake's refusal of respect. Not only does he avoid them at nightclubs, barely acknowledging them at the Copacabana until he receives Tommy's summons, but they take offence that Jake, a neighbourhood boxer, thinks he can win the middleweight championship entirely on his own. Jake has 'become an embarrassment,' Tommy tells Joey: 'I'm lookin' very bad. I can't deliver a kid from my own neighbourhood.' Thus, partly as a show of power Tommy forces Jake to throw a fight in exchange for the title shot. From this perspective the mob may seem only criminally self-interested, as in those many films depicting the boxer's struggle against its corrupting influence. The local gangsters may also appear cast in a role contrary to that of local priests, as false mediators of salvation – the boxing title – portrayed in a mode of analogical parody. Immediately after throwing the fight, Jake weeps in his dressing room over this deep but unavoidable wound to his integrity.

Nonetheless, as self-serving as Tommy Como may be in dealing with Jake, the moral complexity of *Raging Bull* requires recognition that the mob, for all its evil, also promotes order, helpfulness, and respect within the community it dominates. The mob not only looks out for old people but settles quarrels between younger men such as Joey and Salvy. Despite their desire to exploit Jake criminally, Tommy Como and the mob regard him as a neighbourhood hero and sincerely desire his success. Paying his respects to Jake at his gym, Salvy compliments him: 'You're lookin' good, Jake'; and later at the Copacabana Tommy Como sends drinks to Jake's table in a gesture combining self-interest with real admiration and support. Subsequently Tommy and other well-wishers arrive at Jake's hotel just before his first championship bout, once again combining self-interest, as they have bet on Jake, with sincere encouragement. Jake's grief over throwing a fight, which from one point of view seems to express wounded integrity, may also reflect his wounded pride and vanity over his being forced into dependence upon other persons. Whatever its mixed motives, the mob can teach Jake the value of *rispetto* in the sense of a community standard of behaviour outside the autonomous god-like self. That gangsters provide such instruction does not discredit the lesson taught, since, from the Catholic viewpoint, it does not require priests to be communicated but can be understood from even parodic analogies.[73]

For all his titanic hubris and pretentions to autonomy, Jake suffers feelings of abjection that no project of godhood can appease or overcome. Not potency or plenitude but a deep-rooted sense of ontological deprivation fuels his desire for god-like victory and the masochism it entails. Jake's fears of personal inadequacy appear in an irrational complaint that reveals both a physical and spiritual lack: he laments the 'little girl's' hands that prevent him from fighting Joe Louis, no matter how 'big' he becomes.[74] He is thus depressed to think of an unassailable opponent beyond his 'degree.' Although Lourdeaux argues that such self-destructive thinking results from Jake's hunger for mainstream success, this fails to explain why his life falls apart after his championship victory.[75] His chronic sense of inner emptiness makes it impossible for him to enjoy limited triumph, however substantial. Scorsese subtly suggests the anticlimactic self-dissatisfaction Jake feels even upon winning the championship by recording a key detail of that moment when, after his victory, he is adorned with his championship belt. The tall black man who enters the ring to congratulate Jake, even being photographed beside him, is none other than Joe Louis, who was present that night at Briggs Stadium and whom La Motta sees in imagination as his ultimate rival. Louis's presence at this moment could only remind Jake of the insufficiency of his success as middleweight champion and the impossibility of fulfilling his ever-demanding ego-ideal.

Contrary to the autonomy and self-sufficiency Jake seeks to project, his impoverished sense of being reduces him to dependence upon the desires of his boxing audience and rivals. On the one hand, he wants to satisfy the sadistic appetites of the crowd, whose approval carries the promise of escape from self-detestation into success.[76] Yet Jake's desire to surmount his ontological insecurity also leads him into mimetic rivalries with his boxing opponents, with whom he engages in retaliatory and hence imitative cycles of violence in quest of a shared object of desire, namely the middleweight championship. These rivalries become Jake's all-consuming obsession, dominating his life and only intensifying his abjection as they drive him into self-destructiveness that a rational person would avoid.

The inevitable result of Jake's abjection, and a career devoted to obsessive-compulsive mimetic rivalry, is a masochistic syndrome of ascetic life-denial. He gradually rejects love, sex, and pleasure through an increasing preoccupation with his rivals. Some critics, as mentioned above, hold that his sexual *askesis* indicates latent homoeroticism focused on his male boxing opponents, yet the scene of Jake's and Vickie's interrupted lovemaking indicates that, at this point at least, he is interested in and capable of heterosexual activity. Nonetheless, he forces himself to resist desire because two other motives – self-punishing abasement and egoistic desire for prepotency – have totally focused his mental and physical energies upon the upcoming fight with Robinson, his chief rival.[77]

The longer Jake remains in the fighting game, the more anhedonic and life denying he becomes. In her initial appearance, Vickie is identified with water, the life-giving substance, and subsequently Jake and Vickie enjoy glasses of water at Jake's parents' apartment. At this point he is only an up-and-coming fighter, while the drinking of water, besides being required by his training regimen, suggests the purity of his and Vickie's romance, which is about to ensue. Likewise, in Jake's home movies the happiness of his domestic life is suggested in the shot of Vickie throwing him into the swimming pool.[78] However, in a preceding scene Jake had poured ice over his genitals in order to suppress his sexual desire for Vickie, on the eve of his fight with Robinson. After he loses the fight he plunges his fist into a bucket of ice. Water's fluid and life-giving freshness are becoming ice-hard, also betokening Jake's increasing coldness towards Vickie as well as his sadistic insensitivity towards his ring opponents. A further indication of his changing personality is that, after his defeat by Robinson, Jake refuses to be consoled or nursed by Vickie, unlike in the bedroom scene, but sits in his dressing room looking at his mirror image. His self-reflection in the mirror symbolizes the mimetic rival or double, in whom the subject unwittingly sees himself, and who becomes the object of all-absorbing admiration, envy, hatred, and aggression. Thus Vickie is being crowded out of the picture. Soon Jake is occupied with another boxing rival, Tony Janiro, whom he massacres. Following that victory, Jake skips rope in a steam room so as to 'make weight' and thus continue his ring conquests. When he vainly asks his trainer for no more than a sliver of ice to place on his tongue, both his parching agony and the solitariness of his regimen reveal his increasing distance from the fullness of life as symbolized by Vickie on the one hand and, on the other, water as the life-giving feminine substance. In a later scene, by which point boxing has consumed Jake's life, his trainer sponges him with water mixed with blood, an image that, apart from its religious associations, suggests contamination of the sources of vitality and renewal. Nor is it any better for Jake when, after his retirement, he yields to long-resisted temptations. Whereas in his parents' apartment Jake and Vickie had drunk water, with Jake saying 'Salut'' in southern Italian style, he later makes the same toast as emcee of his Miami Beach nightclub, where his audience consists not of Vickie but a local crowd, where he philanders in her absence, and where his glass contains alcohol.

Although originating in feelings of abjection and unworthiness perhaps beyond explanation, Jake's masochism is fed by more immediate psychic causes, namely the personal guilt he shares with Jake La Motta the autobiographer. As we have seen, the young La Motta mistakenly believed that he had killed a bookie, and therefore regarded the physical torments of boxing as an expiation of guilt over the murder. These autobiographical elements may inspire the scene in which, having lost to Robinson, Jake regrets his misdeeds: 'I've done a lotta bad things, maybe it's coming back to me.'[79] This suggests that Jake's masochism as a boxer is motivated by a desire for expiation. In the film as in the autobiography his 'nemesis' is Sugar Ray Robinson, from whom he received many beatings.[80] But unlike the autobiography, Scorsese does not assign guilt a predominating role in Jake's behaviour.

Jake's masochism is partly explicable by his Italian Catholic environment, which calls to mind such Scorsesean characters as J.R. and Charlie Civello. Notwithstanding Jake's apparent lack of religiosity, he has grown up amid a type of Catholicism that, in its emphasis on suffering, often exhibits an extraordinarily masochistic and penitential cast. As Michael P. Carroll notes, the chief object of southern Italian worship is not Christ, whose role is curiously marginal, but the madonna and a host of saints, who conjoin beneficence and positive sadism. Carroll speaks of the southern Italian 'madonnas that maim.' Whereas in northern Italy the Counter-Reformation terminated public displays of ritualistic masochism, Catholic rituals in southern Italy have up to recent times included public self-mutilation and self-flagellation. This may reflect the fact that, for southern Italians, Christ represents the ideal of the good son, 'truly and continually penitent,' or the martyred child for whom the madonna sorrows.[81]

Such spirituality is suggested by the crucifixes appearing in Jake's own as in his parents' bedroom, each placed directly above the bed. His parents' bedroom also contains an icon of St Francis of Assisi, whom Charlie Civello extols in Mean Streets, and whose stigmata signify faithful imitation of the suffering Christ. In view of these images, it can be argued that Jake, like J.R. and Charlie, has come to overestimate martyrdom and suffering as signs in themselves of closeness to Christ, greatest of sufferers.[82] This helps to explain why Scorsese invests the boxing ring with Christian overtones, as in the final fight with Robinson, where Jake allows himself to be beaten mercilessly. Not only is he doused with a mixture of blood and water, calling to mind the Crucifixion, but the scene concludes with a shot of his blood dripping from the ropes.[83] These masochistic moments are best undertood as a secularized version of the public self-flagellations in certain forms of southern Italian Catholicism.

One should not think that, even in these displays of victimization, Jake lacks egoism and vanity. What impels him is masochism not simply as desire for punishment but, paradoxically, as the vehicle of spiritual pride and hubristic prepotency. For to become a victim is one way of achieving godhead, at least in primitive religions. In Jake's masochistic interpretation of Christianity, Christ figures not only as his model for suffering but as his inevitable rival and obstacle, who at once surpasses him in the capacity to endure pain and tortures him by withholding salvation in the form of either the middleweight championship or his actual redemption. Jake's goal is that of challenging Christ so as to equal or outdo him in suffering, that is, public displays of inhuman stoicism. During the final fight with Robinson, he taunts his opponent with the reminder that he has not yet been knocked down. The ring announcer comments: 'How he can survive 'em [Robinson's blows] nobody knows; no man can endure this pummelling.' If no man can endure such an assault, only one conclusion is possible – Jake La Motta is not a man but a god, equalling or surpassing the Christ who outlived the crucifixion. However, Jake's final fight with Robinson is the most extreme example of his masochistic behaviour. His middleweight championship defence against Laurent Dauthuille is more typical in that Jake allows himself initially to absorb an enormous beating, apparently to expiate his recent beating of Vickie, and follows this with a miraculous last-minute knockout. As the announcer says, this is 'one of the most remarkable comebacks in boxing history.'[84]

Another manifestation of Jake's masochism is his sexual jealousy, an immiserating preoccupation with male rivals whom he finds everywhere, even among his boxing opponents. Not only do critics see Jake's boxing violence as displaced homoeroticism; they find his preoccupation with male rivals to be a disguised indicator of the same impulse. Actually, his behaviour is explicable without reference to repressed instincts within the psychology of rivalry as elucidated by Girard.

A clue to Jake's behaviour is provided by J.R. in *Who's That Knocking?* Although J.R. adopts a pose of masculine autonomy and self-sufficiency, he suffers feelings of ontological deprivation that make it hard for him to desire for himself. He therefore clings to his peer group, constantly depending on his friends' mimetic cues to suggest to him objects of desire – usually 'broads.' J.R.'s desires are thus modelled and dependent, however unconsciously, upon those of others. Jake La Motta behaves similarly except that, just as his insecurity surpasses J.R.'s, so his ontological deprivation yields more harshly masochistic results.

To an even greater degree than J.R., Jake depends for his desires upon those of other people, who inevitably become his models. This is shown in those scenes in which the image of the desired object, namely Vickie, is occluded by that of the model – Joey, Salvy, even Tommy Como – whose presence is required to make that object desirable. In the first of these scenes, which takes place at the neighbourhood swimming pool, Jake fleetingly glimpses Vickie for the first time only to have his line of vision blocked by Joey as he moves from right to left across the frame. Jake then observes Vickie smiling beamingly at Joey as he walks past her. To a person as suspicious and insecure as Jake proves to be, so open and pleasant a smile might well appear as evidence of sexual favours either promised or given. However, Jake learns from Joey that he had dated Vickie a few times but that, since she is no 'broad,' he had failed to 'bang' her.

Jake's attention then shifts from Joey to the group of local gangsters, including Salvy, who have gathered with Vickie at poolside, and with whom she, as the adored fifteen-year-old beauty, innocently associates. When Jake inquires of Joey, 'Does she go with them?' Joey answers in the negative, and further informs the intensely inquisitive Jake that Vickie is not to be confused with the beautiful blonde Salvy is known to have dated, as Jake had feared. It is evident that Jake, for all his professed disdain for Mafiosi, is already envisioning these gangster 'big shots,' especially Salvy, as mysteriously fascinating and formidable rivals, a mystique that can only be enhanced by their power of lethal violence as well as the influence they wield within the neighbourhood. Thus as Jake converses anxiously with Joey, the viewer sees from Jake's point of view Salvy as he puts on his dark glasses. These are a symbol of that inscrutable prepotency and provocative remoteness with which high-ranking gangsters are identified, and which is no less characteristic of the model-mediator in Girard's analysis of triangular desire. Indeed, even at this point Jake is interested not simply in wooing Vickie but in punishing these supposed gangster rivals whom he imagines, thanks to a special magnetism he fears he lacks, to be the secret recipients of her love. As he remarks, he would welcome the chance to confront Salvy and his 'tough guy' friends without their guns, so as to be able to 'smack 'em around' and rob them of their status as big shots. In a subsequent scene that takes place at the Webster Hall ballroom, Jake again struggles to gain a glimpse of Vickie, whose image now appears elusively in the midst of a milling crowd of unknown males – for Jake, a host of potential rivals. When Jake observes Salvy, Vickie, and their entourage drive off from the ballroom in Salvy's car, the near-occlusion of Vickie's image by Salvy fires Jake's fixation on the model as the key to desire. At the same time, Jake's frustration over having failed to attract Vickie's attention issues, as previously, in compensatorily violent impulses that in this case are deflected from Salvy, the real object of his anger and hatred, to arbitrarily chosen targets. Thus without provocation Jake willingly participates in the scuffle that takes place outside the ballroom, helping the bouncer to expel a group of 'fuckin' greaseballs,' that is, recently arrived Italian immigrants who had misbehaved. Yet having seen Vickie riding in Salvy's expensive convertible, Jake immediately has his brother introduce him to Vickie so as to take her for a drive in his own new convertible, which he seems to have bought for the occasion. For some critics, Vickie's visual occlusion by her male admirers indicates Jake's desire for the latter, but I have argued that this strains belief. What Scorsese dramatizes, sometimes in slow motion so as to suggest Jake's transfixed attention, is the process by which Jake fixates on the model and absorbs the model's desire through mimetic suggestions.[85] The implied presence of the mediator, as necessary designator of desire, is evident even during Jake's first date with Vickie, as he drives with her alongside him in the front seat: 'Do you know how beautiful you are? ... Yeah, you do. People tell you all the time how beautiful you are.'

A major hazard of such desire is that the model who designates the desirable object is likely to turn into a rival and, ultimately, a soul-lacerating obstacle whose very presence the subject finds to be both a frustration and a goad. This is all the more likely to occur when the subject, like Jake, is a masochist, eager to inflict self-punishment by finding obstacles where none exist. His pain becomes even more intense when the model-rival-obstacle is close to home, embodied in a boxing opponent like Tony Janiro, whom Jake, on the basis of a meaningless remark by Vickie, imagines seriously as a sexual competitor: 'Do you ever think of anybody else when we make love? How come you said that thing about Janiro?' (She had merely described him from hearsay as a 'good-looking kid.')[86] The more Jake's suspicions mount, the greater his sexual withdrawal from Vickie, which is already being fed by his preoccupation with his boxing rivals. In another scene, in which Jake's jealousy exhibits unprededented paranoia, Joey tells him: 'You're killing yourself.' What makes Jake's jealousy especially pathological is that his suspicions now focus on his brother, whom he beats up in the false suspicion that Joey had betrayed him with Vickie. Apparently, Jake has never forgotten that the idea of desiring Vickie had first come to him in association with Joey, his original model, who had received from Vickie a beaming smile, and had also confessed to having tried to 'bang' her. Joey is thus most likely to become the most serious of Jake's rival obstacles, if only in his paranoid imagination.

The masochistic relation between desiring subject and model-rival-obstacle has another aspect. As Girard notes, such a relation in its aggravated form can take on a 'homosexual' dimension, giving a false impression of homosexuality. As Girard remarks of Dostoyevsky's *The Eternal Husband*, some forms of homosexuality result from obsessive fascination with a sexual rival or 'other' as the presumed embodiment of power and superiority.[87] The model-rival-obstacle becomes so fascinating in the subject's eyes that the originally desired object is gradually obscured. Scorsese captures the initial stages of this phenomenon in those scenes where Vickie's image is concealed by the presence of her male admirers, as they dominate Jake's attention. The same phenomenon appears in Jake's remark concerning the boxer Tony Janiro: 'I gotta problem if [whether] I should fuck him or fight him.' And finally, this phenomenon appears in Jake's fears of his brother's supposed adultery with Vickie, which some critics identify as a sign of homosexuality, but which is better explained in terms of the model-obstacle relationship and its ensuing paranoia.

Still another factor in Jake's behaviour is the Mediterranean (and hence southern Italian) cult of honour, which, in fostering constant anxiety towards rivals sexual and otherwise, as well as fears of sexual debasement by rivals, contains a potentially homoerotic component. Consistent with Girard's description of triangular desire, the Mediterranean male exhibits an intense fascination with his male rival or rivals, sometimes to the occlusion of his interest in the originally desired feminine object. The potentially homoerotic element in the Mediterranean cult of honour is reinforced by the homophilic bonding in these societies, and allegedly by the male's repressed 'pre-Oedipal' fascination with the mother, against which *machismo* is claimed to be a reaction formation. This is not to say that there are 'more latent homosexuals' in

Mediterranean countries, but that their social structure produces conditions that can lead to such behaviour.[88]

Nor should one forget the spiritual role of the model-rival-obstacle in the economy of Jake's masochism. As noted, he interprets the *Imitatio* as a masochistic rivalry in which Christ figures as his divine model and obstacle, and in which salvation is the long-withheld reward. Since Jake regards suffering as a sign that he continues to receive divine attention, his boxing opponents and sexual rivals qualify as divine emissaries, though in the form not of angels but of torturers, and entirely within a twisted logic of deviated transcendence. So long as Jake confronts a torturer, whether physical, sexual, or psychological – Janiro, Joey, or Sugar Ray – he not only continues to desire the withheld object – salvation or Vickie, as the case may be – but remains assured of the interest of the divine, conceived as a punishing obstacle. Likewise, in continuing to be tortured he hopes that the obstacle will someday either yield or relent, allowing him to enjoy what had long been denied.

Raging Bull opens with an unforgettable summative image – what Scorsese would call a 'master image' – of Jake as the sadomasochistic god.[89] Accompanied by the intermezzo to Mascagni's *Cavalleria Rusticana*, the film's credits are superimposed upon a slow-motion image of Jake alone in the ring, oblivious to his audience, sparring with invisible enemies. His imitation tiger-skin robe calls to mind predatory cats; the powerful thrust of his head, shoulders, and haunches, and the tail-like belt behind him, indeed suggest a raging bull. In ancient Mediterranean patriarchy the bull signifies Dionysus, god of natural energies, as well as Zeus, father of the gods, who metamorphoses into a bull to commit rape and violence.[90] It is perhaps worth mentioning that in ancient times the bull symbolized the southern Italians in their failed revolt against the Roman she-wolf.[91] Yet this image suggests its opposite, for the robe's peaked hood and long, flowing folds resemble a monk's cowl and cassock and thus signify Jake's monastic self-denial, the opposite of physical potency.[92] This initial identification of Jake with ideas associated with the animal, human, and divine realms defines him as a kind of monster, a being marked for victimization or apotheosis or both. Finally, in underscoring Jake's solitariness among ghostly opponents, Scorsese implies that Jake is his greatest enemy and worst obstacle. His clinching uppercuts seem aimed at not others but himself.

Jake's life begins to disintegrate during his and his family's residence in Pelham Parkway, New York, just after he wins the middleweight championship. Ignoring his upcoming title defence, he appears in his living room eating a hero sandwich while attempting unsuccessfully to repair his television set. Not only does Jake's gluttony imply lack of self-control, but the hero sandwich functions as in three of Scorsese's other Italian American films, as a deflation of the main character's fantasies of prepotency.[93] The no less serious characterological flaws disclosed in this scene include Jake's blindness to reality and, as its chief cause, his by now pathological sexual paranoia, which comes to centre on his brother. The confusion on his television aptly suggests Jake's mixed-up perception of things. His sexual paranoia is subtly conveyed when, bending down in an attempt to adjust the set, he is positioned so that its two antennae seem to project directly from his head, as if he had suddenly grown horns. What Scorsese is symbolizing quite unobtrusively is Jake's self-destructive fantasy of himself as the *cornuto* or cuckold, whose wife denies him due *rispetto* by betraying him with other men. Now much neglected by her husband, Vickie returns home from a movie theatre where she had seen Vincente Minnelli's *Father of the Bride* (1951). This tasteful upper-middle-class comedy concerned with relatively minor premarital tribulations and difficulties seems worlds away from the cauldron of southern Italian jealousy seething in Jake La Motta. In shooting Jake and Joey in a series of one-shots, rather than placing them within the same frame, Scorsese accentuates their growing emotional distance as a prelude to their division. For as Jake needs the most punishing obstacles to satisfy his masochism, he entirely without justification now openly accuses Joey of having betrayed him with Vickie. What drives this accusation is made evident in Jake's prior annoyance over Joey's having given him what he characterizes as a 'dirty look.' This is as much as to say that, from Jake's perspective, Joey has cast upon his brother the *mal occhio* or evil eye, which Phyllis H. Williams describes as a more malicious version of what in English-speaking countries is known as a 'dirty look,' and whose underlying cause is understood by southern Italians always to involve envy, in this case Joey's supposed envy of Jake's beautiful wife.

The scene in which Jake, having beaten up his wife, assaults his brother without explanation or justification culminates the theme of profanation.[94] Cain and Abel, Eteocles and Polyneices, Romulus and Remus, these feuding fraternal 'doubles' symbolize the collapse of familial, social, and ritual order through undifferentiating violence.[95] This theme is initiated in the sparring matches between Jake and Joey, followed by the scene in which Jake brings Vickie to his apartment. He shows her a photograph of Joey and himself both smiling at the camera yet confronting each other with fists raised. Since the photograph appears between Jake and Vickie in an over-the-shoulder shot, it foreshadows their troubled future, in which Jake's preoccupation with his rivals divides him from his wife. Yet whereas the feuding brothers of mythology compete for the same object, the rift between Jake and Joey results only from Jake's suspicion.[96] Indeed, when Joey discovered Vickie in the company of Salvy at the Copacabana during Jake's absence, he beat up Salvy on the false assumption of adultery, despite Salvy's quite credible protestations of innocence.[97]

Although Jake reconciles temporarily with Vickie after assaulting her, his relations with Joey seem permanently broken, for when at her suggestion Jake phones Joey with the aim of reconcilation, he cannot muster sufficient humility to speak. Several years after winning the championship, Jake moves his family to Coral Gables, Florida, and retires from boxing. His declining discipline and material excess can be read in his chubby children, expensive suburban house, swimming pool, and driveway filled with expensive cars, the size of which is exaggerated by means of a sidelong close-up, so that their bulky, foreshortened forms dominate the frame. Jake's persistent self-centredness reveals itself when he interrupts Vickie during a newspaper interview conducted alongside his swimming pool. It is likewise revealed in the name of his Miami Beach nightclub – Jake La Motta's. Playing master of ceremonies on opening night, Jake jokes about the sin of adultery, which, one suspects, he is committing. Ironically, when in an early scene Jake's first wife Irma accused him of adultery, he told her tauntingly of his intention to 'fool around' only after winning his championship belt. Jake is subsequently jailed for admitting a deceptively made-up fourteen-year-old girl into his nightclub, where he had not only kissed her as a 'test' of her age but had allowed her to mingle with male patrons. Curiously, he fails to see that she is a prostitute. Jake thus becomes inadvertently what he had despised in Tommy Como and the mob: a corrupting mediator, a procurer or pimp, one who enables and facilitates other's desires. And yet, in his nasty conversations with Tommy, Salvy, and other gangsters at the Copacabana, Jake had anticipated such a role in telling Salvy insultingly of his plan to have Salvy engage in sex with Tony Janiro, Jake's boxing rival. A joke he tells at the opening of his nightclub concerns a husband who makes a mockery of marriage by singing the praises of his wife and then offering her to a friend. This joke marks the second appearance in Scorsese's Italian American films of a theme that is introduced in *It's Not Just You, Murray!* and which would subsequently appear in *GoodFellas*, namely that of the *contento cornuto* or contented cuckold, and more particularly a man who willingly offers his wife to another person. Jake's affinity for the role of procurer is that, being afflicted with mimetic desire, he knows what objects attract his fellow sufferers. The scene in which Jake displays his 'jailbait' to male customers reverses yet resembles the scene in which he meets the fifteen-year-old beauty Vickie, whose attractions are magnified in his eyes by the presence of mob admirers, 'bigshots' with guns.

Jake's conviction on a morals charge coincides with the collapse of his marriage when Vickie files for divorce and wins custody of the children and family home. After announcing her plans to divorce, she drives off into the Miami dawn as the debauched Jake stands alone in the dusty parking lot of his nightclub, where he had caroused into the morning hours. To round up money for bail, he foolishly tears apart his championship belt for sale in individual pieces – a symbol of his self-destructiveness. He then learns from a jeweller that an intact championship belt would have brought far more money, since it is a 'very rare item.' This only underscores Jake's material but more especially personal loss.

Legally, morally, spiritually, Jake reaches rock bottom in a cell of the Dade County Stockade, whose emptiness and darkness embody the psychopathic isolation he had been skirting. Yet Jake's abjection now holds the possibility of the purgation of false desire, rather than the misguided masochistic *askesis* that had fuelled his assaults on Robinson, Janiro, and other imagined obstacles. 'Why? Why? Why?' cries Jake, 'Why did you do it?' There is special significance in Jake's cry, uttered in torment: 'I'm not that guy.' First, it implies Jake's repudiation of his former, violent self, as if he were a doppelgänger casting out its bad side. However, the 'other guy' can also be seen as Jake's double in the sense of his real or imagined models of violence, those rivals turned obstacles whose hatreds and brutalities he had imitated at every turn. Now, lacking opponents or rivals upon which to project his anger and self-hatred, Jake pounds his head repeatedly against the prison wall. One cannot fail to recall that the friends of the young and frequently angry Scorsese had described him as a 'wall-puncher.' The violence Jake had formerly unleashed upon others can now be directed only at himself. He dimly understands that, in his god-like presumption and subhuman abjection, obverse sides of the sacred, he had been his own nemesis and victim. His cry, 'I am not an animal,' reaffirms his humanity and terminates his confused quest for godhood and self-victimization. He relinquishes his stubborn false demand for independence in belated acknowledgment of something greater than the self. The light that penetrates the cell represents awakening insight and the descent of grace.[98]

The period of Jake's life following his confinement in the Dade Country Stockade coincides with his regeneration, as he begins to expel his demons. Jake abandons boxing in favour of a new career as a stand-up comedian and nightclub performer. The audience had been prepared for the change of direction in the opening scene, dated 1964, in which he rehearses his comic monologue at the Barbizon-Plaza and in the scenes of his Miami nightclub, where, playing emcee on opening night, he attempts several jokes. After his release from jail he first appears in a sleazy bar, the Carnevale Lounge at the Hotel Markwell, where he is learning his trade. In the final scene, perhaps a continuation of the opening, he is about to perform his routine in a much more upscale New York venue. Some critics, however, find Jake's career change puzzling. Pauline Kael, for instance, terms it 'unexpected and inexplicable.'[99] Actually, it makes perfect sense, for both its resemblances to and differences from boxing.

Boxing and stand-up comedy are performative and mimetic activities whose connection is implicit in the first and second scenes. Having rehearsed his monologue in the first scene, Jake repeats the phrase 'That's entertainment,' whereupon Scorsese cuts to the next scene, which portrays his fight with Jimmy Reeves in 1941. Not only does Jake customarily wear an outrageously theatrical leopard-skin robe before every bout, but following his match with Reeves he orders his handlers to 'put on my robe right!,' thus demonstrating his showmanship. The link between boxing and mimesis is further suggested when, in the final rounds of Jake's fight with Dauthuille, the announcer mentions that Jake had been 'playing possum,' only to defeat his opponent with a last-minute barrage of punches – a comeback that, whatever its masochistic motivations, can only make Jake's performance more effective theatrically. As Friedman observes, 'Ringside tables at a nightclub evoke boxing's ringside seats in tacit acknowledgement of the affinity between two forms of show biz.'[100] This is not to forget the differences between stand-up comedy and boxing, as a comedian normally encounters neither a physical opponent nor a crowd screaming for blood. Nor is there the same degree of violence in comedy, in which hostility and aggression are controlled and sublimated, with words substituting for fists. Nonetheless, *Raging Bull* shows that even stand-up comedy can trigger mimetic hostility between comedian and audience. It furthermore shows that performers and audiences are bound reciprocally by contradictory impulses of dependency and aggression, so that popular entertainment carries an often unrecognized potential for violence. The comedy scenes in *Raging Bull* thus anticipate Scorsese's deeper exploration of this theme in *King of Comedy*.

The comic performer craves the approval of his audience and tries to please it by taking as his model its desire for amusement. This, however, may create a level of demand the performer cannot meet. Even as he hopes to satisfy an audience, he may secretly resent its disapproval and feel hostility towards it. He may also resent his own slavish dependency upon audience favour and expectations. Whatever his attitude, his self-estimation depends on the crowd, which can apotheosize, savage, or abandon an entertainer. A comedian is left with two possibilities. One is to 'knock 'em dead,' a phrase that, like 'punchline,' calls to mind boxing while implying a degree of latent hostility towards the audience. Boxers know something of this experience when, with the audience urging them on, and driven by adrenalin, they close in for the kill. The other, less desirable alternative is to disappoint an audience, with the comedian becoming the object of its aggression, amid catcalls, the pitching of rotten tomatoes, and rotten reviews.[101] As a precaution against this, a comedian employs strategies to lessen or even recoup the failure of a joke. He may pre-empt hostility by calling attention to the joke's poor quality, so that humour is salvaged through self-deprecation. Yet this can backfire, especially if done too frequently, in which case the audience's annoyance may intensify. The comedian may also express hostility towards the audience by deflecting attention from a poor routine to persons in the audience who seem especially suitable for ridicule, with the others being invited to join in. This can be standardized in the form of the comic straight man or aptly named 'sidekick.'

All of these comic strategies appear in *Raging Bull* in the comedy routine at the Copacabana before Jake's fight with Janiro. Having made a poor joke, the comedian attempts to recover by pointing to its poor quality: 'I thought that was my best joke,' he says, winning enough laughs to justify the effort. Having fizzled again, he deflects his annoyance unexpectedly upon a peculiar-looking member of the audience and transforms her into an object of ridicule: 'Come on, lady, laugh it up, I laughed when you came in.' This comedian also makes fun of more clearly victimary types, including the sexually deviant and the handicapped. Thus, he interrupts his routine in order to call attention to a passing waiter whom he insults gratuitously as a 'bald-headed fag.' The audience finds it mildly amusing. In another joke he mentions a person who 'hit me with a right hook – no hand, just a hook he had.' Not only does this reinforce the connection between comedy and aggression in the film, but it refers to two forms of violence familiar to Italian American neighbourhoods in those times: boxing, obviously, but also the mob, as gangsters have sometimes sought to intimidate their enemies by wounding them with steel hooks attached to their fists – the type used by delivery men to cut the cords holding newpaper bundles. Indeed, one of the most famous instances of the use of this weapon occurred at four in the morning in the Copacabana.[102] The link between comedy and mob violence is further suggested by the presence in the audience of Jake La Motta, top middleweight contender, and mob boss Tommy Como, who sits with his underlings. Nor is it accidental that Joey brawls with Salvy at the Copacabana, as it only actualizes the violence latent in the entertainment offered there.

It may indicate Jake's having learned from the Copa comedians that during the inauguration of his nightclub he resorts to similar comic strategies. Yet consistent with his still bellicose and provocative personality, his initial object of aggression is his entire audience, as if it substituted for his ring antagonists and were now his enemy, rival, and obstacle. No sooner has Jake opened his monologue than he is insulting the guests he should be welcoming: 'I haven't seen so many losers since my last fight in Madison Square Garden. ... You're all full of shit.' When another joke misfires, partly from his unpractised delivery, Jake says, 'Did I say that?' and receives a few laughs. On this special occasion his audience apparently humours him out of good will, while for the viewer Jake will perform no further comedy routines until after his release from jail. There, far from rivals, models, and the demanding crowd, Jake is for the first time alone with himself and God. There too he comes to terms with himself, as the chief cause of his misery.

A change in Jake's character is signalled in the first scene following his release from jail. He has now resumed his comedy career – on the same bill as the aging and highly buxom stripper Emma 48s, with whom he is conducting an affair – in a sleazy, almost tunnel-like Manhattan nightclub filled with drunks and hecklers. For all its constriction and squalor, mirroring the narrowed possibilities of Jake's life, this setting resembles the Copacabana, where the comic traded insults with his audience and deflected his aggression onto harmless waiters and funny-looking women. The shadowy figure who taunts Jake from the depths of the nightclub abstractly embodies all his foes, rivals, and obstacles, is the vague and dwindling projection of the violence Jake must now conquer not outside but within himself. When Jake muffs a joke, the heckler is impatient: 'Come on, let's go, let's go,' to which Jake replies: 'Pal, you're gonna force me to make a comeback.' His antagonist mocks him as 'Funny man,' whereupon Jake answers with: 'Give him a drink ... and piss in it for me.' Despite the retaliatory content of Jake's statements, his response is weary, perfunctory, muted, yet oddly relaxed. Although insulted and challenged, he avoids falling into a mimetic exchange and possibly violence with this unknown provocateur; and he does so out of not cowardice but self-control. Instead, in a gesture of goodwill out of keeping with his former personality, Jake introduces Emma 48s to a potentially hostile audience: 'Give her a warm welcome, I know you're all capable of it.' Scorsese comments: 'He has found a kind of peace with himself. He's no longer the same man. Of course it's not ideal but he could have fallen even lower.'[103]

This scene is a fitting prelude for Jake's unexpected encounter with his brother, who has never forgiven Jake for beating him up. Jake's break-up with Joey had stemmed from his masochistic need to find obstacles where none exist – a compulsion he is now surmounting. Since the break-up Joey has grown a moustache and seems older, thinner, and less happy. At Jake's approach he moves away, still feeling resentment, but Jake, saying 'Let's forgive and forget,' follows him into a parking garage where he embraces and kisses him with great emotion.[104] For some critics, Jake's behaviour is plainly homoerotic or latently homoerotic. Wood sees this moment as Jake's delayed recognition of his own homosexuality, which had formerly been masked by aggression against the naked male body, and whose chief object is Joey. Indeed, the film self-consciously revises the traditional happy ending of Hollywood romances, with the male couple substituting for the banalities of boy-girl reconciliation. Actually, there is an anthropologically and sociologically credible explanation for Jake's behaviour. His display of affection has no homosexual import but simply exemplifies, under pressure of extreme regret and apology, traditional southern Italian and Italian American homophilism. What Wood sees as the homoerotic 'aggressiveness' of Jake's feelings for his brother is Jake's attempt to make up not only for the beating he had given Joey but for their many years of separation. The intensity of emotion in this scene is not much greater than one might witness between two deeply bereaved male relatives at an Italian American funeral. Wood, whose abstract notions of homoeroticism take little account of ethnology, fails to grasp the ethnic realities underlying Scorsese's portrayal of masculinity. It remains unclear, though, whether Joey reconciles with his brother, although he promises to call him.

Like a number of Scorsese's films, the conclusion shows the protagonist in a distanced relation to his own past life. Practising his comedy routine in his dressing room before taking the stage, Jake seems more natural and fluent than in the film's opening, so that the scene may mark a later point in his career. However, the placement of the ashtray, tissue box, crumpled paper bag, and folded newspaper is identical to that in the opening scene, which suggests that this is its continuation. Jake sits before a mirror and recites the taxicab speech from Elia Kazan's *On the Waterfront*, in which former boxer Terry Molloy (Marlon Brando) reproaches his brother and fight manager Charlie (Rod Steiger) for having fixed the fight that ended Terry's career. A pawn of gangsters who had wanted the 'short-end' money, Charlie had ordered Terry to take a dive in Madison Square Garden. Terry reminds Charlie: 'I coulda been somebody, I coulda been a contenda.' Yet he ended up with a 'one-way ticket to Palookaville.' When an attendant, played by Scorsese, enters to ask Jake whether he 'need[s] anything,' Jake replies that he needs nothing, adding: 'I'm sure.' This statement may imply that Jake, who had pretended to autonomy, has gained a measure of it. When he inquires concerning the size of the audience, the attendant replies, 'it's crowded'   an improvement over the Carnevale Lounge. After the attendant leaves, Jake assumes a crouch, makes animal noises, punches an imaginary opponent, and says to himself: 'Go get 'em champ. I'm the boss, the boss.' One recalls that, in an early scene with his first wife Irma, Jake in reference to his advancing career had boasted that 'they know who's the boss.' That statement had been filled with obsessive egotism, provocation, and violent competitiveness, and should not be confused in its import with its echo in this scene, which implies a degree of hard-won self-mastery. After Jake leaves the dressing room, the camera lingers on the mirror, inviting the audience to see itself in La Motta.

Although an artist need not have the last word regarding his work, Scorsese comments usefully on the ending of *Raging Bull*. Consistent with his statement that Jake had found a 'kind of peace' performing in a Manhattan dive, Scorsese observes that 'we should all have such peace' as Jake possesses in the final scene. In another interview he says of this scene that 'you feel him finally coming to some sort of peace in front of that mirror.' Scorsese states of *Raging Bull* as a whole: 'It's really a straight, simple story, almost linear, of a guy attaining something and losing everything, and then redeeming himself. Spiritually.'[105]

Nonetheless, critics question the degree of Jake's mental and spiritual awareness at the conclusion. Morris Dickstein writes that Jake's 'torment' leads to 'so little self-understanding or dramatic resolution' that one must doubt his redemption: 'This is not how the movie feels. If La Motta's cri de coeur in the jail cell is some kind of catharsis, the final dressing-room scene feels almost posthumous.'[106] Michael Bliss questions Jake's spiritual lucidity: 'We are supposed to see in *Raging Bull* ... the progress of an unreflective, unself-conscious character towards wisdom and self-awareness. Unfortunately, while this is clearly the film's intention, it is at variance with its effects.' For Bliss, Jake remains the 'blind, egotistical oddity he had been throughout the film.'[107] Because Jake's final gestures and animal noises recall his earlier aggressiveness, Colin Westbrook, Jr concludes: 'Yet while everything has changed for him, nothing has changed'; he is still shadow-boxing as at the film's beginning, as if still pursued by invisible demons.[108] Likewise for David Friedkin, Jake seems not to have undergone redemption or salvation.[109]

Critics also object to the seemingly implied parallel between the brothers La Motta and the brothers Molloy, assuming that Jake, in repeating Molloy's rebuke of his brother, has Joey in mind. Like Louis Menand, Friedkin notes a key difference between Jake and Terry Molloy, as Jake wins a championship rather than being banished to Palookaville.[110] The irony of Jake's imitating Terry Molloy's speech, notes Ehrenstein, is that he became a contender because he agreed to take a dive for short-end money.[111] Admittedly, Charlie Molloy and Joey La Motta are their brothers' fight managers, but the resemblance stops there. Unlike Charlie, Joey always kept his brother's interests in mind. His strategy in arranging the Janiro bout well suited Jake's egoistic desire for autonomy: 'You'll do it the way you want, your own way.' Even when Joey arranged for Jake to throw a fight, he did so from necessity, as a step to the championship. If Jake feels resentment towards Joey, he has no reason for it. In Michael Peterson's view, Jake achieves no insight into himself during his imitation of Brando's speech, as he fails to comprehend what he is saying, including the difference between Joey and Charlie Molloy. Similarly, Leger Grindon finds Jake's self-examination 'qualified,' since he is practising a stage routine delivered so flatly and detachedly that it 'slides into ambiguity,' his 'response' to his own monologue being impossible to fathom.[112]

Scorsese's comments on the conclusion are justifiable if one realizes that he makes only modest claims for Jake's spiritual recovery. Just as Jake has gained only a 'sort of' or 'kind of' peace, rather than peace itself, so he has only redeemed himself, which is not the same thing as achieving redemption. He advances spiritually relative to his former masochistic abjection. Yet he has a long way to go, having attained only partial lucidity. That he remains spiritually embattled is suggested by his shadow-boxing, recalling the earlier Jake. Hence Scorsese's statement: 'Maybe it's a little pretentious to talk about redemption. More than anything, it's about learning to accept yourself.' Scorsese further observes that Jake finally learns to be 'kind to himself' and to 'some people around him.'[113]

Such acceptance of self requires abandonment of that sadomasochistic and guiltily penitential Christianity that had tormented J.R. and Charlie Civello, Scorsese's earlier protagonists. More specifically, it involves a recognition lacking in those two characters but that the slower-witted La Motta miraculously achieves, however dimly: 'God is not a torturer.' This translates into greater kindness towards others as towards oneself.

Not accidentally, such an insight coincides with Jake's abandonment of his own sadomasochistic preoccupation with rivals both inside and outside the ring. He has given up soul-lacerating jealousy, the hunt for punishing obstacles, the frustrated mimesis of his boxing and sexual rivals real and imagined. Instead, he substitutes for violent mimetic boxing rivalries another, much less injurious form of mimesis – solo acting. He has substituted words for fists, a step forward in civilization and peaceableness. In the ring, the model-rival is so close as to invite not simply imitation but violent retaliation. The actor, by comparison, is more detached from his models, which are either imaginary or absent and which normally inspire non-violent mimesis, while stage violence is typically simulated rather than real. As Jake proclaims: 'though I can fight, I'd rather recite ... the thing ain't the ring it's the play ... I'd rather hear you cheer when I delve into Shakespeare.' The difference between the older, violently mimetic Jake and the new Jake of the stage is suggested by Scorsese's point, ignored by most critics, that Jake in the 'Terry Molloy part' of his monologue never accuses Joey.[114] No longer falsely denouncing his brother, Jake prefers to imitate Marlon Brando imitating Terry Molloy as he accuses his brother Charlie, but without confusing these fraternal roles.[115] Through the mimetic art of acting Jake has gained distance from his impulses of anger and aggression, coming to terms with them by putting them to a better use, instead of remaining in their grip.[116] Jake thus doubles for Scorsese, who uses the mimetic art of film to gain a distanced perspective on violence, including his own.[117]

The epilogue to *Raging Bull* derives from the Gospel According to John and refers to the man whose blindness Christ had cured and whom the Pharisees then questioned. Ignoring their characterization of Christ as a sinner, the blind man says that he knows nothing of his sinfulness. What he knows is that he had once been blind and, thanks to Jesus, now can see.[118] There follows Scorsese's tribute to his mentor at the NYU film school and co-worker on *Who's That Knocking?*: 'To the memory of Haig Manoogian, teacher, with love and resolution, Marty.'

Many critics find the epilogue inorganic – bafflingly inappropriate for La Motta and the film as a whole. Although Paul Schrader takes it to refer to Jake and to imply his salvation, he disavows responsibility for it. Not only does he find it inexplicable, he holds that Jake has received whatever redemption he hopes to gain through the violence he has already suffered – the precise masochistic view of Christianity Scorsese questions. For Schrader, the epilogue is 'purely Marty,' as Scorsese 'is just imposing salvation on his subject by fiat.' Lawrence Friedman finds Schrader's 'bafflement' to be 'understandable if redemption is a corollary of wising up.' Michael Bliss likewise sees the biblical quotation as applying to Jake, but since in his view Jake is not in the least transformed, much less saved, he finds it unconvincing. Gary Arnold also doubts the relevance of the biblical quotation to Jake: 'Does Scorsese really believe that he has granted La Motta a form of artistic redemption?' For Friedkin, the quotation is unjustified, as Jake falls short of 'personal redemption and salvation.'[119]

That the epilogue must refer to Jake is a false assumption, as it may apply solely to Scorsese. Yet if it refers to Jake, one should recall Scorsese's point that Jake enjoys only a kind of peace and that he is only on his way towards salvation. One should also remember that, as Scorsese sees himself in Jake, so Jake is reflected in the Scorsese who comments on the epilogue: 'I never spoke of redemption, I used the word "resolution."'[120] As applied to Jake, the epilogue implies his ongoing struggle towards a higher spiritual state. Notwithstanding Friedman's claim that he has failed to 'wise up,' the theme of recovered sight in the biblical passage implies that Jake, however inarticulately, has gained a degree of spiritual lucidity whose dimensions should now be evident.

Yet the biblical passage applies chiefly to Scorsese, as he is, metaphorically, the blind man whom Christ enabled to see. This miracle was accomplished in Scorsese's own life through two individuals. First there was Manoogian, who encouraged him to make *It's Not Just You, Murray!* (1964) and who subsequently helped him to complete his first feature film, *Who's That Knocking at My Door?* Manoogian taught Scorsese not only the art of film, but the necessity of making films based on his own life and experience – which happened to be of New York's Italian American community.[121] As Scorsese says, the film is dedicated 'to the one who gave me, at the same time as a camera, eyes to see.' The second participant in the miracle is Jake La Motta. As has been noted, Scorsese began *Raging Bull* after a two-year personal crisis during which his career collapsed as he wandered self-destructively into drugs and divorce amid displays of violent rage. But then in La Motta he found a parallel and clue to his miseries: 'I unconsciously found myself in Jake,' remarks Scorsese, 'I felt that his character was a bringer of hope.' The making of the film, so stressful that Scorsese was hospitalized for pneumonia after completing it, enabled him to comprehend and abandon a false existence. 'Jake La Motta,' says Scorsese, 'at least as he appears in the film, is someone who allowed me to see more clearly.'[122]

Scorsese's former blindness seems to have been that, as a sickly boy, as a candidate for the priesthood, and even as an adult, he had felt a mimetic attraction to violence and the seeming autonomy embodied in the 'bigshots' – hoodlums, mob bosses, boxers – of his neighbourhood. J.R., Scorsese's alter ego in *Who's That Knocking?*, is drawn to models of masculine prepotency, enslaved imitation of his peer group, thuggish brutality, mimetic and retaliatory violence, disdainful and meaninglessly impersonal sexual encounters with 'broads,' and periodic bouts of guilty penitence fed by a masochistic version of Catholicism. In *Mean Streets*, whose main character is torn between the mob and religious scruples, Scorsese plays 'Shorty,' in whom Charlie Civello observes 'delusions of grandeur' and whom Michael enlists as his gunman in the film's final scene. But then, in La Motta, Scorsese found a vivid exemplum of the difference between deviated transcendence through mimetic violence and true spiritual transcendence as written in the Gospels. Of all people, the belligerent and foul-mouthed La Motta was the vehicle of Christian truth and helped Scorsese to exorcise his demons. Yet if to this extent La Motta performs a Christ-like role, Scorsese has shown the greater peace, resolution, and understanding.

7 The Society of Transgression: *GoodFellas*

Scorsese's *GoodFellas* is based on Nicholas Pileggi's *Wiseguy*, a work of journalism published in 1985 and consisting mainly of the recollections of Henry Hill, a small-time gangster associated with New York's Lucchese crime family.[1] Pileggi gladly agreed to Scorsese's request that they collaborate on the film, so that *GoodFellas*, whose script was completed in 1987 over a five-month period and after eleven or twelve drafts, marks the first film since *Mean Streets* in which Scorsese receives credit as a scriptwriter. The title of Pileggi's work, having been used by Brian De Palma in a 1983 film, had to be replaced by the more or less synonymous current title, as Italian American gangsters use both 'wise guy' and 'goodfella' in referring to themselves.[2] The role of Henry Hill went to Ray Liotta; Robert De Niro was assigned that of Jimmy 'The Gent' Burke, Henry's friend and mentor, who appears as Jimmy Conway; and Joe Pesci took the role of Tommy DeVito, another friend of Hill's whose real name was Tommy DeSimone.[3] Filmed in and around Astoria, Queens, and other locations in metropolitan New York, the film won general acclaim upon its release in 1989.

Born in the Bronx to an Irish father and Sicilian mother, Henry Hill at an early age aspired to be a gangster, and by his early teens was being recruited for small jobs by Paulie Vario, a *caporegime* of the Lucchese family. Played by Paul Sorvino under the name of Paulie Cicero, Vario was like a second father to Hill. Among its many criminal activities, the Lucchese family controlled much of the area around Idlewild (later John F. Kennedy) Airport, including a thriving hijacking operation.[4] Following his first arrest for trafficking in stolen goods, Hill became a Lucchese associate with a specialty in hijacking. His frequent accomplices were Burke, an older Irish American gangster who served as his mentor, and DeSimone, both of whom were associates rather than members of the Lucchese family. All three men participated in the Air France heist of October 1967, which yielded nearly half a million dollars. Early in his career Hill married a young middle-class Jewish woman with whom he had two children and who appears in the film as in the book as 'Karen' (Lorraine Bracco). On 1 November 1972 Hill and Burke were sentenced to ten years in prison for beating a mob debtor in Tampa, Florida. Hill was sent to Lewisburg Federal Penitentiary in Lewisburg, Pennylvania, where he lived comfortably with other Lucchese family members. Released for good behaviour in July 1978, Hill resumed his criminal career under the cover of a no-show union job provided by Vario. Now directly violating the bosses' orders, he was continuing the drug trafficking he had already begun in prison. According to Volkman and Cummings, by 1973 Hill more resembled a junkie than a 'street-wise moneymaker.'[5] Upon leaving prison in 1978, his accomplice Burke entered a work-release program and was soon bookmaking and loan-sharking with Vario's help.

Having fallen on hard times, the Vario crew needed a major success. The opportunity came when Marty Krugman, an associate of Burke and Vario, relayed them the information he had received from Lufthansa employee Louis Werner in payment of a loan-sharking debt. The cargo area of the Lufthansa offices at Kennedy Airport was vulnerable to robbery by professionals. Yet whereas the film suggests that Burke led the robbery, Vario was its guiding force. It also required permission from the Gambino family representative in airport operations, John Gotti. The operation was largely planned at Robert's Lounge, a Brooklyn dive frequented by Burke, DeSimone, and Hill. On 11 December 1978 Burke personally orchestrated the Lufthansa heist, in which over ten criminals participated, and in which about eight million dollars in cash and nearly a million dollars in jewels were stolen; Hill, however, was occupied elsewhere with his drug trade.

Large amounts of the haul were claimed by Vario and Burke, their disgruntled underlings having to content themselves with small portions. Although the film suggests that Burke alone elimininated his accomplices out of greed and fear of witnesses, Vario was partly responsible for these executions. Of the seven men who performed the heist, six were murdered, while at least thirteen people connected to the case are believed to have been killed. On 14 January 1979 Tommy DeSimone and his 'pimpmobile' pink Cadillac disappeared forever. A participant in the heist, he was probably eliminated by the Lucchese family, which, under the pretence of making him a member, killed him in retaliation for his suspected murder of Gambino family member Billy 'Batts.'

The authorities were now attempting to track down the robbers and their loot, not a cent of which was recovered. On 11 May 1980 Hill was arrested for drug trafficking and, under threat of a long jail sentence and possible murder by the mob, entered the Witness Protection Program. Burke went to jail in 1981 on the strength of Hill's testimony, which concerned not Lufthansa but Burke's interstate racketeering and fixing of basketball games. In 1984 Vario was convicted of parole fraud for having arranged Hill's no-show union job. A year later a five-year investigation into Mafia operations at Kennedy Airport led to the indictment of eleven persons, including Vario, on charges of racketeering, extortion, and conspiracy. Given long sentences through Hill's testimony, Burke and Vario both died in prison. Hill and his family were transferred to Washington state, where they received a new home and false identities. More recently Hill, who is now divorced, has become a minor talk-show celebrity.[6]

Notwithstanding his low status in the Lucchese family, which, because of his half-Italian, half-Irish ancestry, never officially inducted him, Henry Hill holds for Scorsese the same attraction he held for the FBI. Pileggi describes Hill as a 'prize beyond measure ... He was only a mechanic, but he knew everything. He knew how it [the mob] worked. He knew who oiled the machinery. He knew, literally, where the bodies were buried.'[7] Hill differed from the vast majority of soldiers within the functionally segregated world of the mob in having access to nearly all levels of its hierarchy up to the bosses. This resulted from the fact that, as a half-Italian, he was, to quote Scorsese, 'somewhat of an outsider' and therefore exempt from the restrictive and isolating protocols to which most gangsters are subjected. Another advantage for Hill was that, as Scorsese remarks, he was 'able to be a better front man' than most other gangsters, not only because he 'looked a little nicer' but because, to quote Pileggi, he 'spoke coherently and fairly grammatically.'[8] For Scorsese, Hill's story enabled one to observe a crime family from the perspective of someone both within and outside it, and thus lent itself to that tone of simultaneously passionate involvement and ironic detachment that is Scorsese's signature, especially in his films on the mob. A further reason for Scorsese's interest in Hill is that his story belongs 'to the same period as *Mean Streets*, the early sixties, to the world I grew up in.'[9] A member of Scorsese's generation, Hill exempli-

fies the criminal career choice Scorsese shunned in favour of the priesthood and finally of cinema.

Like *Mean Streets, GoodFellas* is almost an 'anthropological study' of
the mob in those decades.[10] 'I was hoping it was a documentary,' says
Scorsese: 'Really, no kidding. Like a *staged* documentary, the *spirit* of a
documentary.'[11] Thus there are frequent voice-overs and titles giving
the date and locale of major scenes. Consistent with his predominating
view, Henry is assigned most of the voice-overs, but Karen's voice is
also heard. There is a certain 'anthropological' fitness in the use of
voice-over, for just as the mob eschews the written word for fear of
leaving traces, so Scorsese attempts to recapture the orality of that
story-telling streetcorner culture to which he had once belonged. 'Literally,' says Scorsese, '*GoodFellas* is the way I heard stories on the
streetcorner, with asides and everything.'[12] The shots of ritualistic
Mafia banquets and Sunday feasts, or of the gangsters' clubhouses,
where they drink, eat, and play cards, or of their hideously decorated
suburban houses, or of the no-less-tasteless apartments where they
rendezvous with their tastelessly dressed girlfriends, reveal Scorsese's
painstaking effort to record the shapes, colours, and textures of this
world.

Yet *GoodFellas* also typifies Scorsese's equally strong countertendency
towards expressive stylization. There are quite a few point-of-view
shots, two of the most memorable being that of the pistol Karen points
directly into Henry's face and Tommy's brief glimpse of the empty
clubhouse just before his execution. Red filters convey an infernal mood
in the scenes concerning the murder of Billy Batts. Freeze-frames with
voice-over are used sparingly yet effectively, as when Henry, fleeing
from the cabstand he has just destroyed, reports on his increasing status
as a gangster, or in the scene in which Henry realizes Jimmy's intention
to kill Morrie, or his realization that Jimmy intends to have him executed. However, the most vivid testimony of Scorsese's expressionism
is his use of an extremely mobile camera so as to produce 'as much
movement as possible' and thus a 'very speeded, frenetic quality,' with
the style 'kind of break[ing] down by the end.' In Henry Hill's 'last day
as a wise guy,' the 'whole picture' is intended to seem 'out of control,'
and to 'give the impression' that Henry is about to 'spin off the edge
and fly out.'[13] In some scenes the camera pans dizzyingly, while in
others Scorsese's long tracking shots of entrances into restaurants and
night clubs enable one to participate vicariously in the intoxication of
the gangster life. As in Scorsese's earlier films, music often comments

ironically on the action. At the same time, the soundtrack implies a degeneration in popular music parallelling that of the gangsters from the 1950s into the 1980s.[14]

Another distinctive feature of *GoodFellas* is its careful formal organization, which was necessary to maintain points of reference and meaning amid increasingly chaotic action. The film's opening event, in which Henry, Jimmy, and Tommy transport the murdered Batts to a secret burial place, repeats somewhat before the film's mid-point, where it initiates the 'goodfellas'' decline. Their reckless murder of Batts, an important gangster, defines the film's main axis, in relation to which its opening and concluding sections are situated through parallelism or contrast. The high point of the first section, professionally speaking, is the robbery of Air France, the corresponding moment of the second part being the Lufthansa heist in which the 'take' has vastly increased. As Henry's wedding to Karen, to which all of his associates are invited, precedes the murder of Batts, so in the second section the leading guests will either be killed or betrayed. Before Batts's murder Henry and Karen visit the Copacabana in premarital exhilaration, but after the murder Henry appears there with his girlfriend Janice Rossi. When government agents appear routinely at Henry's house before Batts's murder, they are carelessly ineffectual; but in its aftermath government and local authorities hound Henry like a fate, surprising him in Tampa and later in a drug raid upon his home. At the beginning of the film Henry is arrested for the first time; following Batts's murder the FBI arrests him unexpectedly; and towards the end he is arrested for drug trafficking. But whereas after his first arrest he observes *omertà*, in the third he informs on his friends. In the opening scene a solitary Henry spies enviously upon neighbourhood gangsters; in the final scene he is again alone, but now he has betrayed his friends and amounts to a government spy.

The question arises to what extent *GoodFellas* belongs to the tradition of the crime and gangster film. At the conclusion, after the destruction of his gang, the dead Tommy DeVito unexpectedly reappears to fire a pistol at the audience. Not only does this scene allude to the final shot of Edwin S. Porter's silent film *The Great Train Robbery* (1903), the inception of the crime genre, but it recalls the scene in which, seen from Henry's point of view, Karen Hill points a loaded pistol at her husband's face.[15] It is implied that the crime film – embodied in Tommy DeVito as *revenant* – will renew itself as long as the criminal life seduces ordinary people like Henry and Karen.[16]

Regarding the classical form of the gangster film, which had its brief heyday in the early 1930s, *GoodFellas* shows fewer resemblances than dissimilarities. As Robert Warshow argues, the protagonist of the classic gangster film may belong to a group or organization, yet remains an individualist whose career is 'brutality' and whose success requires the 'establishment of an individual preeminence that must be imposed on others.' He 'always dies because he is an individual,' and the final bullet makes him a 'failure.' The rhythm of the classic gangster film is one of 'enterprise and success ending in precipitate failure' just before ultimate triumph. Hardly applicable in all instances, Warshow's paradigm fits film gangsters such as Rico Bandello (*Little Caesar*, 1930), Tony Camonte (*Scarface*, 1932), and Cody Jarrett (*White Heat*, 1949).[17] A resemblance also exists between these urban desperadoes and the gunslinging Western hero, as if the latter had been transferred to the city; for like the classic gangster, the Westerner stands between the law and rival gangs.[18]

Although some gangster films continued to celebrate individuals like Al Capone, Baby Face Nelson, and Mad Dog Coll, the classic type yielded in the 1940s and especially the 1950s to its 'syndicate' variation, so that the 'more naive and romantic original' was displaced, and the 'classic lone wolf' became an 'organization man.'[19] This change is reflected in *GoodFellas*, whose title emphasizes a collectivity, and whose main character, Henry Hill, is very much a joiner-conformist who, as he says, wants desperately to 'belong' to the mob. The disapproval of excessive individualism within the Lucchese crime family is shown in the film when Paulie Cicero downgrades Tommy DeVito as a 'cowboy,' the Mafia term for a recklessly violent and undisciplined gangster.[20] Far from suffering the classic gangster's violently dramatic downfall at the climax, Henry undergoes gradual deterioration into drug-taking and mental confusion, his decline and that of his friends taking up approximately two-thirds of the film. Nor does *GoodFellas* pay much attention to the physically courageous if immoral exploits portrayed in most gangster films. As Scorsese acknowledges, 'most gangster movies focus on the big gunfights,' but his film eschews the 'overdramatic' so as to treat the 'day-to-day life, the tedium' of gangster society.[21] The two airline robberies offer a chance for tough-guy action, yet Scorsese refuses it. Just as the gangsters, provided with a key, saunter in and out of the Air France storage room, so what might have been the film's dramatic high point, the dangerous and suspenseful Lufthansa heist occurs offstage, with Henry, a non-participant, hearing of it over the radio while in the shower. There is less excitement in the heists themselves than in their planning, as the gangsters grow drunk on their greed. The emphasis falls not on the Lufthansa heist but on its aftermath, a series of corpses. Nor does Scorsese opt for the conventionally moralistic ending of many gangster films, for not only does Henry Hill, the 'rat,' survive, he does so unrepentantly, regretting his loss of the gangster life.

Another point of comparison is Coppola's *Godfather* and *Godfather, Part II*, with which Scorsese's film bears little resemblance. Unlike Coppola's romanticizing treatment of the mob, and his attempt to extenuate its activities on the implied basis of its virtual identity with capitalism, Scorsese offers a realistic and ironic interpretation in which self-interest conquers honour and loyalty, brutality replaces heroism, and the largely law-abiding, work-oriented, and productive values of everyday society are flouted by the transgressive, parasitic consumerism of its criminal antagonists.[22] Henry's hectic, disordered, irrational antics at the conclusion are a far cry from Coppola's apocalyptic shootouts, being closer in spirit to the Keystone Cops.

Seen in the perspective of Scorsese's other Italian American films, *GoodFellas* forms the second installment of what Pileggi terms a gangster 'trilogy' beginning with *Mean Streets* and ending with *Casino*. As such, the film marks something like an intermediate stage in the history of the Italian American mob from the 1960s into the 1980s. In *Mean Streets* the young Italian American gangsters have not yet escaped Little Italy into the suburbs, which seem to them alien territory. Nor have they challenged the mob hierarchy and its system of *rispetto*, which dominates their urban neighbourhood. In *GoodFellas* the Northeastern mob appears in its new yuppified manifestation, having transplanted itself to the suburbs of New York City, and is shown extending its operations to Pittsburgh and Florida, the latter being its favoured vacationland. This geographical expansion coincides with an increasingly reckless involvement, particularly by the younger gangsters, with the narcotics trade, in violation of the bosses' orders.[23] Such transgressions lead ultimately to the betrayal of the bosses by informants like Henry Hill, who seems to exemplify an argument very much alive since the 1980s, that the Mafia is declining because of a loss of father-loyalty and mother-respect; a scarcity of reliable, pure-blooded Italian American recruits; and a disregard of *omertà* by the new breed of American-born gangsters.[24] It remains for *Casino* to portray the mob as it expands into the new frontier of Las Vegas, where the crime families are initially successful. Yet here too the bosses encounter betrayal, until the law drives them from the oasis, leaving them with only memories of their paradise lost.

Whatever their differences, these films resemble each other in many ways. Like its companion pieces, *GoodFellas* centres on Italian American criminals dedicated to social transgression and the exploitation of both their fellow ethnics and Americans generally. The members of this homophilic criminal society constantly indulge in drinking, gambling, eating, sex, and both real and recreational gunplay inspired by Western film heroes akin to the desperadoes of the Sicilian past. This helps to explain the concluding reference to *The Great Train Robbery*, a film about Western outlaws.[25] At the same time, the subculture in *GoodFellas*, as in its companion films, is ostensibly a hierarchy ruled by *rispetto* and its prohibitions, although these are honoured more in the breach than in the observance. It is therefore only a matter of time before this gangster society, like that in *Mean Streets* and *Casino*, collapses from within, incapable of containing its own transgressive violence.

As the film begins the credits rush by from right to left, the first sign of its recurrent interest in rapid movement and hectic pacing. The title 'New York, June 11, 1970' is followed by a shot of the rear of a car that, as it travels by night down a highway, switches from the left to the right lane. As we soon learn, the car trunk contains the recently murdered Billy Batts, a 'made man' of the Carlo Gambino family. Seen from the front through a filter, the car's bright-red interior discloses the three gangsters who had murdered Batts that very night: Henry Hill, the driver; Jimmy Conway asleep alongside him; and Tommy DeVito, dozing in the back seat. Unexpectedly disturbed by noises, Henry and his friends quickly trace them to the trunk. After parking the car on a deserted side road, Henry opens the trunk to reveal Batts, still in his death throes. Tommy then stabs him repeatedly with a knife, and Jimmy finishes him off with a revolver. There is irony (though not regret) to Henry's voice-over: 'As far back as I could remember, I always wanted to be a gangster.' The opening of Tony Bennett's version of 'Rags to Riches' blares forth on the soundtrack, whereupon the title appears in red: *GoodFellas*.[26]

The opening anticipates major developments in theme, narrative, and character. The colour red, used for the title, is by now a Scorsesean signature, recalling the titles of *Mean Streets* and *Raging Bull*. Its associations are blood, violence, suffering, and passion, although *GoodFellas* lacks overt Catholic emphases. Reiterating this chromatic register, the car's red interior not only suggests an infernal world but prepares for other instances where red appears. Batts's bloodied face; the ketchup in which the unfeeling Jimmy Conway drowns his breakfast after Batts's murder; the rich red tomato sauce at the gangsters' banquets; Henry's red prison garb; Karen's red dress; the interior of the Bamboo Lounge, a casualty of Mafia arson; and the hellish light of a forest clearing where Batts's body is exhumed nocturnally for reburial. The shifting of lanes also has major symbolic significance, being repeated about a third of the way into the film following Batts's murder. In doubling the film back upon itself, Scorsese pinpoints that killing as the moment when the three friends go off track in their careers, Tommy by killing Batts, Henry and Jimmy by participating in this violation of mob protocols. The Tony Bennett song typifies a film that not only abounds in popular music but uses it for ironic commentary. In this case the irony is that, whereas the singer celebrates a love beyond materialism, Henry and his friends incarnate greed and violence. And finally, the opening already suggests Henry's ambiguous relation to the Mafia, at once within and outside it. To be sure, he is an accomplice to Batts's murder and even drives the body to its hiding place. Yet whereas Tommy and Jimmy had assaulted Batts earlier that evening, Henry had not committed physical violence against him. Likewise, when his friends finish off Batts, Henry does no more than open the trunk, after which he stands back to watch them stab and shoot him. Stepping forwards to close the trunk, Henry looks away with a troubled look, as if disturbed by the night's events. The trunk edge momentarily crosses Henry's face diagonally, as if to suggest his divided consciousness towards the gangster life.

Scorsese cuts to a close-up side view of the young Henry Hill's right eye as, concealed behind window blinds in his family apartment, he watches the comings and goings of neighbourhood gangsters. Identified as 'East New York, Brooklyn, 1955,' this scene calls to mind not only the young Scorsese, who first glimpsed Little Italy from the window of his grandmother's apartment on Elizabeth Street, but the zoom-and-pan shot of that very street at the opening of *Who's That Knocking at My Door?* Besides indicating that *GoodFellas* will unfold from Henry Hill's perspective, the shot of Henry behind window blinds implies his moral blindness as well as his distance from the world he observes.[27] Again one thinks of Scorsese, who was within and outside gangster society. In Henry's case such distance has its analogue in his mixed Sicilian and Irish background, which barred him from the mob's inner sanctum, but also gave him a detached perspective upon it. For al-though Henry's remoteness in this scene implies awed respect for the gangsters he observes, the fact remains that, hidden by blinds, he is spying on them. This suggests transgression, and indeed foreshadows his betrayal of his gangster colleagues when he becomes a real spy and FBI informant. His betrayal culminates dramatically at the moment when, at the trial of his former associates, in which he figures as pri-mary witness, and in an unexpected violation of the film's realistic norm, Henry leaves the witness box in order to deliver his incriminat-ing testimony directly to the audience, face to face, eye to eye.

This scene, however, is chiefly concerned with Henry's mimetic fasci-nation with and attraction to gangsters. Scorsese emphasizes the direc-tion of Henry's gaze and with it the force of his desire by tracking an unnamed local as he walks across the street – Henry's chosen path – to the gangster hangout at the pizzeria. The gangsters are Henry's models, whose seemingly god-like plenitude fuels his insatiable desire to enter their way of life.

Not infrequently, gangster films imply that a gangster chooses his career largely or partly through the influence of a flawed social and familial environment.[28] In Henry's case one is tempted to attribute his criminality to a squalid, overcrowded, penurious home life, including a disgruntled and punitive father who beats him for skipping school in order to run errands for the mob.[29] Pileggi's *Wiseguy*, which provided Scorsese with information on Henry's family, reports on the upbringing of Jimmy Burke, a foundling who, beaten and abused as a child, was shunted from home to home, reform school to reform school.[30] Yet despite Henry's father's apparent tendency to abuse his children, the Hill household contains an image of the Last Supper, which at the very least implies that Henry has undergone a measure of Christian teaching contrary to the ways of the mob. The presence of this religious image may also import Henry's betrayal of his father, not only by lying but by associating with gangsters of whom his father disapproves. Alterna-tively, it may imply that, in beating Henry, his father has failed to live up to the standard of forgiveness exemplified by Jesus; for in the Catho-lic perspective, Jesus provides the analogical measure by which one can evaluate in terms of likeness and contrast the behaviour of mortal fathers. In any case, in *GoodFellas* as in his other films Scorsese refuses to blame society for a character's criminality – an attitude reminiscent of the classical gangster film.[31] Nor do Scorsese's characters complain of their unhappy home lives and other social pressures. To quote Henry on his abusive father: 'Everybody takes a beating sometime ... My father had to work at eleven years old.' Regarding the freeze-frame that fixes Henry's father as he beats him, Scorsese observes: 'This isn't to make the usual point that his father beat him, therefore he was bad.'[32] Scorsese challenges the mentality that would automatically link anti-social behaviour to environmental deficiencies through his portrayal of Henry's wife Karen who, despite her comfortable upper-middle-class suburban Jewish background, shares Henry's attraction to the gangster lifestyle.[33] If anything, the characters become gangsters because they are disposed characterologically to that lifestyle, intoxicated by its excitement, materialism, freedom, and power.

Commenting in voice-over on his initial attraction to the gangster life, Henry mentions the special distinction his neighbourhood conferred on Mafiosi. 'For me it was better than being president ... It meant being somebody in a world of nobodies. They weren't like anybody else.' The gangsters' distinctiveness depends on both the enormity of their transgressive desires and their overwhelming force in asserting them: 'They did whatever they wanted. They double parked in front of a hydrant and no one ever gave them a ticket. In the summer when they played cards all night nobody called the cops ... If we wanted anything we just took it, hit anybody who complained.' The ideal of self-sufficiency essential to the gangster mystique in no way entails a reduction or economizing of desires so as to moderate painful feelings of lack, envy, or jealousy. Rather, it means surrender to an importunate multitude of desires that, at least ideally, never awaken feelings of dearth or privation since, reminiscent of those ancient gods who lack for nothing, those desires always find immediate satisfaction. As Henry reveals in his concluding testimony: 'Anything I wanted was a phone call away.' At the same time, self-sufficiency in this world means freedom to act on one's desires without fear of transgression or punishment, as if invulnerable. A man who does so receives the respect (*rispetto*) of the neighbourhood, becoming an object of attraction but also fear. Accordingly, most locals maintain a respectful distance, as if in the presence of the sacred, if only in its deviated form. In Henry Hill, however, attraction overcomes fear: 'Even before I wandered into the cabstand for an after-school job I knew I wanted to be a part of them. It was there that I knew that I belonged.'

Henry is drawn initially to the gangster life through mimetic cues by which gangsters communicate the sacred aura of violence and untouchability surrounding them. From his window he sees them arrive at the pizzeria in a boat-like new Cadillac, which, as they disembark, bounces upward with the removal of their weight. The image is a visual pun, as these men qualify as *pezzonovanti*, Mafia (and Italian American) slang for heavyweights. Tony Stacks and Ronnie are big, strong, well-fed criminals who bask in their power, freedom, and inner plenitude. However, our first glimpse of them is limited to their shoes – highly polished, of fine Italian make – as they leave the car. Reminiscent of *It's Not Just You, Murray!*, Scorsese's first film on the Italian American underworld, the camera mimes the admiring gaze of an observer who, with awe and respect, takes in these figures from toe to head. Their shoes are so well polished they seem almost metallic, protecting even the least dignified parts of the gangster's body from the grimy street, where others are condemned to wallow. These shoes are like mirrors in which the gangster looks down to admire his reflection and thus confirm the admiring gaze with which lowly humanity honours him.[34] The theme of the shoe shine reappears when Batts confronts Tommy DeVito and, as an insult, reminds him of his days as a shoeshine boy, when he made customers' shoes 'shine like fuckin' mirrors.' This image in turn relates to Henry's earlier glimpse of the gangsters, transforming them into mirrors of his own desire.

Following the shot of the shoes, and still miming the gaze of the awed observer, the camera takes in the gangsters' upper bodies. They are immaculate, perfectly groomed, clean shaven, silk shirted, well tailored with a certain flashiness, and adorned with pinky rings – an image of self-confidence and satisfied desire. Yet though they resemble splendid apparitions from another world, the more awe-inspiring revelation occurs moments later, when Paulie Cicero comes to the door of the pizzeria as if from his inner sanctum and, merely by a look of displeasure, terminates the mock fisticuffs and noisy *passatella* (trading of ritualized insults) between these visitors and his brother Tuddy, whom they had earlier greeted with kisses and embraces. Entangled in mimetic fascination, Henry has found his gods and tremendum, along with its special rituals and privileged pleasures – the form the sacred takes within his world of deviated transcendence.[35] On the other hand, the gangsters' pretended exchange of punches looks forward ironically to the climax, when an actual and bloody conflict among Henry's associates precipitates his decision to inform against them. Likewise, Tony Stacks's and Ronnie's trading of blame for the sidewalk disturbance for which they are both responsible anticipates the recriminations Henry will ultimately launch against his former friends so as to ensure his own survival.

Permission to enter this world comes only after long initiation. Henry's desirability as a recruit is that he is half Sicilian, while his mother's willingness to permit him to hang around Tuddy's cabstand after school is decisively determined by the fact that his family and the Ciceros derive from the same Sicilian village – a detail suggesting that *campanilismo* was alive in some Italian American neighbourhoods after the Second World War. Unaware that her son has become chronically truant in order to serve his apprenticeship with the mob, his mother reminds him to bring back milk on his return from school; the idea is picked up later, when Henry, now a full-fledged gangster, gives Karen a bloodied pistol to conceal in her mother's milkbox. Henry begins as an enthusiastic errand boy for Paulie, parking cards, running numbers, conveying messages, and serving food. Of special importance analogically is the scene in which the barely adolescent Henry, in his job as valet parker, receives the keys of a gangster's car. The shot of the keys, magnified in close-up so as to emphasize their importance, indicates analogically that, for Henry, these are the very keys to his kingdom of deviated transcendence, which Scorsese defines implicitly in ironic contrast to the 'keys of the Kingdom of Heaven.'[36] In a similar vein of analogical parody is Henry's exultant recollection to have been 'just a little kid ... parking Cadillacs' for Mafiosi. The irony lies in the biblical statement, equally applicable to *Mean Streets*, that one must become as little children to enter the kingdom of heaven. In other instances keys serve to represent symbolically all the possibilities of material desire, mobility, and gratification available to Henry. These include the key that he and Tommy receive from Frenchy to pull off the Air France caper as if it were a walk in the park. There are the car keys that Karen throws out of her and Henry's bedroom window, in the vain hope of preventing him from visiting his mistress. And lastly, at the conclusion, there are the car keys Henry misplaces on the drug-strewn kitchen table of his latest mistress's apartment, and whose misplacement portends not only the possibility of his permanent immobility under a prison sentence, but his ultimate denial of access to the gangster life, which amounts to his 'heaven.'

An important moment in Henry's apprenticeship is the blowing up of a rival cabstand with Tuddy, his mentor, cheering him on. The importance of this event is signalled by the freeze-frame of Henry as he runs from the explosion, as if terrified to discover his capacity for violence.[37] Besides representing Henry's baptism by fire, parodic of the biblical version, this scene prefigures his terrified flight from the mob when he informs against it. One thinks too of *Mean Streets*, in which Johnny Boy flees the explosion he has set off in a mailbox, although Henry lacks Johnny Boy's unruliness. The importance of Henry's act of sabotage is emphasized in voice-over: 'People looked at me differently. They knew I was with somebody. I didn't have to wait in line on Sunday morning and wait for fresh bread. The owner knew who I was with.' Henry adds that, with his increase in reputation, people avoided parking in the Hill's driveway, though the Hills had no car and that neighbourhood children now carried Henry's mother's groceries 'out of respect.' By now Henry is sufficiently successful as a neophyte criminal to afford his own gangster-style suit, which elicits his mother's shocked cry: 'You look like a gangster.' Reminiscent of the gangsters' arrival at Tuddy's pizzeria, the newly suited Henry is shot from the head downward as if basking in the awe his appearance produces.[38]

In at least one instance the young Henry seems to lack the toughness the gangster life demands over the long run. When Henry, while working at the pizzeria, aids a wounded man who unexpectedly begs for help at the door, Tuddy not only bars him from the restaurant but objects that Henry has 'wasted' eight aprons by playing Good Samaritan. 'We have to toughen this kid up,' says Tuddy, and Henry recalls wondering whether he had been right. Nonetheless Paulie continues to groom Henry, whose desire to be a gangster is only intensified by the fact that the mid-1950s, the time of his initiation, brought unprecedented prosperity to the mob. The scene in Paulie's clubhouse shows Henry playing gofer for the assembled gangsters, who eat, drink, and gamble in confident jubilation. Henry comments that this took place 'before Apalachin,' when local police surprised a meeting of mob bosses in upstate New York in 1957, and also before 'Crazy Joe' Gallo and his brothers challenged gangland hierarchy.[39] Henry's comment, that Paulie's clubhouse is where he 'met the world,' allows for a biblical reading, as an implicit contrast is suggested between Christ's Kingdom, which is not of this world, and the 'kingdoms of the world,' with which Satan tempted Christ.[40]

The clubhouse is also where Paulie introduces Henry to Jimmy Conway, whose protégé he becomes. Apart from his charisma and legendary toughness, Jimmy appeals to Henry because his Irish background also places him inside and outside the mob. Jimmy teaches

Henry 'to keep the drinks comin',' to gamble recklessly, and to tip lavishly as evidence of personal plenitude, as when Jimmy, on their first meeting, gives Henry twenty dollars merely for handing him a drink. Henry behaves similarly when he is old enough to take women to the Copacabana. Jimmy provides lessons in hijacking, the disposal of stolen goods, and, not least, the proper way of reacting to a 'pinch' or an arrest. After Henry evades a charge thanks to a corrupted judge and lawyer, the avuncular Jimmy compliments his protégé for having revealed nothing to the authorities, rewarding him with a large tip as 'graduation present.' With his arm around Henry's shoulder, Jimmy reminds him of the 'two most important things in life': 'Always keep your mouth shut, and never rat on your friends.' Subsequently the assembled wise guys greet Henry with kisses and embraces of the homophilic rather than homoerotic type, while Paulie cries jubilantly: 'You broke your cherry!'[41] The courthouse staircase upon which this jubilant meeting takes place reinforces the idea of Henry's 'graduation.' However, Scorsese concludes this scene of celebration with a freeze-frame in which Paulie Cicero appears with his eyes closed, implying the blindness of a man who has unwittingly initiated the youth who will betray him.

Henceforward Henry appears as the adult gangster played by Ray Liotta. The time is 1967, the scene Idlewild Airport, which Henry and his associates regard as their privileged domain.[42] Henry stands with Tommy DeVito outside a diner, waiting to hijack a truck about to be handed over to them by a corrupted driver. The camera scans them from the ground up, taking in their expensive alligator shoes, suits, ties, and jewelry – an image of formidable self-sufficiency and confidence. At the same time Henry is presented from a low angle so as to exaggerate his height and with it his power. The soundtrack consists of Hoagy Carmichael's 'Stardust Memories,' a nostalgic pastoral evocation of early love that figures ironically as the life of urban crime. Not impossibly, a homoerotic bond between Henry and Tommy is suggested in the Johnny Mercer lyric referring to the 'nightingale' that 'sings its fairy tale,' but the irony is more likely directed at the truckdriver's story – a fairy tale – that not Henry and Tommy but 'two niggers' had stolen his truck.

Part of the brilliance of the first half of *GoodFellas* is its evocation of Henry Hill's mimetic seduction by the gangster life – his becoming addicted, in effect. Yet once Henry has become a full-fledged gangster, he can exert upon others the same mimetic power his models had exerted upon him. This happens between Henry and his Jewish girlfriend Karen, as he becomes the model of her desire. Initially Henry had ignored her on their blind date because of pressing business elsewhere. Yet nothing more powerfully incites the desire of another person than indifference. After he again stands her up through a misunderstanding, she tracks him down to his neighbourhood where, dressed in passionate red and with dark eyes flashing, she denounces him before his fellow wise guys: 'Who do you think you are, Frankie Valli or a big shot?' Her suggestion that he falls short of being a big shot wounds his *amour propre* and inspires his desire to prove her wrong during their date at the Copacabana. He would awaken her attraction to him so as to satisfy his self-love – an amatory strategy consistent with Henry's weak ego and overall narcissism.

Henry and Karen's visit to the Copacabana qualifies as a pilgrimage to a major cultural shrine of the gangster world, where a wise guy's proximity to the hallowed stage testifies to his worth within the professional pecking order.[43] With the leading bosses and wise guys in attendance, the gods of wise guy culture provide the entertainment – Henny Youngman, 'King of the One Liners,' and Bobby Vinton, the 'Polish Prince,' whose song, 'Roses Are Red, My Love' (which he [impersonated by his son] sings in a later scene), reveals sentimentality as the obverse of gangster violence. For Henry and Karen to be admitted through the Copacabana's side door, a privileged entrance, allowed to move freely through the inner sanctum, and finally seated next to the stage marks the twenty-one-year-old Henry Hill's professional arrival.

Scorsese captures the intoxication of Henry and Karen's date at the Copacabana by rendering it in a long forward-tracking shot that follows them through the side door into a labyrinth of corridors and rooms and finally into the dining area by the stage. To quote Scorsese, the scene 'had to be done in one sweeping shot, because it's his seduction of her, and it's also the lifetyle seducing him.'[44] The scene also appears to be a more extended and elaborated version of the scene in *Mean Streets* in which Charlie enters Tony's bar and, following a similarly intricate route symbolic of his moral errancy, finds himself at last in front of a stage deep in the bar's interior. Before Henry and Karen enter the club, he mentions that he prefers the side door to standing in line, in contrast with all the frustrated nobodies on the sidewalk. Henry having thus identified himself as a god, an aura of privilege envelops him as the side door opens seemingly automatically, as if the waiter had anticipated their arrival. Henry rewards him with a large tip. Proceeding further, they pass a tall, robust, and formally dressed employee named Gino who, while taking a bite of food, acknowledges Henry by his first name. For an employee to be seen eating in the dining area would be unseemly, a violation of its sacred space, but to see Gino munching behind the scenes is a privilege enjoyed only by those permitted to observe the inner workings of the sacred, which for the ordinary visitor remains invested with remoteness and mystery. In terms of analogical parody, the difference is roughly that between standing in line to receive communion and being invited into the sacristy to see or participate in its preparation. Ostentatiously conveying his familiarity with these fascinating interior spaces and those who move amid them, Henry says jokingly to two employees kissing in the corridor: 'Every time I come here ... Every time I come here ... Don't you two work?' He advertises for Karen's benefit his familiarity with the inner sanctum, emphasizing that, for the privileged, like themselves, the Copacabana represents perpetual leisure and pleasure, where neither patience nor exertion is necessary to the gratification of one's desires.

Upon entering the dining room, Henry is recognized by the host, who ushers him and Karen obsequiously to a place 'right up front' while fending off the complaints of less favoured patrons. 'Anything you need, Henry, just let me know,' says the host, with ostentatious familiarity, indicating that Henry and Karen shall not want. He then summons 'Anthony' the waiter, who brings to the stage area a circular table covered by a tablecloth that, as he carries it, sways and flutters slightly as if touched by a spiritual breath. Accentuating the mood of privileged intimacy, the host brings Henry and Karen a bottle of wine offered as a gift by the high-ranking gangster 'Mr Tony,' who also sits close by the stage with his cronies. Further to show his freedom from want and need, and also to make a yet stronger impression on his date, Henry offers twenty-dollar tips to the two waiters and the host, who pockets his bonus as discretely as possible.

However captivating, Karen's visit to the Copa introduces her only superficially to the gangster life and its world of *rispetto* founded on violence. Her addiction to this lifestyle requires a more awe-inspiring encounter with its tremendum, and this occurs through her exposure to violence, and more particularly Henry's gun, which is both terrifying and attractive, like the sacred. Her opportunity comes after she is physically abused by a next-door neighbour and sexual rival of Henry's, whereupon he pistol-whips the would-be boyfriend in the latter's driveway in broad daylight. Returning to Karen, he places the blood-stained gun in her hands, so that she touches it before hiding it in a milkbox.

Now intimate with the sacred, she feels an intensified sense of being: 'I have to admit there are women like my best friends who would have gotten out the minute their boy friend gave them a gun to hide ... [But] I have to admit the truth. It turned me on.'[45] Henceforward Henry will mediate violence to Karen, enabling her to enjoy it vicariously, yet sheltering her from it.

Although Henry imitates older wise guys, and although Karen receives her desires from him, his gangster models are hardly autonomous, but copy models of their own. To a large extent they copy each other's behaviour or else generally defined notions of how a tough guy acts and sounds. The performance Tommy gives in the Bamboo Lounge, and which impresses and amuses his friends, seems like an impersonation of a tough guy, being intended to prove Tommy's menace, disdain of the police, and stubborn refusal to give information. By the same token, a chief reason for the outrage Tommy later shows after having been insulted by the high-ranking gangster Billy Batts, is that in his eyes Batts is nothing but a 'fake old tough guy.' One recalls Pileggi's description of Tommy DeSimone, the original of Tommy, who 'always had to show that he was tougher than anyone around.'[46] Or as Paulie Cicero later says of Tommy, 'he's got too much to prove.' Tommy also finds his models in the heroes of Western films, thus confirming a characteristic feature of Scorsese's other Italian American works as of the gangster genre generally.

Robert Warshow was among the first to see the resemblance between the Old West gunfighter-outlaw and the modern gangster. In *Who's That Knocking at My Door?* J.R. fixates upon Western gunmen played by John Wayne and Lee Marvin and uses them to define his masculine code; in *Mean Streets*, Charlie Civello is equally fascinated by John Wayne's heroic characterizations in the films of Ford and Hawks. Contrastingly, Pileggi's *Wiseguy* largely ignores the parallel of Western gunman and gangster, except to report that Jimmy Burke perversely named his two children after Jesse and Frank James.[47] However, the film brings out this parallelism, portraying not only Jimmy's young son in a cowboy suit at his birthday party, but Tommy DeVito's fantasy of being a Western gunman. During a hijacking Tommy demands the 'strongbox' from the truck driver, whom he vilifies as a 'fuckin' varmint.' He next jumps into the front seat with gun in hand and announces, 'I'm riding shotgun.'[48] He then orders Henry, whom he calls a 'sidewinder,' to drive the 'loot' back to the 'hideout'; Tommy extends his arm out the window and fires a revolver into the air. This, though, is only a prelude to the scene in which Tommy, Henry, Jimmy, and other wise guys gather round a clubhouse table. When Tommy asks his friends to identify Humphrey Bogart's only Western role, Jimmy's mention of *Shane* elicits derision, as these gangsters, and least of all Tommy, could hardly identify Bogart with the sanitized hero of that film. Rather, the film in question is Lloyd Bacon's *The Oklahoma Kid* (1937), in which Bogart plays a killer gun-slinger-outlaw dressed in black – just the type to appeal to Tommy. Yet what no one anticipates is the intensity of his identification with the hero of Bacon's film, for within moments he is waving his pistol in the air, proclaiming, 'I'm the Oklahoma Kid, I'm the Oklahoma Kid.' He then shoots the gofer Spider in the foot, simply because he had been slow to bring him a drink. In the end, having been labelled by Paulie Cicero as a 'cowboy,' Tommy is punished for his excesses. Yet even as he goes unwittingly to his death in a faked induction ceremony, he identi-fies his induction with images of grandeur drawn from the Wild West, for after asking an aged sponsor when he himself had been inducted, Tommy remarks: 'Pike's Peak was a fuckin' pimple then, wasn't it?'

Generally speaking, scholars hold two competing views of organized crime. Some regard it as an essentially deviant, parasitic, predatory, and conspiratorial activity, with extortion, violent or otherwise, being the gangster's chief aim. These scholars distinguish between the upper- and underworlds and sometimes judge the latter rather naively in morally absolutist terms. Such assumptions are often conjoined with the belief that, as organized crime wars against the morality of legiti-mate society, so it has an isolable origin external to that society, within particular ethnic groups or foreign countries, such as Italy. The earlier proponents of the theory of organized crime as essentially deviant include criminologist Edwin Sutherland, who sees it as socially para-sitic and corruptive of the body politic. He believes, though, that the greatest demand for criminal goods and services comes from the under-world itself. During the mid-1960s a report of the Oyster Bay Confer-ence denounced organized crime as, to quote Annelise Anderson, a 'malignant parasite which fattens on human weakness.' The Presiden-tial Task Force, in its report of 1967, saw organized criminal groups in total opposition to society. For Thomas Schelling, extortion is the underworld's chief activity, although gangsters prey largely on under-world victims.[49]

Such interpretations have been challenged by scholars who see orga-nized crime as existing in symbiotic relationship with society, providing it with demanded goods and services that, being illicit, are otherwise unavailable. Avoiding naive moralism, these critics embrace the sociologically functionalist argument that organized crime performs a needed social role, without which it would not exist. Some scholars stress that organized crime operates only with the tolerance or consent of the authorities, whom criminals bribe and corrupt.

Already in the 1930s Walter Lippman described the underworld as the public's 'servant' insofar as it responded to its needs and thus performed a social function. For Lippman, organized crime exists because it serves powerful interests. Contemporaneously, Al Capone made this typically self-justifying statement: 'Prohibition is a business ... All I do is to supply a public demand. I do it in the best and least harmful way I can.' The founder of the crime family that Francis A.J. Ianni designated fictitiously as the Lupollos held the same view. In 1963 police detective Raymond V. Martin asserted that crimes initiated by organized criminals would greatly diminish save that corruption 'burrowed deeply into the fabric of society.' Donald Cressey noted the paradox that the public wanted to eradicate organized crime yet also desired its services and products. Morris and Hawkins saw it as supplying widely demanded consumer goods and services. Citing Durkheim and Robert Merton, Joseph L. Albini attributed to organized crime a function integral to the larger society: far from being society's external enemy, the Mafia supplied illegal goods and services by no means forced upon the public. Ianni similarly stressed the symbiotic and functional role of organized crime, while Henner Hess showed both its relation and its resemblance to legitimate government and business. Contrary to the President's Task Force, which portrayed organized criminals as absolute deviants, Frederic Homer saw them as similar to other individuals in their assumptions and behaviour. Like Gay Talese, Nicholas Pileggi addressed the issue in the early 1970s, concluding that Mafiosi were, to quote Stephen Fox, 'regular guys in a land of expediency,' the suppliers of needed goods and services. A self-appointed debunker of what he termed the 'Mafia mystique,' Dwight C. Smith held that organized crime was so enmeshed in society, business, and politics that the upper- and underworld were now inseparable. FBI agent William F. Roemer observed that the mob, whose predatory mentality he recognizes, requires the help of public officials, police, judges, labour leaders, and legitimate businessmen, thus spending enormous amounts on graft. The same conception of organized crime as 'symbiotic' appears in writings by Lupsha, Lyman and Potter, Kappeler and his collaborators, Block, and Kelly. Sometimes such arguments serve the end of ethnic exculpation, as in Iorizzo and Mondello's claim that the Mafia was called into being by the public's insatiable thirst for illegal products, services, and activities.[50]

In assessing the merits of these competing views on organized crime – one stressing parasitism, externality, extortion, and transgression, the other its symbiosis with society – it is worth noting the difficulties deconstructionists discover in the concept of the 'parasite.' Noting that this is a word 'in para,' J. Hillis Miller finds the 'parasite' to exhibit a threatening confusion and uncertainty in the eyes of the closed community in which it appears.[51] Conventionally, the parasite is identified with a dangerously threatening superfluity or excess – the unnecessary, extraterritorial, and non-functional. Yet in its actual operations the parasite undermines the community's (or text's) operative meanings and distinctions, the laws and limits of its self-identity. Neither within nor without the community and its domestic economy, neither totally desirable nor totally useless, neither totally other nor acceptably familiar, but moving freely across (and thus transgressing) margins, the parasite uncannily makes the familiar strange and the strange familiar, and thus destabilizes the conventional meanings on which a social or textual order depends. Since the parasite is not the sheer other of the community, no matter what the community believes, its mystery and confusion cannot be entirely foreign. Rather, the parasite is the community's uncanny double, whose presence reveals the confusion and uncertainty that a community (or text) seeks to conceal. Although the accusation of parasitism often serves the goal of differentiation and exclusion, whether from a community, home, or text, and although the parasite is thus conceived as marginal or adventitious, such a strategy is called in question not simply by the parasite's prior existence within the community but by its indispensability to social differentiation. The parasite is not only within and beyond the social margin; it is the margin itself. Thus in American society the idea of the 'parasitic' gangster would serve to create the actually permeable distinction between the 'organic' community and that which is perceived to corrupt or confuse its values. From this perspective, to exclude organized crime as a 'parasite' would smack of bad faith.

If one moves from the realm of semantic paradox to an empirical consideration of organized crime, its designation as symbiotic seems highly one-sided, as there is much to show that, in normal language, its operations are often parasitic, predatory, and transgressive. As Howard

Abadinsky notes in *The Criminal Elite*, if organized crime chiefly provided goods and services, most of its activities would be consensual. Yet those activities are a mixed bag, the fact being that since around 1930 organized crime has extended beyond the provision of goods and services to extortion, making mob licensing and protection necessary for legal and illegal businesses to operate. Organized criminals demand heavy protection from gamblers, who can otherwise expect to be 'trunked' or killed. Many if not most of organized crime's activities are extortionate. Nor is the boundary between the provision of a good or service and parasitism clearly delineated in organized crime, since criminals who provide gambling and other illicit goods and services such as loan-sharking are often forced into a relationship with gangsters. Regarding legal businesses, Stephen Fox insists that organized criminals create their own demand, squeezing the public through the extortion of protection money. Jonathan Kwitny similarly rejects the 'willing victim' theory of organized crime. More than simply the servants of a hypocritical society, the mob intimidates and manipulates legitimate businesspeople.[52]

What helps to make Scorsese's films so refreshing is their lack of naive moralism, as he grasps the frequent resemblance and interdependence – the symbiosis – between the upper- and underworlds. This awareness appears in *GoodFellas*, yet has its fullest moral and documentary expression in *Casino*. The later film exposes the hypocrisy of a state and society that at first prosper through their covert reliance upon the goods and services of criminal pariahs, in particular gambling, but that subsequently expel their criminal helpers after those have served their purpose. Scorsese also comprehends the socially beneficial aspects of organized crime, which brings a measure of order and security to urban neighbourhoods. And yet, like the later Pileggi, Scorsese does not exaggerate the similarities or mutual dependence between organized crime and its host society. Not only does he focus in *GoodFellas* on the enormous waste resulting from organized crime, but he exposes its essentially parasitic and extortionate character, refusing to extenuate its transgressions. In this film, predation figures as the chief motive of a fundamentally deviant subculture proud of its own deviance.

GoodFellas depicts a true underworld, a pariah realm whose values are reinforced through deliberate self-segregation. This is predictable if one considers the risks criminals run in socializing with law-abiding people. Karen mentions preferring the insularity of wise guy families, noting

that 'we were very close. There were never any outsiders around.'
Likewise, 'we always did everything together and we were always in
the same crowd – anniversaries, christenings.' Inserted snapshots from
photograph albums show Henry's and Jimmy's families on vacation or
playing cards together, with Karen commenting that, when babies came,
Jimmy's wife Mickey was always first at the hospital. The viewer's
sense of the unity of this underworld society is subtly reinforced through
the frequency of the colour blue in the portrayal of its members' domestic get-togethers.[53] Within their subculture it is expected, according to
southern Italian tradition but also for reasons of security, that a husband
will work and his wife will stay at home, limiting her daily social
contacts to other Mafia wives. Scorsese conveys this in the scene in
which, as Henry leaves for work in the morning, Karen appears separated from him within an enclosed kitchen area that Henry then enters
in order to provide her with a generous cash allowance, the fruit of his
depredations outside the home. A mood of inbred intimacy is further
evoked in the scenes of Paulie's family get-togethers, to which Henry
and Karen are invited as his unofficial nephew and niece, and in the
early scene in the Bamboo Lounge, where the introduction of a series of
picturesque mobsters by their obligatory nicknames affords a rare
glimpse of a highly specialized subculture.[54] So insular is this society
that it is in some ways unaware of its difference from the larger world.
Yet the more it adheres to its subcultural ideal, the greater its contempt
for the world outside, its values, customs, and institutions. Born partly
of ignorance and fear of outsiders, such contempt also reflects a disdainful refusal to live by mainstream norms.

The wise guys regard legitimate society mainly as a field for plunder.
An intruder upon their world, the state no less than the surrounding
society inspires hatred and contempt. Whereas Paulie's system of communication works like a charm locally, the wise guys steal mail and
place a mailman's head in a pizza oven to discourage unwelcome
deliveries. Their contempt for the state reflects the fact that its representatives often collude with the mob, such as the policemen who receive
free (stolen) liquor at the cabstand or turn a blind eye to hijacking in
exchange for cigarettes. Thanks to a corrupted judge and lawyer, Henry's
first arrest is dismissed, and later, while in prison, he and his friends
receive special quarters, rich foods and liquors, and other privileges
from bribed prison officials. Henry even bribes them to ignore his drug-
trafficking. Appropriately, Paulie's brief prison stint penalizes him for
'contempt.' Of all governmental agencies, the wise guys most despise

the FBI, partly because its agents routinely harrass them in search not so much of information as pay-offs. Yet whereas the other Mafia wives spit on their own floors when the agents show up, Karen treats them amicably and sends them off with Al Jolson singing 'Toot Toot Tootsie Goodbye' on television, with bird twitterings supplied by Jolson. Towards the conclusion, Jimmy recklessly dares two napping FBI agents to keep up with him in an early-morning car chase.[55] Ironically, Henry will have no choice but to forsake the mob for the government, his only chance for help, protection, and a 'new life.' The Jolson twitterings during the FBI's visit to Henry's house anticipate not only his becoming a stool pigeon – the moment when he, like Jolson, 'sings' – but his farewell to crime. Yet the salvation provided by the bureaucratic state only parodies salvation in its Christian form.

Religion may appear to be honoured by the wise guys, for not only do Henry and his associates wear crucifixes, but Tommy's mother has an icon of the madonna as well as a representation of the Last Supper in her dining room. Indeed, she even paints what Tommy terms 'religious pictures.' The gangster Johnny 'Roastbeef' and his wife adorn the dashboard of their brand-new pink Cadillac with a statuette of the Virgin Mary. The wise guys attend church on special occasions, such as Henry's Catholic wedding, to which his associates and their families are invited, and the baptisms of their children, where the families are again present. As Karen learns upon entering this world, gangsters customarily name their children after saints. Nonetheless, these pieties are only formal and external, as the wise guys flout Catholicism.

After smashing a glass in the face of a restaurant owner who had attempted to collect a seven-thousand-dollar tab, Tommy remarks laughingly that a week earlier the owner had invited him to christen his child; he compounds the insult by announcing his intention to charge the same amount as a godfather. Following the concealment of Batts's body in Henry's car, one sees in the same frame an icon of the madonna on a windowsill in Tommy's mother's house and, in the background, the trunk of the car where Batts suffers his last agony. That religion means nothing to Tommy is shown when, on the day of his assassination, he tells his mother complacently that she must stop painting religious pictures, the point being that, with Tommy supposedly about to become a mob inductee, she no longer needs divine protection. Henry's contempt for religion is implicit in his remark that, thanks to his increasing power of intimidation, he no longer has to 'wait in line on Sunday morning for fresh bread.' Such behaviour analogically parodies the Eucharistic service, in which humble worshippers line up to receive the freshly made bread of the communion wafer. The cross around Henry's neck is only a cultural or ethnic badge, like the flashy jewellery favoured by gangsters. Vinnie, Henry's roommate in prison, who is played by Charles Scorsese, also wears a cross. Henry reveals his indifference to this Catholic symbol when, not to offend Karen's Jewish mother on their first date, he allows Karen to conceal it. He appears at the first of his two weddings, a Jewish ceremony, wearing a yarmulke. *GoodFellas* thus differs from *Who's That Knocking?*, *Mean Streets*, and *Raging Bull* in the impact Catholicism has upon its characters. J.R.'s mentality is Catholic, while his true 'home' proves to be the church; Charlie Civello attempts, inconsistently, to follow Catholic teachings; and Jake La Motta, for all his animality, exhibits an unthinking religious awareness in his masochistically penitential behaviour. The world of *GoodFellas*, by contrast, is desacralized, without conscience or remorse.

 GoodFellas portrays two other pariah groups within American society, with whom the wise guys come in frequent contact and towards whom they feel varying degrees of respect or disdain: Jews and blacks. Unlike Henry Hill, Tommy DeVito sees Jewish women only as sexual spoil, as when he invites Henry on a double date: 'I'm tryin' to bang this Jew broad.' A minor cultural clash ensues when Tommy's date declines anisette, which prompts his contemptuous remark that she would probably prefer Manischewitz. This cultural contrast subsequently surfaces at Karen's country club when Henry declines to sign a tab for fear of leaving evidence. This contrasts Jewish business probity, in which all is 'above board,' with the wise guys' unwillingness to leave written records. A similar contrast appears between Karen's Jewish would-be boyfriend, outfitted and equipped for tennis, and Henry, who conceals the handgun with which he pistol-whips his rival. When Karen's mother complains of her son-in-law's late hours, Karen replies with a hint of disapproval of her unadventurously uxorious father, 'Daddy never went out at all.' Henry's neglect to phone Karen during his all-night excursions (a failing of which his mother also complains) contrasts with the remark of Belle, the Jewish wife of the Jewish gangster Morrie, Henry's associate, that even during his nocturnal excursions Morrie had never failed to call her. When at dawn Karen's mother confronts the belated Henry with the lesson, 'A married man doesn't stay out like this,' he laughs in her face and drives off with Tommy.[56] Subsequently, an Italian American women who forms part of Karen's new society of gangster wives casually describes Miami as 'Jew heaven,' oblivious to her Jewishness. Like Italian American gangsters of old, the wise guys admit Jews as associates, most notably the nearly omnipresent Morrie Kessler.[57] Nonetheless, anti-Semitism is perhaps suggested when Jimmy denies Morrie a share in the Lufthansa loot that his information had made possible, and even more so by his charging the irate Morrie three points above the 'vig' on a loan. This turns the tables on the stereotypes of the Jewish usurer gouging gentile clients.[58] The wise guys' general contempt for sanctity is shown by Frenchy's delighted realization that the Air France heist is best scheduled so as to take advantage of a Jewish holiday.

For Henry, as for his friends, blacks are more contemptible than Jews. Early in the film, in order to allay Karen's fears that he may land in prison, Henry reassures her that 'only nigger stickup men go to jail.' In the confrontation between Billy Batts and Tommy DeVito, the latter is most outraged that, in reminding the company of Tommy's days as a shoeshine boy, Batts has compared him to a servile black, as is implied by the derogatory play on 'shine.' During the 'girlfriend's Friday night' at the Copa, Tommy shows considerable annoyance when his girlfriend mentions the appeal of black entertainer Sammy Davis, Jr. This is not to deny that, just as the wise guys have Jewish associates, so they rely on the minor services of the black criminal hanger-on Stax Edwards. As Henry says, the Lufthansa heist included 'even' Stax. Yet this places him at the bottom of the barrel. When Tommy is later sent to silence Stax, he casually remarks that he had expected to find him with one of his black 'bitches.'[59]

The contempt of wise guy society for the surrounding world leads inevitably to a general flouting of everyday standards of the permissible and forbidden. Driven by their constantly incited desires, at once urgent, boundless, and unrestrained, the wise guys with their wives and mistresses constitute a veritable society of transgression that cannot but have enormous potential for violence and victimization. One way of defining the transgressiveness is to say that this society ignores the Ten Commandments, which Scorsese takes very seriously as a moral code,[60] three of which it violates in performing its most characteristic activities. Contrary to the sixth commandment, 'Thou shalt not kill,' Henry notes that 'hits never bothered Jimmy' and that 'for most of the guys the killings were just accepted. They were a part of everyday. They were routine ... You got out of line, you got whacked.'[61] The eighth commandment, 'Thou shalt not steal,' which encompasses robbery as well as theft, is violated in the goodfellas' hijacking operations, extortion of restaurateurs, demand for 'protection,' usurious loan-sharking under threat of violence, and so on. Although the wise guys expect fidelity of their wives, they dishonour the seventh commandment in their obligatory adulteries with their girlfriends, whom they set up in apartments and take to the Copacabana on specially reserved Friday nights.[62] Henry lies to Karen brazenly when she suspects his betrayal, shows no remorse over it, and ultimately takes up with a new girlfriend to replace the one Karen had forced him to abandon. His unthinking conformity with the approved patterns of underworld behaviour is reflected in the fact that in two successive instances he takes as a girlfriend a woman who, from the point of view of looks and intelligence, seems decidely inferior to his wife. The first of these girlfriends, Janice Rossi, whom Karen denounces publicly as a 'whore,' stands out especially for her dullness, as when she remarks gushingly of Sammy Davis Jr's impersonations that 'you'd think it was the real people!'

For the wise guys, it is a point of honour openly and boastfully to violate prohibitions. Indeed, the very existence of such prohibitions provokes their transgression, and the wise guys are never more pleased than in knowing they have transgressed. Although the film only implies such attitudes, Pileggi's *Wiseguy* shows the special enjoyments transgression affords. When Pileggi says that the wise guys 'exulted in the pleasures that came from breaking [the law],' he could be describing Jimmy Conway who, to quote Henry, 'loved to steal. I mean, he enjoyed it.' According to Henry, Paulie Vario most loved to pay for a lavish dinner with a stolen credit card or 'Muldoon,' even if this meant taking a big and, for Paulie, uncharacteristic risk. 'It was just that stuff that was stolen always tasted better than anything bought.' To which Henry adds that 'if you knew wise guys you would know right away that the best part of the night for Paulie came from the fact that he was getting over on somebody.' Tommy DeSimone, the model for Tommy, 'was the kind of guy who was being so tough he managed to find a bootleg hooch,' Royal Canadian whiskey, then illegal for sale in the United States, as his favourite drink 'thirty years after Prohibition.'[63]

Unlike the American work ethic, which defines disciplined, patient, and productive labour as the proper means of gain, and which exalts such related virtues as thrift and honesty, Henry and his associates view robbery, theft, and extortion as the better path to riches. 'For us to live any other way was nuts,' says Henry, dismissing as already 'dead' those 'goody good people who worked shitty jobs for bum paychecks and took the subway to work every day and worried about their bills.' They were suckers, they had no balls. If we wanted something we took it.'[64] The wise guys further violate the principle of honest work through their involvement in and addiction to gambling, for besides profiting from the numbers game, they constantly wager money themselves. As Henry recalls, 'I'd bet twenty to thirty grand over a weekend,' typically losing the entire amount. In short, he and his fellow wise guys reject production and saving in favour of unbridled spending fed by criminal predation or sheer luck: food, clothes, cars, houses, furniture, and whatever else their hyperstimulated desires demand. With no sense of irony, Karen feels 'proud' of her husband who 'was willing to go out and risk his neck to get ... [her] the little extras,' which include cavernous closets stuffed with clothes.

It is insufficient to say that the wise guys consume rather than produce. Their daily activities, though focused on superconsumption, also result repeatedly in waste – of goods, money, energy, the possibility of use and productivity, human potential, humanity itself. These various kinds of waste, and the capacity to 'create' and indulge in them, testify to the wise guys' personal potency and privilege, their autonomy in the sense of ontological plenitude and freedom from material need, and not least their limitlessly transgressive appetites, eager to swallow up anything and everything though always with the pretense of god-like casualness and indifference.

The theme of waste appears early in the film, when Henry blows up a rival cabstand. Subsequently he and Tommy carry out Paulie's orders by burning down the Bamboo Lounge restaurant, Paulie having previously tricked the owner Sonny into a partnership and then robbed him blind.[65] Both scenes ironize Henry's statement to Karen that he works in 'construction.' Previously the restaurateur had asked Paulie for help with his business, in which Paulie had first feigned lack of interest: 'I don't know how to make a restaurant. I only know how to go in and order the food.' This shows his preference for consumption over production, his love of power ('order'), its connection with his desire to consume, and not least his inability to create. Like the wise guys, Henry is captivated by the mystique of tipping, which he has learned from Jimmy Conway. For these gangsters, throwing away money demonstrates autonomy in the sense of self-sufficiency, for who discards money except one who has no need of it? Such a gesture of indifference is intended, falsely, to suggest an inexhaustible supply of personal resources, implying that 'there's more where that came from.' At the same time, the film identifies waste with sheer material excess driven by consumeristic extravagance – waste in the sense of owning more than one can use. Henry and Karen's bedroom closet is bursting with clothes, and indeed their originals fought over closet space. On the darker side, waste includes the destruction of humanity, whether through drugs or murder. At the finale, as the Lufthansa heist goes sour, Jimmy shows his contempt of human life by disposing of his victims in a garbage truck.[66] Yet the film also inverts ordinary notions of waste by presenting the opposing wise guy viewpoint, as when Tuddy complains that Henry has 'wasted' eight aprons on a wounded man seeking refuge at the pizzeria.

The wise guys reject not only disciplined labour but the American ideal of a routinized life in which long bouts of work alternate with small amounts of recreative leisure or 'free time' – recreative, that is, in refreshing one for more productivity.[67] As Karen remarks of the Mafia wives: 'We weren't married to nine to five guys.' Ignoring the distinction between work and play, the wise guys seek excitement at all times. Their workdays run round the clock and, largely unscheduled, consist of a series of impromptu attempts to 'score.' They gamble continually, whether at cards, the track, or whatever. Like gambling, the wise guys' other typical activities during work – drinking, drug-taking, sex, gunplay simulated and actual – qualify as play and more specifically *ilinx*. The constant intoxication afforded by these activities can only intensify their addiction to a lifestyle that transports them irresistibly into the vertiginous experience of spinning upwards and outwards and out of control.

This lifestyle has its chief setting in bar-restaurants such as the Bamboo Lounge, where the wise guys congregate, where stolen goods are sold to 'respectable' citizens, and where work and play merge in constant celebration.[68] The Air France and Lufthansa heists are plotted in such places, where Jimmy and friends anticipate their spoils in a rush of excitement. These settings also affirm the social values of the criminal community, for here they meet with girlfriends, spend money freely, and eat enormous quantities of lavishly prepared food, as if symbolically consuming the bodies of their victims.[69] As these communal banquets betoken gangster solidarity, so the ability to consume large amounts of food in the face of constant dangers proves a person's worthiness to live the gangster life. Paulie and his associates gorge on sausage sandwiches as he conducts his daily business, with no effect on his appetite. As the wise guys drink and play cards in Paulie's clubhouse, Henry brings sandwiches from a buffet table laden with bread, meats, and cheese. After their murder of Batts, Tommy, Jimmy, and Henry sit down to a large impromptu breakfast at Tommy's mother's house. When Tommy tells his mother her food 'is great but it's like lead,' he seems not to recall that he had shoved his gun into Batts's mouth and made him 'eat lead.' Having slathered his breakfast with ketchup, oblivious to its resemblance to blood, Jimmy pronounces the food 'delicious.' When Tommy, Jimmy, and Henry are later required to exhume the dead Batts, Tommy pretends ghoulishly to feast on the rotted body: 'My mother's gonna make some fresh pepper and sausages ... Here's a leg and a wing ... [Do you want] the heart or the lungs?' A later scene in a diner shows that Jimmy's appetite is never heartier than on the day Tommy is to become a 'made man.' Contrastingly, loss of appetite signals the inability to enjoy the gangster life, as in the final meeting of Jimmy and Henry in the same diner, where they pick at a scanty, bland breakfast.[70]

Normally, though, the appetitive Italian American gangster contrasts with the ordinary citizen, whose weak stomach cannot endure proximity to danger. Thus Karen's mother says of her father that he is so disturbed by Henry's late hours that 'he hasn't been able to digest a meal in six weeks!' In view of the joke that the Jewish comedian Henny Youngman tells at the Copa, in which he mentions having invited his wife to take her vacation in the kitchen, a 'place she's never been before,' Karen's mother's remark may be intended obliquely as the scenarists' unfavourable comment on the quality of Jewish as opposed to Italian cuisine. However, the film depicts a Jew, Morrie Kessler, perfectly capable of matching the wise guys' display of appetite, as when he seconds their idea of concluding an all-night party with 'Danish.' Yet Morrie pays for his strong stomach, as he is murdered seconds later. This is not to imply, though, that all wise guys are equal in appetite. Not only does Henry pick at his food after Batts's murder, but he is nauseated by the latter's exhumation, which Tommy turns into a mock cannibalistic feast.

Among the film's major ironies is that the pariahs come to see their lives as little different from that of the mainstream society they prey upon – a rationalization typical of deviant groups. The more Karen becomes immersed in the mob, the easier it is for her to explain away her involvement in it. 'After a while it got to be all normal,' says Karen. 'None of it seemed like crimes. It was more like Henry was enterprising and that he and the other guys were making a few bucks hustling while the other guys were waiting on their asses for handouts.'[71] She acknowledges that 'our husbands weren't brain surgeons, they were blue-collar guys. The only way they could make extra money, real extra money was to cut corners.' What helps in this delusion of normality is that, unlike the ghetto-dwelling gangsters of *Mean Streets*, those of *GoodFellas* represent the mob in its new and yuppified manifestation, amid such tokens of the American dream as one-family houses, driveways, parked cars, garages, lawns, and domestic chores – though the latter include the hosing out of a malodorous car trunk recently occupied by the dying Billy Batts. As Henry goes off to work in the morning as if he were a typical office worker, dressed in jacket and tie, he gives Karen the thick wad of money she requests of him, for which she immediately awards him with oral sex.

This scene discloses the unbroken connection throughout the film between sex, money, and violence. First comes Karen's discovery of the material and sexual exhilaration of the Copacabana, where her boyfriend demonstrates a purchasing power beyond his twenty-one years, although he has not yet demonstrated his combination of violence and sexual magnetism. This comes when Henry pistol-whips Karen's rejected suitor after he abuses her. When Henry asks Karen to hide his gun in a milkbox, she experiences not fear but sexual excitement. Following their marriage, there occurs the scene of fellatio where Karen consumes her husband's power at its very source. For her, Henry's sexual organ is symbolically equivalent to his pistol, as each provides her with thrills and money. In this scene her efforts yield her a large number of bills representing more or less the equivalent in exchange to Henry's gun and his seminal substance. It is further implied that Karen behaves similarly to a prostitute, which lends irony to her later denunciation of Henry's mistress as a 'whore.' In a subsequent scene, rightly suspecting Henry of adultery, Karen points a pistol at his face as he awakens on their bed. But then he overpowers Karen, throws her to the floor, and points the gun at her; she lies prostrate with exposed legs bent and up as if preparing for sexual penetration. To complete the series, there is the later scene in which, during an FBI drug raid on her home, Karen hides Henry's pistol in the crotch of her panties.

The foregoing description of the gangster ethos needs qualification. It does not reject the idea of the mob as a pariah society dedicated to licentious desire and transgressive violence as it preys on its mainstream counterpart. Yet gangster society cannot permit itself to be licentious or transgressive within its own confines, lest it become a Hobbesian war of all-against-all, which would in turn necessitate an equally Hobbesian appeal to the state, the institution gangsters despise beyond all others. Connelly therefore errs in saying that in *GoodFellas* 'there is no code of honour or dignity as there is in Coppola's *Godfather* trilogy.'[72] Rather, this society requires not only its own government and hierarchy but a code of sanctities, prohibitions, internal punishments, and controls.[73] Whatever contempt it shows to the outside world, its survival demands that its members treat each other in accordance with the society's internal code, so that everyday behaviour takes on aspects of the sacred. Among other things the code includes the requirement of secrecy, which, for this kind of organization, is the *sine qua non*.[74] Its government allocates power, maintains hierarchical deference among its members, administers violence in a controlled fashion, prevents needless and potentially dangerous rivalries from disrupting the system, and punishes code violators. Only if these values are honoured can the perpetual carnival of gangster life continue. The government of the Mafia family thus resembles a state, the key difference being, perhaps, that the former is invisible.[75] At the same time, the Mafia reveals a weakness typical of secret societies: the constant temptation of individual members to transgress against the formal code. All the more attractive to criminals owing to their normally transgressive habits outside the group, this is the temptation to which Henry Hill succumbs.[76] His career as a future Mafia informant is anticipated as well in the scene in which Sonny the restaurateur, commenting on the frequency of Henry's visits to his restaurant, a Mafia hangout, remarks that were he to spend 'another few fucking minutes' there he 'would be a stool.'

Within the underworld the terrain of predation is mapped out and assigned to individual crime families, each having its *capo* or superleader and sub-boss; the next rank is that of *caporegime*, the head of a crew of wise guys.[77] In *GoodFellas* the highest-ranking gangster is Paulie Cicero, modelled on Paulie Vario, a leading Lucchese *caporegime*.[78] At the level of parodic analogy, Paulie equals God or is at least a god, and thus shows traits identified with the divine. Consistent with Elias Canetti's observation that secrecy lies 'at the very core of power,' Paulie projects an image of unapproachability and silence that fills lesser Mafiosi with fearful respect.[79] He further knows that absolute secrecy in his activities will save him from detection by the police. As Henry remarks, Paulie 'didn't talk to more than six people in one day.' He never goes to conferences, totally avoids the telephone, speaks only in one-on-one situations, and gives orders through flocks of messengers, errand boys, and numbers runners. A large man, Paulie conveys his authority through his massive silent presence. This is seen when, merely by appearing at the door of the pizzeria, he terminates the mock fisticuffs of two Mafiosi who might otherwise disturb the neighbourhood. When his underlings place a mailman's head threateningly in a pizza oven, Paulie watches in silent approval. His silence becomes an object of humour, as when he tells Sonny, the restaurateur who seeks his protection against Tommy's abuses: 'They never listen,' says Paulie, 'I tell them a thousand times but they don't listen.' Ironically, Paulie's last name, Cicero, is identical to that of the greatest Roman orator. Another 'divine' feature to go along with his silence is his ponderous immovability, which he has acquired through constant eating. He seems to parody the unmoved mover in Dante, never exerting himself but always relying upon others to come to him with tribute or requests for favours. The essence of Paulie's power is that he remains unmoved while compelling others to move. To quote Henry: 'Paulie was slow because he didn't have to move for anybody.' This immobility connects with his refusal to be affected by the mayhem around him, however intimate his involvement in it. At the crime family backyard cookout Paulie sits quietly in his chair, chewing deliberately on bread and sausage, as if concealing his secrets and devouring his enemies.[80] With his totemic bulldog at his feet, he dominates Henry's world of deviated transcendence.[81]

Paulie's gang members are as capable of creating as of preventing disturbances in the local neighbourhood. As Henry mentions, during the summertime the card-playing wise guys made a racket late into the night, but the residents could do nothing about it. Nor has Paulie any compunction about extorting from local businessmen, as is shown when the restaurateur Sonny asks him for protection. The fate of his restaurant is foreshadowed at their meeting, in which Paulie's presence crowds the frame, as if he were taking over the space. Inciting Sonny's desire for protection by first pretending unwillingness to give it, Paulie finally agrees to 'try to help,' for which he receives a 'Bless you, Paulie,' as if he were a priest. Sonny fails to realize that this partnership entails protection payments that will drive him into bankruptcy. This occurs, though, only after Paulie has drained his partner of his assets. In this world 'protection' and 'help' signify destruction.[82] Although Nicholls believes that Henry arranges Sonny's meeting with Paulie in order to save him from Tommy's brutal mistreatment, a gesture that would dissociate Henry from the world of violence around him, the truth is that Henry is far from innocent in this scene, as he is only pretending helpfulness in order to lure the restaurateur into Paulie's clutches.[83] A close resemblance exists between Paulie's exploitation of Sonny and Uncle Giovanni's takeover of Groppi's restaurant in *Mean Streets*.

Nonetheless, in *GoodFellas* as in *Mean Streets* and *Raging Bull*, the presence of organized crime in the Italian American neighbourhood helps to preserve order and harmony. Like Uncle Giovanni and Tommy Como, Paulie exerts a pacifying role like that of a priest, and is perhaps more effective.[84] Not only does he subdue the boisterous Mafiosi outside the pizzeria, but, having heard Karen's complaints of Henry's adultery, he informs Henry that he must return to his wife: 'Do the right thing ... Go home to the family.' What Paulie objects to is not adultery itself, a virtual underworld institution at least for males, but the fact that, unlike the properly discrete Mafia husband, Henry has allowed his wife to discover and advertise his unfaithfulness.[85] Paulie realizes that Karen's marital scandal sets a bad example for Mafia wives, by inviting retaliatory infidelities with all their potential for mistrust, mimetic violence, serial betrayal, and breaches of mob security. As he tells Henry: 'We don't know what she's gonna do.' Paulie's intervention is thus motivated not by morality but by a desire to 'keep up appearances' so as to maintain in-group harmony.[86]

Perhaps the most important means by which crime families control violence between and among themselves is the institution of the 'made man,' a phrase suggesting the bosses' god-like power to confer privileged status upon individuals. As Henry reports, a made man is a gangster elected to permanent membership in a mob family, and whose induction is legitimated by a secret swearing-in ritual attended by leading family members.[87] Typical of secret societies, such rituals produce a feeling of community not only by accentuating, as Georg Simmel says, the 'exceptional position' of the person 'enshrouded' in secrecy, but by suggesting to the initiate the 'possibility of a second world alongside the obvious world.' Induction and the ritualization of behaviour within the Mafia make total claims over the 'whole man' comparable to those of military and religious communities. The Mafia initiation oath establishes, under threat of violent punishment of the least lapse of secrecy, those bonds of mutual trust without which the society could not endure.[88] The made man is free to administer violence as he sees fit upon gangsters lacking permanent membership in a family. The made man is also normally immune to violence from other people, who need special permission to kill him. The induction ritual contributes to the control of violence within the family in that made individuals become untouchable, virtually sacred figures from whom lesser gangsters, however attracted to them, must maintain a respectable and fearful distance. To quote Henry: 'It is the highest honour they can give you. It means that you belong to a family and a crew. It means that nobody can fuck around with you. It also means that you can fuck around with anybody just as long as they aren't also a member.' He compares it to a 'licence to steal, ... a licence to do anything.'[89]

Mob families further limit violence by protecting individuals who, because of their crimes, cannot go to the police. Though such a person may be punished by his protectors, for instance, for failing to make protection payments, he is shielded by the mob family from violence by other parties.[90] As Henry remarks, Paulie offers to the isolated wise guy 'protection from other guys looking to rip them off ... protection for the kinds of guys who can't go to the cops ... the police department for wise guys.' The crime families demonically parody state and police, monopolizing violence in order to contain it.

Lacking the status of made men, Henry Hill, Jimmy Conway, and Tommy DeVito are crime family associates who receive from Paulie Cicero the protection they need to operate. With his permission they devote themselves to the family's day-to-day business, which includes gambling, running numbers, fencing, loan-sharking, selling hot cars, and hijacking. Besides being forbidden to harm made men, a Mafia member or associate is required to surrender a substantial portion of his criminal earnings to the *caporegime*, who in turn yields a percentage to those of higher rank.[91] After Henry, Jimmy, and Tommy 'score' in the Air France heist, they do what Henry calls the 'right thing' in giving Paulie his 'tribute,' on which his protection depends. 'Hundreds of guys depended on Paulie and he got a piece of everything that they made,' remarks Henry. A further prohibition is that members and associates must not traffic in drugs, which thus fall under a sacred prohibition. Like other bosses, Paulie objects to such activity because drug convictions bring long sentences and thus provide underlings with an incentive to 'rat' in exchange for a reduced sentence.[92]

Strictly speaking, Henry Hill is a mob underling of no special distinction, as are Tommy and Jimmy. His status is reflected in the jobs he is assigned as well as in his half-Irish and half-Italian (or Sicilian) background, which prevents him from becoming a made man. By contrast, Tommy as a full-blooded Italian can aspire to that honour. Yet despite Henry's marginal role within the mob, his position as a relative outsider affords him advantages unknown to his Italian American counterparts.

Because the typical Italian American wise guy belongs to a professional hierarchy that, governed by an elaborate system of protocols and taboos, prevents him from moving either above or below his level, he has little or no contact with mob bosses and knows little of family operations as a whole. Typical of secret societies, such secrecy within the mob hierarchy is intended to protect the family and more especially the higher-ups against informants.[93] Henry, however, in not being a full-blooded Italian, escapes these restrictions and can thus move throughout the hierarchy. He fraternizes with soldiers like Frenchy, Frankie Carbone, Anthony Stabile, and Johnny Roastbeef, but he also rooms with bigshots like Paulie and Johnny Dio in Lewisburg prison.[94] The scope of his awareness makes him unsurpassed as a betrayer of the world to which he bears witness, as Paulie sadly discovers.[95] The only underworld character of comparable mobility in Scorsese's Italian American films is 'Ace' Rothstein in *Casino*, whose Jewishness enables him to move freely among the mob bosses, and whose advantage as a protagonist is that, like Henry Hill, he provides an unusually broad perspective on mob operations.

GoodFellas charts the progress of a subcultural group as it rises, peaks, declines, and disintegrates. Its high point is perhaps Henry and Karen's Mafia wedding, a communal event in which nearly all levels of gangster society, from *capos* to ordinary soldiers, from Christians to Jews, are present. The wedding guests include Paulie and family, Jimmy and his wife Mickey, Tommy and his mother, Mr and Mrs Frankie Carbone, Morrie and his wife Belle, and others. Something of the wedding's joyous mood persists in the snapshots of Henry's and Jimmy's family in their get-togethers. Yet within two decades this society will collapse through transgression, rivalry, jealousy, scandal, betrayal, and mutual violence. Every person at the wedding's main banqueting table will by the conclusion have been informed against, arrested, or murdered. What *GoodFellas* depicts, more thoroughgoingly than any of Scorsese's previous Italian American films, is a sacrificial crisis, as the last vestiges of social order and decency are obliterated in a flood of undifferentiating violence.

A major reason for this collapse is the prevalence of mimetic desire and its ensuing rivalries, which lead to envious hostility and retaliation. These circumstances are aggravated by mob-imposed taboos that, though intended to promote *rispetto*, provoke contrary impulses of transgression in a community already accustomed to violating mainstream norms.

Another factor driving the gangsters into rivalry is the limited supply of *rispetto*, to which they assert competing claims, and the desire for which makes them abnormally sensitive to insult. Further contributing to this witches' brew is the wise guys' gambling, which impels them towards self-destruction as they take greater and greater risks. Finally, their constant thrill-seeking so disorients them that they lose all sense of stable identity and spin out of control.

An early scene at the Bamboo Lounge adumbrates both the potential conflicts within this gangster society and its inability to control internal violence. Seated before an audience of wise guys gathered round a restaurant table, Tommy, after telling a series of well-received jokes, unexpectedly seems to take offence at Henry for describing him as 'really funny.' Tommy apparently interprets Henry to mean that he himself, rather than his joke-telling, is an object of humour. He also seems to think that Henry has singled him out as a peculiarly laughable individual, and perhaps even as a candidate for the 'funny farm.' If so, Henry has committed an insult for which he could forfeit his life right on the spot. This scene of jubilant laughter seems about to descend unexpectedly into violence as Tommy pressures Henry to explain his use of 'funny.' For Tommy, the increasingly tongue-tied and intimidated Henry resembles a 'stuttering prick,' stuttering being for Tommy the mark of fear. What makes the scene still more disconcerting is that Tommy seems if only fleetingly to suspect his own psychopathology, the anomalousness of his superviolent personality even within the underworld. However, he was only pretending to have been insulted, and his annoyance turns out to have been a joke – although the line between laughter and violence seems precariously thin. The terror having passed, Tommy remarks half-seriously to Henry that 'someday you may fold under questioning' – a fulfilled prediction. Yet that Tommy's violence has not yet been fully appeased is seen when, in a fit of annoyance, he smashes a glass into the face of the restaurant owner, who had been badgering him over a large unpaid bill. Tommy transforms even this act of violence into a joke, which receives its share of laughs from the wise guys.

As with *Who's That Knocking at My Door?* and *Mean Streets*, one must call on anthropology to explain the recurrent interplay of anger and laughter, violence and celebration in *GoodFellas*, this being the chief source of what Scorsese calls its 'black humor.'[96] Above I outlined how, according to Girard, rituals originate in the socially salvific climax of the sacrificial crisis, when the embattled community united unexpectedly in newfound harmony around the scapegoat. Rituals and their accompanying festivals also attempt as closely as possible to reproduce in orderly fashion those violent events through which society returned to order and prosperity. Not only are such celebrations marked by joyful laughter among the participants, but they promote collective happiness through their innocuous mimicry of violence, which awakens amused delight within the community to the extent that it is recognized as make-believe. But all these effects ensue only if no participant substitutes actual violence for its controlled mimetic version – an increasingly likely possibility in *GoodFellas*.

How then to explain those scenes in which, amid escalating violence, and in contrast with the raucous guffaws that greet Tommy's finally controlled display of violence in the Bamboo Lounge, violence and even murder appear in conjunction with jubilant laughter? For Tommy's wise-guy friends, his crippling and subsequent killing of Spider is no more than a joke that briefly interrupts their card game. Tommy's remorselessly mechanical murder of Stax is preceded by his joking remark to Carbone, ordering him to make coffee, as if they intended to join their victim over breakfast. Similarly, Henry pretends to laugh when Jimmy wraps a telephone cord around Morrie's neck, with every intention of strangling his creditor, and Tommy's subsequent murder of Morrie elicits a joyful 'good riddance' among the wise guys. In each case, the victim is marginal to wise-guy society and thus a good conductor of the violence threatening it from within. Manifest before, during, and after these scenes of victimization, the wise guys' ebullient laughter either anticipates or directly expresses the joy felt by the embattled community when, at the conclusion of the crisis, it stands reunited around the murdered scapegoat, typically identified with monstrosity and deformity. Hobbes recognizes the cruelty often present in laughter in defining it as an expression of superiority felt in the contemplation of another person's deformity or imperfections.[97]

The murder of Billy Batts by Tommy, Jimmy, and Henry marks the turning point in their criminal careers, when reckless violence carries them off track and their perpetual festival begins to go wrong. This murder also affords a case where, in the unpredictable play of violence and laughter, the latter fails to control the former. The setting is the bar of Henry's Suite Lounge on 11 June 1970. A made man of the Gambino family,[98] then at the height of its success, and thus a kind of sacred figure, Batts (Frank Vincent) is throwing a party in celebration of his release from prison after six years. His unpopularity is suggested by the fact that fewer than five people attend his party, including Henry and

Jimmy, and that its decorations consist of a few pathetic streamers and coloured balloons. Nonetheless Batts is expansive – 'Good to be home,' he says – and, having suffered the humiliations of prison, he is all the more eager to assume his long-suspended prepotency. His opportunity to demand *rispetto* comes with the arrival of Tommy, who, with his date, finds himself unexpectedly amid the festivities.

'All grown up and doin' the town,' says Batts to Tommy condescendingly, though pretending amity. In ordering Tommy to 'come here,' Batts resembles those gangster gods who, like Paulie, will not move for anyone but expect others to come to them. Embracing the rather short Tommy with a gesture too aggressive to be termed a hug, the much taller Batts laughingly addresses him with insincere affection as 'you little prick,' adding, 'Don't get too big on me.' The wounding impact of the last statement may be gauged from the fact that in an earlier scene, while regaling his friends with comic stories at the Bamboo Lounge, Tommy had admitted to them a desire to be 'big just once' – an admission that also helps to explain Paulie's later observation that Tommy has 'too much to prove.' Unlike Tommy, Batts is allowed by mob protocols to treat underlings overbearingly; the *rispetto* he enjoys depends partly on disrespect for others. Naturally Tommy is annoyed by Batts's dominating embrace, well aware of the animosity underlying it, and embarrassed to be mocked and mistreated while in the company of friends. Thus the audience unexpectedly feels sympathy for Tommy in this as in several other scenes, notwithstanding that he is a cold-blooded psychopathic killer. Yet because Tommy realizes Batts's privileged status, he can only ask him to refrain from 'breaking his balls,' to which Batts protests that Tommy mistakes good will for hostility: 'If I wanted to break your balls I'd tell you to go home and get your shine box.' Further to belittle Tommy, Batts recollects his days as a shoeshine boy: 'He was great. I used to call him Spit Shine Tommy. I swear to God he'd make your shoes shine like fucking mirrors.'[99]

The force of this insult can be measured by those earlier scenes in which expensive and perfectly polished shoes signify a gangster's power, remoteness, and self-sufficiency. Henry's original gangster models are revealed from the shoes up, and Henry is shot from his head down to his shoes when he shows off his first gangster-style suit to his mother. It is a humiliation for Tommy to be reminded in public of those days when, as a boy, he waited slavishly yet enviously upon gangsters like Batts, looking up at them from a seemingly insuperable distance. It is no less humiliating to have performed work commonly associated with lowly and despised blacks, as is implied by Batts's reference to 'Spit Shine Tommy,' 'shine' being a common term of abuse for blacks.[100] The polished surfaces of Batts's shoes are like mirrors in which he admires his own image, seeing himself as he appears from the shoeshine boy's lowly perspective. At the same time, the reference to mirrors imports the double, and more specifically Batts and Tommy as the doubles of mimetic violence. Conscious of his own disgrace, which rankles him all the more owing to his short stature and hopes of incarnating the intimidating gangster in his own right, Tommy with barely suppressed anger reminds Batts that he no longer shines shoes, adding that his jokes sound like insults. 'You're gettin' fuckin' fresh,' rejoins Batts, as if Tommy were an obnoxious child, but then returns to the bar as if letting the matter rest.

Instead Batts, without looking at Tommy, takes a drink and announces: 'Now go home and get your fuckin' shine box.' Tommy then moves threateningly towards Batts but is restrained by Jimmy and Henry. Trusting to his apparent invulnerability as a made man, Batts tells his few guests to 'relax,' 'don't get nervous,' as he surrounds them with a protective shield against Tommy's menace. Yet unwilling to act merely defensively, Batts taunts Tommy: 'Come on. You feel fuckin' strong?' – the implication being that Batts wields the greater strength. Yet though Batts's confidence seems justified when the enraged Tommy leaves the bar, it is tacitly understood by Henry and Jimmy that they will take revenge against Batts later that night.

After Tommy's departure, Jimmy lulls Batts into a false sense of security by apologizing for Tommy: he 'gets a little loaded' but 'doesn't mean any disrespect.' For his part Batts blames Tommy for the altercation: 'He doesn't mean any disrespect? Are you nuts? Teach this kid a little fuckin' manners ... What's right is right ... We're huggin' and kissin' over here and two minutes later he's actin' like a jerk.' Jimmy replies: 'You got a little out of line yourself, you insulted him a little bit,' accompanying this statement with slight movements of his head indicating his long experience in calculating the minutest degrees of insult. But actually he realizes that his friend has suffered a major insult. Turning to the small gathering of party guests, who are relieved that the confrontation is over, Batts remarks casually of Tommy that 'I fucked kids like that in the can [in prison]. In the ass' – a statement indicating that, from Batts's point of view, his mistreatment of Tommy amounts

symbolically to a homosexual degradation to the passive feminine position. Nor is there any doubt that this is how Tommy perceives it, as he
has been deeply dishonoured in the presence of his friends and date.
After Jimmy announces drinks on the house, Batts denounces Tommy
for 'fuckin' breakin' up my party' and resumes the festivities.

Hours later, as the party winds down, and Donovan's 'Atlantis' starts
up on the jukebox, Jimmy distracts the by now quite drunk Batts at the
bar as Tommy enters the barroom alone. Henry ushers out the last
patrons and locks the door as Tommy collars Batts from behind and is
joined by Jimmy in beating and kicking him mercilessly. The Donovan
lyric 'Way down below the ocean, where I wanna be, she may be'
evokes the 'oceanic feeling,' death or nirvana as the unacknowledged
goal of the gangster life. Tommy then places a gun in Batts's mouth in
simulated homosexual disgrace and pulls the trigger. In an overhead
shot Batts appears sprawled on the floor in his own blood as Tommy
strips a table of its covering, which now serves as a makeshift cerement.
One recalls the scene at the Copa, when the waiter brings Henry and
Karen a circular table covered by a tablecloth that billows slightly as if
enchanted. Tommy's removal of the tablecloth implies an exposure of
all the false allurements of the gangster life, a revelation of the brutality
behind its materialistic seductions. Again one feels some sympathy for
Tommy, who has been provoked to murder, and who tearfully apologizes to Henry for bloodying his floor. Fleetingly one sees the vulnerable shoeshine boy behind Tommy's tough-guy facade. Yet he and his
two accomplices have reason for fear, for as Henry remarks in *Wiseguy*:
'If the Gambino people ever found out that Tommy killed Billy, we were
all dead ... Tommy had done the worst possible thing he could have
done, and we all knew it. Billy's body had to disappear.'[101]

An ironic commentary on Batts's murder is provided by the next
scene, in which, with Batts dying in the trunk of Henry's car, the three
friends visit Tommy's mother's house in quest of a shovel with which to
bury him at a secluded site. Unexpectedly they awaken Tommy's mother,
who, not having seen her son in a long time, provides the trio with a
lavish early-morning breakfast. During the meal Tommy asks her for
the loan of a large kitchen knife, which he intends for Batts's burial, but
which he pretends to need in order to amputate the hoof of a deer
trapped on the highway. To do otherwise, Tommy says, would be a
'sin.' That the goodfellas, with the exception of the troubled Henry, eat
heartily after their butchery of Batts proves their fitness for the gangster
life, whose enjoyments require a strong stomach. The religious imagery

in the dining room – the Last Supper on the wall, an icon of the Virgin on the windowsill – contrast with Batts's murder and his concealed agony in the driveway outside the window. At the same time, Christ's betrayal by Judas finds its analogue in the lie Tommy has told his mother in order to conceal the murder he and his friends have just committed.

However, the deeper ironies of this scene are revealed in the conversation at the dining-room table. Tommy's mother tells a Sicilian story concerning a man who was 'two-timed' by his wife but did nothing about it: *content' cornuto*, content to be a cuckold, a phrase common in Sicily.[102] A possible revenge scenario thus fizzled owing to the unwillingness of the offended person to retaliate, notwithstanding that, among southern Italians, the greatest shame a male can suffer is to be dishonoured by an unfaithful wife. This too is Tommy's view, as he translates the Sicilian for his friends as meaning 'content to be a jerk,' adding that such a person 'doesn't care who knows' of his disgrace. In Tommy's world view not to retaliate is to be a jerk, and thus a deserving object of ridicule. He further implies that, had he been cuckolded, he would have avenged himself without hesitation. The mother's story thus parallels Tommy's encounter with Batts, except that Tommy, meeting with an insult, had killed his enemy. Yet the alternative interpretion of the mother's story is that the 'jerk' has taken the Christian path. He avoids retaliation, resists the pressures of the community that attempts to shame him, and avoids the self-destructive violence that ultimately claims Tommy.

The conversation concludes with a discussion of an enigmatic wall painting rendered amateurishly by Tommy's mother. Although the picture lacks overt religious content, it invites such an analysis given that Tommy, before his execution for killing Batts, tells his mother not to paint any more religious pictures. The painting depicts an elderly, distinguished, patriarchal-looking man with white hair and beard standing in a boat against a serene pastoral landscape. Before him on the boat are two standing dogs rendered in profile and virtually identical in size and shape. Thinking of the white-haired Batts, Tommy and Jimmy are amused by his resemblance to the old man. According to Bliss, the painting juxtaposes 'religion with violence ... the man in the boat looks like a patriarch and is situated in a placid, almost biblical scene. The religious connotation of the painting operates in violent contradiction to what's going on right outside the mother's kitchen window.'[103] Actually, what is most crucial is not the patriarch but the two dogs, calling to mind the animal ferocity displayed by Batts and Tommy as well as the brutality of the film's other gangsters. Yet unlike Batts and Tommy, who in their confrontation become unacknowledged doubles of each other's violence, these dogs not only look in opposite directions but are related to the surface of the painting in differing parallel planes, one behind the other, as if refusing confrontation and its ensuing loss of differences. Lowly contemptible creatures, the dogs carry the same message as the cuckold in Tommy's mother's story, the lesson of non-retaliation as the key to God's tranquil kingdom depicted in the painting.

Batts's murder coincides with an escalation in violence in the wise guys' already murderous world. For it is not only Henry, Jimmy, and Tommy who go off-track, but their whole society. 'For most of the guys,' observes Henry, 'killing got to be accepted. Murder was the only way everybody stayed in line. But sometimes even if people didn't get out of line they got whacked. I mean hits became such a habit with some of the guys.' He adds that they 'would get into arguments over nothing and before you knew it one of them was dead. They were shooting each other all the time.' This state of affairs is exemplified by Tommy's wounding and subsequent killing of Spider.

To understand Tommy's motivation in this unprovoked murder, one must consider the mimetic element in his murderous psychopathology. Taking his models of masculinity from both leading Mafiosi and video action heroes, Tommy has difficulty dissociating real from simulated violence, but responds to both with the same cold detachment. His behaviour must also be understood mimetically in relation to his recent killing of Batts and its psychological effect upon him. As the motif of the mirror suggests, Tommy and Batts become mimetic doubles of each other as they vie for *rispetto* as a combined power of magnetism and intimidation. That they are doubles is also suggested by the fact that Tommy dreams of becoming a made man, which would make him equal to Batts while providing him with the same envied prerogatives. Thus, even if Batts had provoked his own murder, Tommy can only feel exultation in having killed him. It is as if, in taking Batts's life, he has also won his prepotency, and thus prepared for his own coveted induction within a crime family. Having 'become' his victim, Tommy wants to imitate Batts, to project the same intimidating remoteness, to exert his power as unmoved mover upon human beings, to demand and compel their awestruck gaze, and not least to find an object of contempt identical to what he himself, the despised shoeshine boy, had been for Batts: a mirror in which to admire his own power. On the other hand, Tommy can never be more offended than when a nonentity fails to show him respect. All this adds up to a formula for the crippling and killing of Spider.

Both scenes of violence occur in a clubhouse bar and game room where Tommy, Henry, Jimmy, Anthony Stabile, and Frankie Carbone sit around a circular card table drinking, smoking, and playing cards. Their gofer, Spider, is a young, thin, gangling, and not very intelligent Italian American male whose name suggests a betwixt-and-between creature, despised, excluded, and, unprotected. In the first scene Spider fails to hear Tommy's request for a a drink, which elicits Tommy's angry question: 'What am I, a mirage?' He adds: 'You been doin' this all night ... You got me on a pay-no-mind list.' For Tommy, who dreams of god-like status, to suffer impatiently an unsatisfied need is as insupportable as going unacknowledged by a person like Spider. He proceeds to intimidate the gofer, whom he denounces as a 'bumblin', stutterin' little fuck,' mocking his stuttering speech. Batts had previously called Tommy a 'little prick,' a phrase Tommy applies twice to Spider. As Batts had insulted Tommy by comparing him to a black shoeshine boy, so Tommy complains that Spider walks like Stepinfetchit, the first of several references to video in this scene. Self-intoxicated, like Batts and Paulie, with the role of unmoved mover, Tommy orders Spider to 'run, dance. Move it, you little prick.'[104] Then, with increasing excitement, he asks his friends to remind him of the only Western film in which Humphrey Bogart appeared. The film having been identified as the *Oklahoma Kid*, the eponymous hero of which is played by James Cagney and in which Bogart actually plays the black-clad villain Whip McCord, Tommy removes his gun from his belt, waves it in circles as if to menace his cronies, and cries out deliriously: 'I'm the Oklahoma Kid, I'm the Oklahoma Kid!' A *mise-en-abîme* of mimeticism suggests itself if one considers that Tommy the gangster now imitates not just made men like Batts but an Irish American actor who played gangsters more often than cowboys and whose role in the film Tommy confuses with that of a Western villain played by an actor better known for impersonating urban tough guys. It is as if Tommy, in his mimetic delirium, were moving progressively out of reality into violent fantasy. Yet unlike Cagney's and Bogart's portrayals, in which violence is only simulated, Tommy suddenly shoots Spider in the foot to the cry of 'Yahoo, motherfucker!' The site of Spider's crippling wound consorts with his despised and excluded social position, as a limp or injury to the foot is one of the classic victimary signs of the scapegoat, as witness Oedipus, Hephaistos, and Matthew Arnold's Empedocles.

Normally more sensitive to bloodshed than his friends, Henry is shocked and appalled by Spider's crippling and calls for a towel to staunch his wound. One recalls the scene in Tuddy's pizzeria, when the young Henry 'wasted' eight aprons on a wounded man. Yet Henry's cronies are scarcely more affected by Spider's misfortune than is Tommy. Uttered amid general laughter, 'Nice fuckin' game' is Carbone's only response to the shooting. Another wise guy, absorbed in the game, insensitively announces, 'I've got a good hand,' as if Spider's wounded foot resulted from bad luck. The wise guys refuse compassion in a world where suffering amounts to disgrace. More out of common sense than sympathy, Jimmy recommends that Spider be taken to a local doctor, but Tommy wants him to 'crawl there, like he crawls for the drinks.' He adds, in another psychopathic confusion of reality with video, that he should be treated by Ben Casey, a television doctor of the 1960s. Dismissing the shooting as an 'accident,' Tommy objects that Spider wants to 'make a big fuckin' thing out of it.' The scene concludes with the continuation of the card game, as one of the players casually announces, 'I'm in,' which implies the distance between the charmed in-group and the excluded world of losers like Spider.

The scene of Spider's murder in the same clubhouse begins as, with bandaged foot, he waits on the same group of wise guys. When Tommy refuses to offer Spider sympathy, the gofer weakly mutters, 'Go fuck yourself' as he walks away, whereupon the wise guys burst into laughter, including Henry. With his fine sense of proportion in retaliation, Jimmy notes the ludicrous disparity between the seriousness of Spider's injury and his feeble answer to it. Then, in a mingling of comedy and violence typical of the film, he remarks ironically to Tommy: 'You gonna let him get away with that? What's the world comin to?' – to which Tommy, taking him seriously, responds immediately by killing Spider with six deafening pistol shots to the chest. In order to emphasize the completeness and finality of Spider's banishment from the gangster society to which he aspires, Scorsese cuts from a claustrophobic shot of Tommy at the table, firing his pistol as he sits among his astonished and frightened friends, to a long shot in which the mortally wounded Spider, falling backward from right to left across the screen, is carried by the bullets' impact a considerable distance from the place where the gangsters have assembled. Tommy then explains to the stunned Jimmy: 'I didn't know if you were kiddin'.' Tommy justifies the killing as punishment administered to Spider's 'family of rats,' informers being the lowest entities of the underworld.

Although Spider stands totally apart from the gangster in-group, there is reason to think that, for Tommy at least, Spider not only doubles for Henry Hill but displaces Tommy's unacknowledged hostility towards his friend. Tommy has already shown antagonism towards Henry at the Bamboo Lounge, where Henry's characterization of Tommy as 'really funny' provokes the latter's resentment, and with it his attempt to intimidate Henry with the threat of violence – an encounter whose confusion of comedy and violence anticipates Spider's crippling and death. That Tommy's murder of Spider targets an innocent victim with violence he might otherwise direct against his friends is suggested by that fact that, immediately before crippling Spider, he waves his pistol in circles in the air, as if repeating the shape of the circular card table, the implication being that he is capable of shooting at any of the persons seated around it, including Henry. The table would then become a wheel of fortune, consistent with the theme of random, undifferentiating violence. Moreover, the resemblances between Spider and Henry are too many to be coincidental. Not only was the young Henry himself a mob gofer, serving food and drink to wise guys gathered at card tables, but his slender, gangling physique and long, thin face during his adolescence had somewhat resembled Spider's. Yet fortunately for Henry in his career as a gofer, he had never forgotten the first order Jimmy Conway had given him, namely to 'keep the drinks comin'' – precisely what Spider fails to do in serving Tommy. As Tommy vilifies Spider as a 'stutterin' prick,' so he says the same thing to Henry during the scene of intimidation at the Bamboo Lounge. So too, Tommy's identification of Spider with a 'family of rats' is paralleled by his earlier claim that Henry 'may fold under questioning.' And finally, Henry and Spider share a certain marginality even if for different reasons, as Henry, in being half Italian, is a bearer of questionable difference and is thus also a candidate for ostracism. Nor is it surprising that Henry alone among his colleagues treats Spider with a certain politeness, and that he sympathizes with him after his crippling and death.

In *GoodFellas*, as in *Who's That Knocking?*, *Mean Streets*, and *Casino*, chance exerts an increasing power over the main characters, partly because of their absorption in risk-taking and thrill-seeking. Thus Tommy, whom Paulie schedules to accompany Jimmy to Florida for the purpose of debt collection, is replaced at the last minute by Henry, who helps Jimmy force the debtor into payment. What they fail to realize is that their victim's sister works for the FBI, so that, after gambling away their weekend at the track, they are both unexpectedly arrested, tried, and sentenced to ten years in prison. Continuing the downward trend begun by Batts's murder, the wise guys grow increasingly reckless as their society unravels.

Reduced to six years thanks to good behaviour, Henry's prison term proves reasonably comfortable thanks to the corruptibility of the authorities. To quote Henry: 'Everybody else was doing real time.' Housed with Paulie and other criminal associates in special living quarters, Henry and his friends enjoy many of their former pleasures, including delectable meats, shellfish, and alcohol smuggled in from outside.[105] The running outfit Henry wears as an inmate gives the impression of a leisurely pastime, as if he were still in the suburbs. As previously at the Copa, Karen has no need to stand in line when she visits Henry in prison, but receives special consideration by officials. Nonetheless prison transforms Henry's gangster career, for now he can support Karen and family only by selling drugs, which he had previously avoided, and which she now provides him from outside.[106] He also acquires a drug habit, partly to ease his boredom but also for the thrill of it. By dealing drugs Henry begins to part company with the older gangsters, including Paulie, and has started on the path that will force him to abandon the gangster lifestyle. In one scene, the older gangsters are gathered at a table while Henry, isolated significantly in a one-shot, sits on a bed as he covertly removes drugs from a sack. Next, in an overhead shot he walks past his friends out of the frame, remarking to Paulie and the others: 'Catch you guys later.' The overhead shot suggests the ultimately dominating surveillance of the United States government. Following his later arrest for drug-trafficking, Henry not only leaves the mob but betrays Paulie to the government, thus 'catching him later.'

Henry's entry into the drug trade suggests that a criminal society devoted to transgression also harbours the seeds of its undoing, since its own laws are bound to be violated sooner or later. Admittedly, the gangster code shows some flexibility, as Paulie tolerates Henry's drug-dealing while in prison as his only means of supporting his family. But after Henry's release Paulie states flatly that he wants 'no garbage here,' meaning drugs. Unwilling to be held accountable for his underling's drug traffic, Paulie knows that narcotics convictions bring long prison terms, as in the case of his friend 'Gribbs,' an older Mafioso likely to die in prison because of his purely circumstantial association with drugs.[107] Paulie further warns Henry against Jimmy and Tommy, the first a 'good earner, but wild,' the second a 'cowboy.' The insincerity of Henry's disavowal of risk-taking is exposed in the next scene, in which he mixes cocaine with a pair of playing cards. Having resumed the Pittsburgh drug connection he had begun in prison, Henry seems to excuse his transgression in noting that Paulie, who wants 'no garbage *here*' (my italics), will remain ignorant of his activities *there*, as if, technically, Paulie's order had not been violated.[108] In another violation, Henry enlists Tommy and Jimmy as his helpers.

The remainder of the film focuses on three parallel narratives that, though minimally related, chart the declining fortunes of Henry's criminal society. There is the Lufthansa heist at Kennedy Airport, the most lucrative in history. There is the murder of Tommy DeVito under the pretext of inducting him into a crime family. And there is Henry's drug-trafficking, a major reason for his loss of control and professional betrayal, as Paulie had feared.

Suggested by Morrie Kessler, the Jewish wig salesman, loan shark, and small-time hood and executed by a large gang under Jimmy's direction, the Lufthansa heist exposes the boundless greed and ambition of these criminals. By comparison with the earlier looting of Air France, Lufthansa's yields more than eight million dollars – an increase of over sixteen times. According to Henry, who is too occupied with his drug business to participate in the heist and who contents himself with a small cut as a Christmas present from Jimmy, this robbery should have been the gang's 'ultimate score,' with 'more than enough to go round.' This triumph is accentuated ironically by its coincidence with the sanctities of Christmas, when the robbers plunge into an orgy of spending that parodies yet oddly resembles the American dream. To quote Henry: 'I bought the most expensive tree they had.'

The ensuing mayhem results partly from the fact that the crew members and their wives, being addicted to mimetic display, cannot curb their consumption. Johnny 'Roastbeef,' who appears at Jimmy's Christmas party with a new bride and a newly purchased pink Cadillac, and Carbone, whose wife arrives wearing a white mink coat, trigger not just Jimmy's angry displeasure but his fear that the FBI will be alerted to these expenditures. As he remarks to Carbone: 'Did I not tell you not to attract attention?' Or as Morrie puts it in commenting enviously upon the division of the loot among the other gangsters: 'Everybody's flashing stuff ... They're wearing it [the loot] ... It's poison in my eyes.' Jimmy thus decides to kill Roastbeef and Carbone. Stax, the black driver on the heist, must also be removed for having failed to destroy the getaway van. His surprise execution by Tommy, who shoots him in the back of the head, ironizes Henry's comment that 'everybody loved Stax' during his days as a Mafia wannabe at Robert's Lounge. Yet the chief cause of all this violence is Jimmy's desire to claim nearly all the loot for himself. To quote Henry: 'I knew Jimmy. He had the cash. It was his. It made him sick to turn money over to guys that stole it. He'd rather whack 'em.' This motivates his murder of Frenchy, Joe Buddha, and Morrie, whose demands for their share of the money – to the tune of five hundred thousand dollars – Jimmy finds intolerable. Indeed, he apparently never intended to reward Morrie for the information that had made the heist possible.[109]

Like Scorsese's previous Italian American films, yet with unequalled scope and intensity, the later scenes of *GoodFellas* exemplify the 'holiday-gone-wrong,' engulfed in a vortex of acquisitive rivalry, transgression, and retaliation. A hallmark of this mini-version of the sacrificial crisis is the unpredictable proliferation of violence and hence the predominance of chance. Such violence in turn produces social undifferentiation by undermining formerly honoured distinctions among individuals. Ultimately, conventional categories are submerged in a tide of violence from which no one is immune and against which the dishonoured traditional sanctities can no longer provide protection.

Random violence is already manifest in the murder of Batts, whose execution is hardly envisioned in his party agenda, and it appears too in Spider's victimization. His crippling and subsequent death occur unexpectedly amid a card game played at a circular card table that – in a familiar Scorsesean motif – becomes his fatal wheel of fortune. A similar unpredictability characterizes the fate of Morrie, for up to his last moment it remains uncertain whether Jimmy will kill him. When Henry first realizes this possibility, he hopes that Jimmy will change his mind during that evening's card game, in which Morrie and Tommy participate. In yet another mingling of laughter and violence, Tommy regales Morrie with a comical story that, for those aware of Tommy's mental habits, holds potentially lethal implications. The butt of Tommy's joke is the 'stutterer,' whom he had intimidated into silence. The story calls to mind Tommy's mock-violent and actually violent encounters with Henry and Spider respectively, both of whom he had identified with fearful stuttering. That this story signals Morrie's end may be suspected from the fact that Jimmy and Tommy are fed up with his constant demands for his share of the Lufthansa loot. However, during the card game Henry infers from a remark of Jimmy's that Morrie's assassination has been cancelled, whereupon Henry breathes a sigh of relief. Yet as it turns out, the audience shares in Jimmy's deception of Henry, for Morrie is murdered by Tommy that night, an event whose unexpectedness drives home the unpredicability of his execution. Jimmy has apparently misled Henry deliberately so as to prevent him from warning Morrie – an act of deception that also forecasts Jimmy's scheme to murder Henry. In a later scene, in which Karen visits the warehouse where Jimmy stores his stolen goods, Jimmy, out of growing fears that Henry and Karen will turn informant, urges her to enter a storeroom 'on the corner' for the purpose of choosing from the expensive dresses kept there. Not only is the dark room filled with burly, dangerous-looking men, but the sidewalk leading to it is lined with old pinball machines, suggesting not only the ricochet of bullets claiming innocent victims but the possibility of the violent death awaiting Karen within. Fearful of being 'cornered,' she flees the scene in her car amid the sound of screeching tires.

The theme of the loss of distinctions is most evident in that the wise guys become each other's unacknowledged doubles through mutual violence. In other instances violent transgression results in a blurring of social boundaries, a confusion of categories normally kept separate and thus protected from mutual contamination.[110] Though concentrated in the later part of *GoodFellas*, such moments appear almost from the beginning.

Not only do Tuddy's henchmen place a mailman's head in a pizza oven, as if he were to be cooked and eaten, but Henry brings a large collection of stolen coats to the Bamboo Lounge, whose owner puts them in his refrigerator for safekeeping. After Henry beats up Karen's disgruntled admirer, she hides his pistol in her milkbox; towards the film's end, he and she leave a large cache of guns in her mother's garage; and at the climax she places Henry's pistol in the crotch of her panties to conceal it from narcotics agents. Having hidden Batts in a car trunk, Tommy borrows his mother's kitchen knife to finish him off. His grisly task represents the contamination of the sacred space of the domus by the bloody world outside. He had previously entered his mother's house with his white shirt covered with Batts's blood, in which condition he had embraced her all the more ironically in full view of an icon of Christ with open arms. Later, when news arrives that condominiums will be built on the site of Batts's grave, Tommy and his friends must remove his corpse. In this scene, Tommy jokes about the putrefied remains as if he were about to indulge in a cannibalistic feast. In addition to its incongruous mingling of comedy and murder, Spider's death is precipitated by Tommy's delirious confusion of real and make-believe. Towards the conclusion the bodies of Frenchy and Joe Buddha show up in a garbage dumpster, having been consigned to an under-world which, in its total disposable heterogeneity, collapses all bound-aries.[111] After his murder of Morrie, Tommy apparently chops him up as if he were a dead animal. At first a participant and then a victim in these killings, Frankie Carbone is found frozen in a meat truck, hanging from a hook like all the other carcasses. He dangles without a coat, frozen stiff like one of the damned in the last circle of the Inferno. Not only does the forward-tracking shot into the meat truck recall the Steadicam shot of Henry and Karen entering the Copa, save that now the camera's progress ultimately discloses a sacrificial reality ignored in the jubilation of that festive moment, but it inflects in a demonic register the earlier scene in which a restaurant refrigerator had served to hide stolen coats. At the same time, one recalls the earlier scene in Lewisburg prison, in which Paulie, Henry, and their fellow inmates had stored lobsters and choice steaks in a makeshift freezer hidden by a curtain. Having been reduced to a slab of meat, Carbone exemplifies the loss of distinction between man and beast that typifies the sacrificial crisis. This confusion had appeared earlier when Jimmy and Henry had threat-ened to feed a defaulting creditor to a lion in the Tampa Zoo – an act that only ironizes Paulie's observation regarding his underlings: 'we're not *animali*.'

Sitting across from Henry in their favourite diner, Jimmy remains confident, self-possessed, and altogether untroubled by the murders he has set in motion following the Lufthansa heist. Nothing better indi-cates his state of mind than his healthy appetite, as if he were consum-ing his victims – the true mark of the gangster being the ability to eat heartily amid circumstances repellent to other people. Yet the chief cause of Jimmy's confidence is that Tommy is about to be ritually inducted into a crime family. Henceforward, thinks Jimmy, he and Henry will enjoy the protection of Tommy and his organization.

What Jimmy learns in sorrow and disappointment is that Tommy, on the pretence of induction, had been executed in the house of a Mafia boss. His death pays for his transgressive murder of the made-man Batts, whom he ought to have avoided. Moreover, Paulie is involved in Tommy's murder, a role foreshadowed when he criticizes his underling as a 'cowboy,' and still earlier when, in response to Sonny's complaints of Tommy's behaviour in his restaurant, he remarks: 'Tommy's a bad kid, a bad seed. What am I supposed to do, shoot him?' To which Sonny responds, 'That wouldn't be a bad idea.' Admittedly, the film never spells out Paulie's participation in the killing, but *Wiseguy* states that Paulie gave the Gambino family his approval to execute DeSimone.[112] In the film, Tommy's execution is carried out by Vinnie and Paulie's brother Tuddy, two underlings in Paulie's criminal family.

As Tommy's mimetic absorption in Batts persists up to his last moments, so Tommy's feigned induction and assassination carry reminders of his murder of Batts, thus indicating a retaliatory symmetry between these events. Evidently, following Batts's murder Tommy had aspired to resemble his victim as closely as possible, thus treating Spider as Batts had treated him, as the equivalent of a black gofer. Tommy has also learned from Batts how a made man, when facing the threat of violence, projects absolute confidence in his supposedly invulnerable position, especially while in the presence of lesser-ranked gangsters. During his exchange with Tommy, Batts had smugly told his anxious party guests, 'Don't get nervous,' as if he were untouchable. When Tommy learns he is about to be 'made,' he shows off his soon-to-be privileged position in telling Henry and Jimmy not to 'worry,' despite increasing pressure stemming from the Lufthansa heist. The made man feels a god-like autonomy that, besides intimidating others, makes him feel impervious to fear, as if shielded by an impenetrable aura of sanctity.

Tommy's murder of Batts comes to mind when Tommy, as he leaves his mother's house on the day of his 'induction,' tells her not to paint any more religious pictures. This refers to the earlier scene where Tommy notices that the elderly figure in his mother's painting closely resembles Batts yet fails to grasp the painting's pacifistic message, which would have prevented Batts's murder. When Tommy and his two drivers arrive at the place of initiation, their car is shown from the back as it enters the garage so as to remind the viewer of Batts's concealment in a trunk. When Tommy is led into the game room for his supposed initiation, he fleetingly glimpses before his murder the far wall of the room where, directly above the card table, hangs a swordfish. This marine motif calls to mind the Donovan song on the jukebox during Batts's murder, 'Way down below the ocean, where I wanna be, she may be.' One thinks too of the violence associated with swordfish, of the traditional saying of Mafiosi that their dead enemies 'sleep with the fishes,' and of Jesus's statement to Peter: 'Those who live by the sword die by the sword.'[113] Yet this swordfish also evokes Christ as the fisher of men, now Tommy's only hope of salvation. The final shot from above of Tommy dead with blood spreading from his head wound over the floor parallels the overhead shot of Batts mortally wounded in Henry's Suite Lounge, with Tommy apologizing tearfully for bloodying the floor.

This scene implies a more subtle resemblance between Tommy and Spider, founded on more than the fact that, in another gaming room less exclusive than that of the made men, Tommy taunts and kills Spider. Like the young Tommy, Spider is an aspiring gangster who seeks acceptance by a clubhouse in-group at its card table, but who instead receives insult, contempt, and ostracism. His biggest mistake is to have inadvertently insulted Tommy by failing to bring him his drink, which the latter takes as a breach of *rispetto*, or evidence that Spider regards him as a 'mirage.' I have suggested that as a result of Tommy's sudden violence, the circular card table becomes for Spider his fatal wheel of fortune. In the later scene, as Tommy is being escorted to his execution, Vinnie, his driver and sponsor, tells him: '*Buona fortuna*, Tommy.' Then, upon entering the game room with the expectation of being greeted by his peers, Tommy unexpectedly sees the world from Spider's point of view. For here too is the sacred and desired circular card table, where Tommy hopes to sit with the chosen few, where he has often sat in fantasy, and where, realizing in the briefest moment his permanent exclusion from this society, he now sees a void, as no one is there to greet him. Tommy's vanity having lured him to destruction, he now sees himself and all his hopes as a mirage, the ephemeral thing he had accused Spider of seeing.

While Jimmy and Tommy pursue their independent careers, Henry Hill sinks deeper into criminality and domestic disorder – a lifestyle all the more bizarre against its backdrop of suburban conventionality. By now Henry has become a drug addict and communicated his taste for narcotics to Karen. Although she had demanded Henry's dismissal of Janice as the absolute limit of his adulteries, he has set up his new girlfriend Sandy in an apartment where, apart from having sex, he mixes and packages cocaine for his Pittsburgh connection with Sandy as his assistant. Since Paulie had forced Henry to end the affair with Janice for the sake of his family, his taking up with Sandy flouts authority. Not only does she snort cocaine herself but, as if in mockery of domesticity, she refuses to use the new dishwasher for fear of ruining her nails, thus leaving cocaine traces all over the kitchen. Henry's inability to find his car keys on the cluttered dining-room table portends his possible loss of mobility under a prison sentence. For drug deliveries he relies on his former babysitter, Lois Bird, who travels by plane with borrowed babies as her cover, and never without her lucky hat. Karen's comment to Lois that one of these babies 'looks just like you' prepares the viewer for the infantile behaviour by which Lois will help to sink Henry's operation.

Henry's lifestyle climaxes disastrously on 11 May 1980. This is the final result of his thrill-seeking, gambling, and drug-taking, his bondage to that 'intoxication of the moral order' that is *ilinx*. Now his frenzied life carries him over the edge and out of control. Although *ilinx* had been portrayed in *Who's That Knocking?* and *Mean Streets*, the conclusion of *GoodFellas* captures that experience with special vividness by means of rapid cutting, mobile camera work, and scenes of hectic activity. As in those earlier films, and subsequently in *Casino*, the descent into chaos is identified with a spinning or whirling movement, an all-engulfing vortex. The result is indistinction, general disorientation, and the total loss of priorities and hierarchies – a mirror of Henry's state of mind. Yet though his chaotic experience resembles that of his wiseguy friends, now caught in the midst of undifferentiating violence, and though Henry's life is never far removed from gunplay, the fact remains that he never fires a gun or kills anyone in the film, and never seems entirely to belong to his associates' world of mayhem. Henry's disorientation results not from violence but from his submission to a host of mimetic passions that, each with an equal claim on his attention, crowd each other out and leave him drained and bewildered. His life becomes a frantic, ever-eddying tumult of desire.

When in a voice-over Henry recalls 11 May – 'I was going to be busy all day' – he sounds like an average suburbanite burdened with weekend tasks. Yet beginning with a hit of cocaine and ending with an abortive drug run, this is no ordinary day in the suburbs, and it grows increasingly harried and nerve wracking. Henry's anxieties arise with the nagging suspicion that his car is being followed by a helicopter whose rotating propeller, shot from below, calls to mind the constant whirl of his desires as well as the wheel of fortune that, in *GoodFellas* as in Scorsese's other films, carries associations of violence and fatality. The theme of desire is again explicit in the accompanying lyric by The Who: 'I want it, I want it, I want it.' When Henry attempts to sell Jimmy guns, the latter angrily refuses them because they are incompatible with his silencers; however, Henry thinks he can find another buyer. As

Henry replaces the guns in his car trunk, his distorted image appears
fleetingly on the fender's curved metallic surface – a sign that his
materialism and child-like attraction to flashy surfaces have transformed
him unwittingly into a human grotesque. Still suspicious of the helicopter, he barely avoids a traffic accident and then picks up his invalid
brother, that evening's dinner guest, at the local hospital. Following a
long description of the dinner's ingredients and his methods of preparing it – as if these weighed equally with gun sales, drug-running, and
police surveillance – Henry rushes off with Karen to find a buyer for the
guns, but not before reminding his brother to keep stirring the tomato
sauce.[114] This gesture reiterates the idea of circular movement, the all-
engulfing *turba* of desire. Thus Scorsese describes the characters as
'getting caught up in a vortex of passion.'[115]

Convinced that the helicopter is following them, Henry and Karen
must conceal the guns temporarily at her mother's house, where they
leave a small arsenal in her garage. The mimetic compulsiveness of
Henry's behaviour, and indirectly that of his wife, is suggested by the
accompanying Rolling Stones' song, 'I'm a Monkey.' Like those of an
ape imitating a human being, Henry's movements are determined by
the pursuing helicopter. Yet the song lyric also identifies Henry implicitly with both the mimetic compulsions of the gangster life and the
constant aping of the consumer culture that inspires and supports it. At
the same time, the lyric exemplifies that confusion of man and animal
that appears elsewhere in *GoodFellas*. There is, moreover, a thematic
resemblance between the soundtrack of *GoodFellas* and that of *Mean
Streets* as each film rushes to its conclusion. In the finale of the earlier
film, Johnny Boy performs a rock and roll war dance to the tune of
'Mickey's Monkey,' referring ironically to the fact that Johnny Boy,
ostensibly the film's free spirit, is trapped in a violent mimetic agon
with Michael, who now governs Johnny Boy's desires and movements.

The helicopter apparently having vanished, Henry and Karen unload
the guns with a buyer. Before rushing to Sandy's apartment to collect a
shipment, Henry phones his brother with the familiar advice, 'Keep
stirring,' which applies as much to the narrative as to the tomato sauce.
The visit to Sandy involves obligatory 'quickie' sex (naturally too hasty
to satisfy either party) and a big hit of cocaine followed by a return
home to make dinner. Unfortunately Sandy, in annoyance over Henry's
departure, has thrown cocaine all over the apartment, while Lois, against
Henry's orders, has revealed details of her upcoming drug delivery
during an outside call from Henry's house. Lois then announces her

inability to make the drug run without her 'lucky' hat, so that Henry must take her home. This marks the height of his and his accomplices' irrationality, their inability to evaluate priorities and to maintain a sense of proportion. Before Henry and Lois are out of his driveway, they are arrested not by local police pursuing Henry for his connections with the Lufthansa heist, as the helicopter had led him to think, but by narcotics agents. Having lost touch with his own world, Henry had not even considered that likely possibility. When the agents raid his house, his operation goes under.

Now in jail, Henry faces the severest test of his loyalty to the code that Jimmy had instilled in him years before: 'Never rat on your friends, and always keep your mouth shut.' Since Henry has already violated orders by running drugs, Paulie has every reason to think that he will 'rat' on Paulie to save his own skin. In short, one act of betrayal implies another. For Henry, a further cause for worry is that Jimmy may want to eliminate him so as to conceal from Paulie his own involvement in the drug trade. Henry must therefore bail himself out of jail and, if possible, repair his relations with both men.

Paulie's role as Henry's provider is underlined by the fact that he is frying sausages in his restaurant when the tearfully contrite Henry appears before him, avowing his trustworthiness henceforward. Nonetheless Paulie cannot forgive Henry's betrayal, for as he says, he has been 'treated like a jerk' – the mistreatment against which Paulie had warned Henry upon his release from prison. The sympathy one feels unexpectedly for Paulie in this scene depends very much on the Catholic analogism underlying Scorsese's portrayal of his betrayed trust. Noting the persistent influence of Catholic modes of thinking upon him, Scorsese finds a close resemblance, both conceptual and experiential, between religious faith and the faith he invests in other people. For him, his faith or trust in another person is largely a spiritual matter.[116] Nor is Scorsese the first to propose such an analogy, which appears in Simmel's 'The Sociology of Secrecy and of Secret Societies.' Simmel writes of 'another type of confidence, which ... falls outside the bounds either of knowing or not knowing ... the type which we call the faith of one person in another. It belongs in the category of religious faith.' He adds that, 'just as no one has ever believed in the existence of God on grounds of proof ... so we have faith in another person, although this faith may not be able to justify itself by proofs of the worthiness of the person.'[117] That Paulie by his own lying and cheating has betrayed the trust of many law-abiding people does not alter the fact that, in being betrayed by his virtually adoptive son, he is able to comprehend, however dimly and by antithesis, something of the religious significance of trust and faith.

Their friendship having terminated, Paulie gives Henry a little over three thousand dollars as severance money. This, however, is only a salve for Paulie's conscience, for in complaining that the amount can hardly pay for his coffin, Henry knows he is marked for death. The fried sausages that Paulie prepares imply symbolically that he is ready to devour Henry and conceal him in his capacious stomach. The same fate awaits Karen, who is bound to be killed as a potential informant or else to punish her husband.

Henry's meeting with Jimmy in their favourite diner is fraught with mutual suspicion. For Henry, the question is whether he will be 'whacked'; for Jimmy, whether Henry will 'rat.' Henry sees through Jimmy's smiling amity, for as he says, when the mob marks a man for death, his murderers come to him 'with smiles, as friends,' without the dramatics of the movies.[118] Such false cheer only adds to the mood of belatedness and irony investing this scene. Now past his prime, Jimmy Conway is grey haired and wears glasses. Whereas formerly he had eaten heartily in celebration of his worst crimes, now he eats sparingly, as if he had indigestion or ulcers, and Henry's appetite is no better. An ironic counterpoint to their lack of appetite is provided by the sign, reading 'Hero Sandwiches,' on a building seen through the diner window. One recalls *Mean Streets*, where the low mimetic characters Charlie and Johnny Boy pass a storefront window with 'Hero Sandwiches' inscribed upon it. As in that film, the gangsters of *GoodFellas* are far from being heroes, and furthermore their appetites by this point no longer qualify as 'heroic.' At the same time, consistent with the quasi-cannibalistic code of the underworld, Henry is about to be eaten.

Although Jimmy is too cunning to declare his lethal intentions, Henry infers them. The revelation comes when Jimmy requests that he travel to Florida 'with Anthony' in order to murder an informer. A freeze-frame fixes Henry's face as he realizes that Jimmy had never asked him to do such a thing before, that the target is himself, and Anthony is his assassin.

Jimmy's plot to murder Henry carries an ironic comment on the gangster life – a recognition not only of its delusions but of its potential for self-destruction. For this is the meaning implicit in the name of the proposed gunman Anthony, to whom Scorsese calls attention. 'Who is Anthony?' he asks, apparently regarding him as a generic 'hit-man.'[119]

Yet one can give a more precise answer. The person in question is probably Anthony Stabile, a minor gangster who first appears in the long tracking shot in the Bamboo Lounge, and who associates with Henry on several occasions, including the card games involving Spider. That this Anthony qualifies as one of Henry's friends, and is thus well suited to betrayal, is evident from the fact that he speaks up on Henry's behalf when Tommy pretends to be angry with Henry at the Bamboo Lounge. Yet Anthony is also the name not only of the host at the Copacabana but of the waiter who, during Karen's introduction to the gangster life at that nightclub, brings her and Henry their table, the tablecloth fluttering magically, and who waits upon their every need. Next comes the fleeting appearance of 'Mr Tony,' the mob bigshot from whom Henry and Karen receive a free bottle of wine. Thus, at the film's conclusion 'Anthony' stands for those purveyors of desire and violence whom Henry has admired, imitated, solicited, and wooed throughout his career, all those who had led him into 'the life.' At the same time, like a fate, Anthony the waiter-gunman symbolizes the drugged-out Henry's death wish, the extinction that very possibly awaits him.

Living on borrowed time, Henry joins the Witness Protection Program and learns that he must move to another state under a new identity. Soon the authorities have convinced Karen that she and the children must join him, for not only has she participated in his drug traffic, but the family will be open to threat and violence. As Bill McDonald, the Witness Protection Program officer who plays himself in the film, tells Karen: 'What it comes down to is we're your only salvation. We're gonna save your life and his life. We're gonna keep you outta jail.' Consistent with his entirely secular mentality, Henry's 'salvation' is provided not by priests but by the state, whose representatives, unlike Paulie Cicero, show absolute impersonality and even indifference to their wards, treating them as mere instruments of law enforcement. Scorsese perhaps implies in a Hobbesian vein that not religion but only the bureaucratic state can control the violence of modern society. If so, then *GoodFellas* anticipates the conclusion of Scorsese's *Gangs of New York*, where the state, with its monopoly of violence, provides the only remedy to the warfare among the Irish gangs of Manhattan's Lower East Side in the 1860s.

Like *Mean Streets, Raging Bull,* and *Casino,* the conclusion of *GoodFellas* exemplifies Scorsese's ability, very possibly rooted in his Catholic background, to elicit concern for morally flawed or unacceptable characters. In the scene of Batts's murder, Tommy's tears momentarily reveal the humiliated, vulnerable shoeshine boy long concealed beneath the tough-guy pose. Yet an equal sympathy is reserved for the swaggering, over-bearing Batts, not only for the brutality he suffers but for the fact that, just before the surprise assault against him, he informs Jimmy of his responsibilities on leaving prison, including 'fucking mouths to feed.' When Jimmy learns of Tommy's execution he is reduced to tears, and Henry grieves too for the loss of their friend. As questionable or unat-tractive as these characters are, the audience is made to share in their sorrow, at least up to a point. Similarly, the concluding announcement of Paulie's and Jimmy's harsh prison sentences awaken sympathy not only for the poker-faced Paulie but for Jimmy, who holds back tears, and his wife Mickey, Karen's good friend, all of whom feel the sting of Henry's betrayal.

Henry Hill, however, invites a less-than-sympathetic response at the conclusion, though he has helped the state and achieved 'salvation.' Part of the difficulty in sympathizing with him is his opportunism, as he has betrayed his friends only to save himself. No moral awareness or contrition accompanies his decision to inform. Rather, he regrets that in ceasing to be a gangster he has become a 'schnook,' like the ordinary people he despises. 'The hardest thing to do was leaving the life. I still love the life. We were movie stars with muscle. We had it all for the asking.' He goes on: 'When I was broke I'd go out and rob some more ... We paid everybody, ran everything. Everybody had their hands out. And now it's all over,' this being the 'hardest part.' Henry's voice-over is accompanied by a shot of a bulldozer excavating the suburban subdi-vision in which he now lives, where the geometrical sameness of the houses implies the conformism and predictability of his new existence. This excavation, which calls to mind the murder of Batts, whose body had to be reburied lest it come to light during the building of new condominions, implies the insubstantiality of Henry's personality, as his own identity has been recast with an efficiency equal to that of the bulldozer in transforming the natural landscape. Nor is this surprising, for just as Henry had concealed his crucifix in order to court his Jewish girfriend Karen, so he had married her in successive Jewish and Catho-lic ceremonies. One of the few remaining connections between Henry and the social world he had formerly inhabited is the *New York Times*, a copy of which he picks up from his doorstep in his farewell scene. Further to underscore the moral void of his personality, Henry remains at the level of hedonistic impulse, as when he arranges with McDonald to join the program. That Henry smokes even as he complains of his bronchial condition, and yet demands that he be sent to a warm climate, proves his continuing enslavement – or addiction – to desire. Similarly, his final words have nothing to do with morality but rather complain of the unavailability in his new location of a good spaghetti with marinara sauce. A fraudulent restaurant had given him egg noodles with ketchup.

8 Pariahs of a Pariah Industry: *Casino*

It is not too much to say that the whole question of organized crime in American society cannot be understood unless one appreciates the distinctive role of organized gambling as a function of a mass consumption economy.

Daniel Bell, 'Crime as an American Way of Life'

The inspiration for *Casino* appears to have come to Scorsese through Nicholas Pileggi, who immediately upon the completion of the *GoodFellas* script began thinking of a film on organized crime in Las Vegas.[1] Pileggi alerted Scorsese to newspaper articles on the professional and domestic problems of Frank 'Lefty' Rosenthal, a Las Vegas casino manager and a leading mob representative in that city during the 1970s. Like Pileggi, Scorsese saw in these materials the basis of a film on the fall of Italian American crime families in Las Vegas in the period when its casinos were being corporatized. Scripted by Pileggi and Scorsese, *Casino* was not inspired by Pileggi's book of the same title, as the screenplay and book were written concurrently.[2] Based on research and interviews, the book is a factual account of the decline of the mob in Las Vegas, with a focus on Rosenthal. A fictionalized treatment of its subject, the film alters characters' names, modifies details, and transforms and transposes events. Yet there remains a close congruity between book and film. Pre-production began in June 1994, and by September Scorsese was filming in Las Vegas, with technical advisers from both the mob and FBI on hand to ensure accuracy. Scorsese wanted to conclude what Pileggi describes as his 'great trilogy' on Italian American organized crime by depicting its expansion into the Far West and the troubles it encountered there.[3]

Scorsese remarks that 'the actual place, and the gaming, were new to me. What interested me was the idea of excess, no limits.'[4] *Casino* thus calls to mind *Raging Bull*, whose ostensible subject, boxing, held no interest for Scorsese, but which attracted him as a form of extreme behaviour. Yet it was not just the excess of Las Vegas that interested Scorsese, but the gambling world in the decisive decade of the 1970s. His film resembles *GoodFellas* in its documentary and even 'anthropological' dimension, as witness its voice-overs, titles, and meticulous rendition of the gambling milieu with its distinctive social code and atmosphere. Scorsese's description of his *The Age of Innocence* (1993) applies to *Casino* as much as to *GoodFellas*: 'What seems to be description is in fact a clear picture of that culture, built up block by block – through every plate and glass and piece of silverware, all the sofas and what's on them.'[5] Yet one should not exaggerate the documentary element in *Casino*, for like *GoodFellas* it employs a highly mobile and expressive camera so as to evoke a world that, as it succumbs to its own excesses, finally spins out of control.

Unlike Scorsese's other Italian American films, *Casino* has received a mainly lukewarm or dismissive response, as critics tend to regard it as overly dependent, even parasitic, upon Scorsese's earlier works, especially *GoodFellas*. To quote Douglas Brode, *Casino* received 'respectable' reviews but is considered 'inferior' to its predecessors. Peter Bondanella describes the pairing of Robert De Niro and Joe Pesci as the leading male characters as 'old territory already traveled.' For Lawrence Friedman, *Casino* is '*GoodFellas* removed to Las Vegas.' 'So striking' are their similarities that the '*raison d'etre*' of the former work remains unclear. Commenting on *GoodFellas*, Jim Sangster writes that 'Scorsese wanted to do something different ... to look at the "family" aspect of organized crime but also to look at the bigger picture, including everyone in the chain.'[6] Thus, when Ian Christie observes that, for 'skeptics,' *Casino* is only '*GoodFellas II*,' the implication is that, though shifting its terrain to Las Vegas, the film simply repeats the themes, materials, and situations of its predecessor by relating the crime family to the larger social chain, but all too obviously.[7] At the same time, *Casino* is 'often cruelly known' as *GoodFellas II* because of its editing, for as in the earlier film, the 'camera is moving almost constantly: flash photography cuts, freeze-frames,' and a long Steadicam tracking shot into and out of the counting room, reminiscent of Henry and Karen's side-door visit to the Copacabana.[8] Critics further complain that *Casino* overdoes voice-overs and documentary information. The latter, remarks Brode, 'made *Casino* fascinating at the level of documentary, yet none of the characters was properly developed, nor were their relationships comprehensible.' He adds that, with its 'gorgeous but chilly surface,' *Casino* leaves you 'hungry for drama.'[9] 'It's hard to be enthusiastic about *Casino* for all its wonders,' observes Sangster, for not only is it 'very light on plot,' but the 'first half-hour of screen time seems to be taken up with background detail while the rest of the film seems to be a string of anecdotes' less entertaining than those of *Mean Streets* or *GoodFellas*. He adds that 'ultimately, there's a strong feeling that, despite the new characters and setting, we've seen it all before.'[10]

Other critics treat *Casino* disdainfully. Terence Rafferty notes that 'Scorsese certainly hasn't forgotten how to make a movie; what he appears to have forgotten is *why*.'[11] Complaining of the all too familiar 'face-off' between De Niro and Pesci, Marilyn Yaquinto describes the film as an 'unintentional diamond-studded sequel to *GoodFellas*,' indeed, as '*GoodFellas* goes Vegas.' Regarding the film's theme, Yaquinto writes: 'Las Vegas ... [as] metaphor for a crass, decaying America besieged by corporate takeovers and a loss of honor – even among mobsters – is well-worn turf.' For Scorsese to put Las Vegas at 'center stage ... is uninspired and disappointing.'[12]

Were these judgments accurate, Scorsese's gangster trilogy must end anticlimactically. Actually, *Casino* has never been examined in detail sufficient to reveal its beauties, subtleties, and complexities. Nor have critics grasped its relation to either Scorsese's other Italian American films or his Catholic and Italian American sensibility. The label *GoodFellas II* is inappropriate, as the situation treated in *Casino* – the relation of organized crime to state and society – differs from that depicted in its predecessor. The voice-overs and documentary details, especially in the first hour, are necessary to clarify a moral situation so complex and ambiguous that it has no parallel in the other Italian American films, including *GoodFellas*.[13]

As noted earlier, crime experts regard organized crime as either parasitic or predatory upon the larger society or else as existing functionally in symbiosis with it. Contrary to the 'willing victim' theory of organized crime, which stresses its symbiosis with mainstream consumers, many organized crime operations are predatory or extortionate. Although *GoodFellas* acknowledges a symbiosis to exist between organized criminals and society, including the government, it emphasizes predatory criminality, so that the viewer's final moral evaluation is comparatively simple. *Casino*, however, focuses painstakingly on organized crime in its most intimate relation not only to its social environment but to the state, which, by supporting casino gambling, has condoned and even allied secretly with the mob. The details or 'blocks' by which Scorsese portrays Las Vegas are indispensible to the revelation of the moral ambiguity of the gambling world as well as the characters' involvement in that world. Once one realizes Scorsese's success in both elucidating and dramatizing this moral sitation, there is only one answer to Ian Christie's statement: 'Only time will tell whether *Casino* is indeed another hard-won masterpiece.'[14] It fully merits such a description, being one of Scorsese's richest efforts and a worthy climax to his Italian American films.

Banned in Nevada in 1910, gambling was legalized in 1931 by a state government desperate for revenue and became big business in the 1950s and 1960s. This was remarkable given the difficulty of financing casinos. Banks and other financial institutions shunned the gambling industry because of its stigma, the heavy cash flow involved, and fear of embezzlement by organized crime. The state preferred, partly for moral reasons, to approve individual licensees rather than deal with corporate shareholders, and thus forbade corporate investment in and ownership of casinos. Although casinos found some legitimate investors, they inevitably attracted others connected with the mob.[15]

Organized crime found gambling less profitable than bottlegging during Prohibition, notwithstanding that criminals like Al Capone owned gambling houses. But after Prohibition, organized crime began to reap enormous profits from gambling, partly because members of the increasingly prosperous middle class demanded a service less stigmatized than previously. As gambling became more sophisticated, technologized, and industrially organized, mob-controlled casinos began to appear in resort areas, with satellites in the metropolises. For organized crime, gambling was proving more lucrative than both prostitution and industrial racketeering.[16] Humbert S. Nelli notes that the Second World War afforded a major impetus to underworld gambling operations, including horse racing, dog racing, bookmaking, numbers, and casinos. In Bell's view, the 'most significant transformation in the field of "institutionalized" crime in the 1940s was the increasing importance of gambling.' By the early 1950s gambling had become organized crime's major cash crop, bringing in twenty million dollars gross and seven million net.[17] It also provided the mob with a useful means of money laundering. By 1997 organized crime made roughly between twenty-nine and thirty-three billion dollars through illegal gambling.[18] In no given year did Italian American crime families claim all the profits, although, for many decades, they are believed to have taken the lion's share.

Mob investors dominated the Las Vegas gambling industry from the mid-1940s into the early 1980s.[19] Preceded in the early 1940s by the El Rancho and The Last Frontier hotel casinos, which introduced under legitimate ownership gambling resorts to what came to be known as the Strip, Bugsy Siegel's Flamingo Hotel represents the mob's first major inroad into the city. Himself a major gangster, Siegel was backed by mob investors in the east, including the New York and Chicago crime families and Meyer Lansky, but having overspent on the hotel and failed to deliver demanded profits, he was murdered in June 1947, six months after its opening. Not only did the Flamingo prove profitable after being taken over by Lansky and the New York mob, but it was also evident that the construction of hotel casinos afforded unparalleled opportunities for in-house skimming, that is, theft of pre-tax profits from the gambling take, a method recently perfected in the mob's Havana casinos. The operation's success depended on hidden ownership, lest the mob come under legal scrutiny; each owner would receive 'points' or shares of the profits. Organized crime had thus found its 'Promised Land.'[20]

Following Siegel's murder, the mob designated Las Vegas as an 'open city' – that is, open to investors from any of the Italian American crime families. The status 'open city' also referred to the fact that Las Vegas was off-limits to mob violence, which was seen as bad for business; mob assassinations were to be performed in the surrounding desert so as not to alarm tourists.[21] Despite these provisions, the Chicago mob or 'Outfit' became the chief and at last the unchallenged criminal power in Las Vegas. Its hegemony was made official in 1976, when the 'commission' of crime families assigned Las Vegas to Chicago and Atlantic City to the New York mob.[22]

Already by 1949 Mo Dalitz, former leader of the Cleveland mob, had become involved in the Flamingo, and he later won prominence in building hotel casinos on the Strip, including the Desert Inn in 1950; Wilbur Clark served as front man for Dalitz, who in turn fronted for Frank Costello and Lansky. Begun by Tony Cornero, the Stardust hotel casino remained unfinished for nearly two years after his death in 1955 but opened in 1958 under the Outfit's hidden ownership. Only marginally involved in Las Vegas up to that point, the Outfit leased the Stardust to the United Hotel Corporation and its director Dalitz, who later bought the resort with due provisions for the Outfit's interests.[23] The Stardust came to acquire a record of continuing controversy surrounding its owners. Other hotel casinos built in the 1950s, including the Riviera, Sands, Sahara, Dunes, and Tropicana hotels, were controlled by organized crime behind the scenes. New York crime boss Frank Costello held a share in the Tropicana, while New York mob investors controlled the Sands. The Riviera, Tropicana, and Dunes became moneymakers only in the long run. The most lucrative mob-held casinos were 'carpet joints,' catering to a wealthy or middle-class clientele, but the Stardust, the mob's flagship hotel on the Strip and the second most profitable, was a 'grind joint' with a clientele mainly of low rollers and slot-machine players. In the late 1950s Sam Giancana sent the suave Johnny Rosselli to protect the Outfit's interests at the Sands, Tropicana, Riviera, and Stardust; he was later replaced by John 'Marshall' Caifano, whose high-profile ferocity displeased the mob and the law.[24] The mob's chief source of profit in Las Vegas was the 'skim,' a steady flow of virtually untraceable tax-free dollars garnered through rampant cheating within the casino – lying on fill-slips, overstatement of losses, reports of IOUs as losses, and outright stealing from the countroom. Skimming amounts to about triple the reported casino profits, or about 20 per cent of the 'handle,' the total amount of money bet. In 1963 Reid and Demaris found the reported casino gross of two hundred million dollars in the preceding year to be unbelievably low.[25]

It has been estimated that by 1963 the mob had invested three hundred million dollars in Las Vegas. Most of these funds derived from loans received from the International Brotherhood of Teamsters, from which the mob began borrowing heavily in the late 1950s. James Riddle Hoffa, head of the IBT, who rose to power with the help of such gangsters as John Dioguardi and Tony 'Ducks' Corallo, provided the mob with money, jobs, and political clout. In 1955 Hoffa negotiated the union's first pension plan, known as the Central States Pension Fund (CSPF); he was assisted by Paul 'Red' Dorfman, a corruptor of labour unions and supplier of insurance policies to the IBT. By 1957, with Allen Dorfman, the son of Paul Dorfman, in the role of consultant to the fund's trustees, Hoffa was transforming the Teamsters' pension fund into the 'bank of the underworld.' The chief borrowers were Midwestern crime families dominated by the Chicago Outfit.[26]

Under Dorfman the pension fund made many high-risk loans to crime families for the purchase or refurbishment of such Las Vegas hotel casinos as Caesars Palace, the Sands, Dunes, Landmark, Stardust, and Desert Inn, which were financed entirely or largely through the CSPF.[27] Mo Dalitz, a close friend of Hoffa, received the first CSPF loan in 1959; he later received another to refinance the Stardust, Desert Inn, and Fremont hotels in the early 1960s. Jay Sarno, allegedly connected with Hoffa and Dorfman, borrowed twenty million dollars in 1961 for the building of Caesars Palace; he later financed Circus Circus with forty-three million dollars from the same source.[28] The United States Justice Department estimates that pension fund loans to Las Vegas ultimately totalled three hundred million dollars, or one-sixth of the fund's total assets, all of which, claims Gus Russo, was paid back. Several casinos also took out insurance with Dorfman's company. Not only was Dorfman widely rumoured to receive kickbacks and pay-offs, but there were complaints that his borrowers received low interest rates, and that sometimes the loans were never repaid.[29] In 1972 Dorfman served ten months in prison for having received fifty-five thousand dollars in kickbacks in order to secure a 1.5-million-dollar loan from the fund. Sometimes the funds were invested in fraudulent or failing businesses, the borrowers simply pocketing the money. In 1974 Dorfman and several Chicago gangsters were charged with fraud in another pension fund loan, but were acquitted when the chief witness was murdered.[30]

Suspicion surrounded Nevada's gambling industry in the 1950s and 1960s because of alleged links to organized crime. Yet the exposure of the skim through FBI wiretaps in 1961 proved fruitless owing to the illegality of such methods of investigation. Hopes for the purification of Las Vegas's image rose once more when Howard Hughes invested heavily in Las Vegas in the mid-1960s, buying up seventeen casinos. However, not only was Hughes prevented from establishing a monopoly, but he failed to control the mob in his own establishments. Optimism again awakened in 1969 with the Corporate Licensing Act, which promised to lure corporate investors to Las Vegas since casino shareholders no longer had to to be licensed individually. It was believed, justifiably, that corporate ownership would help the reputation of casinos through new security systems, more accurate tax accountancy, and other measures. Thus began the process that culminated around 1977 – the corporations' rise to dominance in the gambling industry.[31] Nonetheless, during this decade the mob continued to finance and control casinos. Thanks partly to Scorsese and Pileggi, the most notorious example of mob control is the Argent Corporation and

its chief executive, Allen R. Glick. In 1974, having purchased the Hacienda hotel casino, the thirty-one-year-old Glick received a CSPF loan of
nearly sixty-three million dollars, which the Kansas City and Milwaukee families gave him to purchase the Stardust and other hotels. Glick
had been a housing and real estate investor in San Diego and at the time
of the loan knew nothing of casino gambling. Yet he and his newly
formed Argent Corporation would ultimately receive about 160 million
dollars from the mob, with Dorfman as intermediary. Glick later claimed
that he was drawn into the deal without realizing that it entailed submission to the mob. Others saw Glick as a willing front man, chosen for
the 'squeaky clean' appearance that easily qualified him for casino
licensing. Officially the licensee of the hotel and its chief executive,
Glick answered to Frank 'Lefty' Rosenthal, an instrument of the Midwestern mob. Expert cheater Carl Wesley Thomas calculated that the
Stardust skim amounted to four hundred thousand dollars a month,
although it was probably higher. The film represents it as seven hundred thousand per month.[32]

The Argent Corporation and Stardust Hotel were plagued by suspicions of hidden ownership, skimming, and other links to organized
crime and the Teamsters fund. During the mid-1970s the U.S. government noted a large increase in supposedly mob-linked murders and
disappearances in and around Las Vegas. When in 1975 Tamara Rand
unexpectedly proved her limited partnership with Glick in the Stardust,
she won the right to subpoena the Teamsters books. Although Rand
was killed mysteriously, the Teamsters' role was in the open.[33]

On 18 May 1976 a raid on a number of Las Vegas hotels, including the
Stardust, uncovered the biggest slot machine skim in the city's history.
Skimming operations were shut down, and some hotel executives,
upon their nomination to the Gaming Control Board's infamous Black
Book, were excluded from Nevada casinos. To escape prosecution, Glick
claimed to have been embezzled. A year later the federal government
forced the Central States Pension Fund to relinquish control of its
lending activities. According to Roemer, the real 'crumbling' began on
19 June 1978, with a sweeping search of casino books, sports betting,
and loan-sharking. Yet already in April of that year FBI wiretappers in
Kansas City had accidentally uncovered the mob's role in Las Vegas.
These events initiated the first two 'Strawman' cases: Strawman I,
focusing on the Tropicana Hotel, controlled by the Kansas City mob,
and Strawman II, which targeted the Argent Corporation and its back-
ers. Nick Civella, Joey Aiuppa, Carl 'Tuffy' DeLuna, and other Mid-

western bosses were charged with the skim in November 1981. Civella died before the trial, while Glick, already fined and deprived of his licence, traded testimony for legal immunity. Around this time the FBI was implementing 'Operation Pendorf' against Allen Dorfman, who still controlled the CSPF following Hoffa's disappearance in 1975. The bugging of Dorfman's offices exposed the fund and its relations with the mob. In May 1981 a federal jury indicted five defendants, including Dorfman, for conspiring not only to bribe Nevada senator Howard Cannon but to defraud the CSPF; the defendants were convicted in December 1982. Fearing Dorfman's betrayal, the bosses eliminated him on 20 January 1983. When their trial began later that year, Glick proved a devastating witness, as did Angelo Lonardo, former Cleveland mob boss. On 5 December 1983 federal agents took over the Stardust. The mob's power in Las Vegas was terminated in January 1986 with the conclusion of 'Strawman III,' in which several mob bosses were convicted of skimming two million dollars.[34] As Pileggi puts it, by the 1970s Las Vegas 'was much too big to be dominated, or even influenced,' by mobsters.[35]

In the film as in Pileggi's book, the Las Vegas gambling industry provides the context for a narrative focusing on two of its more important people: Frank 'Lefty' Rosenthal, gambler and casino manager, and Anthony 'The Ant' Spilotro, gangster and leader of a burglary ring.

Born in 1929 and raised in northwest Chicago, Rosenthal was initially a gambler and bookmaker in that city. Thanks to his handicapping skills, he established ties with the Outfit and compiled an extensive record of bookmaking in the later 1950s and 1960s. Contrary to Steven Brill's view of Rosenthal as a 'lower-echelon bookmaker,' Roemer and Pileggi believe that his knowledge of bookmaking, handicapping, and numbers operations made him a 'troubleshooter' in the bosses' gambling schemes. He was arrested for bookmaking in 1959, ultimately forfeiting his horse- and dogtrack licence in Florida because of gambling arrests. In 1961, during a McClellan Committee investigation, Rosenthal took the Fifth Amendment thirty-seven times; he was suspected of bribing players in an Oregon–Michigan football game. A year later he was charged with conspiracy to bribe a New York University basketball player, but escaped conviction. The Outfit subsequently sent Rosenthal to Florida to run a sports gambling operation, which soon became one of the largest in the country. While there, he got into trouble for fixing a basketball game in North Carolina. In 1969 he barely avoided indictment in an interstate gambling and racketeering case.[36]

The year previously Rosenthal had started a new life in Las Vegas, where he became important in the gambling world. With Glick as the mob's front man, Rosenthal controlled the Stardust and other casinos under the title of public relations director. The deception was necessitated by the fact that Rosenthal's gambling record had prevented him from receiving the state licence required for the directorship. Formerly managed by gambler Johnny Drew, who was connected with the Outfit, and located almost in the centre of the Strip, the Stardust had always been the Chicago mob's flagship casino. Rosenthal's main job as 'Mr. Inside' was to implement and protect a major skimming operation. Some claim that his goal was to drive Glick into bankruptcy, whereupon the mob would claim Argent. Despite suspected mob connections, Rosenthal was a capable casino manager whose financial success won him local prestige. In 1969 he married Geri McGee, a former high-priced call girl, with whom he had two children. Yet Rosenthal could not continue to conceal his role under fictitious job titles. To maintain his status as a key casino employee, he had to be licensed by the state. On 15 January 1976 the Nevada Gaming Control Board denied him a licence because of his gambling record. The mob immediately replaced him with the Mormon Carl Wesley Thomas, who was ordered not only to watch over the skim but to prevent in-house cheating. Upon the discovery of the skim a few months later, Rosenthal was suspected of having masterminded it. Although he denied involvement, this seems unlikely; had the skim occurred without his knowledge, he would have been a poor manager indeed.[37]

Rosenthal's licensing problems resulted partly from the arrival in Las Vegas in 1971 of Tony Spilotro, his fellow gangster and long-time friend. Born in 1938 and raised in northwest Chicago, Spilotro dropped out of high school and, despite his short stature, was known for ferocity as a member of a burglary ring. He subsequently joined the Grand Avenue crew, which, originating in the 1920s, specialized in burglary under the direction of *caporegime* Joe Lombardo. During this period Spilotro became friends with Rosenthal. By the late 1950s Spilotro had been arrested thirteen times but evaded conviction. A master jewel thief, he served as enforcer for 'Mad Sam' Di Stefano, Chicago's most notorious loan shark, and sometimes partipated in the torture of debtors in De Stefano's basement. Spilotro is also believed to have performed, on the bosses' orders, the punitive murders of Billy McCarthy and Jimmy Miraglia, placing the head of the former in a vice until one of his eyes popped out – an episode portrayed in *Casino*. Sponsored by 'Milwaukee Phil' Alderisio, Spilotro became a made man around the age of twenty-five and is believed to have subsequently carried out many mob hits. In 1964 he was sent to Miami to assist Rosenthal's gambling operation and there received his first conviction, for resisting arrest; he was fined two hundred dollars and spent ninety days in the Dade County Jail. By 1965 Spilotro controlled Di Stefano's operation, thus becoming Chicago's youngest loan shark. Around this time, during interrogation by FBI agent William F. Roemer, Spilotro received the nickname 'pissant,' which the newspapers shortened to 'The Ant.' After his 1969 arrest for loan-sharking and his appearances on television during loan-sharking hearings, Spilotro was seen as a mob whiz kid and likely stand-in for Alderisio. The bad publicity surrounding his indictment in 1970 for falsification of his employment record contributed to the bosses' decision to send him to Las Vegas the next year. Whereas Rosenthal conducted the skim from within the Stardust, Spilotro was 'Mr. Outside,' an overseer and enforcer protecting the casino from invasion or infiltration. Having been preceded in this by John 'Marshall' Caifano, whose well-publicized savagery had resulted in his banishment from Las Vegas casinos, Spilotro was ordered to keep a low profile.[38]

Spilotro set up a gift shop in the Circus Circus hotel under a fictitious name. He had with him a group of Chicago enforcers who, under his direction and without the bosses' knowledge, soon entered into forbidden activities. Besides extorting unprecedented street taxes from local loan sharks, bookmakers, and prostitutes, Spilotro organized his Hole-in-the-Wall Gang as a jewel theft operation covering much of the Far West. When not long after Spilotro's arrival the dead bodies of loan sharks and cheating dealers began to turn up outside the city, he and his gang were prime suspects. In 1973 Spilotro returned to Chicago in order to murder di Stefano. A year later Spilotro, Irwin Wiener, eight Outfit members, Joe Lombardo, and Dorfman were charged with fraud in a pension fund loan. They escaped conviction when a key witness was murdered, possibly by Spilotro or on his orders. The murder of Tamara Rand, Glick's former partner, occurred on 9 November 1975 and was perhaps carried out by Spilotro, who in the next year opened up a just-off-the-Strip jewellery store, the Gold Rush, as his headquarters and fencing operation. He is presumed to have committed several more murders in the 1970s, as the bosses became increasingly disturbed by his visibility.[39]

While in Las Vegas Spilotro and his wife became close friends with Frank and Geri Rosenthal and pursued an active social life. Not only did the Rosenthals help the Spilotros move in, they sponsored their membership in the Las Vegas Country Club. Nonetheless, relations between Rosenthal and Spilotro grew strained in the late 1970s, as Rosenthal's friendship with a highly publicized gangster was held against him by gambling authorities. For instance, in September 1972 Spilotro used Rosenthal as a character reference after being arrested on a Chicago murder warrant. Nor did it help Rosenthal's reputation that the publicity-hungry Spilotro appeared frequently on television and in the newspapers, often mugging for his fans. Their friendship was played up by the media at the time Rosenthal sought licensing, and is sometimes claimed to have been the chief cause of his denial of a licence.[40]

Observers disagree on Spilotro's role and status in the underworld.[41] The claim of Chicago newspapers that he was sent to Las Vegas to supervise the skim is an error, as that job belonged to Rosenthal, Spilotro being assigned to protect the casino.[42] Nor is there substance to rumours, attributed to Las Vegas authorities, that Spilotro managed the Mafia's casino and real estate interests with Teamsters money.[43] Like Pileggi, Ronald A. Farrell and Carole Case view Spilotro as an underling who used his situation to exceed the bosses' authority. Farrell and Case doubt that he went west to oversee mob interests in the casinos, noting that this supposedly major crime figure was the reputed head of a burglary ring.[44] For Pileggi, Spilotro was a 'minor mob figure' who thought otherwise. Pileggi remarks the failure of FBI wiretaps to confirm Spilotro's control of the Stardust. He was running not casinos but errands for the bosses, trying to win them favours from casino operators. His most embarrassing moment came when the Stardust management refused to give a waitressing job to the relative of a Chicago street boss.[45] Even Roemer, who devotes a whole book to Spilotro, acknowledges his failure to rise officially above the rank of soldier. High-ranking gangster Johnny Rosselli describes Spilotro as 'just a soldier' in whom nothing was confided and who remained Chicago's 'messenger boy, a tool.'[46]

In *The Teamsters* (1978), however, Steven Brill contends that by his thirties Spilotro was 'definitely high up in Chicago's organized-crime family,' even if he had not yet fulfilled his goal of leading the Mafia. By 1971 he was three echelons removed from top boss Tony Accardo, having risen 'as high up on the crime totem pole as any thirty-three year old had a right to expect.' He was transferred to Las Vegas not as a demotion but because Accardo wanted 'someone high up and tough on the scene there.'[47] Roemer similarly holds that despite his official status as a soldier, Spilotro's actual power in Las Vegas was substantial, this being the result of his ambition, his clandestine violations of mob rules, and the inability of the bosses to keep watch on him.

The seriousness of Spilotro's criminal activity in Las Vegas has also been doubted. Citing the limited evidence against him and his non-conviction for major crimes, Farrell and Case find his criminal record greatly exaggerated. In their view, Spilotro's bad reputation reflects media hype and anti-Italian prejudice, the authorities having made him a scapegoat to restore confidence in the gambling industry.[48] Yet for Pileggi, Spilotro had been 'arrested many times' for a 'series of infractions considerably more minor than the ones he had actually committed.' Like many observers, Pileggi believes that for all intents and purposes Spilotro was the city's mob boss, whom FBI wiretaps reveal to have ordered numerous murders, burglaries, and shakedowns.[49] Without doubt Spilotro controlled criminal activity on the streets, directed and participated in burglaries, and used the Gold Rush as his fencing operation. He was probably responsible for the increase in murders and disappearances in the Las Vegas area between 1975 and 1978. Carl Sifakis thinks that Spilotro figured in more than twenty-five execution-style killings; Roemer, Abadinsky, Rosselli, and Fratianno would probably accept that estimate, though Spilotro was never convicted.[50]

Forced to leave the Stardust, Rosenthal directed its casino from his home for a time, and then, after a brief stint as columnist for the *Valley Times*, a local newspaper, returned as food and beverage director, which required no licence. Having decided to appeal the Nevada Gaming Board's decision, and threatening to take his case to the U.S. Supreme Court, Rosenthal used his own television show, broadcast from the Stardust, to impugn the gaming authorities' fairness. This only angered the state and the mob bosses. The Gaming Control Board's refusal in December 1978 to reinstate Rosenthal's gaming licence was followed by a Gaming Control Board hearing in which Rosenthal charged Harry Reid, board commissioner, with corruption. Rosenthal's judicial victory over the board in the aftermath of these televised hearings was subsequently overruled.[51]

The late 1970s spelled trouble for Spilotro. In 1978 law enforcement authorities placed microphones in the Gold Rush, and arrest warrants were issued for Spilotro and other gang members in May of that year. Another warrant was issued in the same month for Spilotro in connection with a large sports betting and loan-sharking operation in Las Vegas as well as his involvement in illegal betting throughout southern

Nevada. Accardo warned Spilotro to shape up. In 1978 or 1979 he was barred from Las Vegas casinos upon his entry in the Gaming Control Board's Black Book. However, he kept the authorities at bay for five years as he and his lawyer Oscar Goodman appealed the Black Book's constitutionality. Indeed, even after his entry he was caught in a casino in violation of gaming regulations, yet he never served time or paid the fine. In 1980, with the Hole-in-the-Wall Gang still riding high, Spilotro was alleged by the IRS to have extorted a percentage on all organized illegal activity in Las Vegas. Very likely he was dealing in narcotics secretly.[52]

By now Spilotro and Rosenthal had fallen out through jealous rivalry. While Rosenthal was offended that Spilotro's reputation had jeopardized his own appeal, Spilotro resented Rosenthal's higher status within the mob and retaliated by having an affair with his alcoholic and drug-addicted wife. One morning Geri appeared at her suburban home and pulled a gun on Rosenthal, who held her off until the police arrived. She requested that they take her to her and Rosenthal's bank, from which she disappeared with a large quantity of cash and jewels. Rosenthal subsequently complained to the Midwestern bosses that Spilotro's adultery with Geri should be punished as a violation of *omertà*. Because the skim was working, and because Rosenthal, as a Jew, had no official family membership, the bosses ignored his complaint. When Rosenthal and Geri were divorced in 1981, he received custody of their two children; she died in Los Angeles of a drug overdose on 6 November 1982 at the age of forty-six.[53]

In July 1981 Spilotro and his gang were arrested during a heist. Two weeks later he was arrested and charged with racketeering, conspiracy to deal in stolen property, possession and concealment of stolen property, and illegal bookmaking; the Gold Rush tapes had told their tale. Upon the defection of Frank Cullotta, Spilotro was indicted as leader of the Hole-in-the-Wall Gang. As more indictments followed, it became increasingly obvious that the bosses had failed to keep an eye on him. When in late 1982 a number of bosses were themselves indicted, they deplored the bad publicity generated by their underlings and were eager to eliminate possible witnesses. This may explain the 4 October 1982 car bombing in which Rosenthal nearly died – although Roemer blames Spilotro. Rosenthal left Las Vegas and relocated in Orange County, California, in 1983, the year Spilotro's appeal was turned down, a landmark case affirming the constitutionality of the Black Book. The murder of Allen Dorfman in January 1983 was very possibly Spilotro's handiwork. Now spending much of his time in Cook County Jail, he was indicted in October of the same year but avoided trial temporarily because of a heart condition. However, the bosses held him responsible for the defection of mobster Joe Agosto in their 1983 trial. On 26 January more top bosses went to jail, but Spilotro won a retrial on the grounds of jury tampering. Joe Ferriola, the new leader of the Outfit, shared the view that Spilotro was chiefly responsible for their failure in Las Vegas along with related indictments, trials, and convictions. Spilotro and his forty-one-year-old brother Michael were lured to an Indiana cornfield where they were beaten and buried alive around 14 June 1986; their bodies were found over a week later. Rosenthal was entered in the Black Book in 1988, with citations of felony convictions, an unsavory reputation, and links to Glick and Spilotro.[54]

Although the film *Casino* is based on these characters and events, there have been alterations, omissions, shifts of emphasis. Rosenthal, Spilotro, and Geri McGee become Sam 'Ace' Rothstein (Robert de Niro), Nicky Santoro (Joe Pesci), and Ginger McKenna (Sharon Stone) respectively.[55] Allen R. Glick doubles as Philip Green (Kevin Pollak), Allen Dorfman as Andy Stone (Alan King). Murray Ehrenberg, an associate of Rosenthal's, perhaps suggested the character Billy Sherbert (Don Rickles), Rothstein's *fidus Achates*. The mob bosses Nick Civella and Joe Aiuppa seem combined in Remo Gaggi (Pasquale Cajano); Frank Cullotta, Spilotro's henchman, has been renamed Marino (Frank Vincent). Carl Wesley Thomas appears as Nance, while Harry Reid, a state senator who chaired the commission that rejected Rosenthal's licensing request in the late 1970s, may seem to resemble the corrupt senator (Dick Smothers) who turns down Rothstein.[56] The big-mouthed Carl 'Tuffy' DeLuna, whose obsessive record-keeping sank his confederates, provides the idea for Piscano.[57] Oscar Goodman, the lawyer who defended Rosenthal and Spilotro and who became mayor of Las Vegas in 1999, portrays himself. The hotel chain, comprising the Stardust, Hacienda, Frontier, and Marina, becomes the Tangiers. The film's casino scenes were shot at the then-closed Landmark or Riviera, depending on the source.[58]

In reality, the raid on the Stardust preceded the wiretaps leading to the bosses' indictments, but the film depicts these events as occurring nearly simultaneously so as to intensify the climax. Whereas Rosenthal's marriage quickly went downhill, and was marked by his many infidelities and physical abuse of Geri, Rothstein's marriage fails because of his coldness and Ginger's addictions.[59] Nor does Ace suffer the ignominy of nomination to the Black Book, as did Rosenthal in 1988. Unlike Rosenthal, whose gambling past cost him a licence, Ace fails to receive one largely because of Nicky's scandalous behaviour. Spilotro was entered in the Black Book in 1978, two years after Rosenthal's denial, and permanently entered in 1983. In the film, Nicky is already in the Black Book when Ace is denied. This change stresses that Nicky had hurt Ace's chances to become licensed.

Casino is the final installment of Scorsese's gangster trilogy. More powerfully than in *GoodFellas*, *Casino* depicts the decline of the mob through internal disloyalties and inability to compete at the corporate level. It appears as a casualty of modernization, typified by impersonal corporations. Scorsese's portrayal of the mob contrasts with Francis Ford Coppola's comments on his *Godfather I*, which attempts to show, in Coppola's dubious interpretation, that little difference exists between American corporations and Italian American crime families.[60] More broadly, *Casino* calls to mind *Raging Bull*, *The Last Temptation of Christ*, *GoodFellas*, and *Kundun*. Like them, *Casino* depicts a closed society that, with its own obsessive rituals, ceremonies, symbols, codes, taboos, and punishments, must defend itself against the hostile mainstream. In this, *Casino* exemplifies Scorsese's fascination with outsiders, pariah figures who originate or take their place on the social margins. It also reflects Scorsese's Catholic analogical sensibility, alert to vestiges of the sacred in the secular world. In *Casino*, gambling exemplifies the persistence of the sacred in modernity.

Johann Huizinga traces all culture to the play instinct. Play is a free activity pursued at leisure and without concern for material profit. It is performed within carefully defined spatial and temporal limits, a consecrated spot endowed with a 'sacred' aura: the arena, card table, and the like. Rituals, sacrifice, and other religious ceremonies are finally indistinguishable from play, being rooted in its 'primeval' soil. Not only are these activities voluntary, leisurely, and rule bound, they are performed in a sacred, staked-out area. A close connection exists between ritual and games, particularly games of chance, which thanks to their 'serious side' are included in ritual. As Huizinga observes, the 'ideas of happiness, luck, and fate seem to lie very close to the realm of the sacred.' In the *Mahabharata*, the ancient religious epic of India, the main action hinges on a throw of the dice and simple rules drawn on the ground. So too, the play character of dicing gives it a special place in ritual, thus subsuming ritual in play.[61]

Roger Caillois lauds Huizinga's conception of play as a free activity performed within a special 'sacred' area. Yet whereas Huizinga focuses more on the spirit of competition (*agon*) than on games generally, Caillois notes that many games of chance are not agonistic. Huizinga also ignores the fact that forms of play like gambling and betting involve material interest, and says little about games of chance played for money. These omissions inspire Caillois's attempt to define the cultural function of games of chance. Rejecting Huizinga's conflation of play with the sacred on the grounds of their formal relations, Caillois insists that, unlike the pure formality of play, ritual is rich with meaning. The sacred may include gaming elements, but is not a game – it is dead serious.[62]

For Caillois, the sacred exists outside everyday life and exhibits a strangely unpredictable doubleness in all the many objects, beings, places, and occasions with which it is associated. Although enhancing and rejuvenating, it is also a dangerous and potentially lethal power of chaos and destruction. Taboos are needed if humanity is to reap benefits from the sacred while repelling its bad effects. Whereas pariah status falls upon the individual who violates taboos, and whose expulsion repurifies society, the task of mediating the sacred to humanity falls to the priest, an expert in ritual. However temporary in the life of society, the topsy-turvy world of festivals also affords contact with the sacred through violations of the social order. Games of luck and chance form part of the disorderly atmosphere of festivals, and signify the gods' power to deliver good and bad unpredictably and impartially.[63]

To revisit his theory, which inverts that of Huizinga, René Girard defines ritual as society's chief means of controlling violence, the essence of the sacred. The bad or profane form of violence stems from ongoing mimetic rivalries among individuals. As these issue in open, escalating hostility, the antagonists fall into imitative cycles of retaliation and thus become each other's unacknowledged doubles. More and more people are swept up by mimetic contagion into a seemingly uncontrollable vortex of retaliatory violence. If left unchecked, such internal strife must level all cultural distinctions and differences, including those rituals, taboos, and laws whereby social order is maintained. As violence becomes increasingly random everyone is at risk, yet each antagonist would strike the final divine blow that would end the chaos. Girard's term for this state of social undifferentiation is the 'sacrificial crisis.'[64]

At the height of the crisis, an individual is singled out arbitrarily, heaped with false accusations, and transformed into the monstrous embodiment of the crisis in all its confusion. The unacknowledged double of his or her accusers, such an individual is chosen from among persons isolated whether on the margins or at the center of society – which also qualifies as a marginal place – and who therefore not only fit the pariah role but recall the indistinction of the crisis itself. This individual is the scapegoat, whose seemingly miraculous elimination is followed by a return to order. Yet because society cannot accept its origins in human sacrifice, the murder is concealed by mythical distortions. The scapegoat becomes a god-saviour; the gods, identified with 'good' violence, are extolled for ending the crisis; and ritual is established with animal victims substituting for the scapegoat. Mediated by priests, attended in orderly fashion by the community, ritual is the controlled mimesis, in disguised form, of those chaotic, unpredictable events out of which social order is miraculously returned. Thus is defined the difference between sacred and profane violence.[65]

For Girard, ritual distinctions underlie the whole differential system of culture. Ritual is the origin of play, whose relation to the sacrificial crisis is shown in the arbitrary nature of prizes in games. Likewise, games of chance first appear in ritualized form, and only later do they lose most of their sanctity. The link between ritual and chance is that the sacrificial crisis encompasses a levelling of distinctions through random violence, arbitrary victimization, and the community's miraculous recovery, interpreted as divine. The function of games of chance in ritual is to commemorate the crisis safely – its inebriating, vertiginous atmosphere of hope and panic and the unpredictable potential of violence for destruction or salvation. Themes and motifs of chance appear in myths and festivals, which simulate the crisis so as to rejuvenate the community.[66]

Games of chance are among the many bearing traces of their sacrificial and ritual origin. Such games often occur in a quasi-ritualized environment outside the ordinary world, and within whose consecrated space all actions conform to strict rules. Also present in many forms of gambling is the crowd, which typifies both the sacrificial crisis and ritual. The crisis also resembles two types of games defined by Caillois: *agon*, or competitive rivalry, in which victory depends mainly on will, effort, and skill; and *alea*, in which each player abdicates his will to pure chance, whose decision he awaits on a 'democratic' level with other players. Although some forms of gambling, such as poker, blackjack, bridge, and backgammon, combine chance and skill, the home of the *agon* is the playing field, while that of *alea* is the racetrack, lottery, pari-mutuel, and casino. Among these games are roulette, slot machines, dice, and heads or tails, each presupposing resignation to chance and renunciation of work, patience, and thrift in favour of fortune. The worshipper of *alea* desires 'submission to the divine power of chance,' which is rooted in the sacred, and which induces such sacred symptoms of self-abandonment as trance, possession, and hypnosis.[67]

The relation between gambling and the sacred is recognized by Pileggi and Scorsese. Pileggi's *Casino* refers to Las Vegas as a 'magical place' where the 'average guy had a shot at a miracle' and a thousand dollars buys 'canonization.' In this 'money-happy Lourdes ... pilgrims got to hang up their psychic crutches and start life anew.'[68] Scorsese observes that 'people become successful' in Las Vegas as in no other city, thinking that 'with one throw of the dice their whole life will be changed.'[69] Ace describes the city as a 'morality car wash' that 'washes away your sins' and offers 'what Lourdes does for hunchbacks and cripples.' For Ace, as for Pileggi, the count room is the 'the holy of holies,' the 'most sacred room in the casino.'[70]

Scorsese and Pileggi are by no means the first to identify the sacred with the Las Vegas casino. As Skolnick remarks, gambling is seen as a vice and is therefore not simply evil, but evil and pleasurable, attractive and repulsive. Such duality typifies the sacred.[71] Reid and Demaris note that 'within the casino, the gambler is protected from secular distractions ... There is only the cacophony of the *action* which imbues the gambler with a sense of eternal life.' Characterizing the casino as a 'little sanctuary,' they also see its dark side, for here the 'go-brokes instantly become lepers.' And since 'there is no place for them in Vegas,' impoverished losers receive state-provided bus tickets to carry them – as pariahs – over the state line. Reid and Demaris conclude that 'there are eighty-one places of worship in Las Vegas, but there is only one true god – money.'[72] In *Inside Las Vegas*, Mario Puzo complains of those 'obnoxious winners' who 'claim their success comes through God's love, [and] then spend their holy lucky winnings on booze, whores, and more gambling.' He mentions 'graven images of roulette wheels' and 'gaily colored, ritualistically sequenced playing cards.' For Puzo, to buy lottery tickets is 'some sort of religious act.'[73]

That the mob as well as the Las Vegas police regard the city as a sacred place is shown by their shared attitude towards violence committed within its limits. Despite its transgressions against mainstream culture, the mob has its own government and code whose aim is to determine and enforce within its community the distinction between permissible or 'sacred' violence and that of the unacceptable or 'profane' type. Thus, as noted above, the mob designates Las Vegas an 'open city' in which no violence is to be committed for fear of scaring away tourists. Violence is carried out only in the desert, the realm of pariahs and scapegoats; and here too the police prefer to dispose of their extralegal victims. This taboo explains why Nicky Santoro, like Spilotro, became anathema to the bosses, whose sacred city had become polluted by his transgressions.[74]

There remain differences between modern gambling and the sacred. Unlike the sacrificial crisis and ritual games of chance, where pure luck predominates, the casino is a business with a small profitable advantage. To quote Pileggi: the players are given the 'illusion that they have a chance.' Or as Ace says: 'It's all been arranged just for us to get *your* money ... In the end, we get it all.'[75] The frequency of cheating in casinos suggests that their prohibitions lack the power of the sacred to control behaviour. And whereas rituals and festivals occur at a leisurely pace, modern gambling has been contaminated by work. Not only are some gamblers professionals, but many devote to gambling the grim earnestness of the workplace. In the past, festivals revivified societies, but the modern world treats the festival and its gambling elements as a meaningless 'parenthesis' in routine. Such activities are confined to the private vacation or holiday, which lacks collectively renewing power.[76]

Gambling's vestigial sanctity is owed not only to its salvific and beneficent features but to its identification with violence, disorder, randomness, and loss of social boundaries. These negatives explain why many communities stigmatize it as immoral and taboo; even where commercial gambling is legal, it has long been what Skolnick terms a 'pariah industry.'[77] Gambling owes its immoral reputation in American society largely to its violation of the Protestant ideal of success as the result of hard work, productivity, punctuality, prudence, self-discipline, self-sacrifice, thrift, and sobriety. For even if modern gambling is contaminated by work, a casino provides partial escape from industrial discipline. Within its world of excess, unrelenting hedonism is promoted for twenty-four hours a day in a hermetic, windowless setting where no clocks are allowed and unchanging illumination suggests a place out of time. Here one pursues a wasteful, unproductive activity holding out the slim yet tempting prospect of effortless riches. This perpetual holiday offers endless banqueting and abundant alcohol, drugs, and prostitutes.[78] Another reason for gambling's stigma is that, as an illegal or quasi-illegal 'pariah' activity, it has attracted pariahs, especially Italians and Jews of the underworld.

Being a pariah, gambling has been banished to the social margins – not simply as a parenthesis in relation to routine activity, but in its geographical setting. Caillois remarks those 'specialized metropolises' and 'abnormal cities' where commercial gambling has been permitted.[79] Until recent decades the 'proper' habitat of gambling has been the frontier, or what remains of it – the borderland between law and order, where sudden riches, wide-open gunplay, claim-jumping, drinking, prostitution, and gambling are normal. As the United States' gambling culture arose on the frontier, so it continues to be identified with those far western locales where it most flourished, chiefly California and its vicinity with their Gold Rush origins. In twentieth-century America gambling's chief home has been a former frontier state, Nevada, which borders on five other states and which, in sites close to its own boundaries, maintains the gambling traditions of its California predecessor.[80] As was most evident in the early days of Las Vegas's gambling industry, when Western themes predominated in the city's decor and advertising (by contrast with the 'diversity of images' introduced by Bugsy Siegel at the Flamingo Hotel), Las Vegans have sought to recreate a 'frontier atmosphere' – the mood if not the reality of misrule.[81]

Commenting on *Casino*, Ian Christie notes its 'Western' plot concerning a 'bad man who strikes lucky in the West and marries a saloon girl,' with Las Vegas figuring as an 'obscene parody of the American myth of the Frontier-as-Promised Land.'[82] Consistent with Nicky's notion of Las Vegas as the 'fuckin' Wild West,' his Gold Rush jewellery store has wooden-planked sidewalks and hitching posts. This is the home of his Hole-in-the-Wall Gang, named after the Western outlaws led by Butch Cassidy and the Sundance Kid.[83] The climactic encounter between Ace and Nicky occurs against a desert landscape reminiscent of a cowboy film.

Nonetheless, Nevada has had deep reservations towards casinos. The puritanical ethos of the Mormons who form much of the population and powerfully influence the state government conflicts with the hedonism of gambling culture. Yet Nevada has had to accept legalized gambling not only because it has a gambling culture but because its ongoing 'fiscal crisis,' to use Skolnick's phrase, has forced it to rely on casinos for tax revenues. Although banned in 1910, gambling was legalized in 1931, and since then many Mormons have been major financial supporters of the industry. The Bank of Las Vegas, which began in 1955 and is perceived as a 'Mormon' bank, has lent large sums to major hotel casinos for expansion and remodelling. Nevada's political and civic leaders have also supported hotel casinos. By the late 1970s the gaming industry had long been fiscally indispensable to the state, with taxes on gambling and gambling-related entertainment providing roughly one-half of its revenue. Without them, many businesses would suffer enormously.[84]

The legalization of gambling implies that a vice has been divested of pariah status and rendered indistinguishable from ordinary business. Yet because anxieties over gambling persist in Nevada, the state has chosen not simply to legalize but to regulate it – to make it good, and keep it good. During the 1950s casino regulation was assigned to the Gaming Control Board, the state becoming a partner in all gaming enterprises. This arrangement could only be morally ambiguous. Whereas upon legalization the division between gambling and the community seemed to vanish, regulation implies that traditional moral distinctions still need protection. Thus, a pariah industry will not necessarily lose its stigma through legalization. The problem for state regulators has been to maintain moral boundaries between normal society and an economy based on vice – one that attracts and employs disreputable people.[85]

The state's regulation of the gambling industry has been compromised because until recently the pariahs have been very much part of it. Despite public anxieties, the state has needed the mob to support and operate casinos. Skolnick thus refers to the 'ambiguities of organized crime infiltration and control' within the industry.[86] A pariah industry also attracts pariah lenders, especially the mob. Farrell and Case show that the first major investors in casinos had backgrounds in bootlegging and illegal gambling, and that many were grandfathered in.[87] Organized crime has concealed its ownership of Las Vegas casinos, while those who operate, manage, and work in them have included people with criminal records. As Skolnick notes, the state has allowed illegal gamblers to remain because people trained to such work are gamblers who 'gained their experience in illegal settings.' Nor are illegal bookmakers or former illegal bookmakers, or those who employ them to bet across state lines, necessarily excluded. The legal gambling industry reconciles expertise with illegality 'by imputing standards of morality to illegal conduct.'[88]

If the mob is indirectly a partner of the state, which side is it on, its own or that of the state?[89] Like many casino owners, the mob has often used casinos to launder money. It has also used people in the gambling industry to bribe officials into relaxing regulations or conferring special favours and licensing. Most important, control of casino management has enabled the mob to embezzle tax revenues. The skim is accomplished by rigging machines and especially through infiltration of the casino's count room, where earnings are tabulated, and from which owners are barred because of their record of cheating. The Stardust management hired George Jay Vandermark, the greatest of all slot machine cheats, to run its slot machine skim. The most larceny, however, occurs in the casino's 'sacred count rooms,' where money is stolen despite all precautions.[90] In the film, Nicky's comment that the mob sought to skim the Tangiers 'dry' is accompanied by a leisurely Steadicam shot of Nance, the bosses' Mormon helper, entering the count room, filling his suitcase with cash, and then leaving the casino after bribing the security guard. Lazy and relaxed, though hinting at a bored suburban malaise, the theme from *Picnic* evokes the smoothness of the theft. The subsequent scene puns visually on the idea of the skim in depicting Nance's delivery of the suitcase to the Kansas City bosses, who greet him welcomingly as Artie Piscano dips a piece of bread into a pot of tomato sauce freshly prepared for Nance's arrival. Just as, in Italian America, tomato sauce is often called 'gravy,' so Roemer terms the skim as 'pure gravy for the mob.'[91]

Not only do the mob's hired cheats in the count room steal money from the mob, but cheating is endemic on the gaming floor among players, dealers, and other employees. This includes stolen chips, tampering with equipment, glancing at the hole card, switching dice, and so on. Former cheats often receive management and lesser positions because they can best detect cheating on the floor. Dealers submit to strict controls, while pit bosses and floormen observe their moves. The best-known example of surveillance is the 'eye-in-the-sky,' a large overhead room permitting a view of each table through one-way mirrors. Yet anti-cheating measures have been ineffectual.[92] Though the mob 'had a thousand eyes' it 'still came up empty,' as 'it is almost impossible to keep a casino from leaking cash.'[93]

Despite legalization, the casino remains a scene of vice, where drinks are free and prostitution is built in. Indeed, its illegality enables casinos to control prostitutes' activities legally within their confines. Since the purpose of prostitution is to lure premium customers to the gaming tables, management encourages prostitutes to frequent casino bars by offering them complimentary drinks. Prostitutes typically pay off security police, bellman, bell captains, taxi drivers, and bartenders, all of whom act as procurers.[94] The film depicts the senator with a prostitute in the Tangiers presidential suite, while Ace describes Ginger as a 'queen' who 'brought in high rollers and helped them spread around a lot of money.' Well aware that Las Vegas is 'Kickback City,' Ginger passes money to floor managers, dealers, pit bosses, and especially those car valets who 'could get you anything and take care of anything.' Nicky likewise has tipsters all over town, from whom he receives information regarding possible victims. For instance, a hotel receptionist's tip enables Nicky and his gang to ransack a hotel room in the guest's absence.[95]

Nor do law enforcement officials escape the moral ambiguity of Las Vegas. Nicky mentions that there are 'a lot of holes in the desert, and a lot of problems are buried in those holes.' But while this is how the mob disposes of its victims, the police do the same – a carryover, perhaps, from the city's frontier times. Ace tells the recently arrived Nicky that the Las Vegas sheriff is a 'real cowboy,' and 'even the coppers aren't afraid to bury people in the desert out here.'[96]

After legalizing gambling, the state of Nevada left the collecting of fees and granting of licenses to individual counties. Yet ever since Bugsy Siegel's murder the public has charged that legalized gambling gives undesirables a cloak of respectability. Henceforward the state involved itself in the licensing process and sought to regulate the gambling industry so as to discourage hidden ownership and skimming. The Kefauver and McClellan committees intensified fears that organized crime had infiltrated casino gambling in Nevada. It was even believed in the 1950s that federal intervention might be necessary.[97]

The bulwark of gambling control has been licensing. In 1948 the Nevada Tax Commission was empowered to investigate, licence, and monitor all applicants, yet despite occasional toughness, many people with underworld ties were licensed in the early 1950s. To deal with the problem, which was revealed in justified allegations of syndicate interests in the Thunderbird Hotel, Nevada instituted its five-member, governor-appointed Gaming Control Board in 1955. Not only was it to serve as the Tax Commission's investigative and enforcement unit, it was empowered to grant or deny casino licence applications. Yet by now it was too late to banish the underworld from Las Vegas.[98] The problem from 1955 onward, writes Skolnick, was to maintain 'gangster-generated revenue' while dissociating the state from their disrepute.'[99]

Disturbed by continuing fears of mob infiltration, Governor Grant Sawyer in 1959 approved a new Gaming Commission, a state agency operating independently of the Tax Commission and concerned solely with gambling issues and regulation. The five-member governor-appointed commission was responsible for all policy related to the enforcement of gaming laws and rules. It also had the last word in licence revocations. The Gaming Board continued as an investigative and enforcement arm, submitting recommendations to the Gaming Commission.[100]

In Nevada one cannot operate casino games or slot machines without state and local licences. Regarding licensing as a privilege, the state schedules public hearings periodically for the examination of applicants, who must prove themselves untainted by connections with stigmatized persons. Since these are show-cause hearings, proof rests with the applicant. A licensee may neither cater to criminals nor associate with them, and licences may be revoked if these conditions are not met.[101]

The more dramatic method of control is the Black Book, which originated not with Al Capone, as Ace and Nicky imply, but on 13 June 1960. The most powerful instrument of gaming control, the book lists those whom the state excludes from casinos and hotel casinos because of their 'notorious or unsavory reputation.' Nicky repeats this description (substituting 'and' for 'or') upon his nomination. Casino licensees must banish such persons from their premises, lest their licences be revoked. Inclusion in the Black Book follows upon an individual's failure to clear his or her name before the commission in a public, show-cause hearing. A nominee faces criminal prosecution if he or she enters a casino. Most nominees are thought to be linked to organized crime.[102]

The criteria of selection are inconsistent in both methods of control. Noting that most licensing applicants have criminal histories, Farrell and Case complain that the fine distinctions made in the licensing process lack objective criteria. According to Findlay, licences are given to former gamblers and even former convicts if they are 'not too shadowy.' Yet others have been denied merely for remote associations with gangsters. The problem of vague licensing standards is compounded by the fact that, since those most qualified for casino work gained their experience illegally, the state often licenses former illegal gamblers to run legal casinos. Licensing thus fails to eliminate disreputables, but legitimates the permeability between the respectable and pariah worlds. Nor does licensing eliminate larceny, as employees often collude with cheaters.[103]

The criteria for inclusion in the Black Book are inconsistent, being tainted by ethnic prejudice. That the regulators are mainly native Nevadans of Anglo-Saxon Protestant and Mormon background explains why the Book contains very few people of this type. Since the regulators falsely assume that the moral threat emanates externally, certain outgroups are consistently singled out on the basis of social 'stereotypes of evil.' The vast majority of nominees have been Italian Americans, targeted prejudicially because their group is identified with organized crime, and also because the state believes in an Italian American criminal conspiracy. Contrastingly, Jews have enjoyed preferential advantage over Italians in the gambling industry because of their reputation for business acumen and probity as well as their philanthropic contributions to Las Vegas.[104] Nonetheless, the Black Book has not kept criminal elements from the gambling industry. Farrell and Case remark that if all those who endanger the name of gambling were nominated, the industry would close down. Carl Wesley Thomas's lawyer argued the arbitrariness of his client's placement in the Black Book, since many convicted felons had been licensed in the preceding fourteen years. In defending Frank Rosenthal, Oscar Goodman noted the inconsistency of excluding a white-collar criminal while licensing convicted murderers, child molesters, drug users, and rapists.[105]

What functions do licensing and the Black Book really serve? When fears of criminal infiltration threaten to undermine public confidence in legalized gambling, regulators must prove their ability to purify it by theatrical, ritualistic, and symbolic means. Based on the assumption that more drama means more control, hearings over licensing and entry into the Black Book are highly dramatic media events. They aim to enact symbolically the industry's purification by denouncing and expelling a contaminating individual. Thus is supposedly retraced what the public feared to have become blurred, the boundary between good and evil. But since such acts neither define nor protect moral boundaries, the public commits *méconnaissance*. Indistinguishable from those whom society accepts, the banished individual is the arbitrary victim of exclusionary violence – a scapegoat.[106]

Yet is the gambling industry still a pariah? In the last four decades the public, business, and state have increasingly embraced legalized gambling – a change reflecting the decline of the Protestant work ethic amid a new culture of consumption and leisure. In 1984 voters' support of every lottery initiative demonstrated general acceptance of the funding of government expenditures through state-operated lotteries. Pari-mutuel betting is also highly popular. Now that gambling is increasingly controlled by publicly owned corporations, with credentials like those of many businesses, it is less identified with organized crime. Besides owning and operating lotteries and off track betting, the state blesses the corporations' gambling enterprises and even cooperates in the lottery business. Gambling is now an enormous leisure industry integrated with the mainstream. For all these reasons it can no longer be seen as a pariah or deviant, or as a 'parenthesis' outside work. Not only does gambling now qualify as conventional behaviour, but commercial gambling is a legitimate business, the institutionalization of what had been a vice.[107]

As late as 1985 Vickie Abt and her colleagues acknowledged that commercial gambling was still seen as a pariah, but they attributed this to the lag of social norms behind behaviour. They also conceded that public approval did not yet extend to casinos, which still struggled for long-term financing. Despite the triumph of casinos in Atlantic City since 1976, the failure of many casino initiatives in the next decade proved that historic questions concerning casino gambling, including the role of organized crime, the political and economic influence of casinos, and their social and economic implications, still troubled mainstream America. Yet more recently casinos have become increasingly accepted.[108] This has resulted from corporate investment and sponsorship, and the public's perception that the criminal element is far less influential than in the past. Now losing what remains of their stigma, casinos no longer suffer the pariah status they bore in the 1970s, when Las Vegas witnessed the agon between Rosenthal and Spilotro.

Situated between the underworld and the upperworld, Ace Rothstein embodies the moral ambiguity of the gambling industry. Not quite illegal nor yet fully legal, the industry stands geographically and morally on the margins of society; and, to quote Mary Douglas, 'all margins are dangerous.'[109] Not surprisingly, casino gambling as formerly practised in Las Vegas has been compared to a 'scapegoat,' an entity being typically located on the social margins.[110] Douglas further remarks the danger and hostility directed at individuals occupying an undefinable, marginal place within the social structure, and who thus threaten its system of distinctions.[111] All this applies to Ace, whose transformation into a scapegoat reflects his interstitial position between the mob and the state. Belonging to neither of the powers he is required to satisfy, he is finally left unprotected against them.

Being both a Jew and a gambler with a record of arrests, Ace bears two stigmas. A stigma, writes Erving Goffman, is a social attribute so 'deeply discrediting' that it reduces its bearer 'from a whole and usual person to a limited, discounted one.' People believe that the 'person with a stigma is not quite human,' and 'on this assumption we exercise varieties of discrimination, through which we effectively ... reduce his life chances.' Yet a stigmatized person often possesses special desirable skills and qualities.[112] Pileggi refers to Lefty Rosenthal as the 'man who set the odds, a perfectionist.'[113] Ace describes himself pridefully as a 'hell of a handicapper ... I could change the odds for every bookmaker in the country.' Suffering from two social handicaps, Ace calculates and compensates for defects so as to equalize the game for all participants. Similarly in Las Vegas, he tries to nullify his own social handicaps so as to become socially respectable.[114]

Though socially stigmatized, Ace enjoys privileged status in the world of the mob – a world that, as the object of awe, fear, and reprobation, partakes of the sacred. Mobsters are associated with violence, fearfully unapproachable secrecy, and indifference to suffering. The criminal's 'very impurity' renders him sacred, says Caillois.[115] Mobsters also project a personal autonomy and power that is often seen as god-like. Indeed, the screenplay for *Casino* calls for a vignette of the bosses 'surrounded by food and wine like the gods of Olympus.'[116] They appear in a warmly mellow light at a banqueting table, where they receive visitors and underlings. In their unflappable self-confidence and tranquil enjoyment of their self-created plenitude, they ignore the violence they inflict elsewhere. One recalls Caillois's point that 'power confers new qualities upon the person,' sanctifying him 'no less than the priesthood,' so that 'one who accepts or seizes it becomes pure.' Accordingly, the 'possessor of such power is himself kept in splendid and strict isolation,' since contact with him would 'strike down the imprudent.'[117] Girard writes of the 'fascination of superior violence' which confers a 'semidivine prestige' upon the 'man who strikes the hardest.' Whether in sex, sports, or games of chance, the victor exhibits a god's 'triumphant majesty.' Yet unlike the gods, one enjoys this 'only fleetingly' and *'always at the expense of other men.'*[118]

Having been welcomed by those he himself calls 'gods,' Ace owes his success to his gambling skills, which win the bosses plenty of money. For Nicky, he was a 'money-maker, a tremendous earner for these guys; as soon as he took over [the Tangiers], he doubled the drop [total gambling earnings]. The bosses couldn't be happier.' Ace's relation to the bosses resembles that of Rosenthal, whom they invited to their homes and called 'messiah' because of his gambling genius.[119] Normally a stigma, Ace's Jewishness gives him the same advantage Lefty had enjoyed in the underworld, for unlike ordinary gangsters and even made men such as Nicky, he can consort with the bosses without asking permission. He is, to quote Nicky, the mob's 'Golden Jew.' All this reflects the logic of the sacred, for though the scapegoat is usually reviled, it is sometimes revered and sanctified.

Needing someone they can trust, the bosses ask Ace through Andy Stone to manage the Tangiers. When Ace worries that his gambling record will prevent him from receiving a licence, Stone reassures him that Nevada has no desire to 'lock us out,' especially when the mob is 'puttin' a hundred million into this desert here.' Stone further suggests that Ace operate under changing job titles, thus postponing his licensing hearing indefinitely. Yet what Ace most desires is Stone's reassurance that he will be allowed to run the Tangiers 'my way,' without mob interference and with complete autonomy. In this prideful ambition Ace already shows signs of the self-destructive egotism and vanity to which he succumbs increasingly while in Las Vegas. At the same time, in demanding complete control over the hotel casino, Ace calls to mind other hubristic characters in Scorsese's Italian American films: Charlie Civello, who would worship and do penance 'my own way'; the egotistical and hard-headed La Motta, who, to quote Joey, wants to do things entirely '[his] way'; Henry Hill, whose cinematic biography concludes with Sid Vicious's monstrously parodistic version of Frank Sinatra's 'My Way'; and Nicky Santoro, who tells his former friend Ace that he plants 'my own flag' in Las Vegas.

Ace takes over the Tangiers under the false description of public relations director. Nominally, Philip Green is chairman of the board, but the real bosses are Ace and Stone. Ace's chief job is to supervise the skim while convincing regulators that the Tangiers conforms to state law so as to provide its share of tax revenue. He must also satisfy corrupt but influential officials such as the senator, to whom Ace gives such 'comps' as the presidential suite, an expensive call girl, and a pouch filled with one-hundred-dollar chips. Yet *Casino* does not convey the extent to which Lefty Rosenthal tried to appease the state. Not only did the highly innovative sports booking operation Lefty introduced at the Stardust make large profits for both the state and casino, but he even appeared before the state legislature to explain its advantages.[120]

Ace is perfectly suited to bring regularity and discipline to gambling because his values are partly those of non-gambling society. Whereas most gamblers submit to the mysterious powers of chance, Ace approaches gambling rationally so as to counteract it. Pileggi says that Rosenthal 'believed in everything but luck. Luck was the potential enemy, ... the temptress, the seductive whisperer taking you away from the data.' Thus Lefty 'had to take even the remotest possibility of chance out of the process.'[121] Nicky similarly observes that Ace 'had to know everything,' even wind velocity to predict field goals, and bet only on games he knew thoroughly. 'Season after season,' says Nicky, Ace 'always made money' and 'was the only guaranteed winner I ever knew.' Or as Ace puts it, in a phrase reflective of his emotional temperature: 'I had it down so cold.'

Like Rosenthal, who immediately punished lazy employees at the Stardust, Ace introduces hard work and strict routinization to the casino world.[122] Approaching his job entirely as a businessman, he imposes upon the Tangiers an American ethos of managerial, bureaucratic discipline, and thus illustrates the point that work now contaminates play. Ace is an anhedonic, naysaying workaholic whose compulsive attention to job details gives him ulcers, and whose office displays an enormous 'No' dwarfing a very small 'Yes.' Nicky rightly observes that Ace 'ate, slept, breathed gambling, ... working on this shit from morning to night' and that he was 'so serious about it all that I don't think he ever enjoyed himself.' Although he indulges in such luxuries as lavish houses, expensive suits and watches, jewellery, and the like, he does so chiefly for social status and self-advertisement. His behaviour distinguishes him not only from casino players but from Nicky and the bosses, who, whatever their flaws, *do* enjoy themselves. Ace calls to mind Coppola's portrayal in *Godfather II* of financial wizard Hyman Roth, another anhedonic, business-oriented Jew out of place among the pleasure-seeking mafiosi.[123]

Hard work brings Ace not just wealth but social rehabilitation, as the aberrant community of Las Vegas rewards and accepts him for his labours: 'Anywhere [else] in the country I was a bookie, a gambler, always looking over my shoulder, hassled by cops day and night. But here I'm Mr. Rothstein.' He understands that 'for guys like me, Las Vegas washes away all your sins. It's like a morality car wash.' At a ceremony held in 1974 at the Vegas Valley Country Club, Philip Green praises Ace as 'indispensable' to the 'gaming community.' Then welcoming him as a club member, Green hands him a 'certificate of appreciation' from the Charitable Foundations of Greater Las Vegas as photographers record the event. This citation indicates, punningly, that Ace has appreciated in personal and social value. 'Back home,' he comments, 'they would have put me in jail for what I'm doing. But out here, they're givin' me awards.' He now belongs to what the screenplay terms the city's 'power elite.'[124] Though temporary, Ace's legitimation somewhat resembles that of the much more successful Jew Mo Dalitz. A former bootlegger and leader of organized crime in Cleveland, Dalitz moved to Las Vegas in the mid-1950s and became a wealthy casino owner highly esteemed for contributions to local charities.[125]

For Ace, legitimation means acceptance by what Scorsese terms the 'American WASP community'; indeed, it means becoming something of an upper-class WASP himself.[126] Playing host to the senator at the Tangiers, Ace refers to his Jewish aide Billy Sherbert as 'William' to give the occasion a more genteel, Anglo-Saxon tone. Nor is it coincidental that Ace marries a blonde, WASPy woman. Yet it is Nicky who notices his most ludicrous fantasy of ethnic metamorphosis, remarking that Ace is 'fuckin' walkin' around [his house] like John Barrymore' with a pink smoking jacket and cigarette holder – a disdainful aristocratic WASP pose.

As Ace sees it, the bosses have given him 'paradise on earth.' Its joys include participating in their wealth and violence, a portion of which comes with the Tangiers. His comment on the bosses' loan to Green, that they are the 'only kind of guys that can actually get you that kind of money,' breathes awe. Yet what most pleases Ace is to run his casino without interference. So great is his desire for control that he complains of the hotel's breakfast muffins, demanding that each muffin contain a sufficient number of blueberries – a scene based on an incident in Rosenthal's life.[127] 'I have to let them know,' says Ace, '[that] I'm watching all the details, all the time.' This dream of total control centres on the gaming floor, where the rituals of play must be scrupulously observed and all infractions punished. In one shot Ace blows on a pair of dice to test their balance; in the next, he weighs them in a micrometer. Caillois notes that the transformation of 'defilement into benediction' and impurity into the 'instrument of purification' requires the 'mediation of the priest,' whose sanctity enables him to approach the sacred 'without fear of impurity.' He 'knows the rites that preserve him' from such impurity while giving him the power and knowledge to 'turn the malign power of infection toward good.'[128] As the priest, through ritual, transforms profane violence into beneficent, so Ace's expertise saves gambling from corruption and thus makes it acceptable. That Ace analogically parodies the idea of a priest is suggested by the early shot in which, surveying his vast casino and its idolatrous worshippers, he appears with his back to the audience and then turns to look towards it as he lights a cigarette. He calls to mind a priest who, in performing the mass, alternately faces and turns his back to the parishioners. He is furthermore shot from a low angle, so as to seem tall, remote, and imposing – the same angle from which a priest would appear to someone kneeling at an altar rail, ready for communion.

Ace's managerial methods confirm Skolnick's description of a casino as a 'totalitarian state' that maximizes surveillance to achieve total control. This requires conditions of regularity and visibility through 'ritualization of the action.' Dealers are required to communicate with floormen through ritualized nods and moves. The angle of cards dealt, the order of the collection of discards, the placement of currency in the drop-box, must be performed correctly. The floorman observes deviations from normality, which requires great knowledge of gambling. Colour coding is assigned to the pit or shift boss. The ultimate measure is the eye-in-the-sky, giving management a god-like view of everything invisibly.[129]

For Ace, cheating is the greatest affront not only to his power but to the bosses and the state. As sacred beings, the bosses may cheat the state as they please, but cheating against them must be prevented or punished lest their sanctity drain away. Yet Ace must also punish non-mob cheaters who covet the state's tax earnings. As he and his colleagues watch the floor for cheats, dealers, players, pit bosses, and floor bosses exchange wary glances beneath the eye-in-the-sky. Ace chastises a dealer: 'Where the hell did you learn how to deal?' He watches approvingly as Nicky drives two cheaters permanently from the Tangiers before they can claim their winnings; it would have been worse for them save that they belong to another crime family and deserve 're-spect.' One system of sanctity, the mob, thus takes precedence over another, the casino. In another scene, the most appalling example of Ace's total control, he detects two cheaters at cards. After a security guard fells one cheater with a cattle prod, he is taken to a private room where another guard prepares to remove his dealing hand with a power saw. However, Ace orders his hand to be broken with a mallet, warning that the power saw will be used next time. The two cheaters are thrown into the street, too terrified ever to return.[130] Ace claims such extralegal right of punishment because, using ex-policemen as his security guards, he partakes of the bosses' god-like power. Ironically, he has taken the law into his own hands to protect the state's interests. The state surely knows this, but will not admit it.

The film's opening shows Ace looking out like a king over his casino. Confident of the authority and protection given him by the bosses, and of the violence he is permitted to exert, Ace exhibits the same contempt of others and remoteness from emotion that had characterized Rosenthal. Glick describes Lefty as the 'kind of man who held out his cigarette and expected it to be lit. He could be withering with people.' According to Murray Ehrenberg, Lefty 'never wanted to show his emotions.' Frank Cullotta recalls that 'nobody liked Lefty,' whose ego became so inflated that he would hardly acknowledge anyone.[131] Ace similarly cultivates an image of ontological plenitude, the autonomy and self-possession of a god or one favoured by the gods. He seems not so much of the casino world as unapproachably above it. As Ace stands with his back to the audience, the camera is required to circle round him in order to view his face, as if miming the behaviour of an obsequious underling whom he has shunned. Yet such evasiveness is also that of a man who fears the scrutiny of the gaming authorities. Meanwhile the soundtrack blasts the nasty blues song 'Hoochie Coochie Man,' whose boastful, bellicose, and provocative refrain expresses Ace's state of mind: 'I got seven hundred dollars, so don't you mess with me.' That paltry sum foreshadows ironically what Ace ultimately discovers, that he has not the means to face down the mob or the state. For the time being, he embodies the arrogance typical of Scorsese's characters in their quest for god-like superiority – Jake La Motta, Travis Bickle, the gangsters in *GoodFellas*. To quote Scorsese, Ace reached 'the point where he didn't want people to smile at him or say hello. You can see it in the way he stands and looks around.' Yet Ace's pose of self-autonomy masks an ontological lack manifested in his obsessive concern for the favourable opinion of others; to quote Scorsese, he is always 'on display.'[132] In *Casino*, as in Scorsese's other films, the quest for divinity proves to be self-destructive.

For all his impassivity, Ace anxiously realizes that he needs to qualify for a gaming licence. To do so he must overcome his gambling past by shunning disreputable activities and associations. Above all, he must not call attention to what the public and the state ignore, that legalized gambling is a form of immorality in which they participate. Were he to do so, he would become a *scandal* in the sense of a public object of both mimetic repulsion and attraction, since the scandalous person affronts society as a reminder of the moral deficiencies it normally conceals.

Such a person also risks opprobrium and sacrifice as the community's dishonest means of convincing itself of its moral distinctions.

The worst danger for Ace is Nicky Santoro, whose resentment of him originates in Chicago. When Nicky observes that Ace 'made more' for the bosses 'on a weekend than I could do heisting joints for a month,' he acknowledges Ace's superior status. While Ace's money-making and Jewishness enable him to move freely among the bosses, Nicky is not only bound by protocols but ordered by the bosses to protect their 'Golden Jew.' Nicky's mocking phrase suggests jealous resentment of his privileged non-Italian friend. Nicky's humiliation is manifest when top boss Remo Gaggi kisses Ace in the Italian manner and then tells him to keep up the 'good job, my boy.' After ordering Nicky to *'vien aca'* (come here),' Gaggi orders him to keep a 'good eye' – as opposed to the *mal occhio* – on Ace, whom Gaggi wants to 'continue makin' a lot of money for us.' Gaggi then disparages Nicky's 'fuckin' friends ... without brains,' which reflects badly upon Nicky.

Subsequently Nicky goes to Las Vegas to safeguard the skim and, in his words, 'to make sure that nobody fucked with Ace.' Certainly it was not the bosses' intention, Nicky realizes, for him 'to have a good time.' Yet he regards the city with a covetousness that makes Charlie Civello of *Mean Streets* look angelic: 'I couldn't wait to get my hands on Vegas.' What makes it all the more attractive is that the bosses are barred from the city, and cannot observe Nicky's operations. In contrast with Ace's anhedonia, Nicky, to quote Ace, 'enjoyed being a gangster.' Although Ace urges him to keep a low profile, he rejects discrete and measured calculation. Instead, he immediately imposes a street tax on numbers, narcotics, and prostitution. As a loan shark he charges three points of interest per week; a typical loan shark charges a point. When Nicky wins on his bets he collects, but when he loses he tells his bookies to 'go fuck themselves.' As Ace remarks, the word quickly spread that Nicky, the 'real gangster in town,' had become the 'new boss of Las Vegas.' Nor is Nicky troubled to profit from activities which the bosses forbid for fear of bad publicity. When Nicky and his gang are all too obviously cheating high-stakes cardplayers at the Tangiers, Ace warns that law enforcement officers are close by and that he endangers the casino. Yet Nicky can only complain of Ace's joyless scruple. As Ace realizes, it is useless to mention Nicky's behaviour to the bosses, since Nicky, a made man, enjoys privileges that Ace, as a Jew, can never claim. Whereas Ace doubles the Tangiers's earnings, remaining what Nicky terms a 'money machine' and a 'tremendous earner' for the bosses, Nicky lets his tribute to the bosses dwindle to a trickle, keeping most of it.[133] He thus rejects the sacred rule that Ace honours, that the gods receive their share from mortal suppliants.[134] A publicity hound, Nicky woos the media and rubs shoulders with celebrities like Steve Allen and Jayne Meadows at his Tower of Pizza Restaurant, whose name signals Nicky's hubris and impending fall. His nomination to the Black Book he dismisses as a 'bunch of bullshit,' resenting it most immediately as an obstacle to his natural appetites. For now he is unable, as he complains, 'to go in the restaurant which happens to be in the casino to get one of those sandwiches I like.' His statement testifies to the scenarists' intimate yet casual familiarity with the gangster mind. Undismayed by his nomination, Nicky organizes a band of seasoned Midwestern robbers – the new Hole-in-the-Wall Gang.[135] By now Ace is avoiding Nicky, so as not to ruin his chance for a licence.

Yet though Ace sees Nicky as his sheer opposite, unacknowledged resemblances unite them and only increase as they descend into rivalry and scandal. Ace too has an enormous ego, extreme ambition, and a desire for prepotency. When Jake is quoted in a newspaper headline as saying, 'I'm the Boss [of the Tangiers],' one thinks of the identical statement by Jake La Motta at the conclusion of *Raging Bull*. Yet whereas in that film it implied a degree of self-mastery, in *Casino* it betokens Ace's overweening pride and futile desire for domination. Like Nicky, Ace cultivates a pose of autonomy and self-sufficiency, and he too enjoys the power conferred by the bosses. Both men crave publicity and admiration, and each would embody something of that fascination which defines the sacred.

As with Nicky, Ace's egotism exceeds reasonable limits. This is apparent in his frequent changes of clothes and attention to their quality, tailoring, and cleanliness. He views wrinkle-free sartorial perfection as the necessary complement to the unflappable self-satisfied demeanour of a 'god.' Scorsese concurs 'absolutely' with Ian Christie's description of Ace's succession of expensive outfits as the 'visible sign' that Jake is 'going off the rails.'[136] Meanwhile, Ace's professional success increases his thirst for publicity. Noting that Ace could be a 'very touchy guy, especially when he got bigger in this town,' Nicky attributes his inflated ego partly to his having hired 'Jonathan and David and their tigers,' an animal-taming act, away from the Palace Hotel by 'buildin' them a new stage and then givin' them a new Rolls-Royce.'[137] One sees Ace being photographed while presenting the car. As the proverbial loyalty of the

Old Testament friends ironically counterpoints the growing antagonism between Ace and Nicky, so the entertainers' mastery of beasts
contrasts with their failure to control the violence within and around
them. In *Mean Streets* one of the few characters exempt from violence is
Tony, the only one sufficiently confident to step into a lion's cage.
Another sign of Ace's egotism is that, just before his licensing hearing, a
reporter tempts him to describe his role as that of the 'real boss' at the
Tangiers, thus damaging his chances for a licence.[138]

As Ace's hearing approaches, the media speculate that his 'boyhood
friendship' with Nicky may jeopardize not only his licence but the
'integrity of the state gaming laws.' As a news report is being telecast,
Nicky slips into Ace's house through the back door, and their first
confrontation ensues. This encounter exhibits classic signs of the
undifferentiation that portends and accompanies the sacrificial crisis.
The close friends Ace and Nicky resemble those feuding brothers whose
mimetic rivalry makes them symbols of the crisis *par excellence*. This is
because their mutual antagonisms and identical desires have transformed them into unacknowledged doubles of each other. According to
Girard, Greek tragedy represents this situation by means of *stichomythia*,
in which two characters exchange a series of identical angry accusations and counter-accusations. Although each persists in opposing the
other, they fail to realize that their reciprocal violence and the symmetry of their accusations render them morally indistinguishable. Although
cinematic realism prevents Pileggi and Scorsese from using *stichomythia*
in the rigidly symmetrical form characteristic of Greek tragedy, whose
purpose is to underscore the unrecognized identity of the feuding characters, Ace's and Nicky's exchange contains unmistakeably stichomythic
features.[139]

Initially Nicky finds Ace consulting with banker Charlie Clark, whom
Nicky threatens to kill if he fails to return him a sum of money. After
Clark flees in terror, Ace tells Nicky that Clark will run to the FBI; he
further complains that he now has to straighten out yet another problem caused by Nicky.[140] When Ace states that his responsibility to his
employees demands that he receive a licence, Nicky says that Ace has
no need for one, since Nicky plants his 'flag' in Nevada. This statement,
and Nicky's refusal to ask the bosses' permission for 'every little thing,'
leads Ace to suspect that he aims to take over the mob. Ace, however,
wants no part of it. 'I just want my licence. I want everything nice and
quiet,' says Ace. Up to this point Ace seems the sober businessman

threatened by Nicky's loud, exhibitionistic egotism. But then Nicky
mentions the magazine article in which Ace's love of publicity drove
him to to reveal, imprudently, his control of the Tangiers:

NICKY: You mean, quiet like this? 'I'm the boss.' That's quiet?
ACE: Everytime you're on television, I get mentioned. That looks
   bad. That looks bad.
NICKY: What the fuck happened to you? Will you tell me?
ACE: What happened to me? What happened to you?
NICKY: Yeah.
ACE: You lost your control.
NICKY: I lost control?
ACE: Yes, you lost your control.
NICKY: Look at you. You're fuckin' walkin around like John
   Barrymore [he refers to Ace's pink robe and cigarette holder] ... *I
   lost control?*

Nicky next mentions the assault Ace had ordered on Lester Diamond
(James Woods), his wife's old boyfriend. For Nicky, this mauling typifies Ace's 'disrespect' for many people, including Ginger, who had
complained to Nicky of Lester's mistreatment. It makes no difference to
Nicky that Ginger and Lester had disrespected Ace, nor is he troubled
by Ace's annoyance over having to vouch for Nicky whenever he runs
afoul of the law. As Nicky leaves he tells Ace that 'your fuckin' head is
gettin' bigger than your casino ... You better check yourself.'
   Girard finds the essence of tragedy in those stichomythic moments
when two characters' mutual recriminations leave nothing to choose
between them.[141] Notwithstanding Nicky's anger, fantasies of revolt,
and threat to Ace's career, he rightly disbelieves Ace's claim to want
only quiet, just as he credibly denies primary responsibility for Ace's
marital and other difficulties. Not only has Ace revealed his role at the
Tangiers, he has used on Lester the strong-arm methods Nicky favours.
Nicky also notices signs of Ace's hubris – pink robe, cigarette holder,
aristocratic pose. And yet the egoistic and megalomaniac Nicky is
hardly in the best position to complain of Ace's undeniably 'big head,'
and he has an equally weak justification for rebuking his friend for
ordering the assault on Lester, as Nicky had participated in it. In short,
Nicky and Ace see only each other's flaws, not their mutual resemblance. Their symmetry is suggested by their parallel accusations: 'What
happened to you?'/'What happened to you?'; 'You lost your control'/

I lost control?' The theme of the doubles later appears in Ginger's identification of Ace as a Gemini, which signifies twins or 'duality.' This
theme is further suggested in the advertisement of *Casino*, in which
Nicky, looming above Ace and Ginger, holds two dice cubes between
his thumb and index finger. The visible side of each cube shows a one,
so that together they signify doubles. This may evoke the pairing of
Ginger and Ace, which Nicky comes to control, or it may allude to the
doubling of Ace and Nicky in their struggle for dominance.

The other destructive figure in Ace's life is Ginger, a former prostitute. In marrying her, Ace diverges from the sexual attitudes and
behaviour of Scorsese's Italian American characters, who equate 'good'
or respectable femininity with the virginal bride while regarding the
'broad' and prostitute as suitable only for sex. Although Ace is chiefly
responsible for his own downfall, it also results from the disappointment of his ill-advised marriage. A seeming life-figure, Ginger offers
him only domestic chaos and emotional frigidity. Ace's attraction to her
testifies to his seduction by the excess and self-intoxication that is Las
Vegas – a spirit that, like Ginger, promises exultation but leads to the
depths.

Ginger ill suits Ace because she is too unlike him, although this partly
explains her fascination. Unlike Ace's love of order and calculation, she
entertains astrological superstitions, including the notion of Ace as a
'triple Gemini.' In addition to duality, this sign represents the snake,
and as Ginger says, 'you've got to watch a snake.'[142] Ironically, she
imputes infidelity to a man who struggles against all odds to trust her.
While Ace follows certain rules, Ginger disdains all restrictions, including those of Ace's casino.[143] She consorts with an old boyfriend while
married and betrays Ace with Nicky. This intolerance of rules is inextricable from her descent into drug and alcohol abuse.

Ginger embodies two closely related kinds of play. One is *alea* or
chance, typified by the throw of the dice: she is throwing dice at the
moment Ace falls for her. Caillois describes *alea* as an unproductive
activity in which the individual 'lets himself drift and becomes intoxicated through feeling directed, dominated, and possessed by strange
powers.' A 'special kind of vertigo seizes both lucky and unlucky players,' who are 'scarcely conscious of what is going on around them.'
Entranced by the game's uncertain outcome, such players 'lose all
objectivity and sometimes gamble more than they have.' *Alea* shares
these features with *ilinx*, the most primitive form of the play spirit.
Meaning 'whirlpool' and implying vertigo, *ilinx* is a whirling move-

ment that produces a 'sense of falling, projection into space, rapid rotation, sliding, spreading, acceleration of vertilinear movement, separately or in combination with gyrating movement.' *Ilinx* is also a 'vertigo' or 'intoxication of the moral order' propelling one into a childish state of destructiveness and confusion. Like Ginger, a person captured by *ilinx* adapts vertigo to daily life and thus experiences a permanent need for intoxication through drugs or alchohol. *Ilinx* presumes a world without rules, where the player constantly twists and improvises in a 'guiding fantasy or supreme inspiration,' neither of which can be regulated. He or she lives always on the edge, in a topsy-turvy panic-driven state where exultant whirling vertical movement at ever-increasing speed promises total triumph but leads to self-destructive collapse. 'The individual pursuit of anxiety and panic,' writes Caillois, 'conquers man's discernment and will. He becomes a prisoner of equivocal and exalting ecstasies in which he believes he is divine and immortal, ecstasies which in the end destroy him.'[144] Ginger's bondage to both *alea* and *ilinx* is reflected in the advice she gives a dealer as she leaves a gaming table: 'Drive fast and take chances.'

Why does Ace fall in love with Ginger?[145] A possible answer lies in the scene where he falls in love. Although it is based on Pileggi's report of this moment in Rosenthal's life, the film heightens its dramatic and emotional significance with a change of detail. In the book Rosenthal is visiting another casino, the Dunes, when he sees Geri plying her trade at a gaming table. With an income between three hundred and five hundred thousand dollars per year, she earns part of it as a chip-hustler, a prostitute who steals her client's chips. Not only is she rolling dice for her rich client and winning him large sums of money, she is snitching his black, one-hundred-dollar chips and putting them in her purse.[146] Although casino management expects prostitutes to keep their clients playing, since the odds are with the house, chip-hustling is a 'sin.'[147] Yet as much as Geri's conduct typifies her disdain of rules, no one could have predicted her next act. After her client refuses to tip her, she demands from five to seven thousand dollars of that night's earnings. When he accuses her of stealing chips and reaches for her purse, she tosses all his chips into the air. To quote Rosenthal: 'Suddenly, the whole casino is raining hundred-dollar black chips and twenty-five dollar green chips. They're falling and bouncing off the tables, people's heads and shoulders, and rolling along the floor.' 'Within seconds,' adds Rosenthal, 'everybody in the casino is diving for chips ... players, dealers, pit bosses, security guards.' The high roller 'is screaming and scooping up as many [chips] as he can,' while the 'security guys and dealers are handing him six and pocketing three. It's a wild scene.' As for Lefty, 'At this point I can't take my eyes off [Geri] ... [who is] standing there like royalty.' She and Lefty are the only ones left standing. As she leaves, Geri asks him, 'You like that, huh?' – the moment Rosenthal realizes he has fallen in love.[148]

In the film, Ginger wins big for a high roller from whom she steals chips, and when he refuses her a generous tip because of her theft, she plunges the casino into confusion by throwing rack after rack of chips high into the air. Amid the general scramble, Ace has his eyes fixed on the ecstatic, manic Ginger. Yet the film also shows that Ginger causes Ace to violate his professional code. Whereas in Pileggi's account this scene occurred at the Dunes, the film transfers it to Ace's own hotel. Furthermore, when in the film Ace observes Ginger incite disorder, he is with two Tangiers executives whom he would normally want to impress with his managerial discipline. Yet he neither rebukes nor punishes Ginger for stealing chips and disrupting the gaming floor. He only says: 'What a move ... I fell in love with her right there.' The immaturity of Ace's feeling for Ginger is reflected in the soundtrack, consisting of Mickey and Sylvia's 'Love Is Strange,' which, with its sophomoric lyrics and intentionally cloying vocals, expresses ironized puppy love. What further underscores Ace's lack of realism is the female singer's avowal to her 'loverboy' that 'You're the one' – not what one expects to hear from a prostitute who, as it turns out, maintains her former habits after becoming a wife. Nonetheless Ace lauds Ginger as a 'queen around the casino,' presumably because she compensates for her chip-hustling through the generosity of her kickbacks and the prodigality of her clientele.

Ginger has made a chaos of the ritualized world of the gaming table. The chips flying upwards suggest *ilinx* in its reckless thrill-seeking and intoxication, an experiential 'high' that Scorsese evokes by placing the camera directly overhead, with the chips rushing toward it. As for why Ace falls in love, the answer lies in the scene itself. On the one hand is total confusion, with nearly everyone scrambling for chips – an undignified display of desire whose participants descend to the same level of commonness. Yet two people rise above this emotional squalor like unmoved deities, free from and contemptuous of the desire engulfing the others. One is Ginger, who walks away careless of the disorder she has produced, exempt from rules and punishment and indifferent to the 'john' whom she has refused to accompany to his room. The other is

Ace, who finds in her a narcissistic reflection of his own haughtiness. She also carries the further fascination of possible indifference since she flouts the order Ace lives by.

Ginger's dangerous duality is implicit in her name, which sounds like 'danger,' and which Pileggi and Scorsese smartly alter from the sexless 'Geri.' The name 'Ginger' derives from 'Virginia' yet so little resembles it in sound and spelling that it well suggests the distorted road she has travelled from girlish innocence. Yet 'ginger' also refers to a spice or medicine that helps or harms depending on dosage. Though ginger enhances the flavour of food, it also causes nausea and stomach ulcers. It is in short a *pharmakon*, at once remedy and poison, hence partaking of the doubleness of the sacred. This is suggested by the fact that the word *pharmakon* is related to *pharmakos*, which refers to the scapegoat who poisons the community yet cures it upon expulsion.[149] Fittingly, Ace's wife has the ambiguous attraction of sacred things. Like ginger, whose colour recalls her brownish-blonde hair, she adds spice to life though only in careful doses, beyond which she is poisonous. She must be dealt with cautiously or *gingerly*, an adverb implying the substance's dangerous properties.

Ginger shows her vitalizing yet destructive power when she plies her clients with drugs so as to keep them awake gambling night after night, until their bodies are drained and their wallets empty. In one scene she walks contemptuously and hatefully away from her victim from left to right across the screen, her right profile to the viewer, her left revealed fleetingly in the hotel-room mirror. The doubling of her profile suggests duality (and duplicity), the very flaw she claims to find in Ace. Her left-to-right movement across the screen is anticipated in the earlier scene in which she walks away from the chaos she has produced at the gaming table. As the two-faced Ginger plunders and abandons her luckless, exhausted, drugged-out johns, so she will do the same to Ace, notwithstanding his protest: 'I am not a john, you understand.' Nor is it incidental that Ace, while married, takes medicine for ulcers. It is as if too strong a dose of Ginger had caused Ace to bleed from within; and she will deplete him in still other ways.[150]

Why should a man seeking respectability marry a prostitute, even if a top-of-the-line hooker? A stigmatized person like Ace will want to remove someone else's stigma as well as his own. This is all part of what he terms the Las Vegas 'morality car wash.' Another explanation for Ace's marriage suggests itself if one realizes that his haughty indifference and seeming self-sufficiency conceal his obsessive concern with both the desires and approval of others. Not only does he crave to make a favourable public impression, but his sensitivity to the public's desires is intensified through his role as both the Tangiers's casino manager and its director of food, beverages, and entertainment. Ace's closest analogue among Scorsese's characters is Jake La Motta, who pretends cold indifference and god-like self-sufficiency yet really feels ontological emptiness, which he tries vainly to fill up by imitating other people's desires. As Jake's attraction to Vickie is kindled in the presence of her mob admirers, so the only woman to awaken Ace's passion is she who has attracted many men yet yielded them only her body. For strictly speaking, a prostitute is seen not as desiring but as desired. Her sleeping with everybody is like sleeping with nobody, and typifies the indifference of sexual promiscuity. Such seemingly god-like indifference fascinates, as when Ace observes Ginger at the gaming table. For Ace, the most attractive woman must be the one who does not love, since he would make her love him. In this masochistic enterprise Ace resembles La Motta, but in the sphere of eroticism. Like Jake, Ace seeks the ultimate obstacle whose conquest will supposedly crown his vanity, but which, in its unshakeable indifference, delivers him ultimate punishment.

'Want to take a chance?' asks Ace of Ginger on proposing marriage. As a 'guy who likes sure things,' to quote his self-description, Ace realizes that to marry a woman who admits she does not love him is to bet 'the rest of ... [his] life on a real long shot.' Yet though he claims to be 'realistic' in believing she will love him someday, and that he can trust her with his life and fortune, Ace catches Ginger stealing from him (and lying about it) even before their marriage. To quote Ace: Ginger's 'mission in life was money.' When Ace, early in their marriage, presents Ginger with Bulgari jewellery as a gift, she cries out, 'Oh my God!' as if recognizing her deity. These stones resemble her in their cold, hard loveliness, and seem like fragments fallen to earth of the astral bodies she worships. In another scene she and her two-year-old daughter appear in a bank viewing room, where Ginger ecstatically examines the lavish jewellery collection Ace has set aside for her in a bank vault, the things that, as he says, 'really moved her.' The bank vault also contains in a safe-deposit box a million dollars in cash that Jake has reserved as ransom money. Increasingly uncontrollable, and gripped increasingly by drug addiction, Ginger later commits adultery with Nicky in the hope of manipulating him into stealing the safe-deposit box; when this stratagem fails, she steals the key from Ace and runs off with it herself.

Ginger has already plotted Ace's murder unsuccessfully, and after their divorce dies of a drug overdose in a cheap hotel. The proposal of the ironically named ex-pimp Lester Diamond, Ginger's off-and-on-again boyfriend, that they elude Ace by fleeing to Europe, where Ginger is to undergo plastic surgery, implies the monstrous deformation of her identity. One recalls *GoodFellas*, in which Henry Hill's face appears grotesquely distorted in its reflection upon the chrome of his car fender.

Yet does Ace love Ginger? At points he seems a devoted and caring husband, as when he offers to enter her in a drug rehabilitation program, or in his despairing statement: 'As hard as I tried, I could never reach her. I could never make her love me.' Nonetheless Scorsese says that Ace is 'responsible for [her] ... emotional alienation,' and that 'something' in his character 'ultimately destroys everything.'[151] The scene of Ginger in the bank viewing room concludes with Ace's voice-over: 'I was able to concentrate on what I knew best.' The workaholic Ace devotes himself to 'eighteen-hour days,' neglecting Ginger emotionally and distracting her with money and jewellery. The same neglect is suggested when, in order to guarantee the most desirable seat, Ginger identifies herself to a restaurant host as Mrs. Sam Rothstein, whereupon Nicky's wife comments, 'Well, you might as well get somethin' out of it.' What Ace gets out of it is the fantasy of being king of Las Vegas. Production designer Dante Ferretti gives his and Ginger's bed and bedroom an 'imperial' look, though in vulgar taste.[152] Ace can also parade his trophy wife at his country club. 'My greatest pleasure,' he recalls, 'was watchin' my wife, Ginger, work the room ... She could be the most charming woman you ever saw. People loved to be around her.' Scorsese comments that Ace and Ginger are 'on display all the time,' since for them 'appearance *is* everything.'[153] But when a young casino executive compliments Ginger too boldly, Ace fires him the next day.

A major instance of Ace's hubris – his insistence on doing it 'my way' – occurs just before his licensing hearing, when he fires casino employee Don Ward for either incompetence or suspected cheating. The danger of firing Ward lies not only in the fact that casino management normally gives such jobs to Mormons so as to appease the local powers, but that Ward is the son-in-law of Pat Webb, the county commissioner, who has influence with the state licensing board. That Ace's decision is motivated more by self-destructive egotism than professional integrity is suggested immediately before he meets with Webb, who is pleading for reinstatement. Ace sits at his desk, dressed save for his pants, which he has hung in a closet to keep from wrinkling; only when Webb is announced does he put them on. Jake's excessive concern for his appearance gives the impression that pride and vanity determine his subsequent decision. In rejecting Webb's request, Ace has the pleasure of punishing the Mormons who despise him and whom he despises. To quote Ace, without casino employment, Ward and his 'cowboy' friends would still be 'shovellin' muleshit.' Ace also refers to the state senator as one of the 'yokels [who] ran the state.' Now Ace is making Ward and Webb feel as unwelcome in his casino as he has been made to feel in Las Vegas.[154] However, in reminding Ace that he and his friends are only 'guest[s]' of Nevada, Webb hints at possible exclusion. When Webb learns of Ace's primacy at the Tangiers, he tells gaming officials that 'we may have to kick a kike's ass out of town.' Ace is now becoming the Jewish outsider Gentile society will not tolerate.

Ace, his attorney Oscar Goodman, and other interested parties meet before the gaming commission on the day of his hearing. It is headed by the senator whom Ace had previously honoured with the presidential suite, free chips, and an expensive prostitute. Apparently the senator had reassured Ace regarding his licensing prospects. But now, without allowing Goodman to speak, the senator rushes through a vote of denial and adjourns the insultingly brief meeting. Ace has been refused the preferential treatment often received by Jews in the licensing process.

Ace's hearing calls to mind Huizinga's observation that the court 'is still ... the sacred circle within which [judges sit] ... Every place from which justice is pronounced is a veritable sacred spot.' Huizinga adds that the 'juridical contest,' which follows restrictive rules, 'can be regarded as a game of chance, or contest, or a verbal battle.'[155] Yet while Ace has risked confrontation with his judges, they violate the agonistic spirit of the occasion by disallowing battle within the court's sacred space. His promised hearing is that only in name.

Unlike the single hearing in the film, Rosenthal attended two hearings in Carson City in January 1976, the second of which was for an appeal of his denial. In the first, far from having been silenced, Rosenthal hurt his case by saying too much and explaining too little.[156] The altercation in the film between Rothstein and the commission members is inspired by Lefty Rosenthal's accusatory confrontation with Senator Harry Reid at another hearing conducted in the late 1970s. But the chief discrepancy between the historical record and the film appears in Pileggi and Scorsese's implicit explanation for Ace's denial. Its chief cause is that Nicky's behaviour becomes too scandalous for Ace as his hearing approaches. In one scene, federal agents are tracking Nicky from a plane when they run out of gas and land on Ace's backyard lawn as he meets with representatives of the gaming board. Scorsese highlights Nicky's destructive influence on Ace's career because their agon is his dramatic focus. Yet Skolnick finds that it was not Spilotro's bad reputation that ruined Rosenthal's chances, but his own gambling past. Having drawn a distinction between those who behave illegally but ethically and those who act both illegally and unethically, the board willingly licensed former gamblers like Rosenthal. What sank him was that he had attempted to fix games, thus behaving illegally and unethically.[157] Hal Rothman contends that had Rosenthal applied for a licence before 1970, his gambling record would have posed no obstacle, as Nevada still needed mob investors and operators in the gambling industry. But in 1976, the year Rosenthal lost his casino job, mainstream money was pouring into Las Vegas and it was possible to dispense with him, as a detriment to the city's new, purified image.[158]

Both the hearing and its portrayal in the film illustrate Farrell and Case's point that the state organizes such events as dramatic, symbolic, and ritualized acts of exclusion in which certain individuals are singled out arbitrarily so as to 'purge' gambling of its bad elements, although the typical excluded individual is indistinguishable from many others whom the state accepts. As Farrell and Case argue, Rosenthal's record resembled that of many industry employees. This is why he accused the commissioners of hypocrisy and a disgraceful lack of jurisprudence, reminding them that, as he said upon his inclusion in the Black Book in 1988, some people in the industry 'made him look like a choirboy.'[159]

Ace's response at his hearing is likewise to challenge the decision. Realizing that Nevada is rejecting him as a guest within its 'home,' he tries to counter this by reminding the senator that he had often been a 'guest' at the Tangiers. Ace thus ties the senator to the moral corruption he condemns. But the senator insists that Ace, as usual, is lying, and admits only that he had dined at the Tangiers. Unfortunately for Ace, television cameras record his behaviour, which the next day's news report slants unfavourably: 'What should have been a routine licensing hearing turned into bedlam yesterday when the flamboyant [Rothstein] ... accused the state's top gaming officials of corruption and hypocrisy.' As the meeting breaks up, Ace chases another commissioner who had promised him a fair hearing after receiving comps at the Tangiers but who now wants only to avoid him. The newscaster's report of Ace's 'wild and unprecedented outburst' accompanies a shot of him crying 'bullshit' to reporters. Next, he addresses the commissioners: 'My past is no worse than yours ... If you look at your own lives you'd be in jail.' The newscaster adds that Ace had long been suspected of running the Tangiers without a licence, and that his 'checkered personal history' had raised doubts about his qualifications. His charges of hypocrisy go ignored because television is more interested in scandal and a seeming freak show than in serious discussion of legalized gambling.

Reminiscent of Lefty Rosenthal, Ace returns to the Tangiers as its entertainment director and is soon hosting his own television talk show, 'Aces High,' on hotel premises.[160] Suggesting an abundance of Aces, as if he has an endless supply up his sleeve, or as if his ontological plenitude enabled him to call forth a multitude of selves, the title implies Ace's capture by the 'high,' the *ilinx* of Las Vegas. The show's musical theme, the bombastic opening of Strauss's *Also Sprach Zarathustra*, casts Rothstein as Nietzschean *Übermensch*, underscoring ironically the titanic hubris behind his recklessness. In describing Ace as a 'man who will take you inside the real Las Vegas as no one has ever done before,' the show's announcer implies that Ace is the ultimate insider, and hence impossible to exclude from the industry. The announcer's statement coincides with the moment when, in the show's video promo in colour, a Las Vegas chef slices into a juicy round of prime beef, with blood pouring from it – an apt reminder of Las Vegas as a scene of carnivorous predation, to which Ace holds the secret. For although his show spotlights minor celebrities like Frankie Avalon, its purpose is to charge the gaming authorities with hypocrisy: 'It's a pity in this ... state,' says Ace during airtime, 'that we have such hypocrisy. Some people do whatever they want. Other people have to pay through the nose.' A master handicapper, Ace would transform his unequal judicial relation to the commissioners into a purely agonistic one, with the public as judge.

Determined to exhaust every possible legal strategy, Ace challenges the commission's verdict in an appeal to the U.S. Supreme Court. Farrell and Case observe, however, that his show only antagonized the authorities, while Pileggi shows that the bosses became increasingly angered by Lefty's attention-grabbing litigiousness.[161] In the film, Gaggi hands Andy Stone a Las Vegas newspaper report of Ace's behaviour at his hearing. Outraged that Ace has attacked 'friends of ours' while making 'all this mess,' Gaggi orders him to take another job title and 'keep quiet.' Yet in the next scene Ace introduces his new talk show.

Having again been ordered to keep Ace quiet, Stone confronts him, only to be told that the U.S. Supreme Court will hear his case. Stone explodes, describing Gaggi's order as a 'papal bull.' Like Rosenthal, Ace has not anticipated offending both the state and the mob. His formerly protected position is becoming one of vulnerable isolation – the position of the scapegoat.

Meanwhile the conflict between Ace and Nicky intensifies through rivalry for the bosses' favour. With Stone as intermediary, Ace complains to the bosses that his licensing problems are caused by Nicky, whom he wishes they would order out of town for a while. Yet though Ace sees the scandal Nicky makes for him, he is blind to the one he is creating for himself and others. Now under constant police surveillance, Nicky resents Ace for having communicated with the bosses behind his back, and is certain that he wants to banish him. The two rivals meet in a desert setting fit only for pariahs and scapegoats. Their confrontation differs from the earlier one in Ace's house, for now their antagonism verges on violence, and each is now pushed to the social margins though trying to deny it.

The scene in the desert opens with a long shot of its sun-baked waste devoid of human presence, with an irregularly peaked mountain range far off, and a large prominently displayed bush in the left foreground. Ace edges onto the screen from the right, as if reluctant to occupy what he calls the 'scary place,' where murdered men are placed in hastily dug holes, and where 'everywhere I looked could have been a hole.' Ace calculates a fifty-fifty chance of surviving the meeting. That he enters an initially empty frame implies his increasing marginality in Las Vegas. At the same time, Ace is shot at such a distance that he seems puny and forlorn, dwarfed by the vast space around him, with the line of mountains oppressing him with their horizontal. Contrastingly, Nicky drives to the meeting eagerly and aggressively, his car cutting a dusty path away from the viewer and into the heart of the desert, his penetration of its interior being emphasized by a remote aerial shot. As Nicky arrives at the meeting, his car thrusts its rapid and forceful diagonal towards the viewer and into the foreground. Unlike Ace's timid response to this space, Nicky wants to dominate it, just as he wants to dominate Las Vegas. In the succeeding exchange Nicky holds the physical and psychological advantage and, despite his short stature, seems to crowd the shrunken and nearly cringing Ace out of the frame.

Nicky's anger towards Ace is partly justified, for he rightly denies total responsibility for Ace's licensing difficulties. Nor can he accept Ace's claim that he went on television solely to be able to 'hang around' the casino. Concurring with the bosses that Ace has 'gone batshit,' Nicky insists that Ace wants to be on television, for he could have kept his casino job without doing so. Though Ace concedes this point, he adds that television provides him with protection: 'That way, I'd have a forum. I could fight back. I'm known, people see me. They know they can't fuck with me like they could if I was an unknown.' Ace grasps that the likelihood of his becoming a scapegoat decreases in proportion as he is perceived capable of fighting back, the scapegoat being by defini-tion a defenceless, unprotected victim whose death can thus end the community's cycles of violence. A further motivation for Ace's televi-sion show is suggested by Ian Christie, who notes a parallel with the character Rupert Pupkin in Scorsese's *King of Comedy* (1982).[162] Pupkin shrewdly uses his kidnapping of talk-show host Jerry Langford to blackmail the authorities into allowing him to perform his comedy routine on television. Because the scandal that accompanies this perfor-mance makes Pupkin more fascinating to the public, he becomes a celebrity and is punished only minimally. The film thus implies that the media possess a sanctifying and protective power that enables celebri-ties to commit scandal with impunity, and even to be rewarded for it – as if they were gods outside normal rules. Ace would similarly become an 'untouchable' minor deity whose misconduct is excused because of his celebrity. What he fails to see is the two-sidedness of his publicity-mongering, as he continues to anger his former protectors, the bosses, by making what Nicky terms a 'big fuckin' spectacle of himself.' Ace also fails to grasp that the public delights as much in tearing down as in building up a 'sacred' celebrity, whose special isolation from society sometimes only increases the chance of his or her victimization.

Yet though Nicky, as before, recognizes Ace's reckless egoism, he continues to ignore his own. Earlier, responding to the bosses' distur-bance over the disorder in Las Vegas, Nicky had complained to Marino of doing 'all the work' and then proposed a 'fuckin' war' with the bosses. Nicky's vauntings contrast ironically with the lowly bus stop bench where he and Marino sit. In the desert, when Ace errs in suggest-ing that Nicky had asked his permission to come to Las Vegas, Nicky announces that he is 'what counts out here,' as Ace exists only because of him. In another prideful fantasy, he warns Ace to get 'your own fuckin' army.' After being insulted as a 'Jew motherfucker,' Ace is told that without Nicky's protection 'every fuckin' wiseguy skell around'll

take a piece of your fuckin' Jew ass. Then where you gonna go?' (A skell
is the 'lowest form of wiseguy [Italian American gangster] – a drunken
bum.')[163] In this fantasy, Ace is the unprotected victim of collective,
expulsive violence administered by the dregs of the mob. His Jewishness
is now his victimary sign.

To describe Nicky as absolutely evil is excessive, as he has a more
attractively human side. Ace mentions that after his nocturnal preda-
tions Nicky unfailingly returned to make breakfast for his son, whose
Little League exploits he cheers on as would a typical American father.
In another scene Nicky rebukes a compulsive 'degenerate' gambler
who squandered family income at the gaming tables, and to whom
Nicky gives money accompanied by the threat to stop gambling or
suffer a severe penalty. Admittedly the egoistic Nicky enjoys playing
'godfather,' protector of the local Italian American community, yet his
outrage over the man's domestic irresponsibility seems genuine. However, in most other instances Nicky exemplifies the male witch and
practitioner of the evil eye.[164]

In southern Italy, the witch is located on the margins of the community and is often thought to harbour secret or active hostility against it.
Witchcraft is identified with envy and jealousy, as the witch covets
goods or advantages possessed by better-placed or more fortunate
people. Witches are believed to go abroad nocturnally to perform their
evil works, so that it is wise to sleep with doors and windows tightly
closed. However, not all witches are bad, nor are they exclusively
female; a male witch is known as a *stregone*. Closely related to witchcraft is the so-called evil eye or *mal occhio*, generally attributed to its
possessor's conscious or unconscious envy or jealousy. Otherwise known
as *jettatura*, from the verb 'to throw,' the evil eye is cast at a person out of
envy of his or her possessions or advantages. Apart from magical
devices, such as amulets and talismans, the best protection against the
evil eye is to have a powerfully influential patron who can warn off a
covetous party. A person who lacks a patron is vulnerable to the malice
of the *jettatore*.

Inextricable from the social dynamics of *Mean Streets*, these phenomena also help to explain *Casino*, especially Nicky's relation to Ace. That
the concept of the witch bears upon this relation is suggested by the
remark of Ace's banker Charlie Clark, who, amid the scandal of Ace's
association with Nicky, attempts to minimize it with a statement whose
implications exceed what Clark intends: 'It's just a political witch hunt.'
As he says this to Ace, Nicky enters Ace's house through the back door.

The relevance of the evil eye to Nicky's and Ace's friendship had previously been suggested when Remo Gaggi, top mob boss in Kansas City, tells Nicky to keep a 'good eye' on the mob's money-making Jewish associate. Nicky must watch over and protect Ace, bestowing upon him the absolute antithesis of the evil eye and its malice – the terrifying look that Italian American gangsters are known to cultivate as a means of intimidating their enemies.[165] The clubhouse scene exemplifies the idea that the best protection against the evil eye is a powerful patron like Gaggi. Yet the possibility that Nicky's good eye for Ace will turn into evil is suggested by his annoyance in having to play Ace's watchdog, his implicit resentment of Ace's superior earning power within the mob, and his awareness that Ace, its 'Golden Jew,' enjoys an intimacy with the bosses that is denied to Nicky, an inductee.

These seeds of envy and jealousy bear fruit in Las Vegas, where Nicky and Ace descend into hateful rivalry. That Nicky qualifies as a version of the *stregone* is suggested by the fact that, being a robber, he is driven by uncontrollable envy. As southern Italian witches prefer to fly nocturnally, so most of Nicky's depredations take place at night, when he and his gang steal into houses or else bore holes in their walls with drills and explosives. What feeds his envy of Ace is that Ace enjoys the publicity Nicky craves, and that his hubris exceeds all bounds. Ace's high status in Las Vegas galls Nicky all the more because of his own mediocre mob status, although he pretends to be Ace's creator-protector.[166] Nicky shows his envy of Ace in his frustrated desire for his safe-deposit box as in his successful seduction of Ginger, which seem motivated by both greed and a desire to humiliate. Yet what is more notable about Nicky's growing malice towards Ace, who can do little to repel it, is that it coincides with that phase of Ace's career when the mob and state – formerly his two most powerful patrons working in secret alliance – are withdrawing protection, thus leaving him, like Nicky, to fend for himself. Ultimately the state and the mob will become the enemies of both men, and seek their elimination in one way or another.

At the ironically named Jubilation Nightclub, an actual hot spot of those days, Ace and his fawning entourage ignore the resentful Nicky and his friends, who pretend to have a good time. Typical of Scorsese's films, this scene exemplifies the 'holiday-gone-wrong,' spoiled by boredom, malaise, and bad blood.[167] The symptoms of impending violence include Nicky's affair with Ginger, who tells Ace publicly that she is 'fuckin'' her 'new sponsor.' Ace realizes that her adultery could lead to the execution of all three parties, for the bosses interdict sexual rivalries among gangsters so as to forestall vendetta. 'There's one thing about these old timers,' says Marino, 'they don't like fuckin' around with the other guys' wives. It's bad for business.' Marino therefore lies to the bosses about Ginger's infidelity during his visit to Kansas City. Another ominous sign is that Ace's Jewishness is held against him increasingly. At the Jubilation, Nicky complains of the clannishness of Ace and his Jewish friends, which shows that Ace is a 'damn Jew motherfucker' and that 'fuckin' Jews stick together.' Ironically, Nicky says this while sitting with two Italian American associates. Later, pretending that Ace wants 'to start a fuckin' war or somethin',' Nicky informs Marino that when he wants Ace killed he will tell Marino to 'go see the Jew.' Even Ginger wants Nicky to kill that 'Jew bastard.'[168]

All this turmoil coincides with an unforeseen threat to the bosses. Formerly masters of chance, they become its victims when the FBI, seeking information about a homicide, bugs a Kansas City grocery and unexpectedly learns of the skim. Further wiretaps expose the mob presence in Las Vegas, followed by a federal raid on the bosses and the Tangiers. It was 'Tuffy' DeLuna whose unthinking loquacity and book-keeping, which his superiors had forbidden, gave away the show – a role assigned in the film to the buffoonish Piscano.[169] Soon the bosses are under indictment and must protect themselves against possible informants.

The climax of *Casino* closely resembles that of many of Scorsese's earlier films, including *Mean Streets*, *GoodFellas*, and *Cape Fear*. Again the increasingly hectic pace matches the intensity of the sacrificial violence engulfing the screen. Having formerly been checked by social rituals, taboos, punishments, and sacrificial substitutions, violence now threatens crowds of victims. These films depict miniature versions of the sacrificial crisis, in which proliferating murderousness becomes increasingly unpredictable, and social relations regress to those primordial antagonisms from which ritual, like gambling, derives. Like Scorsese's other films, *Casino* symbolizes such violence in the form of a circle.

The climax of *Mean Streets* coincides with that of the San Gennaro festival, where crowds mill about brightly lit wheels of fortune. These commemorate the unpredictable foundational violence of the sacrificial crisis, for which they provide a preventive ritualistic substitute. Nonetheless, this festival exemplifies the 'holiday-gone-wrong,' as violence explodes elsewhere in the city among the Italian American protagonists, even claiming two innocent victims. In *GoodFellas*, as the gangster in-group gathers at a circular card table, Spider, the waiter, is shot in the foot without provocation by Tommy DeVito. Thus crippled, Spider bears a classic victimary sign of the scapegoat. Later, as the gangsters again sit at their table, Tommy falls into a sudden delirium, waves his gun in circles pretending to be a cowboy, and shoots Spider through the heart. For Spider the card table has become a fatal wheel of fortune. At the climax of *Cape Fear*, Max Cady aims to kill Sam Bowden and his innocent wife and daughter on their houseboat. The symbol of the circle appears when, as Cady prepares to attack, a hurricane arises and an untended steering wheel spins out of control. Itself a circle or vortex that sweeps up everything, the hurricane resembles the *turba* or milling crowd of violence during the sacrificial crisis – a crisis that the monstrous and psychopathic Cady has attempted to incarnate in himself.[170]

In *Casino*, the spread of random, retaliatory violence begins when Nicky disregards his inclusion in the Black Book and plays blackjack at the Tangiers, thus not only risking a fine and jail sentence but jeopardizing the casino's legal standing.[171] Angered by a losing streak, Nicky menaces the dealers as he demands new cards and a large extension of credit. Summoned from home to meet the emergency, Ace gives Nicky less credit than he had wanted. Ace then prudently leaves, but not before Nicky refers to Billy Sherbert as a 'Jew motherfucker.' Nicky then beats up Billy, whom he calls a 'bald-headed Jew fuck.' The sacrificial component in this unforeseen assault is that Billy substitutes for Ace, whom he, as a Jew, resembles.[172] Nor is it insignificant that Nicky's violence accompanies his violation of gaming rules. Ace had tolerated Nicky's cheating at the Tangiers, but as Huizinga notes, a cheat still honours rules while breaking them.[173] In this scene, Nicky is no longer a cheat but a spoilsport, rejecting gaming rules, which no longer check violence. To quote Ace, Nicky and his gang had gone 'over the edge' to 'rock bottom.' With its alcohol, drugs, and women, Las Vegas had made them 'stupid,' 'sloppy,' and careless – prey to *ilinx*. One of Nicky's gang members, Blue, is killed by a policeman who mistakes the aluminum wrapper of his hero sandwich for a gun.[174] Employees at Nicky's brother's restaurant had previously spit into a sandwich they then served to local policemen; Blue's killing suggests a symbolic if not conscious retaliation. The cycle continues when Nicky's crew retaliates by shooting a policeman's house to smithereens.

As pressure upon them intensifies, the bosses' decision to eliminate potential informants leads to a rash of murders. A Tangiers executive is shot and killed in his new Lincoln. Two other men from the Tangiers are killed and buried in the desert. The most chilling assassinations, however, are those in which chance prevails. Nance, the mob's Mormon errand boy (whose name sounds as if the first two letters of 'chance' had been replaced by a negative prefix signifying bad luck), is tracked down and killed, yet he might have lived except for his son's recent arrest on a drug charge. The bosses decide to kill Nance lest he trade his son's freedom for testimony.[175]

The more memorable assassination, because it reintroduces the symbol of the circle, is that of the Jewish gangster Andy Stone. At a recess in their trial, the bosses sit around a table pondering his fate. Consistent with mob custom, each boss offers his opinion, yet the process need not run full circle, as one negative vote spells doom.[176] 'Stone is a good kid,' says one boss, a 'stand up guy, just like his old man.' Another describes him as 'solid ... a fuckin' marine.' For another, 'He's okay. He always was.' But then Gaggi asks: 'Why take a chance?' Their empire ruined by bad luck, the bosses attempt to exert their former god-like power over chance. For Stone, this means ill chance. Reminiscent of Spider's death, the bosses' round table becomes his fatal wheel of fortune.[177]

Stone's murder contains an element of calculation, however. Its rationale lies in his marginality as a Jew in relation to the Italian American in-group. Ironically, Stone's Jewishness would have given him, as it had given Ace, preferential advantage over most Italian American gangsters in dealing with the bosses. Exempt from mob protocols, Stone would have been able to speak with them without asking permission, and even have been invited to their homes. Yet during a crisis, his Jewishness is a liability. Assuming that Italians feel greater loyalty to fellow ethnics than Jews could ever feel towards Italians, the bosses sacrifice Stone as an outsider. 'As much as they liked him,' says Nicky, 'he wasn't one of us. He wasn't Italian. Otherwise he might still be alive.'

The same anti-Semitism helps to explain the climactic car bombing of Ace – a plot engineered by Nicky or the bosses, but that Ace attributes to Nicky. For Ace is now as unprotected as Stone. The car bombing is anticipated at the opening in a freely imaginative treatment, with Ace pitching high in the air. Ironically, his show had been called 'Aces High.' To quote the screenplay, 'His body twists and turns through the frame like a soul about to tumble into the flames of damnation.'[178] Scorsese relates this imagery to hubris, comparing Ace's fate to the 'grandeur of Lucifer ... expelled from heaven for being too proud.'[179] Although such a comparison may seem inflated, Scorsese thinks in terms of parodic or contrasting analogies. This double perspective on Ace's torment is reflected in the soundtrack, as his agonized movements are accompanied first by Bach's *St. Matthew Passion* and then by the decidedly less spiritually exalted music of Louis Prima, the Las Vegas lounge performer. At the same time, Ace's twisting and turning flight represents the final result of his submission, half-reluctant, half-eager, to chance. He tumbles like a randomly falling dice cube, while his vertical propulsion, with its twisting and turning, suggests *ilinx* in its vertiginous, whirling uncertainty. Like Nicky, Ace has been swept up by the 'high' of Las Vegas and pitched over the edge, seemingly to self-destruction. Yet the fire-bombers could not have known that 'that model car was made with a metal plate under the driver's seat,' says Ace. 'It's the only thing that saved my life.' The ambulance driver tells him, 'You sure are lucky, mister.' The man who had to dominate chance survives by pure luck.

Not all Italian gangsters are exempt from sacrifice by the mob. In the concluding sequence, Nicky and his brother Dominic are beaten and buried alive in a Midwestern cornfield. Theirs is the film's final sacrifice. Yet why does Scorsese accentuate the plenitude of this agricultural landscape with a long and high angle shot? He hints at a pagan theme of violence, death, and rejuvenation – a Frazerian sacrifice to ensure the crops' fertility. If this is so, such symbolism also applies to the quasi-documentary coda, summarizing the demolition of the old Las Vegas and its replacement by the grander city of the corporations – a phoenix 'rising out of ... [its] ashes.'[180]

The transformation of Las Vegas began in 1969 with the Corporate Licensing Act, which opened the city to mainstream investment capital far beyond what the mob could muster. The corporations' arrival was all the more welcome for the fact that, into the middle 1970s, banks and insurance companies shunned the gambling industry because of its association with organized crime, pension fund corruption, and the skim. But by 1977 corporations were taking over the industry, and since then have prospered enormously. The new casinos are highly expensive corporate entities, funded and built by companies such as Hyatt, Hilton, Ramada, Harrah's, MGM, and Bally's.[181] Paralleled and partly inspired by the proliferation of corporate-controlled casinos elsewhere in the United States, the corporatization of Las Vegas's gambling economy has coincided with the decline of mob influence in the gambling world generally. With the bosses' indictment in 1983, the mob suffered a crippling blow. It was no longer the 'main muscle' in Las Vegas casinos, as junk bonds became the primary source of financing.[182]

Casinos were now 'just another service' provided by publicly owned leisure conglomerates. Vast sources of mainstream wealth had enabled the Las Vegas gaming industry to undertake a major expansion through which casinos acquired a new, more broadly middle-class clientele. Already by 1983 slot machines had surpassed gaming tables as revenue producers, indicating that casinos had lost their stigma and solidified a wide appeal. Over the next decade the most important urban development was the mega-resort, which proliferated exclusively along Las Vegas Boulevard, or the Strip.[183] Promoted with the mastery of a Hollywood blockbuster, the new hotels were complexes for the whole family, where children's amusements were highlighted, where shopping, dining, and spectacular entertainment received unprecedented emphasis, and where casinos had ceased to be the main attraction, although commercially they remained the most important. This trend is partly explained by the fact that, with the widespread legalization of gambling in the United States, Las Vegas had to offer something unavailable elsewhere.[184]

Las Vegas's 'Mirage phase' began with the opening of the Mirage in 1988. Described by builder Steve Wynn as the symbol of the 'new Las Vegas,' it came with a volcano that erupted every half hour. The Excalibur, completed in 1990 for a modest 290 million, took as its theme Arthurian fantasy. When in 1993 MGM opened the biggest hotel in the world at the cost of a billion dollars, it included a casino and a vast theme park. Another mega-resort, the Luxor, built for 375 million in the shape of an enormous pyramid, and with over 2,500 rooms, offered not just a hotel casino but simulated Nile cruises. It too opened in 1993, as did Treasure Island, another Wynn venture, which boasted a mock pirate battle staged several times a day in a water-filled tank in front of the hotel. Next came such mega-resorts as New York, New York in 1996, with its popular roller coaster; the Bellagio in 1998, costing about two billion; and, a year later, the Venetian and Paris.[185] In appealing to broader audiences, Las Vegas had become a sort of Disneyland with gaming.[186] Yet Findlay finds the new corporatized Las Vegas 'faceless' as compared with the hoodlum era. Or as Pileggi puts it, it is now an 'adult theme park,' where dealers no longer know your name and arriving at a hotel resembles 'checking into an airport.'[187]

Casino depicts the transformation of Las Vegas by combining shots of the MGM Grand, its entrance in the form of an enormous lion head, with footage of the demolition of the Dunes hotel casino, one of many casualties among the city's antiquated landmarks.[188] These scenes are presented from the viewpoint of Ace Rothstein, who, like La Motta and Henry Hill, has escaped the wreckage of his life. Living in Orange County, California (Rosenthal fled to San Diego), Rothstein has sufficient detachment to evaluate his past. Yet whereas La Motta achieves some spiritual illumination and resolves to better himself, and whereas the amoral Henry Hill regrets only his removal from the underworld, Ace seems chastened and subdued following his years in Las Vegas, abandoning them with the matter-of-factness of a born handicapper, the profession to which he has returned. 'And that's that,' he says unfeelingly – the same unsentimental phrase that follows reports of major loss in Scorsese's other Italian American films.[189]

Of Las Vegas, Ace comments that 'the town will never be the same,' as corporations 'took it all over' and today it looks like 'Disneyland.' His voice-over accompanies a slow-motion shot of tourists as they enter a vast casino, as if stupefied by the holy of holies. These are the 'living dead,' whose regimented pleasures lack the anarchic vitality and spontaneity of the gangster founders. Next a crowd gathers at Treasure Island to watch a mock pirate ship in a water tank, sinking under an assault from the British navy: the state triumphs once more over Hobbesian anarchy. This is but one of the many attractions of the family-style Las Vegas where, to quote Ace, 'Mommy and Daddy' squander house payments and 'Junior's college money.' Simultaneously with a shot of the Excalibur, Ace complains of the corporate impersonality of the new hotels, where 'if you order room service, you're lucky if you get it by Thursday,' and where a 'whale,' or high roller, instead of receiving special treatment, must provide a company-trained employee with his social security number.[190] Ace adds that after the Teamsters 'got knocked out of the box,' the corporations tore down the old casinos, using junk bonds to 'rebuild the pyramids.' The sequence concludes with a nocturnal image of the Luxor, a giant glass pyramid thirty storeys high with a huge sphinx outside. The lion at the MGM Grand, the volcano at Treasure Island, and the pyramid and sphinx at the Luxor: these typify what Scorsese calls the 'spiritual wasteland' of Las Vegas architecture, which recycles as monstrously cartoonish advertising gimmicks images once invested with sublimity and sanctity.[191]

Girard observes of gambling that it originates in ritual and is then divested of its sanctity until it becomes almost entirely secularized. The question thus arises whether gambling can retain anything of that sanctity after being integrated with mainstream society to the point of becoming an ordinary fixture of business routine. With the dismantling of gambling prohibitions, casinos have taken their place alongside family entertainments. As the taboos against gambling have faded, so the end of its pariah status has coincided inevitably with the disappearance of its former criminal overlords from the scene, which is thus bleached of its fascination and terror. In losing its last vestige of sanctity, gambling becomes just one more neutral practice of the technicized world – one more casualty of modernity and its assault on the intimidating, seductive, and provocative system of prohibitions that is the sacred. Hence the mechanization, dullness, and impersonality of which Pileggi, like Ace, complains.

Yet that the gambling industry continues to be touched by the system of the sacred is evident in the fact that, even as it undergoes its resoundingly successful modernization, it relies on those means by which past societies have concealed, distorted, commemorated, and sanctified the chaotically violent origins to which they owe their order and prosperity. Besides portraying the elimination of Nicky, outcast of the bosses and the state, *Casino* depicts the state's expulsion of the bosses from Las Vegas and the near-murder of another pariah, Ace, who leaves the city. These purgations prepare the audience for images of the old Las Vegas, the pariah city, being demolished to make way for the clean, 'purified,' and more prosperous city of the corporations. It is as if, just as the state has expelled the underworld, so the corporations have sought to remove every tainted remainder of the earlier era. Yet they cannot conceal the fact that the pariahs and scapegoats had made the new Las Vegas possible by laying its foundations. Findlay leaves no doubt that mob investors and illegal gamblers provided not only the skills but the necessary financial support for the plant and infrastructure of the Las Vegas gambling industry. Without the immensely productive contribution of the hated, expelled mobsters, the wealthy desert oasis could not have existed.[192] They are its foundation victims. Yet though the corporations and public will not acknowledge openly that their present prosperity and enjoyments have depended upon and even originated among the violent pariahs, they commemorate that originating violence in a disguised, mimetic form. Thus the make-believe depredations of pirates fighting in a tank are a dim reminder of those real pirates, Tony Spilotro and his Hole-in-the-Wall Gang; the pyramid shape of the Luxor evokes, though in distorted fashion, the countless bodies still buried in the surrounding desert; while the sphinx outside the Luxor calls to mind the riddle that haunted that other scapegoat Oedipus, of the inextricable connection between social health and social violence.

Conclusion

Martin Scorsese holds a unique position in contemporary cinema, at once for the abundance and quality of his achievement and his special, manifest relation to his ethnicity. Unlike earlier Italian American directors such as Frank Capra and Vincente Minnelli, who for various reasons largely avoided the undisguised portrayal of Italian America in their films, Scorsese is without doubt the chief exemplar of Italian American cinema, for which the main criterion is that a director of Italian American descent treat his ethnic group in and of itself on screen. This is not to deny that, in some cases, a non–Italian American can do justice to Italian American themes, as witness Tennessee Williams in his play *The Rose Tattoo*, which even Sicilians have praised for its keen insights into their regional character. But apart from such rare exceptions, one must acknowledge that an enormous difference exists between a work such as Delbert Mann's *Marty*, which treats Italian American subject matter from the outside and with a certain condescension, and the far more knowing, assured, and therefore more authentic treatment of a comparable ethnic terrain in Scorsese's *Mean Streets* or *Who's That Knocking at My Door?*

It would also be an exaggeration to claim that ethnicity is the *sine qua non* even of Scorsese's Italian American films, which owe much to his formal and technical brilliance and his reworking of film history. Yet the fact remains that a substantial part of the content of these works, with their rich repository of Italian American signs, cannot be grasped apart from a real understanding of the characters' ethnic background and the ways in which it informs their assumptions, behaviour, and life choices. One needs to know the codes of the ethnic community, the role of the family, domus, and godparenthood, the significance of the ethnic neighbourhood and the place of the church within it, the value of *rispetto* in its familial and other ramifications, the peer group in its various manifestations, and the character of masculine bonding. One needs as well to comprehend the conflicting impulses of conformity and transgression within this sometimes highly conflicted ethnic world. Nor can one forget in assessing these works the continued influence upon the characters of the immigrant generations and their values. In short, Scorsese has created a group of films whose most basic thematic unity is provided by their common focus on his ethnicity.

These films are grounded in the experience of a third-generation Italian American who was born in an urban ethnic enclave in which he lived for over two decades, following which he underwent a surprisingly rapid assimilation through mainstream success. Having been himself an 'urban villager,' and having chosen Italian American urban villagers as the main characters of his early films, Scorsese portrays them as living in a hybrid world largely cut off from the core society and in which Old World Italian and mainstream American influences and habits are strangely mingled. Thus in *Mean Streets* young local hoodlums drive boat-like cars and follow other standard American consumption patterns, yet also suspend red-pepper horns or *corni* from their rear-view mirrors, these being Old World talismans against the evil eye. Yet if the experience of the urban village awakened in Scorsese a strong identification with the ethnic as outsider, which becomes a characteristic concern of his Italian American films and more particularly those on the Mafia, his accelerating experience of assimilation from his late twenties onward could only have intensified his awareness of the ongoing decomposition of his ethnic group, as a direct result of the assimilatory process in which he himself participated.

Taken together, Scorsese's Italian American films chart the group's transition from the urban neighbourhoods to the suburbs, from in-group to out-group marriage, from vestigial Old World solidarities to mainstream forms of individualism and mobility, and as such they reflect the 'twilight' of Italian American ethnicity amply documented by Richard Alba and James A. Crispino. Even at the time of the making of his early films, *It's Not Just You, Murray!* and *Who's That Knocking at My Door?*, Scorsese was aware of the imminent passing of his old neighbourhood and used both works partly as a means of recording it before its extinction, which has now essentially occurred. The same impulse to memorialize the way of life in those ethnic enclaves helps to explain the frequent documentary impulse in later films such as *Mean*

Streets, Raging Bull, and *GoodFellas.* It is not surprising but rather consistent with Hansen's law of ethnicity – which says that the third generation remembers what the second generation forgot – that the most vivid portrait of Italian American ethnicity, that of Martin Scorsese, should have been achieved in the midst of its asymptotic twilight. Scorsese's sense of removal from his ethnic past seems to inform the disengaged and retrospective mood that marks the characters, as well as the conclusions, of his final two Italian American films.

The interest of Scorsese's Italian American cinema is in no way limited to its ethnic themes and subject matter. What enables these films to transcend their parochial origins is chiefly his Catholicism, for though no longer a practising Catholic, Scorsese has sought to imbue his films with Catholic values and modes of representation, as a means of endowing their characters and situations with a universal rather than merely ethnic significance. Although such an assertion most obviously applies to the films preceding *GoodFellas,* from which point Scorsese may appear to depict a thoroughly secularized and desanctified world, his continuing commitment to Christian teaching is reflected in an observation made as late as 1997, that if you break the Ten Commandments they will surely break you.

The key to grasping the persistence of Scorsese's religious perspective in all his works lies in his characteristically Catholic immanentism and analogism, which permits him not only to envision the material world as pervaded by the divine spirit, but to discover within persons, things, and events analogues of divine truth, to which they are related in terms of either resemblance or ironic parody. Thus the Catholic ideals of divinity and sanctity underly Scorsese's awareness of modern life and behaviour as a realm of 'deviated transcendence' in which falsely divinized persons and no less falsely sanctified objects become the envied idolatrous substitutes for an authentic spiritual consciousness, and in this delusive fetishized form provoke transgressive violence stemming from covetous, imitative rivalries. Being thus sensitive to the mechanisms of social violence, Scorsese acknowledges the role of Catholic ritual, and of ritual generally, in the control of human conflict. On the other hand, he is aware of the problematic nature of ritual-based taboos, which by their very nature as prohibitions tend to provoke transgression. In each of his Italian American films the ultimate moral test of all behaviour is the *Imitatio Christi,* that is, the ideal of Christ as the unapproachable model of pacificism, non-retaliation, and non-acquisitive desire. Scorsese's Catholicism also seems to underly one of his typical qualities as a director, namely an unexpected degree of sympathy for his characters, even including cruel and malicious criminals who to some viewers might seem not to deserve it.

Catholicism provides Scorsese with a standard by which to analyse and evaluate the southern Italian ideal of masculinity, and more particularly the code of masculine honour that the immigrants brought to the New World. Not only did this code serve as a behavioural model for many Italian Americans of earlier generations, including those among whom Scorsese grew up, but in some ways it amounts to an ethnic analogue of the so-called American imperial self, which may help to explain the inexhaustible mainstream fascination with the Mafia. Many southern Italian immigrants passed on to their children their image of the ideal male as an autonomous individual who, unwilling to bend to the rules of both the ethnic and core societies, insists on doing things his way and therefore refuses to tolerate any opposition. Haughty, aloof, impassive, self-contained, and seemingly indifferent to virtually everything, as if he occupied a special transcendental sphere, yet at the same time capable of retaliating violently against all perceived offences to his honour and that of his associates, and thus investing himself with an aura of both danger and fascinated attraction, such a man appears to embody individualism to excess and in this way comes to acquire a god-like aspect among the ordinary downtrodden souls of his society. In his sexual conduct he takes for granted the rigid southern Italian distinction between respectable women and whores, treating the former as candidates for marriage and the latter as convenient objects of sexual exploitation. So far as Italian American society is concerned, the residue of these social ideals sometimes takes the form of what has been called the 'Sinatra Syndrome,' which, as the name implies, has its chief exemplar in the legendary singer, whose signature song was 'My Way,' whose social behaviour and presentation more or less conformed to the above description, and who became a behavioural model for many Italian American males from the 1950s onward.

To judge from both the sociological literature and the testimony of Scorsese's films, this older ideal of Italian American masculinity is flawed, and by its very structure undermines its pretensions to individualism and personal autonomy. For one thing, the reputation of the so-called man of honour is conferred by the community according to the value system of what qualifies as a shame culture. Far from being his own master, the ideal man of honour is both well aware of the evaluation of his behaviour by others and ever conscious of the need to maintain or adjust his honourable image so as to conform with their expectations – a state of affairs that can in actuality cause him to lose self-mastery by driving him to act against his own real interests. By the same token, not only is such a man likely to become obsessed over possible offences to his honour, particularly of the sexual type, but the very pose he strikes of superior, god-like aloofness surrounds him with a bubble of false sanctity that is in itself likely to provoke first envy and then transgressive rivalry in a host of imitators covetous of his power and aura. This in turn is bound to entrap the man of honour in a constant defence of that honour against a potentially endless host of rivals, as a result of which his autonomy dissolves in a compulsive flood of retaliatory mimesis, and he becomes indistinguishable from his opponents by virtue of their shared hostility.

Such a cult of masculine honour in its more extreme manifestations can easily lead to a loss of mastery and even unwitting self-destruction on the part of the so-called autonomous individual. What is no less ironic is that, in those ethnic urban communities in which this southern Italian masculine ideal appears to have enjoyed the greatest appeal, the persons most likely to succumb to its mystique were equally likely to belong to all-male peer groups whose members exhibited neither true individualism nor self-mastery, but a conformist adherence to the non-individualist values of both their communities and the peer group itself, to the point where their displays of 'individuality' consisted of no more than a solicitation of group approval. Under these circumstances, individuality becomes a function or reflex of the group, and always bears reference to it. This description would seem to apply as much to Sinatra's fabled Rat Pack as it does to the pack-like behaviour of J.R. and his friends in *Who's That Knocking at My Door?*

As seen through Scorsese's Catholic optic, the southern Italian ideal of masculinity in its most extreme forms represents a project of quasi-self-divinization and thus exemplifies the pride and vanity that Scorsese, like many southern Italian Catholics, regards as the worst of sins. Those who adhere to this ideal as a model of behaviour implicitly choose it as a substitute for the *Imitatio*, against which it stands in obvious competition as its absolute antithesis. The ideal of Christ as the supreme exemplar of pacifism and forgiveness is rejected in favour of the idolatrous worship and emulation of fascinating masculine exemplars of egotism, unfeeling cruelty, awe-inspiring terror, and unstinting vengeance. As the *Imitatio* functions socially to control envious rivalries and the mimetic violence to which they give rise, so the southern Italian cult of masculine honour in its most extreme versions is shown in Scorsese's films to issue all too frequently in the contrary forms of envy, violent rivalry, and unforgiving violent retaliation. Thus the most extreme form of the Italian American masculine ideal lies not in the Rat Pack, which when all is said and done was always something of a send-up and publicity stunt, but rather in the highly malicious criminal 'families' known as the Cosa Nostra or Mafia, which, with their codes of honour, respect, sanctity, and transgression, form the main focus of Scorsese's Italian American cinema. Contrary to the view of some critics, who believe Scorsese to have glorified the Mafia or celebrated it for his own commercial purposes, he has never attempted to romanticize criminality in any form, nor has he ever embraced the simplistic and indeed false notion favoured by Francis Ford Coppola in his commentary on *The Godfather*, that the Mafia is essentially indistinguishable from the capitalist mainstream society surrounding it. Such films as *Mean Streets*, *GoodFellas*, and *Casino* treat the Mafia in a distinctly ironic mode, as a virtual parody of Catholicism, in which the basic elements of Catholic teaching are inverted in a demonic register.

This is not to imply that Scorsese's Italian American films uncritically embrace Catholicism in every aspect – an unlikely possibility given his own falling away from the official church and self-description as a 'Catholic layman.' For all his appreciation of the respect for the individual that characterizes Catholic teachings on sexuality, Scorsese's earliest feature film, *Who's That Knocking at My Door?*, implies that a major negative result of those teachings is a radical and unrealistic division of women into the mutually exclusive categories of madonna and whore; and moreover that such distinctions can only prove impracticable and immiscrating under the test of real life. Nor does the confessional or any of the other Catholic conventions of penance or ritual resolve the sexual and moral torment of the film's main character. As a further point of criticism, Scorsese repeatedly calls in question what he comes with increasing clarity to see as perhaps an inadvertent tendency within Catholicism to overemphasize the Passion and Crucifixion and more generally physical torment as the sign and model of spiritual election. In the case of some Italian Americans, these tendencies are aggravated by their espousal of masochistic forms of Catholic religiosity carried to the United States from the Mezzogiorno. The result is the promotion of the kind of masochistic spirituality that the young Scorsese seems to have identified mistakenly as a path to salvation, and that also misleads such characteristically Scorsesean characters as J.R., Charlie

Civello, and Jake La Motta. For La Motta, the conquest of this syndrome comes with the recognition that 'God is not a torturer,' to quote Scorsese's favourite line from Bresson's *The Diary of a Country Priest*.

Still on a note critical of Catholicism, the scene in *Mean Streets* in which neophyte Mafioso Charlie Civello shakes hands with the local priest or those of the Mafia church weddings in *GoodFellas*, whose Mafiosi customarily wear crucifixes around their necks and hang icons of the madonna from their rear-view mirrors, suggest an all too fluid connection between the world of the church and the world of the mob – the very accommodationism that has long existed in Sicily and that Scorsese himself had complained of in Manhattan's Little Italy. Yet it is a measure of Scorsese's street-wise realism that he also grasps that, for all its deviation from Catholic teaching, the mob has often played a role equal to that of the church in keeping the lid on violence in Italian American urban communities. Indeed, the outbreak of mayhem at the conclusion of *Mean Streets* takes place in the middle of a street festival, thus signalling the failure of conventional religion to perform its traditional function of pacifying the neighbourhood. In *Raging Bull* the abundant rosaries, crucifixes, and other religious icons do nothing to quell the rampant mood of domestic violence. In the later Italian American films, *GoodFellas* and *Casino*, as in Scorsese's more recent *Gangs of New York*, only the state with its legal monopoly of violence seems capable of checking human hostility and aggression.

Ultimately, the quality of Scorsese's Italian American films is less a matter of their ethnic interest or religious advocacy than the brilliance of their art. As Scorsese's Catholic perspective includes and in some cases transcends the more parochial ethnic value system portrayed in his Italian American films, so the value of those films cannot finally depend on their ethnic signs or religious meanings, which viewers are free to take or leave as they see fit. They depend, rather, on the formal and technical skill by which Scorsese deploys and weaves together his ethnic, religious, and other themes, varying them from work to work, with each work exhibiting its own unique fusion of form and content and each, in the consistency of its tone, mood, and imagery, producing the impression of a unified aesthetic whole.

Although the artistic claims of the Italian American films remain paramount in any judgment of them, these works in their developmental trajectory can also serve to illuminate Scorsese's biography in at least two of its aspects: first, his spiritual development, and second, his increasing assimilation into mainstream society, which, in his case as in that of the majority of his fellow Italian Americans, could only lead to an increasing removal from ethnicity. Each an on-screen alter ego of the young Scorsese, the characters J.R. and Charlie Civello in his first two feature films belong as he did to the Italian American urban village and know virtually nothing of the world outside it. Both characters are trapped in the sterile conformism or pack-like behaviour of their peer groups, which robs them unwittingly of the personal autonomy they so much desire. Their models of action and desire are taken from Hollywood Western heroes or local gangsters who exemplify both cold, virtually god-like remoteness from other human beings and a masculine cult of personal honour. Yet whereas J.R. and his peers limit their violence to minor gang warfare, Charlie as a mob aspirant necessarily embraces or at least accepts the code of the underworld even as he attempts to convince himself of the sincerity of his Catholicism. In their sexual attitudes both characters view the majority of women after the manner of Sinatra and his Rat Pack, as contemptible objects to be exploited. And even if they counter their violent models of behaviour with Christian spirituality, J.R. and Charlie confuse the *Imitatio Christi* with self-inflicted torments that they pursue not simply out of guilt but under the mistaken identification of pain with spiritual election. Charlie's worship is especially compromised by such egoism. At the conclusion of each film the main characters remain trapped within their constricting ethnic neighbourhoods and self-destructive value systems; indeed, they are both engulfed by traumatic experiences that leave them morally confused and directionless.

In *Raging Bull*, Scorsese's next Italian American film, the characterological and spiritual infirmities of the earlier characters are projected onto a colossal plane – that of the sadomasochistic boxer Jake La Motta, the greatest of Scorsese's creations. Obsessed with violence as both the vindication of personal honour and sign of god-like supremacy and autonomy, the egoistic and even solipsistic La Motta allows his social and sexual life to become absorbed in a quest to dominate his boxing rivals, a mimetic obsession that, as it leads him deeper and deeper into cycles of retaliatory violence, actually deprives him of the self-sufficiency to which he pretends. However, as an abject being overwhelmed by his own sense of ontological insufficiency, La Motta also depends for his sexual desires on the imitation of those whom he regards as more favoured persons, who, having first become his models, then become in his own eyes his punitive obstacles and rivals. Not only does he torment himself through unjustified fantasies of having been dishonoured by an unfaithful wife but, partly as an expiation of guilt, and also because of his mistaken identification of physical agony with spiritual election and the continuing possibility of salvation, he deliberately submits himself to superhuman punishment in the ring.

Apart from its artistic superiority, what makes *Raging Bull* the crucial moment in Scorsese's Italian American cinema is that it represents a resolution to the spiritual miseries and confusion that had afflicted his earlier Italian American protagonists. Ultimately experiencing a moment of Christian grace in a Miami jail cell, an illumination denied to J.R. and Charlie, La Motta abandons his obsession with mimetic rivalry and violence and with this the false identification of higher spirituality with masochistic self-sacrifice – all in accordance with the idea that 'God is not a torturer.' The conclusion of *Raging Bull* portrays a no longer bellicose La Motta who can look upon his former life with a detachment akin to that of an artist, as he no longer exemplifies immersion in the violent mimesis of boxing rivalries, but rather the more benign and humane mimesis of stand-up comedy. He has also gained a degree of self-mastery unknown to Scorsese's earlier protagonists, who remain submerged in spiritual confusion. At the same time, La Motta differs from J.R. and Charlie in that he has taken a non–Italian American wife and moved out of the urban enclave, first to the Northeastern suburbs and ultimately to Florida, which marks him as a figure of ethnic assimilation through professional success.

Besides having enabled Scorsese to diagnose and resolve the kindred spiritual and behavioural miseries that had up to that point afflicted his main characters, *Raging Bull* freed him from any need to concentrate further on such characters and themes, and thus gave him the chance to develop in subsequent films a different approach to Italian American cinema. In the earlier films Scorsese had concentrated empathically and painstakingly on the spiritually troubled ethnic protagonist whose difficulties have very much to do with the persistence within his restricted ethnic milieu of Old World patterns of religiosity, masculine honour, and sexual behaviour. This holds true even for Jake La Motta, notwithstanding his apparent entry into the mainstream. Yet ten years elapsed between *Raging Bull* and *GoodFellas*, a period during which Scorsese was maturing a new approach to Italian America. In his remaining two Italian American films, the protagonist either lacks the psychological depth of his predecessors, to the point of seeming almost to be without real interiority, or, in the second instance, almost entirely repels the viewer's feelings through his emotional coldness and opacity. Nor is either protagonist a full-blooded Italian American. Because of their comparative separation from the ethnic environments in which they are nonetheless immersed, both characters afford a highly revealing perspective on the criminal groups to which they belong and that now become Scorsese's chief interest. The spiritual and sexual crises of J.R., Charlie, and Jake La Motta give way to a more diffuse, objective, ironically bemused, and even satiric treatment of Italian American criminals as they, like their fellow ethnics, encounter the difficulties of assimilation in a terrain far outside the ethnic enclaves of old, and where the older ethnic values have little chance of surviving amid ongoing Americanization. The theme of the outsider so dear to Scorsese now modifies subtly, for whereas his earlier films had been mainly concerned with Italian Americans emarginated in relation to mainstream society, now the focus is on an individual who, though not entirely cut off from the ethnic world, remains in some way or other removed from it from the very beginning.

Although raised in an Italian American neighbourhood, Henry Hill in *GoodFellas* is only half-Italian, and as such always something of an outsider in relation both to Italian America and the Mafia families of which he is an associate. On the other hand, his ambiguous relation to the group provides him with privileged access to many of its otherwise inaccessible secrets and thus makes him the perfect government informant. Not only does Henry flee the city for the suburbs out of a desire for upward mobility and assimilation, but he marries a Jewish woman and allows himself to be married in a Jewish ceremony. Indifferent to the ethnic and professional (and even religious) loyalties that previous generations had honoured, he ends up spying on and finally betraying his mob associates, in a violation of the traditional Sicilian ideal of *omertà*. Certainly his addiction to American-style consumerism is a stronger force in his life than the values of the ethnic past. In Henry's final appearance as a protected witness his assimilation is complete, ironically in the form of his physical removal from the ethnic Northeast to a faceless, standardized suburb where he is obliged to conceal his name and identity and where he can only lament the permanent loss of his criminal career. Yet Ace Rothstein, the protagonist of *Casino*, if anything surpasses Henry Hill in marginality and distance from the Italian American world. For though he has close connections with the Italian American mob, the fact of his Jewishness makes him much more of an outsider than Henry, especially in crisis situations in which his Jewishness is likely to be held against him. Reminiscent of *GoodFellas*, the ending of *Casino* portrays Rothstein physically at a far remove from his former Las Vegas environment, contemplating with cold matter-of-factness the ethnic culture with which he had long been intimately associated, and which had collapsed around him under the pressure of Americanization, consumeristic greed, and the loss of those Old World loyalties that had formerly unified the Italian American underworld.

It is not difficult to see the pattern of the Italian American films, and more particularly the differences between those of Scorsese's early and later career, as distanced reflections of the developing inner as well as social life of the director himself. Like J.R. and Charlie Civello, the young Scorsese while growing up in the isolated world of Little Italy no doubt felt the conformist pressure of the male peer group and streetcorner society, although he participated in them only intermittently owing to his asthmatic condition. He had also shared the fascination of J.R. and Charlie Civello with cowboy heroes and local gangsters, seeing in them models of masculine honour and prepotency. Yet as a result of his Catholic upbringing Scorsese was also drawn to the *Imitatio Christi* as the ideal of the Christian life. The conflicting claims of these two models, the one extolling inhuman coldness, violent retaliation, and sexual and other forms of cruelty, the other pacifism, compassion, and benevolence, warred within the young Scorsese and found cinematic expression in the anguished struggles of his earliest protagonists between these incompatible value systems. What all the more complicated his personal crisis was the fact that, like his protagonists, Scorsese was attracted to a masochistic form of Catholicism, partly southern Italian and partly American Irish, in which suffering and self-abnegation tended to be seen as being in themselves signs of spiritual superiority or worthiness. Yet though Scorsese's conflicts found expression in these early films, there is nothing in the films or in his personal life to suggest that they had been resolved at least into the late 1970s.

In this light one can grasp the importance of *Raging Bull*, which, partly through the revelatory example of Jake La Motta but also through the re-evaluation of Scorsese's severe conception of Christianity, enabled him at once to diagnose and to exorcise his own demons of anger, retaliatory violence, and masochism, and thus to place his life and career on a new, more stable footing. As La Motta in the film exchanges the real-life violence and retaliatory mimesis of the boxing ring for the more benign forms of stand-up comedy and solo acting, in which violence is sublimated if not fully renounced, Scorsese henceforward will exemplify a comparable detachment, channelling his own violent obsessions into the mimetic forms of art rather than allowing them to obstruct his creativity. His resolution to his crisis, and with it his detachment from his former self and the urban village that helped to shape it, also coincide with his deepening *éloignement* from the ethnic environment as a consequence of his own assimilation. This personal circumstance seems in turn to have been reflected in *GoodFellas*, which Scorsese conceived from the point of view of the assimilating half–Italian American Henry Hill, at once inside and outside his group. The removal from the mob subculture that Hill experiences at the end of that film finds its loose analogue in Scorsese, who has achieved a similarly disengaged (though much more insightful) point of view towards his own ethnicity. Finally, Scorsese's ongoing assimilation in the 1990s may help to explain his interest at that time in a character such as Ace Rothstein, a non–Italian American who, though he maintains connections with the ethnic criminal world, remains essentially outside it, and is finally cut off from it altogether after his banishment from Las Vegas.

The question naturally arises of where to situate Scorsese's Italian American films in relation to the larger body of his work. Do they, by virtue of their ethnic focus and inclusion of such a wealth of Italian American themes and behaviours, form a separate and unique whole within the totality of his oeuvre? Are they to be confined to a special category or subset so compartmentalized as to be impermeable to communication with the themes, narratives, symbolism, and other elements of Scorsese's non–Italian American films? If the answer in both cases is a resounding negative, the reason is partly that, without being specifically concerned with ethnic subject matter, Scorsese's works on non–Italian American subjects in some instances bear the probable imprint of interests, attitudes, and values traceable in one way or another to his ethnicity. This, though, is not the same as saying that these films are to be comprehended most profitably as expressions of Scorsese's ethnicity in a disguised form. The resemblance and intercommunication among the films is rather to be found on a more universal religious and anthropological level, in Scorsese's Catholic perspective, his persistent concern with the various forms of the sacred, his awareness of the role of the sacred in the prevention but also the incitement of violence, his equal awareness of its intimate and paradoxical connection with religious and social ritual, his preoccupation with art and violence as two related yet ultimately contrasting forms of imitative behaviour, and quite a few other concerns that may implicate the director's ethnicity even while being in no way reducible to it.

As *Mean Streets* portrays the failure of traditional southern Italian religious festivals to inoculate society against its own random violence, so *Kundun* depicts a Tibetan society vainly resorting to its own traditional rituals in order to stem a violent internal crisis set off by an impending Chinese invasion. The turning wheel of fortune in *Mean Streets* constitutes a mimetic representation of random sacrificial violence for which it is intended to serve as the disguised substitute and preventive; the ritualized whirling movements of the Tibetan dancers in *Kundun* are intended to avert the hurricane-like descent of violence by turning it against itself. In *Raging Bull*, as we have seen, the pacification of Jake La Motta coincides with his abandonment of the brutality of boxing rivalries in favour of the no less mimetic yet more civilized arts of comedy and acting. In short, art forestalls and contains violence. This conclusion has its analogue in that of *After Hours*, in which the main character, persecuted as a scapegoat by a bloodthirsty mob, allows a local artist to cover him with papier mâché and thus turn him into a work of art, as a result of which he is able to deceive and evade his pursuers. Again, art is seen as a means of deflecting and in a way of cheating violence. Yet *Raging Bull* is no less sensitive to the subtle ways in which the comic art conceals and expresses social hostility, and this theme is subsequently taken up and amplified by Scorsese in *King of Comedy*, in which Rupert Pupkin's adoration of comedian and talk-show host Jerry Langford causes the worshipped model to become Pupkin's obstacle and rival and finally the object of his nearly lethal envy. Not only in *Mean Streets* but at the conclusion of most of Scorsese's Italian American films, the escalation of random violence within the group is symbolized by the circle, and more particularly the rotating circle – the fearful passing around of a gun, players gathered round a card table, the whirling of helicopter blades, the stirring of spaghetti sauce. This calls to mind *Cape Fear*, in which, with a monstrous hurricane and the murderous, revenge-driven Max Cady having descended simultaneously on the Bowden family's houseboat, Scorsese cuts to a shot of its steering wheel spinning out of control – an image that also captures the rhythm of both *GoodFellas* and *Casino*. Like Jake La Motta, Cady is driven by what might be characterized as delusions of divine autonomy, a syndrome that, in Cady as in La Motta, manifests itself in a desire unflinchingly to absorb superhuman amounts of punishment, with the aim of demonstrating personal divinity.

Strange as it may seem, the codes and rituals of the Italian American underworld, which specify the limits this subculture places upon violence as well as its rules of inclusion and exclusion, find their upper-class analogue in the late-nineteenth-century Manhattan society depicted in *The Age of Innocence*, in which the malicious strategies of social acceptance, conformity, containment, and ostracism take not an overtly violent form, as with the mob, but lie concealed beneath the courtesies and benignities of social ritual. The continuity of Scorsese's Italian American films with his other works is apparent in as recent a film as *The Aviator*, in which his familiar themes of prohibition, transgression, contamination, and the containment of violence are transferred from their more familiar social contexts to the mind of a single phobic individual, Howard Hughes (Leonardo DiCaprio), pathologically fearful of impurity and pollution assaulting him from without. Hughes's horror of airborne diseases epidemic in low-lying miasmal areas triggers his own obsession with aviation in the upper reaches of the skies where, safe against contamination by persons and things, he seals himself as the monarch of his own private world within the sleekest and most technologically advanced aircraft. Like human societies confronting similar perceived threats of invasive violence, Hughes resists the supposedly omnipresent microorganic assault upon his being by a kind of self-quarantine, which causes him to isolate himself increasingly from the world. He does so as well through the systematic ritualization of his own life, performing the least gestures self-consciously as if they were exercises in industrial standardization, while meticulously arranging in row after row carefully collected bottles of his own urine, each indistinguishable from the other. Thus in *The Aviator* as in Scorsese's other films ritual figures as a defence against the danger of violence, but in this instance at the cost of condemning the individual to a life of obsessive-compulsive repetition beyond all hope of change. It may also be that Scorsese is making a comment upon the repetitive rigidity of ritualized societies generally.

The final question to be asked is whether the cycle of Scorsese's Italian American cinema has already reached its conclusion with *Casino*. It is now ten years since that film's release, and in the interim Scorsese has not treated Italian America in any of his films. Rather, he has treated Buddhist Tibet, paramedics in New York, and Manhattan's Irish gangs of the mid-nineteenth century. To be sure, ten years also elapsed between *Raging Bull* and *GoodFellas*, but Scorsese seems not to have any Italian American projects in sight, having apparently abandoned the film on Dean Martin upon which he had been working over a decade ago. Moreover, Scorsese himself leads one to think that, with the completion of *Casino*, he had made up his mind to treat only subjects outside Italian America.

As Scorsese remarks to Ian Christie in a *Sight and Sound* interview in January 2003, he had been born into a society of Sicilian ethnics that, in contrast with the culture of Sicily, stopped evolving around 1920, and in which he grew up with his 'father and the family.' He adds that this world is 'what I finally blew up in the explosion at the end of *Casino*. That was an end to it. I don't think that I could do anything further on that.' As a comment on both Italian American ethnicity and the Italian American underworld, Scorsese's statements cannot be taken at face value, as it is known that both ethnicity and underworld developed in various ways upon American soil following 1920, even as they continued to maintain many points of contact with Old World tradition. What is most important about Scorsese's statement is its apparent dismissal of Italian America henceforward as a subject for his films. He seems further to imply that, just as the older Italian America and its underworld have reached their historical closure, so his films not only chronicle the slow extinction of that world but complete their cycle exactly coincident with the conclusion of a distinctly demarcated phase in the history of the ethnic group as a whole.

It would be hard to disagree that Scorsese's Italian American films hang together by virtue of the continuity of their themes and interests, including Catholicism, the exploration of violence, southern Italian masculinity, and the underworld. They give the impression of a unified whole that might be risky to tamper with, especially after the apparently definitive closure of *Casino*. It must also be acknowledged that, as the chief allegiance of the ethnic or any other artist is to the imagination and its necessities, an Italian American director or writer is under no obligation to treat his ethnicity in his work, and should not be faulted for turning his focus elsewhere. Nonetheless, in assessing these films one may note the omission thus far of certain potentially fruitful themes and interests that might be made up for in future efforts. One can also speculate suggestively upon possible projects enabling Scorsese to tackle Italian American subjects of a wider and more varied scope than those that have up to now occupied him, yet that in their own way are consistent thematically with the basic concerns of his Italian American films as of his cinema as a whole.

Pellegrino d'Acierno rightly notes that Scorsese (and Coppola as well) have up to this point been unable to tell the story of Italian America to mainstream America without having recourse to the underworld or gang behaviour as subject matter. Indeed, these figure centrally in at least four of Scorsese's Italian American films. This is not to forget that Scorsese treats ordinary working-class Italian Americans in his portrayal of his parents in *Italianamerican*; however, he does so only in the form of a documentary rather than fictional narrative. Yet so far as the Italian American films are concerned, they seem thin in their handling of the theme of the relation of ethnic parents to their children, and this may be counted as something of a deficiency in a director who has so often undertaken to depict an ethnic group whose centrepiece, perhaps more than in any other, has been the family. Parents are largely absent from the majority of these films, while the Italian American mother, normally played by Mrs. Catherine Scorsese, is rendered fleetingly as a downright caricature or as something close to stereotype. It would therefore be highly interesting were Scorsese to portray the domestic lives of ordinary non-criminal Italian American families of the now-dwindling urban villages, particularly with a focus on husbands, wives, children, and peer groups. It would be no less interesting were he, like Don DeLillo, in some ways his novelistic counterpart, to treat the state of mind of contemporary middle-class, suburbanized, and assimilated third-generation Italian Americans of the non-criminal type, suspended between melancholy recollections of the ethnic past and a mainstream reality that encourages no more than 'low-cost' demonstrations of ethnicity. To my knowledge, the only film directors to have tackled this theme in a compelling fashion have been Phil Karlson in the little-known *The Brothers Rico* (1957), starring Richard Conte as a Florida suburbanite with troubling professional and familial ties to both the mob and Manhattan's Little Italy, and Francis Ford Coppola in *Godfather II* and *III*, in the portrayal of Michael Corleone and his gradual alienation from his ethnic (and Mafia) origins as a consequence of his entry into the American mainstream. However, it is obvious that both these films handle their similar subjects by recourse to the underworld, the very thing one hopes Scorsese would avoid in his continuing treatment of Italian America.

Nor are these the only possible projects by which Scorsese might add to and enrich his Italian American oeuvre. In the last two decades he has on occasion remarked his interest in making a film about Mother Frances Xavier Cabrini, who was born in northern Italy in 1850 and who, as the founder of the Missionary Sisters of the Sacred Heart, came to the United States in 1889, where she and her sisters became famous for their work of charity among the Italian immigrants of the first and second generations. Mother Cabrini died in 1917 and in 1946 was canonized as the first American saint. Her cinematic biography would intersect with the themes and concerns of Scorsese's earlier films while opening up for him new territory within Italian America. First of all, it would provide him with an opportunity to portray directly the world of the immigrants, which up to now he has handled only by report in *Italianamerican* or by implication in his other Italian American films, in which the characters' behaviour reflects their distant Old World origins. The character of Mother Cabrini, 'Patroness of the Immigrants,' would also enable him to focus, within the ethnic context, upon an individual who attains the saintly status to which Scorsese's alter ego, Charlie Civello in *Mean Streets*, aspires yet never even remotely attains. And whereas up to now Scorsese's portrayal of women, though convincing as far as it goes, has always been undernourished and peripheral by comparison with his predominant concern with male characters and societies, a film on Mother Cabrini would present Scorsese with the challenge of portraying a single feminine religious consciousness as his main subject.

Of all the possible Italian American projects available to Scorsese, that which most cries out for completion is the Dean Martin biography upon which he had been working with Nicholas Pileggi in the early 1990s, but which he apparently abandoned for other projects because of various difficulties in bringing it to the screen. To be sure, the success of such a project would finally hinge on the small possibility of finding an actor as variously talented as Martin. Yet apart from that difficulty, the Martin biography would permit Scorsese to expand and enrich the scope of his Italian American oeuvre and at the same time to maintain a strong continuity with its earlier themes. For Martin was associated in widely varying degrees with two spheres that Scorsese treats in his Italian American films and in which Italian Americans have been especially prominent – crime and entertainment. Thus in the Martin biography Scorsese's attention would switch from crime *to* entertainment, the latter having been for many Italian Americans not only a more reputable means of social advancement and assimilation, but a chief vehicle for the popularization of their own version of ethnicity within the mainstream from the late 1950s onward. Because he has up to now examined the theme of Italian American upward mobility and assimilation mainly within the context of the mob, Scorsese has never done justice to the world of Italian American entertainment, which would introduce an element of indirect autobiographical interest.

No less important, the Martin biography would interrogate the *lontananza* and *menefreghismo* that make Martin – along with Frank Sinatra – the exemplary figure in popular culture of one of the characteristic modes of Italian American masculinity. This is the form of behaviour that Scorsese, from a Catholic perspective, subjects repeatedly to withering diagnosis in his gangster films. However, in the Martin biography it would reveal itself in a non-criminal, and indeed, an individual whose persona was that of the more or less typical Italian American male. As Scorsese remarks, he is interested in Martin's gradual coming to terms with himself and, with this self-understanding, his gradual abandonment of the homophilic conformism and antics of the male peer group that, in Martin's case, took the deluxe form of the Rat Pack. One cannot fail to note that Martin thus exemplifies the spiritual malady that afflicts J.R., the hero of the first of Scorsese's Italian American feature films, *Who's That Knocking at My Door?* The crucial differences between the characters are that Martin suffers his version of that affliction in a more upscale context and at a later stage of life than J.R.; that his ethnically coded behaviour acquired iconic status for much of mainstream society in those days, which in itself says something about that society; and that Martin apparently extricated himself from his former pattern of behaviour and thus acquired a measure of autonomy not to be seen in the earlier character. Thus the Martin biography would complete Scorsese's Italian American oeuvre, bringing it full circle with a deeper exploration and amplification – and a still deeper understanding – of the themes with which it originated.

Appendix

Because Italian American gangsters often figure in Scorsese's Italian American films, it seems essential to clarify both the role of members of the ethnic group in organized crime and the nature of the criminal organizations themselves.

Italian American criminal organizations were not imported wholesale from southern Italy, but developed in response to American conditions. Yet though the Sicilian Mafia afforded no organizational blueprint for its American counterpart, Sicilian immigrants held certain attitudes towards state and police, family and society, loyalty and honour, along with distinctive ideals of manliness and secrecy, that lent themselves to the formation of tight-knit, self-perpetuating, internally loyal, and resilient criminal organizations. In Sicily, the Mafioso has an acknowledged and integral role within a personalistic society that shares his values of honour and respect and that, besides being exploited by the Mafioso, has relied on him for social services and benefits left unprovided by the state. Thus the Sicilian Mafia has been honoured and trusted even more than local political authorities. In the United States, however, Italian American criminal organizations encountered a society that, lacking the personalistic values of honour and respect, regarded their typical activities as illegal and transgressive. Though Italian American criminal organizations were supported initially by the ethnic community, which retained the values of the homeland and for which the organizations performed valuable services, this criminal subculture gradually corroded through Americanization, until the Sicilian Mafioso became no more than a gangster on American soil.

Alan A. Block observes that much of Mafia 'history' relies on superficial scholarship, journalistic speculation, or sensationalism. It appears, however, that the earliest Italian American criminal groups limited their activities to the small-scale local ethnic community. These organizations combined an interest in profits with a paternalistic concern for the social and economic welfare of their members. Yet owing to distrust and rivalrousness, the groups were often at each other's throats. The major transformation of Italian American organized crime occurred when, in the early 1930s, and under the inspiration of earlier Chicago-based gangsters such as Johnny Torrio and Al Capone, Lucky Luciano and his associates replaced the paternalistic model with 'family-based' syndicates. These new crime groups, the origin of the Mafia or Cosa Nostra, not only cooperated with each other but, adopting at least some of the impersonal values of modern business, extended their activities into the larger society, a process already initiated by Torrio during Prohibition.

Up to about 1950 crime experts and law enforcement officers concentrated on criminal organizations individually. Yet though the Mafia attracted little attention in the 1920s, by the late 1930s the term 'Mafia' was taken to refer to an organized criminal conspiracy. In the next decade, as organized crime was increasingly identified with ethnic conspirators, speculation on the existence of the Mafia revived. By 1940 the idea of a national crime syndicate was in the air, Frank Costello supposedly pulling the strings. Fears of a national criminal conspiracy only intensified thanks to the five-man Senate Special Committee to Investigate Organized Crime in Interstate Commerce, chaired by Senator Estes Kefauver of Tennessee. Between 1950 and 1951 the committee conducted interviews in various parts of the country, including Nevada, Florida, and New York City. Having interrogated New York crime boss Frank Costello in the final round of hearings, Kefauver concluded that the United States was threatened by a national organization of Italian American gangsters – the Mafia. He seems to have pushed this argument at the insistence of the Federal Bureau of Narcotics.

On 25 November 1957 New York State police officers interrupted a major meeting of Italian American crime bosses at the estate of Joseph Barbara in the small rural community of Apalachin, New York. This meeting seems to have been arranged in order to discuss urgent questions raised by the recent failed assassination attempt on Frank Costello, the more recent assassination of crime boss Albert Anastasia, and the involvement of family members in the narcotics trade, which carried long prison sentences and thus threatened underworld security as an incentive to defection. Of the approximately seventy gangsters rounded up at Apalachin, not one was convicted. Nonetheless, the Apalachin cookout has been called the 'biggest mistake' and 'worst day' in the history of Italian American criminals. Following the Apalachin fiasco, FBI director J. Edgar Hoover, who had denied the existence of the Mafia for years, now regarded it as a major threat.

The Senate Select Committee on Improper Activities in the Labour Management Field, extending from 1957 to 1963 and chaired by Senator John J. McClellan of Arkansas, focused on labour racketeering but also intensified public fears of a national crime conspiracy. Its chief counsel was Robert Kennedy, who, during his subsequent term as attorney general, declared war on the Mafia, which he, like many others, now firmly believed to exist. This belief was strengthened by the testimony of low-level Italian American gangster Joseph Valachi to the Permanent Subcommittee on Investigations of the Senate Committee on Government Operations in 1963–4. Informing on his criminal associates in exchange for protection, Valachi discussed in extensive if questionable detail the inner workings of a far-flung criminal organization of which he claimed to have been a member. He called it 'Cosa Nostra' or 'our thing,' a label that now often substitutes for 'Mafia.' At the 1967 Oyster Bay Conference crime experts affirmed the existence of the Mafia or Cosa Nostra not as a nationally centralized or hierarchical organization, but as a national 'confederation' of twenty-four cartels each organized, as Valachi had claimed, on a family basis. In the same year the Task Force Report of the President's Commission on Law Enforcement and Administration of Justice endorsed Kefauver's conclusions in characterizing the Mafia as a national organization of twenty-four crime groups. By this point many Americans were coming to identify organized crime entirely with Italian American organizations, as if no others existed.

Published in 1952, Ed Reid's *Mafia* was a journalistic work short on evidence. In 1954 Sid Feder and Joachim Joesten claimed in their biography of Lucky Luciano that a national syndicate had existed for over two decades but had only recently become international. Frederic Sondern's *Brotherhood of Evil* (1959) asserted the Mafia's existence but only as a loosely knit organization. Police detective Raymond V. Martin, who witnessed the 'Gallo-Profaci war' in the early 1960s, differed from his New York police colleagues at that time in arguing for the existence of the Mafia as a national crime syndicate. In Martin's view, a Mafia 'commission' divided up territories, maintained leading contacts in the legitimate world, coordinated local with national and international operations, and adjudicated in major mob disputes. Yet Martin saw the Mafia not as a 'tight military organization but a system of verbal agreements between tribal chiefs.' This view contrasts with that of Peter Maas in *The Valachi Papers* (1968), which characterized the Mafia as a state within a state, painstakingly structured. Maas did not see it, though, as synonymous with organized crime.

Criminologist Donald Cressey's widely influential *Theft of the Nation* (1969) portrayed the Cosa Nostra or Mafia as a nation-wide cartel of twenty-four closely allied groups, each arranged in a strictly hierarchical family-based pattern and operating under a rigid code of conduct and governance administered and enforced by an all-powerful national commission. The Mafia thus substituted for the state and its legal system. According to Cressey, each family boss enjoyed absolute authority. Beneath him was a *sottocapo*, the family's vice-president or deputy director. The boss also employed a *consigliere* or counsellor, while the soldiers formed contingents each directed by a *caporegime*. As Cressey conceived it, the Cosa Nostra amounted to a formal bureaucratic organization marked by a complex division of labour, the close coordination of activities, and top-down channelling of commands – a thoroughly rationalized arrangement aiming at announced objectives. Thus Cressey likened the Cosa Nostra, at least structurally, to a legitimate business corporation. Although he found remarkable resemblances between the Sicilian and American Mafia, he regarded the latter as a special response to American conditions. The Cosa Nostra in its post–Second World War manifestation had originated following the Castellamarese War of 1930–1, when Lucky Luciano restructured Italian American criminal groups in a close approximation to American business practices. Never identifying the Mafia with the whole of organized crime, Cressey nonetheless believed it to make up the greater part.

Published in the same year as Cressey's book, Ralph Salerno and John Tompkins's *The Crime Confederation* not only traced the organization of the Mafia to the Castellamarese War, but portrayed it as a centralized syndicate of families ruled over by a national commission. Salerno and Tompkins saw the mob boss as the equivalent of the chief executive officer of a business corporation and likened the underboss to an executive vice-president; the remaining slots were assigned to lower-level bosses and soldiers. Salerno and Tompkins acknowledged, though, that informal relations within the families were sometimes more important than official job designations. The work of a government informant with close ties to the New England mob, Vincent Teresa's *My Life in the*

Mafia (1973) described Italian American crime in the Northeast as dominated by a 'ruling council of bosses from different areas who made decisions on rules and policy involving mobs across the country.' Yet the commission 'didn't interfere in local affairs' except in extreme cases, and then only for the purpose of giving advice. In the 1970s Nicholas Gage, Fred J. Cook, and Anthony Villano all referred to the Mafia as a national syndicate.

The belief in a centralized criminal organization called Mafia or Cosa Nostra did not go unchallenged. Already in 1951 crime expert Virgil Peterson argued only for a 'loose arrangement' among crime syndicates, hesitating to speak of 'Mafia.' In the same year Burton Turkus and Sid Feder claimed that organized crime was neither directed by an individual person nor limited to a single ethnic group; it consisted of a 'syndicate' in the sense of cooperation among national crime groups. Kefauver's conspiratorial notion of the Mafia was a folk myth, while the term 'Mafia' applied only to old-style Sicilian immigrant criminals who were replaced in the early 1930s by the more efficient, ruthless, and inter-ethnic 'Unione Siciliano,' as they termed the syndicate. Two years later Daniel Bell complained that Kefauver had failed to prove the existence of a national criminal network; he later doubted the conspiratorial significance of the Apalachin meeting. Giovanni Schiavo's little-known book *The Truth about the Mafia* (1962) dismissed conventional notions of the Mafia as mythical, as it amounted to a state of mind rather than an organization. In *The Italians* (1964), Luigi Barzini similarly defined 'Mafia' not as an organization but as a state of mind shared by Sicilians, which led them to aid one another, side with friends against common enemies, distrust law and authority, exact vengeance outside the law, keep secrets, and maintain familial loyalties. In 1969 E.J. Hobsbawm found the Sicilian Mafia to have been reproduced in America as a loosely linked ritual brotherhood of independent and uncoordinated 'families' based not on real blood ties but on fictitious kinship, each hierarchically organized.

The arguments of Cressey, Salerno, and Tompkins continued to meet a chorus of objections in the 1970s. According to Henner Hess, in neither Sicily nor the United States has the Mafia ever consisted of a centralized and efficiently led organization defined by statutes and branch offices – an imaginary super-cartel, as he called it. Instead, 'Mafia' refers to a social state of mind and behaviour characteristic of Sicily and transplanted to the United States, and also to the criminal method used by loose, flexible, and clique-like organizations. Similar views appear in later studies by Blok and Arlacchi. Norval Morris and Gordon Hawkins's *Honest Politician's Guide to Crime Control* rejected the Kefauver Commission's findings, dismissed Apalachin as mysteriously inconclusive, noted Valachi's inconsistencies, and found the evidence for an all-American crime confederation to be nil. The Mafia amounted to a myth or fantasy of the media and law enforcement agencies. A year later Joseph L. Albini argued that just as Italian American criminal groups have never been nationally organized in their history, so there is no Mafia in the sense of a centralized bureaucratic organization. Instead, Italian American criminal groups practised 'syndicate crime,' which allows for considerable structural variation and flexibility in operations from group to group. In *A Family Business* (1972), Francis A.J. Ianni focused on a single crime family, the fictionally named Lupollos, whose 'clan' or kinship organization he assumed tentatively to typify other Italian American criminal groups. Rather than a formal membership organization, Ianni found the Lupollos to operate entrepreneurially through a network of social relationships, the entire structure being traditional rather than rational or bureaucratic. What counted was a state of mind manifest in a kinship-based pattern of duties and mutual loyalties among patrons and clients. Nor did Ianni discover a large-scale, centralized, and bureaucratically administered syndicate ruling over individual crime families, which were linked only to some extent by blood ties.

The conspiracy theory of the Mafia was increasingly submerged in a tide of scepticism during the 1970s. Notwithstanding his description of Frank Costello, his former client, as 'Boss of Bosses,' lawyer George Wolf denied that the Mafia was organized as a business corporation, and even acknowledged that Costello had to consult with other bosses on key decisions. In *Guns and Garlic* (1974), Frederic Homer complained that the conspiracy theorists ought instead to have seen informal networks of interaction within a decentralized confederation. Besides exaggerating the Italian American presence in organized crime, Cressey wrongly supposed a national commission to exist. William Howard Moore showed that, despite their failure to prove the existence of a national, centrally organized criminal syndicate, Kefauver and his associates had successfully promoted a conspiratorial as opposed to socio-economic environmental interpretation of organized crime, so that the reality of the Mafia was accepted by government officials, politicians, judges, police, and the general public.

Dwight C. Smith's *Mafia Mystique* (1975) saw the Mafia as a mythological construct that falsely reassured Americans that organized crime derives from alien rather than native sources. The myth had encouraged officials to concentrate almost exclusively on Italian American gangsters, although other ethnic groups participate in organized crime. For Smith, 'Mafia' means a state of mind rather than a centralized conspiracy. The Kefauver and McClellan committees, Apalachin, and Valachi's testimony all lack credibility. Humbert S. Nelli's *The Business of Crime* (1976) denied that Lucky Luciano had transformed Italian American criminal groups into a centralized, impersonal, bureaucratic organization, even if inter-group conferences occurred occasionally. In *The Business of Organized Crime* (1979), Annelise Graebner Anderson noted that though recent wiretapping evidence (the 'DeCavalcante tapes') had revealed the existence of an Italian American crime commission in the Northeast, no evidence existed for a national commission in charge of all Italian American crime operations. Regarding the organization of crime families, Anderson discerned a structure similar to what Cressey described yet lacking the complexity of a large corporation. In her view, Italian American crime families more closely resembled governments than business firms, since individual members offered tribute to members in exchange for the privilege of conducting their criminal businesses. Offended by the identification of Italian Americans with the Mafia, Iorizzo and Salvatore Mondello denied its existence as a centralized national syndicate. More prudently, James Inciardi found the issue to require 'added data.'

In the 1980s and 1990s critics continued to express scepticism about the Mafia as a national, centralized organization. W. Richard Scott saw Italian American organized crime as a 'natural system' whose members structured their activities informally so as to secure their common survival. Ovid Demaris's *The Last Mafioso* reports gangster Johnny Rosselli's statement that the boss of each family enjoys separate but equal powers with every other boss, even if excluded from the 'commission.' This consisted of the bosses of the leading ten families, to whom Rosselli attributed only the power of settling familial disputes. In *A Man of Honor* (1983), crime boss Joseph Bonanno explained the failure to describe the Cosa Nostra satisfactorily by saying it did not exist as a formal organization. As if conversant with contemporary criminology, Bonanno (or his ghostwriter Sergio Lalli) defined 'The Mafia' as not an institution but a process, a special set of relationships. The commission of family bosses had no executive power, but only exerted influence over the families.

Rejecting Cressey's corporate model of organized crime as a nation-wide bureaucratic structure characterized by a high degree of goal-oriented rationality, Howard Abadinsky's *The Criminal Elite* found it to be not a comprehensive coordinated hierarchy based on traditional relationships but a loose and simple arrangement allowing for pragmatism and spontaneity. Not only was there no evidence for a national cartel under a chief executive officer, or for a ruling commission, as in a corporation, but individual family hierarchies often showed discrepancies between an individual's job title and status and his actual power. In other instances gangsters were jacks-of-all-trades. In contrast with a business, gangsters were not salaried employees but private entrepreneurs; had crime families been bureaucratically organized, they would have had more success in banning members from the drug trade. Nor could individual families operate except haphazardly, as they were prevented from using elaborate systems of record-keeping, accounting, and long-distance communication typical of business bureaucracies. Instead, they relied on an informal network of friendships along with a patrimonial model of kinship and patron-client relations extending through the hierarchy. Such haphazardness and lack of bureaucratic organization parallels that of the Sicilian underworld, contrary to what Cressey believed. Regarding rules of conduct, the Americans had replaced Sicilian traditionalism based on family ties – Ianni's model for Italian American crime groups – with a more rational, formal, and impersonal system. Whereas in Sicily family loyalties have led to violence and vendetta, in the United States violence as a response to family dishonour was held in check, and a member of a crime organization might be expected to murder a relative so as to prove his greater loyalty to the criminal organization. Abadinsky reiterates these ideas in the seventh edition (2003) of his *Organized Crime*.

In *Italian Americans* (1985), Richard Alba acknowledged Italian American gangsters' rise to primacy in the 1930s, yet he rejected the notion that organized crime consisted only of Italian Americans. He also questioned the validity of referring to it as a centralized bureaucratic organization on a national scale. Twenty-four Italian American crime families operated independently, relying on a commission only for the solution of jurisdictional disputes among families. According to Robert J. Kelly, crime families by their very nature cannot integrate themselves into larger centralized organizations. Peter A. Lupsha noted that the 1967 Oyster Bay Conference had used the term 'confederation' to refer to the loose and open texture of crime group interaction, rather than thinking in terms of a national business syndicate.

Mangione and Morreale's sensitivity to ethnic slurs perhaps inclined them to accept Smith's dismissal of the 'Mafia mystique' in their history of Italian Americans, *La Storia* (1993). In the same year Victor Kappeler and his colleagues noted that nearly every empirical study over two decades had disproved the reality of the Mafia by showing Italian American criminal groups to be loosely structured, informal, and open entities held together by flexible and adaptive networks. For them, organized crime amounted to a series of fragmented investment and joint business ventures. These were pretty much the views of criminologists Block, Michael Lyman, and Gary W. Potter. In 2000, Ben Lawton described the Mafia as an arbitrary and highly prejudicial construct capable of meaning virtually anything. He noted the low percentage of Italian American criminals within the Italian American population as well as the fact that organized crime remains multi-ethnic. He even denied that it had ever been dominated by Italian Americans. Reiterating his view of the Mafia as a prejudicial myth, Iorizzo was pleased to report what he saw as the Italian Americans' displacement and emargination from organized crime.

Notwithstanding these sceptics, police, prosecutors, and criminologists now believe the Mafia to exist, even if not in the rigidly complex form required by the conspiracy theorists. Thus the long-standing assumptions of law enforcement agencies, folk mythology, and Hollywood have been vindicated. Admittedly only a very small percentage of Italian Americans participate in organized crime. Nor is the Mafia a rationalized bureaucratic organization with a nationally centralized command and formalized communications. In thus defining the Mafia, the conspiracy theorists clouded the issue, enabling their opponents to deny its reality with large and convincing bodies of evidence. Apparently, it is no longer deemed necessary for the Mafia to take a rigidly bureaucratic, hierarchical, and centralized form in order to exist. It is now seen as a fluid combination of loosely organized units that work together or independently, but with sufficient integration, cooperation, solidarity, durability, directive authority, and commonalty of values and interests to constitute a discernible entity. In short, it makes more sense to believe in the existence of the Mafia than to deny it. Contrary to the claim that Italian Americans have never dominated organized crime, the Mafia has been for many decades the most significant criminal combination, enjoying power and influence far beyond its size. It owes its success to ethnic traditions of loyalty and kinship and the solidity and tenacity of the organization based upon them.

In 1976 Francis A.J. Ianni noted that the wiretaps of New Jersey crime boss Sam DeCavalcante in the late 1960s had pointed to an Italian American crime 'commission' in the New York–New Jersey area. In *The Business of Organized Crime*, Annelise Graebner Anderson found these tapes possibly to support the existence of Cosa Nostra. In the same year Jonathan Kwitny's *Vicious Circles* cited the tapes as evidence of the Mafia while lambasting academic sceptics for self-deception. Nonetheless, Kwitny represented a minority viewpoint at this time.

Although Peter Reuter rejected the idea of the Mafia as a centralized, large-scale organization, speaking instead of the complicated interdependence of Italian American criminal 'families,' and although he doubted that these groups monopolized illegal markets even in their own designated areas, he did not hesitate to characterize them as 'the Mafia.' As the 1980s drew to close, FBI agent William F. Roemer acknowledged that the Italian American 'mob' lacked a 'national organization' and single corporate leader, yet he referred to a national ruling body known through FBI wiretaps as early as 1959. This was a grouping of heads of families in major parts of the country, who had formed a board of directors called the 'commission.' Though it ruled over organized crime nationwide, it refused to interfere with a crime family in a particular area. Writing in 1989, Stephen Fox found that, after so many recent prosecutions of gangsters, FBI undercover operations, and gangster memoirs, the existence of the Mafia could no longer be denied. That it constituted a state of mind and cultural process rather than a centralized organization was no reason to deny its reality. Indeed, its circumstances made a centralized bureaucratic organization unwieldy and dangerous.

In 1990, Ernest Volkman and John Cummings held that the Mafia had come to be seen as a coalition of twenty-four separate groups or 'families' throughout the United States, with membership restricted to Italian Americans, and with a ruling 'commission' arbitrating disputes between families. According to Block in *The Business of Crime* (1991), law enforcement agents and scholars had found, if not a 'big' or nationwide conspiracy, then 'certainly ... conspiracies and plenty of interaction among primarily Italian American criminal syndicates.' Indeed, 'the endless weaving of criminal conspiracies is the meaning of organized crime,' and it is 'not likely that belonging to a syndicate is a restraint ... upon the activities of the criminals.' The debate over the Mafia had altered greatly since the 1970s, as the sceptics had to acknowledge the confirmation of Valachi's testimony by federal wiretaps. In a 1988 memorandum Rudolph Giuliani, U.S. attorney for the Southern District of New York, stated that the existence of the Cosa Nostra as a nationwide criminal organization could no longer be credibly disputed. He mentioned a ruling council or 'commission' of Mafia or Cosa Nostra families in the 'Commission case,' adding that judges presiding at prosecutions of Teamsters officials and Mafia figures had recognized the Cosa Nostra.

James B. Jacobs's *Busting the Mob: The United States v. Cosa Nostra* appeared in 1994 after two decades of government warfare against organized crime through electronic surveillance, undercover activities, mob informants, the Witness Security Program, and vigorous use of new anti-racketeering statues. As Jacobs remarked, Italian American criminals suffered grave setbacks in the 1980s and early 1990s, including the 'Commission case,' in which four of the five most important family leaders were convicted of bribery and extortion; the Pizza Connection case, leading to the conviction of leading heroin traffickers between the United States and Sicily; the Teamsters Local 560 case, a civil racketeering suit; the case of *United States v. the International Brotherhood of Teamsters*, exposing Mafia corruption in that organization; and the sentencing of Gambino family crime boss John Gotti to life imprisonment without parole. In Jacobs's view the government had conclusively rebutted all arguments denying the reality of the Mafia, which had turned out to correspond surprisingly closely to the image enshrined in Hollywood and folk mythology. He cautioned, though, that the organization was not yet understood in all its workings and dimensions. Subsequent commentators, including William Kleinknecht, Ernest Volkman, Robert J. Kelly, Vincenzo Ruggiero, Mark Haller, and Thomas Reppetto, hold views similar to those of Jacobs.

Notes

Preface

1 Mary Pat Kelly, *Martin Scorsese: The First Decade* (Pleasantville, N.Y.: Red-grave, 1980), 18, 19, 42–56, 76, 96–7, 100, 122, 124–8; Mary Pat Kelly, *Martin Scorsese: A Journey* (New York: Thunder's Mouth Press, 1991), 9–13, 28–35; Richard A. Blake, SJ, 'Redeemed in Blood: The Sacramental Universe of Martin Scorsese,' *Journal of Popular Film and Television* 24, no. 1 (1996): 2–9; Paul Giles, *American Catholic Arts and Fictions: Culture, Ideology, Aesthetics* (Cambridge: Cambridge Univ. Press, 1992), 298, 335–49; Leo Braudy, 'The Sacraments of Genre: Coppola, de Palma, Scorsese,' *Film Quarterly* 39 (Spring 1986). 17–28; Les Keyser, *Martin Scorsese* (New York: Twayne, 1992), 4–10, 25–8; Lee Lourdeaux, *Italian and Irish Filmmakers in America: Ford, Capra, Coppola, and Scorsese* (Philadelphia: Temple Univ. Press, 1990), 220–1, 222, 234, 241, 243; Andrew Greeley, *The Catholic Imagination* (Berke-ley: Univ. of California Press, 2000), 18, 19, 48–9, 111–17; Richard Gambino, 'Despair, Italian Style,' *Village Voice*, 23 May 1974, in Kelly, *Martin Scorsese: First Decade*, 174–6; Lynn Garafola, 'On Italian-Americans,' in Kelly, *Martin Scorsese: First Decade*, 109–19.

2 Johann Wolfgang von Goethe, *Italian Journey*, trans. Robert R. Heitner, in Thomas R. Heitner and Geoffrey L. Sammons, eds., *Collected Works* (New York: Suhrkampf, 1989), 6:203. Goethe's view of Sicily is shared by Luigi Barzini, *The Italians* (New York: Bantam, 1965), 262. The idea of Sicily as the key to understanding Italy would seem to clash with Francis A.J. Ianni's by no means unusual assertion that Italy is divided into two distinctively northern and southern zones, the former focused on wealth as a source of power and prestige and thus characteristically European, the latter obsessed with honour and power as the source of wealth and thus essen-

tially Mediterranean. Such a distinction perhaps has greater justification in modern times, when the differences between north and south have become more marked. In any case, Ianni holds that the state of mind or 'spirit' known as *mafia* 'represents the quintessence' of southern Italian culture and in its central emphasis on honour and family provides the basis for the more extreme manifestation of Mafia in the sense of criminal organizations. See Ianni, *A Family Business: Kinship and Social Control in Organized Crime* (New York: Russell Sage Foundation, 1972), 16, 25.

3 Lesley Stern, *The Scorsese Connection* (Bloomington: Indiana Univ. Press, 1995); Leighton Grist, *The Films of Martin Scorsese, 1963–77: Authorship and Context* (London: St. Martin's, 2000); Lawrence S. Friedman, *The Cinema of Martin Scorsese* (New York: Continuum, 1997); Mark Nicholls, *Scorsese's Men: Melancholia and the Mob* (North Melbourne: Pluto Press, 2004); Peter Brunette, introduction in Brunette, ed., *Martin Scorsese: Interviews* (Jackson: Univ. Press of Mississippi, 1999), ix.

4 Richard Gambino, *Blood of My Blood: The Dilemma of the Italian Americans* (New York: Doubleday Anchor, 1975), 277–8; Gambino, 'Italian Americans: Today's Immigrants, Multiculturalism, and the Mark of Cain,' in Pellegrino d'Acierno, ed., *The Italian American Heritage: A Companion to Literature and Arts* (New York: Garland, 1999), 70; Ben Lawton, 'The Mafia and the Movies: Why Is Italian American Synonymous with Organized Crime?' in Anna Camaiti Hostert and Anthony Julian Tamburri, eds., *Screening Ethnicity: Cinematographic Representations of Italian Americans in the United States* (Boca Raton, Fla.: Bordighera, 2001), 72.

5 Pauline Kael, 'Every Inferno,' *New Yorker*, 8 October 1973, in Kelly, *Martin Scorsese: First Decade*, 166.

6 Robert Philip Kolker, *A Cinema of Loneliness: Penn, Kubrick, Scorsese, Spielberg, Altman* (New York: Oxford Univ. Press, 1988), 171–3; Lourdeaux, *Irish and Italian Filmmakers*, 221, 228, 232–4, 241, 243; Robin Wood, *Hollywood from Vietnam to Reagan – and Beyond* (New York: Columbia Univ. Press, 2003), 219, 221–31; Michael Bliss, *Martin Scorsese and Michael Cimino* (Metuchen, N.J.: Scarecrow Press, 1985), 31–5, 68–70, 73; Bliss, *The Word Made Flesh: Catholicism and Conflict in the Films of Martin Scorsese* (Lanham, Md.: Scarecrow Press, 1998), xv, xvi, 1–2, 6–7, 13.

7 This statement does not apply to Peter Bondanella. See Bondanella, *Hollywood Italians: Dagos, Palookas, Romeos, Wiseguys, and Sopranos* (New York: Continuum, 2004).

8 On this point, see Carlos E. Cortes, 'The Hollywood Curriculum on Italian Americans: Evolution of an Icon of Ethnicity,' in Lydio F. Tomasi, Piero Gastaldo, and Thomas Row, eds., *The Columbus People: Perspectives in*

Italian American Immigration to the Americas and Australia (Staten Island, N.Y.: Center for Immigration Studies, 1994), 102. Scorsese states that his portrayal of Italian Americans (including gangsters) in *Mean Streets* was intended 'to be as accurate as possible ... I wanted to make them look the way I saw them'; see Cortes, 'Hollywood Curriculum,' 108n.

9 Philip V. Cannistraro, 'The Italians of New York: An Historical Overview,' in Cannistraro, ed., *The Italians of New York: Five Centuries of Struggle and Achievement* (New York: New-York Historical Society, 1999), 19.

10 Jerre Mangione and Ben Morreale, *La Storia: Five Centuries of the Italian American Experience* (New York: HarperCollins, 1992), 416–18. Atypically of the older generation, Jack Valenti, former president of the Motion Picture Association of America, praises *GoodFellas'* artistry while insisting upon its fundamentally moral viewpoint. See Paolo Casella, *Hollywood Italian: Gli italiani nell'America di celluloide* (Milan: Baldini & Castoldi, 1998), 269.

11 Luisa del Giudice, Introduction, in del Giudice, ed., *Studies in Italian American Folklore* (Logan: Utah State Univ. Press, 1993), 5.

12 Frank P. Tomasulo, 'Italian Americans in the Hollywood Cinema,' *VIA* 7 (Spring 1996): 70. See also Tomasulo, 'Raging Bully: Postmodern Violence and Masculinity in *Raging Bull*,' in Christopher Sharrett, ed., *Mythologies of Violence in Postmodern Media* (Detroit: Wayne State Univ. Press, 1999), 180, 181.

13 Fred Gardaphe, *Italian Signs, American Streets: The Evolution of Italian American Narrative* (Durham, N.C.: Duke Univ. Press, 1996), 9–10, 14, 15, 19.

14 On this conflict, see Thomas Belmonte, 'The Contradictions of Italian American Identity: An Anthropologist's Personal View,' in *Italian American Heritage*, ed. d'Acierno, 8.

1. The Immigrant Generations: Italianamerican

1 The following discussion is based largely on Andy Dougan, *Martin Scorsese: The Making of His Movies* (New York: Thunder's Mouth Press, 1998), 7–10; Kelly, *Martin Scorsese: A Journey*, 18; Marie Katheryn Connelly, *Martin Scorsese: An Analysis of His Feature Films, with a Filmography of His Entire Directorial Career* (Jefferson, N.C.: McFarland, 1993), ix; David Ehrenstein, *The Scorsese Picture: The Art and Life of Martin Scorsese* (New York: Carol, 1992), 33; Keyser, *Martin Scorsese*, 3–4. On Polizzi Generosa, see Teresa Maggio, *The Stone Boudoir: Travels through the Hidden Villages of Sicily* (Cambridge, Mass.: Perseus, 2002), 62–74.

2 See Frank J. Cavaioli, 'Corona,' in Salvatore La Gumina, Frank J. Cavaioli,

Salvatore Primeggia, and Joseph A. Varacalli, eds., *The Italian American Experience: An Encyclopedia* (New York: Garland, 2000), 148–9. Unlike Little Italy, with its multi-storey apartment houses, Corona contains many one- and two-family residences on small plots of land and is quasi-suburban.

3 On the uncertain reasons for the return, see Ehrenstein, *Scorsese Picture*, 33. Ben Nye mistakenly claims that the family left Elizabeth Street because of an economic reversal. See Nye, *Scorsese Up Close* (Lanham, Md.: Scarecrow, 2004), 1.

4 Peter Biskind, *Easy Riders, Raging Bulls: How the Sex-Drugs-and-Rock-'n'-Roll Generation Saved Hollywood* (New York: Simon and Schuster, 1998), 227.

5 Robert F. Foerster, *The Italian Emigration of Our Times* (1919; rpt., New York: Russell and Russell), 1968, *passim*; Samuel L. Baily, *Immigrants in the Land of Promise: Italians in Buenos Aires and New York City, 1870–1914* (Ithaca: Cornell Univ. Press, 1999), 25–6; Mangione and Morreale, *La Storia*, 69.

6 Richard Alba, *Italian Americans: Into the Twilight of Ethnicity* (Englewood Cliffs, N.J.: Prentice-Hall, 1985), 22; Joseph Lopreato, *Italian Americans* (New York: Random House, 1970), 12.

7 Foerster, *Italian Emigration*, 16; James A. Crispino, *The Assimilation of Ethnic Groups: The Italian Case* (Staten Island, N.Y.: Center for Migration Studies, 1980), 22. According to Foerster, between 1887 and 1906 a total of 2,092,821 Italian American immigrants were admitted to the United States.

8 Gianfausto Rosoli, 'The Global Picture of the Italian Diaspora to the Americas,' in *Columbus People*, ed. Tomasi et al., 309; Humbert S. Nelli, 'Italians,' in Stephan Thernstrom, ed., *Harvard Encyclopedia of American Ethnic Groups* (Cambridge: Harvard Univ. Press, 1980), 545; Lopreato, *Italian Americans*, 13, 17; Baily, *Immigrants*, 89.

9 Nathan Glazer and Daniel Patrick Moynihan, *Beyond the Melting Pot: Negroes, Puerto Ricans, Jews, Italians, and Irish of New York City*, 2nd ed (Cambridge, Mass.: MIT Press, 1970), 185; Foerster, *Italian Emigration*, 327.

10 Anna Maria Martellone, 'Italian Immigrant Settlement and Repatriation,' in Humbert S. Nelli, ed., *Italy and the United States: The First Two Hundred Years* (Proceedings of the Ninth Italian American Historical Association) (Staten Island, N.J.: American Italian Historical Association, 1997), 147; Foerster, *Italian Emigration*, 48–50; Humbert S. Nelli, *From Immigrants to Ethnics: The Italian Americans* (New York: Oxford Univ. Press, 1983), 19–35; Joseph Lopreato, *Peasants No More: Social Class and Social Change in an Underdeveloped Society* (San Francisco: Chandler, 1967), 47–8.

11 Leonard Covello, *The Social Background of the Italo-American School Child* (Totowa, N.J.: Rowman and Littlefield, 1972), 34–44; Lopreato, *Peasants No More*, 53–8; Foerster, *Italian Emigration*, 51–63.

12 For the 'agrotown,' see Gustav Schachter, *The Italian South: Economic Development in Mediterranean Europe* (New York: Random House, 1965), 55–9; Covello, *Social Background of Italo-American School Child*, 65–7; Jane Schneider and Peter Schneider, *Culture and Political Economy in Western Sicily* (New York: Academic Press, 1776), 32–3, 51, 52. The Schneiders accept Anton Blok's argument that the Sicilian agrotowns arose because major landowners held large tracts of land near the settlement, thus forcing peasants to aggregate in a common residence.

13 Nelli, *From Immigrants to Ethnics*, 20, 22; Tommaso Astarita, *Between Salt Water and Holy Water: A History of the Italian South* (New York: W.W. Norton, 2005), 288; Schachter, *Italian South*, 32, 106, 107–8, 113; Foerster, *Italian Emigration*, 65–79; Schneider and Schneider, *Culture and Political Economy*, 59–61, 117–19; Pino Arlacchi, *Mafia, Peasants, and Great Estates: Society in Traditional Calabria*, trans. Jonathan Steinberg (Cambridge: Cambridge Univ. Press, 1983), 16, 134–6.

14 Foerster, *Italian Emigration*, 81–2, 87–8; Anton Blok, *The Mafia of a Sicilian Village, 1860–1960: A Study of Violent Peasant Entrepreneurs* (New York: Harper and Row, 1974), 53.

15 Schachter, *Italian South*, 107–8, 111; Foerster, *Italian Emigration*, 68, 77; Lopreato, *Italian Americans*, 24, 31; Schneider and Schneider, *Culture and Political Economy*, 63–4; Arlacchi, *Mafia, Peasants, and Great Estates*, 16, 17, 35.

16 Astarita, *Between Salt Water and Holy Water*, 288.

17 Schneider and Schneider, *Culture and Political Economy*, 119–20; Lopreato, *Italian Americans*, 25; Lopreato, *Peasants No More*, 23; Schachter, *Italian South*, 31.

18 Micaela di Leonardo, *The Varieties of Ethnic Experience: Kinship, Class, and Gender among California Italian Americans* (Berkeley: Univ. of California Press, 1994), 50–1; Thomas Kessner, *The Golden Door: Italian and Jewish Immigrants in New York City, 1880–1915* (New York: Oxford Univ. Press, 1977), 15; Josef Barton, 'The Edge of Modernity: Immigration in the United States,' in *Columbus People*, ed. Tomasi et al., 326, 328–30.

19 Martellone, 'Italian Immigrant Settlement,' 148; Lopreato, *Peasants No More*, 24; Schneider and Schneider, *Culture and Political Economy*, 122–3; Kessner, *Golden Door*, 15.

20 Nelli, *From Immigrants to Ethnics*, 23–4; Astarita, *Between Salt Water and Holy Water*, 288, 301; Lopreato, *Peasants No More*, 23, 24; Lopreato, *Italian Americans*, 25.

21 Schneider and Schneider, *Culture and Political Economy*, 123; Mangione and Morreale, *La Storia*, 80–1; Blok, *Mafia of a Sicilian Village*, 121–7; Baily, *Immigrants*, 33.

22 John Briggs, *An Italian Passage: Immigrants to Three American Cities, 1890–1930* (New Haven: Yale Univ. Press, 1978), 9–10; Mangione and Morreale, *La Storia*, 90; Arlacchi, *Mafia, Peasants, and Great Estates*, 183–9. Poverty was only the main 'push' factor in the decision to emigrate. There was also a psychological 'pull' factor, namely the immigrants' initiative and future orientation as active participants in bettering their lives. See Briggs, *Italian Passage*, 67–8, 272.

23 Covello, *Social Background of Italo-American School Child*, xxv; Martellone, 'Italian Immigrant Settlement,' 147; Donna Gabaccia, *From Sicily to Elizabeth Street: Housing and Social Change among Italian Immigrants, 1880–1930* (Albany: State Univ. of New York Press, 1984), 54; Rosoli, 'Global Picture of Italian Diaspora,' 308; Mangione and Morreale, *La Storia*, 89–90.

24 Mangione and Morreale, *La Storia*, 33, 68; Gabaccia, *From Sicily to Elizabeth Street*, 54; Lopreato, *Italian Americans*, 35. One and a half million Sicilians left Italy between 1876 and 1925, 1900 to 1914 being the peak years. See Schneider and Schneider, *Culture and Political Economy*, 124–5.

25 Rudolph J. Vecoli, 'The Search for an Italian American Identity,' *Rivista di Studi Anglo-americani* 4–5 (1984–5): 33; Martellone, 'Italian Immigrant Settlement and Repatriation,' 152; Foerster, *Italian Emigration*, 23–43, 374; Mangione and Morreale, *La Storia*, 88, 94–5, 159; Lopreato, *Italian Americans*, 14–15; Arlacchi, *Mafia, Peasants, and Great Estates*, 59–60; Baily, *Immigrants*, 26, 28, 93–4; R.A. Schermerhorn, *These Our People: Minorities in American Culture* (Boston: D.C. Heath, 1949), 246–7; Nelli, *From Immigrants to Ethnics*, 42–4; Donna R. Gabaccia, 'Peopling "Little Italy,"' in *Italians of New York*, ed. Cannistraro, 47.

26 Crispino, *Assimilation*, 23; Lopreato, *Italian Americans*, 40; Gabaccia, 'Peopling "Little Italy,"' 45–6, 47; Nelli, 'Italians,' 547; Virginia Yans-McLaughlin, *Family and Community: Italian Immigrants in Buffalo, 1880–1930* (Urbana: Univ. of Illinois Press, 1982), 57–8, 60–1, 70–1.

27 Cannistraro, 'Italians of New York,' 5; Betty Boyd Caroli, 'Italian Settlement in American Cities,' in *United States and Italy*, ed. Nelli, 154; Alba, *Italian Americans*, 47; Nelli, *From Immigrants to Ethnics*, 47–56; Foerster, *Italian Emigration*, 363–73; Lopreato, *Italian Americans*, 36–7.

28 Alba, *Italian Americans*, 47; Lopreato, *Italian Americans*, 37–8; Blok, *Mafia of a Sicilian Village*, 48.

29 Schermerhorn, *These Our People*, 232; Gabaccia, *From Sicily to Elizabeth Street*, 67.

30 Humbert S. Nelli, 'Italians in Urban America,' in Silvano S. Tomasi and Madeline Engel, eds., *The Italian Experience in the United States* (Staten Island, N.Y.: Center for Migration Studies, 1970), 79; Lydio F. Tomasi, *The*

Italian American Family: The Southern Italian Family's Process of Adjustment to Urban America (Staten Island, N.Y.: Center for Migration Studies, 1991), 10; Rosoli, 'Global Picture of Italian Diaspora,' 311; George Pozzetta, 'Italian Americans,' in *Reference Library of European America*, Vol. 2, *Ethnic Essays: Irish Americans to Welsh Americans* (Detroit: Gale Research, 1998), 333.

31 Crispino, *Assimilation*, 25; Foerster, *Italian Emigration*, 393–4; Lopreato, *Italian Americans*, 41–2; Vecoli, 'The Coming of Age of the Italian Americans, 1945–1974,' *Ethnicity* 5 (1978): 123–4.

32 Kessner, *Golden Door*, 16.

33 Gabaccia, *From Sicily to Elizabeth Street*, 61, 79, 105, 106, 108, 127; Baily, *Immigrants*, 132–3.

34 Nelli, 'Italians in Urban America,' 80; Lopreato, *Italian Americans*, 105; Gabaccia, 'Peopling Little Italy,' 49–50; Kessner, *Golden Door*, 157–9.

35 Nelli, *From Immigrants to Ethnics*, 42, 75, 77, 87; Alba, *Italian Americans*, 51; Lopreato, *Italian Americans*, 103; Kessner, *Golden Door*, 36, 52.

36 Crispino, *Assimilation*, 26; Gabaccia, *From Sicily to Elizabeth Street*, 64; Briggs, *Italian Passage*, 112–13; Foerster, *Italian Emigration*, 334–5, 349–60; Nelli, *From Immigrants to Ethnics*, 75, 86–7; Gabaccia, 'Little Italy's Decline: Immigrant Rentiers and Investors in a Changing City,' in David Ward and Oliver Zunz, eds., *The Landscape of Modernity* (New York: Russell Sage Foundation, 1982), 240–1.

37 Foerster, *Italian Emigration*, 329–37, 340–1, 345–53; Briggs, *Italian Passage*, 113, 164–6; Kessner, *Golden Door*, 33; Cannistraro, 'Italians of New York,' 7.

38 Elizabeth Ewen, *Immigrant Women in the Land of Dollars: Life and Culture in the Lower East Side, 1896–1925* (New York: Monthly Review Press, 1985), 25, 100–2, 106, 121–6; Baily, *Immigrants*, 100; Briggs, *Italian Passage*, 116; Nelli, *From Immigrants to Ethnics*, 87–9, 160; Kessner, *Golden Door*, 71–5; Nelli, 'Italians,' 551; Virginia Yans-McLaughlin, 'Italian Women and Work: Experience and Perception' and Miriam Cohen, 'Italian-American Women in New York City, 1909–1950,' both in Milton Cantor and Bruce Laurie, eds., *Class, Sex, and the Woman Worker* (Westport, Conn.: Greenwood Press, 1977), 107, 111–12, 122–6.

39 Foerster, *Italian Emigration*, 339; Nelli, *From Immigrants to Ethnics*, 73–4, 75–6, 82–6.

40 Gabaccia, *From Sicily to Elizabeth Street*, 62, 63, 64, 93, 94, 95, 106.

41 Nelli, *From Immigrants to Ethnics*, 57–8; Nelli, 'Italians,' 548; Gabaccia, 'Little Italy's Decline,' 237, 240; Nancy L. Green, 'Sweatshop Migrations: The Garment Industry between Home and Shop,' in *Landscape of Modernity*, ed. Ward and Zunz, 220; Ewen, *Immigrant Women*, 150.

42 Mangione and Morreale, *La Storia*, 134, 143; Gerald Meyer, 'Italian Harlem:

Portrait of a Community,' in *Italians of New York*, ed. Cannistraro, 58; Ewen, *Immigrant Women*, 150.

43 Foerster, *Italian Emigration*, 382, 384; Gabaccia, 'Peopling Little Italy,' 51.

44 Mangione and Morreale, *La Storia*, 143n, 144; Foerster, *Italian Emigration*, 382, 383, 384, 385; Robert A. Orsi, *The Madonna of 115th Street: Faith and Community in Italian Harlem, 1880–1850* (New Haven: Yale Univ. Press, 1985), 29.

45 Crispino, *Assimilation*, 26; Nelli, *From Immigrants to Ethnics*, 60–5, 70–1; Gabaccia, 'Peopling Little Italy,' 52–3; Gabaccia, 'Little Italy's Decline,' 240.

46 Gabaccia, *From Sicily to Elizabeth Street*, 12–13, 21, 24, 29–30, 32, 34, 51, 54, 66, 68, 71, 72, 74; Gabaccia, 'Little Italy's Decline,' 238, 240. For living conditions on Elizabeth Street in the early 1900s, see Ianni, *Family Business*, 68.

47 Gabaccia, *From Sicily to Elizabeth Street*, xvi, 50–1, 74, 75, 76, 77, 78, 80–2, 83–4, 87, 92, 107, 108; Gabaccia, 'Little Italy's Decline,' 237, 246, 247; Green, 'Sweatshop Migrations,' 220, 223.

48 Alba, *Italian Americans*, 30–5; Tomasi, *Italian American Family*, 8 (quoting Foerster, *Italian Emigration*, 95), 11; Phyllis H. Williams, *South Italian Folkways in Europe and America* (New Haven: Yale Univ. Press, 1938), 73; Danilo Dolci, *The Man Who Plays Alone*, trans. Antonia Cowan (London: MacGibbon and Kee, 1968), 126; Francis A.J. Ianni, 'Organized Crime and the Italo-American Family,' in Francesco Cordasco, ed., *Studies in Italian American Social History: Essays in Honor of Leonard Covello* (Totowa, N.Y.: Rowman and Littlefield, 1975), 32.

49 Leonard W. Moss, 'The Family in Southern Italy: Yesterday and Today,' in *United States and Italy*, ed. Nelli, 187; Tomasi, *Italian American Family*, 8–9; Charlotte Gower Chapman, *Milocca: A Sicilian Village* (Cambridge: Schenkman, 1971), 68–9; Herbert S. Gans, *The Urban Villagers: Group and Class in the Life of Italian-Americans* (New York: Free Press, 1965), 211.

50 Tomasi, *Italian American Family*, 10; Williams, *South Italian Folkways*, 79–80; Alba, *Italian Americans*, 34–5; Gambino, *Blood of My Blood*, 30–3; Carlo Levi, *Christ Stopped at Eboli: The Story of a Year*, trans. Frances Frenaye (New York: Farrar, Straus, 1947), 89.

51 Gabaccia, *From Sicily to Elizabeth Street*, 4–5, 28, 114–15; Ianni, 'Familialism in the South of Italy and in the United States,' in *United States and Italy*, ed. Nelli, 194; Gans, *Urban Villagers*, 200.

52 Gans, *Urban Villagers*, 200, 210; Yans-McLaughlin, *Family and Community*, 61–2; Edward C. Banfield, *The Moral Basis of a Backward Society* (Glencoe, Ill.: Free Press, 1958), 153.

53 Lopreato, *Peasants No More*, 67–8; Gabaccia, *From Sicily to Elizabeth Street*,

4–5, 10, 28, 69–70; Banfield, *Moral Basis*, 118–19; Nelli, *From Immigrants to Ethnics*, 134–5. Although Virginia Yans-McLaughlin assigns a more significant role to the extended family than does Donna Gabaccia, she acknowledges that the nuclear family often prevailed in southern Italy, and that the extended family was difficult to establish. See Yans-McLaughlin, *Family and Society*, 61–2.

54 Chapman, *Milocca*, 37, 73–5, 78, 79; Williams, *South Italian Folkways*, 76; Nelli, 'Italians,' 555; Covello, *Social Background of Italo-American School Child*, 158, 193–4, 214; Yans-McLaughlin, *Family and Community*, 182; Nelli, *From Immigrants to Ethnics*, 132–4; Tomasi, *Italian American Family*, 9; Schneider and Schneider, *Culture and Political Economy*, 93–4; Crispino, *Assimilation*, 21–2. The prohibition of agrarian work for women does not hold true for Lucania, the area of Calabria called the Cosentino, and other regions. See Ann Cornelisen, *Women of the Shadows* (Boston: Little, Brown, 1976), 15–16, 23; Arlacchi, *Mafia, Peasants, and Great Estates*, 26; Cohen, 'Italian-American Women,' 121.

55 Tomasi, *Italian American Family*, 9; Nelli, *From Immigrants to Ethnics*, 132–4; Moss, 'Family,' 187; Pozzetta, 'Italian Americans,' 339; Covello, *Social Background of Italo-American School Child*, 154, 207–8, 210, 212, 213, 236; Yans-McLaughlin, *Family and Community*, 84.

56 Chapman, *Milocca*, 37; Covello, *Social Background of Italo-American School Child*, 213, 219–20; Williams, *South Italian Folkways*, 77; Orsi, *Madonna*, 133, 134; Lopreato, *Italian Americans*, 58.

57 Tomasi, *Italian American Family*, 9; Covello, *Social Background of Italo-American School Child*, 236; Nelli, *From Immigrants to Ethnics*, 133; Mangione and Morreale, *La Storia*, 233.

58 Carla Bianco, *The Two Rosetos* (Bloomington, IN.: Indiana University Press, 1974), 30; Alba, *Italian Americans*, 32, 33–4; Covello, *Social Background of Italo-American School Child*, 152–3; Williams, *South Italian Folkways*, 81–2; Ianni, 'Familialism,' 192.

59 Simone Cinotto, *Una famiglia che mangia insieme: Cibo ed etnicità nella comunità italoamericana di New York, 1920–1940* (Turin: Otto, 2001), 392; Orsi, *Madonna*, 114; Gambino, *Blood of My Blood*, 4; Chapman, *Milocca*, 76.

60 Tomasi, *Italian American Family*, 8; Donald Tricarico, *The Italians of Greenwich Village: The Social Structure and Transformation of an Ethnic Community* (Staten Island, N.J.: Center for Migration Studies, 1984), 8; Pozzetta, 'Italian Americans,' 336; Alba, *Italian Americans*, 56.

61 Vecoli, 'Contadini in Chicago: A Critique of "The Uprooted,"' *Journal of American History* 51 (December 1964): 405, 409, 410; Tricarico, *Italians of Greenwich Village*, 8, 21, 30–1; Kessner, *Golden Door*, 71; Thomas Sowell, *Ethnic America* (New York: Basic Books, 1981), 116.

62 Tricarico, *Italians of Greenwich Village*, 21; Gabaccia, *From Sicily to Elizabeth Street*, 59, 60, 103; Yans-McLaughlin, *Family and Community*, 62–3.

63 Tricarico, *Italians of Greenwich Village*, 24, 27–8, 30; Gabaccia, *From Sicily to Elizabeth Street*, 10, 54, 79, 103, 104.

64 Nelli, *From Immigrants to Ethnics*, 29, 149–50.

65 Cinotto, *Una famiglia che mangia insieme*, 87–8; Lopreato, *Italian Americans*, 78–9; Ianni, *Family Business*, 139–40; Vecoli, 'Contadini in Chicago,' 405.

66 Nelli, *From Immigrants to Ethnics*, 145–8; Covello, *Social Background of Italo-American School Child*, 241–74; Alexander DeConde, *Half Bitter, Half Sweet: An Excursion into Italian-American History* (New York: Scribner's, 1971), 108–9; Pozzetta, 'Italian Americans,' 339; Sr Mary Fabian Matthews, CS, 'The Role of the Public School in the Assimilation of the Italian Immigrant Child in New York City, 1900–1914,' in *Italian Experience*, ed. Tomasi and Engel, 128; Briggs, *Italian Passage*, 38, 41–5, 191–3, 215–17, 219–20, 222–4. Contrary to general opinion, Briggs believes that many southern Italians valued education. In his view, not only is illiteracy a questionable indicator of indifference to schooling, but southerners sought alternatives to the poor schools their children attended. Briggs, *Italian Passage*, 22, 24, 25, 38, 41–5, 47–9, 50–4, 242.

67 Covello, *Social Background of Italo-American School Child*, 258, 259, 403–4; Nelli, *From Immigrants to Ethnics*, 145–6; DeConde, *Half Bitter, Half Sweet*, 110; Schachter, *Italian South*, 77; Pozzetta, 'Italian Americans,' 339; Chapman, *Milocca*, 148.

68 Covello, *Social Background of Italo-American School Child*, 244–7; Matthews, 'Role of Public School,' 127; Foerster, *Italian Emigration*, 343; Pozzetta, 'Italian Americans,' 334. Seventy per cent of southern Italians were illiterate in 1900. See Gambino, *Blood of My Blood*, 106; see also Sowell, *Ethnic America*, 103. Forty-seven per cent of Italian immigrants were illiterate, but the figure is affected by the twelve per cent illiteracy rate for northern Italians. See Kessner, *Golden Door*, 40.

69 Kessner, *Golden Door*, 84–5, 96, 99; Nelli, 'Italians in Urban America,' 98–9; Glazer and Moynihan, *Beyond the Melting Pot*, 199; Covello, *Social Background of Italo-American School Child*, 289; Ewen, *Immigrant Women*, 95, 193; Alba, *Italian Americans*, 60–1. Citing Stephen Steinberg, Orsi warns against exaggerating the role of a purely cultural factor such as family orientation in impeding the upward mobility of Italian Americans, which was affected as well by their lack of industrial skills upon their arrival in the United States; when they acquired these skills, they advanced economically. According to Micaela di Leonardo, scholars have overemphasized the

family as the source of the immigrants' difficulties. See Orsi, *Madonna*, 98; di Leonardo, *Varieties of Ethnic Experience*, 19–21, 47.

70 Kelly, *Martin Scorsese: A Journey*, 21. Mrs. Scorsese would have entered high school at the onset of the Depression, a possible factor in her non-attendance. Her age group, consisting of women who had reached from twenty-five to forty-five years of age by 1940, has been studied by Miriam Cohen. She finds in it an increase in the number of years of high school attendance by comparison with foreign- and native-born groups of Italian American women among Mrs. Scorsese's contemporaries. Within her group 55 per cent completed at least one year of secondary education and 29 per cent graduated. Mrs. Scorsese's low educational level is perhaps reflected in the fact that she and her husband, who never finished high school, remained urban villagers rather than exhibiting occupational and territorial mobility. See Cohen, 'Italian American Women,' 129, 131.

71 Glazer and Moynihan, *Beyond the Melting Pot*, 200; Alba, *Italian Americans*, 2, 59–60; Covello, *Social Background of Italo-American School Child*, 318–19; Kessner, *Golden Door*, 95–6.

72 Nelli, 'Italians in Urban America,' 98–9; Nelli, 'Italians,' 554; Alba, *Italian Americans*, 61; Caroline F. Ware, *Greenwich Village, 1920–1930: A Comment on American Civilization in the Post-War Years* (Boston: Houghton Mifflin, 1935), 174. Lopreato and Briggs contend that Italian American immigrants appreciated education and desired it for their children, but that various factors prevented them from taking advantage of it. See Lopreato, *Italian Americans*, 154–7; Briggs, *Italian Passage*, 55, 56, 59, 60, 64, 240, 243, 274.

73 Puzo, qtd. in Stephen R. Fox, *Blood and Power: Organized Crime in the Twentieth Century* (New York: W. Morrow, 1989), 369. See also Gardaphe, *Italian Signs, American Streets*, 1–2.

74 Bianco, *Two Rosetos*, 138; Gans, *Urban Villagers*, 20, 188–9, 194. Gans's observations do not suggest television-centered families. Although the family television was 'always on,' even if no one was watching, viewing itself was 'intermittent.' At the same time, 'excessive' television viewing was discouraged among adults, although children could watch as much as they liked. Yet they were 'not home often enough to be tied to the set.'

75 Glazer and Moynihan, *Beyond the Melting Pot*, 201; Sowell, *Ethnic America*, 120–1; Ware, *Greenwich Village*, 341. In samples gathered in Rochester, Utica, and Kansas City, John Briggs finds Italian American school performances equal to those of other immigrant groups. Regarding truancy, he argues that Italian American parents customarily enrolled their children in school at a later age than did other ethnic groups, and that upon leaving

school for the workplace at the legal age of fourteen their children were hounded by truant officers demanding that they complete the legally required years of coursework. Thus truancy, retardation, and non-achievement resulted largely from factors other than dis-esteem for education. See Briggs, *Italian Passage*, 229, 230, 232, 234–8, 243.

76 DeConde, *Half Bitter, Half Sweet*, 333; Nelli, 'Italians,' 554; Pozzetta, 'Italian Americans,' 339.

77 Henner Hess, *Mafia and Mafiosi: Origins, Power, and Myth*, trans. Ewald Osers (New York: New York Univ. Press, 1998), 16, 32–3; Bianco, *Two Rosetos*, 127; Chapman, *Milocca*, 155–7; Lopreato, *Peasants No More*, 20–1; Levi, *Christ Stopped at Eboli*, 76–7; Ianni, *Family Business*, 19.

78 Kelly, *Martin Scorsese: A Journey*, 26. Scorsese asserts that the challenge of mere survival combined with the experience of repeated foreign invasions had made Sicilians suspicious of government, police, and clergy; instead, they trusted only their families, their 'own blood.' See his *Il Mio Viaggio in Italia* (videorecording) (Burbank, Calif.: Buena Vista Home Entertainment, 2001).

79 Lopreato, *Peasants No More*, 21; Hess, *Mafia and Mafiosi*, 17, 27, 29, 31; Humbert S. Nelli, *The Business of Crime: Italians and Syndicate Crime in the United States* (New York: Oxford Univ. Press, 1976), 3; Foerster, *Italian Emigration*, 433.

80 Covello, *Social Background of Italo-American School Child*, xxv, 87, 161–3, 172–3; Lopreato, *Peasants No More*, 20–1, 67–8, 116; Dolci, *The Man Who Plays Alone*, xi, 103–4, 126, 127; Tomasi, *Italian American Family*, 10; Orsi, *Madonna*, 102.

81 Schachter, *Italian South*, 59; Covello, *Social Background of Italo-American School Child*, 152, 173, 175–6; Nelli, *Business of Crime*, 5–6; Sowell, *Ethnic America*, 117. However, Briggs argues that the theories of sociologist Edward C. Banfield have led many scholars to ignore the evidence for the southern Italians' capacity for voluntary associations, including the mutual aid societies that existed in many parts of the Mezzogiorno during the period of immigration. See Briggs, *Italian Passage*, 15–16, 17, 18, 20, 21, 33, 36, 279–80, 284n.

82 Banfield, *Moral Basis, passim*.

83 Gans, *Urban Villagers*, 203–4; Gabriel A. Almond and Sidney Verba, *The Civic Culture: Political Attitudes and Democracy in Five Nations* (Boston: Little Brown, 1965), 38, and *passim*; Glazer and Moynihan, *Beyond the Melting Pot*, 195; Lopreato, *Peasants No More*, 66; Schachter, *Italian South*, 68, 200, 200n; Nelli, 'Italians in Urban America,' 77–8, 88–9; Kessner, *Golden Door*, 172; Robert D. Putnam, *Making Democracy Work: Civic Traditions in Modern*

Italy (Princeton: Princeton Univ. Press, 1993), 88–9, 91–2, 144, 177, 222n, and *passim*. Notwithstanding the contrast Putnam finds between northern and southern Italy in their civic cultures, Dean Peabody observes that Italians normally do not expect fellow Italians to act universalistically, according to general as opposed to personalistic standards, and that they even expect particularism in state officials. However, Peabody acknowledges that these traits, to which he largely attributes the atmosphere of social mistrust in Italy, are more pervasive in the south than in the north. His views of the south are indebted to Banfield, whose thesis he entirely accepts. See Peabody, *National Characteristics* (Cambridge: Cambridge Univ. Press, 1985), 137, 142; see also 206. For a more recent critique of Italian familism, personalism, and particularism as major factors in the comparatively low level of 'civic-ness' within the nation as a whole, see Carlo Tullio-Altan, *Una nazione senza religione civile: le ragioni di una democrazia incompiuta* (Udine: Istituto Editoriale Veneto Friuliano, 1985), xii, 2–3, 12, 18, 30–1, 69–70, 75.

84 Chapman, *Milocca*, 138–40, 146, 149, 157, 161. However, Chapman noted the villagers' limited cooperation and weak identification with the village considered as an economic unit.

85 Paul T. Campisi, 'Ethnic Family Patterns: The Italian Family in the United States,' in Francesco Cordasco and Eugene Bucchioni, eds., *The Italians: Social Backgrounds of an American Group* (Clifton, N.J.: A.M. Kelley, 1974), 312, 315. Campisi's essay first appeared in *The American Journal of Sociology* 53 (May 1948). 443–49.

86 Sydel Silverman, 'Agricultural Organization, Social Structure, and Values in Italy: Amoral Familism Reconsidered,' *American Sociologist* 70 (1968): 1, 2, 8–11, 15, 16, 17; Arlacchi, *Mafia, Peasants, and Great Estates*, 1–7, 48–9; Hess, *Mafia and Mafiosi*, 16, 37–8, 143; Bondanella, *Hollywood Italians*, 332n.

87 John Davis, 'Morals and Backwardness,' *Comparative Studies in Society and History* 12 (1970): 346–50; William Muraskin, 'The Moral Basis of a Backward Sociologist: Edward Banfield, the Italians, and Italian-Americans,' *American Journal of Sociology* 79 (1974): 1484n, 1489, 1491; Anthony H. Galt, 'Carnival on the Island of Pantelleria: Ritualized Community Solidarity in an Atomistic Society,' *Ethnology* 12 (1973): 325, 326, 327–8, 336, 337–8; Moss, 'Family,' 185; Gabaccia, *From Sicily to Elizabeth Street*, 1–10, 49, 55, 56–7, 139, 140. For further objections to Banfield's thesis, see Mangione and Morreale, *La Storia*, 74–5n; Tomasi, *Italian American Family*, 11; Maureen Giovannini, 'Female Chastity Codes in the Mediterranean,' in David D. Gilmore, ed., *Honor and Shame and the Unity of the Mediterranean* (Special Publication of the American Anthropological Association, no. 22) (Wash-

ington, D.C.: American Anthropological Association, 1987), 63; Alessandro Pizzorno, 'Familismo amorale e marginalità storica, ovvero perchè non c'è niente da fare a Montegrano,' *Quaderni di Sociologia* 3 (1967): 247–62; Filippo Sabelli, 'A Different Way of Knowing: A Research Note on the Real "Montegrano,"' *Italian Politics and Society* 44 (Fall 1995): 18–25; and the extensive gathering of sociological essays excerpted in the Italian edition of Banfield's book, entitled *Le basi morali di una società arretrata* (Bologna: Il Mulino, 1976). According to Loredana Sciolla in a recent book, surveys have established that at the present time familism is more prevalent in northern Italy and other parts of Europe than in the Italian south, and, moreover, that northern Italians place less trust in institutions than do their southern counterparts. According to Sciolla, these findings explode what has been a false antithesis between familism and 'civic-ness.' See Sciolla, *Italiani: Stereotipi di casa nostra* (Bologna: Il Mulino, 1997), 14–19, 20, 23–5, 28. For a recent evaluation of the debate over amoral familism, see Alessandro Cavalli, 'Reflections on Political Culture and the "Italian National Character,"' *Daedalus* (Summer 2001): 119–38.

88 Covello, *Social Background of Italo-American School Child*, 161, 162, 279–81.

89 Tomasi, *Italian American Family*, 13.

90 Gans, *Urban Villagers*, 93–5, 106–7 120–1, 199–204. For a contrasting example, see Tricarico, *Italians of Greenwich Village*, xvii.

91 Yans-McLaughlin, *Family and Community*, 109–10; Vecoli, 'Contadini in Chicago,' 405; Crispino, *Assimilation*, 20–1; Alba, *Italian Americans*, 140.

92 Gabaccia, *From Sicily to Elizabeth Street*, 79; Barton, 'Edge of Modernity,' 327–30, 334, 335.

93 Rosoli, 'Global Picture of Italian Diaspora,' 312.

94 Yans-McLaughlin, *Family and Community*, 62–3, 65, 67, 71, 72, 74, 76–7, 79, 80–1; Gabaccia, *From Sicily to Elizabeth Street*, 27–8, 54–7.

95 Denise Mangieri DiCarlo, 'Italian Festa: The Italian Festa in the United States as an Expression of Ethnic Pride,' in *Columbus People*, ed. Tomasi et al., 84.

96 Gans, *Urban Villagers*, 18, 33, 199–200, 204–5, 207, 208, 210, 229.

97 Vecoli, 'Contadini in Chicago,' 417. In a later essay Vecoli stresses the continuity between the first and second generations. See Vecoli, 'Search for an Italian American Identity,' 37–40.

98 Glazer and Moynihan, *Beyond the Melting Pot*, 12–13; Yans-McLaughlin, *Family and Community*, 20; Gabaccia, *From Sicily to Elizabeth Street*, 1, 10, 100, 112, 113; Humbert S. Nelli, *Italians in Chicago, 1880–1930: A Study in Ethnic Mobility* (New York: Oxford Univ. Press, 1970), 5–6, 157.

99 Glazer and Moynihan, *Beyond the Melting Pot*, 16; Luisa del Giudice, Introduction to *Studies in Italian American Folklore*, ed. del Giudice, 2, 7; in the same volume see Paola Schnellenbaum, 'Stereotypes as Cultural Constructs: A Kaleidoscopic Picture of Italian Americans in Northern California,' 156. See also Ware, *Greenwich Village*, 156, 170; Alba, *Italian Americans*, 9–10; Michael Fischer, 'Ethnicity and the Post-Modern Arts of Memory,' in James Clifford and George E. Marcus, ed., *Writing Culture: The Poetics and Politics of Ethnography* (Berkeley: Univ. of California Press, 1986), 195.

100 See *The Invention of Tradition*, ed. Eric Hobsbawm and Terence Ranger (Cambridge: Cambridge Univ. Press, 1983), 1–2; Nelli, *Italians in Chicago*, 6.

101 Nelli, *From Immigrants to Ethnics*, 131, 135; Gans, *Urban Villagers*, 46.

102 Gans, *Urban Villagers*, 38–41, 74; Alba, *Italian Americans*, 93.

103 Gabaccia, *From Sicily to Elizabeth Street*, 100–1; Covello, *Education of Italo-American School Child*, 333–4; Orsi, *Madonna*, 107–49.

104 Mangione and Morreale, *La Storia*, 224–5; Covello, *Education of Italo-American School Child*, 279–80; DeConde, *Half Bitter, Half Sweet*, 113; Alba, *Italian Americans*, 55.

105 Tomasi, *Italian American Family*, 13, 15, 16; Pozzetta, 'Italian Americans,' 339; Ware, *Greenwich Village*, 341; Ewen, *Immigrant Women*, 187.

106 Campisi, 'Ethnic Family Patterns,' 313; Tomasi, *Italian American Family*, 13–15; Cinotto, *Una famiglia*, 63–4; Nelli, 'Italians,' 555. It seems, however, that first-generation women who entered the workplace continued to think of themselves as dependents of their husbands. See Yans-McLaughlin, 'Italian Women and Work,' 116.

107 Covello, *Social Background of Italo-American School Child*, 333–45; Nelli, *From Immigrants to Ethnics*, 136, 137; Foerster, *Italian Emigration*, 395–6; Ware, *Greenwich Village*, 116; Alba, *Italian Americans*, 56.

108 Alba, *Italian Americans*, 57; Tomasi, *Italian American Family*, 15, 16; Ewen, *Immigrant Women*, 190, 233; Orsi, *Madonna*, 111, 115–17, 125, 136–9; Ware, *Greenwich Village*, 181–2; Gary R. Mormino and George Pozzetta, 'Italian Americans in the 1940s,' in *The Italians of New York*, ed. Cannistraro, 144. John Briggs believes the culture conflict between the first and second generations to have been exaggerated, and doubts that it was largely caused by the exposure of Italian American children to American schools (as opposed to non-Italian classmates). He cites the neglected study by Joseph Wilfred Tait, *Some Aspects of the Effect of the Dominant American Culture upon Children of Italian-Born Parents* (New York: Teachers College, Columbia Univ., 1942). See Briggs, *Italian Passage*, 244, 321.

109 Glazer and Moynihan, *Beyond the Melting Pot*, 188–9; Gans, *Urban Villag-*

428 Notes to pages 26-8

ers, 36–9, 65–9; Orsi, *Madonna*, 110, 123; William Foote Whyte, *Street Corner Society: The Social Structure of an Italian Slum* (Chicago: Univ. of Chicago Press, 1981), *passim*; Ewen, *Immigrant Women*, 106.

110 Cinotto, *Una famiglia*, 43–7; DeConde, *Half Bitter, Half Sweet*, 112–13; Lopreato, *Italian Americans*, 67, 108.

111 Alba, *Italian Americans*, 56–7.

112 Campisi, 'Ethnic Family Patterns,' 312–16; Cinotto, *Una famiglia*, 64, 67–8; Crispino, *Assimilation*, 26, 27–8. Rudolph Vecoli holds that historians such as Oscar Handlin exaggerate the conflict between first and second generations, since basic southern Italian familial forms and attitudes persisted. See Vecoli, 'Contadini in Chicago,' 409.

113 Irvin L. Child, *Italian or American?: The Second Generation in Conflict* (New Haven: Yale Univ. Press, 1943). On the second-generation response, see also Tomasi, *Italian American Family*, 16–18; Lopreato, *Italian Americans*, 68–73, 76; Nelli, *From Immigrants to Ethnics*, 149; Pozzetta, 'Italian Americans,' 339; Orsi, *Madonna*, 98–9, 112–13, 125–7, 143.

114 Child, *Italian or American?*, 71–116.

115 Child, *Italian or American?*, 151–73. See also Lopreato, *Italian Americans*, 76–7.

116 Child, *Italian or American?*, 118–48. See also Lopreato, *Italian Americans*, 77–8.

117 Gans, *Urban Villagers*, 208; Alba, *Italian Americans*, 92–5; Tomasi, *Italian American Family*, 6–7; Campisi, 'Ethnic Family Patterns,' 311, and *passim*. Ware claims that the Italian pattern remained intact save for a new acquisitiveness. See Ware, *Greenwich Village*, 152, 173–4. Rudolph J. Vecoli emphasizes the continuity in values between the first and second generations. See Vecoli, 'Coming of Age of the Italian Americans,' 135–6.

118 Tomasi, *Italian American Family*, 16; Campisi, 'Ethnic Family Patterns,' 314; Nelli, *From Immigrants to Ethnics*, 150; Nelli, 'Italians,' 555; Ware, *Greenwich Village*, 188; Gans, *Urban Villagers*, 63–5.

119 Campisi, 'Ethnic Family Patterns,' 315; Gans, *Urban Villagers*, 54, 74–5.

120 Tomasi, *Italian American Family*, 17, 18; Nelli, *From Immigrants to Ethnics*, 144, 145, 150; Tricarico, *Italians of Greenwich Village*, 24; Campisi, 'Ethnic Family Patterns,' 314; Alba, *Italian Americans*, 56–8; Crispino, *Assimilation*, 29; Nelli, 'Italians,' 555; Gans, *Urban Villagers*, 77.

121 Tomasi, *Italian American Family*, 17; Nelli, *Italians in Chicago*, 69–72; Nelli, *From Immigrants to Ethnics*, 144; Alba, *Italian Americans*, 57. Although the increasing appreciation of education among Italian Americans is often attributed to American cultural influences, in the case of women it may have more to do with economic practicality. In New York City the dis-

placement of the garment industry and other forms of manufacturing by commercial and bureaucratic establishments from about 1930 onward made it advantageous for young women to complete their high school educations so as to meet the requirements for clerical and secretarial positions, which also had the advantage of being more secure than factory work. At the same time, homework came to be legally restricted and truant officers became increasingly effective. See Cohen, 'Italian American Women,' 120–1, 129–35.

122 Kelly, *Martin Scorsese: A Journey*, 23.
123 Gans, *Urban Villagers*, 33; Crispino, *Assimilation*, 48, 66.
124 Cinotto, *Una famiglia*, 31, 38–40, 43–7, 67–70, 73–4, 87–8, 91–9, 100–1, 359–60. See also Gambino, *Blood of My Blood*, 17; Frances M. Malpezzi and William M. Clements, *Italian-American Folklore* (Little Rock: August House, 1992), 81.
125 Cinotto, *Una famiglia*, 5, 11–12, 17–18, 32, 213–14, 229–52, 263, 300–1; Nelli, *From Immigrants to Ethnics*, 119–20; Donna R. Gabaccia, *We Are What We Eat: Ethnic Food and the Making of Americans* (Cambridge: Harvard Univ. Press, 1998), 52, 62, 68; Yans-McLaughlin, *Family and Community*, 31; Tricarico, *Italians of Greenwich Village*, 9; Anthony T. Rauche, 'Festa Italiana in Hartford, Conn.: The Pastries, the Pizza, and the People Who "Parla Italiano,"' in Theodore C. Humphrey and Lin T. Humphrey, eds., *We Gather Together: Food and Festival in American Life* (Ann Arbor, Mich.: UMI Research Press, 1988), 207, 208; Mangione and Morreale, *La Storia*, 136; Fabio Parasecoli, *Food Culture in Italy* (Westport, Conn.: Greenwood Press, 2004), 1, 27, 28, 30; Luisa del Giudice, 'Foodways and Food,' in *Italian American Experience*, ed. La Gumina et al., 246.
126 Cinotto, *Una famiglia*, 5, 6, 11, 12, 17–18, 20, 32–3, 213, 214, 263–9.
127 Vidich, Introduction to Tricarico, *Italians of Greenwich Village*, xi, 23; Judith Goode, Janet Theophano, and Karen Curtis, 'A Framework for the Analysis of Continuity and Change in Shared Sociocultural Rules for Food Use: The Italian-American Pattern,' in Linda Keller Brown and Kay Mussell, eds., *Ethnic and Regional Foodways in the United States: The Performance of Group Identity* (Knoxville: Univ. of Tennessee Press, 1984), 73, 83.
128 Gans, *Urban Villagers*, 183; Goode et al., 'A Framework,' 74–5; Malpezzi and Clements, *Italian-American Folklore*, 221.
129 Nelli, 'Italians in Urban America,' 79; Tricarico, *Italians of Greenwich Village*, 13.
130 Nelli, *From Immigrants to Ethnics*, 59–61; Nelli, *Italians in Chicago*, 152–3; Briggs, *Italian Passage*, 75, 81, 83–5, 90, 103, 118, 119, 145; Schermerhorn, *These Our People*, 238.

131 Nelli, *From Immigrants to Ethnics*, 59–60; Nelli, 'Italians,' 554.

132 Nelli, *From Immigrants to Ethnics*, 60, 113, 114, 135, 148–9; Nelli, *Italians in Chicago*, 156.

133 Nelli, *From Immigrants to Ethnics*, 115–17; Nelli, *Italians in Chicago*, ix, 170–5; Mangione and Morreale, *La Storia*, 139–40; Ware, *Greenwich Village*, 141–7, 155; Schermerhorn, *These Our People*, 249; Alba, *Italian Americans*, 49–50; Pozzetta, 'Italian Americans,' 333; Meyer, 'Italian Harlem,' 60–1.

134 Alba, *Italian Americans*, 49–50; Lopreato, *Italian Americans*, 106–7; Briggs, *Italian Passage*, 152, 153, 161; Nelli, 'Italians in Urban America,' 87.

135 Barton, 'The Edge of Modernity,' 334–5; Nelli, *Italians in Chicago*, 91–2; Briggs, *Italian Passage*, 148; Lopreato, *Italian Americans*, 95–7; Orsi, *Madonna*, 25–6.

136 Nelli, *From Immigrants to Ethnics*, 86, 96–103, 115; Lopreato, *Italian Americans*, 47; Schermerhorn, *These Our People*, 252.

137 Nelli, *From Immigrants to Ethnics*, 29, 60, 114; Tricarico, *Italians of Greenwich Village*, 13, 14.

138 Alba, *Italian Americans*, 49. On this point, see also Vecoli, 'Coming of Age of the Italian Americans,' 131–3. Vecoli notes an increase in associations and institutions since 1945, possibly to make up for the loss of family and neighbourhood ties.

139 Yans-McLaughlin, *Family and Community*, 68, 111.

140 Alba, *Italian Americans*, 51; Lopreato, *Italian Americans*, 106, 113–15, 158; Vecoli, 'Coming of Age of the Italian Americans,' 141; Ware, *Greenwich Village*, 170.

141 Alba, *Italian Americans*, 74, 99; Lopreato, *Italian Americans*, 105.

142 Nelli, 'Italians in Urban America,' 6; Gans, *Urban Villagers*, 36–7; Crispino, *Assimilation*, 28.

143 Tricarico, *Italians of Greenwich Village*, 13, 21, 27–8, 32, 37, 39, 41, 42, 49. See also Ewen, *Immigrant Women*, 161–2. However, the social openness noted by Tricarico perhaps only repeats behaviour common to southern Italian villagers. To quote Lopreato, 'even today ... the people of rural southern Italy shut their doors only at night and ... neighbours move about freely in each other's houses, whether they are relatives or not.' See Lopreato, *Italian Americans*, 98n.

144 Tricarico, *Italians of Greenwich Village*, xv–xviii; Ware, *Greenwich Village*, 152, 155, 156.

145 Alba, *Italian Americans*, 84–6.

146 Gans, *Urban Villagers*, 90–6, 91n, 96, 100, 105–9, 163–4, 201–3, 204–5; Tricarico, *Italians of Greenwich Village*, xvii–xviii.

147 Ianni, 'Familialism,' 195; Valentine Rossilli Winsey, 'The Southern Italian

Immigrant Family in the United States,' in *United States and Italy*, ed. Nelli, 204.

148 Nelli, *From Immigrants to Ethnics*, 60. See also Lopreato, *Italian Americans*, 111.
149 Kessner, *Golden Door*, ix–x (Foreword by Richard C. Wade), 47, 48–59, 67, 78–86, 93, 107–9, 111–19. See also Lopreato, *Italian Americans*, 158, 173; Briggs, *Italian Passage*, 113, 115.
150 Nelli, *Italians in Chicago, passim*; Sowell, *Ethnic America*, 122.
151 Cairoli, 'Italian Settlement,' 157–8.
152 Kessner, *The Golden Door*, 78–83, 104–26; Nelli, *From Immigrants to Ethnics*, 145–6, 148. Vecoli stresses the similarity of the first- and second-generation job profiles, both strongly blue collar. See Vecoli, 'Coming of Age of the Italian Americans,' 127–8.
153 Schermerhorn, *These Our People*, 253; John J. D'Allesandre, 'Occupational Trends of Italians in New York City,' Bulletin No. 8, Casa Italiana Educational Bureau, Columbia University, New York, 1935.
154 Cannistraro, 'Italians of New York,' 17; Nelli, cited in Tricarico, *Italians of Greenwich Village*, xvi (see also 17); Orsi, *Madonna*, 42–3.
155 Crispino, *Assimilation*, 97.
156 Lopreato, *Italian Americans*, 76.
157 Lopreato, *Italian Americans*, 77–8.
158 Kessner, *Golden Door*, 95; Lopreato, *Italian Americans*, 77–8.
159 Alba, *Italian Americans*, 92–5.
160 Nelli, *From Immigrants to Ethnics*, 144–5; Alba, *Italian Americans*, 81–4, 89, 99, 117–29; Lopreato, *Italian Americans*, 135; Pozzetta, 'Italian Americans,' 337; Vecoli, 'Search for an Italian American Identity,' 43; Richard Alba, 'Identity and Ethnicity Among Italians and Other Americans of European Ancestry,' in *Columbus People*, ed. Tomasi et al., 24. By 1972 Italian Americans between the ages of twenty-five and thirty-four had reached the national average in years of schooling and closely approximated the national average in completion of college. See Sowell, *Ethnic America*, 127.
161 Alba, *Italian Americans*, 86–8; Nelli, *From Immigrants to Ethnics*, 60; Lopreato, *Italian Americans*, 48–9; Cannistraro, 'Italians of New York,' 18; Vecoli, 'Search for an Italian American Identity,' 43. Vecoli stresses Italian Americans' resistance to suburbanization, claiming impressionistically that they tend to stick together even in the suburbs. See Vecoli, 'Coming of Age of the Italian Americans,' 126.
162 Vecoli, 'Coming of Age of the Italian Americans,' 128–31; Lopreato, *Italian Americans*, 51, 53; Cannistraro, 'Italians of New York,' 18; Sowell, *Ethnic America*, 126.

163 Kelly, *Martin Scorsese: A Journey*, 17.

164 Keyser, *Martin Scorsese*, 3.

165 Kelly, *Martin Scorsese: A Journey*, 17; Michel Henry, 'Una storia orale dell'America: Conversazione con Martin Scorsese,' *Cinema & Cinema* 11 (January–March 1984): 50.

166 Kelly, *Martin Scorsese: A Journey*, 17.

167 Kelly, *Martin Scorsese: A Journey*, 17, 18.

168 On the Italian American habit of 'laying low' so as not to be 'found out,' see Gay Talese, 'Where Are the Italian-American Novelists?' in *Columbus People*, ed. Tomasi et al., 464, 466, 473–4. See also Gardaphe, *Italian Signs, American Streets*, 29.

169 Kelly, *Martin Scorsese: A Journey*, 16.

170 Daniel Aaron, 'The Hyphenate Writer and American Letters,' *Smith Alumnae Quarterly* (July 1964): 213–17; revised in 'The Hyphenate American Writer,' *Rivista di Studi Anglo-Americani* 4–5 (1984–1985): 11–28; Tamburri, *To Hyphenate or Not to Hyphenate: The Italian/American – An Other American* (Montreal: Guernica, 1991), 17.

171 Tamburri, *To Hyphenate or Not to Hyphenate*, 10–11, 17, 18, 28, 43–4, 45, 46n, 47.

172 Aaron notes that with the rise of ethnic consciousness in the later 1960s the hyphen not only came back but 'hardened,' having been transformed from a 'minus' to a 'plus' sign among those flaunting a newly discovered ethnic pride. Meanwhile, assimilation continued and is perhaps reflected in the recent tendency to drop the hyphen. See Aaron, 'The Hyphenate American Writer,' 11–14, 27. For further discussion, see George J. Leonard, 'Preface: Making a Point of It,' in *The Italian American Heritage*, ed. d'Acierno, xl, xli.

173 Poverty was a major external cause of Sicilian emigration, but another factor (which Mrs Scorsese perhaps takes for granted) was the immigrants' initiative to shape their own lives. In *Il Mio Viaggio* Scorsese links emigration to poverty.

174 Gabaccia, 'Peopling Little Italy,' 51; Gabaccia, 'Little Italy's Decline,' 235, 241.

175 In the recollections of the people of Italian East Harlem, the mother's domestic power and importance took on 'heroic proportions.' See Orsi, *Madonna*, 135.

176 In *Il Mio Viaggio* Scorsese mentions having heard about his grandfather's grocery store 'for so many years.'

177 On the frugality of the early Italian Americans, see Sowell, *Ethnic America*, 127.

178 For the 'Shabbas Goy,' see Ernest Volkman, *Gangbusters: The Destruction of America's Last Great Mafia Dynasty* (New York: Avon Books, 1998), 14.

179 For the southern Italian art of storytelling, and its decline as a result of the loss of its social context and competition from the American media, see Malpezzi and Clements, *Italian-American Folklore*, 163–6; Gioia Timpanelli, 'Stories and Storytelling, Italian and American,' in *Italian American Heritage*, ed. d'Acierno, 132, 142.

180 As late as the 1930s the remaining Irish residents of South Greenwich Village, which is not far from Little Italy, regarded their Italian American neighbours as intruders. The hostility between the groups arose from economic competition, with the Italians commonly accusing the Irish of drunkenness. See Ware, *Greenwich Village*, 128–31.

181 One should not exaggerate the 'homogenizing' effects of radio and television on Italian American 'urban villagers.' Herbert Gans reports that the residents of Boston's West End accepted only those messages supportive of their own values. See Gans, *Urban Villagers*, 181–2, 189, 193–4.

182 Malpezzi and Clements, *Italian-American Folklore*, 83, 89. According to Malpezzi and Clements, Christmas is the 'most important event in the Italian American traditional calendar.'

183 The practical joke seems to have been inspired by the legend of La Befana, or La Vecchia di Natale, the folkloric figure identified with the Feast of the Epiphany who 'rewards virtuous children by filling their stockings with candy and fruit but punishes the naughty by leaving them only lumps of coal.' See Malpezzi and Clements, *Italian-American Folklore*, 89. Giuseppe Pitrè discusses the feast of Natale or Christmas as it was celebrated in Cimmina in the later nineteenth century. It was accompanied by highly detailed scenes of the birth of Christ (*presepi*); specially prepared foods, often in elaborate arrangements; much drinking, eating, and card-playing following Mass on Christmas Eve; and the firing of normally interdicted weapons such as shotguns and small cannons by local townspeople in procession round the town. At the centre of the procession was the puppet-like image of the Vecchia di Natale, who was believed to bring gifts to the local children on the following evening. In Polizzi Generosa, where similar seasonal festivities were observed, La Vecchia was believed to make her visit on the evening of 31 January. See Pitrè, *Spettacoli e feste popolari siciliane* (Palermo: Luigi Pedone Lauriel, 1881), 404–5, 437–41, 455.

184 Nelli, *From Immigrants to Ethnics*, 132; Arlacchi, *Mafia, Peasants, and Great Estates*, 22.

185 Italian Americans of those days commonly travelled from Manhattan to comparatively unsettled Staten Island in search of mushrooms and greens for the dinner table. See Tricarico, *Italians of Greenwich Village*, 9–10.

186 On home gardens and the desire for property, see Malpezzi and Clements, *Italian-American Folklore*, 239–43.

187 Malpezzi and Clements, *Italian-American Folklore*, 241.

188 Schneider and Schneider, *Culture and Political Economy*, 93–4; Gans, *Urban Villagers*, 48.

189 Kelly, *Martin Scorsese: A Journey*, 17.

190 Henry, 'Una storia orale dell'America,' 50.

191 The recipe in the concluding title reads (with punctuation added where necessary): 'Singe an onion and a pinch of garlic in oil. Throw in a piece of veal and a piece of beef, some pork sausage and a lamb neckbone; add a basil leaf. When the meat is brown, take it out and put it on a plate. Put in a can of tomato paste and some water. Pass a can of packed whole tomatoes through a blender and pour it in. Let it boil. Add salt, pepper, and a pinch of sugar. Let it cook for a while. Now make the meatballs. Put a slice of bread, without crust, 2 eggs, and a drop of milk, into a bowl of ground veal and beef. Add salt, pepper, some cheese and a few spoons of sauce. Mix it with your hands. Roll them up, throw them in. Let it cook for another hour.'

192 Henry, 'Una storia orale dell'America,' 50.

2. Scorsese as Third-Generation Italian American Artist

1 Vecoli, 'Search for an Italian American Identity,' 49; Gambino, *Blood of My Blood, passim.*

2 Vecoli, 'Coming of Age of the Italian Americans,' 144.

3 Crispino, *Assimilation*, vi (Gans's Preface), 8, 67, 92–3, 146; Alba, *Italian Americans*. Herbert J. Gans believes that Crispino's findings, based on research in Bridgeport, Connecticut, and its surrounding area, can be generalized. See Gans, Preface to Crispino, *Assimilation*, vii–viii.

4 Crispino, *Assimilation*, 134, 145–6. See also Nelli, *From Immigrants to Ethnics*, 186.

5 Vecoli, 'Search for an Italian American Identity,' 50.

6 Crispino, *Assimilation*, v–vi (Gans's Preface), xxii–xxiii, 8, 9, 10, 30, 34–5, 47–94, 145–6, 150–1; Alba, *Italian Americans*, 12, 89, 110–13, 129, 133–4, 138, 139–43, 148–9; Alba, 'Identity and Ethnicity,' 26–7, 33, 34; Tomasi, *Italian American Family*, 19; Nelli, *From Immigrants to Ethnics*, 180–1.

7 Alba, *Italian Americans*, 16, 159–71; Alba, 'Identity and Ethnicity,' 29.
8 Marcus Lee Hansen, *The Problem of the Third Generation Immigrant* (Rock Island, Ill.: Augustana Historical Society, 1938), 6–12. See also Crispino, *Assimilation*, 13, 150; Alba, *Italian Americans*, 8.
9 Will Herberg, *Protestant – Catholic – Jew: An Essay in American Religious Sociology* (Garden City, N.Y.: Doubleday, 1955), 44, 201, 273.
10 Crispino, *Assimilation*, 12–4, 72–3, 164; Alba, *Italian Americans*, 7–8, 15, 101; Nathan Glazer, Introduction to *Columbus People*, ed. Tomasi et al., 18.
11 Crispino, *Assimilation*, vi (Gans's Preface), 72–3, 76, 79, 158–9, 160; Alba, *Italian Americans*, 15, 159–71; Alba, 'Identity and Ethnicity,' 30, 33; Richard Juliani, 'Identity and Ethnicity: The Italian Case,' in *Columbus People*, ed. Tomasi et al., 57.
12 Herbert Gans, 'Symbolic Ethnicity: The Future of Ethnic Groups and Cultures in America,' *Ethnic and Racial Studies* 2 (January 1979): 1–20; Crispino, *Assimilation*, vi, ix (Gans's Preface); Alba, *Italian Americans*, 7, 15, 173; Alba, 'Identity and Ethnicity,' 22. Crispino disputes Glazer and Moynihan's contention that the ethnic revival would provide an economic, social, and political focus for the individual ethnic group. See Crispino, 13–4.
13 Crispino, *Assimilation*, 163.
14 Crispino, *Assimilation*, 89, 99, 164; Alba, *Italian Americans*, 171–3.
15 Anthony DeCurtis, 'What the Streets Mean,' *South Atlantic Quarterly* (Spring 1992), in *Martin Scorsese: Interviews*, ed. Brunette, 161, 163–4.
16 DeCurtis, 'What the Streets Mean,' 178–9.
17 DeCurtis, 'What the Streets Mean,' 162. Paraphrasing an article by Michael Henry (*Positif*, June 1975), Mary Pat Kelly says of Scorsese that in leaving Little Italy he 'manage[d] to escape the "Family" and the Church.' See Kelly, *Martin Scorsese: First Decade*, 149.
18 Scorsese's five wives include, in order, Larraine Brennan, Julia Cameron, Isabella Rossellini, Barbara de Fina, and Helen Morris. Only Barbara de Fina is an Italian American.
19 Gavin Smith, 'The Art of Vision: Martin Scorsese's *Kundun*,' *Film Comment* (January/ February 1998), in *Martin Scorsese: Interviews*, ed. Brunette, 25–6.
20 Kelly, *Martin Scorsese: A Journey*, 15, 18, 20.
21 Jerre Mangione, 'American Artists of Italian Origin,' in *Italy and United States*, ed. Nelli, 212.
22 Pellegrino d'Acierno argues that the concept of Italian American cinema cannot be limited to films by Italian American directors on Italian American subjects, but must be extended to include works in which Italian American directors such as Capra, La Cava, and Minnelli treat subjects having nothing to do with Italian Americans per se. Because, in

d'Acierno's view, ethnic cinema 'always involves the inscription of the doubleness' of a director ambivalent towards his or her own ethnicity and thus divided in allegiances, such ethnicity will manifest itself cinematically where it is not overtly apparent, in repressions, negations, displacements, distortions, and the very strategy of 'passing.' In short, even seemingly non-ethnic films can be read symptomatically, as bearing traces of an original suppression or 'murder' of the director's background. This theory seems to imply that, for a director, ethnicity is inescapable. It is always present even in its apparent absence, and the critic's job is to ferret out traces of the original crime against ethnicity.

From the methodological point of view, this theory has several major weaknesses. To begin with, while it is possible for a director to encrypt or encode a multitude of signifiers of his own ethnic group in a film ostensibly on a different theme, with the film's subject matter thus becoming a pretext for the disguised representation of ethnicity or the expression of ethnic values and attitudes, such a film is not likely to be very good, or even worth making. To the extent that it amounts largely to an excuse for ethnic self-encoding, its director must inevitably lose sight of what is arguably a primary obligation of a work of art, that it focus on the reality of its subject matter, and attempt to remain faithful to it. Yet how can the director hope to do so when the film's characters, situation, and settings turn out to be signs of a disguised ethnicity? Is not the social, cultural, and experiential reality of the characters likely to be betrayed in their very representation? By the same token, when the film's subject matter is primarily a veil concealing some deeper, more authentic ethnic substratum, is not the effort of criticism likely to become a tedious effort in smoking out such arcana?

A further weakness of d'Acierno's proposed methodology is that it encourages critics to 'discover' traces of ethnicity in films where it does not or only barely exists, but into which its supposed vestiges are projected with a confirmatory bias. Such a danger is bound to arise when the critic harbours mistaken notions of what constitutes a particular kind of ethnicity, as witness the errors of Lee Lourdeaux, examined in note 26 below. Similar errors appear in d'Acierno, whose discussion of Capra can be taken as a caution against his proposed methodology. According to d'Acierno, in an argument anticipated by Paola Casella, Frank Capra displaces his vision of the first-generation Italian American family onto the WASPish Vanderhofs in *You Can't Take It with You* (1938). In its anarchism, eccentricity, dilettantism, and hospitality to strangers, this family is alleged to exemplify the Italian American familism of Capra's youth. The father, played by Lionel Barrymore, is a mild, understanding, soft-hearted patriarch; his daughter, having accidentally received a typewriter, has whimsically taken up novel-writing as a substitute for her previous dabbling in painting; one of the granddaughters (Jean Arthur) is a secretary marrying outside her class; another granddaughter (Ann Miller), typically clad in a tutu, performs ballet exercises within the house all day long; her husband is a political radical whose presence in the family helps to awaken in the police suspicions of its anarchist sympathies; a stranger is immediately invited to join the household permanently so as to indulge his crankish fondness for mechanical invention; and an Italian American non-family member, Mr De Pinna, has long resided by invitation in the basement, where he makes firecrackers whose explosions periodically disturb the household.

To be sure, the presence of Mr de Pinna gives the proceedings something of an Italian flavour, for not only have pyrotechnics been a long-standing Italian specialty, but fireworks were a standard feature of the street festivals celebrated in the Italian American communities of those days. Nonetheless, the general impression produced by the Vanderhof household, with its black maid and pervasive atmosphere of dilettantish zaniness rather than work, contrasts almost totally with ethnological reports of the same period, which identify the Italian American family with stern patriarchy; intra-class and endogamous marriage; suspicion of strangers; illiteracy and indifference to reading; silence and solemnity at the dinner table; conformity as opposed to individualism, much less eccentricity; and a utilitarian work-mindedness rather than a dabbling in the arts. Nor could Capra's own, basically materialistic Sicilian immigrant family have provided the model for the Vanderhofs. The fact is that their representation is based upon that of the identically named family portrayed in the stage play by George F. Kaufman and Moss Hart, both Jews, from which the film derives its title and characters, and which Hart's biographer Steven Bach shows to have been inspired by Hart's bookish and eccentric British Jewish relatives. Accordingly, one may argue more credibly that Capra's film encodes not an Italian American but a Jewish family, although probably few viewers have taken the Vanderhofs to be anything but WASPs. What is also curious about d'Acierno's attempt to read the Vanderhofs as Italian Americans is that he characterizes the typical Italian American family of those decades in terms inapplicable to its supposed cinematic counterpart, referring to the father as a man of

'patience' and 'reserve,' and to the mother as a guardian of familial 'seriousness' and 'decorum' – domestic virtues largely absent in *You Can't Take
It with You*.

It is therefore advisable to avoid a theory and methodology such as
d'Acierno's, which, in their reliance on discredited Freudian concepts like
repression, displacement, and symptom, not only tempt the critic to
deposit within the cinematic text ethnic significance not actually present
within it, but encourage notions of ethnicity so loose and malleable that
they can only prove arbitrary in their application. This is not to deny that
some films on non-Italian American subjects can be shown to reflect in
varying degrees their Italian American directors' ethnicity, but such a
demonstration requires great care in defining ethnicity and authorial
biography. As for the definition of Italian American cinema, the safest
methodology confines it to films by Italian American directors on demon-
strably Italian American themes, so as to avoid attributing *italianità* to
films in which it is palpably absent.

Another weakness in d'Acierno's theory lies in his implicit claim that an
ethnic director cannot escape his or her ethnicity, that to do so is some sort
of crime against oneself and one's group, and that one's ethnicity will
sooner or later leak out in the form of a trace or symptom. Admittedly, an
ethnic artist who totally rejects his or her ethnic origins and experiences
runs the risk of not having much to say over the long and perhaps even in
the short run, and is very likely to sink into a sterile, abstract formalism or
slavish copyism of the host culture. This problem is well exemplified in
Gilbert Sorrentino as discussed by John Paul Russo. Nonetheless, one
must always allow for the creative autonomy of the artist, whose chief
allegiance, in the final analysis, is not to ethnicity but to the imagination.
Ideally, nothing should prevent the ethnic artist from treating his or her
own ethnic background – a limitation regrettably endured by Capra, La
Cava, and Minnelli; yet the artist should have the equal right of ignoring
ethnicity when his or her creative interests and necessities dictate otherwise, without having to suffer the imputation of cultural betrayal, crime,
or even symbolic murder. Scorsese has followed this course in his film-
making, and it goes far to explain the unequalled richness of his work
among Italian American directors.

See d'Acierno, 'Cinema Paradiso: The Italian American Presence in
American Cinema,' in *The Italian American Experience*, ed. d'Acierno, 607–
10, 619; Casella, *Hollywood Italian*, 76; John Paul Russo, 'The Choice of
Gilbert Sorrentino,' in Anthony Julian Tamburri, Paolo A. Giordano, and

Fred L. Gardaphe, eds., *From the Margin: Writing in Italian Americana* (West Lafayette, Ind.: Purdue Univ. Press, 1991), 338–56; Steven Bach, *Dazzler: The Life and Times of Moss Hart* (New York: Alfred A. Knopf, 2001), 144–5.

23 Vittorio Zagarrio, 'F.-C.-F.C. Ovvero: *Italian-American-Dream* dal Film muto alle television,' *Cinema & Cinema* 38 (January–March 1984): 37–8; John Paul Russo, 'An Unacknowledged Masterpiece: Capra's Italian American Film,' in *Screening Ethnicity*, ed. Hostert and Tamburri, 293–4n.

24 Frank Capra, *The Name above the Title: An Autobiography* (New York: Macmillan, 1971), xi, 3.

25 For Capra, see Raymond Carney, *American Vision: The Films of Frank Capra* (Cambridge: Cambridge Univ. Press, 1986), 36–42.

26 Lourdeaux contends that whenever Capra's WASP characters reject acquisitive individualism, impersonality, or anti-familialism, they are really Italians or ethnics in disguise – as if these attitudes could not exist in WASP culture. Not only does Jefferson Smith in *Mr. Smith Goes to Washington* supposedly display Italian personalism merely when he cuts through formality and asks a woman's name, but the Christmas celebration in *Meet John Doe* reflects ethnic Catholicism. By this logic, one might claim that Dickens's *A Christmas Carol* is 'Italian' in feeling. Yet Lourdeaux's weakest contention is that Capra's Italian heritage and, more particularly, his distinctly Italian social ethic appear in his depiction of WASP characters who, challenging the aristocratic WASP 'demigods,' attempt to maximize their fellow Americans' participation in institutions such as nation-wide networks of boys' clubs, building and loan associations, and other voluntary organizations. Likewise, when Capra's characters demonstrate 'swift' or 'positive' social action, or implement their vision of America as an extended family, they covertly reveal Capra's Italian heritage. Besides being unaware that voluntary organizations and grass-roots movements are characteristically American, as Tocqueville recognized, Lourdeaux fails to comprehend that Italian Americans, most of whom, like Capra, derive from southern Italy, have rarely been 'joiners,' and certainly not during Capra's heyday. Largely without traditions of political participation or opposition, Italian Americans have been hampered in their political and social involvements by a southern Italian background characterized by vertical hierarchies, clientelism, political repression and injustice, and a one-sided concentration upon familial loyalties. These have resulted in a distrust of society and the state along with political absenteeism or fatalism – although such attitudes have been mitigated in the United States. This social heritage can hardly have inspired Capra's civic ideals of politi-

cal activism and communalism, which he surely derived from his American milieu. Lourdeaux also identifies the extended family with southern Italy when in reality it developed mainly on American soil. Perhaps the best evidence against Lourdeaux's claims for Capra's civic-minded and politically activist ethnic background derives from Capra's autobiography, in which he mentions that his Sicilian family had virtually no ambitions beyond its material survival symbolized by a 'coffee can stuffed with cash, preferably gold': 'The prime challenge an ignorant family faces in a foreign land is to keep alive. Never mind leading the kids to school. Get the moola, the hard jingling cash in the pockets.' Indeed, so civic-minded was Capra's family that, by his own account, it would have been happy had he become a prosperous bootlegger. The characteristic fatalism and suspicion of strangers endemic to Sicily is not likely to have inspired the portrayal of bank president Tom Dickson (Walter Huston) in Capra's *American Madness* (1932), whom Capra describes as 'filled with beautiful optimism and a cheerful trust in man.' It may be objected to this point that Dickson is modelled on an Italian, A.P. Giannini, founder of the Bank of America. Yet not only was Giannini an Americanized Italian, having been born in the United States in 1870, but his family was of northern Italian, that is, Genoese, origin, thus deriving from a region which had been the financial centre of Europe in the late sixteenth and early seventeenth centuries, where the values of social trust and credit essential to high finance were for historical reasons far more deeply rooted than in southern Italy. See Lourdeaux, *Italian and Irish Filmmakers*, 130–3, 139, 140, 141, 144, 146–9, 153–4, 156–62; Capra, *The Name above the Title*, 112, 137–8.

27 Russo, 'Unacknowledged Masterpiece,' 291–321; Casella, *Hollywood Italian*, 76, 77, 78.
28 Zagarrio, 'F.C.-F.C. Ovvero,' 37–40. See also Zagarrio, 'The Italian American Imaginary: The Imaginary Italian American: Genres, Genders, and Generations,' in *Screening Ethnicity*, ed. Hostert and Tamburri, 126–42.
29 Aaron, 'Hyphenate American Writer,' 11–28; Gardaphe, *Italian Signs, American Streets*; Tamburri, *To Hyphenate or Not to Hyphenate*; Thomas J. Ferraro, *Ethnic Passages: Literary Immigrants in Twentieth-Century America* (Chicago: Univ. of Chicago Press, 1993).
30 Aaron, 'Hyphenate American Writer,' 12; Tamburri, *To Hyphenate or Not to Hyphenate*, 28–31.
31 Gardaphe, *Italian Signs, American Streets*, 7; Barolini, discussed in Tamburri, *To Hyphenate or Not to Hyphenate*, 26–7.
32 Aaron, 'Hyphenate American Writer,' 12–13.
33 Gardaphe, *Italian Signs, American Streets*, 9–12, 14, 15, 19–20, 21, 122.

34 Ferraro, *Ethnic Passages*, 2–3, 5–6.
35 Aaron, 'Hyphenate Writer,' 215; Aaron, 'Hyphenate American Writer,'
    12–13, 25–6.
36 In *Il Mio Viaggio in Italia* Scorsese remarks that, thinking of himself as an
    American, he aspired to work in Hollywood in accordance with its direc-
    torial conventions. However, the influence of Italian cinema, which he
    had absorbed while growing up in Little Italy, prevented him from fully
    embracing the standard paradigm of the Hollywood director, so that he
    now finds himself somewhere 'in between' one culture and the other, the
    only place where he feels 'comfortable.'
37 Michel Henry, article in *Positif: revue de cinema* 170 (June 1975), in Kelly,
    Martin Scorsese: The First Decade, 149.

3. The First World of Martin Scorsese

 1 Guy Flatley, 'He Has Often Walked *Mean Streets*,' *New York Times*, 16 De-
    cember 1973, in *Martin Scorsese: Interviews*, ed. Brunette, 6.
 2 'Dialogue on Film: Martin Scorsese,' The American Film Institute, 1975, in
    Martin Scorsese: Interviews, ed. Brunette, 44. In *Il Mio Viaggio* Scorsese
    remarks that, though Elizabeth Street was itself 'Sicily,' each building was
    occupied exclusively by people from the same village, who for a long time
    kept their distance from non-*paesani* in other buildings and only gradually
    came to intermarry with them. Yet to judge from *Raging Bull*, inter-clan
    rivalries persisted in the neighbourhood at least into the early 1940s. As
    Scorsese remarks of the scuffle that breaks out at Webster Hall, the dance
    hall visited by Jake and Joey, the participants derive from two hostile
    clans, the one consisting of acculturated Italian Americans, the other of
    new arrivals whom the bouncer derides as 'greaseballs.' See Michel Henry,
    'Nuit blanche et chambre noire,' *Positif*, April 1981, trans. by Peter Brunette
    as 'Raging Bull' in *Martin Scorsese: Interviews*, ed. Brunette, 92.
 3 Martin Scorsese, 'Confessions of a Movie Brat: Martin Scorsese,' in David
    Pirie, ed., *Anatomy of the Movies* (New York: Macmillan, 1981), 133;
    Dougan, *Martin Scorsese*, 15; Connelly, *Martin Scorsese*, ix.
 4 David Thompson and Ian Christie, eds., *Scorsese on Scorsese* (London:
    Faber and Faber, 1996), 3; Scorsese, 'Confessions,' 132.
 5 'Dialogue on Film,' 44–5.
 6 Kelly, *Martin Scorsese: A Journey*, 26–7.
 7 Taylor, 'Martin Scorsese,' 303; Scorsese, 'Confessions,' 133.
 8 Kelly, *Martin Scorsese: A Journey*, 26.
 9 Tricarico, *Italians of Greenwich Village*, 43, 44, 64–71. Tricarico treats an

Italian American neighbourhood northwest of Manhattan's Little Italy; syndicate activities in both neighbourhoods are likely to have been similar. Robert Orsi finds that the residents of Italian East Harlem were much inclined to disparage the police and judiciary while mythifying and romanticizing local gangsters as protectors and pacifiers of the community. The locals refused to recognize the gangsters' criminality towards the larger society, and more particularly their predation upon some members of the Italian American neighbourhood. Orsi attributes such moral blindness to the community's isolation vis-à-vis the larger society combined with absolute loyalty to the neighbourhood, 'narrowly considered.' See Orsi, *Madonna*, 31, 103–4, 127–8.

10 Dougan, *Martin Scorsese*, 11–12.

11 Kelly, *Martin Scorsese: A Journey*, 27. Typically streetcorner boys or unlucky gamblers, those who have fallen irremediably into debt to a loan shark often face death or serious injury as punishment for non-payment. However, they are sometimes able to pay off the debt by performing or participating in a criminal act or by providing the creditor with information that makes them a criminal accomplice. Debtors may also initiate crimes in order to meet their debts.

12 Amy Taubin, 'Everything Is Form,' *Sight and Sound*, February 1998, in *Martin Scorsese: Interviews*, ed. Brunette, 260.

13 Gavin Smith, 'Art of Vision,' 255.

14 Whyte, *Street Corner Society, passim*, esp. xviii, 255; Gans, *Urban Villagers*, 36–41, 64–5. For Gans, peer group sociability typifies working-class Italian American social life throughout the life cycle; one grows out of one peer group into another. See also Gabaccia, *From Sicily to Elizabeth Street*, 102.

15 Alba, *Italian Americans*, 93; Orsi, *Madonna*, 120, 123.

16 Dian G. Smith, *American Filmmakers Today* (New York: Meissner, 1983), 116; DeCurtis, 'What the Streets Mean,' 170.

17 Keyser, *Martin Scorsese*, 4.

18 Keyser, *Martin Scorsese*, 4; DeCurtis, 'What the Streets Mean,' 173.

19 David D. Gilmore, 'The Shame of Dishonor,' in *Honor and Shame and the Unity of the Mediterranean*, ed. Gilmore, 2–4, and *passim*; see also in the same volume Gilmore, 'Honor, Honesty, Shame: Male Status in Contemporary Andalusia,' 90–1. In this volume, John Davis notes that though the social and cultural unity of the Mediterranean has been identified with the shared values of honour, shame, and vendetta, these can be found elsewhere. See Davis, 'Family and State in the Mediterranean,' 22. Davis remarks the diversity of societies, cultures, religions, and histories in the region, refusing to define it as a homogeneous cultural area; yet he finds

some anthropological significance in the term 'Mediterranean,' as its societies have interacted for millennia and have much in common. See Davis, *People of the Mediterranean: An Essay in Comparative Social Anthropology* (London: Routledge and Kegan Paul, 1977), 11–14, 19, 255.

20 Covello, *Social Background of Italo-American School Child*, 42–3, 65–7, 68, 70, 198–200; George Saunders, 'Men and Women in Southern Europe: A Review of Some Aspects of a Cultural Complexity,' *Journal of Psychoanalytic Anthropology* 4 (Winter 1981): 443–4, 445; Ann Parsons, 'Paternal and Maternal Authority in the Neapolitan Family,' in Parsons, *Belief, Magic, and Anomie: Essays in Psychosocial Anthropology* (New York: Free Press, 1969), 93–4; Chapman, *Milocca*, 38, 39–40, 92; Alba, *Italian Americans*, 23–4; Sydel Silverman, *Three Bells of Civilization: The Life of an Italian Hill Town* (New York: Columbia Univ. Press, 1975), 192–4, 202, 203, 206; Cornelisen, *Women of the Shadows*, 16; Lopreato, *Italian Americans*, 81.

21 Gans, *Urban Villagers*, 38–9, 40, 47–53, 55, 62, 62n, 70; Gabaccia, *From Sicily to Elizabeth Street*, 97; Lopreato, *Italian Americans*, 81; Glazer and Moynihan, *Beyond the Melting Pot*, 189.

22 Tricarico, *Italians of Greenwich Village*, 8, 21, 38; Gans, noted in Lopreato, *Italian Americans*, 81–2. Two studies of the 1970s show that Italian Americans spend much time with their immediate families; among white ethnics they ranked third highest in time spent with children, and first in time spent with wives. See Alba, *Italian Americans*, 93.

23 Gans found Italian males in the working-class community he studied to be awkward with women. He related this to the sexual segregation of southern Italian society and consequent homophilic peer group relations. Gans found some instances of male homosexuality and remarked that the sartorial vanity of males in their peer groups might indicate latent homosexuality; yet he cautioned against such conclusions. Gans, *Urban Villagers*, 37–41, 40n, 47–8, 50–4, 63, 69–70, 80. Gambino writes: 'Even in their playful banter Italian American men display the need for closeness typical of the entire ethnic group. One sees this most clearly in the physical quality of the interplay among the *giovanotti*, the boys and young men. There is a great deal of touching in the form of jabbing, leaning on, poking, ruffling of hair, and playful slaps on shoulders and faces.' *Blood of My Blood*, 147.

24 Gilmore, 'The Shame of Dishonor,' 3; Carol Delaney, 'Seeds of Honor: Fields of Shame,' 36; and Gilmore, 'Honor, Honesty, Shame,' 90–1: all in *Honor and Shame*, ed. Gilmore; Davis, *People of the Mediterranean*, 77–8; J.G. Peristiany, introduction, in Peristiany, ed., *Honor and Shame: The Values of Mediterranean Society* (1966; rpt. Chicago: Univ. of Chicago Press, 1974), 9, 11 (see also in this volume Julian Pitt-Rivers, 'Honour and Social Status,'

21, 22, 24, 27–8, 31, 34–5, 47; Schneider and Schneider, *Culture and Political Economy*, 86–102); Gerhart Piers, 'Shame and Guilt: A Psychoanalytic Study,' Part 1 of Gerhart Piers and Milton B. Singer, *Shame and Guilt: A Psychoanalytic and a Cultural Study* (Springfield, Ill.: Charles T. Thomas, 1953); Peter Burke, *Popular Culture in Early Modern Europe* (New York: New York Univ. Press, 1978), 57; William Ian Miller, *Humiliation: And Other Essays on Honor, Social Discomfort, and Violence* (Ithaca: Cornell Univ. Press, 1993), 116–8; Ianni, *Family Business*, 20.

The distinction between and shame and guilt, and shame and guilt cultures, has long been a commonplace in anthropological and sociological theory. It has also been accepted by classical scholars who, following E.R. Dodds, regard Homeric Greece as a shame culture. Many social and cultural theorists define internalized morality based on the conscience as a historically unique feature of Protestant Europe and the United States. Yet the rigid antithesis between such cultures was questioned as early as 1953 by Milton B. Singer. More recently, Douglas Cairns has argued that these categories are fraught with contradictions and should be applied very cautiously. Emphasizing the difficulty of distinguishing shame from guilt in social practice, Cairns insists that, contrary to the view that shame requires an audience, it sometimes reveals an internalized component. As shame can be internalized, so one can suffer guilt in and as a result of the presence of an audience. For Cairns, some degree of internalized morality is an absolute requirement for any society or culture, since no one can survive by relying solely on external constraints. Yet Cairns acknowledges not only that societies differ in the degree to which they rely on external-ized or internalized standards, but that small, face-to-face societies (like those of the Mediterranean) probably depend heavily on external con-straints, while in impersonal mass societies the internalized conscience predominates. Peristiany and Miller similarly observe that, although all societies evaluate behaviour in terms of honour and shame, some socie-ties, such as the Mediterranean, emphasize it. See Milton B. Singer, 'Shame Cultures and Guilt Cultures,' Part 2 of Piers and Singer, *Shame and Guilt*, 45–53, 55–64; Cairns, *Aidos: The Psychology and Ethics of Honor and Shame in Ancient Greek Literature* (Oxford: Clarendon, 1993), 15–18, 24, 26–47; Peristiany, Introduction to *Honor and Shame*, ed. Peristiany, 10; Miller, *Humiliation*, 116.

Although the cult of honour is entrenched in southern Italy, it plays an important role in masculine and feminine behaviour in Italy generally. Confirming the insights of Luigi Barzini, Dean Peabody finds that Italians tend to rely on external moral sanctions, whereas the Americans and

English rely more on internalized controls. In Italy, an attractive and
esteemed public presentation is known as *bella figura*. However, Barzini
unconvincingly attributes the Italian idea of honour, whose difference
from the ideal of conscience he recognizes, to the comparative absence
in Italy of northern European feudalism. Actually, feudalism existed in
southern and to a lesser extent in northern Italy, as did the imported
traditions of French chivalry, as witness the *pupi Siciliani* (which Barzini
mentions) and the elaborately decorated Sicilian carts depicting the story
of Roland and other French-inspired epics. Yet unlike the religious values
of the medieval period, with their stress on Christian virtue, feudalism
and chivalry were concerned not only with prestigious display but with
such externally determined values as glory, reputation, renown, and
vengeance – a system of honour and shame. It appears that, in the Middle
Ages at least, northern and southern values regarding conduct were
similar. See Peabody, *National Characteristics*, 141–2, 211–13; Barzini, *Italians*, 189–92; Barzini, *From Caesar to the Mafia: Sketches of Italian Life* (New
York: Library Press, 1971), 327; Gloria Nardini, *Che Bella Figura!: The Power
of Performance at an Italian Woman's Club in Chicago* (Albany: State Univ. of
New York Press, 1999), 10–11; Jacques Le Goff, 'Il peso del passato nella
coscienza collettiva degli italiani,' in Fabio Luca Cavazza and Stephen R.
Graubard, eds., *Il Caso Italiano* (Milan: Garzanti, 1974), 541–2; Donald S.
Pitkin, 'Italian Urbanscape: Intersection of Private and Public,' in Robert
Rotenberg and Gary McDonogh, eds., *The Cultural Meaning of Urban Space*
(Westport, Conn.: Bergin and Garvey, 1993), 98, 99; Silverman, *Three Bells*,
39; Hess, *Mafia and Mafiosi*, 37; Marvin Becker, *Civility and Society in West-
ern Europe, 1300–1600* (Bloomington: Indiana Univ. Press, 1988), *passim*;
Curtis Brown Watson, *Shakespeare and the Renaissance Concept of Honor*
(Princeton: Princeton Univ. Press, 1960), 35, 38, 45–6, 47, 63–4; Chapman,
Milocca, 154; Peristiany, Introduction to *Honor and Shame*, ed. Peristiany, 11.
   Does the Renaissance mark the divergence between southern and
northern norms of conduct? Jacob Burckhardt describes the 'sentiment of
honor' among later Italian Renaissance aristocrats as 'that enigmatic
mixture of conscience and egotism which often survives in the modern
man after he has lost, whether by his own fault or not, faith, love, and
hope.' William Kerrigan and Gordon Braden note that during the Renaissance honour was initially identified with socially conferred *dignitas*, but
that Leone Battista Alberti defined it not as the 'result of social success' but
as its 'interior cause.' Nonetheless, they see the Renaissance conception of
honour as a mixture of conscience and such externally influenced traits as
egoism and pride. Italian Renaissance theorists of honour (and duelling)

distinguish between honour as an inner-directed quality, in the sense of virtue, duty, and moral conscience, and as a concern for mere reputation, regardless of one's deeds or conscience. Yet Frederick R. Bryson describes the Italian Renaissance code of honour as 'concerned less with virtue than with reputation.' Like the duel, the Renaissance cult of honour was an almost entirely aristocratic affair. Among the Italian common people, honour was sometimes manifest in assassinations and vendettas, and apparently exhibited a primary concern for public reputation. Nor does sensitivity to honour and shame disappear in Italy during the Baroque period, although, as Peter Burke reports, traditional ideas of honour declined in some sectors of the upper class in the eighteenth century. What needs emphasizing, though, is that these attitudes and behaviours typified not Italy alone but Renaissance Europe, as Curtis Brown Watson shows. Like their Italian counterparts, northern European aristocrats were obsessed with social approval and thus very much concerned with their personal reputation as conferred by public esteem. As enormous attention was devoted to display, so dishonour in the sense of public disgrace was a fate worse than death, especially in sexual matters. Vengeance was also acceptable, even though it violated church teachings. Indeed, Huizinga sees no difference between the Middle Ages and Renaissance with respect to moral conduct. See Burckhardt, *The Civilization of the Renaissance in Italy*, trans. S.G.C. Middlemore (Harmondsworth: Penguin, 1990), 273; William Kerrigan and Gordon Braden, *The Idea of the Renaissance* (Baltimore: Johns Hopkins Univ. Press, 1989), 48; Bryson, *The Point of Honor in Sixteenth-Century Italy: An Aspect of the Life of the Gentleman* (Chicago: Univ. of Chicago Press, 1935), 4–5, 8–9, 12, 14, 36, 45–6, 85; V.G. Kiernan, *The Duel in European History: Honour and the Reign of Aristocracy* (Oxford: Oxford Univ. Press, 1988), 48–9; Peter Burke, *The Historical Anthropology of Early Modern Italy: Essays on Perception and Communication* (Cambridge: Cambridge Univ. Press, 1987), 13–14, 102; Watson, *Shakespeare and the Renaissance Conception of Honor*, 3–4, 11–12, 52, 64, 67–8, 70–2, 92, 127, 140, 141, 150–1, 155–60; Johan Huizinga, *The Waning of the Middle Ages: A Study of the Forms of Life, Thought, and Art in France and the Netherlands in the XIVth and XVth Centuries*, trans. F. Hopman (1924; rpt.; London: E. Arnold, 1967), *passim*.

The divergence of the northern from the Italian idea of honour – a difference not to be exaggerated – probably owes more to the Protestant emphasis on self-examination, internalized morality, and distrust of appearances. For Kerrigan and Braden, the Italian Renaissance conception of honour is inferior ethically to what they see as the more fully internalized morality (and sense of honour) promoted by Protestantism. Although John Addington Symonds questionably attributes the difference between northern and Italian conceptions of honour to the relative absence of chivalry in Italy, and although his terms might be bettered, he shrewdly assesses these antithetical values. The Italian word *onore*, he writes, 'means something different from that mixture of conscience, pride, and self-respect which [in northern Europe] makes a man true to a high ideal in all ... possible circumstances ... Honour with the Northern gentry was subjective; with the Italians *Onore* was objective – an addition conferred from without, in the shape of reputation, glory, titles of distinction, and offices of trust.' Analyzing *onestà* as the feminine counterpart of masculine *onore*, Symonds describes it as 'compatible with secret infidelity, provided ... [a woman] does not expose herself to ridicule or censure by letting her amour be known.' See Kerrigan and Braden, *Idea of Renaissance*, 48; Symonds, *Renaissance in Italy*, Vol. 1, *The Age of the Despots* (New York: Henry Holt, 1988), 481–7.

25 Gilmore, 'The Shame of Dishonor,' 5, 10, 11; Gilmore, 'Honor, Honesty, Shame,' 90–1; Michael Herzfeld, '"As in Your Own House": Hospitality, Ethnography, and the Stereotype of Mediterranean Society,' 75–89: all in *Honor and Shame*, ed. Gilmore. See also George R. Saunders, 'Men and Women,' 439, 441; Peristiany, Introduction to *Honor and Shame*, ed. Peristiany, 11; Pitt-Rivers, 'Honour and Shame,' 29, 31; Schneider and Schneider, *Culture and Political Economy*, 86–7; Maria Pia di Bello, 'Name, Blood and Miracles: The Claims to Renown in Traditional Sicily,' in J.G. Peristiany and Julian Pitt-Rivers, eds., *Honor and Grace in Anthropology* (Cambridge: Cambridge Univ. Press, 1992), 151–5; Arlacchi, *Mafia Business*, 6; Rudolph M. Bell, *Fate and Honor, Family and Village: Demographic and Cultural Change in Italy since 1800* (Chicago: Univ. of Chicago Press, 1979), 2–3.

26 Gilmore, 'The Shame of Dishonor,' 4; Gilmore, 'Honor, Honesty, Shame,' 90, 91; Giovannini, 'Female Chastity Codes,' 61, 63, 65; all in *Honor and Shame*, ed. Gilmore; Gans, *Urban Villagers*, 30, 40, 47–50, 70, 207–8; Covello, *Social Background of Italo-American School Child*, 197–9, 204–5; Chapman, *Milocca*, 39–41, 108; Schneider and Schneider, *Culture and Political Economy*, 2, 89–91; Tomasi, *Italian American Family*, 10; Arlacchi, *Mafia Business*, 7; Bell, *Fate and Honor, Family and Village*, 105; Cornelisen, *Women of the Shadows*, 19, 20; Saunders, 'Men and Women,' 439–40, 445, 446; Parsons, 'Is the Oedipus Complex Universal? The Jones-Malinowski Debate Revisited,' in Parsons, *Belief, Magic, and Anomie*, 22, 45–6. On the honour-shame complex

in Renaissance and Baroque Italy, and the identification of shame or *vergogna* with women, see Burke, *Historical Anthropology of Early Modern Italy*, 13–4.

27 The Piazza della Vergogna in Palermo is better known as the Piazza Pretoria.

28 On the Italian American distinction between 'good' (that is, chaste) and 'bad' girls, based on observations extending from the 1930s into the late 1950s, see Ware, *Greenwich Village*, 111; Gans, *Urban Villagers*, 30, 48–9. The conservative sexual attitudes conventionally attributed to Italian Americans have greatly diminished in the decades after immigration, during which they relaxed their views of adultery, premarital sex, women in the workplace, and male dominance. Alba finds that by the mid-1980s, in addition to having become more tolerant than WASPs towards premarital sex and adultery, Italian Americans often held liberal attitudes regarding divorce and the Old World requirement that women stay at home. He attributes these changes to the fact that Italian Americans live predominantly in urban areas. See Gabaccia, *From Sicily to Elizabeth Street*, 113–14; Alba, *Italian Americans*, 136–8.

29 Gilmore, 'Honor, Honesty, and Shame,' 90–1. Julio Caro Baroja finds Spanish honour not to be exclusively sex based. According to Pitt-Rivers, Andalusian duels have not typically involved sexual honour. See Baroja, 'Honour and Shame: A Historical Account of Several Conflicts,' 79–137; Pitt-Rivers, 'Honour and Social Status,' 39, 63, 77n: both essays in *Honour and Shame*, ed. Peristiany.

30 Gilmore, 'Shame of Dishonor,' 3–5, 10–11; Pitt-Rivers, 'Honour and Social Status,' 46. Anthropologists err in thinking that the *cornuto*'s horns metaphorically represent those of the bull. Anton Blok observes that this symbol originates in the southern Italian (and Mediterranean) identification of the *cornuto* with the vertical-horned billy goat or *becco*, which lets other goats mount its mate and whose behaviour is therefore despised as shameful. The antithesis of the billy goat is not the bull but the ram, which tolerates no rivals and thus stands for masculine honour. A Mediterranean symbol of manliness and power since Homer's time, the ram has been identified with kings as well as with Zeus, Apollo, and Poseidon. As for why southern Italians rarely refer to the ram as a symbol of strength, vigour, and honour, and have largely forgotten that the vertical horn sign (*cornuto*) refers to the billy goat, Blok notes that these meanings became lost as pastoralism yielded to agriculture in the Mediterranean. It seems plausible that, through this change, the bull acquired the symbolic properties of the ram, which it far surpasses in size and strength, being the

strongest of European mammals. See Blok, 'Rams and Billy-Goats: A Key to the Mediterranean Cult of Honour,' *Man* 16 (September 1981): 427–30.

31 Dougan, *Martin Scorsese*, 47.

32 Dougan, *Martin Scorsese*, 11.

33 Giles, *American Catholic Arts and Fictions*, 278.

34 DeCurtis, 'What the Streets Mean,' 178.

35 Scorsese, 'Confessions,' 133.

36 DeCurtis, 'What the Streets Mean,' 178–9.

37 Kelly, *Martin Scorsese: First Decade*, 76.

38 DeCurtis, 'What the Streets Mean,' 178, 179.

39 Dougan, *Martin Scorsese*, 16.

40 Guy Flatley, 'Martin Scorsese's Gamble,' *New York Times*, 8 February 1976, in *Martin Scorsese: Interviews*, ed. Brunette, 57.

41 Keyser, *Martin Scorsese*, 4.

42 Flatley, 'Martin Scorsese's Gamble,' 57.

43 Bella Taylor, 'Martin Scorsese,' in Jon Tuska, ed., *Close-Up: The Contemporary Director* (Metutchen, N.J.: Scarecrow Press, 1981), 296.

44 Flatley, 'Martin Scorsese's Gamble,' 57.

45 Kolker, *Cinema of Loneliness*, 163.

46 Gans, *Urban Villagers*, 252–8, esp. 255.

47 Mangione and Morreale, *La Storia*, 411.

48 Richard P. McBrien, *Catholicism* (San Francisco: Harper-San Francisco, 1994), 10, 13, 15, 78; Peter Berger, *The Sacred Canopy: Elements of a Sociological Theory of Religion* (Garden City, N.Y.: Doubleday, 1969), 111–12, 121; John Paul Russo, 'DeLillo: Italian American Catholic Writer,' *Altreitalie* (July–December 2002): 5–7.

49 McBrien, *Catholicism*, 9–12, 1108–9, 1250; Greeley, *Catholic Imagination*, 1–2; Russo, 'DeLillo: Italian American Catholic Writer,' 5–9.

50 David Tracy, *The Analogical Imagination: Christian Theology and the Culture of Plurality* (New York: Crossroad, 1981), 410, and *passim*; McBrien, *Catholicism*, 15, 46; Greeley, *Catholic Imagination*, 5–8, 50; Russo, 'DeLillo: Italian American Writer,' 7; Giles, *American Catholic Arts and Fictions*, 8, 27–9, 38–9, 55, 57, 69, 85, 109, 119. For Scorsese and analogism, see Giles, 336, 348.

51 Kolker, *Cinema of Loneliness*, 184.

52 Kelly, *Martin Scorsese: A Journey*, 10. See also Blake, 'Redeemed in Blood,' 3, 5.

53 Giles, *American Catholic Arts and Fictions*, 158–9, 338–9.

54 Glazer and Moynihan, *Beyond the Melting Pot*, 202–3; Rudolph J. Vecoli, 'Prelates and Peasants: Italian Immigrants and the Catholic Church,' *Journal of Social History* 2 (Spring 1969): *passim*, esp. 220, 220n; Henry J.

Browne, '"The Italian Problem" in the Catholic Church in the United
States, 1880–1900,' *United States Catholic Historical Society, Historical Records
and Studies*, 35 (1946): 46–72. The 'Italian Problem' was of relatively short
duration, ending with the establishment of 'national parishes.' According
to Lopreato, it has been resolved since the 1930s. See Alba, *Italian Americans*, 91; Lopreato, *Italian Americans*, 92.

55 Ernesto de Martino, *Sud e magia* (Milan: Feltrinelli, 1966), 9, 11, 12, 22, 48–9,
66, 81, 90–1, 92–4; de Martino, *La Terra del Rimorso: Contributo a una storia
religiosa del Sud* (Milan: Mondadori, 1961), 27, 28, 30, 31, 32; Gabriele de
Rosa, *Vescovi, popolo e magia nel sud: Ricerche di storie socio-religiosa dal XVII
al XIX secolo* (Naples: Guida Editori, 1971), 3 (see also chap. 1, 'Problemi
religiosi della società meridionale nel settecento attraverso le visite
pastorali di Angelo Anzani,' 3–92); Giuseppe Pitrè, *Feste popolari in Sicilia*
(1870–1913; rpt. Bologna, n.d.), xxviii, xxix, xxx, lix–lxi, lxiv, 38–4; Pitrè,
Spettacoli e feste, xv–xxi; Vecoli, 'Prelates and Peasants,' 228; Luciano J.
Iorizzo and Salvatore Mondello, *Italian Americans* (New York: Twayne,
1980), 219; Mangione and Morreale, *La Storia*, 170, 327–8; Richard A.
Varbero, 'Philadelphia's South Italians and the Irish Church:
A History of Cultural Conflict,' in Silvano M. Tomasi, ed., *The Religious
Experience of Italian Americans* (Staten Island, N.Y.: American Italian His-
torical Association, 1975), 44; Di Carlo, 'Italian Festa,' 85–7; Silvano M.
Tomasi, *Piety and Power: The Role of the Italian Parishes in the New York
Metropolitan Area, 1880–1930* (Staten Island, N.Y.: Center for Migration
Studies, 1975), 33; Pozzetta, 'Italian Americans,' 339; Bianco, *Two Rosetos*,
84–5, 98–9; Nelli, 'Italians in Urban America,' 96; Alba, *Italian Americans*,
90–1; Michael P. Carroll, *Madonnas That Maim: Popular Catholicism in Italy
since the Fifteenth Century* (Baltimore: Johns Hopkins Univ. Press, 1992),
30–51; Michael P. Carroll, *Veiled Threats: The Logic of Popular Catholicism in
Italy* (Baltimore: Johns Hopkins Univ. Press, 1996), 6–7, 17, 28, 69; Covello,
Social Background of Italo-American School Child, 103–4, 117–20, 122–7, 130–2;
Chapman, *Milocca*, 158–63, 172, 176; David Gentilcore, *From Bishop to
Witch: The System of the Sacred in Early Modern Terra d'Otranto* (Manchester:
Manchester Univ. Press, 1992), 1–2. Carroll remarks that the focus in
studies of Mezzogiorno religion has shifted from syncretism and pagan-
ism to the forms of Christian piety. See Carroll, *Veiled Threats*, 6–7. In 1962
Herbert Gans found that among Italian Americans of Boston's West End
the 'superstitions based on the anthropomorphizing of nature have faded
away.' See Gans, *Urban Villagers*, 35; see also 201.

56 Gambino, *Blood of My Blood*, 215, 217; Bianco, *Two Rosetos*, 86–7, 89–90,
100; Carroll, *Madonnas That Maim*, 67–8, 112–28; Carroll, *Veiled Threats*, 60,

195–6; Pitrè, *Spettacoli e feste*, 81–2, 92–3, 95–6; Iorizzo and Mondello, *Italian Americans*, 220; Mangione and Morreale, *La Storia*, 41, 44, 169–70; Gentilcore, *From Bishop to Witch*, 183–4; Pitrè, *Feste patronali*, xvi; Williams, *South Italian Folkways*, 137–8; Covello, *Social Background of Italo-American School Child*, 105–16; Vecoli, 'Prelates and Peasants,' 229.

57 Varbero, 'Philadelphia's South Italians and the Irish Church,' 36–7, 40, 41n, 43, 45–6; Philip M. Kayal, 'Panelist Remark,' in *The Religious Ex-perience of Italian Americans*, ed. Tomasi, 129; Fr Leonard Bacigaliupo, OFM, 'Some Religious Aspects Involving the Interaction of the Italians and the Irish,' in Francis X. Femminella, ed., *Italians and Irish in America* (Staten Island, N.Y.: American Italian Historical Association, 1985), 118, 127n; Nelli, 'Italians in Urban America,' 93; Russo, 'DeLillo: Italian American Catholic Writer,' 6; Gans, *Urban Villagers*, 113; Vecoli, 'Prelates and Peasants,' 230; Tomasi, *Piety and Power*, 61, 66, 68.

58 Tricarico, *Italians of Greenwich Village*, 51; Sowell, *Ethnic America*, 116; Ware, *Greenwich Village*, 132; Briggs, *Italian Passage*, 132, 199, 201–3, 311.

59 Kelly, *Martin Scorsese: First Decade*, 124; Gans, *Urban Villagers*, 113; Russo, 'DeLillo: Italian American Writer,' 24n; Nelli, 'Italians,' 553; Pozzetta, 'Italian Americans,' 339.

60 Sebastian De Grazia, *Of Time, Work, and Leisure* (New York: Doubleday, 1962), 155.

61 Iorizzo and Mondello, *Italian Americans*, 218–19, 220–1, 225, 229; Vecoli, 'Prelates and Peasants,' 230, 233, 234, 238–9, 245, 255–6, 260, 262; Varbero, 'Philadelphia's South Italians and the Irish Church,' 33, 35, 37–9; Richard Giuliani, 'The Interaction of Irish and Italians: From Conflict to Integra-tion,' in *Italians and Irish in America*, ed. Femminella, 30; Nelli, 'Italians,' 553; Pozzetta, 'Italian Americans,' 339; Tomasi, *Piety and Power*, 1–2, 46, 76–8; Tricarico, *Italians of Greenwich Village*, 12, 13, 46, 48–51; Orsi, *Madonna*, 55; Mary Elizabeth Brown, 'Religion,' in *Italian American Experience*, ed. La Gumina et al., 540, 541.

62 Alba, *Italian Americans*, 90; Francis A.J. Ianni, 'The Mafia and the Web of Kinship,' in Francis A.J. Ianni and Elizabeth Reuss-Ianni, eds., *The Crime Society: Organized Crime and Corruption in America* (New York: New Ameri-can Library, 1976), 45; Bacigalupo, 'Religious Aspects,' 127; Chapman, *Milocca*, 193; Covello, *Social Background of Italo-American School Child*, 137–8; Gambino, *Blood of My Blood*, 229; Vecoli, 'Prelates and Peasants,' 221, 222, 229, 263; Lopreato, *Italian Americans*, 88, 90.

63 Iorizzo and Mondello, *Italian Americans*, 220; Vecoli, 'Prelates and Peas-ants,' 228; Salvatore Primeggia and Joseph A. Varacalli, 'The Sacred and Profane among Italian American Catholics: The Giglio Feast,' *International*

Journal of Politics, Culture, and Society 9, no. 3 (1996): 424; Orsi, *Madonna*, 55; Pitrè, *Feste patronali*, vii; Chapman, *Milocca*, 159, 146–7, 163.

64 Vecoli, 'Prelates and Peasants,' 229, 230; Gambino, *Blood of My Blood*, 212, 219; Levi, *Christ Stopped at Eboli*, 39; Yans-McLaughlin, *Family and Community*, 86; Chapman, *Milocca*, 42–3; Lopreato, *Italian Americans*, 87.

65 Varbero, 'Philadelphia's South Italians and the Irish Church,' 44; Gambino, *Blood of My Blood*, 232–6; Alba, *Italian Americans*, 90, 91; Vecoli, 'Prelates and Peasants,' 224, 230; Bacigalupo, 'Religious Aspects,' 117; Bianco, *Two Rosetos*, 104. Bianco quotes a resident of Roseto in Pennsylvania, which was settled from a town of the same name in southern Italy: 'We don't have that great respect for priests. Our old people here were the same. I think they came with that from Italy.'

66 Gambino, *Blood of My Blood*, 232, 239; see also Chapman, *Milocca*, 228. Chapman relates the response of the Sicilian muleteer Giglia to a pious person whom he met on the road: 'See, there she goes to Mass, and doesn't even have the decency to salute the Christian she meets.' To quote the Schneiders on western Sicily: 'A completely selfless person would be a fool, as would anyone who neglected an opportunity to aggrandize his own position solely out of concern for legality or the common good.' Schneider and Schneider, *Culture and Political Economy*, 83. Micaela di Leonardo (*Varieties of Ethnic Experience*, 35) says that Italian Americans have the lowest church attendance record of any American ethnic group.

67 Vecoli, 'Prelates and Peasants,' 236–7; Iorizzo and Mondello, *Italian Americans*, 227–8; Ware, *Greenwich Village*, 311; Yans-McLaughlin, *Family and Community*, 86; Crispino, *Assimilation*, 63.

68 Gans, *Urban Villagers*, 111–12; Chapman, *Milocca*, 43, 89, 193; Crispino, *Assimilation*, 162; Glazer and Moynihan, *Beyond the Melting Pot*, 204, 205. Crispino reports that in the early 1900s any young Italian American man interested in entering the priesthood risked being disowned by his family; however, Chapman remarks of the Sicilian village she studied that a family was extremely proud to have one son preparing for the priesthood. Not only have southern Italian priests been criticized and ridiculed behind their backs, but their celibacy has been doubted, sometimes with justification. Indeed, priests of the *chiese recitizzie* (local colleges of ecclesiastics outside episcopal jurisdiction) took wives or concubines by whom they had children. See Vecoli, 'Prelates and Peasants,' 229, 240; Schachter, *Italian South*, 69–70; Carroll, *Madonnas That Maim*, 99; Gentilcore, *From Bishop to Witch*, 42, 43, 44, 45, 46, 105; Levi, *Christ Stopped at Eboli*, 99.

69 In 1969 Vecoli argued that the Italians had stuck to their traditional religious beliefs despite opposition and censure from the influential Irish

American element in the Catholic church. See Vecoli, 'Prelates and Peasants,' 268. The period after the Second World War nonetheless witnessed the increasing influence of institutional Catholicism upon second- and third-generation Italian Americans, many of whom attended mass regularly as families, and who increasingly sent their children to parochial schools. Nor were they praying any longer to saints, but to God directly. This transformation, which some see as 'Hibernization,' coincided with the removal of Italian Americans to the suburbs and, to some extent, their adoption of conventional Catholicism as an expression of middle-class respectability. See Glazer and Moynihan, *Beyond the Melting Pot*, 202–5; DeConde, *Half Bitter, Half Sweet*, 336–7; Nelli, 'Italians in Urban America,' 96; Nicholas John Russo, 'Three Generations of Italians in New York City: Their Religious Acculturation,' in *Italian Experience in the United States*, ed. Tomasi and Engel, 209; Alba, *Italian Americans*, 91–2; Lopreato, *Italian Americans*, 91–2; Crispino, *Assimilation*, vi (Gans's Preface), 66, 133, 139, 142; Sowell, *Ethnic America*, 124.

70 Gans, *Urban Villagers*, 115.
71 Keyser, *Martin Scorsese*, 7.
72 Peter Occhiogrosso, *Once a Catholic: Prominent Catholics and Ex-Catholics Reveal the Influence of the Church on Their Lives and Work* (Boston: Houghton Mifflin, 1987), 91.
73 Kayal, 'Panelist Remark,' 129.
74 Primeggia and Varacalli, 'Sacred and Profane,' 437–8, 449.
75 Chapman, *Milocca*, 145–6; Vecoli, 'Prelates and Peasants,' 263; Orsi, *Madonna*, 189, 226; Russo, 'DeLillo: Italian American Catholic Writer,' 6, 8, 9, 10; Nelli, 'Italians in Urban America,' 96; Mangione and Morreale, *La Storia*, 170; Lopreato, *Italian Americans*, 89, 90–1.
76 Orsi, *Madonna*, 57, 69. Orsi writes that after the Second World War the church dominated the *festa*. On the popular as opposed to ecclesiastical emphasis of the *festa*, see Whyte, *Street Corner Society*, 269. Writing in 1994, Denise Mangieri DiCarlo describes *feste* as 'largely commercial endeavors that have lost their original religious and ritualistic tone.' See DiCarlo, 'Italian Festa,' 79. According to Anthony T. Rauche, the commercialization of the Festa Italiana in Hartford, Connecticut, caused community residents to vote for its termination in 1985. See Rauche, 'Festa Italiana in Hartford, Connecticut,' 206–7, 208, 213–14, 216.
77 Scorsese may have attended the Feast of San Ciro, the patron saint of his mother's hometown of Cimmina, which was still celebrated around 1940 but now seems defunct. He mentions having recently seen his family's home movies of the festival. See Scorsese, *Il Mio Viaggio*. Giuseppe Pitrè

discusses the legend and festival of San Ciro as observed in the Sicilian
town of Marineo, which, like Cimmina, is in the province of Palermo. See
Pitrè, *Feste patronali*, 131–8; Pitrè, *Spettacoli e feste*, 98.

78 Peter D'Agostino, 'The Religious Life of Italians in New York City,' in
Italians of New York, ed. Cannistraro, 74; Mangione and Morreale, *La Storia*,
171. See also Williams, *South Italian Folkways*, 140, 150–1. The photographs
adjacent to page 52 of the latter show loaves of bread of ingenious and
varied design, specially baked for the Festival of San Gandolfo by the
Palumbo Bakery, Elizabeth Street. The celebrants invested this bread with
sanctity, as if analogous to Communion.

79 Cinotto, *Una famiglia*, 168–9, 175–6; Primeggia and Varacalli, 'Sacred and
Profane,' 424–5; Orsi, *Madonna*, xxii, 183, 200; Russo, 'DeLillo: Italian
American Catholic Writer,' 9; DiCarlo, 'Italian Festa,' 81–2, 84; Whyte,
Street Corner Society, 269; Mangione and Morreale, *La Storia*, 170; Covello,
Social Background of Italo-American School Child, 130–2.

80 Primeggia and Varacalli, 'Sacred and Profane,' 425, 427, 429; Pitrè,
Spettacoli e feste, 86, 93–5, 98; Rauche, "Festa Italiana,' 207. The Giglio feast
is the subject of *Heaven Touches Brooklyn in July* (2001), a remarkable fifty-
seven-minute documentary by Tony di Nonno.

81 Orsi, *Madonna*, 165, 172–8, 181, 184–5, 228; DiCarlo, 'Italian Festa,' 80;
Mangione and Morreale, *La Storia*, 170–2; Williams, *South Italian Folkways*,
149, 150.

82 Orsi, *Madonna*, 3, 165, 172–8, 181, 184–5; Nelli, *From Immigrants to Ethnics*,
128; Carroll, *Veiled Threats*, 43; Covello, *Social Background of Italo-American
School Child*, 130–2; Pitrè, *Spettacoli e feste*, 264; Vecoli, 'Prelates and Peasants,' 232–3. The pastries made in Sicilian households during festival are
'almost sacramental in significance.' See Williams, *South Italian Folkways*,
151.

83 Orsi, *Madonna*, 221; Russo, 'DeLillo: Italian American Catholic Writer,' 6,
7. See also Malpezzi and Clements, *Italian-American Folklore*, 91–2, 101,
102–3.

84 Orsi, *Madonna*, xix–xx, 75, 77, 226. Orsi derives the term and concept of the
domus from Emanuel Roy Ladurie. See also Chapman, *Milocca*, 229.

85 Orsi, *Madonna*, 83–4.

86 Orsi, *Madonna*, 92 (see also 93–4); Covello, *Social Background of Italo-
American School Child*, 158; Chapman, *Milocca*, 230.

87 Alba, *Italian Americans*, 33–4; Orsi, *Madonna*, 92, 93; Bell, *Fate and Honor,
Family and Village*, 2–3; Covello, *Social Background of Italo-American School
Child*, 156–8; Ianni, *Family Business*, 19, 84; Ianni, 'Familialism,' 193; Russo,
'DeLillo: Italian American Catholic Writer,' 13.

88 Orsi, *Madonna*, 22, 105–6; Covello, *Social Background of Italo-American School Child*, 135–6.

89 Orsi, *Madonna*, 65, 105; Russo, 'DeLillo: Italo-American Catholic Writer,' 13.

90 Orsi, *Madonna*, 173; Gambino, *Blood of My Blood*, 183–4, 187, 188. See also Frances M. Malpezzi and William M. Clements, 'Bread and Wine in Italian American Village Folk Culture,' in *Italian American Heritage*, ed. d'Acierno, 112.

91 Scorsese characterizes the Sicilian fishing scene (the *mattanza*) in Rossellini's *Stromboli* (1949) as the record of an 'ancient ritual of food-gathering' passed down from prehistory through the generations: 'It's about the sanctity of eating as a communal act, and gathering food with the people you know. The food is sacred, a gift of God.' See Scorsese, *Il Mio Viaggio*.

92 Orsi, *Madonna*, 108, 109.

93 Gambino, *Blood of My Blood*, 183–5, 187, 188; Williams, *South Italian Folkways*, 80–2.

94 Gambino, *Blood of My Blood*, 192, 193; Orsi, *Madonna*, 115; Williams, *South Italian Folkways*, 81, 96; Chapman, *Milocca*, 31.

95 Orsi, *Madonna*, 115–16; Bell, *Fate and Honor, Family and Village*, 2; Alba, *Italian Americans*, 33–4. To quote a second-generation Italian American woman: 'You leave the house in a wedding dress or a casket.' See Volkman and Cummings, *Goombata: The Improbable Rise and Fall of John Gotti and His Gang* (Boston: Little Brown, 1990), 18.

96 Marjorie Rosen, 'New Hollywood: Martin Scorsese Interview,' *Film Comment* 11, no. 2 (1975): 43.

97 Orsi, *Madonna*, 92–3, 228. See also Covello, *Social Background of Italo-American School Child*, 159.

98 DeCurtis, 'What the Streets Mean,' 197.

99 Diane Jacobs, *Hollywood Renaissance* (New York: Delta, 1980), 137.

100 Lourdeaux errs in supposing that Scorsese's characters' guilt feelings must derive exclusively from the director's Irish Catholic education, rather than emerging from his own ethnic experience as well. See Lourdeaux, *Italian and Irish Filmmakers*, 228.

101 Carroll, *Madonnas That Maim*, chap. 7, 'Mezzogiorno Masochism,' 129–37; Carroll, *Veiled Threats*, 77–9; Pitrè, *Feste patronali*, xlvi–xlviii, 106–7, 350–6, 364; Pitrè, *Spettacoli e feste*, 82; Levi, *Christ Stopped at Eboli*, 121, 122; Parsons, 'Is the Oedipus Complex Universal?' 17–18. Gabriele de Rosa attributes the severely ascetic, penitential, and masochistic component in southern Italian religion to the longstanding influence of Byzantine,

Islamic, and Christian traditions. In his view, the influence of Eastern monasticism, with its extremely harsh discipline, was still evident in southern Italy at least into the 1800s. Both heroic and superhuman, southern Italian mysticism takes as its model not only the Crucifixion but the martyrization and self-flagellation of the saints. Masochistic punishments are at once proof of one's love of Christ and signs of *materializzazione divina*. For example, the eighteenth-century holy figure Gerardo Maiella submitted his body to the harshest torments in imitation of *Christus patiens*, so as to expiate the guilt of humanity. Macerated willingly to the point of looking like a living skeleton, Gerardo was widely regarded with awe and veneration. See De Rosa, 'Pertinenze ecclesiastiche e santità nella storia sociale e religiosa della Basilicata dal XVII al XIX secolo,' in De Rosa, *Chiesa e religione popolare nel Mezzogiorno* (Rome-Bari: Laterza, 1978), 83, 96–9.

102 Orsi, *Madonna*, 4, 10–11, 202–4, 224–5, 228; DiCarlo, 'Italian Feste,' 81–2; Mangione and Morreale, *La Storia*, 172; Primeggia and Varacalli, 'Sacred and Profane,' 434.

103 Orsi, *Madonna*, 221–5. Belmonte implies that the Italian American emphasis on the suffering Christ reflects Irish American Catholicism. See Belmonte, 'Contradictions,' 16.

104 Orsi, *Madonna*, 203, 221.

105 Gambino, *Blood of My Blood*, 213, 229; Primeggia and Varacalli, 'Sacred and Profane,' 437.

106 Vecoli, 'Prelates and Peasants,' 228, 268; Primeggia and Varacalli, 'Sacred and Profane,' 438. Vecoli characterizes Mezzogiorno Catholicism as 'only a thin veneer.' See 'Contadini in Chicago,' 415, 416. Belmonte apparently thinks that the *contadini* became true Catholics only on American soil. See Belmonte, 'Contradictions,' 16.

107 Russo, 'DeLillo: Italian American Catholic Writer,' 10–12; Carroll, *Veiled Threats*, xi, 5, 7–11. The Church had to reconcile itself with local image cults of the Virgin and saints in many parts of Italy. These cults, which attributed to images a supernatural power to dispense favours, clashed with the more Christocentric type of Catholicism favoured from the Counter-Reformation onward. See Carroll, *Veiled Threats*, 16–76, 79, 189, 195, 200–7, 229–30. According to de Rosa, the presence of magic and other putatively retrograde elements in Mezzogiorno religious beliefs is insufficient to remove them from the orbit of Catholicism. Nor is Carlo Levi justified in proclaiming that 'Christ stopped at Eboli.' See de Rosa, *Chiesa e religione popolare nel Mezzogiorno*, 7–8, 12, 15, 19, 38–9, 98–9, 100–1. See also Gentilcore, *From Bishop to Witch*, 1–2. Carla Bianco writes of official

and southern Italian popular Catholicism in terms of a 'complex ideology of compromise.' See Bianco, *Two Rosetos*, 84.

108 Occhiogrosso, *Once a Catholic*, 90–1; Kelly, *Martin Scorsese: A Journey*, 34. Gans remarks the untroubled use of contraceptives among Italian American Catholic residents of Boston's West End in the late 1950s. See Gans, *Urban Villagers*, 54. See also Alba, *Italian Americans*, 91.

109 Richard Corliss, '... and Blood,' *Film Comment*, September–October 1988, in *Martin Scorsese: Interviews*, ed. Brunette, 113–14; Occhiogrosso, *Once a Catholic*, 90; Keyser, *Martin Scorsese*, 7.

110 Occhiogrosso, *Once a Catholic*, 91; Lourdeaux, *Italian and Irish Filmmakers*, 220.

111 Occhiogrosso, *Once a Catholic*, 91, 92.

112 Flatley, 'He Has Often Walked *Mean Streets*,' 5.

113 Keyser, *Martin Scorsese*, 9; Connelly, *Martin Scorsese*, ix; Kelly, *Martin Scorsese: A Journey*, 9.

114 Occhiogrosso, *Once a Catholic*, 91–2.

115 See Lourdeaux, *Italian and Irish Filmmakers*, 221: 'The Irish nuns at St. Patrick's ... taught that the road to salvation is paved with decisions of conscience ... [which] determine whether one goes to heaven or burns for eternity in hell. The nuns also stressed the painful self-sacrifice needed down the long road to Calvary and salvation.'

116 *Scorsese on Scorsese*, ed. Thompson and Christie, 12; Dougan, *Martin Scorsese*, 18.

117 Kelly, *Martin Scorsese: A Journey*, 29.

118 Kelly, *Martin Scorsese: A Journey*, 9–10.

119 Kelly, *Martin Scorsese: A Journey*, 9, 29.

120 Kelly, *Martin Scorsese: A Journey*, 10.

121 Keyser, *Martin Scorsese*, 9; *Scorsese on Scorsese*, ed. Thompson and Christie, 12.

122 Dougan, *Martin Scorsese*, 16.

123 Greeley, *Catholic Imagination*, 147.

124 *Scorsese on Scorsese*, ed. Thompson and Christie, 12. See also Keyser, *Martin Scorsese*, 9.

125 Occhiogrosso, *Once a Catholic*, 92. In another interview Scorsese states: 'I wanted to be a priest for a long time, and then I realized I ... wanted to be a priest out of ego rather than understanding of what a priest is supposed to be.' See Smith, 'Art of Vision,' 246.

126 *Scorsese on Scorsese*, ed. Thompson and Christie, 9, 12, 48.

127 Keyser, *Martin Scorsese*, 10, 12; Dougan, *Martin Scorsese*, 18; *Scorsese on Scorsese*, ed. Thompson and Christie, 12; Kelly, *Martin Scorsese: A Journey*,

31–2, 295; Occhiogrosso, *Once a Catholic*, 92–3, 99; Lourdeaux, *Italian and Irish Filmmakers*, 223.

128 Dougan, *Martin Scorsese*, 19; Kelly, *Martin Scorsese: A Journey*, 295; Giles, *American Catholic Arts and Fictions*, 333; Occhiogrosso, *Once a Catholic*, 92–3; Scorsese, 'Confessions,' 133. At Cardinal Hayes Scorsese was taught by the Marist Brothers.

129 Occhiogrosso, *Once a Catholic*, 97.

130 Kelly, *Martin Scorsese: A Journey*, 34; Kelly, *Martin Scorsese: First Decade*, 42. The Stations of the Cross are one of the devotions created by the Catholic preaching orders. Combining visual images and the dynamic emphasis of Christocentric Catholicism, they were promoted most actively by the Franciscans. They consist of a series of fourteen plaques, each depicting a scene from the Passion of Christ. The plaques are usually arrayed along the inside walls of churches, though they can be set up out of doors. As they move from station to station, the devout are asked to contemplate the scene depicted. On special occasions, the congregation remains seated while a priest and assistants move from station to station and lead the audience in prayer. See Carroll, *Veiled Threats*, 81, 81n; Carroll, *Catholic Cults and Devotions* (Montreal: McGill-Queen's Univ. Press, 1989), 41–56.

131 Occhiogrosso, *Once a Catholic*, 97–9. See also Keyser, *Martin Scorsese*, 21.

132 Friedman, *Cinema of Martin Scorsese*, 10–11; Michael Pye and Lynda Myles, *The Movie Brats: How the Film Generation Took Over Hollywood* (New York: Holt, Rinehart, and Winston, 1979), 191.

133 Dougan, *Martin Scorsese*, 19, 21, 23, 28; Kelly, *Martin Scorsese: A Journey*, 21.

134 Gans writes of Boston's West Enders that '[they] are a religious people, and accept most of the moral norms and sacred symbols of the Catholic religion,' yet realize that it 'often fails to practice what it preaches. Thus they identify with the religion, but not with the church, except when it functions as a moral agency.' Gans, *Urban Villagers*, 111.

135 Occhiogrosso, *Once a Catholic*, 96, 100; Dougan, *Martin Scorsese*, 85; Flatley, 'He Has Often Walked *Mean Streets*,' 6; Smith, *American Filmmakers Today*, 117; Taylor, 'Martin Scorsese,' 300.

136 Dougan, *Martin Scorsese*, 24, 28; Friedman, *Cinema of Martin Scorsese*, 24; Occhiogrosso, *Once a Catholic*, 100.

137 Michiko Kakutani, 'Scorsese's Past Colors His New Film,' in *Martin Scorsese: Interviews*, ed. Brunette, 103.

138 Occhiogrosso, *Once a Catholic*, 92, 96; Lourdeaux, *Italian and Irish Filmmakers*, 222, 224.

139 Lourdeaux, *Italian and Irish Filmmakers*, 222, 223, 241–3.

140 Occhiogrosso, *Once a Catholic*, 91. From the second generation onward, Italian American Catholicism has tended to undergo 'Hibernization,' as is reflected in increased attendance at Mass, growing respect for priests, enrolment of children in parochial schools, and increased donations. This correlates with Italian Americans' advancement into the middle class. Yet these developments should not be exaggerated, for as late as 1970 Lopreato observed that the 'Italians' tradition of secularism and skepticism toward church authority ... has not disappeared and remains ingrained in the younger generations in the suburbs.' According to Vecoli in 1978, it is an 'error' to describe Italian Americans as 'ersatz Irish Catholics.' Studies of ethnic behaviour 'suggest that the distinctive Italian religious heritage persists beneath an apparently homogeneous surface.' Like Lopreato, Vecoli sees Italian Americans' choice of birth control as indicating independence from church authority. Furthermore, Italian Americans are conspicuous among those leaving the priesthood. Crispino holds that the 'hostility toward institutionalized religion prevalent in the Old Country has been transferred to American soil.' See Vecoli, 'Coming of Age of the Italian Americans,' 133; Lopreato, *Italian Americans*, 93; Crispino, *Assimilation*, 66.

141 Ehrenstein, *Scorsese Picture*, 34.

142 Jacobs, *Hollywood Renaissance*, 137; see also Keyser, *Martin Scorsese*, 8.

143 Friedman, *Cinema of Martin Scorsese*, 24.

144 Occhiogrosso, *Once a Catholic*, 93.

145 Kelly, *Martin Scorsese: A Journey*, 31; Friedman, *Cinema of Martin Scorsese*, 24.

146 Kelly, *Martin Scorsese: A Journey*, 6.

147 Dougan, *Martin Scorsese*, 16–17.

148 Greeley, *Catholic Imagination*, 113.

149 Dougan, *Martin Scorsese*, 16–17.

150 Jacobs, *Hollywood Renaissance*, 137.

151 John J. O'Connor, 'Martin Scorsese as Seen by His Friends and Peers,' *New York Times*, 16 July 1990, C14.

152 Dougan, *Martin Scorsese*, 16.

153 Ehrenstein, *Scorsese Picture*, 35.

154 Kelly, *Martin Scorsese: First Decade*, 96–7.

155 Giles, *American Catholic Arts and Fictions*, 275–7. On the increasing appeal of visual representation, including Catholic ritualism, for nineteenth-century Protestants, see Jenny Franchot, *Roads to Rome: The Antebellum Protestant Encounter with Catholicism* (Berkeley: Univ. of California Press, 1994), xx, xxiii, 7, 9, 11, 16, 17, 24, 119, 197, 216, 237, 241, 270.

156 Keyser, *Martin Scorsese*, 32.
157 Keyser, *Martin Scorsese*, 32.
158 Bliss, *Martin Scorsese and Michael Cimino*, 4, 24–5; Hodenfield, 'You've Got To Love Something Enough to Kill It: The Art of Non-Compromise,' *American Film*, March 1989, in *Martin Scorsese: Interviews*, ed. Brunette, 130.
159 Bliss, *Word Made Flesh*, x.
160 Brunette, Introduction, in *Martin Scorsese: Interviews*, ed. Brunette, xiii.
161 Corliss, '... and Blood,' 122.
162 Richard Goldstein and Mark Jacobson, 'Martin Scorsese Tells All: Blood and Guts Turn Me On!' *Village Voice*, 5 April 1976, in *Martin Scorsese: Interviews*, ed. Brunette, 60–1.
163 Flatley, 'Martin Scorsese's Gamble,' 56.
164 Peter Biskind, 'Slouching toward Hollywood,' *Premiere*, November 1991, in *Martin Scorsese: Interviews*, ed. Brunette, 194.
165 Biskind, *Easy Riders, Raging Bulls*, 238–9.
166 Brunette, Introduction, in *Martin Scorsese: Interviews*, ed. Brunette, xiii.
167 DeCurtis, 'What the Streets Mean,' 169.
168 Amy Taubin, 'Blood and Pasta,' *New Statesman and Society*, 9 November 1990, 13.
169 *Scorsese on Scorsese*, ed. Thompson and Christie, 118.
170 Goldstein and Jacobson, 'Martin Scorsese Tells All,' 61.
171 Lourdeaux, *Italian and Irish Filmmakers*, 222.
172 Occhiogrosso, *Once a Catholic*, 95, 101.
173 Corliss, '... And Blood,' 42, 38, 39.
174 Caillois, *Man and the Sacred*, trans. Meyer Barasch (New York: Free Press, 1959), *passim*; Caillois, *Man, Play, and Games*, trans. Meyer Barasch (New York: Free Press, 1961), 126.
175 René Girard, *Deceit, Desire, and the Novel: Self and Other in Literary Structure*, trans. Yvonne Freccero (Baltimore: Johns Hopkins Univ. Press, 1975), *passim*; Girard, *Things Hidden since the Foundations of the World*, trans. Stephen Bann and Michael Metteer (Stanford: Stanford Univ. Press, 1987), 17, 18, 327, 335–8, 414, 416; Girard, *The Scapegoat*, trans. Yvonne Freccero (Baltimore: Johns Hopkins Univ. Press, 1986), 172; Robert G. Hamerton-Kelley, *Sacred Violence: Paul's Hermeneutic of the Cross* (Minneapolis: Fortress Press, 1982), 19–21; Paisley Livingston, *Models of Desire: René Girard and the Psychology of Mimesis* (Baltimore: Johns Hopkins Univ. Press, 1982), xii; Richard J. Golsan, *René Girard and Myth: An Introduction* (New York and London: Garland, 1993), 1–8, 8n, 10–13, 16–21, 25–7; Robert Casillo, 'Twilight of the Sacred,' *Annals of Scholarship* 11, no. 4

(1997): 407. For an attempt to relate Girard's religious thought to Scorsese's films, see David John Marsh, 'Redeeming Violence in the Films of Martin Scorsese,' in Clive Marsh and George Ortiz, eds., *Explorations in Theology and Film: Movies and Meanings* (Oxford: Blackwell, 1997), 87–95.

176 Girard, *Deceit, Desire, and the Novel, passim*; Girard, *A Theater of Envy: William Shakespeare* (New York: Oxford Univ. Press, 1991), 183; Hamerton-Kelley, *Sacred Violence*, 21; Golsan, *René Girard and Myth*, 47; Casillo, 'Twilight of the Sacred,' 406–7.

177 René Girard, *Violence and the Sacred*, trans. Patrick Gregory (Baltimore: Johns Hopkins Univ. Press, 1977), 1–67, 148–9; Girard, *Things Hidden*, 13; Livingston, *Models of Desire*, 107–12, 120–7; Golsan, *René Girard and Myth*, 30–1.

178 Girard, *Violence and the Sacred*, 5, 36, 64, 92–5, 118, 135–7, 160, 164, 215; Girard, *Scapegoat*, 24–5, 27–8, 32, 35, 37, 38, 54–5, 61–75, 88–93, 97; Golsan, *René Girard and Myth*, 31–8, 61–84; Girard, 'A Venda Myth Analyzed,' 154, 163, 168, 176, 177, 178.

179 Girard, *Violence and the Sacred*, 31, 92, 115, 218–19, 258, 297; Girard, *Things Hidden*, 10, 14, 54–65, 103; Girard, *'To Double Business Bound': Essays on Literature, Mimesis, and Anthropology* (Baltimore: Johns Hopkins Univ. Press, 1978), 105; Paul Dumouchel, ed., *Violence and Truth: On the Work of René Girard* (London: Athlone, 1988), 14; Victor Turner, *From Ritual to Theater: The Human Seriousness of Play* (New York: Performing Arts Journal Publications, 1982), 10–11, 92, 106–10.

180 Girard, *Violence and the Sacred*, 311–15 (see also 149); see also Girard, *Things Hidden*, 49.

181 René Girard, *I See Satan Fall Like Lightning*, trans. James G. Williams (Maryknoll, N.Y.: Orbis, 2001), 14.

182 Casillo, 'Twilight of the Sacred,' 419–23.

183 Casillo, 'Twilight of the Sacred,' 425.

184 Girard, *Things Hidden*, 37, 126, 141–223; Girard, *Scapegoat*, 101–24, 165–6, 190–1, 198, 199–200; Raymond Schwager, 'Christ's Death and the Prophetic Critique of Sacrifice,' *Semeia: An Experimental Journal for Biblical Criticism* 33 (1985): 110; Golsan, *René Girard and Myth*, 85–105, 130–1, 174–5. Peter Berger links religion with masochism, identifying its 'key characteristic' with 'the intoxication of surrender to an other.' He relies on Sartre's idea of religion as a masochistic project destined to failure and riddled with bad faith and lack of personal responsibility. Noted in Giles, *American Catholic Arts and Fictions*, 20. See also Berger, *Sacred Canopy*, 55–8, 193n, 194n.

185 Girard, *Things Hidden*, 180–229, 326–35; Girard, *Scapegoat*, 126, 200–1;

Girard, *Job: The Victim of His People*, trans. Yvonne Freccero (Stanford: Stanford Univ. Press, 1987), 158–9; Golsan, *René Girard and Myth*, 25; Hamerton-Kelly, *Sacred Violence*, 69–70, 146–9.

186 Primeggia and Varacalli, 'Sacred and Profane,' 424–5, 427, 428, 430. For competition among participants in Sicilian festivals, see Pitrè, *Feste patronali*, xlv, 17. For Italian American examples, see Malpezzi and Clements, *Italian-American Folklore*, 102, 105.

187 Orsi, *Madonna*, xxii, xxiii, 2, 8, 9–11, 173, 178, 193–5, 200, 202–3. In addition to general observations on festivals and carnivals, Richard M. Swiderski's study of the Italian American feast of St Peter in Gloucester, Mass., which he observed in 1970, discloses many features similar to those found by Orsi in its Manhattan counterpart. See Swiderski, *Voices: An Anthropologist's Dialogue with an Italian American Festival* (Bowling Green, Ohio: Bowling Green State Univ. Popular Press, 1987), 11–17, 39, 68–74, 77, 86–8, 90–2, 100, 107–8, 110, 114–15. See also Mangione and Morreale, *La Storia*, 171–2; Victor Turner, 'Carnival, Ritual, and Play in Rio de Janeiro,' in Alessandro Falassi, ed., *Time Out of Time: Essays on the Festival* (Albuquerque: Univ. of New Mexico Press, 1987), 76; David D. Gilmore, *Carnival and Culture: Sex, Symbol, and Status in Spain* (New Haven: Yale Univ. Press, 1998), 4, 10, 14, 23–5; Furio Jesi, 'Corrosibilità della Festa'; Karoly Karenyi, 'Religione e Festa': both in Jesi, ed., *La Festa: Antropologia, etnologia, folklore* (Turin: Rosenberg and Sellier, 1977), 7, 8, 33, 34, 36, 37; Antonino Buttita, 'L'Immagine, Il Gesto, e il Tempo Ritrovato'; Pietro Clemente, 'Maggiolata e Sega-le-Vecchia nel Senese e nel Grossetano: Note Sulla Festa'; Alfonso di Nola, 'Varianti semiotiche della festa e interpretabilità marxiana': all three in C. Bianco and M. del Ninno, eds., *Festa: Antropologia e semiotica* (Florence: Nuova Guaraldi, 1981), 31, 35, 46, 89. Buttita mentions Easter representations of the Passion of Christ in Polizzi Generosa, the Sicilian town where Scorsese's father's family resided. For the carnival in early modern Europe and its decline in later modernity, largely through what Norbert Elias terms the 'civilizing process,' see Burke, *Popular Culture in Early Modern Europe*, 24–5, 26, 27, 57, 178–243; Natalie Zemon Davis, *Society and Culture in Early Modern France* (Stanford: Stanford Univ. Press, 1975), 97, 103, 119, 120, 122–3, 124, 128, 131, 134, 136, 140–1, 143, 143n, 144. For the carnival as a scene of potentially liberating inversion, transgression, and criticism of the existing social order, see Mikhail Bakhtin, *Rabelais and His World*, trans. Helene Iswolsky (Cambridge, Mass.: MIT Press, 1968), *passim*; Peter Stallybrass and Allon Lewis, *The Politics and Poetics of Transgression* (Ithaca: Cornell Univ. Press, 1986), 6–19; Alessandro Falassi, 'Festival: Definition and

Morphology,' in *Time Out of Time*, ed. Falassi, 3; Barbara Babcock, ed., *The Reversible World: Symbolic Inversion in Art and Society* (Ithaca: Cornell Univ. Press, 1978); Galt, 'Carnival on Island of Pantelleria,' 328, 331–4, 336.

188 Mangione and Morreale, *La Storia*, 172. In Sicilian towns and villages, angry disputes often arose when the supporters of the preferred saint in one neighbourhood attempted to increase the prestige or territory of their favourite at the expense of some other holy figure popular in another part of town. See Pitrè, *Feste patronali*, xlviii–lvi, liii–liv, 131–2, 320–2, 331, 349–2. For parallels in Italian America, see Vecoli, 'Prelates and Peasants,' 230; 'Cult and Occult in Italian American Culture: The Resistance of a Religious Heritage,' in Randall M. Miller and Thomas D. Marzik, eds., *Immigrants and Religion in Urban America* (Philadelphia: Temple Univ. Press, 1977), 29, 30, 31. The immigrants formed many regional societies that honoured local saints with celebrations. Yet though the Feast of the Madonna of Mount Carmel began as an intensely Neapolitan festival, already by the mid-1880s it had become a great popular event peaceably bringing together southern Italian immigrants from many regions. See Orsi, *Madonna*, 34. See also D'Agostino, 'Religious Life of Italians,' 75: '[The] integration of feasts into established national parishes which often had a different madonna or patron saint was a difficult process that often brought Italian immigrant mutual aid societies which controlled the feasts into conflict with clerical authorities.' As village rivalries declined, the *feste* gained a broader appeal.

189 Mangione and Morreale, *La Storia*, 170. See also Rauche, 'Festa Italiana,' 206; Malpezzi and Clements, 'Bread and Wine,' 116; Malpezzi and Clements, *Italian-American Folklore*, 100, 106; Swiderski, *Voices*, 39, 42, 43.

190 Barzini, *From Caesar to the Mafia*, 326–7; Hess, *Mafia and Mafiosi*, 1–2, 3, 52, 52n; Barzini, *Italians*, 253–4, 263–5; James J. Inciardi, *Careers in Crime* (Chicago: Rand McNally, 1975), 113; Hess, 'The Traditional Sicilian Mafia: Organized Crime and Repressive Crime,' in Robert J. Kelly. ed., *Organized Crime: A Global Perspective* (Totowa, N.J.: Rowman and Littlefield, 1986), 114. Some scholars argue not only that the Sicilian Mafia had already formed a criminal network by the 1870s, but that recent government investigations have proved that it existed as a large and complex organization for most of the twentieth century into the present. See John Dickie, *Cosa Nostra: A History of the Sicilian Mafia* (New York: Palgrave Macmillan, 2004), 13–24, 19, 47, 84, 91–2. More cautiously, Diego Gambetta holds that into the 1950s Sicilian Mafia families belonged to no collective structure but consisted of a 'constellation' of independent groups. In that decade a degree of systematization was introduced with the formation of several

cartels in which individual families worked together under more regulated and administered conditions than previously. Nonetheless they remained independent of each other, while the Sicilian Mafia 'commission' lacks executive power. See Diego Gambetta, *The Sicilian Mafia: The Business of Private Protection* (Cambridge: Harvard Univ. Press, 1993), 100–2, 104–5, 107–10, 112–16, 136, 259–61, 291n, 295n.

191 Joseph L. Albini, *The American Mafia: Genesis of a Legend* (New York: Irvington, 1971), 107; Hess, *Mafia and Mafiosi*, 109; Ianni, *Family Business*, 25; Howard Abadinsky, *Organized Crime*, 7th ed. (Belmont, Calif.: Wadsworth/Thomson Learning, 2003), 146. John Dickie holds that *omertà* is now generally accepted as deriving from *umiltà* (*umirtà* in Sicilian), meaning humility; it is humble not to inform on one's friends. See Dickie, *Cosa Nostra*, 50.

192 Abadinsky, *Organized Crime*, 146; Barzini, *Italians*, 253–4.

193 Hess, *Mafia and Mafiosi*, 71–2, 110–11, 112; Schneider and Schneider, *Culture and Political Economy*, 193–4; Dolci, *The Man Who Plays Alone*, 69, 108; Albini, *American Mafia*, 107.

194 Barzini, *From Caesar to the Mafia*, 327; Nelli, *Business of Crime*, 13; Schneider and Schneider, *Culture and Political Economy*, 192–3; Abadinsky, *Organized Crime*, 146; Norman Lewis, qtd. in Fred J. Cook, *Mafia!* (Greenwich, Conn.: Fawcett, 1973), 28; Barzini, *Italians*, 263–4.

195 Joseph Bonanno, *A Man of Honor: The Autobiography of Joseph Bonanno* (New York: Simon and Schuster, 1983), 87, 171; Gambino, *Blood of My Blood*, 193; see also 130, 131.

196 Hess, *Mafia and Mafiosi*, 10–11, 72.

197 Hess, *Mafia and Mafiosi*, 10–11, 109–10, 132–3; Barzini, *Italians*, 263–4; Albini, *American Mafia*, 109; Ianni, *Family Business*, 25–6; Pino Arlacchi, *Mafia Business: Mafia Ethic and the Spirit of Capitalism*, trans. Martin Ryle (London: Verso, 1986), 3, 6.

198 Hess, *Mafia and Mafiosi*, 10–11.

199 Hess, *Mafia and Mafiosi*, 56; Robert J. Kelly, *The Upperworld and the Underworld: Case Studies of Racketeering and Business Infiltration in the United States* (New York: Kluwer Academic/Plenum, 1999), 35–6.

200 Hess, *Mafia and Mafiosi*, 72–3; Blok, *Mafia of Sicilian Village*, 111, 112.

201 Hess, *Mafia and Mafiosi*, 11.

202 Arlacchi, *Mafia Business*, 4, 18, 19. Arlacchi states that the Mafioso's reputation 'casts a haze of glory over every murderous act and over its agents and accessories' (19).

203 Barzini, *From Caesar to the Mafia*, 328; Barzini, *Italians*, 263; Ianni, *Family Business*, 20.

204 Hess, *Mafia and Mafiosi*, 51, 52, 52n.
205 In receiving respect the man of honour 'is obliged to project a public self of some sort.' See Kelly, *Upperworld and Underworld*, 35–6.
206 Barzini, *Italians*, 264; Hank Messick and Burt Goldblatt, *The Mobs and the Mafia* (New York: Galahad, 1972), 7.
207 Ianni, 'Mafia and Web of Kinship,' 45; Donald Cressey, *Theft of the Nation: The Structure and Operations of Organized Crime in America* (New York: Harper, 1969), 214, 216–17.
208 Gambino, *Blood of My Blood*, 130, 131, 193. In distinguishing the southern Italian ideal of masculinity from *machismo*, by which he apparently means the Spanish masculine ideal, Gambino apparently implies that the latter is of a contrasting 'florid' type, extravagantly and passionately exhibitionistic rather than aloof and reserved. Actually, the two styles are similarly 'Mediterranean,' the *macho* being thought of as an autonomous person 'closed up in himself' and stoically indifferent to passion and desire – or at least seemingly. The *macho* also resembles the Mafioso in avoiding physical domination by or emotional exposure to another human being. On the *macho*, see Octavio Paz, qtd. in Scott Donaldson, *By Force of Will: The Life and Art of Ernest Hemingway* (New York: Viking, 1977), 189.
209 Hess, *Mafia and Mafiosi*, 72.
210 Bonanno, *Man of Honor*, 87.
211 Arlacchi, *Mafia, Peasants, and Great Estates*, 113–15.
212 Hess, *Mafia and Mafiosi*, 40, 57, 71, 72.
213 Arlacchi, *Mafia, Peasants, and Great Estates*, 113.
214 Hess, 'Traditional Sicilian Mafia,' 118–19; Hess, *Mafia and Mafiosi*, 72; Schneider and Schneider, *Culture and Political Economy*, 101.
215 Barzini, *From Caesar to the Mafia*, 326–7, 328.
216 Hess, *Mafia and Mafiosi*, 61. See also Arlacchi, *Mafia Business*, xii–xiii, xvi, 12, 14, 51, 154–60. As competition among Mafiosi often drives them into new criminal activities, ambitious, rivalrous men pose a problem for Mafia leaders, who try to co-opt them through rapid advancement. See Schneider and Schneider, *Culture and Political Economy*, 180, 182, 190–1. Lopreato notes the limited supply of goods in Sicilian society, where one gains wealth or honour only at another's expense. See Lopreato, *Peasants No More*, 67–8.
217 Arlacchi, *Mafia, Peasants, and Great Estates*, 113–14; Arlacchi, *Mafia Business*, 21–2, 26–8, 31–8.
218 Hess, *Mafia and Mafiosi*, 163.
219 Ralph Salerno and John S. Tompkins, *The Crime Confederation: Cosa Nostra and Allied Operations in Organized Crime* (New York: Doubleday, 1969), 108.

220 Dougan, *Martin Scorsese*, 17.

221 Dougan, *Martin Scorsese*, 104.

222 Girard, *Violence and the Sacred*, 125.

223 Scorsese's films afford analogues to a situation Hess finds typical of the Sicilian Mafia. In his view, 'the root cause of enmity between *mafiosi* is the shortage of positions of power, while its immediate cause is frequently private affairs of honour, a quarrel over a woman, the refusal of a marriage proposal, disputes which grow into vendettas and bloody political clashes.' These vendettas sometimes have far-reaching consequences, as the two antagonistic mafiosi become 'nuclei' of 'two hostile factions.' Often individuals who belong to neither faction are drawn into the conflict, 'for example, the doctors whose loyalty and discretion could become vitally important in the treatment of any wounded and the issuing of death certificates, the village authorities, the lawyers, the bandits, and above all the small criminals.' See Hess, *Mafia and Mafiosi*, 95–6.

224 *Scorsese on Scorsese*, ed. Thompson and Christie, 4, 42.

225 Caillois, *Man, Play, and Games*, passim.

226 For the epigraph and treatment, see Kelly, *Martin Scorsese: First Decade*, 42. In dismissing this quotation as 'sentimental, hopeful,' Keyser mistakes its significance. See Keyser, *Martin Scorsese*, 40.

4. 'Where's the Action?': Early Projects and *Who's That Knocking at My Door?*

1 Lourdeaux, *Italian and Irish Filmmakers*, 224. This, however, was not Scorsese's first film; the previous year he made a nine-minute film entitled *What's a Nice Girl Like You Doing in a Place Like This?*

2 Kelly, *Martin Scorsese: A Journey*, 39; Jim Sangster, *Scorsese* (London: Virgin, 2002), 8, 9; Biskind, *Easy Riders, Raging Bulls*, 229; Dougan, *Martin Scorsese*, 24.

3 Kelly, *Martin Scorsese: First Decade*, 14; Yaquinto, *Pump 'em Full of Lead*, 119; Sangster, *Scorsese*, 8.

4 Kelly, *Martin Scorsese: First Decade*, 14, 16; *Martin Scorsese: A Journey*, 42.

5 Kelly, *Martin Scorsese: First Decade*, 16. See Manoogian's comment in the same volume, 62: 'He was never able to end that movie.'

6 Useful sources include Donald Cressey, *Theft of the Nation*, 57–60, 64–5, 110–15, 162, 163; Salerno and Tompkins, *Crime Confederation*, vii–viii, 83–93, 155, 289; Frederic Sondern, *Brotherhood of Evil: The Mafia* (New York: Farrar, Straus, and Cudahy, 1959), 7, 17, 167–9; Raymond V. Martin, *Revolt*

in the Mafia (Duell, Sloan, and Pearce, 1963), 5, 26, 108, 111, 259; Volkman
and Cummings, *Goombata*, 45; Burton B. Turkus and Sid Feder, *Murder,
Inc.: The Story of 'The Syndicate'* (New York: Farrar, Straus, and Young,
1951), xiii, xiv, 3, 4–5, 6, 7, 15, 20, 22, 74–7, 80–9, 97–9, 101; Lopreato, *Italian
Americans*, 129; Carl Sifakis, *The Mafia Encyclopedia* (New York: Facts on
File, 1987), vii, viii–ix, 18–20, 206; Peter Maas, *The Valachi Papers* (New
York: Bantam, 1972), 181, 260–6; Ianni, *Family Business*, 1–14, 16, 29–30, 41,
43, 48, 56–9, 61, 63, 72, 83–4, 104, 107–11, 139, 151, 153, 155; Francis A.J.
Ianni, Preface to *Crime Society*, ed. Ianni and Reuss-Ianni, xiii, xiv;
'President's Crime Commission: Organized Crime,' in *Crime Society*, ed.
Ianni and Reuss-Ianni, 18–19; Gambetta, *Sicilian Mafia*, 140, 142, 278n, 297;
Nelli, *Business of Crime*, xii, 5–6, 136, 206–8, 210, 212, 261, 262; Peter A.
Lupsha, 'Organized Crime in the United States,' in *Organized Crime*, ed.
Kelly, 36–8; Frederic Homer, *Guns and Garlic: Myths and Realities of Orga-
nized Crime* (West Lafayett, IN: Purdue Univ. Press, 1974), 6, 9, 10, 12, 13,
41–43, 118–21, 124–30; Fox, *Blood and Power*, 7, 62–4, 67–8, 70, 325–7, 367–8,
378–81; Michael Lyman and Gary W. Potter, *Organized Crime*, 2nd ed.
(Upper Saddle River, N.J.: Prentice-Hall, 1997), 3–4, 14–15, 27, 28, 30–1,
48–9, 50, 138, 142–3; Gus Russo, *The Outfit: The Role of Chicago's Underworld in the Shaping of Modern America* (New York: Bloomsbury, 2001), 22–
3; Hess, *Mafia and Mafiosi*, viii–ix, xi, 11–12, 79, 85, 95, 97–8, 107, 108, 132,
161, 165, 166–7; Hess, 'Traditional Sicilian Mafia,' 113, 119–22, 126–7, 127;
Blok, *Mafia of Sicilian Village*, 125–6n, 145, 146; Arlacchi, *Mafia Business*,
44–50, 57–61, 83–92, 94–100; Victor E. Kappeler, Mark Blumberg, and Gary
W. Potter, *The Mythology of Crime and Criminal Justice* (Prospect Heights,
Ill.: Waveland Press, 1993), 75–8, 81–4; Dwight C. Smith, *The Mafia Mys-
tique* (New York: Basic Books, 1975), *passim*; Dwight C. Smith, 'The Mafia
Mystique,' in Luciano J. Iorizzo, ed., *An Inquiry into Organized Crime*
(Staten Island, N.Y.: American Italian Historical Association, 1970), 69–87;
Annelise Graebner Anderson, *The Business of Organized Crime* (Stanford:
Hoover Institution Press, 1979), 10–11, 12, 13, 16, 47; Graebner Anderson,
'Organized Crime, Mafia, and Governments,' in Gianluca Fiorentini and
Sam Peltzman, eds., *The Economics of Organized Crime* (Cambridge: Cam-
bridge Univ. Press, 1995), 33, 39, 40; Peter Reuter, *Disorganized Crime: The
Economics of the Visible Hand* (Cambridge, Mass.: MIT Press, 1983), x, xi, 4–
5, 6–7, 157–8; Cook, *Mafia!*, 19; Nicholas Gage, *The Mafia Is Not an Equal
Opportunity Employer* (New York: McGraw Hill, 1971), 25–7; Bonanno,
Man of Honor, 159, 164, 219, 222; Alan A, Block, *Space, Time, and Organized
Crime*, 2nd ed. (New Brunswick, N.J.: Transaction, 1994); 3–13, 21, 22–5,
28, 29, 58n; Block, 'Introduction: The Business of Organized Crime,' in

Block, ed., *The Business of Crime: A Documentary Study of Organized Crime in the American Economy* (Boulder, Colo.: Westview, 1991), 11–14; Anthony Villano, *Brick Agent: Inside the Mafia for the FBI* (New York: Quadrangle, 1977), 41; Norval Morris and Gordon Hawkins, *The Honest Politician's Guide to Crime Control* (Chicago: Univ. of Chicago Press, 1970), 203–5, 208–9, 211, 213–20, 231; Vincent Teresa, *My Life in the Mafia* (Garden City, N.Y.: Doubleday, 1973), 87; Inciardi, *Careers in Crime*, 104–5, 107–8, 109–13, 119–21; Mangione and Morreale, *La Storia*, 260–3; Howard Abadinsky, *The Criminal Elite: Professional and Organized Crime* (Westport, Conn.: Greenwood, 1983), 6, 81–2, 83, 93, 95–6, 97, 101–2, 103, 108, 109, 158, 159, 163n; Albini, *American Mafia*, 16, 85, 87, 126, 136, 153–4, 221, 223, 235, 243, 244–5, 246; Daniel Bell, 'Crime as an American Way of Life: A Queer Ladder of Social Mobility,' in Daniel Bell, *The End of Ideology: On the Exhaustion of Political Ideas in the Fifties* (New York: Collier, 1961), 138–41, 140n; Iorizzo and Mondello, 'Italian Americans and Organized Crime,' in Iorizzo and Mondello, *Italian Americans*, 193, 195, 197, 198, 201, 203, 205, 207, 211, 212; Luciano J. Iorizzo, 'Crime and Organized Crime,' in *Italian American Experience*, ed. La Gumina et al., 157–9; DeConde, *Half Bitter, Half Sweet*, 346–7, 349; William Howard Moore, *The Kefauver Committee and the Politics of Crime, 1950–52* (Columbia: Univ. of Missouri Press, 1974), x, 6, 21, 24, 32, 57, 70, 76, 78–9, 88–90, 109, 112, 113, 114, 117–27, 130, 131–4, 184, 211, 237–8, 239, 239–40n, 241; Richard Scott, *Organizations: Rational, Natural, and Open Systems* (Englewood Cliffs, N.J.: Prentice-Hall, 1987); Ianni, 'Mafia and Web of Kinship,' 59; Ianni, 'Organized Crime and Italian American Family,' 29, 36; Kelly, 'Criminal Underworlds,' 15; Alba, *Italian Americans*, 96–8; Kelly, *Underworld and Upperworld*, 11–14; Ovid Demaris, *The Last Mafioso: The Treacherous World of Jimmy Fratianno* (New York: Times Books, 1981), 18; George Wolf, *Frank Costello: Prime Minister of the Underworld* (New York: Bantam, 1974), xii, 178, 234–5; William Kleinknecht, *The New Ethnic Mobs: The Changing Face of Organized Crime in America* (New York: Free Press, 1996), 43; Ralph Blumenthal, *Last Days of the Sicilians: At War with the Mafia: The FBI Assault on the Pizza Connection* (New York: Times Books, 1988), 8; Jonathan Kwitny, *Vicious Circles: The Mafia in the Marketplace* (New York: Norton, 1979), 49–61; James B. Jacobs, *Busting the Mob: United States v. Cosa Nostra* (New York: New York Univ. Press, 1994), 5, 7–8, 83, 89–91, 95–6, 226; William F. Roemer, *Roemer: Man against the Mob* (New York: Donald I. Fine, 1989), 23–4, 42; William F. Roemer, *War of the Godfathers: The Bloody Confrontation between the Chicago and New York Families for Control of Las Vegas* (New York: Donald I. Fine,

1990), 272–3; Lawton, 'Mafia and Movies,' 69, 70, 77–8, 87; Volkman, *Gangbusters*, xii, 55, 73, 198; Abadinsky, *Organized Crime*, 18–31, 67–73, 87–102, 108–16, 148; Vincenzo Ruggiero, *Crime and Markets: Essays in Anti-Criminology* (New York: Oxford Univ. Press, 2000), 18; Thomas Reppetto, *American Mafia: A History of Its Rise to Power* (New York: Henry Holt, 2004), x, 141–2, 151.

7 After the Second World War the two most common prejudicial stereotypes of Italian Americans were the buffoon and the mobster. By Rudolph J. Vecoli's estimate, a content analysis of mass media presentations shows that 90 per cent of criminal references are to Italian Americans, who thus receive the 'stigma of criminality.' Known jokingly as 'The Italian Hour' or 'Cops and Wops,' *The Untouchables* was only one of many demeaning television and cinematic portrayals of Italian American criminals that elicited protests from such organizations as Americans of Italian Descent, the Italian-American Coalition, the Columbus Coalition, the Joint Civic Committee of Italian Americans, and the Sons of Italy. Not only were law-abiding Italian Americans offended by *The Untouchables*, but so too were Italian American gangsters, who resented its misrepresentation of Ness as a major racketbuster, and who thought seriously of assassinating Desi Arnaz, the show's producer. See Vecoli, 'Coming of Age of the Italian Americans,' 138, 140; Gambino, *Blood of My Blood*, 274, 275, 277; DeConde, *Half Bitter, Half Sweet*, 348–9; Crispino, *Assimilation*, 117; Lopreato, *Italian Americans*, 130. On the Mafia's response to *The Untouchables*, see DeMaris, *Last Mafioso*, 122 3; Russo, *Outfit*, 352–4. For Ness's 'wildly melo-dramatized' exploits, see John Kobler, *Capone: The Life and Career of Al Capone* (New York: Putnam, 1971), 278.

   For discussion of negative Italian American stereotypes in the national media, see the following essays in Randall M. Miller, ed., *Ethnic Images in American Film and Television* (Philadelphia: The Balch Institute, 1978): Joseph Papaleo, 'Ethnic Pictures and Ethnic Fate: The Media Image of Italian-Americans,' 93–6; Richard N. Giuliani, 'The Image of the Italian in American Film and Television,' 99–104; Michael Parenti, 'The Italian American and the Mass Media,' 106–7; Joseph L. Monte, 'Correcting the Image of the Italian American and Television,' 109–10. See also Mirella J. Affron, 'The Italian American in American Films, 1918–1978,' *Italian Americana* 3 (Spring/Summer 1977): 232–55; Karen Szczepanski, 'The Scalding Pot: Stereotyping of Italian American Males in Hollywood Films,' *Italian Americana* 5 (Spring/Summer 1979): 196–204; Anthony L. LaRuffa, 'Media Portrayals of Italian Americans,' *Ethnic Groups* 4 (July

1982): 191–206; Cortes, 'Hollywood Curriculum,' 89–108; Tomasulo, 'Italian Americans in Hollywood Cinema,' 65–77; Teresa Carilli, 'Still Crazy After All These Years: Italian Americans in Mainstream U.S. Films,' in Yahya Kamalipour and Teresa Carilli, eds., *Cultural Diversity and the U.S. Media* (Albany, N.Y.: SUNY Press, 1998), 111–24; Casella, *Hollywood Italian*, 15.

8 Scorsese assigned the name 'Murray' to his main character because Mel Brooks, who much influenced *It's Not Just You, Murray!*, had used it, and also because it had been applied as a nickname to Sicilians whom Scorsese had known. See Kelly, *Martin Scorsese: First Decade*, 14.

9 To quote Lucky Luciano: 'No matter what anybody says, I was a good American and I always think of myself as a good American.' Antoinette Giancana, daughter of Chicago mob boss Sam Giancana, recalls that her father's predecessor, Paul 'The Waiter' Ricca, often stated 'how proud he was to be an American.' Testifying before the Kefauver Committee, crime boss Frank Costello avowed, 'I love this country' – an understandable sentiment since, as Thomas Reppetto remarks, 'America had been very good to men like him.' Consistent with these statements are the political attitudes of dethroned crime boss Johnny Rocco (Edward G. Robinson) in John Huston's *Key Largo* (1948). Offended by his deportation, as if he were no better than a communist, Rocco regards himself as a patriot. In Coppola's *The Godfather* (1971), crime boss Barzini (Richard Conte) proclaims at a Mafia summit meeting: 'We're not communists.' Italian American gangsters have thus shared the tendency of their ethnic group to idealize the United States as the land of freedom, equality, and opportunity. Borrowing Melvin Tumin's phrase, Joseph Lopreato characterizes this as a 'cult of gratitude.' During the 1960s many Italian Americans also turned from liberalism to conservatism, while some Italian American criminal organizations, to extrapolate from the example of the 'Lupollo' family studied by Ianni, came to espouse 'Americanism' of the ultraconservative type. Glazer and Moynihan trace the ethnic group's growing conservatism to insecurity, but Lopreato links it to the 'cult of gratitude' and upward mobility. See Martin A. Gosch and Richard Hammer, *The Last Testament of Lucky Luciano* (New York: Dell, 1974), 232; Bondanella, *Hollywood Italians*, 218; Antoinette Giancana and Thomas Renner, *Mafia Princess: Growing Up in Sam Giancana's Family* (New York: Morrow, 1984), 131; Reppetto, *American Mafia*, 161; Lopreato, *Italian Americans*, 119, 172, 173–4, 175; Ianni, *Family Business*, 84.

10 Since the inception of the genre, gangster films have portrayed underworld connections with show business, as witness *Broadway* (1929), *The*

Roaring Twenties (1939), *Party Girl* (1958), *The Godfather* (1984), and many others.

11 See Kelly's discussion of these scenes in *Martin Scorsese: First Decade*, 156–7.

12 In 1951 Senator Estes Kefauver of Tennessee confused the Mafia with the Black Hand. As New York Police lieutenant Joseph Petrosino already understood in the first decade of the twentieth century, no connection existed between the Black Hand and any criminal organization whether Italian or American. See Reppetto, *American Mafia*, 36–8, 46; Nelli, *From Immigrants to Ethnics*, 93–4; Sid Feder and Joachim Joesten, *The Luciano Story* (New York: Da Capo, 1994), 85; Turkus and Feder, *Murder, Inc.*, 75–6; Sifakis, *Mafia Encyclopedia*, 258; Kobler, *Capone*, 46; Ianni, *Family Business*, 49–52 (quoting Z.W. Zorbaugh, *The Gold Coast and the Slum: A Sociological Study of Chicago's Near North Side* [Chicago: Univ. of Chicago Press, 1929], 71).

13 Heavily parodistic as it may seem, Murray's mother's injunction to 'eat first' has a parallel in the highly successful Chicago 'Outfit' – a mainly Italian American criminal organization – as reported by Gus Russo. A lawyer who defended Outfit boss Tony Accardo reports that, even under pressure of the most urgent legal conferences, with court appearances scheduled for the next day, 'we had to eat before we conducted business. Everything revolved around food.' As a result of one 'mandatory cook-fest,' as Russo calls it, for which the gangsters bought and prepared the food, the gang left its get-together at five in the morning with no work completed. Gangsters and counsel simply 'faked it' at a hearing only four hours later. According to Russo, 'the "eat first" ritual typifies the Outfit.' See Russo, *Outfit*, 321.

Murray's Italian American mother incarnates a cinematic stereotype perhaps originating in Howard Hawks's *Scarface* (1932), in which the mother of gangster Tony Camonte (Paul Muni) plies him with spaghetti. However, the identification of the Italian American gangster with this dish goes back at least as far as Mervyn LeRoy's *Little Caesar* (1930), whose protagonist, played by Edward G. Robinson, eats spaghetti in a diner after committing his first major crime. In Robert Siodmak's *Cry of the City* (1948), the mother of imprisoned gangster Martin Rome (Richard Conte) brings him minestrone.

14 Among the most important unwritten rules of the Mafia is that, for reasons of security, a husband should never discuss Mafia matters in the presence of his wife. These are understood to be *fatti suoi*, his business alone. The rule makes sense, as the wives of two major gangsters, Vito

Genovese and Tommy 'Trigger Mike' Coppola, testified against them. See Volkman and Cummings, *Goombata*, 63; Gambino, *Blood of My Blood*, 7; Salerno and Tompkins, *Crime Confederation*, 118; Teresa, *My Life in the Mafia*, 275; DeMaris, *Last Mafioso*, 131; Ianni, *Family Business*, 84; Giancana and Renner, *Mafia Princess*, 8, 17; Gambetta, *Sicilian Mafia*, 121.

15 Scorsese in his recollections of Little Italy comments on the cordiality and mutual respect that existed between priests and gangsters; the latter attended mass and donated to neighbourhood churches, and were delighted when the priests blessed their expensive cars. In *Mean Streets* Charlie Civello's house contains religious objects and images, as does his Uncle Giovanni's cafe restaurant. In *GoodFellas* Henry Hill wears a crucifix and is married in a Catholic ceremony. Antoinette Giancana, daughter of Chicago crime boss Sam Giancana, recalls that most Mafia families of her acquaintance had 'religion and faith' and practised the Catholicism they had brought from Sicily. Having adopted Catholicism in order to marry his devout fiancée, Sam Giancana subsequently learned the mass flawlessly, and in his daughter's opinion believed in God. Giancana's wife customarily said grace at the dinner table; the family eschewed meat on Fridays, Christmas Eve, and Good Friday; and Antoinette attended a parochial school. According to Raymond V. Martin, crime boss Joseph Profaci 'was a religious man' who worshipped faithfully at his neighbourhood church, befriended the pastor, and donated handsomely to charities. When a crown of jewels was stolen from a local religious icon, the thief returned it upon Profaci's orders, but was killed for having removed three of the jewels. Nicholas Pileggi, who collaborated with Scorsese on *Good-Fellas* and *Casino*, mentions a gangster who faithfully attended the feast of the Madonna of Mount Carmel in Italian Harlem. See Giancana and Renner, *Mafia Princess*, 59, 62; Martin, *Revolt in the Mafia*, 68–9; Orsi, *Madonna*, 103; Kelly, *Martin Scorsese: Journey*, 268. To judge from Diego Gambetta's and John Dickie's reports, even closer relations exist between the Catholic Church and the Mafia in Sicily. Besides sponsoring festivals and processions in honour of saints, Mafiosi are married and buried in church and in some cases are alleged to be priests themselves. Their generous donations to the church perhaps help to explain its hesitation in excommunicating them. See Gambetta, *Sicilian Mafia*, 49–52, 129; Dickie, *Cosa Nostra*, 32.

16 Bliss, *Word Made Flesh*, xvi; Kelly, *Martin Scorsese: First Decade*, 16, 18, 42; Kelly, *Martin Scorsese: A Journey*, 46; Keyser, *Martin Scorsese*, 21; Sangster, *Scorsese*, 15. The film's title derives from Jesus's words in Matthew 23:37: 'O Jerusalem, Jerusalem, thou that killest the prophets, and stonest them

which are sent unto thee, how often would I have gathered thy children together, even as a hen gathered her chickens under her wings, and ye would not!'

17 Kelly, *Martin Scorsese: First Decade*, 16. For excerpts from the treatment of *Jerusalem, Jerusalem*, see Kelly, *Martin Scorsese: First Decade*, 37–56.

18 Kelly, *Martin Scorsese: First Decade*, 42.

19 Weldon Thornton, *Allusions in Ulysses* (Chapel Hill: Univ. of North Carolina Press, 1968), 11; Don Gifford, with Robert J. Seidman, *Ulysses Annotated: Notes for James Joyce's Ulysses*, 2nd ed. (Berkeley: Univ. of California Press, 1988), 12–13, 12–13n.

20 In Sicily St Martin is honoured with a feast day celebrated on 11 November. See Pitrè, *Spettacoli e feste*, 409–14.

21 Kelly, *Martin Scorsese: A Journey*, 46–7; Lourdeaux, *Italian and Irish Filmmakers*, 232.

22 Scorsese, 'Confessions,' 13; Kelly, *Martin Scorsese: First Decade*, 16.

23 Sangster, *Scorsese*, 15; Kelly, *Martin Scorsese: First Decade*, 59, 62–32; Kelly, *Martin Scorsese: A Journey*, 51; Biskind, *Easy Riders, Raging Bulls*, 229; Grist, *Films of Martin Scorsese*, 30; 'Dialogue on Film,' 15; Scorsese, 'Confessions,' 134.

24 Kelly, *Martin Scorsese: First Decade*, 63–4; *The Motion Picture Guide, W–Z, 1927–1984*, ed. Jay Robert Nash and Stanley Ralph Ross (Chicago: Cinebooks, 1987), 3839.

25 Kelly, *Martin Scorsese: First Decade*, 5, 16, 63–8, 159–64; Kelly, *Martin Scorsese: A Journey*, 51–4; Sangster, *Scorsese*, 15; 'Dialogue on Film,' 15–6; *Motion Picture Guide: W–Z*, ed. Nash and Ross, 3839–40.

26 DeCurtis, 'What the Streets Mean,' 162. To quote Scorsese, the film 'was done over such a long period of time that there's no transition between scenes. You have no idea where people are. The only thread of it is the characterization ... [He used] jump cuts because we had no time to shoot establishing shots.' See 'Dialogue on Film,' 15.

27 Jacobs, *Hollywood Renaissance*, 133; Grist, *Films of Martin Scorsese*, 28; Friedman, *Cinema of Martin Scorsese*, 22, 23–4; Taylor, 'Martin Scorsese,' 310; Kolker, *Cinema of Loneliness*, 165–6.

28 Kolker, *Cinema of Loneliness*, 170–1; Friedman, *Cinema of Martin Scorsese*, 32; Grist, *Films of Martin Scorsese*, 32, 35; *The Motion Picture Guide, W–Z*, ed. Nash and Ross, 3840.

29 Gans, *Urban Villagers*, 28–32. Compare Whyte's description of Italian American streetcorner-society attitudes of a previous generation: 'A corner boy is not expected to be chaste, but it is beneath him to marry a girl who is "no good."' Whyte, *Street Corner Society*, 15.

30 The Pleasure Club calls to mind the adolescent peer groups of Boston's West End, who rented club rooms for gambling, drinking, dancing, and after-hours sex. See Gans, *Urban Villagers*, 67.

31 For these symbols of confinement, see Bliss, *Word Made Flesh*, 6.

32 The streetcorner boys of an earlier generation operated within a radius of three hundred yards of their chosen corner, to which they always returned. Whyte attributes this to their social insecurity. See Whyte, *Street-Corner Society*, 256.

33 Noting the differences in class between J.R. and The Girl, and their extreme difficulty in communication, Rebecca West hints at the film's chief problem in credibility, namely the improbability of their entering into a long-term romance, whatever their mutual sexual attraction. They have too little in common, and J.R. especially lacks the means to break down the social and experiential barriers between them. See Rebecca West, 'Scorsese's *Who's That Knocking at My Door?*: Night Thoughts on Italian Studies in the United States,' in *Romance Languages Annual*, Vol. 3, ed. Jeanette Beer, Charles Ganelin, Anthony Julian Tamburri (West Lafayette, Ind.: Purdue Research Foundation, 1992), 331–8.

34 Peter Burke, *The Art of Conversation* (Ithaca: Cornell Univ. Press, 1993), 10.

35 *Marty* originated as a teleplay. See Paddy Chayefsky, *Marty*, in Chayefsky, *Television Plays* (New York: Simon and Schuster, 1955). The film won the Best Picture Oscar in 1955.

36 These are Hammer's words at the conclusion of Spillane's *I, The Jury*.

37 The scene is Elizabeth Street as viewed more or less from Scorsese's grandmother's apartment window, from which he often looked out as a child. See Ehrenstein, *Scorsese Picture*, 33.

38 After leaving his teaching duties at NYU, Scorsese worked as an editor in Hollywood, where he was nicknamed 'The Butcher.' See Kelly, *Martin Scorsese: A Journey*, 64. Lesley Stern writes: 'If cinema does not simply reconstitute a presence of bodies, but if it participates in the genesis of the "bodily," then it can also dismember bodies, disperse bodily fragments like Actaeon, torn limb from limb by his hounds and scattered in pieces through time and space.' See Stern, *Scorsese Connection*, 12.

39 Lourdeaux, *Italian and Irish Filmmakers in America*, 236.

40 Scorsese says that Michael Powell's *Peeping Tom* (1960) 'shows the aggression of it, how the camera violates.' See *Scorsese on Scorsese*, ed. Thompson and Christie, 20.

41 The heavy-handedness of Chayefsky's script appears in the frequent repetition of words and phrases – for instance 'tomatoes,' referring to Marty's fantasies of ripe women as well as to the maternal tomato sauce

he substitutes for them; the refrain 'Whaddya wanna do tonight, Marty?,' underlining ad nauseam the futility of his life; and the encomiastic 'Micky Spillane, he sure can write,' bludgeoning home the low cultural level of the peer group. Harry Warren's best-known hit was the recently revived *Forty Second Street.*

42 See Bliss, *Scorsese and Cimino,* 34–5.

43 Scorsese observed a streetfight in which a Puerto Rican kissed a knife; see Keyser, *Martin Scorsese,* 8.

44 Bliss, *Word Made Flesh,* 1, 4. See also Friedman, *Cinema of Martin Scorsese,* 25–6; Bliss, *Scorsese and Cimino,* 31, 34.

45 Grist, *Films of Martin Scorsese,* 24–5, 26; Bliss, *Scorsese and Cimino,* 31–2.

46 Bliss, *Word Made Flesh,* 2, 13; Bliss, *Scorsese and Cimino,* 32–3.

47 DeCurtis, 'What the Streets Mean,' 163.

48 Mark S. Massa, SJ, *Anti-Catholicism in America: The Last Acceptable Prejudice* (New York: Crossroad, 2003), 7.

49 See Keyser, *Martin Scorsese,* 28; he cites Gambino, *Blood of My Blood,* 17.

50 On concupiscence as a malicious, acquisitive, and violent attitude towards another person, see Wilhelm Ernst, 'Marriage as Institution and the Contemporary Challenge to It,' in Monsignor Richard Malone and John R. Connery, SJ, eds., *Contemporary Perspectives on Christian Marriage: Propositions and Papers from the International Theological Commission* (Chicago: Loyola Univ. Press, 1984), 49–50, 53; G.J. McAleer, *Ecstatic Morality and Sexual Politics* (New York: Fordham Univ. Press, 2005), 31, 41, 46, 49, 94–5, 118, 125–9; Michael G. Lawler, *Marriage and the Catholic Church: Dispute Questions* (Collegeville, Minn.: Liturgical Press, 1989), 1–2, 71; Mary G. Durkin, *Feast of Love: Pope John Paul II on Human Intimacy* (Chicago: Loyola Univ. Press, 1983), 104, 110, 112, 113–14, 115, 142–4, 148, 153–4; John S. Grabowski, *Sex and Virtue: An Introduction to Sexual Ethics* (Washington, D.C.: The Catholic University of America, 2003), 38–9, 71, 86–7, 89, 111–14.

51 Ernst, 'Marriage as Institution,' 52, 53, 55, 64, 65; Grabowski, *Sex and Virtue,* 10, 11, 38–9, 46, 47, 78–9, 80, 82, 85–7, 88, 89; McAleer, *Ecstatic Morality and Sexual Politics,* 20–1, 23, 31, 41, 124, 125, 128, 129, 130, 134, 136; Lawler, *Marriage and the Catholic Church,* 5–7, 8, 14, 15, 18–23, 32, 33–6, 37, 70–3, 141, 152; Durkin, *Feast of Love,* 104, 105, 110, 114, 137, 142, 158–9. The current emphasis within Catholicism on marriage as an interpersonal union, rather than as an institution established primarily for the purpose of procreation, owes much to the work of Dietrich Von Hildebrand and Herbert Doms in the 1920s and 1930s, and finally came into its own following the Second Vatican Council in 1968. At present the older, procreative model of marriage competes with that of marriage regarded as

a form of mutual love instituted for the well-being of the partners, with
sex serving as the legitimate expression and vehicle of that love, and
within which the goal of procreation remains a highly valued though not
the sole major component. Yet it must be acknowledged that, consistent
with its traditional suspicion of the sexual impulse, Catholicism up to 1968
tended to regard all sex, including the marital variety, as tainted with lust.
Scorsese has often remarked that he had been raised as a Catholic in the
decades preceding Vatican II, and that his religious training very much
inclined him to regard all forms of sexual desire with anxiety and guilt.
See Ernst, 'Marriage as Institution,' 53; Lawler, *Marriage and the Catholic
Church*, 18–20, 32, 33–7; Durkin, *Feast of Love*, 105, 108–12, 133–4, 135;
Grabowski, *Sex and Virtue*, ix, 10–11, 47, 76–8, 80, 84–6.

52 Ernst, 'Marriage as Institution,' 74–8, 86; Durkin, *Feast of Love*, 148;
Grabowski, *Sex and Ethics*, 95, 112.

53 Mary Durkin makes no mention of mediated desire per se, but she acknowledges the powerful role of the contemporary media in the incitement of sexual desire. She also mentions pornography and prostitution
along with what she terms the 'social exploitation of people through their
sexual desires.' Grabowski refers similarly to the current commodification
and packaging of sex, whereby pornography, which inherently disrespects
the dignity of persons, no longer remains confined to its underground
existence. See Durkin, *Feast of Love*, 116, 147; Grabowski, *Sex and Virtue*,
8–9, 20, 116.

54 Durkin, *Feast of Love*, 148, 149.

55 Gans, *Urban Villagers*, 190–1.

56 Gambino, *Blood of My Blood*, 2. The *passatella* is a 'peasant tournament
of oratory, where interminable speeches reveal in veiled terms a vast
amount of repressed rancor, hate, and rivalry.' See Levi, *Christ Stopped at
Eboli*, 178.

57 On the trading of insults as a form of mimetic reciprocity resulting in a
loss of differentiation between or among characters, to the point where
they become each other's unacknowledged doubles, see Girard, *Violence
and the Sacred*, 44, 150–1. Girard mentions *stichomythia* in Greek tragedy, in
which the characters exchange similar or identical insults each consisting
of a line of verse, so that the characters' unacknowledged resemblance is
accentuated by the repeated symmetry of their responses.

58 Stern notes Edwards's uncanny resemblance to his Indian enemies, but
does not relate his mimeticism and loss of identity to J.R.'s situation. See
Stern, *Scorsese Connection*, 44–5, 58–60.

59 Girard, *Deceit, Desire, and the Novel*, 1–4.

60 J.R. and his friends resemble those action-seeking adolescent peer groups that Gans observed in Boston's West End in the late 1950s. What was 'most satisfying' to them was the 'search for action by the group as a whole,' which might consist of a fight, sexual adventure, cards, athletic contests, or in some cases juvenile delinquency. Indeed, the West End male adolescent felt himself 'active only with his peer group; outside it, he [was] ... a quiet and almost passive individual.' For Gans, the peer group demanded a high degree of conformity yet allowed sufficient room for individualistic display to keep its members satisfied with the arrangement. Gans calls this 'person-oriented individualism,' in which one desires to be a person within a group, and in which the patterns in which individualism expresses itself are group products. See Gans, *Urban Villagers*, 65, 86, 88, 89–103.

61 Keyser, *Martin Scorsese*, 27.

62 Bliss fails to see that Joey's remark indicates the distance between the world of the priest and that of the peer group; he takes it only to imply worldly savvy, which values money over the cheapness of confession. See Bliss, *Word Made Flesh*, 3.

63 J.R.'s bachelor peer group exemplifies, in arrested form, the sexual attitudes Herbert Gans found typical of Italian American adolescent males of Boston's West End, but which the majority abandoned during the mature phase of courting, when their peer groups inevitably broke up: 'The hold of the group is so strong that only rarely did the boy have an individual date. West Enders noted that boys rarely left the group for a girl, and that a male group seldom broke up because of conflicts over a girl ... If a boy should leave the group for a girl, he is likely to be accused of disloyalty, and must either give her up or leave the group. I am distinguishing here between a date and a "good girl" who may be a potential wife, and the continuous search for sexual relations with complaisant "bad girls." It is dates with the former that result in accusations of desertion. Dating the latter, however, is a much sought-after experience.' See Gans, *Urban Villagers*, 70–1.

64 Girard, *Violence and the Sacred*, 57.

65 A study of the Italian Americans of Boston's West End in 1958, Herbert Gans's *Urban Villagers* was published in 1962. According to Gans, probably the most popular entertainer among the West Enders was Frank Sinatra, whom young adults 'almost worshiped.' Sinatra was admired partly because he was proud of his ethnicity and also because, far from deserting his peer group, he consorted in public with gangsters. In addition to his loyalty to friends, Sinatra was admired because of his refusal to bend to

middle-class notions of respectability. Like some West Enders Sinatra qualifies as an 'action-seeker' – one who gambles, plays the horses, drinks, stays out late, enjoys various women, and acts generally on emotion and impulse. It was another plus for Sinatra that in his films he often played rebellious characters like himself with whom male West Enders readily identified. At the same time, Sinatra had the best of both worlds, as his brash nonconformism won him great success in the core society, whose money and women he seemed to plunder at will. The same favourable image of Sinatra prevailed in Greenwich Village after the Second World War. See Gans, *Urban Villagers*, 192–3, 193n; Nelli, *From Immigrants to Ethnics*, 188–9; Tricarico, *Italians of Greenwich Village*, 19; Richard Connolly and Pellegrino d'Acierno, 'Italian American Musical Culture and Its Contribution to American Music,' in *Italian American Heritage*, ed. d'Acierno, 425, 427–8; Gay Talese, 'Frank Sinatra Has a Cold,' in *The Gay Talese Reader: Portraits and Encounters* (New York: Walker, 2003), 41.

66 Sinatra has been called an 'Italian American imperial self' who rejected the 'Other-induced self' imposed by mainstream culture. See Connolly and d'Acierno, 'Italian American Musical Culture,' 425, 428.

67 The original Rat Pack gathered informally at the Holmsby Hills, California, house of Humphrey Bogart and Lauren Bacall around the time of Bogart's terminal illness. This group, which in addition to Sinatra numbered Spencer Tracy, Katharine Hepburn, Judy Garland, David Niven, and John Huston, was famous for late-night drinking and irreverence towards Hollywood convention. Following Bogart's death in 1957, Sinatra became the leader of a reconstituted and much noisier Rat Pack that flourished into early 1960s. Its male members included Dean Martin, Sammy Davis, Jr., Peter Lawford, and Joey Bishop, with Tony Curtis, Eddie Fisher, songwriter Jimmy Van Heusen, Milton Berle, and others on the periphery; its leading female members, who served as mascots, were Shirley MacLaine, Angie Dickinson, and Jill St John; like their husbands, Curtis and Fisher respectively, Janet Leigh and Elizabeth Taylor were on the margins of the group. In 1958 *Life* magazine characterized Sinatra and his cronies as the social pace-setters in Hollywood, a development all the more remarkable in view of Sinatra's and Martin's refusal to conceal their ethnicity. Sinatra and his crowd disdained conservative Hollywood and flouted the 'squares' by pursuing a free-wheeling, devil-may-care lifestyle, indifferent to a normal nine-to-five world. To quote Bacall, who named the original 'Rat Pack' and with whom Sinatra flirted with marriage soon after Bogart's death, they were 'thumbing their noses at Hollywood.' Bondanella says that they rejected the 'staid morality of the Eisenhower years.'

Otherwise known as 'The Clan' and 'The Kings of Cool,' and so insular that it acquired its own grotesque lingo, the Rat Pack attracted enormous publicity in the early 1960s. It owed its fascination to the constant thrill-seeking reflected in the group's motto: 'Where's the action?' They drank, gambled, played childish practical jokes, drove fast cars, bedded (but did not marry) beautiful women, and generally fulfilled their idea of a hip and macho existence. In view of Bogart's role in the formation of the Rat Pack, and also in view of his great popularity among Italian Americans as reported by Gans, it is appropriate that Connolly and d'Acierno character-ize Sinatra's behaviour as 'Italian American Bogartism.' Known for bad manners on occasion, as witness his fistfight with a parking lot attendant, Sinatra not only dressed and swaggered thuggishly but was known to be friends with leading gangsters. He is claimed to have said: 'I'd rather be a don of the Mafia than president of the United States' – on which Eddie Fisher commented, 'I don't think he was fooling.' In Scorsese's *GoodFellas*, Henry Hill prefers membership in a mob family over the American presi-dency. The quasi-gangland image attaching to the Rat Pack was strength-ened by its close connection with Las Vegas, where Sinatra, Martin, and Davis often performed and where Sinatra and Martin owned shares or 'points' in the Sands Hotel casino. The height of the Rat Pack coincided with the 1960 film *Ocean's Eleven*, which was shot at the Sands, and whose cast consisted of Sinatra's friends in roles reminiscent of their real-life personae. Known as the 'summit conference of cool,' the film concerned a Las Vegas casino robbery. Accompanied by heavy drinking, joking, and improvisation on the set, the production exemplified the mingling of work and play that typified the Rat Pack during this period. Many people came to Las Vegas simply to be in its vicinity. Nick Tosches compares these fans' 'imitation of cool' to the 'imitatio Christi.' Gans describes the Rat Pack as a middle-aged version of 'street-corner boys,' thus implying that ethnicity, or rather (in his view) their lower-class origins, continued to influence the members' behaviour. For Quirk and Schoell, its attraction lay in its mem-bers' ability to live life as they wished and never to fear the consequences. However, the Rat Pack's reputation for revolutionary nonconformism is unjustified, as it exemplifies 'arrested development' and calls to mind 'irresponsible, irrepressible college boys.' In any case, resemblances exist between the Rat Pack and J.R.'s peer group, whose refrain 'What do you wanna do tonight?' distantly and pathetically echoes the hip slogan 'Where's the action?' See Daniel Bell, 'America as a Mass Society: A Cri-tique,' in Bell, *The End of Ideology*, 35; John Howlett, *Frank Sinatra* (New York: Simon and Schuster, 1980), 113, 114, 116; Connolly and d'Acierno,

'Italian American Musical Culture,' 428, 433; Earl Wilson, *Sinatra: An Unauthorized Biography* (New York: MacMillan, 1976), 129–3; Lawrence J. Quirk and William Schoell, *The Rat Pack: Neon Nights with the Kings of Cool* (New York: Avon, 1998), *passim*; Richard Gehman, *Sinatra and His Rat Pack*, *passim*; Nick Tosches, *Dino: Living High in the Dirty Business of Dreams* (New York: Dell, 1992), 333 (see also 151, 155, 159, 165–6, 168, 211, 242–3, 321–2, 338, 348–9, 360, 361); Gans, *Urban Villagers*, 192, 193, 193n; Nelli, *From Immigrants to Ethnics*, 188; Ed Reid and Ovid Demaris, *The Green Felt Jungle* (New York: Trident, 1963), 89–91; Russo, *Outfit*, 369; Bondanella, *Hollywood Italians*, 147–9, 152–61; Donald Clarke, *All or Nothing at All: A Life of Frank Sinatra* (New York: Fromm International, 1997), 146–8, 167–8, 208–9, 219–29; Gilbert L. Gigliotti, *A Storied Singer: Frank Sinatra as Literary Conceit* (Westport, Conn.: Greenwood Press, 2002), 94, 109, 112, 145n; Leonard Mustazza, Introduction, in Mustazza, ed., *Frank Sinatra and Popular Culture: Essays on an American Icon* (Westport, Conn.: Praeger, 2002), 17; Talese, 'Frank Sinatra,' 19.

68 The sexual attitudes of the Rat Pack closely resemble those not only of J.R.'s peer group but of many Italian American males of Sinatra's generation. Commenting on the favourable response of the males of Boston's West End to Sinatra's widely publicized sexual exploits, Gans notes that he was said to 'make the traditional Italian distinction between the good and bad girl,' the second of whom is preferred for sex. He was also said to be 'unwilling to become emotionally involved with his sexual partners.' This is confirmed by Sinatra biographies and chronicles of the Rat Pack. With cocked hat and insouciant swagger intentionally reminiscent of the Mafioso, Sinatra already appears on the album covers of his Capitol period as an insolent, self-confident exploiter of women. He and his Rat Pack cronies were male chauvinist misogynists for whom most women were only 'broads.' Adopting a love-'em-and-leave-'em attitude, Sinatra always returned to the emotionally undemanding male peer group. His preference for emotionally independent women and unwillingness to commit himself to a stable relationship during his Rat Pack period, his romance with Juliet Prowse being the only exception, is sometimes attributed to his fear of betrayal. Although Sinatra demanded fidelity from a wife, he is known to have committed adultery. His first marriage to Nancy Sinatra grew ever more troubled in the early 1940s as he spent increasing time away from home, often with other women, though he promised to reform. Ultimately he divorced Nancy, although continuing to provide handsomely for her and his children. Dean Martin also committed adultery repeatedly during his first marriage and, though remarried during

the Rat Pack period, still carried on (as did the married Peter Lawford) as a playboy. Besides hinting that Sinatra hired prostitutes, his biographers note that while filming on location he and Martin would rent large houses that they turned into the equivalent of bordellos, as during the making of *Four for Texas*. Sinatra is said to have thrown a woman out of a window on one occasion.

However, another aspect of Sinatra's masculinity and sexuality calls to mind J.R.'s romance with The Girl. As Roger Gilbert points out, even as Sinatra was expressing sexual swagger, aggressiveness, and insouciance in his songs and films of the 1950s, he was allowing himself in some films to play weak, fearful, and self-pitying characters. Moreover, in some of the most celebrated albums of the Capitol period, such as *Only the Lonely* (1958) and *No One Cares* (1959), Sinatra appears in a much more muted and self-communing fashion as a male torch-singer whose songs evoke masculine sexual vulnerability of the most poignant type – that of a man, to quote Gilbert, 'invaded by feminine otherness.' Sinatra's tumultous and disappointing failed marriage to Ava Gardner probably influenced these masterly performances. However, to judge from Gans's *Urban Villagers*, the Italian American males of Boston's West End were unimpressed by these torch songs, preferring those in which Sinatra's sexual confidence and effrontery gave no hint of psychic disturbance below the surface of ceaselessly projected and satisfied desire. As Gans says, the songs were interpreted 'as arousing the audience to action.' He adds that Sinatra's 'singing style has a teasing quality which suggests to West Enders that he is making fun both of the song and the outside world ... To them, he seems to be putting something over on the outside world, while at the same time taking its money and attractive women.' Yet though J.R. and his peer group can likewise be expected to prefer Sinatra in his mystique of autonomy and emotional detachment, J.R.'s failed and traumatizing affair with The Girl shows him 'invaded' by 'feminine otherness.' The same may be said of Jake La Motta in Scorsese's *Raging Bull*, whose desperate longing for his future wife Vickie (Cathy Moriarty) is evoked through the accompaniment of the first of Sinatra's hit songs, 'All or Nothing at All,' in which he already expresses sexual vulnerability. Ironically, during his visit to The Girl's apartment in *Who's That Knocking?*, in a final attempt to renew their relationship, J.R. in thumbing through her record collection shows no interest in a Sinatra album of the 1950s but requests records by Percy Sledge, a black 1960s soul singer. J.R. may be thinking of Sledge's 1966 hit, 'When a Man Loves a Woman.' The irony is that not J.R. but his former girlfriend appreciates Sinatra the male torch-singer.

See Gans, *Urban Villagers*, 192–3; Bondanella, *Hollywood Italians*, 154, 157, 159; Quirk and Schoell, *Rat Pack, passim*; Gehman, *Sinatra and Rat Pack, passim*; Clarke, *All or Nothing at All*, 167; Roger Gilbert, 'The Swinger and the Loser: Sinatra, Masculinity, and Fifties Culture,' in *A Storied Singer*, ed. Mustazza, 38–47; Tosches, *Dino*, 152, 176, 179, 190, 262–3, 266, 404; Connolly and d'Acierno, 'Italian American Musical Culture,' 424–5.

69 Gans, *Urban Villagers*, 193n.

70 To quote Scorsese: 'I love him [Dean Martin], I love Sinatra, and that's my period, that's when I was coming of age.' He adds that, although *Mean Streets* 'pretends' to take place in the 1970s, its date is '1963, before the Beatles' and nearly contemporaneous with *Who's That Knocking at My Door?* As this suggests, the personae of Sinatra and Martin influenced Scorsese's portrayal of Italian American youth in the later as in the earlier film.

Whereas most commentators on the Rat Pack mention the pack-like – that is, conformist – behaviour of its members, and thus their resemblance to each other, Nick Tosches attempts to argue for Martin's distinct individuality and essential distance from the group from the very beginning. In Tosches's view, Sinatra was captivated by the image of Mafiosi, whom he sought to emulate, while Sammy Davis, Jr., and Peter Lawford were in Martin's eyes nobodies who slavishly copied Sinatra. For his part, Martin imitated no one, being secure in the inborn *lontananza* and *menefreghismo* that he shared with true Mafiosi, and that Sinatra, with his continuing sensitivity to insult and periodic vulnerability to women, was never able to achieve to anywhere near the same degree. Thus not Sinatra but Martin is for Tosches the true king or hero of 'cool.' Yet just as *lontananza* and *menefreghismo* often turn out to be carefully studied poses that fail to hold up under the storms of life, so Tosches's portrayal probably overestimates Martin's detachment from the Rat Pack, in which he participated for many years, and many of whose attitudes and behaviours, particularly towards women, he seems to have shared. On the other hand, Scorsese's view of Martin very possibly diverges from that of Tosches, at least to judge from reports of the Martin biopic that Scorsese was making plans to film in the late 1990s, and which was to have focused on the 1940s into the 1970s, with an emphasis on the Rat Pack. Apparently Scorsese intended to show Martin's gradual detachment from his peer group in 'finally ... coming to terms with himself,' but circumstances prevented the project, on which he had begun work with Nicholas Pileggi. See Smith, 'Art of Vision,' 253, 254; Tosches, *Dino*, 267, 323; Connolly and d'Acierno, 'Italian American Musical Culture,' 432.

71 One of the 'best known' of Italian games of chance 'was *morra* or "throw-

ing fingers," called by the ancient Romans *micare digitis*. This pastime for two people, usually played for money, required each person at a given signal to hold out one or more fingers and call as quickly as possible a guess of the total the two had extended.' See Williams, *South Italian Folkways*, 108. However, the game played by J.R. and his friends follows different rules.

72 Grist, *Films of Martin Scorsese*, 37; Keyser, *Martin Scorsese*, 27. Keyser quotes Holly McClennan, who says that the male characters 'are really only capable of loving each other,' adding that the 'tragedy is that theirs is a world without woman.'

73 Giuseppe Prezzolini, *Come gli americani scoprirono l'Italia, 1750–1850* (Milan: Fratelli Treves, 1933), 226.

74 Girard, *Deceit, Desire, and the Novel*, 46, 47, 50; Girard, *'To Double Business Bound,'* 52–4, 66.

75 Bliss, *Word Made Flesh*, 11; Bliss, *Scorsese and Cimino*, 5, 43.

76 Grist, *Films of Martin Scorsese*, 31.

77 Girard, *Violence and the Sacred*, 138, 166–8.

78 Maria T. Milioca reads the thrown deck of cards as a symbolic ejaculation signifying J.R.'s mastery of the supine women. This interpretation neglects the more obviously symbolic connection of cards with the theme of chance as manifest as well in Morrison's song and J.R.s related fantasies of sexual promiscuity. See Milioca, *The Scorsese Psyche on Screen: Roots and Themes and Characters in the Films* (Jefferson, N.C.: McFarland, 2004), 71.

79 Scorsese acknowledges the film's anomalousness. See DeCurtis, 'What the Streets Mean,' 163.

80 Girard refers to the hierarchy of desires in Stendhal, who though he first believes that the 'strongest desires are the passionate desires,' finally realizes that 'strength of desire' correlates with mediation and vanity. See Girard, *Deceit, Desire, and the Novel*, 19–21.

81 Bliss, *Scorsese and Cimino*, 41.

82 Bliss misinterprets this scene: '[J.R. is] on the verge of realizing what a (Catholic-influenced) orientation towards death (as symbolized by the sunset) and enclosure represents.' See Bliss, *Scorsese and Cimino*, 42. Lourdeaux reads the scene correctly: 'Atop a steep, tree-covered hill, J.R. stands transfixed by the grandeur of Nature, struck as in *Jerusalem, Jerusalem* by the sacrament and artistry of God's creation.' See Lourdeaux, *Italian and Irish Filmmakers*, 237. Nyce mistakenly regards the scene as superfluous, a mark of Scorsese's inexperience as a director. See Nyce, *Scorsese Up Close*, 10.

83 DeCurtis, 'What the Streets Mean,' 163.

84 Compare the Italian American males studied by Gans: 'The Western or detective hero ... who is conquered by the woman is scorned ... The hero who can "love-em-and-leave-em" was admired.' See Gans, *The Urban Villagers*, 190.

85 Bliss, *Word Made Flesh*, 9–10.

86 To use a phrase of Julian Pitt-Rivers in his study of the Spanish version of the Mediterranean cult of masculine honour, J.R. has become a 'retroactive cuckold.' See 'Honour and Shame,' 51.

87 According to David D. Gilmore, 'a tendency to split woman symbolically in two, into good and bad, is probably a universal male tendency, at least in Western culture.' He cites Freud and Nancy Chodorow on this phenomenon. Yet Gilmore correctly observes that, 'though ubiquitous, this symbolic splitting of the feminine in male thinking achieves its fullest expression in Mediterranean Catholicism.' See Gilmore, *Carnival and Culture*, 57–8, 69–70. For examples of this dichotomy in Western civilization, including traditional Hollywood cinema, see Leslie Fiedler, *Love and Death in the American Novel* (New York: Stein and Day, 1966), *passim*; Sharon W. Tiffany and Kathleen J. Adams, *The Wild Woman: An Inquiry into the Anthropology of an Idea* (Cambridge, Mass.: Schenkman, 1985), *passim*; Laura Mulvey, 'Visual Pleasure and Narrative Cinema,' in Mulvey, *Visual and Other Pleasures* (Bloomington: Indiana Univ. Press, 1990), 14–26.

88 To quote Robert Warshow's 'Movie Chronicle: The Westerner': 'Those women in the Western movies who share the hero's understanding of life are prostitutes (or, as they are usually presented, barroom entertainers) – women, that is, who have come to understand in the most practical way how love can be an irrelevance, and therefore "fallen" women.' See Warshow, *The Immediate Experience: Movies, Comics, Theatre, and Other Aspects of Popular Culture* (New York: Atheneum, 1970), 138.

89 Girard, *I See Satan*, 14.

90 Grist, *Films of Martin Scorsese*, 37.

91 Jonathan Taplin recalls that the young Scorsese gave 'full rein' to his 'bad temper' only in the company of women. This anger had its masochistic side, for as a girlfriend recalls, Scorsese never hit her but was a 'wall puncher.' See Biskind, *Easy Riders, Raging Bulls*, 238–9.

92 Pitrè, *Spettacoli e feste*, 424–30; John T. Delany, *Dictionary of Saints*, 2nd ed. (New York: Doubleday, 2005), 388; *Butler's Lives of Patron Saints*, ed. Michael Walsh (San Francisco: Harper and Row, 1987), 291.

93 On Saint Lucia, see Williams, *South Italian Folkways*, 135; Leonard W. Moss and Stephen C. Cappanari, 'Mal'occhio, Ayin ha ra, Occhio fascinus, Judenblick: The Evil Eye Hovers Above,' in Clarence Maloney, ed., *The Evil*

Eye (New York: Columbia Univ. Press, 1976), 11. Pitrè relates the saint's legend to Matthew, 5:29: 'If the eye offendeth, pluck it out.' See Pitrè, *Spettacoli e feste*, 426.

94 The song carries 'overtones of popular Catholic iconography in paintings in which Jesus is seen knocking at a door with no handle. The door, in Catholic belief, is the door to your heart, and the handle is on the inside because only you can let Jesus in.' See Dougan, *Martin Scorsese*, 29.

95 Bliss, *Word Made Flesh*, 13; Bliss, *Scorsese and Cimino*, 47. For similar interpretations of Catholicism in this scene, see West, 'Scorsese's *Who's That Knocking?*' 333; Desirée Everts, 'Martin Scorsese and His Young "Girl": Female Objectification in *Who's That Knocking at My Door?*,' *VIA* 7 (Spring 1996): 65–77.

96 Kelly, *Martin Scorsese: First Decade*, 42. See also Friedman, *Cinema of Martin Scorsese*, 30.

5. Season of the Witch: *Mean Streets*

1 Taylor, 'Martin Scorsese,' 321; Kelly, *Martin Scorsese: A Journey*, 54; Scorsese, 'Confessions,' 135.

2 Grist, *Films of Martin Scorsese*, 61–2.

3 Keyser, *Martin Scorsese*, 39; Kelly, *Martin Scorsese: A Journey*, 69, 75.

4 Gavin Smith asks Scorsese whether *GoodFellas* and *Mean Streets* 'serve as an antidote to the ... mythic version of the Mafia' in Coppola's *Godfather* films: 'Yes, yeah, absolutely ... [*Mean Streets*] is really, to use the word loosely, anthropology – that idea of how people live, what they ate, how they dressed. *Mean Streets* has that quality – a quote "real" unquote side of it.' See Smith, 'Martin Scorsese Interviewed,' *Film Comment*, September – October 1990, in *Martin Scorsese: Interviews*, ed. Brunette, 148. Scorsese regarded *The Godfather* as 'bullshit.' See Kelly, *Martin Scorsese: A Journey*, 72. Despite the differences between *The Godfather* films and Scorsese's gangster trilogy, they resemble each other in their geographical drift. As in *Godfather, Part II* Michael Corleone moves his family and criminal businesses to Lake Tahoe and Las Vegas, so Scorsese's trilogy begins in the ethnic neighbourhoods of the Northeast and concludes in *Casino* with the Nevada gaming industry.

5 *Scorsese and Scorsese*, ed. Thompson and Christie, 48.

6 Keyser, *Martin Scorsese*, 39; Kolker, *Cinema of Loneliness*, 165, 168, 173, 176; Kelly, *Martin Scorsese: First Decade*, 88.

7 Keyser, *Martin Scorsese*, 39; Connolly, *Martin Scorsese*, 7; 'Dialogue on Film,' 15.

8 Taylor, 'Martin Scorsese,' 324; Grist, *Films of Martin Scorsese*, 65, 70.

9 Dougan, *Martin Scorsese*, 35.
10 Chandler, 'The Simple Art of Murder,' in Chandler, *The Simple Art of Murder* (Boston: Houghton Mifflin, 1950), 523.
11 *Scorsese on Scorsese*, ed. Thompson and Christie, 38. The title *Season of the Witch* has its merits and is arguably preferable to the present one, being more closely related to the film's themes, narrative, and characters. Such an argument, however, depends partly on the likely possibility that Scorsese grasped the significance of witches, witchcraft, and the related belief in the evil eye or *mal occhio* in both southern Italian and Italian American society. Writing of the Italian Americans of Greenwich Village in the 1930s, Caroline F. Ware noted that the residents continued to believe in witches and witchery and even more so in the evil eye, against which such protective charms as horns, fishes, and red string were still used. Although the younger generation was coming to reject superstitions, some young people retained them, including belief in the evil eye. According to Rudolph J. Vecoli, 'commonly the second-generation [Italian Americans] chose not to transmit the mutilated fragments of oral tradition and folklore to their children.' Carla Bianco's study of the Italian American community of Roseto, Pennsylvania, published in 1974, shows that most children had forgotten much of the folklore, including stories of witches, from the ancestral past. Yet she also found that second- and third-generation Italian Americans held on to Old World traditions 'even when they no longer need to or understand why.' Such cultural retention, as Malpezzi and Clements note, is likely to be strongest outside major urban areas, but as for the third and fourth generations, they had shed most of the 'original import' of the 'evil eye belief,' which they now associated with 'generalized concepts of good and bad luck.' In any case, Sicilian folk traditions persisted in Manhattan's Little Italy during Scorsese's childhood, and it goes without saying that he had an impressionable eye for colour, mystery, drama, and the more bizarre manifestations of the sacred. Even if legends of witches were not transmitted to him directly, they are likely to have come to his attention. What therefore needs clarification is the role of witchcraft and the evil eye in southern Italian and early Italian American society.

   Mary Douglas finds witchcraft to appear at social disjunctions where individuals feel enmity generated by their unfavourable position. It also appears in instances where a social hierarchy is threatened by people from 'inarticulate' and 'unstructured' areas. An 'alleged psychic force,' usually malevolent, witchcraft is identified with specific people in the 'nonstructure' of society, its interstitial spaces. These individuals are regarded

as ambiguous, fearful, unlucky, and envious of those more socially favoured, and are bound to be disliked and even hated. Douglas proposes
two types of witches, the outsider and the 'internal enemy.' The first is
seen as posing little threat to society and normally is neither identified,
punished, nor expelled. The second type appears in more complex societies, where two factions are involved, and is made up of three subtypes.
The internal enemy can be a member of a rival faction, a dangerous deviant needing to be controlled in the name of community values, or an
external enemy with external liasons, who would split the community and
establish a new hierarchy. All of these types are perceived as dangerous,
and the accusations of witchcraft hurled against them serve as warnings.
Since 'witches' are out of control, the accusations produce control where it
would be otherwise hard to establish. Another means of warding off danger is sorcery, a medicinal magic used by the authorities to repel, disarm,
and expel witches. If witchcraft is chiefly identified with unlucky people
struggling within the social interstices, sorcery belongs to the lucky ones
at the top of the hierarchy, who in being lucky only become luckier, and
who in exercising power only grow more powerful. Yet sorcery does not
belong exclusively to the powerful, while luck can operate fluidly and
unpredictably in social conflicts, so that a witch sometimes topples a
sorcerer.

Southern Italian folklore abounds in stories and legends of demons,
ghosts, werewolves, devils, and witches, the belief in which the Catholic
Church in no way officially sanctions. Although witches are typically
feminine, male witches or *stregoni* are not unheard of. Whatever their sex,
witches are not supernatural, but human beings with a dual personality.
The peasantry believe that witches leave their houses at night, when they
turn into animals, and that they enter houses nocturnally to commit theft
and other crimes; one should therefore bolt doors and windows during
the sleeping hours. Christmas affords a rare opportunity to expose witches
to public view. It is further believed that witches possess the power, both
conscious and unconcious, to cast harmful spells, their motivation being
envy or jealousy. As Covello writes: 'The power of human envy operates
to some extent through witches.' Witchcraft affects not only the health of
certain individuals, often adversely, but their love lives, as in the case of a
married witch who caused a young man to fall in love with her, witches
having special knowledge of love potions. However, witches are sometimes healers and herb doctors. Nor is a witch's presence within a community necessarily perceived as threatening.

Another form of southern Italian social behaviour deserves mention as a variation of witchcraft. This is the 'evil eye,' the *mal occhio* or *jettatura*, which, though not confined to the Mezzogiorno, is often identified with it. Another belief without church sanction, the evil eye consists of a malign glance inborn in those who possess it. Operating either unconsciously or consciously, this bad-luck charm physically wastes those upon whom it is 'thrown.' As it is typically motivated by envy or jealousy, the evil eye usually targets people with wealth, beauty, or good fortune. Not only is it dangerous to be pretty or handsome, as this attracts the *jettatura*, but to express admiration of anything can injure it through unconscious envy. As protection against the evil eye peasants resort to such magical practices as amulets of all sorts (beast's horns, claws, teeth, figurines of male hunch-backs), conjurations, incantations, exorcisms, talismans, charms, and spells. Baptism gives immediate protection against the evil eye. Nonetheless, the *mal occhio*, like the sacred generally, has its positive side, for though it is undesirable when used by evil persons, the authorities can use it for social control, defeating or repelling the *jettatore* by homeopathy. Robert Orsi notes that in Italian East Harlem as late as the 1940s older people believed in witches and the evil eye; magical charms and local healers were used to repel them. To judge from Banfield's observations of southern Italy, made in the late 1950s, the belief in witches and the evil eye had greatly declined, at least in some areas.

Vivian Garrison and Conrad M. Arensberg relate the *mal occhio* to societies where, as in southern Italy, goods are scarce and patronage is crucial to success. One finds the typical situation of the impoverished 'gazer' fixing his or her envious eye on the 'gazee,' a more fortunate person whose goods the other covets. The gazee needs to defend or protect him or herself against the other's envious gaze, and can do this only with the help of a powerful patron, whose symbol can then be waved before the gazer as a shield of sanctity. The gazee thereby becomes untouchable, sacred.

Mal occhio and witchcraft are by no means identical. As Garrison and Arensberg suggest, whereas witchcraft normally involves a one-on-one relation between two antagonists, the *mal occhio* often involves three people: the gazer, gazee, and patron. Di Stasi notes that with *mal occhio* there is seldom an attempt to take revenge or find the perpetrator, as with witchcraft. Nonetheless, the close resemblance between these two practices has been noted. Elworthy remarks a 'whole class of operations directly connected with ... [the evil eye], comprehended in the terms Magic, Enchantment, and Witchcraft.' For William Wetmore Story, the evil eye 'bears a curious resemblance to the effects of witchcraft as practiced in

New England.' Douglas views the evil eye as a special case of witchcraft belief, while Richard Swiderski terms it a 'clandestine involvement with dark powers' akin to magic and other 'forbidden practices.' Indeed, the *jettatore* is sometimes a male witch or *stregone*. Ronald A. Riminick places the evil eye within the purview of witchcraft, and Brian Spooner finds them to be 'undoubtedly of the same order of phenomena.' For Leonard W. Moss and Stephen C. Cappanari, witchcraft and the evil eye are 're-lated phenomena,' as is suggested by Willie Appel's description of a *jettatore* bewitching a victim. According to Carla Bianco, witches some-times have the evil eye, and Di Stasi remarks the 'infringement' of the *mal occhio* on the black arts, characterizing witchcraft, spells, and magic as a 'substratum' of *mal occhio*.

That *Mean Streets* encompasses the theme of the evil eye cannot be gainsaid, as Charlie's friend Tony has taken the precaution of attaching a red *corno* to his car's rearview mirror, obviously a protection against the *mal occhio* and its malevolences. In view of the fact that Tony alone escapes the bloody violence that engulfs his friends at the film's climax, the *corno* may be said to have 'worked.' Yet there is much else in the film to suggest that Scorsese comprehends intuitively the whole anthropological and ethnological complex of witches and witchery, social marginality and rebellion, protection and patronage, and not least the *mal occhio* in its inextricable relation to malicious envy.

Since, in southern Italian tradition, witches follow nocturnal habits, it is worth noting that *Mean Streets* takes place almost entirely at night. The film depicts an entrenched social hierarchy, dominated by Uncle Giovanni, which is challenged by the highly deviant and dangerous Johnny Boy, a curiously dressed deadbeat and ne'er-do-well on the margins of local society. Because of his peripheral position, Johnny Boy feels ill-concealed envy of the more aspiring, well-heeled, and successful members of his peer group, Charlie and Michael. Yet his malignant gaze extends to the entire ethnic neighbourhood, which he professes to hate, and even to the whole of Manhattan. As an unpredictably violent force, Johnny Boy must be contained or expelled.

When Johnny Boy, out of envy and contempt for Michael, denies him payment on a debt, he recklessly invites Michael's evil eye. In this world of competition over scarce wealth and even scarcer social prestige, Michael has become the envious gazer, coveting the money (and prestige) Johnny Boy withholds from him, while Johnny Boy is the gazee. Normally the gazee hopes for protection against the gazer's malevolence by appealing to a patron whose talismanic power can ward off the threat – precisely what Johnny Boy attempts to do in asking Charlie to secure Uncle Giovanni's intercession on his behalf. But Charlie for personal reasons refuses to do so, and Johnny Boy is left unprotected against Michael.

Notwithstanding his attraction to Christian morality, Charlie engages in a kind of witchcraft by casting an evil eye against those whose possessions he envies. He practises the evil eye implicitly in his covetous desire for an uptown Italian restaurant that his Mafioso uncle will give him once the current owners have declared bankruptcy after failing to meet the uncle's protection payments. In the terms of Garrison and Arensberg, Charlie is the 'gazer' and the restaurateurs are the 'gazee[s].' The restaurateurs need a patron through whose protection they can ward off Charlie's claim. Unfortunately, their original patron, the only person capable of protecting them, is the uncle who has now withdrawn his favour to further his nephew's interests, and whose 'protection' now means destruction.

Another witch-like character is Teresa, Charlie's girlfriend, who despite his ambivalence exerts a powerful sexual spell over him and whom he describes as a 'Wild Woman.' Teresa qualifies as a witch not only because she tempts Charlie into sex outside marriage but because, in her desire to escape Little Italy, she challenges its male hierarchy while demonstrating antagonistically her marginal role within it. In the eyes of Uncle Giovanni, the Italian American community's authority figure, she is a witch-like deviant. He not only views her as a threat to the social hierarchy, but seems to suspect the competing spell she has cast over Charlie, who may join her social rebellion. Teresa's deviant and socially marginal status is hardly helped by her epilepsy, which Uncle Giovanni reads as mental illness and which in his view underlies her desire to leave the neighbourhood. It bears mentioning that in southern Italy some diseases are traced to witchcraft.

Also belonging to the category of witch is Diane, the long-limbed black dancer at Tony's club, who powerfully attracts Charlie and with whom he entertains an affair. The first nightclub scene includes a shot of Diane's slender hands weaving a witch-like spell of fascination over Charlie. Insofar as Diane, being black, comes from outside the community, and insofar as she tempts Charlie to betray it through a forbidden and career-threatening liaison, she represents a more dangerous version of Teresa.

This witches' gallery is rounded out by Uncle Giovanni. Dominating the social hierarchy, he is not so much a witch as a magus or sorcerer who uses controlled and expulsive violence to keep deviants in line and thus to maintain social order. Accordingly, he casts a baleful – that is, evil – eye upon all who offend him, and, with a wave of his phallic cigar, reminiscent of a magic wand, commands their banishment. This occurs when a young thug violates the Mafia rule of controlled violence by committing an unprovoked murder in a local bar, which Giovanni punishes with expulsion to Miami. Disapproving of Charlie's association with Johnny Boy and Teresa, Giovanni orders his nephew to stay away from them. For failing to heed his uncle, Charlie and his friends are shot by Michael, an unexpected event that can only result in the loss of the uncle's favour. The film thus exemplifies the fluidity of fortune Douglas associates with struggles between witches and sorcerers. It also confirms the identification of witches with bad luck, and of the powerful with augmenting good luck. Appropriately, Uncle Giovanni identifies with Lucky Luciano and vainly attempts to educate Charlie in the ways of that gangster (whose luck, incidentally, ran out).

Since the title *Season of the Witch* seems appropriate to the themes and narrative of what became *Mean Streets*, one wonders why Scorsese rejected it. Its unsuitability lies in the fact that, while witches have a specific significance in southern Italian society and its earlier Italian American offshoots, these meanings would have been lost on most American viewers. Another problem is that, in the Anglo-American world, one normally thinks of a witch as a hideous old lady rather than as a dangerously seductive beautiful woman or sinister male, as in southern Italy. More fundamentally, Americans think of witches as female, but the female 'witches' in the film, even Teresa, are secondary characters, so that the original title would have produced confusion regarding narrative and content. Finally, whereas the word 'witch' is singular, *Mean Streets* portrays several witches, male and female.

See Mary Douglas, *Purity and Danger: An Analysis of the Concepts of Pollution and Taboo* (London: Ark, 1984), 98–9, 101–5, 107–9, 111, 112; Bianco, *Two Rosetos*, 73, 78, 84, 86, 89–98, 100, 151n; Vecoli, 'Search for an Italian American Identity,' 62; Williams, *South Italian Folkways*, 102, 141–4, 142n, 152–5, 157–9; De Martino, *Sud e magia*, 10, 13–4, 17–21, 30–6, 38, 42, 43, 55–65, 81–2, 97–130; Ware, *Greenwich Village*, 189, 190; Moss and Cappanari, 'Mal'Occhio, Ayin ha ra, Occhio fascinus, Judenblick,' 2, 10–11, 13–14; Pierre Bettez Gravel, *The Malevolent Eye: An Essay on the Evil Eye, Fertility, and the Concept of Mana* (New York: Peter Lang, 1995), 5–9; Schneider and Schneider, *Culture and Political Economy*, 101; Lawrence Di Stasi, *Mal Occhio: The Underside of Vision* (San Francisco: North Point, 1981), *passim*; Malpezzi and Clements, *Italian-American Folklore*, 61, 72, 117–28, 130, 132, 145; Frederick Thomas Elworthy, *The Evil Eye: An Account of This Ancient and Widespread Superstition* (New York: Julian Press, 1986), 1–2, 7, 17–28, 44;

William Wetmore Story, *Castle St Angelo and the Evil Eye* (London: Chapman and Hall, 1877), 145–238; Chapman, *Milocca*, 43–4, 200–8, 217; Levi, *Christ Stopped at Eboli*, 9, 14, 104, 151, 206; Schermerhorn, *These Our People*, 242–3; Banfield, *Moral Basis*, 143, 144n; Orsi, *Madonna*, 3, 132; Gentilcore, *From Bishop to Witch*, 146–8, 238, 253, 254; Pamela Goyan Kittler and Kathryn P. Sucher, *Food and Culture*, 3rd ed. (Belmont Calif.: Wadsworth/ Thomson Learning, 2001), 135. See also Willie Appel, 'The Myth of the Jettatura'; Richard Swiderski, 'From Folk to Popular: Plastic Evil Eye Charms'; Ronald A. Reminick, 'The Evil Eye Belief among the Amhara'; Vivian Garrison and Conrad M. Arensberg, 'The Evil Eye: Envy or Risk of Seizure; Paranoia or Patronal Dependency?': all in *The Evil Eye*, ed. Moloney, 17, 28, 29, 96–7, 286–328. Giuseppe Galasso emphasizes a distinction that he believes to have been too often ignored or glossed over, between the *jettatura*, which has to do with unconscious envy and malice proceeding involuntarily from the entire being of the individual, and the *mal occhio*, which he identifies with voluntary and unconscious malice transmitted through the eyes. See Galasso, 'Dalla "fattura" alla "iettatura": Una svolta nella "religione superstiziosa" del Sud,' in Galasso, *L'altra Europa: Per un'antropologia del Mezzogiorno d'Italia* (Milan: Mondadori, 1982), 272, 273n, and *passim*.
12 Tricarico, *Italians of Greenwich Village*, 44.
13 Keyser, *Martin Scorsese*, 40; 'Dialogue on Film,' 14; Kakutani, 'Scorsese's Past Colors His New Film,' 103; Taylor, 'Martin Scorsese,' 302, 326–7; Occhiogrosso, *Once a Catholic*, 92.
14 Compare Scorsese's statements in Lourdeaux, *Italian and Irish Filmmakers*, 222, 223, 241, 243. According to Lourdeaux, Charlie rejects Irish religious legalism.
15 Jim Hosvey, Jacqueline Wollman, and Jesse Ward Engdahl, 'The Passion of St Charles: Martin Scorsese's *Mean Streets*,' in Jody McAuliffe, ed., *Plays, Movies, and Critics* (Durham: Duke Univ. Press, 1993), 180.
16 Matthew 18:3.
17 Hebrews 11:1.
18 Kolker, *Cinema of Loneliness*, 177–8. The victim of the gangland murder in *Little Caesar* is Tony Russa (William Collier, Jr.), whose mother had persuaded him to return to the church after reminding him of his days as an altar boy. Before Tony can confess to Father McNeil, he is shot down by gangleader Rico Bandello (Edward G. Robinson). Gangster Eddie Bartlett (James Cagney) dies from bullet wounds on the steps of a church at the conclusion of Raoul Walsh's *The Roaring Twenties* (1939), one of Scorsese's

favourite films. In *Cry of the City* (1948), Martin Rome (Richard Conte) is shot by police after leaving the church in which he had taken refuge. To quote Stuart H. Kaminsky, 'The church is a place on whose steps the gangster dies.' See Kaminsky, *American Film Genres*, 2nd ed. (Chicago: Nelson Hall, 1984), 37. The deaths of these celluloid criminals call to mind that of Polish Catholic gangster Hymie Weiss, machine-gunned by Al Capone's henchmen in 1926 near Chicago's Holy Name Cathedral. See William F. Roemer, *Accardo: The Genuine Godfather* (New York: Donald I. Fine, 1995), 42. For Pauline Kael, *Mean Streets* qualifies as a gangster film. See Kelly, *Martin Scorsese: First Decade*, 169.

19 Dark glasses are a recent trademark of Mafiosi. See Gambetta, *Sicilian Mafia*, 127, 134.

20 1 Corinthians 13:11.

21 Commenting on Rossellini's *Flowers of St Francis* (1950), Scorsese identifies the saint with compassion and 'unconditional love of every living thing,' as witness the scene in which he embraces a leper. The scene somewhat recalls Charlie's relation to Johnny Boy and even more so Scorsese's childhood interest in Father Damien, who died of leprosy in the leper colony he administered. Scorsese had probably seen Rossellini's film before 1973, when *Mean Streets* was released. See Scorsese, *Il Mio Viaggio*; Lourdeaux, *Italian and Irish Filmmakers*, 229–30.

22 Scorsese played such games during his childhood. See Occhiogrosso, *Once a Catholic*, 91.

23 Friedman, *Cinema of Martin Scorsese*, 32.

24 Taylor, 'Martin Scorsese,' 327.

25 See also Elworthy, *Evil Eye*, 234, on the hand as 'instrument of evil when used by the malignant.'

26 Friedman, *Cinema of Martin Scorsese*, 31, 33; Keyser, *Martin Scorsese*, 40, 44.

27 Hosvey et al., 'Passion of St Charles,' 180, 181. See also Lourdeaux, *Italian and Irish Filmmakers*, 244.

28 Goldstein and Jacobson, 'Martin Scorsese Tells All,' 63. See also Ianni, *Family Business*, 31n.

29 For many historians, Charles 'Lucky' Luciano is responsible more than any other individual for the modernization and expansion of Italian American syndicate crime in the twentieth century. Some writers, however, such as Kobler and McPhaul, assign greater importance to Johnny Torrio, a major Chicago crime boss of the 1920s, while others like George Murray extol, less credibly, Torrio's overpublicized protegé and successor, Al Capone. According to Francis A.J. Ianni, the Jewish gangsters of the

1920s were more powerful and innovative than their better publicized Italian counterparts, although by the 1930s the Italians dominated organized crime.

Born Salvatore Lucania near Palermo in 1897, Luciano came to the United States in 1906 and began his career as a petty hoodlum and racketeer specializing in bootlegging and narcotics. By the late 1920s he held an important position within the criminal organization directed by the Sicilian-born Joseph Masseria, who represented, as against the Americanized Luciano, the traditional Italian American approach to crime. Known as a 'Mustache Pete' or 'greaseball,' Masseria focused his activities on the ethnic community, specializing in extortion, money-lending, and ghetto monopolies. He refused to cooperate with other Italian American, Irish, and Jewish criminal groups, whom he regarded with distrust and hostility.

Impatient with this old-fashioned approach to criminal organization, the young Luciano saw much greater monetary potential in the example set by Torrio, who had branched outside the Italian American colony into the American underworld during the Prohibition era, applying modern business techniques to organized crime, and by Capone, who dominated crime not only in Chicago's Italian neighbourhood but within the city as a whole. Not only had Torrio and Capone perfected the corruption of police and other officials, but they had invested their enormous bootlegging profits in legitimate businesses, which afforded new sources of profits and a cover for their illegalities. Anticipating the inevitable end of Prohibition, they had diversified their operations to include racketeering, prostitution, gambling, and other forms of crime. This, then, was the inspiration for what in Luciano's hands became the Italian American crime syndicate. His admiration for the Chicago model was shared by other aspiring 'Americanizers' within the Italian American mob in the New York area, including Frank Costello (Castiglia) and Joe Adonis (Doto), two of Luciano's closest associates.

Peter Maas asserts that Luciano acquired his nickname after surviving a beating by other hoodlums in the narcotics trade. According to Luciano, the beating had been administered by the henchmen of Sicilian-born gangster Salvatore Maranzano, who had asked Luciano to betray Masseria. Like Masseria, with whom he was embroiled in the 'Castellamarese War' of the late 1920s and early 1930s, Maranzano adhered to the Sicilian tradition of criminal activity focused on the ethnic group. Luciano ultimately betrayed Masseria to Maranzano, who exterminated his rival in a Coney Island restaurant on 15 April 1931, Luciano having disappeared into the men's room just before the assassination. Yet Maranzano's victory was by no means welcomed by Luciano and his friends, as it was followed by Maranzano's proclamation of himself as 'boss of bosses' in a new syndicate organization modelled on the Roman Empire. On 11 September 1931, Luciano eliminated Maranzano in a gangland-style execution. However, this event is no longer believed to have been accompanied by a 'civil war' during which Luciano and his allies purged scores of Maranzano's associates on the same day. Rather, the transfer of power occurred relatively peacefully.

Now at the top of the Italian American criminal hierarchy, Luciano called a meeting of major crime leaders and outlined his plans for a larger, more comprehensive, and more orderly criminal organization. Besides eliminating the position of 'boss of bosses,' which had only created envy, Luciano created a crime commission made up of the five leaders of the major Italian American crime organizations in the New York area. This commission seems not to have acted as a centralized government but as a mediating agency. Although Luciano preferred Americanizers among his associates, he reconciled with traditionalists like Joe Bonanno and Joseph Profaci for the sake of general harmony. Yet he insisted upon a new rule forbidding the traditional Italian American practice of kissing among males as a form of greeting, as he feared it would attract attention. The rule has not lasted in the long run. Another of Luciano's achievements was to have established a policy of peaceful coexistence with non-Italians, including Irish and Jewish criminals. Some scholars even believe that Jewish gangsters were allowed to participate in the syndicate alongside Italians. Not only did Luciano expand Italian American criminal enterprise into the larger American community, in the form of gambling, labour racketeering, prostitution, loan-sharking, and narcotics, but he introduced on a scale larger than that of Torrio and Capone more modern methods of business organization, emphasizing the impersonal value of profitability rather than, as in the past, the paternalistic protection and welfare of each member of the criminal society. These far-sighted innovations enabled Italian American criminal organizations to grow and diversify following Prohibition. They were introduced, however, within the traditional framework of a family or brotherhood structured not as a business bureaucracy but by real and artificial ties of loyalty and respect.

Despite his nickname, Luciano ran afoul of the law in 1936, when he received a prison sentence of thirty to fifty years for participating in the New York City prostitution trade. His nemesis was New York special prosecutor Thomas Dewey, who is alleged to have convicted Luciano illegally. When in *Mean Streets* Uncle Giovanni speaks of Luciano as having been present ('there') 'on the docks' during the Second World War, he refers to what may have been a scheme engineered by Luciano's gang-land allies to have him transferred from the forbidding Dannemora Prison in upper New York State, where he had been confined since his convic-tion. On 11 February 1942 the *Normandie*, a luxury liner transformed into a troop ship, was destroyed in a fire supposedly caused by saboteurs. It was also feared that leakage of information from the New York waterfront had resulted in the loss of United States shipping to German U-boats. Luciano and others have claimed that the mob burned the *Normandie* so as to create the illusion of a threat to the waterfront, which the Mafia had plundered for years, and whose security would then necessitate Luciano's collab-oration with the government in exchange for his release. Actually, the *Normandie* fire was probably accidental. In any case, these real and imag-ined threats resulted in Luciano's transfer to the more pleasant Great Meadow Prison so as to exert control over dockworkers, who were en-listed in the patrolling of the docks for evidence of espionage and sabo-tage. According to Luciano, Dewey concocted the Navy protection operation to distract attention from his illegal methods in convicting Luciano. Doubts have also been raised regarding the value of Luciano's intervention. In 1946 he was deported by order of then-governor Thomas Dewey and spent most of the remainder of his life in Italy, where he died in 1962.

In view of Uncle Giovanni's admiration for Luciano, and also in view of Luciano's preference for Americanized gangsters rather than the old-fashioned type, the so-called Mustache Petes, it may seem ironic that the film portrays the mustached Uncle Giovanni as exemplifying the second-generation crime boss, in contrast with Charlie's peer group, who are largely Americanized in manners and deportment. For instance, whereas Giovanni is associated with old-style Sicilian music sung in dialect, the peer group, save for Michael, is associated with rock and roll.

See Sifakis, *Mafia Encyclopedia*, 200–2; Kobler, *Capone*, 25, 53, 69–73, 142, 145, 237–8, 245–6; Gosch and Hammer, *Last Testament of Lucky Luciano*, *passim*; Nelli, *Business of Crime*, xii, 100–6, 139–40, 180–3, 199–200, 201–8, 239–41, 256–8; Nelli, *Italians in Chicago*, 148–52, 155, 212–15; Feder and Joesten, *Luciano Story*, 37, 64–71, 83, 93–6, 135–6, 176–229; Alan A. Block, 'A Modern Marriage of Convenience: A Collaboration between Organized Crime and U.S. Intelligence,' in *Organized Crime*, ed. Kelly, 65–8; Reppetto, *American Mafia*, 132–61, 172–80; Ianni, *Family Business*, 55–6; Inciardi, *Careers in Crime*, 107–8, 111, 117–18, 119–21; Alba, *Italian Americans*, 63–4, 95–7; Albert Fried, *The Rise and Fall of the Jewish Gangster in America* (New

York: Holt, Rinehart, and Winston, 1980), 120–2, 126–8, 231, 240–3; George Murray, *The Legacy of Al Capone: Portraits and Annals of Chicago's Public Enemies* (New York: G.P. Putnam's Sons, 1975), 18–20; John T. McPhaul, *Johnny Torrio: First of the Gang Lords* (New Rochelle, N.J.: Arlington House, 1970), 23–6.

30 The Mafia is believed to avoid violence wherever possible. To quote Henner Hess, 'No Mafioso, not even a novice, need apply actual physical violence all the time to assert his will. Mostly the realization of the ultimate possibility is enough.' Because the Mafioso is known to have his organization behind him, violence remains his 'last resort.' Although assassination and other forms of violence were fairly standard in the early twentieth-century Italian American underworld, Lucky Luciano and other bosses of the next generation viewed impulsive and sporadic violence as dysfunctional, since it not only required great expense but attracted police and media attention. Accordingly, the Mafia code is thought to limit the use of violence, normally employing it to check violence among its members. The reduction of violence, which Frederic Homer sees as crucial to the development of the Mafia in the twentieth century, was already noted in the 1930s by William Foote Whyte in his study of Italian American streetcorner society. See Bliss, *Scorsese and Cimino*, 68; Whyte, *Street Corner Society*, 115, 117, 121; Homer, *Guns and Garlic*, 9, 51, 109, 110–11; Hess, *Mafia and Mafiosi*, 69, 76; Gambetta, *Sicilian Mafia*, 41–2; Reuter, *Disorganized Crime*, 135–6. Alan A. Block finds the claim of a reduction of violence within the Mafia to be unsupported and in some ways contradicted by known facts. See Block, 'Organized Crime: History and Historiography,' in Block, *Space, Time, and Organized Crime*, 26, 29, 30–8.

31 Scorsese acknowledges the ordering and pacifying role played by Mafiosi in Sicily and its parallels in the early Italian American immigrant settlements, where gangsters frequently mediated in disputes and 'were the law in many different respects.' See Kelly, *Martin Scorsese: A Journey*, 26. Commenting on Sicily, Hess notes that the Mafioso, as *uomo d'ordine*, has a protective mediatory function within society to this day and often intervenes on the side of order (if not of justice). For instance, in the past he protected landowners' property against bandits. Daniel Bell, Volkman and Cummings, and Stephen R. Fox make similar observations regarding Italian American neighbourhoods. See Hess, *Mafia and Mafiosi*, 146–8, 171–2; Bell, 'Crime as an American Way of Life,' 147; Volkman and Cummings, *Goombata*, 113–14; Abadinsky, *Organized Crime*, 37–8.

32 However, the crime bosses studied by Ianni were hard-line 'hawkish' Republicans in contrast with the Democrat Uncle Giovanni. See Ianni,

Family Business, 84. During the period depicted in *Mean Streets*, many Italian Americans were abandoning the Democrats for the Republicans because of the civil rights movement, student protest, and the liberalizing influence of the 1960s.

33 Henry, 'Raging Bull,' 94.

34 Flatley, 'Martin Scorsese's Gamble,' 57.

35 'Skag' is sixties slang for an ugly girl.

36 Douglas Brode, *The Films of Robert De Niro*, 4th ed. (New York: Kensington, 2001), 73; Bliss, *Scorsese and Cimino*, 67–8; Hosvey et al., 'Passion of St. Charles,' 180; Kelly, *Martin Scorsese: First Decade*, 167; Marilyn Yaquinto, *Pump'Em Full of Lead: A Look at Gangsters on Film* (New York: Twayne, 1998), 121.

37 Girard, *Deceit, Desire, and the Novel*, 15–17, 16–17n.

38 Gans, *Urban Villagers*, 40, 63, 65, 80–8. Writing of a streetcorner society of a generation earlier, Whyte remarks 'that the boys valued both "prestige" and "respect," but that the smooth functioning of a group required informal recognition of prestige gradations. There was general annoyance when a member showed too much conceit. Yet though Whyte notes conflicts over prestige and authority among the groups he studied, he reports no violence, which the boys sublimated in bowling competitions. See Whyte, *Street Corner Society*, 3–4, 6, 12, 13, 16, 23, 35, 259, 272.

39 'Dialogue on Film,' 44.

40 On 'mook,' see Goldstein and Jacobson, 'Martin Scorsese Tells All,' 63.

41 Mangione and Morreale, *La Storia*, 416.

42 Lourdeaux, *Italian and Irish Filmmakers*, 218, 229, 230–1, 235, 245, 246.

43 Mark Nicholls ignores the mob's positive role within the ethic community in *Mean Streets*. See Nicholls, *Scorsese's Men*, xiv.

44 Kolker, *Cinema of Loneliness*, 176.

45 Kelly, *Martin Scorsese: First Decade*, 171.

46 On the 'Wild Woman' as an anthropological motif, see Tiffany and Adams, *Wild Woman*, xi, 1–15, 16, 23, 29, 30, 31, 32. The Wild Woman exemplifies primitivism and overt eroticism while transgressing against patriarchal law. A dangerous sexual aggressor well aware of her powers, she causes male anxiety and thus falls victim to resentful masculine domination.

47 Grist, *Films of Martin Scorsese*, 84–5.

48 Grist, *Films of Martin Scorsese*, 85–6.

49 Maxfield, 'Worst Part,' 283. Maxfield, who attributes Charlie's lack of commitment to Teresa to his and Johnny Boy's latently homosexual relationship, claims that Charlie's dream of ejaculated blood equates sex

with pain and thus indicates lack of interest in Teresa. This interpretation mistakenly applies a 'universal' psychology while ignoring the characters' ethnic background. Charlie's dream of blood, like his reference to Teresa as a 'cunt,' reflects Italian Catholic sexual attitudes, which do not keep him from pursuing Teresa sexually but which fill him with guilt for sleeping with a 'bad' girl outside marriage. Maxfield's assumptions cannot explain Charlie's attraction to Diane, in which his impulses again war with his ethnic code. See James F. Maxfield, 'The Worst Part: Martin Scorsese's *Mean Streets,' Literature/Film Quarterly* 23, no. 4 (1995): 283.

50 Grist, *Films of Martin Scorsese*, 84–5. See also Jacobs, *Hollywood Renaissance*, 136, 144.

51 Kolker, *Cinema of Loneliness*, 171–2.

52 Proverbs 2:15, 21:8; Psalms 125:5; Luke 3:5.

53 Girard, 'The Plague in Literature and Myth,' in Girard, *'To Double Business Bound,'* 136–54.

54 'Dialogue on Film,' 36; Grist, *Films of Martin Scorsese*, 76; Taylor, 'Martin Scorsese,' 328.

55 *Scorsese on Scorsese*, ed. Thompson and Christie, 48; Lourdeaux, *Italian and Irish Filmmakers*, 241–2; Kelly, *Martin Scorsese: First Decade*, 125.

56 'There is no fear in love, but perfect love casts out fear.' 1 John 4:18.

57 Bell, *Fate and Honor, Family and Village*, 105–6.

58 Matthew 26:18. Practically speaking, Michael's ambush calls to mind the retaliatory style favoured by the Mafiosi whom Michael emulates: 'His vengeance must on no account be direct or open; it must take place in that mysterious and opaque manner which magnifies the awe surrounding him; it must strike not blindly but deliberately ... he waits until the moment of vengeance arrives.' See Hess, *Mafia and Mafiosi*, 72. In *The Godfather* (1971) Don Vito Corleone's son Santino (James Caan) is killed because he lacks the patience to postpone vengeance.

59 Matthew 25: 31–46.

60 Moss and Cappanari, 'Mal' Occhio, Ayin ha ra, Oculus fascinus, Judenblick,' 8, 9.

61 Ianni, *Family Business*, 18–19; Pitrè, *Spettacoli e feste*, 288, 305, 306.

62 On epilepsy as a 'sacred' disease inviting expulsive violence, see Girard, *Theater of Envy*, 205. On the Sicilian view of mental disorders as diseases, see Chapman, *Milocca*, 217.

63 Gans observes that Italian American women of Boston's West End usually led in the acculturation process through their greater receptivity to education and desire for employment in the white-collar world outside the community. Most West Enders kept the middle-class mainstream at a

distance and would 'reject other West Enders who stray[ed] too far from
the peer group society and adopt[ed] middle class ways.' Two decades
later, in the film *Saturday Night Fever*, the Italian American woman strikes
out from the ethnic neighbourhood while her boyfriend follows hesitantly.
See Gans, *Urban Villagers*, 216, 221–2; Glazer and Moynihan, *Beyond the
Melting Pot*, 198.

64 Girard, *Violence and the Sacred*, 128.

65 One of Scorsese's favourite films, Rossellini's *Flowers of St Francis* (1950),
contains a scene suggestive of the sacrificial crisis, yet so shrewdly manipulated by the saint that the result is neither social discord nor retaliatory violence but the suppression of angry competition for the sake of
peace and reconciliation. In the film's concluding scene St Francis announces to his community of monks that they must now split up to
pursue their preaching duties. Such a situation could conceivably awaken
a bitterly quarrelsome rivalry among the monks, with each demanding his
right to preach in the most attractive regions and cities of Italy. To avert
trouble, St Francis orders each saint to 'spin on the spot where your feet
are planted, as children do when they are playing: don't stop until you
feel dizzy.' At the height of their vertigo they are to fall to the ground, so
that each of their heads points in a different direction of the compass.
Indicating the region of each saint's preaching duties, these randomly
determined directions are interpreted by St Francis as the gift of providence. In his ingenious strategem, the randomness and disorientation that
normally play a role in the escalating vertiginous chaos of the sacrificial
crisis have in a sense been turned against themselves and made to serve
the cause of social harmony. Rather than imploding inwardly in violent
rivalry, whether against St Francis or its other members, the monastic
community radiates outwards so as to extend its peaceful message. Furthermore, St Francis does this by means of a childish game, reminiscent
of Jesus's statement that one must become as little children to enter the
kingdom of heaven.

66 Hosvey et al., 'Passion of St Charles,' 183. Scorsese's idea of Charlie
disguised as Christ was very possibly inspired by Sicilian religiosity. In
theatrical representations of the Passion of Christ performed in Polizzi
Generosa, participants impersonate Christ and other biblical characters.
See Buttita, 'L'immagine, il gesto, e il tempo ritrovato,' 31. According to
Pitrè, from the fourteenth at least into the nineteenth century the celebration of holy occasions in the cities, towns, and villages of Sicily was often
accompanied by sacred dramas, scenic portrayals, and processions portraying biblical scenes, including the life of Christ; of all themes, the most

popular was the Passion. These representations were typical not only of large cities like Palermo and Messina but of smaller centres such as Trapani, Castelbuono, Nicosia, Avola, and Scorsese's ancestral home town of Polizzi Generosa. Pitrè, *Spettacoli e feste*, 4–6, 10, 15–19, 26–9, 31–2n, 35, 37, 80–1, 86–90, 105–8, 110–14, 116–18, 120–2, 124–5, 137, 143, 145, 217–18. *Il Mio Viaggio* contains a photograph of a festival in the home town of Scorsese's father's or mother's family, with an actor in the guise of Christ carried supine on a cross by townsmen.

67 Ehrenstein, *Scorsese Picture*, 35.

68 *Scorsese on Scorsese*, ed. Thompson and Christie, 47; Bliss, *Word Made Flesh*, 35.

69 After gambling, loan-sharking is perhaps the Mafia's most lucrative business, in addition to providing it with a convenient way of putting its cash to good use. It is unclear, though, whether Michael loans money to Johnny Boy as a private entrepreneur or as an associate of a Mafia family, to which he would owe part of his earnings. The latter may seem more likely, as one would not expect a loan shark to operate free of charge in a prized area like Little Italy. Yet Reuter reports many instances in which the mob fails to monopolize loan-sharking in lucrative segments of the New York market. In any case, loan-sharking in urban neighbourhoods is usually based on a usurious rate of 20 per cent per week. For every five dollars loaned at the beginning of a week, the borrower owes six at its end. Probably deriving from the Yiddish 'vigorish,' the term 'vig' refers to each unit of interest or 'point,' usually measured in hundred-dollar amounts. A loan shark, however, is often willing to charge the highest possible rates. If the borrower fails to repay the entire loan, that is, principal plus interest, on the due day, he is still required to pay the interest, which is compounded for the following week. On a hundred-dollar loan charging twenty-dollars interest, the borrower must pay twenty dollars a week later, but this payment does not count against the next week's interest. Thus interest compounds from week to week, and the borrower must pay until the principal and interest are both paid off. What makes loan-sharking so destructive is that a borrower must repay a loan many times over without reducing the principal. The lender will sometimes content himself with repayment of partial amounts if sufficiently ample and steadily forthcoming. If a debtor cannot repay, valuable information may serve as a substitute. The penalty for non-payment or insufficient payment includes broken legs, the rape of a spouse, and even death. The loan shark's customers often consist of gamblers with heavy debts needing quick repayment but who cannot obtain a banking loan. Other typical

victims include burglars, gamblers, thieves who need cash while awaiting their next 'score,' and businesspeople lacking normal sources of credit. The term 'loan shark' is a corruption of 'Shylock' (Homer, *Guns and Garlic*, 153). According to Benjamin Nelson, the modern legitimation of usury in the broad sense of interest on loans marks the end of medieval Christian fraternity and its supplanting by the impersonal capitalist-commercial world of 'universal otherhood.' Although Michael lives in a world in which interest, once known as usury, is permitted, his demand of excessive rates from Johnny Boy – who, as Charlie reminds him, belongs to his Italian American neighbourhood and is thus a kind of 'brother' – imports Michael's alienation from Christian values as well as the deteriorating sense of community in *Mean Streets*. See Homer, *Guns and Garlic*, 153–4; Ernest Volkman and John Cummings, *The Heist: How a Gang Stole 8,000,000 at Kennedy Airport and Lived to Regret It* (New York: Franklin Watts, 1986), 11–12; Sifakis, *Mafia Encyclopedia*, 191–3; Reuter, *Disorganized Crime*, 85, 86, 87, 99, 100, 105–6; Benjamin Nelson, *The Idea of Usury: From Universal Brotherhood to Universal Otherhood* (Chicago: Univ. of Chicago Press, 1969), *passim*; Abadinsky, *Organized Crime*, 237–40; Roemer, *Roemer*, 61–2; William F. Roemer, *The Enforcer: Spilotro – The Chicago Mob's Man over Las Vegas* (New York: Donald I. Fine, 1994), 22.

70 Matthew 5:21–6; Benedict T. Viviano, 'The Gospel according to Matthew,' in Raymond Brown, S.S. Joseph, A. Fitzmyer, SJ, and Raymond E. Murphy, eds., *The New Jerome Biblical Commentary* (New York: Prentice-Hall, 1988), 642; *The Anchor Bible: Matthew*, ed. W.F. Albright and C.S. Mann (Garden City, N.Y.: Doubleday, 1971), 62; *The Interpreter's Bible*, Vol. 7, exegesis by Sherman E. Johnson, exposition by George A. Buttrick (New York: Abingdon, 1951), 294–8.

71 Hand-to-neck movements are associated in the film with Charlie, Johnny Boy, Tony, and Michael. See Friedman, *Cinema of Martin Scorsese*, 36; Bliss, *Word Made Flesh*, 36–7; Bliss, *Scorsese and Cimino*, 77–8. Charlie rubs his neck when Johnny Boy stays over in Charlie's apartment, scratches his neck while talking to Uncle Giovanni in the restaurant, and hits Johnny Boy in the neck in order to make a point. Johnny Boy raises his hand to adjust his collar as he and Charlie leave the cemetery, a gesture anticipating his imminent wound to the neck. Tony rubs his neck in the scene in which Michael confronts Johnny Boy in Tony's bar.

72 'Dunsky' remains part of the mob vocabulary. See Ralph Blumenthal, foreword to Gotti, *Gotti Tapes*, xviii.

73 Keyser, *Martin Scorsese*, 40. Scorsese refers to Charlie's 'stigmata' in the final scene. See 'Martin Scorsese,' in Tony Macklin and Nick Pici, eds.,

Voices from the Set: The Film Heritage Interviews (Lanham, Md.: Scarecrow, 2000), 41.

74 See John 19:34 and 1 John 5:6–9; Blake, 'Redeemed in Blood,' 9n; Ronald S. Librach, 'The Last Temptation in *Mean Streets* and *Raging Bull*,' *Literature/ Film Quarterly* 20, no. 1 (1992): 15.

75 Johnny Boy calls to mind the two criminals who were crucified alongside Jesus, and whose legs were broken before they died.

76 Kelly, *Martin Scorsese: First Decade*, 18.

77 In view of Uncle Giovanni's emulation of Lucky Luciano, it is notable that the latter is mentioned in Lang's film, in which Italian American crime boss Lagana, fearing bad publicity, declares: 'I don't want to land in the same ditch with the Lucky Lucianos.' Lagana alludes to Luciano's deportation in the 1940s, a fate that the low-profile Giovanni has avoided.

78 Gans's point is noted in DeConde, *Half Bitter, Half Sweet*, 330–1.

79 Keyser, *Martin Scorsese*, 40; Librach, 'Last Temptation,' 15.

80 Keyser, *Martin Scorsese*, 40; Bliss, *Word Made Flesh*, x.

81 Bliss, *Word Made Flesh*, 26.

82 Kelly, *Martin Scorsese: First Decade*, 167.

83 'Dialogue on Film,' 15, 36; see also Kelly, *Martin Scorsese: First Decade*, 18. Connelly finds Charlie misguided in trying to help Johnny Boy, whom he ends up hurting unintentionally. See Connelly, *Martin Scorsese*, 4. Maxfield remarks the same irony. See Maxfield, 'Worst Part,' 280.

84 Scorsese remarks the irony in Jacobs, *Hollywood Renaissance*, 138.

6. The Abject God: *Raging Bull*

1 Much of the information in the preceding paragraphs is based on Jake La Motta's autobiography, *Raging Bull: My Story* (Englewood Cliffs, N.J.: Prentice-Hall, 1970), *passim*.

2 Henry, 'Raging Bull,' 84; 'Martin Scorsese Directs,' PBS Television, New York, 16 July 1990; Kelly, *Martin Scorsese: A Journey*, 122, 124; Dougan, *Martin Scorsese*, 64.

3 Dougan, *Martin Scorsese*, 55–8; Kelly, *Martin Scorsese: A Journey*, 117–18, 121.

4 Biskind, *Easy Riders, Raging Bulls*, 377.

5 Biskind, *Easy Riders, Raging Bulls*, 378.

6 Dougan, *Martin Scorsese*, 58; see also 60, 63, 64. See also Biskind, *Easy Riders, Raging Bulls*, 386–7; Occhiogrosso, *Once a Catholic*, 100.

7 Scorsese, 'Confessions,' 138.

8 Peter Biskind, 'Slouching Toward Hollywood,' 193; Dougan, *Martin Scorsese*, 63–4.

9 *Scorsese on Scorsese*, ed. Thompson and Christie, 77; Henry, 'Raging Bull,' 99.
10 Dougan, *Martin Scorsese*, 64; Andy Dougan, *Untouchable: A Biography of Robert De Niro* (New York: Thunder's Mouth Press, 1996), 118.
11 Dougan, *Martin Scorsese*, 64; Kelly, *Martin Scorsese: A Journey*, 124.
12 Kelly, *Martin Scorsese: A Journey*, 124.
13 Dougan, *Untouchable*, 116.
14 La Motta, *Raging Bull*, 13, 14, 53–65, 69–71, 76–7, 88–9, 93, 170–1, 165–6, 173–5, 199, 208.
15 Noted by Henry, 'Raging Bull,' 89. La Motta never asserts a direct causal link between, on the one hand, his juvenile delinquency, bad temper, love of violence, and lack of trust, and, on the other, his brutal father and impoverished upbringing. In his view, he neither indulged in self-pity nor sought compassion. Yet he mentions that he had assaulted bookie Harry Gordon because of his intolerable home environment, of which he also complains to Father Joseph. See La Motta, *Raging Bull*, 1–2, 3, 5, 11, 56–7.
16 Dougan, *Untouchable*, 119; Henry, 'Raging Bull,' 89.
17 La Motta, who managed his own career, assigned his brother a fictional managerial role only because each boxer was required to have a manager. See La Motta, *Raging Bull*, 85.
18 On the self-help theme in the boxing film, see Ronald Bergan, *Sport in the Movies* (New York: Proteus, 1982), 34, 35; Pam Cook, 'Masculinity in Crisis?' *Screen* 23, nos. 3–4 (1982): 42; Leger Grindon, 'Art and Genre in *Raging Bull*,' in Kevin J. Hayes, ed., *Martin Scorsese's 'Raging Bull'* (Cambridge: Cambridge Univ. Press, 2005), 20, 22, 24, 25.
19 Bergan, *Sport in the Movies*, 9, 14, 15, 26, 30, 35; Edward J. Recchia, 'Martin Scorsese: *Raging Bull*: In Violence *Veritas*?' *Aethlon: The Journal of Sports Literature* 7, no. 2 (1990): 22. In *Kid Galahad* (1937), the corrupt Italian American boxing manager Nick Donati (Edward G. Robinson) redeems himself before being shot and killed. In *Somebody Up There Likes Me*, Robert Loggia plays fixer Frank Peppo, who threatens Rocky Graziano's career.
20 As La Motta told his friend Peter Petrella, the mob, which had long interfered with boxing, came to control it in the 1940s. La Motta had to pay the mob twenty thousand dollars for his shot at the middleweight championship, a bout for which, despite his victory, he received only nineteen thousand dollars. Fortunately, La Motta had bet on himself and won sixteen thousand on the side.
   Already in the later nineteenth century the underworld had penetrated boxing, fixing fights and 'owning' fighters. This is partly explained by the fact that boxers and gangsters emerge from the same lower-class urban

environment that, remote from the public eye, affords excellent cover for corruption. After Prohibition the mob became involved increasingly in boxing as a means of expanding its income, and in the 1940s and 1950s it enjoyed a virtual tyranny over the sport.

In La Motta's day the two most influential fixers were West Coast–based gambler Franky Carbo, a former member of 'Murder, Inc.' with close ties to the Lucchese crime family, and his assistant Blinky Palermo, another gambler who ran the Philadelphia numbers game. Their job was to manipulate the odds and outcomes of boxing nationwide so as to ensure the mob its edge. The assignment of fights was almost entirely in their hands, especially in the heavyweight division. Carbo's power lay in his control of the managers in the Boxing Managers Guild of New York, which enabled him to extort large payments from the International Boxing Club and its director, James Norris, who had no choice but to pay Carbo to keep the guild in line so as to ensure a steady supply of boxing dates. Outside New York Carbo colluded with state boxing commissions.

Palermo and Carbo arranged not only the fix in which La Motta 'lost' to Fox but his championship bout with Cerdan two years later. La Motta's 1951 title defence against Robinson came about only after consultation with Carbo. Lightweight champion (1947–50) Ike Williams paid Palermo a great deal of money for fighting opportunities denied to him before he made Palermo his manager. According to Rocky Graziano in testimony given in 1947, gangsters repeatedly attempted to bribe him to throw fights, and he even feigned illness to avoid a fix. For his helpful candour Graziano lost his boxing licence temporarily. Sugar Ray Robinson was similarly approached, and Rocky Marciano claimed to have given half his earnings to the mob.

Carbo was indicted for extortion in 1959 along with Palermo and others. The public was now becoming increasingly aware of the mob's penetration of boxing thanks to the Senate AntiTrust and Monopoly Committee, which was formed in 1960, and before which La Motta testified. Carbo was again convicted in 1961 and sentenced to twenty-five years in prison, where he died. Palermo was paroled in 1971 after serving seven years of a fifteen-year sentence. While in prison he and Carbo continued to fix fights, and even into the late 1980s Palermo influenced boxing.

See Jeffrey T. Sammonds, *Beyond the Ring: The Role of Boxing in American Society* (Urbana and Chicago: Univ. of Illinois Press, 1988), xv, 139–48, 151–6, 168, 171–3, 177–83, 255–7; John Sugden, *Boxing and Society: An International Analysis* (Manchester: Manchester Univ. Press, 1996), 30, 40–3, 49; Turkus and Feder, *Murder, Inc.*, 276–81, 283; Fox, *Blood and Power*, 89–92,

354–8; Bondanella, *Hollywood Italians*, 96–7, 107; Roemer, *Roemer*, 309; Gerald Early, 'The Romance of Toughness: La Motta and Graziano,' in Gerald Early, *The Culture of Bruising: Essays on Prize-Fighting, Literature, and Modern American Culture* (Hopewell, N.J.: Ecco Press, 1994), 90–1; Volkman, *Gangbusters*, 62. See also La Motta, *Raging Bull*, 78, 79, 86, 113–14, 123–4, 156–60, 161–3.

21 *Scorsese on Scorsese*, ed. Thompson and Christie, 80.

22 Steven G. Kellman, Introduction to Kellman, ed., *Perspectives on Raging Bull* (New York: G.K. Hall, 1984), 6.

23 Connelly, *Martin Scorsese*, 71.

24 Friedman, *Cinema of Martin Scorsese*, 115.

25 *Scorsese on Scorsese*, ed. Thompson and Christie, 80.

26 Denby, 'Brute Force,' *New York Magazine*, 1 December 1980, 61–3, in *Perspectives on Raging Bull*, ed. Kellman, 45. For the sake of realism, De Niro trained under Jake La Motta himself, with whom he underwent roughly a thousand rounds of sparring. See Bergan, *Sport in the Movies*, 12.

27 Kellman, Introduction to *Perspectives on Raging Bull*, ed. Kellman, 8. Black-and-white captures the mood and tone of La Motta's life as he experienced it: 'Now, sometimes at night, when I think back, I feel like I'm looking at an old black-and-white movie of myself. Why it should be in black-and-white, I don't know, but it is.' See La Motta, *Raging Bull*, 2.

28 *Scorsese on Scorsese*, ed. Thompson and Christie, 154.

29 Richard Corliss, 'Animal House,' *Time*, 27 November 1980, 100, in *Perspectives on Raging Bull*, ed. Kellman, 40.

30 Henry, 'Raging Bull,' 92.

31 A likely consequence of this syndrome in La Motta's autobiography is his sexual incapacity with 'high class' women, 'not the tramp kind': 'I'd have some block about making them even if they wanted it, like they were too good for me.' See *Raging Bull*, 77.

32 Vickie's portrayal in the style of a forties movie star is perhaps inspired by La Motta's description of her: 'She looked like a beauty-contest winner, like the blonde who plays the lead in one of those movies about the queen of the campus.' See *Raging Bull*, 119.

33 The Debonair Social Club actually existed as a mob hang-out. See *Raging Bull*, 135.

34 Scorsese comments: 'I was happy with [his own cinematic treatment of] the Copacabana and the Debonair Social Social Club, one of those masculine sanctuaries where men can be alone and do their business quietly together.' See Henry, 'Raging Bull,' 88.

35 Whereas Nicholls one-sidedly focuses on La Motta's struggle to maintain

his professional integrity against mob exploitation, Leger Grindon rightly notes that *Raging Bull* eschews stock types of demonic gangsters in favour of a more complex portrayal of Tommy Como as a 'wise grandfather' and 'peacemaker,' so that La Motta's stubbornness is accentuated. See Nicholls, *Scorsese's Men*, xiv, 5, 47; Grindon, 'Art and Genre in *Raging Bull*,' 30.

36 Eric Dunning observes that many sports have 'religious roots,' and that Durkheim's study of the 'collective effervescence' in religious rituals of Australian aborigines calls to mind the 'emotion and excitement generated at a modern sports event.' According to John Sugden, 'formalized versions of unarmed combat were regular features of secular and sacred festivals in the ancient cultures which flourished around the Mediterranean.' Similarly, medieval religious festivals were accompanied by ball games between towns and guilds. In his study of the relation of sport to the 'civilizing process,' Norbert Elias stresses the mimetic character of sporting events, which, in the disciplined and administered world of modernity, produce the emotion of real-life situations for the purpose of a cathartic effect, though without danger for the audience. Elias also observes a reduction of sporting violence in the transition to modernity. For instance, whereas Greek and Roman boxers ignored weight classes and often fought to the death, modern boxing is more 'civilized' owing to a greater concern for fairness and the introduction of rules that limit injury and suffering. Yet unlike the bloodless athletic contests prevalent today, boxing remains a blood sport rather than a sport as the term is now understood.

There is some question, though, whether boxing should properly be seen as ritualistic, whatever its possible ritual origins. Although Mary and Max Gluckman acknowledge that games and athletic contests, like the drama, originate in rituals or in connection with them, they hold that, unlike the regularity and predictability of prescribed forms that typify a religious ritual and are crucial to its efficacy, both athletic contests and drama are much less stereotyped while allowing for spontaneity, variety, and unpredictable outcomes. More recently, however, many anthropologists have adopted what David D. Gilmore terms a 'less restrictive' approach to ritual, defining 'all forms of standardized social action with or without a religious element' as 'secular ritual.' According to Alessandro Falassi, though games have uncertain outcomes, rules are canonic and ritual provides the paradigm. He sees competitive sporting events as a 'corruption' of older ritual combats with fixed obligatory endings. For Victor Turner, modern athletic contests inherit functions from religious ritual.

See Norbert Elias and Eric Dunning, *Quest for Excitement: Sport and*

Leisure in the Civilizing Process (Oxford: Basil Blackwell, 1985), *passim;* Sugden, *Boxing and Society*, 10; Mary Gluckman and Max Gluckman, 'On Drama, and Games and Athletic Contests,' in Sally F. Moore and Barbara G. Meyerhoff, eds., *Secular Ritual* (Amsterdam: Van Gorcum, 1977), 227–41. (See also in the same volume Sally F. Moore and Barbara S. Meyerhoff, 'Secular Ritual: Forms and Meanings,' 3–24; Gilmore, *Carnival and Culture*, 26–7); Falassi, 'Festival: Definition and Morphology,' 5; Turner, 'Carnival, Ritual, and Play,' 76, 77.

37 Tomasulo, 'Raging Bully,' 183.

38 Kelly, *Martin Scorsese: A Journey*, 134.

39 Henry, 'Raging Bull,' 97.

40 The riot immediately following the announcement of Reeves's victory calls to mind Elias's observation that the controlled mimesis of an athletic contest sometimes fails to work, so that, as violence spills beyond the playing field, the distinction between real and staged battles evaporates in a breakdown in the 'civilizing process.' See Norbert Elias, *Sport and Leisure*, 43, 54. See also in the same volume Elias and Eric Dunning, 'The Quest for Excitement in Leisure,' 80.

41 Stanley Kaufman, 'Look Back at Anger,' *New Republic*, 6 December 1980, in *Perspectives on Raging Bull*, ed. Kellman, 49. David Alan Mellor refers to the 'sonic animalism that fills *Raging Bull's* soundtrack with the uncannily abstracted noises of elephants during the fight scenes.' See Mellor, 'The Ring of Impossibility, or, The Failure to Recover Authenticity in the Recent Cinema of Boxing,' in David Chandler et al., eds., *Boxer: An Anthology of Writings on Boxing and Visual Culture* (London: Institute of International Visual Arts, 1996), 82.

42 Denby, 'Brute Force,' 44; Hatch, qtd. in Brode, *Films of Robert De Niro*, 133; Arnold, 'The Boxing Brute of *Raging Bull*,' *Washington Post*, 19 December 1980, in *Perspectives on Raging Bull*, ed. Kellman, 55.

43 David Friedkin, 'Blind Rage and "Brotherly Love": The Male Psyche at War with Itself in *Raging Bull*,' in *Perspectives on Raging Bull*, ed. Kellman, 122.

44 Kolker, *Cinema of Loneliness*, 172; Sarris, 'Mean Fighter from Mean Streets,' in *Perspectives on Raging Bull*, ed. Kellman, 36 (see also 34); Menand, 'Methods and Madnesses,' *Bennington Review* 12 (December 1981): 58–65, in *Perspectives on Raging Bull*, ed. Kellman, 65.

45 Henry, 'Raging Bull,' 89, 93.

46 Richard Coombs, 'Hell Up in the Bronx,' *Sight and Sound* (Spring 1981): 128–30.

47 Arnold, 'Boxing Brute,' 55; Bergan, *Sport in the Movies*, 41; Carroll, noted in Biskind, *Easy Riders, Raging Bulls*, 399.

48 Kaufman, 'Look Back at Anger,' 51.
49 Kolker, *Cinema of Loneliness*, 172.
50 Friedman, *Cinema of Martin Scorsese*, 120.
51 Early, 'Romance of Toughness,' 93–4; Brode, *Films of Robert DeNiro*, 133–4; *Variety* review, 12 November 1980, in *Perspectives on Raging Bull*, ed. Kellman, 26.
52 Joyce Carol Oates, *On Boxing* (Garden City: Doubleday, 1987), 25, 30, 32, 60, 83, 85.
53 See Ronald Levao, 'Reading the Fights: Making Sense of Professional Boxing,' in Joyce Carol Oates and Daniel Halpern, eds., *Reading the Fights: The Best Writing about the Most Controversial of Sports* (New York: Prentice-Hall, 1988), 11.
54 This legend is taken seriously in Stallone's *Rocky* (1976) but poked fun at in *The Main Event* (1979). See Bergan, *Sport in the Movies*, 15–16. La Motta apparently took it seriously. See *Raging Bull*, 96.
55 Lawrence de Garis, 'Be a Buddy to Your Buddy: Male Identity, Aggression, and Intimacy in a Boxing Gym,' in Jim McKay et al., eds., *Masculinities, Gender Relations, and Sport* (Thousand Oaks, Calif.: Sage, 2000), 88, 89, 94, 97, 100.
56 Noted in De Garis, 'Be a Buddy,' 89.
57 Levao, 'Reading the Fights,' 10.
58 See Early, 'I Only Like It Better When the Pain Comes: More Notes toward a Cultural Definition of Boxing,' in *Reading the Fights*, ed. Oates and Halpern, 42–5.
59 George Garrett, 'My One-Eyed Coach,' in *Reading the Fights*, ed. Oates and Halpern, 255, 257.
60 Friedman, *Cinema of Martin Scorsese*, 116.
61 Wood, *Hollywood from Vietnam to Reagan*, 219–31. Even before his interview with Wood, Scorsese had mentioned such a 'subtext.' With the filming of *Raging Bull* about to begin, Mary Pat Kelly remarked to Scorsese that 'a friend who boxed as an amateur told me that sometimes you form such close relationships with the person you're fighting, that at the end you love him. Fighters do hug at the end.' Scorsese replies: 'Oh yes, the film has very much to do with that, very much to do with that confusion, sexual confusion, sexual ambiguity. But not only sexual – the emotional, even more than emotion. Because in the ring that love is more than emotion.' See Kelly, *Martin Scorsese: First Decade*, 32.
62 Michael S. Kimmel, 'Ethnicity and the Erotics of Violence,' in *Perspectives on Raging Bull*, ed. Kellman, 92–3.
63 Friedkin, 'Blind Rage,' 122–9. Nicholls similarly contends that, in urging

Joey to punch him, Jake submits masochistically to a symbolic rape. However, Jake's behaviour is more likely motivated by a desire for punishment for his abuse of Irma, one of those 'bad things' he later mentions guiltily, or, as Nyce suggests, for his recent loss of the fight with Jimmy Reeves. See Nicholls, *Scorsese's Men*, 57, 60; Nyce, *Scorsese Up Close*, 65. Regarding Jake's 'little girl hands,' Stern rightly shows caution: 'We could say that Jake blames the feminine in himself (as embodied in his hands) for preventing him from realizing his ambitions of greatness. But it's not quite as simple. For one thing Jake as character is not so self-conscious; but more to the point, the film never posits masculinity as simply dependent on repressed femininity.' See Stern, *Scorsese Connection*, 24. The scene in which Jake asks Joey to punch him is based on *Raging Bull*, 83–4, in which he asks the same thing of his friend Pete. However, Jake wants only to determine how Pete, whose punch he doubts, could have knocked out an opponent Jake had beaten by decision.

64 Friedman, *Cinema of Martin Scorsese*, 116, 117, 118, 121, 124, 125. For similar arguments, see Nick James, 'Raging Bulls: Sexuality and the Boxing Movie,' in *Boxer: An Anthology of Essays on Boxing and Visual Culture*, ed. Chandler et al., 113–15; Nicholls, *Scorsese's Men*, 47–8, 56, 57, 59; Bergan, *Sports in the Movies*, 15; Dorothée Bonnigal, 'Men in (G)Love(S): Martin Scorsese's *Raging Bull* in Light of Luchino Visconti's *Rocco and His Brothers*,' in *Screening Ethnicity*, ed. Hostert and Tamburri, 146, 147, 149, 150. Bon-nigal contends, dubiously, that boxing reactivates a Freudian Oedipal triangle whereby the child's homosexual desire for the father is re-enacted in the ring in a sadomasochistic ballet in which the boxer incarnates not only the phallus in beating the opponent, but a vaginalized wounded face in submitting to the opponent's beating, thus becoming the defiled woman marked by the phallus. Girardian theory rejects this Oedipal scenario; the mediator need not be, and usually is not, the father. Bonnigal's assumption that masochistic motives pervade boxing shows her ignorance of the fact that a good boxer wants to avoid being hit, both to win the match and to prolong his career. Purely economic or 'rational' motives are usually sufficient to explain why men become boxers. The masochist who enters the ring for the sake of being pummelled in order to become a symbolic defiled vagina has no future in the profession. See Girard, 'The Underground Critic,' in Girard, *'To Double Business Bound,'* 50–6; and, in the same volume, Girard, 'Strategies of Madness – Nietzsche, Wagner, and Dostoevski,' 64–8.

65 An analogue to Wood's error appears in the Italian American underworld as observed by Robert Delaney, an undercover agent of the New Jersey

State Police. Delaney was present at a meeting of major New Jersey gangster Tino Fiumara and six or seven of his associates at a bar tended by a young man new at the job. Before dinner the gangsters exchanged kisses as a form of greeting, and this was repeated as more gangsters arrived. The bartender, who aspired to a comic career, commented: 'What is this, a ... gay bar?' Fiumara became angry and ordered underboss Michael Coppola to enlighten and chastise the young man. Coppola went to the end of the bar, pulled him aside, and spoke to him very severely. 'When the bartender came back,' recalls Delaney, 'he was obviously upset and was having a hard time even figuring out how to pour a drink.' See Abadinsky, *Criminal Elite*, 163n. Misreading Italian American homophilism, Mark Nicholls claims that Jake 'twinks' Joey's cheeks in a 'patronizing but amorous way.' Actually, this is a common non-sexual gesture of affection between male friends and is evident elsewhere in Scorsese's films. See Nicholls, *Scorsese's Men*, 56.

66 Freudian theory has been discredited over the last two decades in an accumulation of studies large enough to make up a small library. For instance, the concept of repression and the related concept of the unconscious as Freud understood it now stand thoroughly discredited. See Frederick Crews, *The Memory Wars: Freud's Legacy in Dispute* (New York: New York Review of Books, 1995), 5, 7–14, 16, 19–20, 23, 28, 33–7, 43, 45–9, 53, 56–73, 107–10, 113–35, 151–5, 295–8. For a sampling of critiques of Freud, see Karl R. Popper, *Conjectures and Refutations: The Growth of Scientific Knowledge* (New York: Basic Books, 1962); Frank Cioffi, 'Freud and the Idea of a Pseudo-Science,' in Robert Borger and Frank Cioffi, eds., *Explanation in the Behavioural Sciences* (Cambridge: Cambridge Univ. Press, 1984); Edward Erwin, *A Final Accounting: Philosophical and Empirical Issues in Freudian Psychology* (Cambridge, Mass.: MIT Press, 1995); Malcolm MacMillan, *Freud: The Complete Arc* (Amsterdam: North-Holland, 1991); Alan Everson, *Seductive Mirage: An Exploration of the Work of Sigmund Freud* (Peru, Ill.: Open Court Press, 1993).

67 Father Joseph noted Jake's almost pathological distrust of people, including himself, and tried to counteract it. La Motta also mentions this trait. See *Raging Bull*, 43, 71, 135.

68 Gail Carnicelli Hemmeter and Thomas Hemmeter, 'The Word Made Flesh: Language in *Raging Bull*,' *Literature/Film Quarterly* 14, no. 2 (1986): 101–5, in *Perspectives on Raging Bull*, ed. Kellman, 72.

69 See *Raging Bull*, 187, where La Motta refers to his 'self-image of indestructibility.' On the desire for indifference and autonomy or self-possession, see Girard, *Deceit, Desire, and the Novel*, 159, 160, 162–7. Father Joseph

recognized La Motta's self-destructive demand for absolute self-autonomy and admonished him that 'no one can stand by himself, not even you, ... none of us can stand all alone.' As a corrective he advised him 'to make your peace with God.' La Motta's discovery of his own power came when he fended off several boys with an ice pick: 'Talk about fear, they took off like they were being attacked by a monster from outer space. It was the first time I can remember really having someone afraid of me. I can still remember that feeling of power flood through me. An icepick in my hand – and I was boss!' The term 'monster' suggests the remote, alien, and sacred. See *Raging Bull*, 4, 53–4, 174.

70 This piece of dialogue modifies Petrella's statement to Nick, the mob boss, at his social club: 'You know Jake like I do. You know when he gets set on something God himself could come down out of heaven and couldn't talk him out of it.' The film script stresses not La Motta's stubbornness but his proud indifference to human and sacred things. See *Raging Bull*, 139.

71 This scene is based on *Raging Bull*, 80, 135–9.

72 La Motta's father and gang boss Nick complain of his lack of respect. See *Raging Bull*, 38–9, 139.

73 Dorothée Bonnigal describes Jake's world as 'ruled by perverted fathers' who compromise his integrity. This one-sided evaluation fails to comprehend Jake's Italian American neighbourhood and its complex, ambiguous value system. See Bonnigal, 'Men in (G)Love(S),' 146.

74 In his autobiography La Motta complains to Petrella of his inability to fight Joe Louis. In the film, Scorsese conjoins this complaint with La Motta's anxieties over his small hands and his demand that Joey punch him repeatedly in the face. See *Raging Bull*, 83–4, 88.

75 Lourdeaux, *Italian and Irish Filmmakers*, 252.

76 In La Motta's autobiography the Reeves fight reveals to him the pleasure he is capable of receiving from a highly supportive crowd, which violently protests Reeves's victory. See *Raging Bull*, 89.

77 Inexplicably, Nicholls contends that the 'arousal of violence in relation to men ... allows him [Jake] to engage sexually with Vickie.' If anything, the scene of interrupted lovemaking indicates that such violent emotions block Jake's sexual impulses. See Nicholls, *Scorsese's Men*, 60.

78 In view of Wood's claim that La Motta constructs his home movies as a fantasy image of himself as a macho – that is, non-homosexual – male, it is curious that La Motta allows himself to appear in them at a backyard barbecue wearing an apron inscribed with the slogan 'Mother's Little Helper.' Is it conceivable that La Motta would have filmed himself in this effeminate and infantilized guise were the purpose of these home movies

to deny his homosexuality and thus to prove his virility, as Wood claims? Yet as a Freudian working within a system whereby even contrary evidence can be whipped into service, Wood has the ready option of arguing that the repressed content of Jake's fantasy is now slipping past his censor. In short, there is no defeating a system in which either the presence or the absence of evidence can be made to mean the same thing.

79 For La Motta's fears of retribution, see *Raging Bull*, see 70–1, 124.

80 La Motta, *Raging Bull*, 112.

81 Carroll, *Madonnas That Maim*, 132–7; Parsons, 'Is the Oedipus Complex Universal?' 17–18.

82 Ronald S. Librach correctly observes that Jake '*tries* to attain martyrdom by the letting of his own blood in the ring.' See Librach, 'The Last Temptation,' 16.

83 The Gospel according to John relates that, at the Crucifixion, the soldiers broke the legs of the two thieves, but because Jesus was already dead they 'did not break his legs. Yet one of the soldiers stabbed his side with a lance, and at once there was a flow of blood and water. This is vouched for by an eyewitness, whose evidence is to be trusted' (19:34). This flow of water most probably represents the fulfilment of Jesus's prophecy that upon his glorification the Spirit would be received by those who believed in him (Compare John 7:38–9). The significance of blood in this passage is clarified in the First Epistle of John (5:6–9): 'This is he who came with water and blood: Jesus Christ. He came, not by water alone, but by water and blood; and there is the Spirit to bear witness, because the Spirit is truth. For there are three witnesses, the Spirit, water, and the blood, and these three are in agreement.' In Brown's interpretation, the water of baptism cannot convey the Spirit, which requires Jesus to shed sacrificial blood. Thus water and blood had to be mingled before the Spirit could give testimony. It was also necessary for Jesus's blood not to have coagulated, so that it could be sprinkled according to Jewish sacrificial law. Finally, Jesus in death makes possible the release of the Spirit as the principle of life. Although the gift of the Spirit, strictly speaking, comes only after the Resurrection, it figures proleptically in the blood-and-water symbolism. For some scholars, the water prefigures the sacrament of baptism and the blood that of the Eucharist, but this is hard to prove.

The requirement that Jesus's blood must flow in order to be sprinkled calls to mind Edward J. Recchia's observations on La Motta's last championship bout: 'When the blood from the blows striking Jake is propelled outside the ring and sprays the ringside observers, they become ... participants in a bloody ritual, and the blood of the ritual victim, sprayed over them like the holy water a priest sprays over the congregation, confirms the link between them and the sacrificial lamb within the ring.'

See *The Gospel According to John (XIII–XXI)*, trans., with introduction, translation, and notes, by Raymond Brown (Garden City, N.Y.: Doubleday, 1970), 946, 949–50, 951–2; *The Epistle of John*, trans., with introduction, notes, and commentary, by Raymond Brown (Garden City, N.Y.: Doubleday, 1982), 576–8, 596, 597–9; Recchia, 'Martin Scorsese's *Raging Bull*,' 21–31.

84 In his 1941 bout with Jimmy Reeves, Jake allowed himself to be battered for much of the fight, believing himself unworthy of victory. Although he made a rousing comeback in the last round, he missed a knockout by seconds. See *Raging Bull*, 88–9.

85 However, the desiring subject's abjection can turn to triumph when, having won the coveted object, and now capable of playing mediator, he parades that object publicly so as to luxuriate in the envy he provokes. As La Motta writes of Vickie: 'I was really nuts for her. Like I said, she was such a looker that I liked to walk behind her when we went into a restaurant or something, just to see the expression on guy's faces as they turned to watch her go by.' See *Raging Bull*, 120. Jake's dependence upon his models calls in question a common interpretation of his behaviour as the expression of animal instinct. David Denby writes of Jake that the 'filmmakers diminish him too much, reducing him to mere instinct.' Scorsese encourages such interpretations, describing La Motta as an animal, as does La Motta himself. See Denby, 'Brute Force,' 44.

86 In La Motta's autobiography sexual jealousy plays no role in the fight with Janiro, although there are mistaken suspicions of a fix. What La Motta fails to mention is that before the Janiro fight he proposed to the mob a deal whereby he would lose to Janiro in exchange for a title shot. The mob refused this arrangement, although it offered La Motta a hundred thousand dollars to lose the fight, which offer La Motta refused. See *Raging Bull*, 152–5; Sammonds, *Beyond the Ring*, 146–7.

87 Girard, *Things Hidden*, 335–47; Girard builds on his earlier work, *Deceit, Desire, and the Novel*. See also Girard, 'Underground Critic,' 52.

88 Gilmore, 'Shame of Dishonor,' 10–11, 12; Saunders, 'Men and Women,' 443–5. Gans notes that the mother's predominance in child-rearing, and her frequent desire to overprotect a child from an authoritarian father, had made some Italian American males doubt their masculinity. See Gans, *Urban Villagers*, 62–4. On this point, see also Belmonte, 'Contradictions,' 6.

89 The opening title of *Raging Bull* achieves perhaps as nowhere else in Scorsese's work what he terms the 'concept of the master image ... the

single shot that represents a whole film.' Suggesting that Scorsese 'want[ed] to come up with a master shot that would sum up [himself]' Gene Siskel speculates that *Raging Bull* meets this requirement, to which Scorsese replies that he was satisfied by the 'opening title shot,' the 'shot that's used over the titles has that quality for me. The sense of desolation, the sense of loneliness, and that sense of that ring being in a way not different from the kitchen or the bedroom or the living room or the street.' See Roger Ebert and Gene Siskel, *The Future of the Movies: Interviews with Martin Scorsese, Steven Spielberg, and George Lucas* (Kansas City: Andrews and McMeel, 1991), 10–11. What Scorsese terms a 'master image' resembles what Noel Burch calls an 'emblematic shot.' See Stern, *Scorsese Connection*, 1–2; Burch, 'A Primitive Mode of Representation?' in Thomas Elsaesser and Adam Barker, eds., *Early Cinema: Space, Frame, Narrative* (London: British Film Institute, 1990), 223–4.

90 La Motta notes the origin of his nickname, the 'Bronx Bull': 'That was because of the way I fought – charge out of the corner, punch, punch, punch, never give up, take all the punishment the other guy could hand out but stay in there, slug and slug and slug. But the bull, of course, is also the symbol of sexual prowess, the all-conquering male that can handle a whole herd of cows, that has to have a barn to himself because of his violence when he gets on the prod.' Besides confessing to his rape of a young woman whose life he apparently ruined, La Motta notes the irony that, notwithstanding his nickname, he suffered long and inexplicable bouts of impotence. See *Raging Bull*, 76–7, 116–17.

91 Ernst Langlotz, *The Art of Magna Graecia: Greek Art in Southern Italy and Sicily* (London: Thames and Hudson, 1965), 12–13.

92 Citing Amy Taubin, Kevin J. Hayes notes the resemblance between Jake and Rossellini's monks in *The Flowers of St. Francis*. See Hayes, Introduction to *Martin Scorsese's 'Raging Bull,'* 9.

93 In *Mean Streets*, Charlie and Johnny Boy are framed by a window advertising hero sandwiches; their comic reduction is probably intended. In *GoodFellas*, gangsters Henry Hill and Jimmy Conway pick at their food in their favourite diner as they contemplate possible imprisonment; across the street an advertisement for 'hero sandwiches' comments ironically on their formerly gargantuan appetites. In *Casino*, the destruction of Nicky Santoro's gang coincides with the killing of the gang member Blue, whose hero sandwich, wrapped in tin foil, the police had mistaken for a gun.

94 Williams, *South Italian Folkways*, 142n.

95 In *Raging Bull*, 146–9, La Motta beats up Petrella and Vickie for suspected adultery.

96　On the feuding brothers, see Girard, *Violence and the Sacred*, 61–5, 71, 109, 150, 158, 203, 279.

97　The fight between Joey and Salvy is based on that between Pete and Salvy in *Raging Bull*, 131–2.

98　On the descent of grace in 'transcendental cinema,' see Paul Schrader, *Transcendental Style in Film: Ozu, Bresson, Dreyer* (Berkeley: Univ. of California Press, 1972), 91–3. Bliss states mistakenly that Scorsese's characters are always 'alone in a universe from which God's grace has been withdrawn.' See Bliss, *Scorsese and Cimino*, 4. This scene is inspired by *Raging Bull*, 206–9. La Motta sees prison as a 'turning point' in his life, initiating his climb 'up.' He repudiates his inhuman qualities and clears his accounts with God, whose existence he now acknowledges through prayer. Although Jake fails to mention it, his prison experience confirms Father Joseph's statement that 'none of us can stand all alone,' without God. See 174.

99　Hemmeter and Hemmeter, 'The Word Made Flesh,' 73.

100　Friedman, *Cinema of Martin Scorsese*, 126.

101　Scorsese's understanding of contemporary comedy in *Raging Bull* as later in *King of Comedy* (1982) is confirmed by William Keogh, who examines the mutual antagonism (which comedians admit to exist) between comic performers and their audiences. Besides noting a resemblance between stand-up comedy and boxing, Keogh finds that, whereas earlier stand-up comics merely told jokes, their contemporary counterparts specialize in verbal aggressiveness aimed at themselves, other people, and their audiences. Anxiously fearing disapproval, the stand-up comic wants to knock his audience 'dead.' However, Scorsese's feeling for the love-hate relationship between performers and audiences may also be rooted in Italian culture. In eighteenth-century Rome audiences often sided for and against performers, sometimes pelting them with missiles. Undaunted, the actors and singers threw stones and tiles back at the audience. To this day Italians similarly abuse losing soccer teams. See William Keogh, *Punchlines: The Violence of American Humor* (New York: Octagon House, 1990), 171–2; Maurice Andrieux, *Daily Life in Papal Rome in the Eighteenth Century*, trans. Mary Fitton (New York: Macmillan, 1968), 161–2.

102　The notorious loan shark Nicholas 'Jiggs' Forlano, a member of the Profaci crime family, used a steel hook to intimidate recalcitrant debtor Sidney Slater, whom he cut just below the eye. See Sifakis, *Mafia Encyclopedia*, 192.

103　Henry, 'Raging Bull,' 97–8. Nyce misreads as bellicose Jake's behaviour in this scene. See Nyce, *Scorsese Up Close*, 167.

104 This scene is based on *Raging Bull*, 209–10.

105 Terence Rafferty, 'Martin Scorsese's Still Life,' *Sight and Sound* 52 (Summer 1983), 186; *Scorsese on Scorsese*, ed. Thompson and Christie, 77; Kelly, *Martin Scorsese: First Decade*, 32.

106 Dickstein, 'Stations of the Cross: *Raging Bull* Revisited,' in *Perspectives on Raging Bull*, ed. Kellman, 78, 79, 82.

107 Bliss, *Word Made Flesh*, 67, 70–1; see also Bliss, *Scorsese and Cimino*, 124.

108 Colin Westbrook, Jr., 'Shadow-boxing: A Fighter's Stance towards Life,' in *Perspectives on Raging Bull*, ed. Kellman, 57.

109 Friedkin, 'Blind Rage,' 130.

110 Louis Menand, 'Methods and Madnesses,' 65–6; Friedkin, 'Blind Rage and Brotherly Love,' 129–30.

111 Ehrenstein, *Scorsese Picture*, 69; see also Friedman, *Cinema of Martin Scorsese*, 124.

112 Peterson, '*Raging Bull* and the Idea of Performance,' in *Martin Scorsese's 'Raging Bull,'* ed. Hayes, 85, 86; Grindon, 'Art and Genre in *Raging Bull*,' 28, 39. For similar views, see Tomasulo, 'Raging Bully,' 183–4.

113 Henry, 'Raging Bull,' 89; 'Martin Scorsese Directs.'

114 Henry, 'Raging Bull,' 98.

115 The mimetic chain is more extensive than it appears. Like James Dean and Paul Newman, Marlon Brando was an acquaintance of La Motta and Rocky Graziano, who became showbiz celebrities in the 1950s, and whose physical manner and speech patterns influenced the young method actors' portrayal of troubled, alienated, antisocial young people. As Bondanella notes, La Motta's monologue before the mirror 'represents more than Robert De Niro imitating La Motta imitating Brando. More accurately, it is De Niro imitating La Motta imitating Brando imitating La Motta and Graziano.' See Bondanella, *Hollywood Italians*, 117–18, which relies on Early, *The Culture of Bruising*, 90.

116 As Grindon notes, art sometimes figures in the boxing film as the antithesis to the ring. In *Golden Boy* (1939), the Italian American Joe Bonaparte abandons boxing for the violin. However, Michael Peterson confuses the nature of this choice by drawing a distinction between what he calls 'forceful performance,' namely boxing, and 'cultural performance,' by which he means art and, in Jake's case, stand-up comedy. Actually, both boxing and art are cultural phenomena, and each exhibits in its own way a mimetic element. Nor is Peterson correct in saying that *Raging Bull* 'as a whole is uncertain about the merits of cultural versus forceful performance,' that is, stand-up comedy as against boxing. For whereas the latter coincides with Jake's spiritual and emotional degradation, the former is identified with his personal recovery and plays an indispens-

able role within it. See Grindon, 'Art and Genre in *Raging Bull*,' 29; Peterson, '*Raging Bull* and the Idea of Performance,' 71–2.

117 Nicholls claims that Jake's dressing-room scenes are filled with a melancholy sense of the loss of his ideal image of himself and his past, that is, his boxing career and the magnificent physique that went with it. Likewise, his clumsy nightclub performances represent a 'pathetic display of primal loss,' and thus contrast lamentably with his ring virtuosity. According to Peterson, Ace's athletic performances are driven by 'masculine animal power ... whereas his stand-up appearances imply a pathetic reduction and confinement of his beastly side.' Hence the film 'can be read conveniently and coherently as a tragedy of macho purity dragged down by the falsity of the modern world.' For Pam Cook, the final scenes depict a bloated Jake whose tragedy leads one to mourn the loss of his beautiful, well-conditioned body and violent virility. Actually, what interests Scorsese in the nightclub scenes is Jake's spiritual advance over his former physical violence inside and outside the ring; his virtuosity and ring triumphs are now irrelevancies. Far from lamenting the reduction and restriction of Jake's 'animalistic' impulses, Scorsese celebrates their abandonment. The loss of Jake's beautiful physique is equally irrelevant, as the older, bloated Jake represents, spiritually speaking, a development beyond his mean-and-muscular predecessor. See Nicholls, *Scorsese's Men*, 46, 70; Peterson, '*Raging Bull* and the Idea of Performance,' 72; Cook, 'Masculinity in Crisis?' 39–40, 42.

118 'So for the second time they summoned the man who had been blind, and said, "Speak the truth before God. We know that this fellow is a sinner." "Whether or not he is a sinner, I do not know," the man replied. "All I know is this: once I was blind, now I can see."' The Gospel According to John, 9: 24 5 (New English Bible as quoted in the title).

119 Friedman, *Cinema of Martin Scorsese*, 114, 122; Bliss, *Scorsese and Cimino*, 129–30; Bliss, *Word Made Flesh*, 70–1; Arnold, 'The Boxing Brute of *Raging Bull*,' 55; Friedkin, 'Blind Rage,' 130.

120 See Henry, 'Raging Bull,' 92.

121 Dougan, *Martin Scorsese*, 20–1, 23–4; Biskind, *Easy Riders, Raging Bulls*, 227–8.

122 Henry, 'Raging Bull,' 90, 99.

7. The Society of Transgression: *GoodFellas*

1 Nicholas Pileggi, *Wiseguy* (New York: Pocket Books, 1990).

2 Dougan, *Martin Scorsese*, 91–2; Mary Pat Kelly, *Martin Scorsese: A Journey*,

259, 260; Ian Christie, 'Passion and Restraint: Ian Christie Talks with
Martin Scorsese,' in Ginette Vincendeau, ed., *Film/ Literature/ Heritage: A
Sight and Sound Reader* (London: British Film Institute, 2001), 67.

3 As Tommy is a protégé of Jimmy Conway, so DeSimone was a favourite of
Jimmy 'The Gent' Burke, upon whom Conway is based. Like Tommy in
the film, DeSimone always hoped to become an inducted member of a
mob family, or 'made man.' He too believed himself to have the credentials for admission, including a number of executions and participation in
major robberies at Kennedy Airport. Again like Pesci's Tommy, DeSimone
was lured to his death under the pretence of being inducted as a family
member. On 14 January 1979, DeSimone's wife reported the disappearance
of her husband, whose body was never found; he was thirty-two years
old.

There are, however, differences between the Pesci character and his
prototype. Unlike Tommy, who in *GoodFellas* seems moderately successful
as a gangster, DeSimone was a poor earner not likely to receive induction
into a Mafia family; indeed, he joined Jimmy Burke in the Lufthansa heist
in hope of a big score. According to Volkman and Cummings, DeSimone
was executed for killing a minor hoodlum favoured by a rising young
capo; in *Wiseguy* and *GoodFellas*, Tommy DeVito and his real-life prototype
are executed for the murder of Billy 'Batts,' a member of the Gambino
family. Physically Tommy DeSimone little resembled the Pesci character,
for whereas Tommy DeVito is short, stocky, and ordinary looking, his real-
life counterpart was tall and dashing and looked like Errol Flynn. He was
known as 'Two Gun Tommy' for carrying two pearl-handled pistols. See
Sifakis, *Mafia Encyclopedia*, xii; Volkman and Cummings, *Heist*, 16, 189–90.

4 The Lucchese was a relatively small but highly successful criminal organization consisting of only about a 110 'made' members and 110 associates,
and taking in about three hundred million dollars yearly. This low-profile
family came into the spotlight only in its decline, with the success of *Good-
Fellas*. Its origins trace to the New York criminal gang led by Joe 'The Boss'
Masseria in the 1920s. The gang's subgroup was led by Tom Reina, with
Gaetano 'Tom' Gagliano and Tommy 'Three Finger Brown' Lucchese
serving beneath him. After Lucky Luciano arranged for Reina's murder,
so as to prevent him from allying with Salvatore Maranzano, Masseria's
rival, the subgroup was assigned to Angelo Pinzolo, a man of filthy habits
whom Gagliano and Lucchese rejected as their leader. Following Pinzolo's
murder, Masseria and Maranzano were exterminated by Luciano, with
whom Gagliano and Lucchese had joined forces, these murders taking
place respectively in April and September 1931. Thus concluded the

'Castellamarese War.' Luciano took over Masseria's crime family, while Gagliano claimed the Reina gang. Gagliano was a moderate traditionalist whom Lucchese served as underboss for two decades. The gang focused on loan-sharking, narcotics, black marketeering, and labour racketeering, including bakeries, wholesale foods, meats, and the garment district, which it took over from Jewish gangsters in the 1930s. During that decade Lucchese grew rich in the kosher chicken racket not only by controlling an important labour union but by establishing an organization that payed him a fixed 'tax' for fixing prices and maintaining labour peace. In 1953, upon the death of Gagliano, leadership passed to the low-key Lucchese, who had strong political connections as well as a reputation for fairmindedness. Henry Hill in Pileggi's *Wiseguy* recalls admiringly Lucchese's visits to the bar-restaurant where the young Henry was employed. A main reason for Lucchese's popularity was that he demanded minimal 'tribute' from family members, allowing them to keep a large percentage of their earnings. In addition to its corruption of Jimmy Hoffa and his Teamsters locals, largely thanks to Johnny Dio (Dioguardi), a Lucchese family member, and its hijacking operations at Idlewild (later Kennedy) Airport, in which Dio played a major role and in which it worked closely with the Gambino family, the Lucchese organization focused on loan-sharking and various extortion and corruption rackets. Once more thanks chiefly to Dio's skills as a corruptor, the Lucchese family penetrated the UAW, of which Dio became regional director in the early 1950s. The family controlled all goods within the garment district and, with the Gambinos, solidified its traditional basis in garment trucking. It also expanded into the manufacturing end of the business in New York and eastern Pennsylvania. After Lucchese's death in 1967, the family's top position went to Tony 'Ducks' Corallo, a highly experienced gangster who presided over its activities in gambling, loan-sharking, trucking, garbage removal, construction, the garment industry (including manufacturing and trucking), labour racketeering, and hijacking at Kennedy Airport; however, he failed to keep family members from dealing in narcotics. Unlike other crime families at this time, the Lucchese enjoyed a considerable degree of harmony that aided in its expansion. Its most prosperous period ended in 1986, when Corallo and other mob bosses were convicted in the 'Commission case.' Henry Hill was already in the Witness Protection Program by this point. Following Corallo's imprisonment, the Lucchese family fell into the hands of two reckless, trigger-happy, and stupid members, Anthony 'Gas Pipe' Casso and Vic 'Little Vic' Amuso, who while fleeing from the law attempted to annihilate large segments of their own family. Its New Jersey division, under Anthony 'Tumac' Acceturo, became the object of a bloody conflict until Acceturo and five associates were convicted of racketeering in 1993. Fearing for his life, acting boss Alphonse d'Arco became an informant in 1991 and by his testimony helped to convict seven crime bosses, of whom four were Lucchese family members. By the mid-1990s the Lucchese family seemed to have disintegrated.

See Sifakis, *Mafia Dictionary*, 110; Lupsha, 'Organized Crime,' 53; Maas, *Valachi Papers*, 85; Kelly, *Underworld and Upperworld*, 61; Volkman, *Gangbusters*, 1–3, 16–26, 35, 41–4, 49, 56–8, 61–2, 122–8, 148–54, 168–233; Abadinsky, *Organized Crime*, 95–7, 263; *Business of Organized Crime*, ed. Block, 97, 98, 99–100, 101–5, 112, 126, 127–8; Gosch and Hammer, *Last Testament of Lucky Luciano*, 77–8, 101, 125, 126–8; Feder and Joesten, *Luciano Story*, 84; Volkman and Cummings, *Heist*, 37–8, 256, 268.

5 Volkman and Cummings, *Heist*, 19.
6 The discussion of Hill and his associates is based on Volkman and Cummings, *Heist*, *passim*; Volkman, *Gangbusters*, *passim*.
7 Pileggi, *Wiseguy*, 2.
8 DeCurtis, 'What the Streets Mean,' 160; see also Pileggi, *Wiseguy*, 4: 'an articulate hoodlum.'
9 Kelly, *Martin Scorsese: A Journey*, 259.
10 Dougan, *Martin Scorsese*, 93.
11 Smith, 'Martin Scorsese Interviewed,' 146. See also Kelly, *Martin Scorsese: A Journey*, 259, 273; Keyser, *Martin Scorsese*, 197, 199. Remarking to Scorsese that 'there is something about social and professional ritual that fascinates you,' Ian Christie proposes that, despite differences in time, class, and setting, *The Age of Innocence* and *GoodFellas* are 'very close,' as they 'both try to be truthful to ... [their] milieu ... and to make you feel the emotion, the allure, the danger is something almost palpable.' Scorsese comments that, while the former work had to achieve 'a saturation of detail,' *GoodFellas* 'was more like a documentary on a lifestyle.' See 'Passion and Restraint,' 69–71.
12 Smith, 'Art of Vision,' 256.
13 Smith, 'Martin Scorsese Interviewed,' 153.
14 Smith, 'Martin Scorsese Interviewed,' 149–50.
15 For this scene, see Pileggi, *Wiseguy*, 149–50.
16 Lesley Stern describes the concluding image of the *Great Train Robbery* as the best-known example of what Noel Burch terms the 'emblematic shot,' which can serve a narrative purpose, but whose strength lies 'in the very autonomy of the shot, in a presentational or monstrative, rather than

primarily narrative, aspect.' The appearance of the image at this point of the film 'suggest[s] a kind of non-closure ... a return of the irrepressible.' See Stern, *Scorsese Connection*, 1–2.

17　Robert Warshow, 'The Gangster as Tragic Hero,' in Warshow, *Immediate Experience*, 132, 133; see also in the same volume 'Movie Chronicle: The Westerner,' 135. See also Thomas Schatz, *Hollywood Genres: Formulas, Filmmaking, and the Studio System* (Philadelphia: Temple Univ. Press, 1981), 86, 90, 93. For the limitations of Warshow's paradigm, see Carlos Clarens, *Crime Movies: An Illustrated History of the Gangster Genre from D.W. Griffith to Pulp Fiction*, 2nd ed. (New York: Da Capo, 1997), 13; Stephen Louis Karpf, *The Gangster Film: Emergence, Variation, and Decay of a Genre* (New York: Arno, 1973), 25–7.

18　Schatz, *Hollywood Genres*, 82, 89; Inciardi, *Careers in Crime*, 170; Eugene Rosow, *Born to Lose: The Gangster Film in America* (New York: Oxford Univ. Press, 1978), 5–7.

19　Schatz, *Hollywood Genres*, 82, 102–3; Kaminsky, *American Film Genres*, 23; Clarens, *Crime Movies*, 231, 234–5, 237, 246; Rosow, *Born to Lose*, 171, 235, 271, 272, 327.

20　Volkman, *Gangbusters*, 183. Pauline Kael's complaint that *GoodFellas* resembles Howard Hawks's *Scarface* but without the 'lead' character implies a too rigid notion of the gangster genre. Responding to this criticism, Scorsese claims that in *GoodFellas* the function of the lead character is assigned to the gangster 'lifestyle.' Nor does he accept the view that this makes it impossible to identify with the characters. See Smith, 'Art of Vision,' 241. On the looseness and inclusiveness of the gangster genre, see Raymond Durgnat, 'The Gangster File: From *The Musketeers* to *GoodFellas*,' as discussed by Phil Hardy, ed., *The Overlook Film Encyclopedia of the Gangster Film* (Westbrook, N.Y.: Overlook Press, 1998), 8.

21　Kelly, *Martin Scorsese: A Journey*, 259.

22　Friedman, *Cinema of Martin Scorsese*, 171, describes the film as Scorsese's 'antidote to the romanticized Mafia' of *The Godfather*. See also Smith, 'Martin Scorsese Interviewed,' 148.

23　Marilyn Yaquinto writes that the gangsters in *GoodFellas* differ from those of the *Godfather* trilogy in being detached from Sicilian traditions of family order and in-group marriage; rather, they typify the 'infiltration' of the Mafia by 'Yuppie nihilism.' See Yaquinto, *Pump 'em Full of Lead*, 169–70.

24　Scorsese remarked in 1990: 'With drugs being the big money and gangsters killing people in the government in Colombia, the Mafia is nothing.' See Smith, 'Martin Scorsese Interviewed,' 151.

　　In his 1953 essay, 'Crime as an American Way of Life,' Daniel Bell advanced the 'ethnic succession' theory of organized crime. According to Bell, organized crime was a traditional means by which ethnic groups such as the Irish and Jews had risen from poverty to professional success and social acceptance. Yet once they had left behind their lowly origins, these groups ceased to prevail in the underworld. The Italian Americans who then dominated organized crime would also advance socially until it would cease to attract them, and criminal leadership would pass to other, less successful ethnic groups. Nonetheless, Italian Americans played a major role in organized crime for decades following Bell's essay.

During the 1960s Glazer and Moynihan noted that the 'natural' succession of organized crime from Italians to blacks and Puerto Ricans had not taken place, perhaps because of the Italians' superior familial organization. Nonetheless, many observers have predicted the decline and ultimate extinction of the Italian American form of organized crime, based on artificial loyalties or 'families.' As Gay Talese reports in *Honor Thy Father* (1971), crime boss Joe Bonanno had complained of a declining organization in the 1960s, when many bosses were retiring and their sons, whether for lack of ability or access to more rapid career options, were failing to provide leadership. Bonanno also found American-born gangsters to lack the coolness and quickness as well as the drive, alienation, and leadership abilities that had impelled their Italian-born predecessors to success. Writing in 1971, Joseph L. Albini seconded Bell's thesis, as did Francis A.J. Ianni a year later in *A Family Business*. According to Ianni, the Mafia must gradually decline not only because the families were moving into legitimate businesses but because the children of Mafia bosses were rejecting criminal careers in favour of professions such as medicine, law, and business. At the same time, Mafia traditions of father-obedience and mother-respect were yielding to the impersonal, corporate, bureaucratic values of American business. Ianni's *Black Mafia: Ethnic Succession in Organized Crime* (1974) predicted the supersession of Italian American organized crime by new, supposedly Mafia-like organizations dominated by blacks and Hispanics using crime as a means of social mobility. Variations of these arguments appear in works by James J. Inciardi, Hank Messick and Burt Goldblatt, and Humbert S. Nelli. Messick and Goldblatt claimed that the Cubans of Miami were driving the Mafia out of the narcotics trade, while Nelli argued that the 'golden age' of Italian American criminal entrepreneurship was over by the mid-1970s.

Belief in the decline of the Mafia only intensified in the 1980s and early 1990s, when the U.S. government dealt Italian American gangsters a devastating series of setbacks. This was achieved partly through improved surveillance and investigative methods, including FBI infiltration, by such undercover agents as Joseph Pistone, or 'Donnie Brasco.' It was also achieved through the government's ability to exploit what some saw as a dissolving Italian American subculture. This was thought to have resulted inevitably from the disappearance of America's Little Italies and the assimilation of Italian Americans. The new type of gangster tended to be flashy, attention grabbing, and selfishly materialistic. Nor was he bound to the same degree by the traditional values of family loyalty, including the code of *omertà*, which forbade the giving of information to government authorities.

The most powerful weapon against the Mafia has been the Racketeer Influenced and Corrupt Organization Act (RICO), legalized in 1970 as part of the Organized Crime Control Act, and which officials learned gradually to use. RICO enables the government to punish enterprise criminality by showing a pattern of racketeering activity. Not only does it extend the scope of electronic eavesdropping and grand jury subpoenas but, by expanding accessorial and conspiratorial liability, facilitates mass trials of gangsters. Indeed, under RICO a crime boss can be charged almost automatically. The new law is based on the idea that officials need to attack not so much individual criminals as organized criminal enterprises. The draconian sentences imposed under the RICO statutes broke down *omertà* and pressured gangsters to cooperate with the government. Protection against mob retaliation through the Witness Security Program, authorized by the 1970 Organized Crime Control Act, afforded gangsters a further incentive to turn informant.

The government has compiled an impressive record against the Mafia over the last two decades. The 'Strawmen' cases, essential context for Scorsese's *Casino*, revealed the central role of the Chicago and Midwestern crime bosses in the skimming of pre-tax money from Las Vegas casinos. Their subsequent conviction and imprisonment dealt a major defeat to organized crime in that part of the country. In the so-called Commission case, or *United States v. Salerno*, the bosses of four of the New York crime families, including Anthony 'Tony Ducks' Corallo, head of the Lucchese family, were convicted and sent to prison on 19 November 1986. Led by Rudolph Giuliani, United States attorney for the Southern District of New York, the government prosecutors proved the bosses' systematic bribery and extortion in the concrete industry. In the Pizza Connection case, begun in 1984 and concluded in 1987, and which amounted to the biggest criminal investigation in FBI history, the government convicted as co-conspirators many leading drug traffickers between the United States and Sicily.

They had been using pizza parlours, cafes, country homes, and apartments as fronts. Another blow was dealt to the Mafia during the 1990s in *United States v. the International Brotherhood of Teamsters*, which showed the mob to have dominated the IBT for the purpose of acquiring money, real and no-show jobs, and political clout. Yet the government's greatest success was the conviction in 1990 of the 'Teflon Don,' John Gotti, head of the Gambino family, who had gained a reputation for invulnerability to prosecution. In his flamboyant and obvious cultivation of publicity, so unlike the behaviour of earlier bosses, Gotti needlessly attracted the attention of the law. He also showed his disregard of Mafia tradition not only in his professed disdain for the rituals of honour and respect, but in his promotion of an individualistic ethos among his followers. Ironically, he was brought down by his right-hand man Sammy 'The Bull' Gravano, the highest ranking of all mob informants.

Not surprisingly, many scholars of the 1980s and 1990s reaffirmed earlier predictions of the fall of the Mafia. Richard Alba's *Italian Americans* (1985) attributed the recent rash of Mafia informants to a loss of respect for the code of familial loyalty. He predicted the gradual decline of Italian American crime families through dwindling recruitment and the disappearance of the social conditions that had fostered them. Formerly an endless source of ambitious and talented recruits, Little Italies were disappearing. Not only were Italian Americans dispersing across the country, but their high rate of out-group marriage signalled the end of that group consciousness and loyalty upon which the Mafia depends. It would become yet another casualty of the 'twilight of ethnicity.' During this decade Nelli pointed to a host of problems very possibly signalling the end of Mafia supremacy in organized crime, a viewpoint more or less shared by Ralph Blumenthal.

Flush from government victories over the Mafia in the 1980s, Rudolph Giuliani and Robert Blakeley anticipated its ultimate extinction. In *The Mythology of Organized Crime and Criminal Justice* (1993), Kappeler, Blumberg, and Potter attributed the Mafia's widely presumed decline to the bosses' advancing age, avoidance of high-risk enterprises, inexperienced recruits, and improved law enforcement. A year later James B. Jacobs noted that, in the face of the government's successes, many were predicting the Mafia's downfall. William Kleinknecht, whose *New Ethnic Mobs* appeared in 1996, envisioned the near collapse of the Mafia and its supersession by ethnic competitors. Like the Irish and Jews before them, the Italians were losing control of organized crime through their upward mobility. As Italian Americans abandoned Little Italies and increasingly entered the professions, the supply of street toughs was drying up and older mobsters were complaining of disloyalty among the younger men. For Kleinknecht, Henry Hill exemplified the old-style street tough once produced by ethnic neighbourhoods (although, given his perfidy, he better represents the new type). Nor were Italian American gangsters intimidating their ethnic competitors any longer. In one respect, however, the ethnic succession theory had failed to hold up, as black gangsters still lacked the durable syndicate organization required for a takeover of the drug trade outside their neighbourhoods. Yet Kleinknecht also noted the growing presence of Chinese, Russian, Columbian, Haitian, Korean, and Ukrainian mobs in organized crime, now transformed into a multi-ethnic tapestry. Four years later Luciano J. Iorizzo proclaimed the virtual elimination of the Cosa Nosta through law enforcement and ethnic succession.

Such predictions were premature. As early as 1974, having found that Italian American crime families were not necessarily vanishing, Frederic Homer attributed the persistence of Italian Americans in organized crime to their ethnic identification and close family ties. They were also ethnically predisposed to crime thanks to their distrust of government carried over from Italy, suspicion of outsiders promoted by a strong family structure, and propensity to form close-knit, secret organizations. Surveying the mob as a protected witness in the early 1970s, Vincent Teresa saw it as thriving. Not only was it continuing to corrupt judges and policemen, but it was inceasing its total power through the recruitment of Sicilian or Sicilian American gangs (known as 'Zips' from their rapid speech in dialect). In 1986 Robert J. Kelly cited government studies suggesting the permanence and uniqueness of the Mafia. Even though most Italian Americans had disavowed it, its basic structure had proved stable and durable. In Carl Sifakis's view, ethnic succession had failed to materialize, for in the 1980s as in the past successful black criminals cooperated with the Mafia. Far from dying, it has continued to expand thanks to an endless supply of young Italian American candidates thirsting for admission. Stephen R. Fox argued in 1989 that black gangs remained confined to their ghettoes for lack of a Mafia-like organization. Moreover, the Mafia continued to corrupt labour unions, while some Italian Americans still wanted to be gangsters – a desire fed by video mythifications.

In 1990 Ernest Volkman and John Cummings found a thriving Mafia highly adaptive to changing conditions and mores. Kappeler and colleagues warned against overconfidence in the battle against organized crime following Gotti's conviction, since the Mafia was very much alive. Jacobs remained uncertain whether federal 'crime busting' of the 1980s and 1990s would prove successful in the long run. Although Kleinknecht had argued that multi-ethnic gangs were supplanting the Mafia, he concluded his book equivocally, acknowledging that Chinese criminals, whose activities focused largely on their own communities, were not likely to equal the Mafia in national significance, that no new ethnic mob had achieved a major takeover, and that Italian Americans continued as major players: 'And yet the Mafia's decline is vastly overestimated. The truth is somewhere in the middle. The Mafia is in very gradual decline.' According to Kelly in 1999, the notion that the law had produced an 'irreversible decline' of the Mafia must be taken cautiously. The imprisonment of mob bosses has not dealt a crushing blow, for the main work of crime depends on their typically resilient and resourceful underlings. More recently, Howard Abadinsky has acknowledged the decimation of some Italian American crime units yet noted that several families had regrouped and recruited new members, so that the Mafia was still quite visible and dangerous despite competition. Middle-class Italian Americans were entering criminal careers through the lingering influence of tradition and a rational desire to join an attractive subculture. Nor were Mafia sons necessarily rejecting their fathers' profession, as Peter Lupsha had shown.

See Daniel Bell, 'Crime as an American Way of Life,' 141–50; Glazer and Moynihan, *Beyond the Melting Pot*, 197, 211; Bonanno, *Man of Honor*, 289–90; Gay Talese, *Honor Thy Father* (New York: World, 1971), xvi, 35, 222–3; Albini, *American Mafia*, 326; Messick and Goldblatt, *Mobs and the Mafia*, 2; Homer, *Guns and Garlic*, 48, 77–80, 84, 88, 92–3; Anderson, *Business of Organized Crime*, 75; Iorizzo and Mondello, 'Italian Americans and Organized Crime,' 207; Ianni, *Family Business*, 49, 74, 76, 82, 99, 127, 132, 192–3; Francis A.J. Ianni, *Black Mafia: Ethnic Succession in Organized Crime* (New York: Simon and Schuster, 1974), 11–21, 279–332, *passim*; Ianni, 'Mafia and Web of Kinship,' 49, 59; Ianni, 'Organized Crime and Italo-American Family,' 36, 39; Volkman and Cummings, *Goombata*, 123, 156, 226–8, 229–30; Nelli, *Business of Crime*, 264–5; Nelli, *From Immigrants to Ethnics*, 190; Nelli, 'Overview,' in *Organized Crime*, ed. Kelly, 8; Lupsha, 'Organized Crime,' 38; Alba, *Italian Americans*, 62, 95, 151–3; Hess, *Mafia and Mafiosi*, 173; Kappeler, Blumberg, and Potter, *Mythology of Crime and Criminal Justice*, 78; Demaris, *Last Mafioso*, ix; Jacobs, *Busting the Mob*, 3–26, 215, 222; Kelly, *Underworld and Upperworld*, 119–34, 133n; Kleinknecht, *New Ethnic Mobs*, 1–22, 85–8, 209, 287–8, 289, 294, 296–7, 301–2; Sifakis, *Mafia Encyclopedia*, 39, 180, 207; Inciardi, *Careers in Crime*, 124, 134; Vincent Teresa, 'A Mafioso Cases the Mafia Craze,' in *The Crime Society*, ed. Ianni and Reuss-Ianni, 155; Kelly, 'Criminal Underworlds,' 23, 29n; Lyman and Potter,

Organized Crime, 492–4, 499–501; Iorizzo, 'Crime and Organized Crime,'
157–9; Fox, *Blood and Power*, 381–2, 413–15, 418–20; Roemer, *Roemer*, 124;
Roemer, *Accardo*, 402–7; Blumenthal, *Last Days of Sicilians*, vii, 7, 11, 12, 15,
24, 26–7, 33, 40, 41–2, 80–3, 271–81, 292–5, 308, 315–18; Gotti, *Gotti Tapes*, 99
(see also Foreword by Ralph Blumenthal, x, xv–xvi, xvii–xviii); Volkman,
Gangbusters, 164–5, 182–3, 185, 189, 190–1, 195, 198; Diego Gambetta and
Peter Reuter, 'Conspiracy among the Many: The Mafia in Legitimate
Industries,' in *Economics of Organized Crime*, ed. Fiorentini and Peltzman,
133–4; Reuter, *Disorganized Crime*, 136; Lawton, 'Mafia and Movies,' 78–9,
81–2; Abadinsky, *Organized Crime*, xv, 26, 36–8, 43, 45–6, 47–50, 96, 129,
318–22; James Finckenauer and Elin J. Waring, *Russian Mafia in America:
Immigration, Culture, and Crime* (Boston: Northeastern Univ. Press, 1998),
26–8.

25 As the violence of the early-twentieth-century urban environment calls to
mind the Western frontier, so the Western cowboy and gunman are now
rivaled in the American imagination by the figure of the urban ethnic
gangster conceived as a rugged individualist shooting his way to the top.
The latter image remains alive notwithstanding that its heyday, the 1920s
and 1930s, is long past, and that the individualistic gangster-outlaw has
largely been replaced by the gangster-businessmen tied to an organization. It is less commonly recognized that many Sicilian immigrants were
peasants originating in a country whose rusticity and lawlessness are
comparable to the Old West.

   Not only did first-generation immigrants grow up among animals, often
living with them in the same rooms, but the hired gunmen of the Sicilian
gabellotti resemble the vigilante groups of the Western frontier. The
gabellotti were estate managers hired by the rich urban-dwelling aristocrats, gentry, and bourgeoisie; their gunmen were employed to protect
their property against peasants, bandits, and state encroachment. These
enforcers were sometimes drawn from the bandit groups they were
intended to repel. They and the *gabellotti* are believed by some scholars to
have provided the nucleus of what became the Mafia, that is, criminal
entrepreneurs who, besides preying upon the peasantry, frequently
reduced the *gabellotti* to subservience through extortion and intimidation.
As the Sicilian economy mingled agriculture and pastoralism, livestock
rustling was and to some extent remains a problem in Sicily, especially its
western areas, where the status of a landowner has been measured by the
splendour of his caparisoned mule trains. A highly important commercial
activity, rustling was organized and financed by the *gabellotti*, who themselves owned large numbers of animals that they grazed on the vast

holdings or *latifundium* they were assigned to supervise. Their activity was typically centred on the *masseria*, a farm complex housing abundant live-stock. As the government held no monopoly on violence, one had to carry guns to protect oneself and one's animals, a practice typical of herdsmen, bandits, estate guards, and owners of large herds. Emanuele Navarro della Miraglia describes a Sicilian animal dealer of about a hundred years ago as 'leaning on the barrel of a rifle with one leg crossed over the other to ex-pose the butt of a revolver in the waistband of his trousers.' It was not unheard of for agricultural workers sleeping overnight away from their village residences to barricade themselves in fortress-like enclosures in order to ward off bandits. Nonetheless the rural folk romanticized the many bandits who ravaged the countryside, sometimes using caves for hideouts. Their popularity may have resulted from the fact that they were often former peasants who had taken to the hills in protest against the political, social, and economic system. One should not exaggerate their rebelliousness, however, as rich landowners also used them against the peasants. Even the interior landscape of western Sicily, with its flat or rolling or sometimes ruggedly mountainous terrain, and with its vast stretches of deforested grazing land, baked by the meridional sun, recalls the deserts of the Old West. Of Pietro Germi's *In Nome delle Legge* (1949), the first Italian film to deal explicitly with the Mafia, one critic writes that the 'parched and mysterious landscapes' of Sicily allow the director to pay homage to his idol, John Ford. According to Diego Gambetta, it is consid-ered preferable for Mafia murders to be photographed with prickly pears nearby, since without the prickly pear they would seem inauthentic and the photographs would be unsellable to news agencies on the Continent. The musical soundtracks of Italian news reports on the Mafia sound vaguely like spaghetti westerns.

Commenting on his Sicilian family, which lived near Castellamare del Golfo in the late nineteenth century, crime boss Joseph Bonanno mentions its holdings in land, cattle, and horses. In his view, the frequent land feuds of those days 'resembled the range wars among cattle barons in the Ameri-can West. In Western Sicily, as on the American cowboy frontier, men fought over cattle because cattle made a man rich.' Not surprisingly 'these conditions almost invited rustling, and thefts of cattle resulted in retalia-tion. One skirmish brought on another,' and there were also ambushes. In his book on the Bonannos, *Honor Thy Father*, Gay Talese assigns these thoughts to Joe Bonanno's son Salvatore (Bill): 'Nevertheless, a kinship of sorts probably did exist between these men and the legendary American cowboy, Bill thought, impressed by the similarity between the tales of the

Old West and certain stories he had heard as a boy involving gun battles between mounted mafiosi in the hills of Sicily.' Talese's book includes a family photograph of the young cowboy-suited Bill on horseback at a riding camp in Arizona, where his father had established a second home. The resemblance between Western and Sicilian codes with respect to masculinity, honour, vengeance, and the treatment of women help to explain not only Scorsese's characters' deep affinity for the American West (as in the films of Ford and Hawks) but that of many Italian Americans. Herbert Gans describes John Wayne as the favourite film star among Italian Americans of Boston's West End in the late 1950s. Dean Martin, who starred in Westerns, including at least two with Frank Sinatra, liked few things better than to watch Westerns on television. Frankie Laine, the singer of Western ballads (including the theme from 'High Noon') was Italian, born Frank Lo Vecchio in 1913.

See Jane and Peter Schneider, *Culture and Political Economy, passim*; Blok, *Mafia of Sicilian Village, passim*; Ianni, *Family Business*, 26–7, 37; Dickie, *Cosa Nostra*, 49; Smith, *Mafia Mystique*, 97–8; Mangione and Morreale, *La Storia*, 35; Chapman, *Milocca*, 220, 225–6; Lyman and Potter, *Organized Crime*, 16; Bonanno, *Man of Honor*, 23, 26, 41; Talese, *Honor Thy Father*, 49–50; *Overlook Film Encyclopedia: Gangster Film*, ed. Hardy, 118; Gardaphe, *Italian Signs, American Streets*, 213–14n; Gambetta, *Sicilian Mafia*, 127–8, 248–9; Tosches, *Dino*, 18–19, 22, 264, 265, 368.

Contrary to the enshrined view that the Mafia originates in the *gabellotti*, Gambetta traces it to the gangs that protected not only agricultural hold-ings outside Palermo but the movement of herd animals to the city's markets. Yet though predominantly an urban phenomenon to the present day, the Mafia has maintained an enduring connection with the country-side. See Gambetta, *Sicilian Mafia*, 83–99, 288n.

26 Citing Stephen Holden, Connolly and d'Acierno characterize the Bennett song as an ethnic anthem. See Connolly and d'Acierno, 'Italian American Musical Culture,' 431.
27 George P. Castellito, 'Imagism and Martin Scorsese: Images Suspended and Extended,' *Literature/ Film Quarterly* 26, no. 1 (1998): 27.
28 Somewhat too restrictively, Scorsese identifies these films with the early phases of the gangster genre, beginning with Raoul Walsh's *Regeneration* (1915). See Scorsese, *A Personal Journey with Martin Scorsese through American Movies* (video recording) (Santa Monica: Buena Vista Home Entertainment, 2000).
29 For this see also Pileggi, *Wiseguy*, 24–5.
30 Pileggi, *Wiseguy*, 94–6.

31 In such early gangster films as *Little Caesar* (1930), *The Public Enemy* (1931), and *Scarface* (1932), and later in *T-Men* (1947) and *Cry of the City* (1948), character provides the criminal's motivation. But in many later films such as *Knock on Any Door* (1949) society takes the blame. See Bondanella, *Hollywood Italians*, 195, 212, 214–15; Schatz, *Hollywood Genres*, 87–8.

32 *Scorsese on Scorsese*, ed. Thompson and Christie, 154. As Howard Abadinsky notes, a young man's choice of a criminal career is often attributed to anomie or social 'strain,' the disparity between the American ideal of social success and the major social and educational disadvantages that limit real opportunities. Another explanation for such a career choice is a morally defective environment, whether familial or communal. Nor does Abadinsky doubt that such factors impel some people into organized crime. Yet like Peter A. Lupsha, he finds that many become criminals through a conscious, rational desire to be, rather than a law-abiding 'sucker,' a deviant with all its thrills and pleasures. This is the attitude of Henry Hill and his associates. See Abadinsky, *Organized Crime*, 34–7, 45–8. According to William Howard Moore, who attributes most crime to social conditions, the conspiratorial view of organized crime came to prevail during the 1950s and 1960s, when politicians, policemen, and the general public embraced the myth of the Mafia as a foreign invasion. See Moore, *Kefauver Committee*, viii–ix, 79.

33 Karen mentions her 'predisposition' for the life of a gangster wife. See Pileggi, *Wiseguy*, 77.

34 Antoinette Giancana, daughter of Chicago crime boss Sam Giancana, describes his footwear: 'his shoes, beautiful, expensive shoes, brightly polished so that you could see your reflection in them.' See Giancana and Renner, *Mafia Princess*, 61.

35 Already in Mervyn Leroy's *Little Caesar* (1930) the aspiring mobster Rico Bandello (Edward G. Robinson) is captivated mimetically by the flashy jewellery and fine clothes of mob boss Pete Montana.

36 Matthew 16:19: 'I will give you the keys of the Kingdom of Heaven.'

37 For this scene, see Pileggi, *Wiseguy*, 27–8. Compare Hess's description of a young Sicilian Mafioso's self-discovery upon performing his first violent act: 'This ... act of violence ... leads to the discovery of power, the discovery that it is possible to manipulate other people and gain not only outward advantage but a deep psychological satisfaction from the imposition of one's own will. And the wish to hold and multiply what has been once discovered, enjoyed, or exploited requires recourse to violent action also in the future.' See Hess, *Mafia and Mafiosi*, 52, 53.

38 In the gangster genre the aspiring criminal's acquisition of an expensive,

well-tailored suit signifies his advancement in the underworld, as witness *Little Caesar* and *Scarface*. What is perhaps original in *GoodFellas* is the shocked maternal response. See Rosow, *Born to Lose*, 36, 185.

39 See also Pileggi, *Wiseguy*, 22. Hill's characterization of the Mafia at this time reflects historical reality. The Second World War opened up a new era of prosperity for Italian American gangsters, including opportunities in gambling that the mob continued to exploit in the post-war period. The emergence of a wartime black market provided a strong incentive to expand operations. By war's end the mob was in what Nelli terms 'strong financial condition,' having catered for four years to the public demand for a wide variety of illegal products and services. The period following the Second World War constitutes in Nelli's words a 'golden age for criminal syndicates' in the United States, when they enjoyed 'unlimited opportunities' in such 'traditional lines of activity' as gambling, loan-sharking, labour and business racketeering, and narcotics. The syndicates began to tap new enterprises such as arson for hire, credit card and real estate frauds, pornography. theft and sale of securities, and bootlegging. There was also significant penetration of legitimate businesses. Although the Kefauver hearings, which were conducted between 1950 and 1951, alarmed the public with news of interstate racketeering and the Mafia, the furore settled down temporarily for lack of evidence.

As the 1950s drew to a close the Italian American syndicates were in trouble. Against the expressed wishes of the bosses, many members, including some of the bosses themselves, had entered the narcotics traffic that, owing to new laws, now resulted in long sentences for offenders. The sentencing of increasing numbers of gangsters in the 1950s endangered the whole organization. Another source of danger was the targeting of crime boss Frank Costello, sometimes known as 'Prime Minister of the Underworld,' by his rival Vito Genovese. An exponent of smooth diplomacy over violence, Costello had taken over Lucky Luciano's organization following the latter's deportation to Italy in 1946. Initially a subordinate of Luciano, Genovese had spent the Second World War in Italy in flight from a murder charge but later established his own increasingly powerful criminal organization in the United States.

Another problem was the greed and power lust of crime boss Albert Anastasia. By the early 1950s, after assuming control of Joe Adonis's crime operations, he had overthrown the leaders of the Mangano crime family and went on to challenge pre-existing mob interests in the Caribbean, including those of Meyer Lansky and Florida crime boss Santo Trafficante. Contrary to the wishes of the other bosses, Anastasia scandalously sold at high prices membership in his crime family. It was widely feared that, because of his greed, stool pigeons were infiltrating the Mafia. Thus its traditional unity and discipline had been shaken, and the issues of narcotics and gambling needed straightening out.

On 2 May 1957 Frank Costello barely avoided assassination in the lobby of his Central Park West apartment building. Although Costello refused to discuss the murder attempt, he realized that he was being threatened by Genovese and sought to ally with Anastasia. However, Genovese succeeded in enlisting Carlo Gambino, Anastasia's second-in-command, in the killing of his boss. On 25 October 1957 Anastasia was murdered by two gunmen in the barber shop of the Park Sheraton Hotel in Manhattan. The execution was probably orchestrated by the Gallo brothers, lowly members of the Profaci family, although they did not perform the execution. Facing an extended gang war, Costello retired from crime after turning over to Genovese what had been the Luciano crime family.

With the Mafia in crisis, a major summit meeting of approximately 113 Mafiosi took place outside New York City in the rural village of Apalachin at the large suburban home of mob boss Joseph Barbara on 14 November 1957. Genovese may have wanted the meeting so as to enhance his recently augmented prestige; his rivals may have agreed to it so as to embarrass him by means of a secretly orchestrated police raid on the meeting. Yet the bosses are also likely to have had an important agenda: to define a new policy on narcotics traffic, forbidding it to all Mafia members, at least temporarily; to determine a successor to Anastasia, a position subsequently assigned to Gambino; to clarify the boundaries among the various mob interests in the Caribbean; and to close the Mafia books officially against new admissions. Before these matters could be discussed, local police descended upon Barbara's property, causing most of the guests to scatter into the woods. About sixty-three gangsters were apprehended, and in 1959 twenty were convicted of conspiracy to obstruct justice; however, this decision was overturned for lack of evidence. The presence of so many Mafiosi at Apalachin still excites controversy, yet what is indisputable is that this fiasco raised strong suspicions among the police and public of an Italian American criminal conspiracy against the nation. As the 'heat' intensified, the Mafia would find it increasingly difficult to operate in the coming decades. Formerly sceptical of the Mafia's existence, J. Edgar Hoover now saw it as the major internal threat to the nation and responded by strengthening the investigative and enforcement branches of the FBI. Already underway at the time of the cookout, the McClellan hearings on interstate racketeering gained added impetus from Apalachin.

To quote FBI agent William F. Roemer, Apalachin marks the 'line of demarcation between the old and the new law enforcement' in the war against organized crime.

For nearly two decades after Apalachin the Mafia experienced considerable turmoil. Vito Genovese was convicted of narcotics trafficking in 1959, possibly in a set-up arranged by Frank Costello and others, and remained in prison until his death in 1969. Joe Valachi, Genovese's cellmate in the Atlanta penitentiary, fearing assassination by Genovese's henchmen, turned informant and in testifying to a Senate investigative committee in 1963 gave information that only increased police and public attention on the Mafia or – as Valachi termed it – the Cosa Nostra. His testimony coincided with the last phases of the Gallo–Profaci war, which had wracked the Brooklyn Mafia for several years as fallout from Anastasia's murder. The war had begun after the Gallo brothers killed Frank 'Frankie Shots' Abbatemarco on the assumption that the boss of their family, Joseph Profaci, the 'olive oil king,' who resented Abbatemarco's delinquency in paying tribute, would give them a substantial portion of their victim's numbers business. When Profaci refused to share the family income, the Gallos kidnapped four members of his organization, whom they released only upon promise of fair treatment. When Profaci again failed to keep his word, the outnumbered Gallos raised a force of gangland dissidents and risked a 'mattress war' so disruptive that mob bosses Carlo Gambino and Tommy 'Three Finger Brown' Lucchese suggested to Profaci that he retire. The balance of power, which was shifting to the Gallos, was recovered when Joe Bonanno announced his support of his in-law Profaci. Although Profaci died in 1962, the war continued for another year, as the Gallos were satisfied only when Joe Columbo became family leader. Yet though Columbo instituted some reforms, the Gallos lost the war, and ultimately conflict broke out between them and the Columbos in the early 1970s, following Joey Gallo's release from prison. The struggle culminated in Gallo's assassination at Umberto's Clam House in Manhattan's Little Italy in the early morning hours of 7 April 1972.

The Mafia was further disrupted during the 1960s by the so-called Banana War, which extended from 1964 to 1969 and which pitted Joe Bonanno's family against the Gambino and Lucchese families. This war would have strongly affected Henry Hill, as he was an associate of the Lucchese family, which was allied to the Gambinos. Many attribute the hostilities to Bonanno's attempt to eliminate Carlo Gambino and Tommy 'Three Finger Brown' Lucchese as part of his plan to take over the drug traffic between the United States and Sicily. Bonanno claims that he simply reacted to his increasing isolation as a result of a power play orchestrated by Gambino, Lucchese, and Stefano Maggadino. After failing to assassinate his rivals, who were forewarned by his betrayer Joe Columbo, Bonanno refused to surrender. He claimed to have been kidnapped on 21 October 1964 and was subsequently spared execution, although he may have faked his own kidnapping to evade both a grand jury investigation and his mob enemies, who during his absence replaced him as family head with Gaspar Di Gregorio. This angered Bonanno's supporters, causing a war to break out within the Bonanno organization. At the same time, Joe Bonanno's enemies tried to wipe out the loyalists. By his own report Bonanno during his captivity had agreed to be replaced as family head, but upon his release he rejected the agreement and resumed the war against Di Gregorio with considerable success. Although Joe Bonanno suffered a severe heart attack in 1968, the Banana War continued in Brooklyn and Arizona, where he resided. He was finally allowed to keep his Western interests but was replaced in the New York area.

One should not exaggerate the internecine strife within the mob over the last five decades. Bonanno regards the Banana War as too small to merit that description. From 1930 onward, underworld wars have always occurred within rather than between crime families, which testifies to the relative stability of the larger organization.

See Nelli, *Business of Crime*, 253, 259–60; Nelli, 'Overview,' 3–4; Wolf, *Frank Costello*, 119; Salerno and Tompkins, *Crime Confederation*, 98, 103, 131–48, 296–300; Martin, *Revolt in the Mafia, passim*; Sondern, *Brotherhood of Evil*, 7, 13–17; Volkman and Cummings, *Goombata*, 45, 92–3; Gage, *Mafia Is Not an Equal Opportunity Employer*, 34–5; Volkman, *Gangbusters*, 76–9; Cook, *Mafia!*, 10–14, 205–37; Fred J. Cook, 'A Family Business: Hijacking, Book-making, Policy, Dice Games, Loan-Sharking and Special Contracts,' in Nicholas Gage, ed., *Mafia, U.S.A.* (New York: Playboy Press, 1972), 347, 348–61; Talese, *Honor Thy Father*, 73–4, 217–22; Sifakis, *Mafia Encyclopedia*, 12, 13, 18, 24–5, 136, 174, 203, 265; Russo, *Outfit*, 270; Cressey, *Theft of the Nation*, 201–3; Abadinsky, *Organized Crime*, 30, 87–8, 92, 100–1; Albini, *American Mafia*, 245; Lyman and Potter, *Organized Crime*, 132; Homer, *Guns and Garlic*, 44, 140–1; Abadinsky, *Criminal Elite*, 100; Roemer, *Roemer*, 23–4; Roemer, *War of the Godfathers*, 74–5; Bonanno, *Man of Honor*, 165–6, 207–93; Teresa, *My Life in the Mafia*, 81–4, 179; Reuter, *Disorganized Crime*, 214–15n; Donald Goddard, *Joey* (New York: Harper and Row, 1974), 5–11, 14, 34–5, 37–8, 69, 71–105.

40 Matthew 4:8: 'the kingdoms of the world and the glory of them.'
41 On Mafia recruitment, see Salerno and Tompkins's description of this

process in *Crime Confederation*, 94–7; Cressey, *Theft of the Nation*, 239–40; Abadinsky, *Organized Crime*, 22–3; Martin, *Revolt in the Mafia*, 60–2.

42 Idlewild Airport promised enormous riches to organized crime in the mid-1960s, as by then nearly thirty billion dollars worth of goods was being transmitted through airline shipping companies. The Lucchese family's ability to exploit this traffic was owed considerably to Johnny Dio, a family member who controlled the labour unions at the airport. His dominance began in the mid-1950s when, with the help of Jimmy Hoffa, Dio transformed Teamsters Locals 295 and 851 into extensions of his family organization. Henceforward the unions were used to extort labour peace, at the cost of huge bribes from shipping companies, and the freight and trucking companies were formed in a price-fixing organization. Union jobs were given to Lucchese representatives who conducted loan-sharking and facilitated hijacking at the airport. Essential to airport hijacking was a network of mob-controlled fences, with the profits proceeding upwards by percentage to Lucchese bosses. As is shown in *GoodFellas*, drivers were bribed to leave keys in the ignition of their trucks. In the film Hill mentions that if the airline companies complained about hijackings, *caporegime* Paulie Cicero (Vario) would threaten to incite a strike. Although the Gambino family had close ties with the Lucchese family, it concentrated less on hijacking than on the corruption of union officials, who, to quote Volkman and Cummings' *Heist*, 'extorted millions each year from frightened shippers eager to keep labour peace.' There was also some tension between families regarding hijacking, as the Gambinos regarded Jimmy Burke, the model for Jimmy Conway, as an overly reckless hijacker who endangered the airport operation. See Volkman and Cummings, *Goombata*, 65, 66; Volkman and Cummings, *Heist*, 37; Sifakis, *Mafia Encyclopedia*, 110, 152; Volkman, *Gangbusters*, 151–2.

43 The Copacabana carries Mafia associations in having once been owned by mob boss Frank Costello, 'prime minister of the underworld.' Police detective Raymond V. Martin writes: 'Everybody knows the Copacabana ... It is ... a top meeting place for the mob. Aside from Joe Profaci, a puritanical killjoy, almost every top mobster in the United States has been there at one time or another ... [It] seems to be a preferred syndicate watering place.' See Martin, *Revolt in the Mafia*, 214; see also Tosches, *Dino*, 161–3.

44 Dougan, *Martin Scorsese*, 94; see also Pileggi, *Wiseguy*, 70–1.

45 Pileggi, *Wiseguy*, 74, 77.

46 Pileggi, *Wiseguy*, 130.

47 Pileggi, *Wiseguy*, 23.

48 Tommy's fantasy of 'riding shotgun' conjoins Old West and Sicilian themes, as the 'technique most frequently associated with Mafia crimes in Sicily is the *lupara*, a spray of lead fired from a shotgun, and traditionally used by shepherds to protect their flocks from wolves (*lupi*).' See Schneider and Schneider, *Culture and Political Economy*, 197.

49 Sutherland, 'Organization of Criminals,' and Thomas Schelling, 'What is the Business of Organized Crime?': both essays in *Crime Society*, ed. Ianni and Reuss-Ianni, 5, 8, 70; Anderson, *Business of Crime*, 10; Abadinsky, *Organized Crime*, 70; Homer, *Guns and Garlic*, 4, 7.

50 See Walter Lippman, 'The Underworld as Servant,' in *Crime Society*, ed. Ianni and Reuss-Ianni, 162–72; Ianni, *Family Business*, 61, 92; Ianni, *Black Mafia*, 331–2; Martin, *Revolt in the Mafia*, 260, 264, 266; Kelly, 'Criminal Underworlds,' 11, 16–17; Cressey, *Theft of the Nation*, 72–3; Lyman and Potter, *Organized Crime*, 3, 502; Albini, *American Mafia*, 9–10, 55–7, 61–2, 305; Abadinsky, *Criminal Elite*, 125, 143; Lupsha, 'Organized Crime,' 33; Kappeler, Blumberg, and Potter, *Mythology of Crime*, 81, 91–2; Smith, 'Some Things That May Be More Important to Understand about Organized Crime than Cosa Nostra,' in *Crime Society*, ed. Ianni and Reuss-Ianni, 62, 65; Smith, *Mafia Mystique*, 67–8, 183; Kobler, *Capone*, 214, 215; Murray, *Legacy of Al Capone*, 147; Homer, *Guns and Garlic*, 4; Roemer, *Roemer*, 88–9; Block, 'Introduction: The Business of Organized Crime,' 2; Nelli, *Italians in Chicago*, 212; Morris and Hawkins, *Honest Politician's Guide to Crime Control*, 210–11; Kelly, Prologue to Kelly, *Upperworld and Underworld*, 2–3; Iorizzo and Mondello, 'Italian Americans and Organized Crime,' 191; Russo, *Outfit*, 270, 491–3.

51 J. Hillis Miller, 'The Critic as Host,' in Harold Bloom et al., *Deconstruction and Criticism* (New York: Seabury Press, 1979), 219.

52 See Abadinsky, *Criminal Elite*, 136, 143–4, 167; Abadinsky, *Organized Crime*, 222–5; Fox, *Blood and Power*, 381; Kwitny, *Vicious Circles*, 67–70. According to Hess, the extortion of 'protection' money has long been practiced by Sicilian Mafiosi: 'The typical form of making money ... is the exacting of tribute for protection allegedly offered; that is, for refraining from causing damage.' See Hess, *Mafia and Mafiosi*, 136. Whereas D'Acierno exaggerates the parasitic character of the Mafia, to the neglect of its symbiosis with the host society, the limitations of the 'willing victim' and functional theories of organized crime appear in the Sicilian Mafia, which customarily extends itself into areas where its 'protection' is not needed. For Schneider and Schneider, this is a 'strong argument against understanding mafia in terms of the "functions" it performed for the state and society.' See d'Acierno, 'Cultural Lexicon: Italian American Key Terms,' in *Italian*

American Heritage, ed. d'Acierno, 737; Schneider and Schneider, *Culture and Political Economy,* 180. Confining his discussion to Sicily, and noting the 'irrational, aggressive aspect of mafia activity itself,' Pino Arlacchi remarks that the 'case of the *mafioso*-entrepreneur clearly demonstrates that there is no automatic correspondence between entrepreneurial activity and the collective good.' See Arlacchi, *Mafia Business,* xv. William Howard Moore says that organized crime in the United States is sometimes 'purely parasitic,' virtually amounting to robbery. See Moore, *Kefauver Committee,* 16. More recently Diego Gambetta has argued that, in many instances, Mafia protection is freely or voluntarily chosen by buyers rather than extorted from them; moreover, that these buyers regard protection not as a threat or imposition but as a valuable service or commodity providing them with a definite functional advantage in their commercial affairs. See Gambetta, *Sicilian Mafia,* 3, 4, 19, 20, 21, 23, 28, 29, 187, 248, 277n.

53 Jimmy Conway is introduced at Paulie's gangster hang-out wearing a blue jacket, and subsequently he and Paulie appear in blue jackets of varying shades. At the hostess party attended by Karen and other Mafia wives, Morrie's wife Belle's face is half covered by a blue cosmetic unguent applied by Mrs Carbone, who wears blue earrings and is dressed partly in blue. Likewise, Mickey Conway wears conspicuously blue eye make-up. The scene is followed by one in which Karen has discarded a blue dress upon her marital bed, and another in which Tommy dresses in a blue overcoat during a hijacking; Henry also wears blue in this scene, as does the truckdriver. In the scene portraying the birthday celebration for Jimmy and Mickey's young son, not only do the boy and his parents wear blue clothes, but the birthday cake is blue and the room contains blue balloons. Blue is also the predominant colour in the inserted snapshots depicting the Hills and Conways amid their weekend and vacation get-togethers. When Karen points a pistol into the face of the sleeping Henry, he wears a blue shirt and lies upon a blue bed. Tommy wears a blue coat when he kills Stax, as does Johnny Roastbeef's wife when she enters the Christmas party after the Lufthansa heist. And this is only a partial list of examples. As for the meaning of these chromatic details, they suggest an undercurrent of melancholy at the core of the gangster life, consistent with the death wish possibly implied by the refrain of the Donovan song that plays on the juke-box during the murder of Batts: 'Way down below the ocean, where I wanna be.'

54 For reasons of security Mafia wives are, to quote Volkman and Cummings, 'not to venture beyond the tight circle of the family and their husbands' friends.' Nor are they allowed careers outside the home, which would also

jeopardize security. Yet Mafia wives usually find it easy to maintain such exclusive friendships, as they are often related by blood. A Mafia family normally patronizes stores and restaurants owned by members of the same professional kinship organization, that is, the Mafia 'family' in the larger sense. See Volkman and Cummings, *Goombata*, 64; Salerno and Tompkins, *Crime Confederation*, 99; Gage, *Mafia Is Not an Equal Opportunity Employer*, 96.

55 The disdainful, insulting behaviour of Jimmy Conway and the Mafia wives towards the FBI typifies the mob. John Gotti was driven 'wild' by the civility that Paul Castellano, whom he overthrew as head of the Gambino family, showed to FBI agents. See Ralph Blumenthal, Foreword to Gotti, *Gotti Tapes*, xvi; see also 13–14.

56 Vincent Teresa reports that a mob hustler works eighteen to twenty hours a day, seven days a week, with little time for home life. See Teresa, *My Life in the Mafia*, 189–90, 199.

57 Morrie is based on Marty Krugman, a hairdresser, bookie, loan shark, and would-be wise guy who, besides owning a hairpiece salon, had associations with Jimmy Burke and other mobsters involved in the Lufthansa heist. See Volkman and Cummings, *Heist*, 18, 68–70, 72–3. As is evident from the character of Morrie in *GoodFellas* and even more so from 'Ace' Rothstein, the protagonist of *Casino*, Scorsese and Pileggi, the second of whom is married to the Jewish writer Nora Ephron, are fascinated by Jewish–Italian relations in organized crime. Many of the earliest lords of Italian American crime, the so-called Mustache Petes or 'greaseballs,' were Sicilian-born Old World types who preferred working with fellow Sicilians and viewed Jewish (and Irish) gangsters unfavourably. Nonetheless, Jews and Irish gangsters attended some meetings of the Italian American crime bosses even in the 1920s. Upon defeating the Mustache Petes in 1931, Lucky Luciano introduced a new Italian American criminal organization in which Jews operated as financiers and distributors for the Italians. According to Sifakis, during the pre-war period organized crime was dominated by two commissions, one consisting of Italian Americans, the other including Italians and Jews and thus being of larger scope and influence. Although the Chicago mob was dominated by Italian Americans in the pre-war period, its chief financial officers were Jake and Sam Guzik, eastern European Jews. The Cleveland syndicates, which were largely Jewish, had close connections with Luciano and his associates, as did Jewish gangsters Meyer Lansky and Bugsy Siegel. The Calabrian-born Frank Costello, Luciano's successor, liked Jews (his wife was Jewish), but Vito Genovese, of Neapolitan background, wanted to sever the Mafia's

Jewish connection. Crime boss Joe Bonanno held similarly that Jews 'could not take part in our Tradition.' For many decades, the Italian American commission has prevailed over its rivals. Although Iorizzo and Mondello refer to Italian American gangsters' participation in multi-ethnic syndicates, as if to imply conditions of equality, Cressey remarks that Italian American gangsters deny Jewish associates any say in major decisions. As 'Ace' Rothstein is the pawn of his Italian American masters in *Casino*, and ultimately suffers the stigma of Jewishness in their eyes, so Rothstein's prototype, Frank 'Lefty' Rosenthal, complained that out of favouritism the mob bosses ignored the wrongs committed against him by Italian American mobster Tony Spilotro. To quote Jewish FBI agent Joe Yablonski: 'When push comes to shove, if it's an Italian against a Jew in the LCN [La Cosa Nostra], you know who's going to win.' Jimmy Fratianno held the same opinion. See Sondern, *Brotherhood of Evil*, 106; Nelli, *Business of Crime*, 212; Volkman and Cummings, *Goombata*, 40, 43; Sifakis, *Mafia Encyclopedia*, 85; Messick and Goldblatt, *Mob and Mafia*, 102; Bonanno, *Man of Honor*, 127; Ianni, 'Mafia and Web of Kinship,' 53; Gosch and Hammer, *Last Testament of Lucky Luciano*, 24, 39–40; Iorizzo and Mondello, 'Italian Americans and Organized Crime,' 211; Cressey, *Theft of the Nation*, 50; Abadinsky, *Criminal Elite*, 86; Roemer, *Enforcer*, 236; Demaris, *Last Mafioso*, 24, 69.

58 However, Jimmy's motivation is perhaps simply greed; in *Casino* the rapacious Nicky customarily lends money at three points of interest or 'vig' to all borrowers.

59 Stax Edwards wanted to join the Mafia (or 'Mafiay' as he called it) but was excluded because of his background. He could do no more than assist in a minor capacity. See Pileggi, *Wiseguy*, 206, 216–18. According to Carla Bianco, the immigrant Italians disdained blacks because they were gratified to find another minority beneath them on the social ladder. Mafiosi, who controlled numbers in black neighbourhoods as late as 1990, refer to blacks as 'niggers.' See Homer, *Guns and Garlic*, 82–3; Sifakis, *Mafia Encyclopedia*, 39, 244–5; Abadinsky, *Criminal Elite*, 162n.

60 Scorsese endorses the theme of De Mille's *The Ten Commandments* (1956): 'You cannot break the Ten Commandments or they will break you.' See Scorsese, *Personal Journey*.

61 See also Pileggi, *Wiseguy*, 127.

62 For this Mafia practice, see Tosches, *Dino*, 165.

63 Pileggi, *Wiseguy*, 19–20, 23, 37, 130.

64 See also Pileggi, *Wiseguy*, 36. Humbert Nelli finds the same disdain of 'suckers' in pre–Second World War gangsters. Nelli, *Business of Crime*, 106–7.

65 For the method of extorting from restaurants, see Pileggi, *Wiseguy*, 59–61.

66 The placement of the dead gangsters in a garbage truck would have been easy for Burke or Vario, as the Mafia has played a role in stabilizing the highly competitive waste-handling industry, in some cases taking over waste management businesses themselves. Thanks to the business acumen of boss Tony 'Tony Ducks' Corallo, Vario's own Lucchese family had been in the forefront of this form of monopolistic racketeering since the 1970s, focusing on Long Island and suburban New York. See Abadinsky, *Criminal Elite*, 137; *The Business of Crime*, ed. Block (see Part 6, 'Criminal Infiltration of the Toxic and Solid Waste Disposal Industries in New York State,' 175–96); Alan A. Block, *Perspectives on Organizing Crime: Essays in Opposition* (Dordrecht: Kluwer, 1991), 79–104; Volkman, *Gangbusters*, 149–51.

67 De Grazia, *Of Time, Work, and Leisure*, 7–8, 15, 22, 63–4, 82, 87, 93, 210, 269.

68 To quote Vincent Teresa: 'Night-clubs are big business for mob guys. They pick them because they like to cabaret, themselves. It gives them a place to meet, rather than, say, on a street corner. A nightclub is a great place to do business.' See Vincent Teresa, *My Life in the Mafia*, 118; Volkman and Cummings, *Heist*, 13. In films such as *Little Caesar*, *I Walk Alone*, and *Angels with Dirty Faces*, the gangster works out of a restaurant or bar. See Kaminsky, *American Film Genres*, 33.

69 Joseph Bonanno recalls that Joseph 'The Glutton' Masseria, an Italian American crime boss of the 1920s and early 1930s, had vowed to 'eat those people,' his gangland rivals, 'like a sandwich.' Commenting on Salvatore Maranzano's plot against Masseria, Bonnano remarks that the latter 'had a limited number of meals left to eat in this life.' In recounting Masseria's murder he states that 'Joe the Glutton was dead. He had eaten his last supper.' In the Mafia, to be victimized is to be eaten, while loss of appetite portends one's victimization. See Bonanno, *Man of Honor*, 101, 103, 122, 123.

70 At least from the early 1930s onward, the gangster film has linked violence to the consumption of ethnic food. In Mervyn Leroy's *Little Caesar* (1930) and Howard Hawks's *Scarface* the protagonists devour spaghetti while speaking pidgin English, heavily accented; Rico, or Little Caesar, has just accomplished a murder. The first *Godfather* depicts the gunman Clemenza enjoying a large meal in an Italian restaurant before driving the stool pigeon Paulie to his assassination, after which Clemenza orders the gunman: 'Leave the gun, take the cannoli.' In *Godfather, Part II* Vito Corleone (Robert De Niro) eats spaghetti as he hints in heavily accented English at the soon-to-be achieved assassination of the extortionist Fanucci. See John Paul Russo, 'The Hidden Godfather: Plenitude and Absence in Francis

Ford Coppola's *Godfather I and II*,' in Joseph L. Tropea et al., eds., *Support and Struggle: Italians and Italian Americans in a Comparative Perspective* (*Proceedings*, 18th Annual Conference, American Italian Historical Association) (Staten Island, N.Y.: American Italian Historical Association, 1986), 264.

71 See also Pileggi, *Wiseguy*, 86. Mafia members typically rationalize their criminal activities to the point of seeing them as legitimate and normative. In the words of federal informant Joe Valachi: 'Well, after you get used to burglarizing and committing crimes, you don't feel these other things are crimes. For instance, I had been in some machines, and I didn't think that was a crime; everyone else had them.' (He refers to the widespread profit-taking on illegal slot machines within the underworld.) Crime boss Joseph Bonanno writes: 'Some family members had illicit businesses such as bookmaking or numbers. In our world, such enterprises are not considered wrong.' Howard Becker observes of outsiders and subcultures that a person labelled an outsider may not accept the insiders' viewpoint. Just as an individual learns to participate in a subculture, so 'deviant groups tend, more than deviant individuals, to be pushed into rationalizing their position' by means of a 'self-justifying rationale (or "ideology").' See Homer, *Guns and Garlic*, 52–3, 113; Bonanno, *Man of Honor*, 149, 223; Howard S. Becker, *Outsiders: Studies in the Sociology of Deviance* (London: Free Press, 1963), 1–2, 4, 8, 31, 38–9, 81; Abadinsky, *Organized Crime*, 35–6.

72 Connelly, *Martin Scorsese*, 139.

73 Salerno and Tompkins observe that, 'as a minority group in a hostile environment, the criminal society needs the stability and protection that law offers. More than a social conveniences, laws are literally the difference between a smooth working organization and violent chaos.' In Ianni's view, the internal rules of Mafia families are of Sicilian derivation and constitute an informal family-based code of behaviour. However, Abadinsky argues more persuasively (in basic consistency with Cressey) that the Mafia's strictly defined rules of conduct emerged under specifically American conditions; moreover, they are administered by an internal government controlled by the bosses and amounting to a substitute for the state. The interests of the Mafia 'family' – typically an artificial entity formed of fictional kinship ties rather than actual blood relationships – take precedence over the actual kinship loyalties of any member. Sometimes to fulfil a judicial sentence but also as a test of his indifference to blood loyalties, a member may be required to murder a blood relative. A new member is required to recite important elements of the Mafia code in his induction ceremony. The organization's internal government is in-

tended to protect the property of individual members, to assign operations to specific territories, to adjudicate in territorial disputes, and to determine when to use its influence over law enforcement officials on a member's behalf.

A conscientious Mafioso refuses the help of the law while observing the code of silence (*omertà* in its narrower sense) in all that concerns his Mafia family, even under threat of imprisonment. The honorific title 'stand-up guy' is given to those who keep quiet under interrogation. A Mafioso must also show a virtually slavish respect for the bosses, rising in their presence, bowing before them, and opening and closing doors for their convenience. The major problem for any Mafia family is to stipulate and enforce rules for the control of internal violence, lest blood feuds reduce it to a 'Hobbesian jungle' or bad publicity jeopardize business operations. Joe Bonanno remarks: 'All societies ... use force, at some level, to enforce the values of that society. No well-ordered society tolerates indiscriminate and arbitrary violence. My world was no exception.' Similar to a centralized state-within-a-state, the government of a Mafia family monopolizes violence within its own realm as does a modern government, determining the distinction between acceptable and profane violence. In his induction ceremony a new member learns that he may not strike another member, and that if he does so, the offended party may retaliate lethally, without asking permission of the governing body. As Joe Valachi says: 'The most important ... [rule] is that you can't put your hands on another member. This is to keep one thing from leading to another.' It is also forbidden to commit adultery with another member's wife; if the cuckold discovers the betrayal, he may kill the man who has dishonoured him, again without asking permission. Normally, however, it is impermissible for members to take the law into their own hands; instead, they must submit to a sit-down with the bosses, who usually settle the dispute amicably and decisively.

According to George Simmel, the more lawless the secret society, the greater the need for hierarchy and unlimited authority, since the excess freedom claimed by its members needs tempering by their submissiveness to authority. 'The carefully considered and clear-cut architecture' of secret societies such as the Mafia furthermore adds to 'their energetic consciousness of their [own] life.' Salerno and Tompkins believe that, because of their working conditions, 'criminals violate their societies' laws less often' than their counterparts in non-criminal society and 'obey the law more carefully.' Yet, as Homer says, 'it would be wrong to imply that control is not a problem in these groups. The conflict between political and economic goals, disputes and disagreements over organizational and social norms, and a "generation" gap weaken internal discipline.' Writing in 1991, Block finds Mafia hierarchies and boundaries of action to have been challenged increasingly in recent decades. He mentions territories and organizations honoured only in the breach, widespread instability, disputes over rackets and turf, competition, and murderous treachery.

Salerno and Tompkins, *Crime Confederation*, 105–6, 111–12, 126–7, 157–8; Cressey, *Theft of the Nation*, 160–220; Abadinsky, *Criminal Elite*, 149, 150–1, 153, 158, 161, 165; Abadinsky, *Organized Crime*, 30–1; Hess, *Mafia and Mafiosi*, 109–10, 112; Anderson, *Business of Organized Crime*, 45; Annelise Anderson, 'Organized Crime, Mafia, and Governments,' and Stergios Skaperdas and Constantinos Syropolous, 'Gangs as Primitive States': both in *Economics of Organized Crime*, ed. Fiorentini and Peltzman, 33–5, 62; Block, 'Introduction: The Business of Organized Crime,' 8; Bonanno, *Man of Honor*, 77, 154–5; Maas, *Valachi Papers*, 207–15; Teresa, *My Life in the Mafia*, 87–9; Dickie, *Cosa Nostra*, 80; Gus Tyler, 'Sociodynamics of Organized Crime,' in *Crime Society*, ed. Ianni and Reuss-Ianni, 120–2; Lyman and Potter, *Organized Crime*, 7, 8; Homer, *Guns and Garlic*, 8–9, 109, 110–11, 139; Ianni, *Family Business*, 135–6, 144, 146–7; Simmel, 'The Sociology of Secrecy and Secret Societies,' *American Journal of Sociology* 11, no. 4 (January 1906): 478, 479, 492.
74 Simmel, 'Sociology of Secrecy,' 480.
75 Schneider and Schneider, *Culture and Political Economy*, 10.
76 Simmel, 'Sociology of Secrecy,' 466.
77 Donald Cressey's influential table of the organization of a typical crime family is largely based on Joseph Valachi's testimony and follows the assumption that Mafia families pattern themselves rigidly after a modern, centralized, rationalized, bureaucratic hierarchy such as a business corporation. At the top stands the boss, comparable to the president of a corporation, and below him an underboss (*sottocapo*) analogous to a vice-president. Acting in conjunction with the two chief executives is the *consigliere* or counsellor. The next administrative rank is that of *caporegime* (captain or lieutenant), of which a family is likely to have quite a few, each with his own crew composed of soldiers of varying status and ability (some of whom are only associates of the family). Mere soldiers have no administrative status and must prove their loyalty and earning power in their effort to rise in the organization. However, Cressey carries his corporate analogy too far, for unlike in a business, official job titles and responsibilities need not coincide in a Mafia family, nor does an exalted job title necessarily indicate a member's real status or power. There is also consid-

erable job overlap in a Mafia organization, whose members are often jacks-of-all-trades.

See Cressey, *Theft of the Nation*, 109–5; Anderson, *Business of Organized Crime*, 15; Salerno and Tompkins, *Crime Confederation*, 93; Teresa, *My Life in the Mafia*, 85–93; Villano, *Brick Agent*, 6; Abadinsky, *Criminal Elite*, 81–3, 95, 96, 101–2, 103, 108, 109; Abadinsky, *Organized Crime*, 18–29; Gage, *Mafia Is Not an Equal Opportunity Employer*, 31; Volkman and Cummings, *Goombata*, 59.

78 For Vario, see Pileggi, *Wiseguy*, 9–11, 34–5, 55–7. According to Ernest Volkman, the Lucchese family's 'most profitable subsidiary' in the 1960s and 1970s was Brooklyn, thanks largely to the 'premier criminal capitalist' Paulie Vario. Before his elevation to *caporegime* Paulie had specialized in illicit gambling and the enforcement of loans. His domain constituted a 'money machine' with enormous proceeds from 'narcotics, loansharking, illicit gambling, labour extortion, auto theft, hijacking, and at least two dozen assorted felonies.' The numbers operation in the black community totalled twenty-five thousand dollars on many days. Yet though Vario rivalled Tommy 'Three Finger Brown' Lucchese, family head up to his death in 1967, as a money earner, Lucchese found his 'notorious crudity' repellent. Vario was known to consume an entire shrimp cocktail by pouring it down his throat. The public visibility of his drunken brawling also angered the low-key, low-profile Lucchese. Vario was charged with income tax evasion on his 1966 and 1967 returns and made a fool of himself during the trial, thus ruining his chance to become Lucchese's successor, he was passed over as family boss in favour of Tony 'Tony Ducks' Corallo. In 1972 Vario suffered the 'first serious assault' against the Lucchese family when authorities placed an electronic bug in the trailer where he did business. Although he received a three-year prison sentence, he continued to direct operations from jail. In *GoodFellas* Henry mentions that Paulie Cicero, who is based on Vario, had received a one-year sentence for contempt. By the late 1970s Vario was performing badly as *caporegime* and, when a narcotics smuggling operation went sour, failed to achieve his 'big score.' His involvement with the Lufthansa heist, from which he received a very healthy cut, was driven by his need to repair his fortunes. This too explains his probable role in the murder of most of the participants, whether as possible informants or as potential claimants to a greater share of the pie, whose size had greatly exceeded expectations. On Vario, see Pileggi, *Wiseguy*, 9–11; Volkman and Cummings, *Heist*, 26–9, 34–45, 84, 103; Volkman, *Gangbusters*, 114–16, 117, 125–6, 146.

79 Elias Canetti, *Crowds and Power*, trans. Carol Stewart (New York: Farrar, Straus, Giroux, 1962), 206–7, 290.

80 On the Sicilians' long-standing preference for silence over garrulity, see the traditional fable reported in Hess, *Mafia and Mafiosi*, 110.

81 The bulldog was perhaps suggested by Volkman and Cummings's description of Vario in *The Heist*, 35: 'Squat, with large hanging jowls that made him look like bulldog.'

82 See Pileggi, *Wiseguy*, 59–61. Although they acknowledge the mob's sometimes helpful and pacifying role in Italian American neighbourhoods, Scorsese and Pileggi see the other side of the picture. To quote Pileggi: 'The wise guys might do little things like pay your rent, but the bottom line is, they are bad, and they are going to victimize you. They have to rob you. It's endemic.' Scorsese reports that in Little Italy crime bosses typically arbitrate disputes so that 'people don't get killed,' and that 'that's where the love comes in ... But ... as my father always pointed out, ... they are basically bloodsuckers. There was a whole group of guys who were doing little more than taking money. In other words, protection.' See Kelly, *Martin Scorsese: A Journey*, 262, 274.

83 Nicholls, *Scorsese's Men*, 105.

84 See Pileggi, *Wiseguy*, 9, 11: 'Vario tried to maintain a certain amount of decorum in a neighbourhood known for mayhem ... [He] had the responsibility for maintaining order among some of the city's most disorderly men. He assuaged grievances, defused ancient vendettas, and settled disputes between the stubborn and pig-headed.' See also 38: 'There were other marginal benefits bestowed upon those who were raised under the protective umbrella of the mob. Street muggings, burglaries, purse-snatchings, and rapes were almost nonexistent in mob-controlled areas.'

85 Italian American gangsters typically have girlfriends as well as wives. This practice apparently reflects the southern Italian sexual double standard distinguishing between the 'good' wife and mother and the 'bad' woman favoured as a sexual partner. See Gage, *Mafia Is Not an Equal Opportunity Employer*, 100; Teresa, *My Life in the Mafia*, 199; Vincent 'The Cat' Siciliano, *Unless They Kill Me First* (New York: Hawthorn, 1970), 21; Pileggi, *Wiseguy*, 140; Turkus and Feder, *Murder, Inc.*, 191; Sam Giancana and Chuck Giancana, *Double Cross: The Explosive, Inside Story of the Mobster Who Controlled America* (New York: Warner Books, 1992), 58, 60, 76–7, 99; Giancana and Renner, *Mafia Princess*, 57. However, Chicago mob boss Tony Accardo disapproved of his underlings' philandering and attempted to promote 'family values' among them. See Russo, *Outfit*, 247.

86 Nicholls claims that in ordering Henry to return to his family, Paulie

shows no concern for business or 'any core aspect of Cosa Nostra' but only for Henry's private spousal obligations. Such an interpretation ignores the convergence in this instance of familial and Mafia values, which Paulie impresses upon Henry. As Gambetta observes, the Mafioso must not become a cuckold, which would endanger group security. See Nicholls, *Scorsese's Men*, 117; Gambetta, *Sicilian Mafia*, 120.

87 In the Mafia the term 'made man' refers to an official member of a crime family. His admission is marked by a secret initiation ceremony in which he avows strict adherence to a code whose main requirements seem to be observed by Mafia families generally. In the past most Mafia families (the Chicago 'Outfit' being an exception) have limited membership to males of Sicilian or Italian ancestry on both sides, the object being to prevent infiltration. Yet in recent years, in response not only to a dwindling supply of recruits but to the Italian Americans' increasing rate of out-group marriage, Italian Americans have also been admitted if only their father was fully Italian. Not only must a candidate be sponsored by a top boss, he must also receive a unanimous vote of bosses and captains. The typical candidate comes from a neighbourhood with a criminal network and is about thirty years old. He is likely to have an extensive criminal record, usually burglary and robbery, and probably one prison sentence. According to Teresa, an inductee is required to have committed a murder, although he noted at least one exception to this rule, which by the 1980s seemed to have lapsed among many families. Instead, the inductee has only to have participated in a murder, without being the trigger man. During John Gotti's leadership of the Gambino family, murder was apparently required for induction, although Gotti wanted 'guys that done more than killin'.'

The practice of a ceremonial initiation into a Mafia family originates in the small, loosely organized criminal groups or secret brotherhoods of nineteenth-century Sicily. In 1916 a Sicilian who was forced to join a criminal group underwent an initiation ritual during which his middle finger was pricked by a needle, and blood was squirted from it in order to soak a small paper image of a saint. After the burning of the image, the inductee, holding the ashes in his hand, had to recite an oath pledging loyalty to his brothers, with the final provision that if he failed to observe *omertà*, he should turn to ashes as did the holy image. This ceremony apparently repudiates Christianity in favour of another system of morality and sanctity, namely the criminal organization. To quote E.J. Hobsbawm, the burning of the image 'may have been designed to bind the novice to the brotherhood by the ceremonial breaking of a taboo: a ritual invoking

the firing of a pistol at a statue of Jesus Christ is also reported' in Sicily.
Not only does the quasi-religious induction ceremony that took place in
1916 closely resemble a ceremony enacted by a Sicilian Fratellanza, a kind
of criminal organization, in 1885, as described by Humbert Nelli; it also
resembles, as Fred J. Cook notes, that undergone by Italian American
criminal Joe Valachi in the United States in the early 1930s. However,
Valachi was also required to swear upon a gun and dagger that he would
live and die by those weapons while pledging undying loyalty to the
organization above family, religion, and country. The gun and dagger
seem to derive not from the Sicilian Mafia but from the Neapolitan
Camorra, and are mentioned as early as 1872. During his induction at
Cleveland's Statler Hotel, Angelo Lonardo, who rose to a high place in the
Cleveland mob, sat at a table as the bosses commanded him never to deal
in narcotics and prostitution; he also had to commit murder if called upon
to do so. The revolver and dagger produced from under the tablecloth
signified willingness to die with those weapons. Next receiving a paper
picture of a saint that was then burned to ashes, Lonardo had his finger
pricked. After he had sucked the blood from the wound, the bosses shook
hands and kissed each other on the cheek: 'You are a member from now
on,' they announced. Jimmy 'The Weasel' Fratianno and four other men
were inducted into the Los Angeles Mafia in 1947 in a similar ceremony.
'I felt like I was in church' recalls Fratianno, and that Jack Dragna, Los
Angeles family crime boss, 'was going to make me a fucking priest.'

Induction ceremonies appear to have varied depending on the families
concerned. Al Capone swore upon a Bible during his initation into the
Chicago mob, whose present induction ceremony Hobsbawm compares to
a luncheon for a new employee, void of Old World dramatics. Reminisc-
ing in the early 1970s, Vincent Teresa recalled that inductions into the New
England Mafia had recently become businesslike. In *The Crime Confederation* (1969), Salerno and Tompkins claimed that the Mafia had replaced
induction ceremonies with banquets. In the view of later commentators
such as Jonathan Kwitny and Stephen Fox, the rituals of bloodletting have
gone out of fashion.

The latter claim is refuted by recent decriptions of induction ceremonies,
such as that of Gambino family underboss Sammy 'The Bull' Gravano in
the mid-1970s. Like Tommy DeVito in *GoodFellas*, Gravano dressed formally for his induction and was driven by other formally dressed Mafiosi
to the house of a family member where, with other gangsters, he was
officially inducted. The lasting fidelity he pledged to the organization
entailed a vow not to inform on fellow members or to pursue their wives.
Trafficking in drugs and the striking of fellow members were likewise

forbidden to Gravano under oath. Yet he was also required to kill for the organization. Not only was the swearing-in ceremony accompanied by finger-pricking and the burning of a saint's paper image, but Gravano was pledged to absolute secrecy lest his soul burn like the paper. However, the pistol and dagger were omitted. In *The Last Mafioso* Jimmy Fratianno describes a Los Angeles crime family initiation in 1976 that hardly differed from his own nearly thirty years before. A Sicilian induction ceremony conducted in 1975, mentioned in Ralph Blumenthal's *Last Days of the Sicilians*, closely resembled that of Joseph Valachi, which was virtually identical to that of a Mafia inductee as secretly tape-recorded by the FBI in Providence, Rhode Island, as late as 1989. Anthony 'Gas Pipe' Casso reports that the traditional induction was still employed by the Lucchese crime family into the 1990s.

Two of the most important components of the oath administered to Mafia inductees apparently originated at the conclusion of the Castellamarese war in 1931, having been introduced by the victor, Salvatore Maranzano, not long before his assassination. Realizing that internal violence could easily get out of hand and undermine the entire organization, Maranzano required all members to pledge never to strike one another. The initiation oath also stipulated that a member should never commit adultery with the wife of another member, lest jealous rivalries lead to internally destructive vendettas.

According to Joseph Pistone, a 'made man' enjoys unbounded satisfaction, for no matter how disliked he may be, he has more respect and protection, thanks to his family connection, than other criminals. No other family can encroach upon his turf without permission, and he can, for instance, start his own gambling operation knowing that no outside competition will be tolerated. Unlike a non-member, a made man can represent himself in person at a table meeting presided over by a top boss. Another advantage is that he is permitted to enter activities from which non-members are excluded. Being on his own, he need not rely on a patron, but has the freedom to set up, for instance, a loan-sharking or numbers business, with assigned territory and underlings from whom he receives tribute but to whom he gives none. A made man may also patronize non-member clients, as did Paulie Vario with Henry Hill, Jimmy Burke, and Tommy DeSimone. Pistone's mentor, Benjamin 'Lefty Guns' Ruggiero, a high-ranking member of the Bonanno family, told him that a non-member must never argue with a made man, much less raise a hand against him. However, Vincent Teresa noted that a Mafia family owns a member 'body and soul,' as he cannot refuse to perform certain actions, such as the murder of blood kindred.

Besides 'made man,' Mafia terms for an official member of a crime family include 'wise guy' and 'goodfellow' or 'goodfella.' Thus the title of *GoodFellas* is misleading, as neither Henry Hill, Jimmy Conway, nor Tommy De Vito is a made man.

See Nelli, *Business of Crime*, 16; Cook, *Mafia!*, 32–3; Homer, *Guns and Garlic*, 114–15; Maas, *Valachi Papers*, 95–6, 207–15; Jacobs, *Busting the Mob*, 102–3, 105, 107, 118–19; Volkman and Cummings, *Goombata*, 59, 73; Joseph D. Pistone, *Donnie Brasco: My Undercover Life in the Mafia* (New York: New American Library, 1987), 64–5; Demaris, *Last Mafioso*, 3–4, 17–18, 326; Sifakis, *Mafia Encyclopedia*, 165; E.J. Hobsbawm, 'Mafia,' in *Crime Society*, ed. Ianni and Reuss-Ianni, 93; Teresa, 'Mafioso Cases the Mafia Craze,' 151; Kwitny, *Vicious Circles*, 63; Fox, *Blood and Power*, 68–9; Kelly, *Upperworld and Underworld*, 35–6, 54; Salerno and Tompkins, *Crime Confederation*, 97–9; Cressey, *Theft of the Nation*, 237–8; Abadinsky, *Criminal Elite*, xiii, 115–23, 154, 167; Abadinsky, *Organized Crime*, 20, 22–5, 30, 129; Roemer, *Roemer*, 168; Gotti, *Gotti Tapes*, 143–8; Dickie, *Cosa Nostra*, 29, 32, 44–5; Gambetta, *Sicilian Mafia*, 146–8, 151, 262–70; Teresa, *My Life in the Mafia*, vii, 87–8, 180; Roemer, *Spilotro*, 47–9; Roemer, *War of Godfathers*, 15; Roemer, *Accardo*, 37–8; Blumenthal, *Last Days of Sicilians*, 31; Russo, *Outfit*, 2; Volkman, *Gangbusters*, xii; Charles Rappleye and Ed Becker, *All-American Mafioso: The Johnny Rosselli Story* (New York: Doubleday, 1991), 27, 124; Nicholls, *Scorsese's Men*, 106.

88 Simmel, 'The Sociology of Secrecy,' 462, 464, 470, 473, 480–2, 484. When a made man introduces a non-initiate to fellow initiates, he says: 'I'd like you to meet a friend of mine.' But in introducing to fellow initiates another made man, he says: 'I'd like to introduce a friend of ours [*amico nostro*].' See Gotti, *Gotti Tapes*, 148. John Dickie remarks certain parallels between religious organizations and the Mafia, including their common requirement of commitment, loyalty, and belief. 'Mafia religion,' observes Dickie, 'generates a sense of belonging, trust, and a set of flexible rules by borrowing words from the Catholic creed.' See Dickie, *Cosa Nostra*, 32.

89 Pileggi, *Wiseguy*, 57, 130–2.

90 One should not exaggerate the mob's helpfulness. As Thomas Schelling contends, not only does organized crime mainly target the underworld, but criminals unable to seek legal protection are the ideal victims. See Schelling, 'What Is the Business of Organized Crime?' 75–80.

91 See Pileggi, *Wiseguy*, 55, 116. A mob family observes a custom of tribute whereby lower-echelon men, having received permission to attempt a 'score,' must give their superiors roughly 10 to 15 per cent of their illegal earnings. These contributions, properly given with 'affection' and a 'show

of respect,' keep the bosses happy. However, members sometimes with-
hold tribute under some pretext or other, which rarely angers the bosses
so long as a reasonable amount is surrendered. Cheating is usually dangerous in the long run, while a perpetually poor earner may face execution. Needless to say, tribute is unidirectional; whereas the boss always
demands a 'piece of the action,' the lower-echelon worker is a private
entrepreneur rather than a paid employee and thus receives no salary.
What he receives from the bosses is permission to operate and some protection in the event of legal troubles. In this respect, the Mafia resembles
not a bureaucracy but a government, with its powers of taxation. Atypical
of the mob, Lucchese family bosses demanded only token tribute from
their underlings. See Abadinsky, *Organized Crime*, 29, 31; Salerno and
Tompkins, *Crime Confederation*, 99; Jacobs, *Busting the Mob*, 103; Nelli,
Business of Crime, 209–10; Sifakis, *Mafia Encyclopedia*, 265; Pistone, *Donnie
Brasco*, 65–7; Abadinsky, *Criminal Elite*, 98, 119, 135–6; Volkman,
Gangbusters, 61, 145–6.

92 Initially the Jewish mob dominated the narcotics trade, but in the 1920s
Lucky Luciano was also active as a drug trafficker, and by the 1930s he
and other Italian American bosses were taking over drug sales at an
enormous profit. Although many bosses, such as Chicago's Paul 'The
Waiter' Ricca, Joe Bonanno, and Frank Costello, frowned on this type of
business, fearing bad publicity, its high profits attracted Mafiosi, and some
bosses such as Lucchese sold drugs clandestinely. By 1950 the five New
York Mafia families enjoyed 95 per cent of the business. What made it
highly attractive was that convictions for narcotics trafficking carried brief
sentences – ten years at the maximum, but rarely more than two or three
years. In 1955, however, the Narcotics Control Act set much stiffer punishments – five to twenty years for a first offence, ten to twenty years for
a second. Over the next eighteen months, 206 drug-trafficking Mafiosi
were imprisoned. The Mafia summit meeting at Apalachin, New York, in
October 1957, which was interrupted by local police, was partly intended
to impose a ban on the drug trade. This was necessary not only to avoid
involvement with erratic Cuban and Puerto Rican gangsters but, more
importantly, to eliminate the possibility that arrested drug traffickers
would exchange information for reduced sentences or immunity. Following the Apalachin fiasco, hoodlum Nelson Cantalops may have been
enlisted by a number of crime bosses, including Carlo Gambino, in order
to present federal authorities with information concerning the involvement of crime boss Vito Genovese in a narcotics deal. In 1959 Genovese
was sentenced to fifteen years in a federal prison, where he died in 1969.

Now the top figure in organized crime, Gambino successfully proposed that New York's five leading crime families prohibit their members from drug-dealing. By the early 1960s, the Mafia had shifted from high-risk drug-smuggling to low-risk wholesale operations. Yet many gangsters disregarded the prohibition, the profits being too tempting. In the 1970s and 1980s the Bonanno family was involved in the Pizza Connection, which dominated heroin traffic between the United States and Sicily.

See Volkman and Cummings, *Goombata*, 78–80; Gage, *Mafia Is Not an Equal Opportunity Employer*, 35; Talese, *Honor Thy Father*, 74; Sifakis, *Mafia Encyclopedia*, 20, 235; Salerno and Tompkins, *Crime Confederation*, 159; Nelli, 'Overview,' 5–6; Nelli, *Business of Crime*, 123; Roemer, *Roemer*, 29–30; Bonanno, *Man of Honor*, 149, 209–10; Volkman, *Gangbusters*, 47–9, 75–7; Blumenthal, *Last Days of Sicilians*, 7, 51, 80–3; Blumenthal, Foreword to Gotti, *Gotti Tapes*, xvi.

93 The ranks within a Mafia family's hierarchy are tightly insulated, as the vast majority of its members know little or nothing of the higher-ups, whom they rarely if ever see. According to Vincent Teresa: 'In the operation of a crime family, there is an orderly chain of command that must be observed. Associate members may talk to soldiers, soldiers seek rulings from captains, captains talk to consiglieres (advisers) or the underboss, and only the underboss talks to the crime leader.' Crime boss Joseph Bonanno never met many members of his organization. See Ianni, 'What Is Organized Crime?' 4; Pileggi, *Wiseguy*, 252–3; Gage, *Mafia Is Not an Equal Opportunity Employer*, 113; Abadinsky, *Organized Crime*, 28; Salerno and Tompkins, *Crime Confederation*, 156–7; Kappeler, Blumberg, and Potter, *Mythology of Crime*, 84; Cressey, *Theft of the Nation*, 226–7; Bonanno, *Man of Honor*, 157; Teresa, *My Life in the Mafia*, 87, 113; Ruggiero, *Crime and Markets*, 3–4. On 'degrees of secrecy' and 'hidden authority' within secret societies, including criminal organizations, see Simmel, 'Sociology of Secrecy,' 488, 489, 493, 494.

94 Portrayed by Frank Pellegrino, Johnny Dio was a highly important member of the Lucchese crime family. Born in 1914 or 1915 as John Dioguardi, Dio began his career under Lucky Luciano as a shake-down racketeer in Manhattan's garment district, forcing manufacturers to employ only those truckers who paid dues to the trucking association dominated by Dio, his brother Vincent Dio, and his uncle James Plumeri. Joseph Valachi recalls that Dio enabled him to carry on a dress-manufacturing business for twelve years without union workers. In 1937 Dio was jailed for extortion and four years later served a six-month jail term for unlawful possession of narcotics. In the mid-1950s he provided essential mob support for James Hoffa's take-over of the International Brotherhood of Teamsters, with

which Dio had close ties. The 1956 blinding of journalist Victor Riesel, whose articles attacked corruption in the Teamsters' Union, was probably ordered by Dio, who escaped conviction by intimidating witnesses. This reckless act likely cost him leadership of the Lucchese family upon the death of Tommy 'Three Finger Brown' Lucchese in 1967. During the 1950s, Senate investigations named Hoffa and Dio as the masterminds behind the 'paper locals' of the union that ultimately took over the airport trucking business in New York City. Dio thus participated crucially in the operations of the Lucchese family as depicted in *GoodFellas*. Besides referring to the family's control of labour unions at Idlewild airport, the film portrays the hijacking operations in which Henry and his associates among the Lucchese soldiers engaged in collaboration with the truckers themselves. As a friend of corrupt union representative Allen Dorfman (who appears in *Casino* as Andy Stone), Dio had a powerful influence on such unions as the Amalgamated Meatcutters and United Automobile Workers, AFL. By June 1954 Dio held the title of business manager of UAW local 102, and subsequently became regional director of UAW. In November 1955 Hoffa chartered seven new Teamsters locals in the New York area, five of which were transferred to Dio's UAW. The auto workers union over which he presided was a shake-down operation directed against employees. In 1958 he was cited by Senator John L. McClellan's investigative committee for corrupting union locals. When called upon to testify, he took the Fifth Amendment 140 times. His close associate in labour racketeering was Tony 'Tony Ducks' Corallo, who became head of the Lucchese family in the 1970s. Imprisoned for tax evasion in 1954, Dio went to jail in 1957 for two years because of a shakedown operation, and in 1962 received a two-year sentence for bribing a judge. He later became highly successful in stock fraud ventures as well as in huge frauds in the kosher meat business. In the late 1960s he was convicted in two cases of stock fraud, and in October 1970 his kosher meat fraud landed him in jail with a long sentence that was lengthened after another trial in 1973. During the mid-1970s Dio and Henry Hill lived together in Lewisburg Prison, where Dio ran his illegal businesses behind the scenes. The prison scene in *GoodFellas*, in which Dio pan fries choice steaks for his fellow inmates, including Paulie Cicero (Vario) and Henry Hill, implies ironically that he is still cheating the United States government, having received these steaks not only by bribing prison officials but through his meat fraud operations. He died in 1979, after repeated failed attempts to commute his sentence. On Dio, see Sifakis, *Mafia Encyclopedia*, 109–10, 283; Kwitny, *Vicious Circles*, 12, 13, 65, 66, 145–6, 155, 213, 267–74, 278, 307–8, 319, 392; Volkman, *Gangbusters*, 124–5, 127–9, 151–2; Maas, *Valachi Papers*,

174–5; Arthur A. Sloane, *Hoffa* (Cambridge, Mass.: MIT Press, 1991), 81–3, 86–7, 98, 119, 127, 156, 161, 403–4; Abadinsky, *Organized Crime*, 256–7; *Business of Crime*, ed. Block, 99, 104, 126, 127–8; Volkman and Cummings, *Heist*, 37–8; Smith, *Mafia Mystique*, 155–6; Goddard, *Joey*, 42.

95 Noted by Pileggi, *Wiseguy*, 252. See also Smith, 'Martin Scorsese Interviewed,' 152. Nicholls contends, inexplicably, not only that Henry Hill is 'significantly outside' the mob but that his ambiguous position as a 'stranger' within it prevents him from knowing its secrets. See Nicholls, *Scorsese's Men*, 102, 104, 124.

96 Kelly, *Martin Scorsese: A Journey*, 259.

97 Thomas Hobbes, *Leviathan*, ed. C.B. MacPherson (Harmondsworth: Penguin, 1975), part 1, chapt. 6, 125: '*Sudden Glory* is the passion which maketh those grimaces called *Laughter*; and is caused either by some sudden act of their own, that pleaseth them; or by the apprehension of some deformed thing in another, by comparison whereof they suddenly applaud themselves.'

98 The organization known as the Gambino family, after its leader Carlo Gambino, who ruled from 1957 to his death in 1976, has a continuous history from the 1920s onward. It originated with Sicilian-born mobster Vincent Mangano, who began with the Mineo crime family, and who assumed Mineo's position after his assassination during the Castellamarese war. Having served in that conflict as an associate of Lucky Luciano, Mangano joined the board of directors of the new crime syndicate Luciano had organized, although he ranked below the top six. Mangano's family concentrated on waterfront rackets and had close ties with Murder, Inc., whose chief executioner, Albert Anastasia, was technically Mangano's underling. However, not only did Anastasia feel closer ties with such Americanized bosses as Costello and Luciano, but he and Mangano had major differences. Ultimately Anastasia eliminated both Vincent and Philip Mangano, taking over the family, with Carlo Gambino as his underboss. In 1957 Gambino secretly arranged with Vito Genovese for the assassination of Anastasia as punishment for his violent temper, sales of Mafia membership, and encroachments in Florida and the Caribbean. Gambino then assumed control of the family and ruled it for nearly two decades. Soon after assuming family leadership, Gambino seems to have participated with other bosses in a plot whereby Vito Genovese was sent to prison for fifteen years for involvement in a drug deal. In his victory over Costello and Genovese, Gambino was supported by Tommy 'Three Finger Brown' Lucchese, head of the Lucchese family, which maintained friendly working relations with the Gambinos. From the late 1950s

onward the two families solidified their base in garment trucking while expanding on the manufacturing side. The provision of exclusive and mandatory trucking services to garment shops proved highly lucrative. Like the Lucchese family, the Gambinos practiced theft and hijacking as well as labour racketeering at Kennedy airport, but with more emphasis on the latter. Upon Gambino's death, control of the family went to Paul Castellano, who was publicly assassinated in 1985 by orders of John Gotti, the new family leader. Gotti escaped conviction for several years but in 1992 was sentenced to life in prison, where he died in 2003. By 1992 the state had ended Gambino dominance of the garment industry. The family remains in disarray after the revelations of Sammy 'The Bull' Gravano, the informer who brought down Gotti, his former boss, and many associates.

See Volkman, *Goombata*, 7; Talese, *Honor Thy Father*, 220; Sifakis, *Mafia Encyclopedia*, 11, 13, 136, 213–14; Abadinsky, *Organized Crime*, 28, 44, 92–3, 95–6, 99, 101, 262–3; Lupsha, 'Organized Crime,' 53; *Business of Crime*, ed. Block, 94, 98, 99, 101–2; Bonanno, *Man of Honor*, 121, 207, 225, 228–9, 234–6, 250–1; Volkman, *Gangbusters*, 58; Volkman and Cummings, *Heist*, 37.

99 The idea of Tommy DeVito as a former shoeshine boy was apparently suggested by the life of Tommy DeSimone. A shoeshine boy during his childhood, he was never without a shine. Yet few dared to refer to DeSimone's former employment in his presence, as he was believed to have murdered a hood who had reminded him of it. See Volkman and Cummings, *The Heist*, 16.

100 For an Italian American of Tommy's generation the idea of being a shoeshine boy may have carried reminders of a degraded ethnic past, for not only did many Italian immigrants take up this occupation beginning in the 1860s, but representations of the group included the stereotype of the bootblack. In the 1915 silent film *The Italian*, the main character Beppo Donati, played by George Beban, becomes a bootblack in America after working in Italy as a gondolier. See Mangione and Morreale, *La Storia*, 134, 223; Tomasi, *Piety and Power*, 63; Lopreato, *Italian Americans*, 147–8; Bondanella, *Hollywood Italians*, 22–8.

101 Pileggi, *Wiseguy*, 131–2.

102 Sicilians believe that to cuckold another person implies superiority in honour, although homicide may result if the victim rejects that claim. Generally, a poor man is assumed to be a passive cuckold, and can be dishonoured in at least two ways. There is either the *cornuto bastionato*, powerless to retaliate, or the *cornuto contento*, 'who in effect sells his wife or daughter to a status superior.' See Schneider and Schneider, *Culture*

and Political Economy, 100–1. On the *cornuto contento*, see also Pellegrino d'Acierno, 'Cultural Lexicon: Italian American Key Terms,' in *Italian American Heritage*, ed. d'Acierno, 719. Nicholls mistakenly takes Tommy's mother's anecdote to refer to a man named Campari rather than to a *compare* or godfather. See Nicholls, *Scorsese's Men*, 109. Scorsese's interest in the *cornuto* owes something to Rossellini's *Stromboli* (1949), in which a Sicilian fisherman (Mario Vitale) is mocked as a cuckold (and also as a *cornuto contento*) on the false suspicion that his wife (Ingrid Bergman) has betrayed him. See Scorsese, *Il Mio Viaggio*.

103 Bliss, *World Made Flesh*, 98.

104 Compare Rico Bandello, the gangster hero of Mervyn Leroy's *Little Caesar*: 'I don't want no dance. I figure on makin' other people dance.'

105 Pileggi, *Wiseguy*, 167–70. Scorsese's portrayal of Henry's stint in Lewisburg Prison may be reasonably accurate. Although Volkman and Cummings describe Lewisburg as a 'forbidding place ... one of the tightest prisons in the entire federal system,' these conditions seem not to have applied to Mafioso prisoners such as Vincent Teresa, who was confined to Lewisburg not long before Hill's arrival. 'As prisons go,' recalled Teresa, 'I didn't find Lewisburg that bad. As a matter of fact, the mob calls it "the country club." Not that it's heaven.' A special advantage of G-Block, or 'Mafia Row,' was that, being absolutely off-limits to other prisoners, it remained free of the racial conflicts elsewhere in the prison. The true ruler of G-block was not the warden but Carmine Galante, a boss in the Bonanno crime family. Incoming prisoners to Mafia Row received quality haircuts, decent prison clothes, and the best jobs. Galante, who liked plants and worked in the prison hothouse, had a small home-made grill and refrigerator and often treated friends to breakfasts and dinners consisting of ham, sausage, pancakes, candy, fine tenderloin steaks, tomatoes, pepper, olive oil, macaroni, peanut butter, and salt and pepper. Some of this food was from the hothouse, but much of it was lifted from the prison farm; the steaks came from the prison butchers, whom Galante bribed, while the salt and pepper was stolen from the officers' mess. Galante also had several pet cats. During his stay in 'Club Lewisburg,' as he called it, Teresa transformed the office where he worked into a furnished clubhouse, although the place was finally raided. Like Galante, Paulie Vario during his term at Lewisburg not only continued to run his criminal operations but often cooked for fellow inmates, his *pasta e fagiole* being regarded as incomparable. According to Volkman, every prison has its 'Mafia Manor' where, in an orderly and trouble-free environment, gangsters remain subject to the rules of the organization, and where they

enjoy sex, special food, and drugs. See Volkman and Cummings, *Goombata*, 68; Teresa, *My Life in the Mafia*, 2, 5, 298–30, 307, 309–10; Volkman, *Gangbusters*, 108–9, 115–16; Sloane, *Hoffa*, 331–4, 342.

106 Some observers hold that an imprisoned Mafioso's family is taken care of by his colleagues. See Salerno and Thompson, *Crime Confederation*, 114. This is not the case in *GoodFellas*, in which Karen complains that during Henry's stay in prison her friends totally neglected her and her children, and in which Henry runs drugs in order to support his family. Yet Henry may have no claim to such help, as he does not belong officially to a crime family. See Pileggi, *Wiseguy*, 178, 183.

107 Actually in the late 1970s Vario was already suffering economically when he failed to bring off a large narcotics smuggling operation. See Volkman and Cummings, *Heist*, 26–9, 35, 40–5.

108 Hill was trading heroin for cocaine supplied by his Pittsburgh connection. See Volkman and Cummings, *Heist*, 73.

109 The 'great Lufthansa slaughter' began when Jimmy retaliated against crew members who had ignored his warnings against overspending. Yet Scorsese and Pileggi allowed themselves some liberty with the facts. The film character Joe Buddha is based on crew member Joe Manri, who answered to that nickname. But no members of Jimmy's crew were named Frankie Carbone or Johnny 'Roastbeef,' as in the film, although 'Roastbeef' may be modelled on a crew member who was very fat. The pink Cadillac that Roastbeef purchases for his wife in his mother's name was probably suggested by the 'pimpmobile' driven by Tommy DeSimone, rather than by the pink Cadillac in the black-and-white film *Hud*, as Lesley Stern suggests. The death of Roastbeef and his wife in their Cadillac conflates the disappearance of crew member Louis Cafora and his wife with the deaths of Joe Manri and Frenchie McMahon, whose bodies were found in a two-door Buick on 16 May 1979 in the Mill Basin section of Brooklyn; they had been shot in the back of the head, a mode of killing reminiscent of Tommy's ice-pick murder of Morrie Kessler, who was probably thrown into the ocean from a plane. Whereas in the film Stax Edwards is killed by Tommy DeVito, who holds him in contempt, the real Stax was killed on Jimmy's orders by Tommy DeSimone, who had been good friends with his victim since their days in prison. See Volkman and Cummings, *Heist*, 121–2, 175, 177, 187–8, 193–4, 195; Stern, *Scorsese Connection*, 144–5.

110 Mary Douglas holds that 'ideas about separating, purifying, demarcating, and punishing transgressions have as their main function to impose system on an inherently untidy experience. Characterizing the 'old

definition of dirt as matter out of place' as a 'very suggestive approach,' Douglas finds it to imply 'two conditions: a set of ordered relations and a contravention of that order. Dirt, then, is never a unique, isolated event … Dirt is the by-product of a systematic ordering and classification of matter.' As prohibitions aim to avoid anomalous, ambiguous, and in-between things that elude classification, so 'pollution behaviour … condemns any object or idea likely to confuse or contradict cherished classifications.' See Douglas, *Purity and Danger*, 4, 35–6, 39, 40.

111   On waste, with reference to differentiation, pollution, and transgression, see William G. Little, *The Waste Fix: Seizures of the Sacred from Upton Sinclair to the Sopranos* (New York: Routledge, 2002).

112   Pileggi, *Wiseguy*, 220.

113   Matthew, 26:52. This is the epigraph to Mervyn Leroy's *Little Caesar* (1930).

114   Scorsese comments on this sequence in *Scorsese on Scorsese*, ed. Thompson and Christie, 160. See also Amy Taubin, 'Martin Scorsese's Cinema of Obsessions,' *Village Voice*, 18 September 1990, in *Martin Scorsese: Interviews*, ed. Brunette, 141.

115   Kelly, *Martin Scorsese: A Journey*, 259.

116   Jacobs, *Hollywood Renaissance*, 137.

117   Simmel, 'Sociology of Secrecy,' 450n.

118   'It was characteristic of the Mafia to use as executioners men who were so close to the intended victim that they could not be suspected.' See Martin, *Revolt in the Mafia*, 131. See also Giancana and Renner, *Mafia Princess*, 45.

119   Smith, 'Martin Scorsese Interviewed,' 146–7.

8. Pariahs of a Pariah Industry: *Casino*

1   The following discussion of *Casino* is based on both the film and Nicholas Pileggi and Martin Scorsese, *Casino* (London: Faber and Faber, 1996), a transcript of the completed film that will be referred to as the 'screenplay.'

2   Sangster, *Scorsese*, 245; Ian Christie, 'Introduction: Stardust in Vegas,' in Pileggi and Scorsese, *Casino*, xi; Dougan, *Martin Scorsese*, 103–4.

3   Brode, *Films of Robert De Niro*, 264, 265.

4   Ian Christie, 'Martin Scorsese's Testament,' *Sight and Sound*, January 1996, in *Martin Scorsese: Interviews*, ed. Brunette, 223.

5   'Passion and Restraint,' 68.

6   Brode, *Films of Robert De Niro*, 266; Bondanella, *Hollywood Italians*, 279; Friedman, *Cinema of Martin Scorsese*, 175; Sangster, *Scorsese*, 245.

7   Christie, 'Introduction,' x.

8   Sangster, *Scorsese*, 247.

9 Brode, *Films of Robert DeNiro*, 267, 268.
10 Sangster, *Scorsese*, 251.
11 Brode, *Films of Robert De Niro*, 266.
12 Yaquinto, *Pump 'Em Full of Lead*, 173–4. See also Nyce, *Scorsese Up Close*, 139, 141, 143, 144.
13 Although Pellegrino d'Acierno notes a close resemblance between *GoodFellas* and *Casino*, he finds in the apparent recycling a 'metacinematic' strategy consistent with the fact that *Casino* 'is essentially about movies – the rules of their game – and about moviemaking as a form of gaming,' so that its 'extravagance of representation' and 'spectacular economy' mirror the gambling world it portrays. Such an attempt to legitimate *Casino* through an appeal to self-conscious formalism and authorial self-reflexivity only trivializes a work that, independently of *GoodFellas*, constitutes a profound meditation on the social and cultural significance of gambling. See d'Acierno, 'Cinema Paradiso,' 652, 656.
14 Christie, 'Introduction,' xi.
15 Ronald A. Farrell and Carole Case, *The Black Book and the Mob: The Untold Story of the Control of Nevada's Casinos* (Madison: Univ. of Wisconsin Press, 1995), 21–2; Jerome H. Skolnick, *House of Cards: The Legitimation and Control of Casino Gambling* (Boston: Little, Brown, 1978), 108, 140–2; Roger Munting, *An Economic and Social History of Legalized Gambling in Britain and the U.S.* (Manchester: Manchester Univ. Press, 1996), 146–7; Vicki Abt, James F. Smith, and Eugene Martin Christiansen, *The Business of Risk: Commercial Gambling in Mainstream America* (Lawrence: Univ. of Kansas, 1985), 79–80; Hal Rothman, *Neon Metropolis: How Las Vegas Started the Twenty-First Century* (New York: Routledge, 2003), xvi, 19. Rothman contends that the requirement, which Nevada officially adopted in 1955, that every stockholder in a gambling operation be licensed by the state, discouraged large corporations from casino investment. It also unintentionally strengthened the mob's power, as its financing became crucial to casino construction.
16 Bell, 'Crime as an American Way of Life,' 130–1.
17 Nelli, *Business of Crime*, 259–60; Nelli, 'Overview,' 3; Bell, 'Crime as an American Way of Life,' 129–32. See also Moore, *Kefauver Committee*, 17–20, 33, 34; Turkus and Feder, *Murder, Inc.*, 91–4; Martin, *Revolt in the Mafia*, 95, 264. In 1983 the FBI could confirm neither that illegal gambling is dominated by the Mafia nor that it is the main source of the Mafia's economic and political power. See Reuter, *Disorganized Crime*, ix.
18 Munting, *Economic and Social History of Legalized Gambling*, 147; Lyman and Potter, *Organized Crime*, 191.

19 John M. Findlay, *People of Chance: Gambling in American Society from Jamestown to Las Vegas* (New York: Oxford Univ. Press, 1986), 123.

20 Eugene P. Moehring, *Resort City in the Sunbelt: Las Vegas, 1930–2000* (Reno: Univ. of Nevada Press, 2000), 44, 46, 47–9, 50; Michael Dear, *The Postmodern Urban Condition* (Oxford: Blackwell, 2000), 201; M. Gottdiener, Claudia C. Collins, and David R. Dickens, *Las Vegas: The Social Production of an All-American City* (Oxford: Blackwell, 1999), 17–19; Robert Lacy, *Little Man: Lansky and the Gangster Life* (London: Century, 1991), 150–9, 218–19, 285, 294–5, 300; Fried, *Rise and Fall*, 249–54, 273–6; Roemer, *Roemer*, 94–5, 130; Sifakis, *Mafia Encyclopedia*, 182–3; Peter Wiley and Robert Gottlieb, *Empires in the Sun: The Rise of the New American West* (New York: G.P. Putnam's, 1982), 193–4, 197–8.

21 Cressey, *Theft of the Nation*, 149; Reid and Demaris, *Green Felt Jungle*, 214; Roemer, *Roemer*, 28, 126, 138, 166; Demaris, *Last Mafioso*, 265. The Mafia ruled against violence in resort areas as early as 1933; see Reppetto, *American Mafia*, 154.

22 Roemer, *Roemer*, 126, 138; Roemer, *War of the Godfathers*, 6–7; Roemer, *Accardo*, 141.

23 Abadinsky, *Organized Crime*, 235; Reid and Demaris, *Green Felt Jungle*, 61–6, 68–70, 79–82; Moehring, *Resort City*, 82–4; Roemer, *Enforcer*, 86, 88, 249; Roemer, *Roemer*, 127–30; Roemer, *Accardo*, 141–3, 172, 174, 245, 461, 462; Rothman, *Neon Metropolis*, 13.

24 Moehring, *Resort City*, 78, 79, 80, 84–5; Roemer, *War of Godfathers*, 61, 64–5, 80, 81; Roemer, *Accardo*, 142–3, 174, 244, 461; Russo, *Outfit*, 299, 307, 382; Reid and Demaris, *Green Felt Jungle*, 70, 81; Rappleye and Becker, *All-American Mafioso*, 161–2, 165; Roemer, *Enforcer*, 83; Demaris, *Last Mafioso*, 106. Rosselli is believed to have secured the purchase of the Stardust for The Outfit.

25 Reid and Demaris, *Green Felt Jungle*, 95–6; Roemer, *Enforcer*, 106; Roemer, *Roemer*, 130–1; Roemer, *War of Godfathers*, 42; Rappleye and Becker, *All-American Mafioso*, 170–1; Sifakis, *Mafia Encyclopedia*, 306–7; Fried, *Rise and Fall of Jewish Gangster*, 275–6.

26 Reid and Demaris, *Green Felt Jungle*, 6; Abadinsky, *Organized Crime*, 258; Sloane, *Hoffa*, 84, 274; Lyman and Potter, *Organized Crime*, 452–3; Kwitny, *Vicious Circles*, 145, 165–71; Roemer, *Enforcer*, 111, 124, 128–9, 216–17; Roemer, *Roemer*, 127, 129; Roemer, *Accardo*, 173–4, 461.

27 Reid and Demaris, *Green Felt Jungle*, 98–109; Sloane, *Hoffa*, 274; *Business of Crime*, ed. Block, 212, 213; Wiley and Gottlieb, *Empires in the Sun*, 200–1; Kwitny, *Vicious Circles*, 171; Rothman, *Neon Metropolis*, 15–17; Russo, *Outfit*, 316, 349–50; Steven Brill, *The Teamsters* (New York: Simon and

Schuster, 1978), 4, 13–14, 189–249. Johnny Rosselli, the Chicago mob's first 'enforcer' in Las Vegas, befriended Allen and 'Red' Dorfman and with their help financed mob interests in Las Vegas. See Rappleye and Becker, *All-American Mafioso*, 169. Neither the Teamsters Union nor the pension funds generally merited charges of criminality. Only the CSPF was controlled by the mob.

28 Sloane, *Hoffa*, 274-5; Roemer, *Enforcer*, 89, 109–10; Roemer, *Roemer*, 128, 130; Roemer, *Accardo*, 462; Moehring, *Resort City*, 116–18; Russo, *Outfit*, 461-2.

29 Russo, *Outfit*, 351; Abadinsky, *Organized Crime*, 257–8; Roemer, *Enforcer*, 191; Sloane, *Hoffa*, 120, 156, 275; Kwitny, *Vicious Circles*, 166–8, 195.

30 Abadinsky, *Organized Crime*, 258; Roemer, *Accardo*, 463; Demaris, *Last Mafioso*, 273, 275.

31 Skolnick, *House of Cards*, 13, 144–5; Munting, *Economic and Social History of Gambling*, 147; Rothman, *Neon Metropolis*, 20–2; Farrell and Case, *Black Book and Mob*, 53–7; Demaris, *Last Mafioso*, 183, 184, 188–9, 202–4; Roemer, *Accardo*, 304–5; Moehring, *Resort City*, 118–19; Gottdiener et al., *Las Vegas*, 23–4, 27–8; Wiley and Gottlieb, *Empires in the Sun*, 201–3, 204; Russo, *Outfit*, 413, 423, 463.

32 The Stardust had been sold by Mo Dalitz to the Parvin-Dorhrmann Corporation, which, running into a public relations problem in the late 1960s, sold it to Delbert W. Coleman, who artificially inflated the company stock. After the bubble burst, Parvin-Dohrmann bought the company back under the new name of Recrion, subsequently selling all shares to Glick and his newly formed Argent Corporation. See Pileggi, *Casino*, 121–6, 129–32; Farrell and Case, *Black Book and Mob*, 57–60; Skolnick, *House of Cards*, 208–10; Brill, *Teamsters*, 225; Roemer, *Roemer*, 135–6; Roemer, *Enforcer*, 101–2, 140; *Business of Crime*, ed. Block, 213; Kwitny, *Vicious Circles*, 167; Lyman and Potter, *Organized Crime*, 452–3; Rothman, *Neon Metropolis*, 22; Demaris, *Last Mafioso*, 203, 223, 269–70, 271; Fried, *Rise and Fall of the Jewish Gangster*, 284–5. Pileggi sees Glick as a 'straight-arrow naif' who was deceived and manipulated by the mob, at least initially. In the film, Philip Green gives the same impression. See Pileggi, *Casino*, 176; Pileggi and Scorsese, *Casino*, 14. Abadinsky speculates that at least fourteen million dollars were skimmed from the Stardust between 1973 and 1983. See Abadinsky, *Organized Crime*, 235.

33 Pileggi, *Casino*, 176, 183, 185–6; Farrell and Case, *Black Book and Mob*, 59–60, 73; Kwitny, *Vicious Circles*, 167; Brill, *Teamsters*, 228–9; Demaris, *Last Mafioso*, 307. In the film Tamara Rand is named Anna Scott and is killed by Nicky.

34 Pileggi, *Casino*, 214–17, 248, 255–60, 268, 319, 336–40; Skolnick, *House of Cards*, 310–18; Farrell and Case, *Black Book and Mob*, 91–6, 103–4; Brill, *Teamsters*, 229–30; *Business of Crime*, ed. Block, 228; Abadinsky, *Organized Crime*, 118, 123, 259; Demaris, *Last Mafioso*, 433–4; Roemer, *Enforcer*, *passim*; Roemer, *Roemer*, 129–30; Roemer, *Accardo*, 348–51, 368–71, 409–10, 464, 465; Abadinsky, *Organized Crime*, 259; Wiley and Gottlieb, *Empires in the Sun*, 203. The Teamsters fund was ultimately restructured and given to outside managers.

35 Pileggi, *Casino*, 14.

36 Pileggi, *Casino*, 29–31, 42–4, 58–9, 61–2, 63, 64–8, 70; Farrell and Case, *Black Book and Mob*, 78–9, 113; Brill, *Teamsters*, 226; Abadinsky, *Organized Crime*, 122; Roemer, *Enforcer*, 66, 137, 138, 139; Roemer, *Roemer*, 135. Skolnick finds 'some question' in allegations of Rosenthal's illegal bookmaking. He notes that his indictment had been dismissed and that he had denied ever having been a bookmaker. Rosenthal claimed to have been principally a sports bettor and professional gambler, a man of that 'moral character.' See Skolnick, *House of Cards*, 211, 219.

37 Pileggi, *Casino*, 13, 17–18, 73, 176, 192–5, 197–9, 206–7; Farrell and Case, *Black Book and Mob*, 78, 80–4; Brill, *Teamsters*, 229; Roemer, *Enforcer*, 1, 101–2, 137, 139–41; Roemer, *War of the Godfathers*, 60, 63, 182; Roemer, *Accardo*, 462; Skolnick, *House of Cards*, 219.

38 Abadinsky, *Organized Crime*, 118, 122; Reid and Demaris, *Green Felt Jungle*, 70, 72; Roemer, *Enforcer*, *passim*; Roemer, *Roemer*, 41–2, 65–6, 135.

39 Abadinsky, *Organized Crime*, 122, 258; Roemer, *Enforcer*, *passim*; Roemer, *Roemer*, 139–40; Roemer, *Accardo*, 309–11, 464; Pileggi, *Casino*, 141, 142, 144–9; Kwitny, *Vicious Circles*, 189–95. Carl Sifakis believes Tamara Rand to have been killed not by Spilotro but by San Diego crime boss and hit man Frank 'Bomp' Bompiensiero. See Sifakis, *Mafia Encyclopedia*, 40–1.

40 Roemer, *Enforcer*, 232; Pileggi, *Casino*, 108, 114–15. See also Frank Cullotta, Tony's henchman, in Pileggi, *Casino*, 144: 'He was in the papers all the time ... Everybody wanted to be around a gangster. Movie stars. Everybody ... I guess it's a feeling of power.'

41 Upon the murder of Sam Giancana in 1975, speculations circulated in Chicago that Spilotro would replace him as boss of the Outfit; in fact Giancana had been demoted by this point, while Spilotro had no chance for such a promotion. See Roemer, *Enforcer*, 132–3.

42 *Chicago Tribune*, cited in Abadinsky, *Criminal Elite*, 140.

43 Kwitny, *Vicious Circles*, 167, 197–8. See also the high estimations of Spilotro's importance by *Time* magazine and a Justice Department official in Roemer, *Accardo*, 343.

44 Farrell and Case, *Black Book and Mob*, 70, 72 (caption); Pileggi, *Casino*, 110–11.

45 Pileggi, *Casino*, 151–2, 239, 241.

46 Roemer, *Enforcer*, 124, 126; Demaris, *Last Mafioso*, 269, 271.

47 Brill, *Teamsters*, 205–6, 210.

48 Farrell and Case, *Black Book and Mob*, 67, 69–74, 76, 78.

49 Pileggi, *Casino*, 103, 317.

50 Farrell and Case, *Black Book and Mob*, 71, 73; Sifakis, *Mafia Encyclopedia*, 5; Roemer, *Enforcer*, 37–8, 51–3, 69–71, 77–8, 142–3, 162, 181, 192, 222; Demaris, *Last Mafioso*, 271, 275, 307, 308, 328.

51 Pileggi, *Casino*, 198–9, 206–7, 224–5; Roemer, *Enforcer*, 140–1, 186; Roemer, *Roemer*, 136; Roemer, *War of the Godfathers*, 181–2; Roemer, *Accardo*, 464; Farrell and Case, *Black Book and Mob*, 86. Rosenthal's television show was 'so bad that people watched it just to see how bad it could get.' See Rothman, *Neon Metropolis*, 23. Despite his disapproval of Rosenthal, Harry Reid, later U.S. senator from Nevada, rejected a 'cops and robbers' stance as chairman of the Gaming Control Board. See Wiley and Gottlieb, *Empires in the Sun*, 205.

52 Roemer, *Enforcer*, 196, 199–200, 210–11, 214, 223–5, 230–1, 239, 245; Roemer, *Roemer*, 140; Roemer, *War of the Godfathers*, 161; Pileggi, *Casino*, 311–12; Farrell and Case, *Black Book and Mob*, 99, 101–4, 141; Abadinsky, *Organized Crime*, 123.

53 Roemer, *Enforcer*, 233–6; Roemer, *Accardo*, 369–70; Pileggi, *Casino*, 207–8, 237–8, 271–7, 281–9, 292–3, 299, 300–2, 304–7; Abadinsky, *Organized Crime*, 123.

54 Roemer, *Enforcer*, 222, 237–8, 239, 241, 242, 245, 253, 257–9, 262, 265, 273, 278, 287, 304–7, 309–13, 318, 321; Roemer, *Roemer*, 140–1; Roemer, *War of the Godfathers*, 161–2, 281; Roemer, *Accardo*, 370, 376, 465–6; Pileggi, *Casino*, 314–17, 340, 344–6; Farrell and Case, *Black Book and Mob*, 113–19; Abadinsky, *Organized Crime*, 122–3. Contrary to his claim in other works that the Outfit killed Spilotro for disobedience and incompetence, Roemer contends in a quasi-fictional work published in 1990 that Spilotro was murdered by the Bonanno family, which in the mid-1980s was supposedly competing for dominance of Las Vegas. And whereas in other writings Roemer holds that Spilotro probably attempted to blow up Rosenthal, he claims in 1990 that Rosenthal was targeted by the Bonannos in retaliation for the Outfit's murder of Mo Dalitz. See Roemer, *War of the Godfathers*, 162, 164–5, 180–3. Pileggi (*Casino*, 348) says that Rosenthal was nominated to the Black Book in 1987.

55 Rothstein's name was perhaps suggested by Hymie the Ace, a legendary

gambler whom Rosenthal admired in his early years. See Pileggi, *Casino*, 26.

56 In 1979 Reid was cleared of allegations that he had accepted bribes for preferential treatment in regulatory matters. See Farrell and Case, *Black Book and Mob*, 98.

57 DeLuna went to jail rather than dying of a heart attack in a police raid, as does Piscano.

58 Sangster, *Scorsese*, 246–7; Brode, *Films of Robert De Niro*, 267. The Tangiers stands for the four main Argent Corporation hotel-casinos, the Stardust, Hacienda, Frontier, and Marina.

59 Pileggi, *Casino*, 165–6, 275, 279–80.

60 Like his character Michael Corleone, Coppola identifies Italian American crime families with legal capitalist organizations, including impersonal corporations. This questionable assertion, made in a 1972 interview with Stephen Farber, has been more or less accepted by Farber, Les and Barbara Keyser, and Thomas J. Ferraro. See Farber, 'Coppola and *The Godfather*,' *Sight and Sound*, Autumn 1972: 218; Les and Barbara Keyser, *Hollywood and the Catholic Church: The Image of Roman Catholicism in American Movies* (Chicago: Loyola Univ. Press, 1984), 88; Thomas J. Ferraro, 'Blood in the Marketplace: The Business of Family in *The Godfather* Narratives,' in Ferraro, *Ethnic Passages*, 1993, 18–52. For a contrary view, see Robert K. Johnson, *Francis Ford Coppola* (Boston: Twayne, 1977), 109–10, 114–16.

61 Johann Huizinga, *Homo Ludens: A Study of the Play-Element in Culture*, trans. R.F.C. Hull (New York: Roy, 1950), 5, 6, 7, 8, 10, 11, 14, 15, 18–19, 20, 22–7, 45, 46, 48, 51, 56, 57, 74.

62 Caillois, *Man and the Sacred*, 152–62; Caillois, *Man, Play, and Games*, vii, 4, 5, 6.

63 Caillois, *Man and the Sacred, passim*; Caillois, *Man, Play, and Games*, 126.

64 Girard, *Violence and the Sacred*, 36–67, 143–68, 312.

65 Girard, *Violence and the Sacred*, 68–118, 119–20, 124, 132, 135.

66 Girard, *Violence and the Sacred*, 154, 311–15. See also Munting, *An Economic and Social History of Gambling*, 4: 'It is easy to find biblical references to gambling and indeed the determination of events by "lot" or chance was seen as being by the hand of God and therefore not to be defiled in mere gambling.'

67 Caillois, *Man, Play, and Games*, 12, 14, 17–18, 19, 40, 41, 73–4, 75, 77, 114, 115, 118.

68 Pileggi, *Casino*, 13, 14, 80.

69 Christie, 'Introduction,' xii.

70 Pileggi refers to the casino's 'sacred count rooms' as the 'sanctum sanctorum,' or holy of holies. See Pileggi, *Casino*, 16.

71 Skolnick, *House of Cards*, 8.

72 Reid and Demaris, *Green Felt Jungle*, 2–5.

73 Mario Puzo, *Inside Las Vegas* (New York: Grosset and Dunlap, 1977), 14, 72. Richard Francaviglia notes that the desert landscapes of the Great Basin are associated with pilgrims, pilgrimage, and spirituality. He also remarks analogies between churches and casinos, where individuals hope fervently to improve their lives by submitting to a higher power. See Francaviglia, *Believing in Place: A Spiritual Geography of the Great Basin* (Reno: Univ. of Nevada Press, 2003), xv, xviii, xix, xx, xxi, 166–7.

74 Reid and Demaris, *Green Felt Jungle*, 214; Roemer, *Enforcer*, 3–4. Ovid Demaris assigns these words to gangster Johnny Rosselli concerning the murder within the city in March 1974 of John Dubeck and his wife Frances Ann, who were to testify against a crooked gambling operation: 'Any idea who clipped them? ... It's against the rules to clip guys in Vegas. That's been the law since Bugsy built the Flamingo.' See Demaris, *Last Mafioso*, 265.

75 Pileggi, *Casino*, 14. On the casino's advantage, see Bill Friedman, *Casino Management* (Secaucus, N.J.: Lyle Stuart, 1974), 18; Skolnick, *House of Cards*, 53–8, 66; Findlay, *People of Chance*, 152.

76 Caillois, *Man and the Sacred*, 11–12, 123, 126, 127, 131, 132, 163–4, 165; Caillois, *Man, Play, and Games*, 44–5, 117, 157, 158. Alfonso di Nola remarks the contamination of the modern festival by work, as it has become primarily a means of profit and the recreation of the labour force, that is, the restoration of its energies for further work. He also notes the festival's role in concealing the *ennui* or *noia* lurking within industrial capitalist society. See di Nola, 'Varianti semiotiche della festa e interpretabilità marxiana,' 89, 90, 92, 93–4.

77 Skolnick, *House of Cards*, 13, 102, 117, 298.

78 Caillois, *Man, Play, and Games*, 5, 66, 115, 157, 158; Findlay, *People of Chance*, 147; Munting, *Economic and Social History of Gambling*, 29; Abt et al., *Business of Risk*, 79, 194–5, 203; Skolnick, *House of Cards*, 20, 35, 36; Reid and Demaris, *Green Felt Jungle*, 2. According to Gottdiener, Collins, and Dickens, Las Vegas 'extolled with pride what other places sought to hide.' Thus it became 'the behavioural "Other," a land where the "victimless" crimes of sex, drink, and gambling were not only condoned, but celebrated.' See Gottdiener et al., *Las Vegas*, 69.

79 Caillois, *Man, Play, and Games*, 117.

80 Daniel Boorstin writes that 'Nevada gambling flourished as a border industry – just over the border from illegality and from other states.' Not only does Las Vegas border on California, Oregon, Idaho, Utah, and

Arizona, but Reno is a dozen miles from the California line while Lake Tahoe virtually straddles it. Wendover, another gambling mecca, is close to the Utah border. Two more recent gambling dens are located at Jackpot, on the Idaho border, and Laughlin, at the southernmost point of Nevada where California meets Arizona. See Daniel Boorstin, *The Americans: The Democratic Experience* (New York: Random House, 1973), 75; Thomas L. Clark, 'Gambling Language and Nevada Law,' in Francis X. Hartigan, ed., *History and Humanities: Essays in Honor of Wilbur S. Shepperson* (Reno: Univ. of Nevada Press, 1989), 138, 154n.

81 Findlay, *People of Chance*, 3, 4, 8, 81, 110–11, 116, 117, 121, 127–8, 131, 143, 170. See also Munting, *Economic and Social History of Gambling*, 29. One of the earliest Las Vegas hotels was the Apache, at the western end of Fremont Street. During the 1930s tourism was promoted through frontier themes embodied in unpaved streets, wooden sidewalks, rodeos, and cowboy parades. Two important pre-Flamingo hotels were El Rancho and The Last Frontier, built in 1941 and 1942 respectively, which have been described as opulent dude ranches with a frontier ambience. The theme persisted in the Thunderbird Hotel, which opened in 1948, and which took its name and facade imagery from a Navajo legend. In 1951 the advertising firm of West-Marquis introduced the neon image of the friendly cowboy, Vegas Vic, whose motto is 'Howdy Podner,' and which still overlooks Fremont Street. See Moehring, *Resort City*, 44, 46, 49, 66; Gottdiener et al., *Las Vegas*, 17–18.

82 Christie, 'Introduction,' x. It is worth noting resemblances between the main characters of *Casino* and those of Howard Hawks's *Rio Bravo*, which figures significantly in *Who's That Knocking at My Door?* The hero of *Rio Bravo* is John T. Chance (John Wayne) who, like Ace, is associated by name with gambling. As Ace falls in love with the prostitute Ginger and gambles on the small possibility of transforming her through marriage, so Chance risks marriage with dance-hall entertainer and card sharp Feathers (Angie Dickinson), who also has a disreputable past. Indeed, Ginger wears feathers in the scene where she plies a customer with anti-soporific drugs to keep him gambling, while Feathers has perhaps been a prostitute. Yet unlike *Casino*, *Rio Bravo* implies that the risky marriage will prove successful.

83 The earlier criminal band was named for the remoteness and obscurity of its hideaway; Nicky's gang is known for knocking holes in buildings in order to plunder them. See Pileggi, *Casino*, 146.

84 Skolnick, *House of Cards*, 9–10; Farrell and Case, *Black Book and Mob*, 19–22; Abt et al., *Business of Risk*, 82; Findlay, *People of Chance*, 121, 172; Wiley and Gottlieb, *Empires in the Sun*, 118.

85 Skolnick, *House of Cards*, 5, 8, 10–12, 31, 39, 98, 115; Abt et al., *Business of Risk*, 81.
86 Skolnick, *House of Cards*, 13.
87 Findlay, *People of Chance*, 122, 123; Farrell and Case, *Black Book and Mob*, 32–5; Skolnick, *House of Cards*, 117, 298.
88 Skolnick, *House of Cards*, 31–2, 117, 176, 211, 217.
89 The question is Herbert Packer's, cited in Skolnick, *House of Cards*, 9.
90 Skolnick, *House of Cards*, 75–6, 127; Pileggi, *Casino*, 16, 177–9; Demaris, *Last Mafioso*, 434.
91 Roemer, *Roemer*, 131. Rosow complains that most gangster films fail to clarify how gambling generates money for organized crime. See Rosow, *Born to Lose*, 319.
92 Friedman, *Casino Management*, 36–44; Pileggi, *Casino*, 15, 92–3; Christie, 'Introduction,' xv; Skolnick, *House of Cards*, 71.
93 Pileggi, *Casino*, 263.
94 Skolnick, *House of Cards*, 37–40; Reid and Demaris, *Green Felt Jungle*, 110–31; Friedman, *Casino Management*, 124; Moehring, *Resort City*, 42, 60–1, 91, 114.
95 Pileggi, *Casino*, 145–6.
96 See Pileggi, *Casino*, 110. According to Mario Puzo, eastern police organizations lack the 'iron hand that the police of the West use so effectively.' See Puzo, *Inside Las Vegas*, 72.
97 Moore, *Kefauver Committee*, 78–9; Findlay, *People of Chance*, 171; Munting, *Economic and Social History of Gambling*, 52; Farrell, *Black Book and Mob*, 23–5, 27; Skolnick, *House of Cards*, 117; Moehring, *Resort City*, 52, 53; Gottdiener et al., *Las Vegas*, 80–1; Roemer, *Enforcer*, 85; Rothman, *Neon Metropolis*, xxi; Brill, *Teamsters*, 198, 205–6; Moehring, *Resort City*, 74, 89; Reid and Demaris, *Green Felt Jungle*, 61–5.
98 Moehring, *Resort City*, 54–5; Wiley and Gottlieb, *Empires in the Sun*, 203–4; Roemer, *Enforcer*, 86, 98, 214; Rothman, *Neon Metropolis*, 18–19. The Thunderbird hotel casino was secretly owned by Meyer and Jake Lansky. See Roemer, *Accardo*, 461.
99 Skolnick, *House of Cards*, 118; Farrell and Case, *Black Book and Mob*, 118.
100 Moehring, *Resort City*, 54–5; Gottdiener et al., *Las Vegas*, 27; Rothman, *Neon Metropolis*, 19.
101 Farrell and Case, *Black Book and Mob*, 80; Skolnick, *House of Cards*, 171–8; Friedman, *Casino Management*, 316–26, 327–48.
102 Friedman, *Casino Management*, 340–1; Farrell and Case, *Black Book and Mob*, xi, 3, 5–7, 9, 10–11; Sifakis, *Mafia Encyclopedia*, 36; Roemer, *Enforcer*, 214; Skolnick, *House of Cards*, 121. Since 1976 the Black Book has been formally designated the List of Excluded Persons so as to avoid offence to African Americans, who had complained of its original title.

103 Farrell and Case, *Black Book and Mob*, 221; Findlay, *People of Chance*, 153; Skolnick, *House of Cards*, 176, 211, 216–17, 233, 240.

104 Farrell and Case, *Black Book and Mob*, *passim*; Alan Balboni, *Beyond the Mafia: Italian Americans and the Development of Las Vegas* (Reno: Univ. of Las Vegas, 1996), 16; Russo, *Outfit*, 347–9. Italian Americans have often worked in Las Vegas as entertainers, dealers, pit bosses, floormen, and shift managers, yet the media's focus on the mob has made it hard for them to rise in the gaming industry, at least up to the 1980s. Yet by comparison with the eastern United States, Las Vegas, like the western states generally, has afforded Italian Americans with an opportunity for more rapid social mobility and assimilation. See Balboni, *Beyond the Mafia*, xviii–xix, 13–15. See also Andrew F. Rolle, *The Immigrant Upraised: Italian Adventurers and Colonists in an Expanding America* (Norman: Univ. of Oklahoma Press, 1968).

105 Farrell and Case, *Black Book and Mob*, 32, 107, 109, 111–13, 144–5, 146–51, 157, 163–4, 171.

106 Farrell and Case, *Black Book and Mob*, 4–5, 9–11, 67, 69, 169, 172, 194, 217, 218, 227. Hal Rothman describes the Black Book as a public relations ploy to clean up the state's image. See Rothman, *Neon Metropolis*, 19.

107 Munting, *Economic and Social History of Gambling*, 4–6, 51–3, 150, 214–15; Abt et al., *Business of Risk*, *passim*.

108 Abt et al., *Business of Risk*, 14, 147–8, 212. As of 1999 some form of gambling was permitted in forty-eight states, whereas in 1994 this was true of only twenty-three states and in 1988 of only Nevada and New Jersey. See Gottdiener et al., *Las Vegas*, 90–2.

109 Douglas, *Purity and Danger*, 121.

110 For casino gambling as a 'scapegoat' for the gaming habits of the nation, incapable until recently of acknowledging its symbiosis with Las Vegas, see Rothman, *Neon Metropolis*, 26.

111 Douglas, *Purity and Danger*, 95–8, 102, 113.

112 Erving Goffman, *Stigma: Notes on the Management of Spoiled Identity* (New York: Simon and Schuster, 1986), 1–5.

113 Pileggi, *Casino*, 12.

114 Goffman discusses the stigmatized person's efforts to correct his condition. See *Stigma*, 10. A minor stigma, left-handedness, is implicit in 'Lefty,' Rosenthal's nickname.

115 Caillois, *Man and the Sacred*, 50.

116 Pileggi and Scorsese, *Casino*, 6.

117 Caillois, *Man and the Sacred*, 90, 92, 93.

118 Girard, *Violence and the Sacred*, 152.

119 Pileggi, *Casino*, 25, 43.

120 Pileggi, *Casino*, 175, 189–92.

121 Pileggi, *Casino*, 23, 24.

122 Pileggi, *Casino*, 91–3.

123 With the exception, that is, of the highly serious, troubled, and anhedonic Michael Corleone.

124 Pileggi and Scorsese, *Casino*, 72.

125 On Dalitz, see Brill, *Teamsters*, 199; and Skolnick, *House of Cards*, 215–16.

126 Christie, 'Introduction,' xiii.

127 Rosenthal fired a Stardust breakfast cook for making watery eggs. See Pileggi, *Casino*, 198.

128 Caillois, *Man and the Sacred*, 45.

129 Skolnick, *House of Cards*, 68, 71–3.

130 This scene parallels Pileggi, *Casino*, 93–5. The punishment of cheaters in *Casino* closely resembles the extremely brutal methods employed by casino manager Gus Greenbaum at the Riviera Hotel in the 1950s. See Reid and Demaris, *Green Felt Jungle*, 52.

131 Pileggi, *Casino*, 134, 277, 294.

132 Christie, 'Introduction,' xxi.

133 Ace doubled not his casino's earnings but its blackjack drop in a year. See Pileggi, *Casino*, 175.

134 Caillois, *Man and the Sacred*, 28.

135 The film suggests that Nicky organizes the Hole-in-the-Wall Gang in vengeance against his inclusion in the Black Book. However, Spilotro's gang was operating at least as early as 1976, three years before his listing, and seems to have started up not long after his arrival in Las Vegas.

136 Christie, 'Introduction,' xx. For Lefty Rosenthal's obsession with perfect tailoring, see Pileggi, *Casino*, 169.

137 'Jonathan and David and their tigers' are inspired by Siegfried and Roy, the magical act Rosenthal lured from the MGM Grand to the Stardust by building them a special dressing room as well as giving them a free Rolls-Royce. See Pileggi, *Casino*, 175–6.

138 In a June 1975 article in *Business Week* Rosenthal stated that 'Glick is the financial end, but the policy comes from my office.' See Pileggi, *Casino*, 192–3; Brill, *Teamsters*, 226.

139 Girard, *Violence and the Sacred*, 44, 45, 63.

140 When Spilotro was picked up for homicide, Rosenthal had to bail him out. See Pileggi, *Casino*, 114–15.

141 Girard, *Violence and the Sacred*, 46–7.
142 Ginger's statements are based on similar ones reported of Geri McGee. See Pileggi, *Casino*, 84.
143 Rosenthal said that his wife refused to accept rules. See Pileggi, *Casino*, 168–9.
144 Caillois, *Man, Play, and Games*, 17, 18, 24, 51, 73, 74–5, 77, 78, 97.
145 Yaquinto finds his attraction inexplicable. See Yaquinto, *Pump'Em Full of Lead*, 175.
146 Pileggi, *Casino*, 76–7.
147 Skolnick, *House of Cards*, 38–9; Pileggi, *Casino*, 76. See also Reid and Demaris, *Green Felt Jungle*, 114: 'The more attractive whores operate strictly from calls from the pitbosses ... Known as "pitgirls," their job is to entertain high rollers while the house empties their pockets. The pit girl ... accompanies [her date] to dinner ... and later stands beside him as he gambles. This is her big opportunity to steal chips. But she has to be very careful, not only of her date but of the eagle-eyed pit boss, who frowns on anyone stealing ... the house's money. If she's experienced she'll find ways of secreting chips from the rack into the specially designed narrow pockets ('subs') inside her fur cape. Her next problem will be to get rid of the chips at one of the cashier's cages before accompanying the high roller to his suite. Most gamblers get angry if they find girls stealing chips from them.'
148 Pileggi, *Casino*, 78.
149 Girard, *Violence and the Sacred*, 296–7.
150 Rosenthal's friends told him Geri McGee 'will empty you out.' See Pileggi, *Casino*, 87.
151 Christie, 'Introduction,' xvi.
152 Christie, 'Introduction,' xxi.
153 Christie, 'Introduction,' xxi.
154 Ace's difficulties with Webb are based on a similar episode that hurt Rosenthal's chances for a licence. Not long before his hearing in 1976, he evaluated the Hacienda, an Argent Corporation hotel, 'from top to bottom.' Finding malfeasance, mismanagement, and glaring violations of Gaming Commission rules, he fired many employees, including a friend of Pete Echeverria, chairman of the State Gaming Commission. Pileggi thinks this 'mistake' helped to prejudice the commission against Ace. However, Echeverria appears not to have confronted Rosenthal in his Stardust office over the firing. See Pileggi, *Casino*, 193; Farrell and Case, *Black Book and Mob*, 90–1.
155 Huizinga, *Homo Ludens*, 77, 78.

156 Pileggi, *Casino*, 197.
157 Skolnick, *House of Cards*, 216–7. Gangster Johnny Rosselli's assessment of the causes of Rosenthal's licensing denial is the same as Skolnick's; see Demaris, *Last Mafioso*, 271. Like Roemer, Farrell and Case attribute Rosenthal's failure to receive a licence in large degree to his association with Spilotro. See Roemer, *Enforcer*, 232; Farrell and Case, *Black Book and Mob*, 79, 80, 83, 86.
158 Rothman, *Neon Metropolis*, 23.
159 Farrell and Case, *Black Book and Mob*, 87–8, 90. Pileggi quotes Rosenthal's remark that 'there were guys licensed in town you wouldn't believe.' See Pileggi, *Casino*, 198.
160 See Farrell and Case, *Black Book and Mob*, 87; Pileggi, *Casino*, 229.
161 Farrell and Case, *Black Book and Mob*, 87; Pileggi, *Casino*, 235–6.
162 Christie, 'Stardust in Las Vegas,' xv.
163 Pileggi and Scorsese, *Casino*, 148n.
164 On the southern Italian belief in witches and the evil eye, see chap. 5, note 11.
165 Gus Russo describes the young Johnny Rosselli (born Filippo Sacco) as he trained to become a gangster: 'Like so many before him, young Sacco spent countless hours at the mirror practicing *malocchio* (the evil eye), or the Look.' To quote Rosselli, the trick was to 'pick a spot on the forehead and zero in.' See Russo, *Outfit*, 63.
166 Compare Pileggi, *Casino*, 237, 239.
167 The scene parallels Pileggi, *Casino*, 237–8.
168 For parallel instances of anti-Semitism, see Pileggi, *Casino*, 288, 291.
169 In order to dramatize the wiretaps and to heighten the pace of the action towards the climax, Pileggi and Scorsese portray the government's bugging operation as the cause of the raid on the skim. Actually, the Stardust raid occurred in May 1976. The wiretaps began more than two years later, in June 1978. The listening devices had been planted in a pizzeria rather than a grocery store. See Pileggi, *Casino*, 255–8. 'Tuffy' DeLuna violated mob practice by scrupulously recording his expenses in travelling and visiting Las Vegas on assignment by the bosses.
170 For the *turba*, see Girard, *Job*, 25–6; *Scapegoat*, 89–94. See also Robert Casillo, 'School for *Skandalon*: Scorsese and Girard at Cape Fear,' *Italian Americana* 12 (Summer 1994): 201–25.
171 A nominee to the Black Book who enters a casino faces a year in jail and a thousand-dollar fine. Yet though Spilotro violated this rule, he never paid for it. See Roemer, *Enforcer*, 230–1.
172 A similar but less violent scene appears in Pileggi, *Casino*, 277–8.

173 Huizinga, *Homo Ludens*, 11.
174 Pileggi, *Casino*, 309–11.
175 Although Carl Wesley Thomas provides the model for Nance, he was not assassinated by the mob. Nance's murder is inspired by that of George Vandermark, whom the Stardust employed to run its slot-machine skim. Chicago mob boss Joey Aiuppa suspected Vandermark of skimming the skim and probably ordered him killed in Central America. Vandermark's son had been murdered by the mob, angered by the father's disappearance. See Roemer, *Enforcer*, 194; Demaris, *Last Mafioso*, 433–4.
176 Pileggi, *Casino*, 320.
177 Stone's murder corresponds to that of Allen Dorfman in January 1983. Dorfman had been convicted of using the Teamsters pension fund in an attempt to bribe Nevada senator Howard Cannon. See Pileggi, *Casino*, 336–7.
178 Pileggi and Scorsese, *Casino*, 3.
179 Christie, 'Introduction,' xxi.
180 See Scorsese in Christie, 'Introduction,' xiv.
181 Skolnick, *House of Cards*, 13; Rothman, *Neon Metropolis*, 18, 22–4; Wiley and Gottlieb, *Empires in the Sun*, 207; Abadinsky, *Organized Crime*, 235; Moehring, *Resort City*, 55, 264.
182 Pileggi, *Casino*, 340, 348; Rothman, *Neon Metropolis*, 25. However, the Excalibur, Luxor, and MGM Grand were built with cash on hand, while other hotels were endangered for a time with junk bond debt. In 1982 Wiley and Gottlieb noted Las Vegas's uneven success in wooing the money markets of New York and California, adding that it remained a 'mob town.' In 1989 William F. Roemer found that members of the Chicago crime family were still in Las Vegas, working in casinos and skimming corporate profits. Yet a year later he described many major hotel-casinos as 'clean,' without 'mob taint.' Farrell and Case hold that, following Spilotro's removal, the Las Vegas authorities still feared infiltration by organized crime, especially the Chicago mob, and vigorously revived the Black Book to discourage mob inroads. At least into the mid-1990s the gaming authorities singled out Italians arbitrarily because of their associations with organized crime, although, contrary to predictions, the Los Angeles, San Diego, and New England crime syndicates failed to claim the territory vacated by Chicago. Nor have they established a hold in corporate Las Vegas. See Roemer, *Roemer*, 143; Roemer, *War of the Godfathers*, 265; Farrell and Case, *Black Book and Mob*, 99, 141, 143–6, 167, 178, 198–201, 205, 206, 208–13, 233; Gottdiener et al., *Las Vegas*, 35–6, 81; Wiley and Gottlieb, *Empires in the Sun*, 209, 214; Abadinsky,

Organized Crime, 235; Iorizzo, 'Crime and Organized Crime,' 158–9. In *War of the Godfathers* Roemer claims that, during the mid-1980s, the Chicago Outfit and Joe Bonanno's crime family fought for control of the Las Vegas gambling industry. The book takes such liberties with fact as the depiction of a turncoat Mo Dalitz poisoned by Chicago gangsters while in the hospital. It also seems doubtful that astute bosses like Bonanno and Accardo could have seriously considered a takeover of Las Vegas after the Strawman cases and in the face of the far superior economic clout of the corporations. See Roemer, *War of the Godfathers*, 6–7, 9, 12–13, 19, 113–16.

183 Abt et al., *Business of Risk*, 99; Pileggi, *Casino*, 340; Rothman, *Neon Metropolis*, xx, xxxiii, 23–4; Gottdiener et al., *Las Vegas*, 30–67; Moehring, *Resort City*, 261, 268–9.

184 Munting, *Economic and Social History of Gambling*, 151; Moehring, *Resort City*, 268, 270–2; Rothman, *Neon Metropolis*, xix, xxiii, xxvii, 26, 38, 45; Gottdiener et al., *Las Vegas*, 64–5. The new mega-resorts were not the first Las Vegas hotel casinos aimed at a family crowd. Opened in 1957, the Hacienda long stood out for catering to such a clientele, to which it offered pools, play areas, and race tracks. In the late 1960s Circus Circus casino provided similar features, becoming a popular family attraction from 1974 onward, with its amusement parks and roller coasters. See Moehring, *Resort City*, 81, 271–2; Dear, *Postmodern Urban Condition*, 203; Rothman, *Neon Metropolis*, 45.

  In the late 1980s, non-gambling profits from Strip businesses made up only 30 per cent of their total revenue. By 1994 the figure was 45 per cent – an increase attributable to corporatization, increased tourism, and the growth of the family market. Gambling has provided less than 50 per cent of Las Vegas's total income since 1996. Treasure Island, opened in 1993, is the first Las Vegas resort intentionally designed to generate a minority of its revenue – 40 per cent – from gambling. Yet gambling revenues have doubled to a figure of 6.2 billion from 1988 to 1997. See Gottdiener et al., *Las Vegas*, 38; Rothman, *Neon Metropolis*, 34.

185 Moehring, *Resort City*, 267, 268, 269, 272–3; Rothman, *Neon Metropolis*, xvii, 25, 45, 46, 79; Gottdiener et al., *Las Vegas*, 35–9; Pileggi, *Casino*, 347. Older hotel-casinos like the Sahara, Circus Circus, Riviera, Frontier, and Stardust were also refurbished and expanded.

186 Munting, *Social History of Gambling*, 151; Rothman, *Neon Metropolis*, 24; Pileggi, *Casino*, 347. The Disneyland model has declined in the decade following the film's release. As the mega-resort owners discovered, theme and amusement parks generated income insufficient to justify the

space assigned them, while shows, games, and spas proved less profit-able than expected. The shift from adult to family-centred resorts in the 1990s was overrated, and recently Las Vegas projects have tended to be upscale, aiming at high rollers and spenders who prefer a luxuriously high-status simulated environment. Thus the Bellagio, Venetian, and Monte Carlo and the highly expensive Forum Shops at the new Caesars Palace. See Moehring, *Resort City*, 273; Gottdiener et al., *Las Vegas*, 64–6.

187 Findlay, *People of Chance*, 201; Pileggi, *Casino*, 347.

188 The Dunes was imploded on 27 October 1994, amid the fireworks spec-tacle shown in *Casino*; it had been failing and was replaced by the Bellagio, priced between 1.6 and 2.1 billion. The Landmark hotel-casino, built in the early 1960s, suffered the same fate in 1995. A year later the Sands, which had opened in 1952, went under, as did the Hacienda, which dates back to 1956. Opened in 1966 and imploded in 1998, the Aladdin was resurrected in much enlarged form but has struggled since reopening in 2000. See Moehring, *Resort City*, 267, 268; Gottdiener at al., *Las Vegas*, 40–2.

189 Reporting her father's death in *Italianamerican*, Catherine Scorsese men-tions that his fig trees never bloomed thereafter, adding without senti-mentality: 'And that's that.' Mafia executioner Vinnie (Charles Scorsese) applies the same phrase to the murdered Tommy DeVito in *GoodFellas*.

190 'The introduction of the corporations significantly changed the face of Las Vegas gaming,' write Gottdiener and colleagues. Cheap buffets, inexpensive shows, and underpriced room rates became casualties of the 'corporate mentality,' which, being concerned with 'bottom-line reports to stockholders, replaced the more personal, informal atmosphere which had characterized the Vegas resorts for decades.' Only the high rollers were given 'comps,' meals, shows, and free rooms. See Gottdiener at al., *Las Vegas*, 30–1; Rothman, *Neon Metropolis*, 27–8.

191 Smith, 'Art of Vision,' 246. The Sphinx of Gizeh with its 'bare feeling for solemn and imposing magnitude' exemplifies the sublime as an expres-sion of the sacred and numinous. See Rudolf Otto, *The Idea of the Holy: An Inquiry into the Non-Rational Factor in the Idea of the Divine and Its Relation to the Rational*, trans. John W. Harvey (New York: Oxford Univ. Press, 1958), 27, 64, 66, 69.

192 Findlay, *People of Chance*, 98, 122–4, 127, 143, 172. See also Lacy, *Little Man*, 296–7, 300–1; Jerome Edwards, Foreword to Balboni, *Beyond the Mafia*, ix; Russo, *Outfit*, 351.

Index

383–400; alternatives to violence
in, 120–2, 387–8; analogism in,
378–9, 385; art as curbing violence,
395; assimilation in, 391–3, 394;
asthma influenced films, 77, 78,
79, 80; Catholicism, critique of,
388–9; state and violence, 389;
chance in, 119–20; chronicles of
Italian America, ix, 36, 67, 180,
384–5; circle as symbol of violence,
160, 165, 319, 364, 376–7, 379, 395;
conflict between Christianity and
code of masculine honour, xvi, 66,
230, 387–8, 393; contradictions of
third generation in, xi; critical
misunderstandings of, xii–xiv;
Dean Martin biography, 399–400,
482n70; documentary impulse,
384–5; domus in, xi, 128; ethnicity,
ix–x, xi–xiv, xv–xvi, 5, 61–2, 65,
66–7, 383, 384, 385; evaluating
artistic merits of, 389; *feste* in, 111;
films avoid sermonizing, 242;
films reveal Scorsese's biography,
389–94; food in, 48; formal/
technical brilliance of, 383, 389;
formal/thematic/spatial pattern
in, 159–60; Girardian analysis of,
108–11, 115–16, 117, 118, 121, 159–
60; Girardian analysis of violence
in, 111, 160, 385–6; homophilia in,
xiii, 73; influence of American
culture, 48–9, 66–8; *Imitatio* as
ultimate moral standard, xvi, 385,
387–8; immanentism in, 385;
influence of Catholicism, x, xi, xii,
xiii–xiv, xvi, 66, 81, 82, 91, 96, 98–
101, 132, 189, 385–6, 387–9, 393;
Italian American films, relation to
oeuvre, 394–6; Italian American

literature, relation to, 63–5; Italian
American reaction to, xiv–xv; Jake
La Motta 'greatest of Scorsese's
creations,' 390; laughter and
violence in, 121, 160–1, 554n97;
Little Italy in, 123; Mafia, xi–xiii,
xvi, 98–9, 116–20, 287, 393; Mafia
becomes focus, 393; Mafia, ironic
treatment of, 388; male sexual
attitudes in, 76–7; markers of
status (clothes, cars) in, 125, 191,
192, 277, 279, 280, 304, 360; as
meditation on violence and the
sacred, xvi, 385, 391; Mediterranean code of masculine honour,
71–2, 386–8 (*see also* names of
individual films); meld underworld and religion, 98–9; no
further Italian American films
planned, 397; peer groups in, 73–
4, 387, 390; penitential suffering,
100–1; pride, 117–18; *Raging Bull* a
turning point, 391–2, 393–4;
recurrent themes/motifs, x, 66–7,
79, 98–9, 100, 101–2, 111, 118, 121,
132, 133, 136, 159–60, 177, 184, 209,
211–12, 213–14, 227, 230, 314–15,
341, 375–6, 385–6, 387–8, 394–6,
397; non-Italian American films,
x–xi, 65–66, 395–6, 438n22 (*see also*
names of individual films); pride
in, 117, 118, 189, 190; rationalizing
of criminality, 128; religious imagery in, 129; sacrificial crisis in, 376;
Sicilian code of masculinity, 116–
18; suggested future themes/
projects, 397–400; sympathy for
flawed characters, 321, 323–4, 386;
thematic gaps, 398–400; theme of
holiday-gone-wrong, 118, 160, 212,

United States Government, 191, 193, 289, 312, 553n94

United States Justice Department, 332

United States Senate, 124, 129, 223, 224, 534n39, 553n94

United States Supreme Court, 338, 371, 372

United States v. International Brotherhood of Teamsters, 411, 525n24

United States v. Salerno, 524n24

The Untouchables, 124, 127, 469n7

urban villagers, 35–6, 51–2, 56–7, 153, 384, 423n70, 458n134, 484n84, 499–500n63

Valachi, Joe, 124, 403, 406, 407, 411, 534n39, 542n71, 543n73, 544n77, 548n87

Vario, Paulie: 266, 267, 268, 292, 297, 298, 536n42, 541n66, 545n78, 546n81, 549n87, 553n94, 556n105, 557n107

Vatican II, 133, 476n51

Venere Oculis, 176

Venice Film Festival, 142

vertigo, 160, 364, 379

Vietnam War, 97, 204, 211, 213

violence: art as control on, 395; and chance, 106, 110, 119–20, 213, 216–17, 234, 314, 342–3, 378; circle as symbol of, 160, 165, 319, 364, 376–7, 379, 395; controls on in Scorsese's films, 107–8, 120–2, 385, 387, 389, 395–6; controls on within underworld, 299–300; economy in use of, 115, 191, 497n30, 499n58; and *feste*, 109–11; *Imitatio* as alternative to, 107–8, 120, 385, 387; Girardian analysis of, 111; link

with laughter, 121, 160–1, 302–3, 554n97; of Mafia, 113, 114, 115, 116, 191, 296–7, 299–300, 322, 465n216, 466n223, 497n30, 499n58, 531n37, 543n73; Mafia bans in resorts, 330, 344–5, 560n21; and masculine code of honour, xvi, 74, 75–6, 77, 111, 113, 114, 115, 116, 118, 197–8; psychology of, 531n37; ritual fails to control, 395–6; ritual sacrifice as 'good' violence, 105–6; rivalry leads to, 75–6, 111, 118, 155–8, 161–2, 197–8, 212, 230, 375–6, 387; and the sacred, xvi, 104, 102–10, 389, 395; and social collapse (sacrificial crisis), 104–6, 110, 154, 233–4, 314–15, 342–3, 376, 500n65; and social undifferentiation (mimetic doubles), 103–5, 152, 153–4, 155–6, 157, 212–13, 235, 301, 314, 315, 316, 319, 320, 342, 343, 361, 362–3; of wise guy society, 291; and women, 161, 162, 165, 166, 172–3, 212, 235, 296; wheel of fortune portends, 311, 314, 319, 376

Virgin Mary, 81, 83, 84, 85, 90, 93, 136, 137, 138, 145, 148, 167, 170, 199, 231, 289, 307, 456n107

Wayne, John, 67, 153, 154, 155, 156, 168, 173, 174, 175, 187, 283, 566n82

West End (Boston), 19, 24, 33, 35, 71, 73, 86, 153, 433n181, 450n55, 457n108, 458n134, 474n30, 477n60, 478n65, 480n68, 481n68, 499–500n63, 530n25

What's a Nice Girl Like You Doing in a Place Like This?, 466n1

Who's That Knocking at My Door?, 10, 67, 73, 132, 141–78; American culture/media in, 153–5, 156, 165, 166, 170–2, 173–4; camera, use of, 143, 144, 148, 157, 158, 164, 165; Catholicism in, 149–52, 166, 175–8; Catholic sexual morality in, 150–2; characters/milieu of 143–5; cinematic precursors of, 145–7; domus in, 149–50; Girardian analysis of peer group violence, 155–8; homosexuality vs. homophilia in, 162–3; imperfect technique of, 143; J.R. as Scorsese's alter ego, 390; J.R. compared to Jake La Motta, 249–50; J.R.'s relation with 'The Girl,' 144–5, 167–70, 175; loss of individuality in, 387; madonna/whore dichotomy in, 148, 150, 170–2, 388; making of, 141, 142–3; mimetic desire, 161–2, 249–50; mimetic violence, 152–5; music in, 149, 150, 156, 177; scene in loft, 163–6; sexual violence in, 172–4; Sinatra as model, 158–9; theme of entrapment/escape, 144, 148–9, 166–7,

175, 178, 390; theme of holiday-gone-wrong, 159–60; title, 142, 161, 485n94

wheel of fortune, 216, 311, 314, 318

White Anglo-Saxon Protestant, 36, 63, 83, 351, 356, 436n22, 437n22, 439n26, 448n28

Wild Woman, 199, 498n46

Wiseguy (Pileggi), 275, 283, 292, 306, 317, 519n3, 520n4

witchcraft. *See under* superstition

Witness Protection Program, 268, 323, 520n4

Witness Security Program, 411, 524n24

women: attitude to education, 33, 78, 428n121; constrained by spousal jealousy, 11, 12, 44; domestic expectations of, 11, 16, 44; role in church, 85; role in Mafia, 288, 538–9n54; and shame, 75–7, 111; as wage-earners, 11, 12, 44–5

You Can't Take It with You (Capra), 436–8n22